Indonesia
a country study

Federal Research Division
Library of Congress
Edited by
William H. Frederick
and Robert L. Worden

On the cover: A two-masted *pinisi*—a modern adaptation of traditional Indonesian watercraft. Based on photography by Tim Hornby and with permission of Explore Worldwide, Farnborough, Hampshire, United Kingdom. This artwork and the images used on the chapter title pages were chosen to represent the diversity of watercraft used in the archipelagic waters of Indonesia.

Sixth Edition, First Printing, 2011.

Library of Congress Cataloging-in-Publication Data

Indonesia: a country study / edited by William H. Frederick and Robert L. Worden. -- 6th ed.
   p. cm.
   Includes bibliographical references and index.
   ISBN 978-0-8444-0790-6 (alk. paper) -- ISBN (invalid) 978-0-8444-9503-3 (alk. paper) 1. Indonesia. I. Frederick, William H. II. Worden, Robert L. III. Library of Congress. Federal Research Division.
   DS615.I518 2011
   959.8--dc23

                   2011038834

AUTHENTICATED
U.S. GOVERNMENT
INFORMATION
GPO

Use of ISBN

This is the Official U.S. Government edition of this publication and is herein identified to certify its authenticity. Use of the ISBN 978-0-8444-0790-6 is for U.S. Government Printing Office Official Editions only. The Superintendent of Documents of the U.S. Government Printing Office requests that any printed edition clearly be labeled as a copy of the authentic work with a new ISBN.

For sale by the Superintendent of Documents, U.S. Government Printing Office
Internet: bookstore.gpo.gov Phone: toll free (866) 512–1800; DC area (202) 512–1800
Fax: (202) 512–2104 Mail: Stop IDCC, Washington, DC 20402–00001

ISBN 978-0-8444-0790-6

Foreword

This volume is one in a continuing series of books prepared by the Federal Research Divison of the Library of Congress under the Country Studies/Area Handbook Program, formerly sponsored by the Department of the Army and revived in FY 2004 with congressionally mandated funding under the sponsorship of the Joint Chiefs of Staff, Strategic Plans and Policy Directorate (J–5).

Most books in the series deal with a particular foreign country, describing and analyzing its political, economic, social, and national security systems and institutions, and examining the interrelationshps of those systems and the ways they are shaped by historical and cultural factors. Each study is written by a multidisciplinary team of social scientists. The authors seek to provide a basic understanding of the observed society, striving for a dynamic rather than a static portrayal. Particular attention is devoted to the people who make up the society, their origins, dominant beliefs and values, their common interests and the issues on which they are divided, the nature and extent of their involvement with national institutions, and their attitudes toward each other and toward their social system and political order.

The books represent the analysis of the authors and should not be construed as an expression of an official U.S. government position, policy, or decision. The authors have sought to adhere to accepted standards of scholarly objectivity. Corrections, additions, and suggestions for changes from readers will be welcomed for use in future editions.

David L. Osborne
Chief
Federal Research Division
Library of Congress
Washington, DC 20540–4840
E-mail: frds@loc.gov

Acknowledgments

This edition supercedes *Indonesia: A Country Study*, published in 1993. The authors wish to acknowledge their use of portions of that edition in the preparation of the current book.

Various members of the staff of the Federal Research Division of the Library of Congress assisted in the preparation of the book. Sandra W. Meditz made many helpful suggestions during her review of all parts of the book and managed the editing and production of the book. Catherine Schwartzstein edited the manuscript, made many very useful suggestions, and helped clarify obscure points. She also performed the final prepublication editorial review and compiled the index. Vincent Ercolano also edited parts of the manuscript in its early stages. Sarah Ji-Young Kim provided valuable assistance in checking facts, reviewing and revising maps and figures, collecting illustrations, and assisting with updating the Country Profile and revising the Bibliography. Janie L. Gilchrist performed word processing and formatting of text.

The authors also are grateful to other individuals in the Library of Congress who contributed to the book. Kathryn Wellen, former Indonesia Reference Specialist in the Asian Division, provided advice and clarifications on many points. William Tuchrello, director of the Library's Overseas Office, Jakarta, and his staff assisted in providing photographs and published information from Indonesia.

Jennifer Foley compiled draft editions of the maps and identified many of the photographs used in the book. Graphics support was provided by Christopher Robinson, who prepared the book's graphics and also performed the photocomposition and preparation of the final digital manuscript for the printer. Both he and Katarina David of the Federal Research Division performed digital conversion of photographs and illustrations used in the study.

Thanks go to Harris Iskandar, education and cultural attaché of the Embassy of Indonesia in Washington, DC, for providing useful research information on his country. Finally, the authors acknowledge the generosity of individuals and public and private organizations who allowed their photographs to be used in this study; they have been acknowledged in the illustration captions.

Contents

Joel C. Kuipers

Blair A. King

List of Figures

Preface

This edition of *Indonesia: A Country Study* replaces the previous edition, published in 1993. Like its predecessor, this study attempts to review the history and treat in a concise manner the dominant social, political, economic, and military aspects of contemporary Indonesia. Sources of information included books, scholarly journals, foreign and domestic newspapers, official reports of governments and international organizations, and numerous periodicals and Web sites on Indonesian and Southeast Asian affairs.

To avoid confusion over the spelling and pronunciation of Indonesian names and terms, the so-called new spelling (*ejaan yang disempurnakan*—EYD—perfected spelling) of 1972, which replaced an earlier system based in part on pre–World War II Dutch spellings, has been used throughout, even when it differs from the personal preference of individuals. The usage and alphabetization of Indonesian names may also pose problems for those familiar with Indonesian cultures as well as the preferences of individuals and fashions of any given period. The procedure followed in this volume is to alphabetize according to the last name of the individual when two or more names exist. Thus, works by the historian Sartono Kartodirjo are listed under "Kartodirjo, Sartono." The military figure Sarwo Edhie Wibowo is alphabetized under "Wibowo." This procedure is at odds with some earlier Indonesian practices, but it has the advantage of being easily understood internationally and is becoming more common in Indonesia itself. Some individuals are generally referred to using the first element(s) of their name—such as "Sarwo Edhie" rather than Wibowo—and others by the last element, such as Ibnu Sutowo, who is referred to as "Sutowo" or "Colonel Sutowo" or "Colonel Ibnu Sutowo" but not as "Ibnu." Some individuals, such as former presidents Sukarno and Suharto, used only one name, and former president Megawati Sukarnoputri is always referred to as Megawati and not Sukarnoputri, which is a contrived surname. Thus, the late President Abdurrahman Wahid is referred to as President Wahid and President Susilo Bambang Yudhoyono as President Yudhoyono. In this regard, this book follows the practices observed in contemporary Indonesian discourse and print media, even if these themselves are, in a few instances, inconsistent. Some Islamic terms familiar to readers in transliteration from Arabic are spelled here in transliteration according to EYD.

The spelling of contemporary place-names conforms in most cases to the system approved by the U.S. Board on Geographic Names (BGN);

spellings of some names, however, cannot be verified, as the BGN itself notes. Indonesian spellings are given for all modern province names, such as Jawa Tengah (Central Java). Similarly, the names Sumatera Utara (North Sumatra) and Papua Barat (West Papua) are used to refer to provinces on the islands of Sumatra and Papua, respectively. Conventional spellings of names referring more generally to portions of Java, for example, are given in lower case and the form "eastern Java," "southern Sumatra," and so on.

Because of the widespread use of acronyms and contractions in Indonesia, the ones used in this edition are listed in a table along with an English translation at the front of the book (see table A). A chronology of major historical events also is provided (see table B). Measurements are given in the metric system; a conversion table is provided to assist readers wanting to convert metric measurements (see table C).

Readers are encouraged to consult the chapter bibliographies at the end of the book, which include a number of general and specialized, primarily English-language-source bibliographies that will lead readers to further resources on Indonesia. Also, brief comments on some of the more valuable and enduring sources recommended for further reading appear at the end of each chapter. A glossary also is included.

The body of the text reflects information available as of July 2010. Certain other parts of the text, however, have been updated: the Chronology and Introduction discuss significant events that have occurred since the completion of research, and the Country Profile and portions of some chapters include updated information as available. Indonesia completed its decennial census in May 2010, but the full results were not available for inclusion in the main text of this book.

Table A. Selected Acronyms and Contractions

Acronym or Contraction	Full Name
ABRI	Angkatan Bersenjata Republik Indonesia (Armed Forces of the Republic of Indonesia); used from 1962 to 1999 and included the National Police; thereafter TNI (*q.v.*) has been used.
AEC	ASEAN (*q.v.*) Economic Community
AFTA	ASEAN (*q.v.*) Free Trade Area
AIDS	acquired immune deficiency syndrome
AJI	Aliansi Jurnalis Independen (Alliance of Independent Journalists)
Akmil	Akademi Militer (Military Academy)
Apodeti	Associação Popular Democrática Timorense (Timorese Popular Democratic Association)
APRI	Angkatan Perang Republik Indonesia (Armed Forces of the Republic of Indonesia); successor to APRIS (*q.v.*) in August 1950, used until 1962; APRI was identical to TNI (*q.v.*), which was the more commonly used term.
APRIS	Angkatan Perang Republik Indonesia Serikat (Armed Forces of the Federal Republic of Indonesia [RIS, *q.v.*]); used in 1949 and early 1950, when APRIS merged with KNIL (*q.v.*).
ARF	ASEAN (*q.v.*) Regional Forum
ASA	Aksi Stop AIDS (Stop AIDS [*q.v.*] Action)
ASEAN	Association of Southeast Asian Nations (see Glossary)
ASNLF	Aceh Sumatra National Liberation Front
Babinsa	Bintara Desa (village NCO, *q.v.*)
Bais	Badan Intelijens Stratejis (Armed Forces Strategic Intelligence Body)
Bakin	Badan Koordinasi Intelijen Nasional (National Intelligence Coordinating Board)
BAN–PT	Badan Akreditasi Nasional Perguruan Tinggi (National Accreditation Agency for Higher Education)
Bappenas	Badan Perencanaan Pembangunan Nasional (National Development Planning Board)
Bareskrim	Badan Reserse Kriminal (Crime Investigation Agency); also see Kabareskrim
Bimas	Bimbingan Massal (Mass Guidance System)
BIN	Badan Intelijen Nasional (National Intelligence Agency)
BKKBN	Badan Koordinasi Keluarga Berencana Nasional (National Family Planning Coordinating Agency)
BKPM	Badan Koordinasi Penanaman Modal (Capital Investment Coordinating Board)
BKR	Badam Keamanan Rakyat (People's Security Forces); used August 22–October 5, 1945, when it was succeeded by the TKR (*q.v.*).
BPK	Badan Pemeriksa Keuangan (Finance Audit Board)
BPPN	Badan Penyehatan Perbanken Nasional (Indonesian Bank Restructuring Agency; also abbreviated as IBRA, *q.v.*)
BPPT	Badan Pusat Pengembangan Teknologi (Agency for the Study and Application of Technology)
BPS	Badan Pusat Statistik (Central Statistical Office; also referred to as Central Bureau of Statistics and Statistics Indonesia)
BPTRI	Balai Perguruan Tinggi Republik Indonesia (Republic of Indonesia Institute for Higher Education)
BPUPK	Badan Penyelidik Usaha–Usaha Persiapan Kemerdekaan (Commission to Investigate Preparatory Measures for Independence)

Table A. Selected Acronyms and Contractions (Continued)

Acronym or Contraction	Full Name
BRI	Bank Rakyat Indonesia (Indonesian People's Bank)
BRR	Badan Rehabilitasi dan Rekonstruksi (Rehabilitation and Reconstruction Agency)
Bulog	Badan Urusan Logistik (National Logistical Supply Organization)
Caltex	California Texas Oil Company
CEMEX	formerly Cementos Mexicanos
CGI	Consultative Group on Indonesia
CIA	Central Intelligence Agency (U.S.)
CMI	Crisis Management Initiative
COHA	Cessation of Hostilities Agreement
DDR	Deutsche Demokratische Republik (Democratic Republic of Germany—or East Germany)
Depdiknas	Departmen Pendidikan Nasional (Department of National Education)
Dephan	Departmen Pertahanan (Department of Defense; since 1999)
DPD	Dewan Perwakilan Daerah (Regional Representative Council)
DPR	Dewan Perwakilan Rakyat (People's Representative Council)
DPRD	Dewan Perwakilan Rakyat Daerah (Regional People's Representative Council)
EU	European Union
EYD	*ejaan yang disempurnakan* (perfected, or new, spelling of Bahasa Indonesia language, adopted in 1972)
FDI	foreign direct investment
FMF	Foreign Military Financing (U.S.)
FMS	Foreign Military Sales (U.S.)
FNC	Fabrique Nationale Carabine (National Factory Carbine, a carbine made by Fabrique Nationale de Herstel, Belgium)
FPI	Front Pembela Islam (Islamic Defenders' Front)
FSPSI	Federation Serikat Pekerja Seluruh Indonesia (All-Indonesian Workers' Union Federation)
Fretilin	Frente Revolucionária do Timor Leste Independente (Revolutionary Front for an Independent East Timor—see Glossary)
FY	fiscal year (see Glossary)
GAM	Gerakan Aceh Merdeka (Free Aceh Movement)
GDP	gross domestic product (see Glossary)
Gerindra	Gerakan Indonesia Raya (Great Indonesia Movement, as in Partai Gerindra or Gerindra Party)
Gestapu	Gerakan September Tiga Puluh (September 30 Movement, also G30S)
GMT	Greenwich Mean Time
Golkar	Golongan Karya (Functional Groups—see Glossary)
GPK	Gerakan Pengacauan Keamanan (Security Disturbance Movement)
Hankam	Departmen Pertahanan dan Keamanan (Department of Defense and Security; prior to 1999)
Hankamrata	Pertahanan dan Keamanan Rakyat Total (Total People's Defense)
Hanura	Hati Nurani Rakyat (People's Conscience Party, as in Partai Hanura or Hanura Party)
HIS	Hollands–Inlandsche School (Dutch–Native Schools)

Table A. Selected Acronyms and Contractions (Continued)

Acronym or Contraction	Full Name
HIV	human immunodeficiency virus
HMI	Himpunan Mahasiswa Islam (Islamic University Student Association)
IAIN	Institut Agama Islam Negara (State Institute for Islamic Religion)
IBRA	Indonesian Bank Restructuring Agency (also BPPN, *q.v.*)
ICMI	Ikatan Cendekiawan Muslim Indonesia (Indonesian Muslim Intellectuals' Association)
IGGI	Inter-Governmental Group on Indonesia
ILO	International Labour Organisation
IMET	International Military Education and Training (U.S.)
IMF	International Monetary Fund
Indra	Indonesian Debt Restructuring Agency (Badan Restrukturalisasi Utang Luar Negeri Perusahaan Indonesia, which in full translates as Agency for Structuring the Foreign Debt of Indonesian Industries)
INTERFET	International Force in East Timor
Interpol	International Criminal Police Organization
IPKI	Ikatan Pendukung Kemerdekaan Indonesia (League of the Supporters of Indonesian Independence)
IPTN	Industri Pesawat Terbang Nusantara (Archipelago Aircraft Industry)
ISDV	Indische Sociaal-Democratische Vereeniging (Indies Social-Democratic Association)
IVS	Indonesische Verbond van Studerenden (Indonesian Student Association)
Jabodetabek	Jakarta, Bogor, Depok, Tangerang, and Bekasi
Jabotabek	Jakarta, Bogor, Tangerang, and Bekasi
JIL	Jaringan Islam Liberal (Network for Liberal Islam)
Kabareskrim	Kepala Badan Reserse Kriminal (head of Crime Investigation Agency); also see Bareskrim
Kasum	Kepala Staff Umum (Chief of the General Staff)
KNIL	Koninklijk Nederlandsch Indisch Leger (Royal Netherlands Indies Army)
KNIP	Komite Nasional Indonesia Pusat (Central National Committee)
Kodam	Komando Daerah Militer (Military Regional Command)
Kodim	Komando Distrik Militer (Military District Command)
Kohanudnas	Komando Pertahanan Udara Nasional (National Air Defense Command)
Komnas FBPI	Komite Nasional Pengendalian Flu Burung Kesiapsiagaan Menghadapi Pandemi Influenza (National Committee for Avian Influenza Control and Pandemic Influenza Preparedness)
Ko–Op	Komando Operasi (Operations Command)
Kopassandha	Komando Pasukan Sandi Yudha (Army Special Forces Command); also see Kopassus
Kopassus	Komando Pasukan Khusus (Army Special Forces Command)
Kopkamtib	Komando Operasi Pemulihan Keamanan dan Ketertiban (Operational Command for the Restoration of Security and Order)
Koramil	Komando Rayon Militer (Military Subdistrict Command)
Korem	Komando Resor Militer (Military Resort, or Garrison, Command)
Kostrad	Komando Strategis Cadangan Angkatan Darat (Army Strategic Reserve Command)
KPK	Komisi Pemberantasan Korupsi (Corruption Eradication Commission)

Table A. Selected Acronyms and Contractions (Continued)

Acronym or Contraction	Full Name
KPPU	Komisi Pengawas Persaingan Usaha (Commission for the Oversight of Business Competition)
KPU	Komisi Pemilihan Umum (General Elections Commission)
LatGap	Latihan Gabungan (Joint Exercise)
Lemhanas	Lembaga Ketahanan Nasional (National Resiliency Institute)
LNG	liquefied natural gas
LSM	*lembaga swadaya masyarakat* (nongovernmental organizations), also sometimes *ornop* (*q.v.*)
Lusi	Lumpur Sidoarjo (Sidoarjo mud volcano)
Manipol	Manifes Politik (Political Manifesto)
Masyumi	Majelis Syuro Muslimin Indonesia (Consultative Council of Indonesian Muslims)
MDMA	methylenedioxymethamphetamine (Ecstasy)
MPR	Majelis Permusyawaratan Rakyat (People's Consultative Assembly)
MPR(S)	Majelis Permusyawaratan Rakyat (Sementara) (Provisional People's Consultative Assembly)
MRP	Majelis Rakyat Papua (Papuan People's Council)
NAD	Nanggroe Aceh Darussalam (State of Aceh, Abode of Peace, a name used from 2000 to 2009)
Nasakom	Nasionalisme, Agama, Komunisme (Nationalism, Religion, Communism)
NCO	noncommissioned officer
NGO	nongovernmental organization; also see LSM and *ornop*
NHM	Nederlandsche Handel–Maatschappij (Netherlands Trading Association)
NICA	Netherlands Indies Civil Administration
NII	Negara Islam Indonesia (Islamic State of Indonesia)
NMDP	national medium-term development plan
OECD	Organisation for Economic Co-operation and Development
OIC	Organization of the Islamic Conference
OPEC	Organization of the Petroleum Exporting Countries (see Glossary)
OPM	Organisasi Papua Merdeka (Free Papua Organization)
ornop	*organisasi nonpemerintah* (nongovernmental organizations); also sometimes LSM (*q.v.*)
OSVIA	Opleidingschool voor Inlandsche Ambtenaren (School for Training Native Government Officials)
P4	Pedoman Penghayatan dan Pengamalan Pancasila (Guide to Realizing and Experiencing the Pancasila)
PAN	Partai Amanat Nasional (National Mandate Party)
panja	*panitia kerja* (working committee)
pansus	*panitia khusus* (special committee)
Panwaslu	Panitia Pengawas Pemilu (Election Oversight Committee)
Parkindo	Partai Kristen Indonesia (Indonesian Christian Party)
Partindo	Partai Indonesia (Indonesian Party)
PasMar	Pasukan Marinir (Marine Corps Group)

Table A. Selected Acronyms and Contractions (Continued)

Acronym or Contraction	Full Name
PBB	Partai Bulan Bintang (Star and Moon Party); also used for Perserikata Bangsa-Bangsa (United Nations)
PBR	Partai Bintang Reformasi (Reform Star Party)
PD	Partai Demokrat (Democrat Party)
PDI	Partai Demokrasi Indonesia (Indonesian Democracy Party)
PDI–P	Partai Demokrasi Indonesia–Perjuangan (Indonesian Democracy Party–Struggle)
PDP	Partai Demokrasi Pembaruan (Democracy Renewal Party)
PDS	Partai Damai Sejahtera (Prosperous Peace Party)
Pelni	Perusahaan Layaran Nasional Indonesia (Indonesian National Shipping Company)
Permesta	Perjuangan Semesta Alam (Universal Struggle); also Piagam Perjuangan Semesta Alam (Universal Struggle Charter)
Pertamina	Perusahaan Pertambangan Minyak dan Gas Bumi Negara (State Oil and Natural Gas Mining Company, but translated as State Oil Company by Pertamina itself)
Perti	Persatuan Tarbiyah Islamiyah (Islamic Educational Movement)
Peta	Pembela Tanah Air (Defenders of the Fatherland)
Petrus	*penembakan misterius* (mysterious shootings) or *pembunuhan misterius* (mysterious killings)—Both terms have been used in the Indonesian press.
PID	Politiek Inlichtingen Dienst (Political Intelligence Service)
PIR	Perkebunan Inti Rakyat (Nucleus People's Estate)
PK	Partai Keadilan (Justice Party)
PKB	Partai Kebangkitan Bangsa (National Awakening Party)
PKH	Perserikatan Komunis di Hindia (Communist Association of the Indies)
PKI	Partai Komunis Indonesia (Indonesian Communist Party; see Glossary)
PKPI	Partai Keadilan dan Persatuan Indonesia (Indonesian Justice and Unity Party)
PKS	Partai Keadilan Sejahtera (Prosperous Justice Party)
PLN	Perusahaan Listrik Nasional (National Electric Company)
PMI	Partai Muslimin Indonesia (Muslim Party of Indonesia)
PNI	Partai Nasional Indonesia (Indonesian Nationalist Party)
PNI–M	Partai Nasional Indonesia–Marhaenisme (Indonesian Nationalist Party–Marhaenism)
Polda	Polisi Daerah (Regional Police)
Polri	Kepolisian Republik Indonesia (National Police of Indonesia)
PP	Partai Pelopor (Pioneer Party)
PPKI	Panitia Persiapan Kemerdekaan Indonesia (Indonesian Independence Preparatory Committee)
PPP	Partai Persatuan Pembangunan (Development Unity Party)
PRD	Partai Rakyat Demokratik (Democratic People's Party)
PRRI	Pemerintah Revolusioner Republik Indonesia (Revolutionary Government of the Republic of Indonesia)
PSII	Partai Sarekat Islam Indonesia (Islamic Association Party of Indonesia)
pungli	*pungutan liar* (illegal levies, that is, kickbacks)
Putera	Pusat Tenaga Rakyat (Center of the People's Power)
RCTI	Rajawali Citra Televisi Indonesia (Hawk Television Indonesia)

Table A. Selected Acronyms and Contractions (Continued)

Acronym or Contraction	Full Name
Repelita	Rencana Pembangunan Lima Tahun (five-year economic development plan; see Glossary)
RIS	Republik Indonesia Serikat (Federal Republic of Indonesia)
RMS	Republik Maluku Selatan (Republic of South Maluku)
ROTC	Reserve Officers' Training Corps (U.S.)
Rp	rupiah (see Glossary)
Satelindo	Satelit Palapa Indonesia
SBI	Sertifikat Bank Indonesia (Bank Indonesia Certificate)
SBSI	Serikat Buruh Sejahtera Indonesia (Indonesian Prosperous Workers' Union)
SBY	Susilo Bambang Yudhoyono
SCTV	Surya Citra Televisi (Sun Television)
Sesko TNI	Sekolah Staf dan Komando TNI (TNI [q.v.] Command and Staff College)
SIJORI	Singapore, Johor, and Riau
SIRA	Sentral Informasi Referendum Aceh (Aceh Referendum Information Center)
SPSI	Serikat Pekerja Seluruh Indonesia (All-Indonesian Workers' Union)
Stanvac	Standard-Vacuum Oil Company
STOVIA	School tot Opleiding van Inlandsche Artsen (School for Training Indigenous Doctors)
Supersemar	Surat Perintah Sebelas Maret (Letter of Instruction of March 11)
TAC	Treaty of Amity and Cooperation in Southeast Asia
TII	Tentara Islam Indonesia (Islamic Army of Indonesia)
Timtas Tipikor	Tim Pemberantasan Tindak Pidana Korupsi (Coordinating Team for Eliminating Crimes of Corruption)
Tipikor Court	Pengadilan Tindak Pidana Korupsi (Corruption Crimes Court)
TKR	Tentara Keamanan Rakyat (People's Security Army); used as of October 5, 1945, as successor to BKR (q.v.); also Tentara Keselamatan Rakyat (People's Security Army) as of January 1, 1946.
TNI	Tentara Nasional Indonesia (Indonesian National Army); from 1947 to 1962 and again starting in April 1999 but now usually translated as Indonesian National Armed Forces; also see ABRI, APRI, and APRIS.
TNI–AD	Tentara Nasional Indonesia–Angkatan Darat (Army of the Republic of Indonesia)
TNI–AL	Tentara Nasional Indonesia–Angkatan Laut (Navy of the Republic of Indonesia)
TNI–AU	Tentara Nasional Indonesia–Angkatan Udara (Air Force of the Republic of Indonesia)
TPI	Televisi Pendidikan Indonesia (Indonesian Educational Television)
TPN	Timor Putra Nasional (National Son Timor)
TRI	Tentara Republik Indonesia (National Army of the Republic of Indonesia); used as of January 24, 1946, as successor to TKR (q.v.).
TVRI	Televisi Republik Indonesia (Television of the Republic of Indonesia)
UIN	Universitas Islam Negara (State Muslim University)
UN	United Nations
UNDP	United Nations Development Programme
UNESCO	United Nations Educational, Scientific, and Cultural Organization
UNICEF	United Nations Children's Fund
UNTAC	United Nations Transitional Authority in Cambodia

Table A. Selected Acronyms and Contractions (Continued)

Acronym or Contraction	Full Name
UNTAET	United Nations Transitional Administration in East Timor
USDEK	Undang–undang Dasar '45, Socialisme à la Indonesia, Demokrasi Perpimpin, Ekonomi Terpimpin, Kepribadian Indonesia (1945 Constitution, Indonesian Socialism, Guided Democracy, Guided Economy, and Indonesian Identity, usually paired with Manipol [*q.v.*] to read Manipol–USDEK)
USINDO	United States–Indonesia Society
UVI	Universiteit van Indonesië (University of Indonesia; later changed to Universitas Indonesia [University of Indonesia])
VAT	value-added tax
VCI	Véhicule de Combat d'Infanterie (Combat Infantry Vehicle [France])
VOC	Verenigde Oostindische Compagnie (United East Indies Company)
YKP	Yayasan Kesehatan Perempuan (Foundation for Women's Health)
ZOPFAN	Zone of Peace, Freedom, and Neutrality

Table B. Chronology of Important Events

By ca. 1.8 million B.C.	*Homo erectus*, an early hominid, living in Java.
By ca. 600,000 B.C.	Fairly sophisticated hominid cultures scattered throughout the archipelago.
Ca. 40,000 B.C.	Earliest verifiable modern human (*Homo sapiens*) remains (Sulawesi and Java).
Ca. 3,000 B.C.	Austronesians begin voyaging from the Philippines into Indonesian archipelago.
Beginning ca. 400 B.C.	Development of regional trade linking present-day China, Vietnam, India, the Mediterranean, and other points to the archipelago.
Ca. A.D. 375	Kutai (eastern Kalimantan) and Taruma (Java) rise as Indian-influenced kingdoms.
Mid-sixth century	Kingdom of Srivijaya rises in southern Sumatra, in later centuries spreads to western Java and the Malay Peninsula.
Ca. 732	Rise of Mataram (central Java) under Sanjaya.
Ca. 770–820	Construction of the Buddhist temple Borobudur (central Java).
Ca. 820–50	Construction of the Hindu temple complex at Prambanan (central Java).
929–1292	Rise of Mataram in eastern Java, followed by Kediri and Singhasari; conflict with Bali and Srivijaya.
1211	Death of Sultan Sulaiman of Lamreh, northern Sumatra, first verifiable Muslim ruler in the archipelago.
1294	Rise of Majapahit (eastern Java) in wake of Mongol incursion.
Mid-14th century	Golden age of expanded Hindu-Buddhist Majapahit kingdom under Hayam Wuruk (Rajasanagara, r. 1350–89) and Prime Minister Gajah Mada (in office 1331–64).
1364	Gajah Mada dies; architect of an expanded Majapahit empire throughout much of archipelago.
1405–33	Seven Chinese maritime expeditions led by Zheng He, some of which land in Java, Sumatra, and points as distant as East Africa.
1511	Portuguese occupy Melaka, on Malay Peninsula, and arrive a year later in Ternate, Maluku, where they build a fort in 1522.
1527	Final days of Majapahit as the small Muslim port state of Demak defeats Majapahit capital at Kediri, eastern Java.
1595–1601	First Dutch ships in archipelago.
1602	United East Indies Company (VOC—see table A) established by Dutch.
1607–36	Rule of Iskandar Muda, sultanate of Aceh, northern Sumatra.
1610–80	VOC gradually extends dominance over eastern archipelago, for example in Ternate, Hitu, and southern Sulawesi.
1613–46	Sultan Agung rules in an expanding Mataram, central Java.
1619–21	VOC establishes control over Jayakerta (present-day Jakarta).
1704–55	Javanese wars of succession, in which the VOC becomes embroiled.
1723	Coffee becomes a VOC monopoly in a forced-delivery system in Priangan, western Java.
1755	Treaty of Giyanti (Java).
1799–1800	VOC charter lapses following bankruptcy; holdings taken over by Netherlands state.
1808–16	Rule of Java and other Dutch territories in the archipelago by French (under Herman Willem Daendals, 1808–11) and British (under Thomas Stamford Raffles, 1811–16).
1816	Dutch control of Java and other territories reestablished.
1821–37	Padri Wars in Minangkabau region of western Sumatra.

Table B. Chronology of Important Events (Continued)

1824	Anglo–Dutch treaty recognizes spheres of influence in Malay Peninsula and Sumatra, respectively.
1825–30	Java War; last Javanese aristocratic resistance to Dutch rule; Prince Diponegoro central figure.
1830	Introduction of the Cultivation System by Johannes van den Bosch.
1870	Sugar Act and Agrarian Act enacted, end of the Cultivation System.
1873	First state-sponsored railroad in archipelago, central Java.
1873–1903	Aceh War.
1890	Royal Dutch Company for Exploration of Petroleum Sources in the Netherlands Indies established.
1901	Ethical Policy inaugurated.
1902	Inauguration of Transmigration Program, in which Javanese move to Outer Islands (see Glossary).
1907	Royal Dutch Shell established through merger of Dutch and British companies.
1908	First modern political organization—Budi Utomo (Noble Endeavor)—established.
1909	Sarekat Dagang Islam (Islamic Trade Association) founded in Surakarta, central Java; becomes Sarekat Islam (Islamic Association) in 1912.
1911	Indies Party (Indische Partij) founded.
1912	Muhammadiyah (Followers of Muhammad) established in Yogyakarta.
1914	Indies Social-Democratic Association (ISDV) founded, forerunner of the Communist Association of the Indies (PKH, 1920) and Indonesian Communist Party (PKI, 1924).
1926	Nahdlatul Ulama (literally, revival of the religious teachers, sometimes referred to as Council of Scholars) founded in eastern Java.
July 1927	Sukarno and others establish the Indonesian Nationalist Union (PNI) in western Java; becomes Indonesian Nationalist Party (PNI) in 1928.
February 1933	Mutiny on Dutch warship De Zeven Provinciën begins a period of greater political pressure.
July 1936	Sutarjo Petition, calling for a conference on the possibility of Indies autonomy within the constitution of the Netherlands, accepted by Volksraad, later rejected by Dutch government.
March 1942	Dutch surrender control of Indies to Japanese military forces, Kalijati, western Java.
October 1943	Beginning of Peta (Java) and Giyugun (Sumatra), Japanese-designed defense force.
September 1944	Japan promises independence.
June 1, 1945	Sukarno announces the Pancasila (see Glossary).
August 15, 1945	Japan surrenders.
August 17, 1945	Sukarno and Mohammad Hatta proclaim independent Republic of Indonesia.
August 18, 1945	Constitution promulgated.
September 29, 1945	First Allied troops (British and British Indian) land at Jakarta.
November 10, 1945	Battle of Surabaya, eastern Java.
November 12, 1946	Linggajati Agreement initialed; recognizes Republican rule on Java and Sumatra and the Netherlands–Indonesian Union under the Dutch crown; Indonesia ratifies May 25, 1947.
July 21, 1947	First Dutch "police action" begins (ends August 4, 1947).
January 19, 1948	Renville Agreement signed.

Table B. Chronology of Important Events (Continued)

September 18, 1948	Madiun Affair erupts in eastern Java, pitching the PKI against the Republic.
December 19, 1948	Second Dutch "police action" begins (ends January 5, 1949).
January 1949	United Nations (UN) Security Council demands reinstatement of Republican rule.
August 23–November 2, 1949	Round Table Conference held at The Hague prepares for formal transfer of sovereignty.
December 27, 1949	Dutch recognize sovereignty of Federal Republic of Indonesia (RIS).
January–April 1950	Separatist revolts begin in western Java and Maluku Islands.
August 17, 1950	RIS and other states form new unitary Republic of Indonesia under amendment to RIS constitution; Sukarno confirmed as president.
April 18–24, 1955	Asia–Africa Conference held in Bandung, Jawa Barat Province.
September 29, 1955	First national elections.
May 8, 1956	Indonesia leaves Netherlands–Indonesian Union.
December 1, 1956	Hatta resigns as vice president in protest against Sukarno's growing authoritarianism; office remains vacant until 1973.
February 21, 1957	Sukarno proposes Guided Democracy concept.
March 14, 1957	Sukarno declares martial law.
December 1957	Dutch nationals expelled; private companies nationalized; armed forces take greater role in economic affairs.
February–May 1958	Anti-Sukarno revolts in Sumatra and Sulawesi; Sukarno accuses United States of complicity.
July 5, 1959	1945 constitution restored.
August 17, 1959	Political Manifesto (Manipol) announced, gives ideological content to Guided Democracy.
March 1960	New legislature organized with control given to functional groups, including the military; PKI emerges stronger.
May 1963	Indonesian authority established in West New Guinea (renamed Irian Barat).
September 23, 1963	Sukarno issues statements threatening independence of new state of Malaysia; three-year Confrontation (see Glossary) begins.
October 1964	Golongan Karya (Golkar—see Glossary) formed by army leaders.
January 1, 1965	Sukarno withdraws Indonesia from the UN.
September 30– October 1, 1965	Abortive, communist-inspired coup launched.
October 1965–March 1966	Decline of Sukarno, rise of Suharto; Guided Democracy eclipsed; mass killings of PKI members and suspected affiliates; tens of thousands jailed.
March 11, 1966	Sukarno transfers authority to Suharto (Supersemar—see Glossary); marks rise of New Order.
March 12, 1966	PKI formally banned.
August 11, 1966	Confrontation with Malaysia ends.
September 23, 1966	Indonesia rejoins UN.
March 12, 1967	Suharto appointed acting president by Provisional People's Consultative Assembly (MPR(S)); New Order era officially acknowledged; relations with China "frozen."
August 8, 1967	Indonesia joins four other countries in founding new Association of Southeast Asian Nations (ASEAN—see Glossary).
October 1967	Demonstrators attack Chinese Embassy in Jakarta, diplomatic relations severed.
March 27, 1968	Suharto elected president by MPR(S).

Table B. Chronology of Important Events *(Continued)*

September 1969	Irian Barat (Indonesian New Guinea) becomes Indonesia's twenty-sixth province following Act of Free Choice among tribal leaders; name changed to Irian Jaya in 1972; in 2001 renamed Papua, and in 2003 divided into three separate provinces (only two of which had been established as of 2010).
July 3, 1971	Golkar wins majority of popular vote in second general elections.
January 1973	Development Unity Party (PPP) and Indonesian Democracy Party (PDI) formed.
March 12, 1973	Suharto reelected to second term as president, and Hamengkubuwono IX elected vice president by People's Consultative Assembly (MPR).
January 15, 1974	Malari Affair, Jakarta.
December 7, 1975	Indonesian armed forces invade East Timor.
July 15, 1976	East Timor becomes Timor Timur, Indonesia's twenty-seventh province.
May 2, 1977	Third general elections; Golkar majority confirmed.
March 22, 1978	Suharto reelected to third term as president, Adam Malik elected vice president by MPR.
May 5, 1980	Petition of 50 accuses Suharto of one-man, antidemocratic rule; group is suppressed.
May 4, 1982	Fourth general elections; Golkar majority maintained.
March 11, 1983	Suharto reelected to fourth term as president, Umar Wirahadikusumah elected vice president, by MPR.
April 1983	Beginning of anonymous "mysterious killings" (*petrus*) of criminals and others in many large cities, especially on Java.
April 23, 1987	Fifth general elections; Golkar majority increases.
March 10, 1988	Suharto reelected to fifth term as president, Sudharmono elected as vice president, by MPR.
July 1990–October 1991	Paris International Conference on Cambodia, co-chaired by Indonesia and France, features Jakarta's role as peacemaker in Cambodia.
August 8, 1990	Indonesia and China reestablish diplomatic relations.
November 12, 1991	Armed Forces of the Republic of Indonesia (ABRI) troops fire on funeral at Santa Cruz Cemetery, Dili, East Timur, killing 50–250.
March 1992	Dutch-chaired Inter-Governmental Group on Indonesia (IGGI—see Glossary) disbanded at Indonesia's insistence, replaced with Consultative Group on Indonesia (CGI—see Glossary) without Dutch participation.
June 9, 1992	Sixth general elections confirm Golkar majority.
September 1992	Indonesia assumes chairmanship of the Nonaligned Movement during Jakarta Summit.
March 10, 1993	Suharto reelected to sixth term as president, General Try Sutrisno elected as vice president, by MPR.
June 21, 1994	Governments bans *Tempo* and other prominent news magazines.
December 18, 1995	Indonesia and Australia sign security cooperation agreement.
July 27, 1996	Government closes ousted opposition leader Megawati Sukarnoputri's PDI headquarters in Jakarta; widespread rioting, looting, and arson ensue in capital and later spread across Java and elsewhere.
May 29, 1997	Seventh general elections confirm Golkar majority.
October 27, 1997	Amidst stock market panic, Indonesia–International Monetary Fund (IMF) agreement leads to closure of 16 Indonesian banks and restriction of credit.
March 3, 1998	Economic crisis deepens as foreign reserves dramatically shrink.
March 21, 1998	Suharto reelected to seventh term as president, Bacharuddin J. (B. J.) Habibie elected as vice president, by MPR.

Table B. Chronology of Important Events (Continued)

May 12–14, 1998	Following shooting of Trisakti University students by security forces, rioting in Jakarta leads to mob-led destruction in Chinese Indonesian community, closure of foreign embassies, and more than 1,000 deaths.
May 21, 1998	Suharto resigns from presidency; succeeded by Vice President B. J. Habibie.
January 28, 1999	People's Representative Council (DPR) approves major changes to election laws, sets scene for June 7 national legislative elections.
June 7, 1999	First democratic parliamentary elections since 1955 held; Megawati's PDI–P wins 34 percent, Golkar 22 percent.
August 30, 1999	78.5 percent of Timor Timur voters in UN-supervised referendum reject broad autonomy from Indonesia, allowing province to become independent.
September 16, 1999	Indonesia abrogates 1995 security cooperation agreement with Australia over latter's involvement in East Timor.
October 20, 1999	Abdurrahman Wahid elected to presidency and Megawati Sukarnoputri to vice presidency by MPR.
February 1, 2001	Wahid censured by DPR for involvement in financial scandals; censured again April 30.
July 23, 2001	Wahid resigns amidst MPR impeachment proceedings; Megawati sworn in as fifth president.
May 20, 2002	Timor Timur Province (East Timor) becomes independent nation of Timor-Leste.
August 3, 2002	MPR amends constitution to allow direct election of president and vice president; provides for new legislative body, the Regional Representative Council (DPD).
October 12, 2002	202 die, more than 300 injured in terrorist bombings in Kuta tourist district in Bali.
August 5, 2003	14 killed, 149 injured in terrorist car bombing at JW Marriott hotel in Jakarta.
April 5, 2004	Elections held for DPD, DPR, and representatives for all provincial, regency, and municipality-level legislatures; Golkar wins 21 percent, PDI–P 18 percent.
July 5, 2004	Initial round of Indonesia's first direct popular election for president and vice president held; Susilo Bambang Yudhoyono wins 33 percent of votes to Megawati's 26 percent.
September 9, 2004	Terrorist suicide car bombing at Australian Embassy in Jakarta, kills 9, wounds 180.
September 20, 2004	Susilo Bambang Yudhoyono receives 60.9 percent of popular votes in presidential runoff election.
October 20, 2004	Yudhoyono sworn in as sixth president of Indonesia, Muhammad Yusuf Kalla sworn in as vice president.
December 26, 2004	Tsunamis devastate coastal areas throughout the Indian Ocean, killing 166,561 persons and displacing 203,817 in northern and western coastal areas of Sumatra.
March 28, 2005	Earthquake strikes Nias and other nearby islands, Sumatera Utara Province, killing 1,300 and displacing 40,000.
October 1, 2005	26 die, 129 injured by suicide attacks in Jimbara and Kuta, Bali.
November 13, 2006	Indonesia and Australia sign security agreements.
September 6, 2007	Russia's President Vladimir Putin signs arms agreement with Susilo Bambang Yudhoyono while visiting Jakarta.
December 3–14, 2007	UN Climate Change Conference held in Bali.
January 27, 2008	Former President Suharto dies in Jakarta hospital.
July 8, 2009	Yudhoyono reelected for second term as president with 60.8 percent of the first-round vote.

Table B. Chronology of Important Events (Continued)

July 17, 2009	Two suicide bombers kill 7, injure 53 at Ritz-Carlton and JW Marriott hotels in Jakarta.
September 30, 2009	7.6-magnitude earthquake strikes Padang, Sumatera Barat Province.
December 30, 2009	Former President Wahid dies in Jakarta hospital.
May 2010	Indonesia conducts national census.
August 2010	According to preliminary census data, population of Jakarta calculated at 9.58 million or nearly 4 percent of the national population of 237.6 million, surpassing all forecasts. Authorities discuss eventually moving government to new satellite town.
October–November 2010	Eruptions of Mount Merapi, Jawa Tengah Province, kill more than 300 and displace more than 135,000. Underwater earthquake of 7.7 magnitude and tsunami near Mentawai Islands, Sumatera Barat Province, kill more than 300 and displace 16,000.
April 15, 2011	Suicide bombing of a mosque inside a police compound in Cirebon, Jawa Tengah, during Friday prayers.
July 2011	Indonesia's two largest Muslim organizations—Nahdlatul Ulama and Muhammadiyah—with combined memberships of 110 million, publically condemn Islamic radicalism and use of violence.
August 2011	Following August 2 rallies in Jayapura, Papua Province, and other locations, condemning 1969 Act of Free Choice and calling for referendum on independence from Indonesia, Free Papua Organization (OPM) attacks Indonesian armed forces troops.

Table C. Metric Conversion Coefficients and Factors

When you know	Multiply by	To find
Millimeters..........................	0.04	inches
Centimeters..........................	0.39	inches
Meters..............................	3.3	feet
Kilometers	0.62	miles
Hectares	2.47	acres
Square kilometers.....................	0.39	square miles
Cubic meters.........................	35.3	cubic feet
Liters..............................	0.26	gallons
Kilograms...........................	2.2	pounds
Metric tons	0.98	long tons
....	1.1	short tons
....	2,204	pounds
Degrees Celsius (Centigrade).............	1.8 and add 32	degrees Fahrenheit

Country Profile

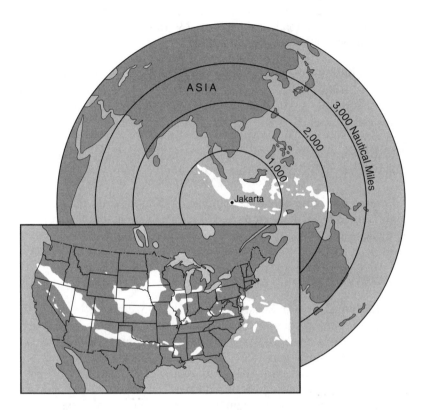

Country

Formal Name: Republic of Indonesia (Republik Indonesia; the word Indonesia was coined from the Greek *indos*—for India—and *nesos*— for island).

Short Form: Indonesia.

Term for Citizen(s): Indonesian(s).

Capital: Jakarta

Date of Independence: Proclaimed August 17, 1945, from the Netherlands. The Hague recognized Indonesian sovereignty on December 27, 1949.

Geography

Size: Total area 1,904,569 square kilometers, of which land area is 1,811,569 square kilometers and water area 93,000 square kilometers. Indonesia claims total sea area of 7.9 million square kilometers, including an exclusive economic zone.

Topography: Largest archipelagic nation in world, Indonesia encompasses 17,508 islands, five main islands, two major archipelagoes, and about 60 smaller archipelagoes. Larger islands are mountainous, with some peaks reaching 3,800 meters above sea level on western islands and more than 5,000 meters on Papua. Highest point is Puncak Jaya (5,030 meters) on Papua. The region is tectonically unstable, with some 400 volcanoes, 100 of which are active.

Climate: Maritime equatorial climate with high, even temperatures and heavy rainfall; temperatures and rainfall vary across the archipelago because of elevation and monsoon patterns. Average temperatures at or near sea level range from about 23° C to 31° C.

Society

Population: 245,613,043 estimated by U.S. government in July 2011 (237.6 million according to preliminary 2010 census figures released in August 2010); annual growth rate of 1.1 percent. In 2011 birthrate estimated at 18.1 births per 1,000, death rate 6.2 per 1,000, sex ratio at birth 1.05 males to each female. Approximately 52 percent of population living in urban areas, about 4 percent in Jakarta. Average population density 135 per square kilometer, with wide regional variation.

Ethnic Groups: About 350 recognized ethnolinguistic groups, 180 located in Papua; 13 languages have more than 1 million speakers. Javanese 41 percent of population, Sundanese 15 percent, coastal Malays 3.4 percent, Madurese 3.3 percent, and others 37.3 percent.

Languages: Official national language Bahasa Indonesia (or Indonesian), a modified form of Malay, with estimated 17 million to 30 million mother-tongue speakers and more than 140 million second-language speakers or readers. At least 731 other languages and dialects also spoken, some by large numbers: Javanese (83 million), Sundanese (30 million), Malay/Indonesian (17 million), and Madurese (nearly 6.7 million). Other languages with more than 1 million speakers each are Acehnese, Balinese, Banjarese, Batak (including Toba), Batawi, Buginese, Minangkabau, and Sasak; also various Chinese dialects. English widely used in government and business circles.

Religion: Indonesia largest Islamic population in world; per 2000 census most Indonesians (86.1 percent) Muslims (mostly Sunni—see Glossary) and observe Islamic practices to varying degrees; another 5.7 percent Protestant, 3 percent Roman Catholic, 1.8 percent Hindu, 3.4 other, including Buddhist, and unspecified religions. Animism practiced in some remote areas.

Health: Life expectancy estimated in 2011 at 71.3 years overall (68.8 years for males, 73.9 for females). Infant mortality 27.9 per 1,000. Recent data unavailable, but figures estimate 0.1 physicians, 0.8 nurses or midwives, and 0.6 hospital beds for every 1,000 inhabitants. Per-capita health expenditure in 2006 was 2.2 percent of gross domestic product (GDP—see Glossary), lowest among members of Association of Southeast Asian Nations (ASEAN—see Glossary).

Education and Literacy: Twelve-year public and private primary and secondary education system; the first nine years mandatory. In 2008 primary and secondary education, both private and public, included: 63,444 kindergartens, 144,228 six-year primary schools, 28,777 junior secondary schools, 10,762 general senior secondary schools, and 7,592 vocational senior secondary schools, enrolling total of 45.4 million students taught by 2.9 million teachers. Special education schools, for the physically and mentally disabled, numbered 1,686, with 73,322 students and 18,047 teachers. Higher education offered in 2,975 colleges, universities, and other tertiary institutions, with more than 4.2 million students. Adult literacy rate 90.4 percent in 2009.

Economy

Major Features: Following fast-paced growth during most of the New Order period (1966–98) and decline during and following 1997–98 Asian financial crisis, Indonesian economy characterized by decade of reform aimed at the financial sector and corrupt politicians and managers. Recent improvements in international trade, aid, and payments; in employment and income development; plus continued reorientation from agriculture to industry; and within the industrial sector itself, from oil and gas production to other manufacturing branches. Services, transportation, and communication sectors making greater contributions to economic growth.

Gross Domestic Product (GDP): In 2010 estimated at US$1.03 trillion; per-capita income based on GDP estimated in 2010 at US$4,200. GDP by sector, based on 2010 U.S. Government estimates, agriculture 15.3 percent, industry 47.1 percent, and services 37.6 percent.

Agriculture: Principal crops: cassava, cocoa, coconuts, coffee beans, corn, palm oil, rice, rubber, tea, and tobacco. Livestock: buffalo, cattle, goats, horses, pigs, poultry, and sheep. Inland and marine fishing valuable sources of domestic protein and export. Forestry also important.

Industry and Manufacturing: Oil and gas, food production, textiles, automobiles and other transportation equipment, electrical appliances, and chemical products.

Natural Resources: Bauxite, coal, copper, gold, natural gas, nickel, petroleum, and tin.

Exports: US$158.2 billion free on board estimated 2010. Major commodities (in order of importance): oil and gas, electrical appliances, plywood, textiles, rubber. Japan, China, United States, Singapore, South Korea, India, and Malaysia largest trading partners.

Imports: Totaled US$127.1 billion (cost, insurance, and freight) estimated 2010. Major imports (in order of importance): machinery and equipment, chemicals, fuels, foodstuffs. Singapore, China, Japan, United States, Malaysia, South Korea, and Thailand main trading partners.

Exchange Rate: US$1=8,481.76 rupiah at the end of July 2011.

Fiscal Year: Calendar year. Prior to 2001, the fiscal year ran from April 1 to March 31.

Transportation and Telecommunications

Inland and Coastal Waterways and Ports: 21,579 kilometers of navigable rivers, canals, and inland waterways. Extensive interisland and coastal maritime routes. Total 379 ports and harbors: deep-sea ports at Tanjung Priok (Jakarta), Tanjung Perak (Surabaya, Jawa Timur Province), Belawan (Medan, Sumatera Utara Province), and Makassar (Sulawesi Selatan Province); other major ports at Cilacap, Cirebon, and Semarang (all on Java), Dumai (Riau), Balikpapan (Kalimantan Timur), Kupang (Nusa Tenggara Timur Province), and Palembang (Sumatera Selatan Province); 127 ports capable of handling international shipping.

Roads: In 2008 total road network estimated at 437,760 kilometers; 59 percent paved, about 32 percent classified as highways.

Railroads: In 2010 some 5,042 kilometers railroad track, all government owned and operated; about 75 percent of railroad track located in Java, a minimal portion electrified. In 2007 some 175 million passengers carried, 17.3 million tons of freight transported in 2005.

Civil Aviation: 684 airports, 171 of which had paved runways, and 64 heliports in 2010. In 2004 more than 263 million kilometers flown, 26.7 million passengers carried (increased to 31 million in 2007), and 2.9 trillion tons-kilometers transported. State-owned domestic and international carrier Garuda Indonesia; subsidiary, Merpati Nusantara Airlines. Twenty-seven privately owned companies.

Pipelines: In 2010 Indonesia had pipelines as follows: 12 kilometers oil/gas/water, 44 kilometers water, 73 kilometers condensate/gas, 812 kilometers condensate, 1,370 kilometers refined products, 5,984 kilometers oil, and 7,165 kilometers gas.

Telecommunications: Some 7,000 local and regional radio stations, only 6 broadcast nationally; 11 national television channels, TVRI state-owned; 100 local television stations (2008). More than 20 million Internet users (2009).

Print Media: More than 50 principal daily newspapers published throughout archipelago, majority in Java; largest readership *Kompas* (Jakarta), circulation of 523,000; largest English-language dailies, both published in Jakarta, *Jakarta Post* and *Jakarta Globe,* both with print runs of 40,000.

Government and Politics

Party and Government: Republic based on separation of powers among executive, legislative, and judicial branches. Constitution of 1945 in force but amended in 1999–2002 to make once powerful, party-centered presidency subject to popular election and limited to two five-year terms. President and vice president elected on single ticket, usually representing coalition of parties; winning ticket must gain more than 60 percent of popular vote in the first round of voting and at least 20 percent of vote in half of provinces. If percentages not met, second-round runoff election held. President both chief of state and head of government. Legislative power vested in People's Representative Council (DPR) and less-powerful upper house, Regional Representative Council

(DPD). People's Consultative Assembly (MPR), which formerly elected the president and vice president, now joint sitting of the DPR and DPD but retains separate powers restricted to swearing in president and vice president, amending constitution, and having final say in impeachment process. Newly decentralized power of subnational authorities enshrined and delineated in amended constitution. Numerous political parties; Democrat Party (PD), Partai Golkar (Golkar Party), and Indonesian Democracy Party–Struggle (PDI–P) gained largest number of DPR seats in 2009 election.

Administrative Divisions: Thirty-three provincial-level units: 30 provinces (*propinsi*), two special regions (*daerah istimewa*; Aceh and Yogyakarta), and one special capital city region (*daerah khusus*; Jakarta). Provinces subdivided into districts, called municipalities (*kota*) in urban areas and regencies (*kabupaten*) in rural areas; below are subdistricts (*kecamatan*), with village (*desa*) at lowest tier. Indonesia in 2009 had 348 regencies, 91 municipalities, 5,263 subdistricts, and 66,979 villages.

Judicial System: Complex system with three inherited sources of law: customary or *adat* law, Islamic law (sharia), and Dutch colonial law. Judicial branch independent and coequal with executive and legislative branches, with Supreme Court and Constitutional Court at apex of judicial system. Four different court systems below Supreme Court: courts of general civil and criminal jurisdiction, religious courts, state administrative courts, and military courts.

Foreign Relations: Founding member of ASEAN in 1967, encourages regional solidarity among members while expanding relations with other regional and global powers. Tenuous but slowly improving relations with immediate non-ASEAN neighbors (Papua New Guinea and Timor-Leste) and working interdependencies with Malaysia and Singapore. Mutual suspicions color relations with Australia. Relations with China, once poor, warmer in recent years; trade important, as it also is with Japan and South Korea. Relations with United States warm and trade important.

National Security

Armed Forces: Indonesian National Armed Forces (Tentara Nasional Indonesia—TNI) had about 302,000 active-duty personnel in 2009, with army (TNI—Angkatan Darat), 233,000; navy (TNI—Angkatan Laut), 45,000, of which 20,000 marines and 1,000 part of naval aviation; and air force (TNI—Angkatan Udara), 24,000, of which 4,000 "quick-action" paratroopers.

Military Budget: US$3.4 billion, just over 1 percent of budget by 2009.

Military Units: Army—12 military regional commands (Kodams), each with one or more battalions, one of which is quick-reaction battalion; and two centrally controlled army strike force commands— Army Strategic Reserve Command (Kostrad) with two divisions and Army Special Forces Command (Kopassus), with three operational groups. Navy—two fleet commands (Eastern Fleet at Surabaya and Western Fleet at Jakarta), marine corps, air arm, and military sealift command. Air Force—three operational commands (Ko-Op I/West, Ko-Op II/East, and National Air Defense Command) and two support commands (Air Matériel Command and Air Training Command); four battalions of "quick-action" paratroopers.

Military Equipment: Army—light tanks, armored reconnaissance vehicles, armored personnel carriers (APCs), towed and self-propelled artillery, air defense guns, surface-to-air missiles, fixed-wing aircraft, helicopters. Navy—submarines, frigates, patrol and coastal combatants, mine warfare ships, amphibious forces ships, non-combatant fixed-wing aircraft, armed helicopters, transport helicopters; marines have light tanks, anti-infantry fighting vehicles, APCs, towed artillery pieces, air defense guns. Air Force—combat aircraft, maritime reconnaissance aircraft, tankers, transports, trainers, helicopters.

Auxiliary Forces: Many former official and unofficial paramilitary forces disbanded or integrated with TNI since 1999. National Police of Indonesia (Polri), since 1999 independent of TNI, numbered 280,000 in 2009.

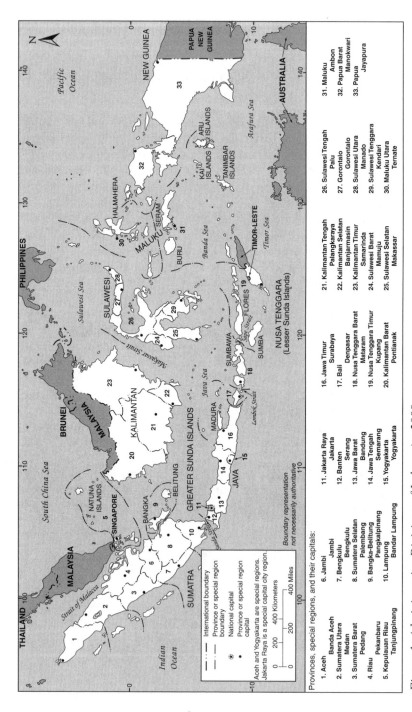

Figure 1. Administrative Divisions of Indonesia, 2009

Introduction

ON THE EVENING OF JUNE 18, 2009, tens of millions of Indonesians settled in front of their televisions to watch three candidates—former Vice President and President Megawati Sukarnoputri, incumbent Vice President Muhammad Yusuf Kalla, and incumbent President Susilo Bambang Yudhoyono—debate major issues prior to the presidential election to be held on July 8. By all accounts, the audience was largely disappointed. Megawati, daughter of Sukarno, the often-radical nationalist and fiery orator who was Indonesia's first leader, discussed the national challenges of getting motorcyclists to wear helmets and government offices to issue identification cards in a timely fashion. Yusuf Kalla, whose background is in business, spoke about the necessity of setting goals and deadlines but mentioned no specifics or priorities. President Yudhoyono, a former army general, emphasized the need for the rule of law, lest Indonesia be compared unfavorably to countries with better legal systems, and he proposed more online systems for identification cards and drivers' licences so that identities could be checked and "people can see what is normal and what is not." Many ordinary people who watched said they were simply bored, missing real clashes of opinion and discussion of large issues such as the economy and human rights. Some, while not especially excited, did say the debates changed how they would vote, while others admitted that, as a result of watching the debates, they had decided to abstain from voting altogether.

The next day, however, popular columnist and media figure Wimar Witular noted that while he agreed the debate had been "neither inspiring nor exciting," that was not the important point. "Eleven years ago," he wrote, "it would have been a Star Trek–like fantasy [to think] that presidential candidates would someday engage in an open debate on national television." However "boring" or overcautious, and despite the failure of the candidates to engage each other on large and substantive matters, it had been a historic event. In contrast to a political history dominated by commanding, larger-than-life figures like Sukarno and Suharto, Indonesian political decisions were now in the hands of a broad electorate, voting for presidential candidates who were undeniably "ordinary" people. This was an impressive step in the nation's journey from authoritarianism to democracy, and should not be forgotten.

It is not entirely clear whom Wimar Witular was intent on reminding, since his article appeared in Indonesia's foremost English-language newspaper, *The Jakarta Post*, and the foreign community, curiously enough, has generally marveled over the changes of the past decade more than Indonesians themselves. Whatever the case, his point was well taken. Since the late 1990s, Indonesia has shifted politically from being the world's largest military-dominated authoritarian state to being the world's third-largest civilian democracy (after India and the United States) and the largest Muslim-majority democracy, holding the world's largest direct presidential elections. It has gone economically from the heights of the "Asian miracle" of the 1960s to the 1990s to the depths of the Asian financial crisis of 1997–98—in which the national currency lost as much as 70 percent of its value, and income per capita fell an estimated 40 percent—and back, by mid-2009, to heights of growth at which it was deemed the best-performing Asian market for the year and third-fastest-growing economy, placed by some analysts in the company of the "emerging giants" of Brazil, China, India, and Russia. Administratively, Indonesia has moved from being one of the world's most centrally controlled regimes to being one of the most decentralized. Finally, contrary to the expectations of many careful observers, both foreign and domestic, Indonesia has succeeded in the past decade in preserving the territorial state virtually intact against the considerable forces of separatist movements. The exception is East Timor—now the Democratic Republic of Timor-Leste—acquired by force in 1976 and relinquished under pressure in 1999. Indonesia has also faced severe ethnic and religious violence, growing internationally influenced Islamic terrorism, tension over—and within—the armed services, and a series of natural disasters of which the most devastating was the 2004 tsunami that killed more than 166,500 Indonesians, mostly in the troubled region of Aceh, in northern Sumatra.

Trying to account for these enormous accomplishments has for some time occupied Indonesia watchers ranging from serious, academic specialists to commentators with varied and comparatively casual interests in the country and its people, to say nothing of Indonesians themselves. One result has been a wave of academic and journalistic writing, much of it sharply divided ideologically and theoretically. Indonesians from the political elite to ordinary citizens have also plunged into a period of unprecedented—and unprecedentedly open—introspection, raising a vibrant public discourse. There is no broad consensus, but the principal analyses tend to fall into four main types.

The first takes a long-term view. According to this explanation, Indonesia's dramatic shift to a successful democratic political process confirms what some had argued all along: democracy began to take root in the years immediately following the National Revolution (1945–49), but this natural, often disorderly development was nipped in the bud by the imposition of Sukarno's Guided Democracy (1957–65) and further suppressed by Suharto's military-backed New Order (1966–98). Proponents of this view dismiss arguments that newly independent Indonesians in the early 1950s were not "ready" for representative democracy, or that democracy along Western lines (what Sukarno called "free-fight liberalism" and "50 percent + 1 democracy") is somehow antithetical to both Indonesia's needs and its traditions. They also suggest that previous governments' attempts to deal with the specter of ethnic and religious conflict by smothering the expression and discussion of differences rather than channeling and protecting them only made matters worse. The fall of the New Order, and with it the fall from favor of the old political elite and the military, made possible what was in fact a kind of "back-to-the-future" movement: returning to what began so promisingly nearly two generations earlier, and this time doing it right. Indonesia's achievement since 1998, then, was as possible 40 years ago as it has now proven to be.

A second explanation looks at matters from a mid-range perspective, focusing on the previous 20 years or so. The success of Indonesia's transformation thus appears due largely to the influence of internal dissidents and progressives—particularly educated young people—during the last half of the New Order and the subsequent period of *reformasi* (reform—see Glossary), coupled with pressure from both a general globalization and specific outside sources. Advocates credit this combination of forces not only with weakening and eventually bringing an end to Suharto's rule, but also, even more important, with persisting during the subsequent period of upheaval in championing and providing the ideas and manpower necessary for genuinely democratic reforms. Seen in this way, Indonesia's post–New Order achievement is to a very large degree a generational one, which, as many reformers are quick to point out, is very much in the tradition of Indonesia's original struggle for independence.

A still shorter field of vision defines a third perspective, which focuses for the most part on the past decade. This view emphasizes the importance of the political and military leadership after the resignation of Suharto in May 1998, arguing that without it Indonesia might easily have continued as previously, under the sway of an authoritarian figure. Instead, as it happened, the individuals who followed the New Order president had neither the inclination nor the opportunity to attempt to reassemble the strongman pattern. Military leaders made conscious decisions to forego any thoughts of reinstating—by force or other means—the armed forces' self-declared dual responsibilities as both governors and enforcers. However great a role the architects of reform may have played, according to this argument, their efforts could have been derailed by powerful civilians and soldiers if they had been so inclined. But they were not derailed, and it is therefore to current military and political leaders, with all their strengths and weaknesses, that the success of the past decade must ultimately be attributed.

A final theory suggests that the great transformation at issue has not (or at least not yet) taken place, and that the changes that have occurred are in many respects superficial. For example, a prominent analyst of Indonesian affairs examined the three pairs of candidates in the 2009 presidential election and found they were all "creatures of Indonesia's past." Yusuf Kalla, a "classic Suharto-esque businessman" and conservative political supporter, was allied with Wiranto, a retired general who was Suharto's former adjutant and was indicted by the United Nations for crimes against humanity in East Timor. Megawati, a "woman longing for a return to the glory days of her father," had as a running mate Prabowo Subianto, another general (and former son-in-law of Suharto), who was dismissed by the military for brutal treatment of political activists. Susilo Bambang Yudhoyono, yet another former general, although one with a reputation for liberal tendencies and indecisiveness, chose as his vice presidential candidate a career government economist—Budiono—who had most recently headed Bank Indonesia. All of this suggests that at best modest and largely cosmetic change has taken place since 1998, and that, furthermore, the prospects for deep, meaningful reforms in the immediate future are perhaps considerably dimmer than most enthusiasts are willing to admit.

Each of these sorts of explanations has strengths as well as obvious weak points, and none can stand entirely on its own. Beyond the op-ed pieces and academic studies, in their everyday thinking most Indonesians probably borrow from all of them in assembling their own conclusions. Even taken together, however, it is startling that in their combined field of vision, the 32 years of New Order governance scarcely figure except as a source of obstacles to political modernization, a decidedly negative force in any effort to explain the advances of the past decade. Recently, however, a handful of commentators have quietly begun to raise the possibility that a powerful explanation of the undeniably rapid, and apparently successful, transformation since 1998 may lie precisely where least suspected: in the policies and realities of the New Order itself.

A full consideration of this fifth theory would require a thorough reexamination of Indonesia's history in the last half of the twentieth century, which has yet to be undertaken. For the present, however, some principal points of the argument seem clear enough. The basic notion is that the "amazing" transformation after 1998 is not quite as amazing as has generally been suggested because the New Order regime was never as powerful and monolithic, in some views even totalitarian, as many believed, and that its ability to control the way people thought and behaved was overestimated. (In the same vein, the military was never as unified or free to assert its will as most assumed.) From this perspective, for example, the New Order censorship about which critics constantly complained was on the whole much milder than portrayed, and at best erratic and incomplete; it certainly did not entirely smother public debate or expressions of discontent. Similarly, the regime's signature efforts to inculcate the ideology of Pancasila (see Glossary), which critics decried as so much self-interested, statist propagandizing, were surprisingly ineffective, producing more cynicism and questioning than acquiescence, and certainly not blind adherence. Individuals' ability to think or act independently in political matters, although indeed limited under the New Order regime, was far less severely damaged than imagined, and did not require a miracle to revive.

This explanation also suggests that the New Order may have contributed to the post-1998 transformation in a more positive manner. It is not, for example, quite so astonishing that Indonesia was able to hold complex and reasonably peaceful elections in 1999, 2004, and 2009 if we recall that, in fact, the nation had practice doing so for a quarter of a century under New Order auspices in 1971, 1977, 1982, 1987, 1992, and 1997. This notion may be repellent to critics who spent years pointing out how the New Order political process was anything but free, manipulated as it was by numerous means, including dishonest management of elections, curtailment of party independence, manipulation of parliament through large appointed memberships, and the like. Nevertheless, elections were routinely held and order maintained until the process became familiar, even taken for granted; it was by no means new in 1999, even though the all-important political context had changed. Furthermore, it seems likely that the millions of Indonesians who participated in those New Order elections came to understand that process's shortcomings and to develop ideas about how it could be improved. There was no dearth of ideas when the time came to make changes, and the journey to democracy required modest hops rather than great leaps.

The larger implication of this fifth sort of explanation is that what took place between roughly 1998 and 2004 in Indonesia was on the one hand not the revolution or near-revolution some saw or wished for, and on the other hand not the ephemeral, surface phenomenon others feared. There was neither miracle nor mirage but rather a complex transition in which continuity figured as importantly as change, and the two were often very closely intertwined. This insight is useful in understanding other aspects of contemporary Indonesia beyond elections and democratic procedure.

One illustration concerns the promotion of Pancasila ideology, a widely criticized hallmark of the New Order that appeared to have been summarily abandoned in 1998. Beginning in about 2002, however, there was a revival of interest in Pancasila and in honoring it as a kind of national creed and summation of national identity. Even prominent intellectuals who had considered New Order leaders' interest in a national ideology an anathema, and the Pancasila itself as shallow and outdated, appeared at symposia and on op-ed pages as advocates of a "revitalization," emphasizing the ways in which the message of the Pancasila is not only appropriate for post–New Order Indonesia, but indeed even necessary. In 2006 President Yudhoyono made a point of giving a major national speech on the then-neglected Birth of Pancasila Day (June 1), recommending that politicized niggling over the historical origins and other details surrounding the Pancasila—which he described as the "state ideology"—cease and that greater attention be paid to its precepts. There were numerous calls for making June 1 a national holiday, and the minister of education said that the Pancasila would remain part of the curriculum. It looked very much as if a key element of the New Order was about to be reinstated.

The president made a special effort, however, to emphasize that he did not intend to return to the past. The authoritarian Suharto government had, he said, "twisted the ideology to promote conformity and stifle dissent" with what he termed "Pancasila brainwashing," which caused the populace to turn against it and its sponsors. But in reality, he said, the Pancasila is "not an absolute doctrine but a compromise reached by the nation's founding fathers," and it should be accepted as such, not as a sacred document used to enforce uniformity. It is a compromise that sees all Indonesians as equal and protects pluralism and tolerance; it supports democratic reform and human rights, at the same time as it promotes a sense of unity under a common sense of social justice. This is precisely what is needed, Yudhoyono argued, at a time when rapid political decentralization and vigorously competing ethnic and religious identities threaten national unity. Whatever the degrees of public trust in Yudhoyono's message, it will, of course, be some time before it is clear where it will lead. Nevertheless, making the effort to see elements of change where continuity is most apparent at least brings observers closer to the realization that an easy, either/or reading is inadequate.

A second illustration concerns contemporary Indonesian public culture. By mid-2009, after a comparatively short period of growth beginning around 2006, by far the most popular television genre in the nation was the reality show—dating shows, talent contests, extreme home makeovers, and the like—which are widely seen as being American in origin (although in fact British and Dutch producers were the true pioneers); nearly 80 different shows of this type were being produced by local companies. To both outsiders and many Indonesians, this seemed to be a sign of an abrupt change. The Indonesian scholar and public intellectual Ariel Heryanto, for example, suggested that the pendulum had swung away from a post-1998 interest in Islamic popular culture, and he talked about American culture being suddenly "in" among Indonesians at all economic and social levels. One reality-show producer even suggested that what viewers consider American values are in fact universal ones, and that Indonesians are now part of a world in which everyone shares "the same dream, no matter who you are and what nationality you are." Not surprisingly, some Western commentators took this as another confirmation that Indonesia had moved definitively into the liberal democratic camp.

There is an important "continuity" side to this story as well. For one thing, as *New York Times* reporter Norimitsu Onishi pointed out, the reality show is not the first American genre to attract attention. American sitcoms ranging from "I Love Lucy" to "The Golden Girls," as well as series such as "McGyver," filled Indonesian television schedules beginning in the mid-1970s but then lost ground to shows with Islamic themes and to telenovelas from Latin America and soap operas from Asia; the current fascination with televised reality shows is thus part of a longer evolution and should be interpreted in that light. The careful foreign viewer might also notice that a number of the most popular Indonesian reality shows focus on themes markedly *not* found in America—for example, transplanting wealthy or upper-middle-class Indonesians into poor, rural settings, and vice versa, focusing on the tribulations each group faces in making adjustments and attempting to understand an altogether different way of life. These productions tend to validate the values of modern, urban middle-class Indonesians at the same time as they highlight the importance of empathy for others, reflecting in part a longstanding mainstream nationalist populism and in part a Muslim morality and sensitivity to the plight of the poor. The analysis that the popularity of such reality shows is evidence of a recent and dramatic social change—"Americanization," even—is neither as accurate nor, truth be told, as interesting as the more complicated view that notices a more complex story of adaptation.

Since the previous edition of this volume in the Country Study Series appeared in 1993, Indonesia has experienced enormous changes of great significance. The purpose of this revised version is not merely to point them out but also to attempt to show them in their proper perspective, in which changes are never without roots and continuities never untouched by innovation. Particularly for a country as large, diverse, and historically intricate as Indonesia, this approach seems both necessary and sensible.

September 16, 2009

*   *   *

As the manuscript for this book was being completed, a number of significant events occurred in or concerning Indonesia, most notably Indonesia's third post-Suharto presidential election, which was held on July 8, 2009. Fifteen days later, the General Elections Commission (KPU; for this and other abbreviations and contractions, see table A) declared the Democrat Party (PD) coalition candidates, incumbent president Susilo Bambang Yudhoyono and former Bank Indonesia head Budiono, the official winners as president and vice president, respectively, for the 2009–14 term. They garnered 60.9 percent of the vote. The election itself was largely peaceful, but not without grumbling in some quarters about how the KPU had managed the process. There were challenges to the results, particularly of massive fraud involving voter rosters. Megawati Sukarnoputri and her running mate, former army general Prabowo Subianto, who placed second with 26.8 percent of the vote, pressed the issue particularly hard, claiming that 28.5 million of her opponent's votes had been rendered invalid. On August 12, however, the Constitutional Court declared that the claims of both Megawati and the Golkar (see Glossary) candidate, Yusuf Kalla, "lacked legal basis," as the court found "no systematic, structural, and massive violations on the KPU's part." Although some observers expected further difficulties, such as violence or new procedural challenges, the court's ruling appeared to have defused a potentially very troublesome issue.

Another development was the ongoing anticorruption campaign. By the time of Yudhoyono's official inauguration on October 20, 2009, his second administration was already darkened by a storm of controversy that had been gathering since well before the election. The central issue was corruption, long considered by Indonesians and foreign observers alike as the nation's most serious problem, and one Yudhoyono was widely seen as having had some success combating by establishing in 2002 the Corruption Eradication Commission (KPK) and Corruption Crimes Court (Tipikor Court). The KPK, which had been given extraordinary powers of investigation (for example, into warrantless wiretapping) and prosecution, earned public respect for achieving a conviction rate of 100 percent in 86 graft cases involving mostly mid- and lower-level bureaucrats and civilians. But by early 2009, the KPK had begun to take aim at more important targets, especially in the higher ranks of the National Police of Indonesia (Polri) and the Attorney General's Office. The KPK also became increasingly involved in investigation of the controversial US$700 million bailout in 2008 of the nation's thirteenth-largest bank—Bank Century—to which the new Yudhoyono government's finance minister, Sri Mulyani Indrawati, and vice president, Budiono, were connected.

These initiatives appear to have persuaded many prominent individuals, perhaps because they themselves were potential targets, that the KPK was too powerful. Representatives of Polri and the Attorney General's Office and groups of legislators launched a seemingly concerted effort to deflate the KPK. The first important victim was the KPK head himself, Antasari Azhar, who in May 2010 was accused of masterminding a bizarre love-triangle murder plot, for which he was later convicted and sentenced to 18 years in prison. (As of late June 2010, the case was still under appeal.) The next major erstwhile targets were two KPK commissioners, Bibit Samad Riyanto and Chandra Hamzah, arrested in October 2009 on accusations of accepting bribes in what by that time had become a bitter feud between the KPK and Polri. (That case, after an even more tortuous journey through the courts, was in limbo more than eight months later.) In addition, the Bank Century case brought accusations of wrongdoing and, implicitly, corruption on the part of a range of principals involved, some of whom were connected to KPK and Polri scandals. In all of these cases, there was widespread public suspicion that many of the targets had been framed by police, as indeed several police officers publicly testified.

The long-term significance of these scandals is still uncertain, but there is general agreement about several consequences. First, President Yudhoyono's standing in many circles was at least temporarily weakened, as he appeared to vacillate in the face of the legal disputes and interdepartmental dissension. Forced by public pressure to take action, he was unable to fully fend off legislators' attacks on the authority of the KBK and Tipikor, which, despite the retention of wiretapping and prosecution rights, was in other ways diluted. Yudhoyono also lost the political battle to keep reform-minded Minister of Finance Sri Mulyani, who resigned in May 2010. (She soon accepted a high post with the World Bank and has been mentioned as a likely future presidential candidate.) The president had repeatedly complained that the scandals were being used to discredit him personally and remove him from office (impeachment was indeed being discussed in the legislature); however, the broad public did not appear to share this conclusion.

Second, and probably of more lasting importance, is the unprecedented degree to which high-level corruption and the struggle against it were opened to public scrutiny. Ordinary Indonesians devoured published accounts and watched televised news programs offering, for example, coverage of court proceedings and sensational whistle-blower testimonies, for up to three hours a day by January 2010, commanding more than four times the earlier viewer share of broadcast news. And it did not escape the notice of government bureaucrats and politicians that the Internet was quickly and skillfully used to mobilize public opinion, generally against government authorities. The most impressive mobilization arose in July 2009 when Polri commissioner general and head of the Crime Investigation Agency (Kabareskrim) Susno Duaji commented derisively to a journalist that the KPK trying to stand up to the police and Attorney General's Office was like a tiny house lizard (*cicak*) confronting a crocodile (*buaya*): opposition was foolish and doomed. Published by *Tempo*, the nation's foremost news magazine and online news source, the remark was endlessly repeated and soon triggered an enormous public reaction. The Internet, Facebook, and Twitter were used to gather hundreds of thousands of supporters of the KPK, while T-shirts and demonstrators' banners appeared with slogans such as "I'm a *cicak*!" and "Say no to the crocodile!" The police were especially humiliated, but public officials everywhere took uneasy notice of a newly powerful public that seemed to know what corruption was when they saw it and that vigorously supported efforts to combat both corruption and the types of authority that allowed it to exist. Sensational turns in the case by mid-2010 led to Susno, recently jailed in a military facility, now being praised as a heroic whistle-blower by some and even suggested as the next head of the KPK. Some people, however, accused him of being deeply involved in graft and other corrupt practices.

How did these developments affect public attitudes generally? According to one respected polling source, in the last quarter of 2009 public distrust of the government was lower overall (28 percent) than it had been in the past five years but higher (33 percent) in the cities. The poll also found that confidence that "democracy is working" was nearly as high as it had ever been (78 percent), but that such confidence suffered slightly more in the cities. The conclusion that corruption was the major problem facing the nation was reached by nearly as many people as ever (86 percent). Polling for the first quarter of 2010 seemed likely to show slippage, which many in the business community feared would, in turn, have unwelcome economic effects.

The power of the Internet was demonstrated not only in the corruption scandals but also in the case of Prita Mulyasari, a young mother whose e-mailed complaints about a large Jakarta hospital's services circulated online beginning in mid-2009. Sued for defamation by the hospital, she was also taken to court in civil and criminal suits under the 2008 antipornography law. Public outcry, organized via Facebook, Twitter, and various blogs and glogs, resulted in her being found not guilty in the criminal suit, but Prita refused to settle the civil suit out of court because she felt that doing so was an admission of guilt. She lost the case in December 2009 and was fined more than US$20,000. An online campaign raised several times that amount in donated coins to pay her expenses and fines. The case underscored in several ways the enormous potential power of social networking in Indonesia, where the number of Facebook users is said to have increased from fewer than 1 million to more than 21 million (compared with Britain's 24 million) between early 2009 and mid-2010.

One government response came from the conservative minister of communication and information, Tifatul Sembiring, who, in February 2010, drafted regulations widely seen as limiting freedom of expression; public outcry was so immediate and forceful that President Yudhoyono felt compelled to warn his minister to tone down the proposed regulations. Some legislators agreed with Tifatul, however, calling for strengthened limitations in laws governing multimedia use, violations of which are already subject to greater penalties than those in print media. There has been considerable pushback on the issue from a variety of groups, among them the Alliance of Independent Journalists, and the debate gathered momentum in May 2010. During the following month, a sensational case developed around an explicitly sexual video allegedly showing the male pop singer Nazril (Ariel) Irham and two female media celebrities (they claimed that the individuals depicted simply looked like them), which was widely circulated on the Internet. Police scrambled to find out who uploaded the clips and whether the photos were indeed of the people everyone thought they were. (In late June, Ariel was arrested and charged with violating the 2008 antipornography law.) Tifatul commented that the public debate over these "sex tapes" was like the dispute between Muslims, who believe that Jesus Christ was not crucified but rather that someone resembling him was, and Christians, who believe that Jesus Christ was crucified. He was immediately engulfed by a barrage of messages from angry Twitterers suggesting, for example, that he had been drunk when he made the comment; Tifatul's response (via his own Twitter account) was that his accuser himself must have been drunk. The controversy escalated so rapidly and in such dangerous directions that President Yudhoyono felt constrained to offer an opinion. In late June 2010, he appeared to back Tifatul's call for, among other things, an Internet "black list" and general regulation of Internet use, lest society and the nation be damaged.

The threat of terrorist attacks against Indonesia continues, but government forces appear to have successfully disrupted some significant sources of terror activity. On "Black Friday," July 17, 2009, a little more than a week after the presidential election, explosions were detonated by suicide bombers at two American-owned hotels in Jakarta, the JW Marriott and the Ritz-Carlton, killing seven (one of whom was Indonesian) and wounding 53. The bombings were widely condemned internationally and within Indonesia itself, where tolerance for terrorism had already been dropping noticeably. President Yudhoyono suggested that the terrorist acts were somehow connected to the election and directed at him, an idea discounted by most analysts. (However, the police discovery in May 2010 of a plot to assassinate Yudhoyono on the coming Independence Day, August 17, lent the earlier suggestion some retrospective credence.) Heightened police efforts in succeeding months after the hotel bombings paid off. In September 2009, commandos killed Noordin Muhammad Top, the Malaysian-born Islamist militant thought by police to have been responsible for major bombings in Indonesia since 2002, including the recent JW Marriott and Ritz-Carlton explosions. In March 2010, counterterrorism forces killed Dulmatin, a Javanese bombing mastermind who played a prominent role in the militant Jemaah Islamiyah and was also connected to the Abu Sayyaf group in the Philippines. The police received widespread approval for these efforts—as opposed to their involvement in various corruption scandals—and it was clear that the militants and their followers attracted little sympathy. Two Javanese villages, whose native sons were followers of Noordin and were also killed, refused to have them buried on village land. Finally, in June 2010 police killed former Indonesian soldier Yuli Harsono, suspected of planning, among other things, an attack on the Danish Embassy in Jakarta, and arrested Abdullah Sunata, wanted for establishing a terrorist training camp in Aceh and suspected of planning to assassinate President Yudhoyono.

Issues having to do with the public practice of Islam continue to feature in national news, especially in the Special Region of Aceh, where implementation of sharia (*syariah* in Bahasa Indonesia—see Glossary) began in 2000 and has caused intense debate since then. During the 2009 elections, Golkar Party candidates attempted to make the wearing of the *jilbab* (Muslim woman's head covering) a political issue, in which the vast majority of Indonesians seemed to show no real interest. Polri announced a plan on August 21, 2009, to monitor sermons given at mosques and public gatherings, presumably for their potential to incite hatred or violence. There was, however, a strong public outcry, and the order was quickly rescinded.

The most sensational development occurred in mid-September 2009, when the Aceh legislative council introduced new Islamic criminal bylaws (*qanun jinayat*), calling for, among other things, adulterers (both Muslim and non-Muslim) to be stoned to death. The bylaws, introduced before the recently elected, more moderate legislature could officially be seated, drew condemnation from many sources, including, in early October, a council of 80 Muslim clerics, who said such laws were foreign and called for a presidential review. Other legal experts suggested, however, that the bylaws were reasonable, in that they reflected Indonesia's effort to recognize diversity in legal sanctions. Under pressure from civil society and both foreign and indigenous human-rights groups, the provisions had not yet been fully enacted and signed by the provincial governor as of mid-2010. The Department of Home Affairs announced its intention of requesting a Supreme Court review of Aceh's Islamic criminal code but had not yet done so, and the law remained officially in a suspended state. In the meantime, however, Aceh's *syariah* police appear to have been emboldened, enforcing conservative standards of women's dress and, in several instances, carrying out public and brutal punishments for suspected moral crimes such as having premarital sex, intrusions the majority of Acehnese appear to resent. The struggle between religious conservatism and more moderate ideas and the search for a less-tense relationship between Aceh's autonomy—extended in 2006 as part of the settlement of the armed conflict there—and the requirements of the Indonesian state and constitution seem likely to continue for some time.

Another controversial legal issue also attracted widespread attention. The controversy concerned Indonesia's 1965 Blasphemy Law, a section of the Criminal Code that prohibits both expression of hostility toward or contempt of the recognized religions and the advocacy of unorthodox interpretations of those religions. The law can be used to hand down sentences of up to five years' imprisonment, and to disband any group deemed unorthodox or heretical. In October 2009, a group of prominent Muslim intellectuals (including former President Abdurrahman Wahid), human-rights activists, and civic leaders requested that the Constitutional Court review the Blasphemy Law, suggesting that it violates guarantees of freedom of religion and threatens the tolerance and pluralism fundamental to maintaining a democratic Indonesia. In April 2010, after several months of public debate and demonstrations, the court refused to conduct a full judicial review of the law, thereby upholding it. An eight-to-one decision by the court argued that, without anything to immediately replace it, the law is necessary in order to maintain social order and prevent religious conflicts. Conservative Muslims, who feared among other things that more liberal interpretations of Islam might be encouraged, were heartened by the decision, but an array of opponents feared that religious freedom, especially of minority groups, would be further threatened. While the Constitutional Court's ruling suggests that legislative review and modification of the law might be pertinent, it seems unlikely that lawmakers will accept such a sensitive undertaking anytime in the near future.

Eastern and western Indonesia have continued to experience repeated earthquakes. The largest of these occurred in western Java in early September 2009 (7.0 magnitude and at least 72 deaths), in Sumatera Barat later the same month (7.6 magnitude with at least 1,100 deaths and more than 2,180 injured), and offshore from Sumatera Utara in April 2010 (7.8 magnitude, no deaths). In Jawa Timur, the notorious Lumpur Sidoarjo (Lusi) mud volcano, which in 2006 killed 13 and destroyed the homes of tens of thousands of residents, was still oozing in 2010. International researchers argued in February that new data confirmed the disaster was man-made and not caused by an earthquake as the gas-exploration company Brantas Lapindo claimed. President Yudhoyono reiterated in March 2010 that he expected Lapindo to adequately reimburse all victims (the government itself had allocated more than US$210 million for the purpose in 2008 and 2009), but the case has been increasingly embroiled in legal and political controversy, and protests by the victims continued.

In May 2010, scientists announced the discovery of previously unknown species of gecko, pigeon, and bat in the remote Foja Mountains in Papua Province, described as "perhaps the least disturbed ... tropical forest block on earth." On the same day, the government of Norway announced a US$1 billion grant to the Indonesian government to reduce deforestation through a series of ongoing, verifiable projects. Days later, President Yudhoyono issued a moratorium on new forest and peatland concessions, considered an encouraging first step in an aggressive, long-term campaign.

Despite the many political and social problems its people face, Indonesia's economy appeared to perform remarkably well in 2009 and early 2010. In May 2010, the International Institute for Management Development in Zürich placed Indonesia thirty-fifth on its annual list of the most competitive economies, jumping it ahead of seven other nations (the Philippines was listed thirty-ninth, and Malaysia was listed tenth). The economy grew a respectable 4.5 percent in 2009, and it was estimated to achieve 5.8 to 6 percent growth in 2010. Consumer expenditures were growing, but even the top strata were spending cautiously; government spending was strong, offsetting declining exports. Average per-capita income rose from US$1,180 in 2004 to US$4,200 in 2010. Most important, statistics indicated that poverty was declining: the nation's poorest stratum, earning US$65 or less a month, declined during roughly the same period, from about 40 percent of society to slightly more than 20 percent. According to the latest Gini index (see Glossary), which measures inequality of wealth, Indonesia enjoyed considerably more equitable income distribution (0.36) than neighboring Thailand (0.42), Singapore (0.43), or Malaysia (0.46), although the gross domestic product (GDP—see Glossary) in all those countries was higher. As had been the case two decades earlier, such figures did not go entirely unchallenged but were widely accepted among economists.

"Culture wars" also were underway. In a series of disputes with neighboring Malaysia over traditional cultural heritage, public voices—many on the Internet—became surprisingly shrill, including character-izations of Malaysia as "a nation of thieves," and threats of war. In mid-2009, a Malaysian Ministry of Tourism advertisement aired internation-ally on the Discovery Channel portrayed a Balinese dance as part of Malaysia's cultural heritage; the government subsequently withdrew the advertisement and apologized for what it said had been a production error. But the uproar nevertheless gathered steam, and by September, despite some Indonesian commentators' dismissal of the issue as trivial and an indication of Indonesian feelings of inferiority, it had become a cause célèbre threatening diplomatic relations. Some of the sharp feel-ings on the Indonesian side were apparently assuaged in October when the United Nations Educational, Scientific, and Cultural Organization (UNESCO) declared batik to be part of Indonesia's intangible cultural heritage, adding to a similar declaration in 2008 for shadow puppet the-ater (*wayang kulit*) and the *keris*, an asymmetrical dagger, which many Malaysians had felt were at least equally theirs.

There also were some prominent deaths. W. S. Rendra, major poet and playwright who achieved fame during the New Order for taking stands against the government, died at age 74 on August 6, 2009. For-mer president of Indonesia Abdurrahman Wahid, who served from 1999 to 2001, died at age 69 on December 30, 2009. Gesang, composer of many *keroncong* (songs), among them the world-famous "Ben-gawan Solo," died at the age of 92 on May 20, 2010. Hasan di Tiro, best known for founding the Free Aceh Movement (GAM), the 1976–2006 movement aimed at achieving Acehnese independence, died at age 84 on June 3, 2010, one day after being officially reinstated as an Indonesian citizen.

July 1, 2010

*   *   *

After the manuscript for this book was completed in the summer of 2010, a number of important events took place. One of the most significant was the ongoing struggle against corruption, particularly that involving politicians and government bureaucrats. Public opinion appeared to stiffen further against corruption. In August 2010, not long before the traditional time of forgiveness at the end of the Muslim fasting month of Ramadan, President Yudhoyono issued pardons and remissions of sentences for a number of individuals convicted of graft, most of whom had served 75 percent or more of their sentences. Although such pardons are generally seen as customary, in this instance Yudhoyono was strongly criticized, and the question was asked more sharply than in the recent past whether he was indeed committed to the struggle against corruption. The Corruption Eradication Commission (KPK), which had been viewed by many as seriously weakened in early 2010 by legislative efforts to rein in its powers, appeared to be holding its own. Despite a call in July 2011 by People's Representative Council (DPR) speaker Marzuki Alie (from President Yudhoyono's own Democrat Party) for the dismantling of the agency, the People's Consultative Assembly (MPR) moved to establish the KPK more firmly with a constitutional amendment.

Meanwhile, the KPK itself continued to pursue suspects and attempt to bring them to justice. The case of former police commissioner Susno Duaji, the self-proclaimed whistle-blower suspected of widespread corrupt practices, proceeded with many sensational twists. Formally charged in late September 2010 as the ringleader in a number of important graft cases, Duaji's trials were just beginning 10 months later in mid-2011. The most important new case was that of Gayus Halomoan Tambunan, a midlevel tax official who said he was a witness who had been prepared to testify against corrupt officials but was betrayed by the KPK. He claimed he altered the tax forms of 149 corporations, including Chevron and Ford, and received Guyanese passports from a U.S. Central Intelligence Agency (CIA) agent working for the KPK. Gayus was sentenced to seven years in prison in one case, but, as of late July 2011, three other cases against him were still pending. Another major suspect in multiple corruption charges was former Democrat Party treasurer Muhammad Nazaruddin, who had spectacularly eluded arrest and even had the entire country scanning television commercial jingles for clues as to his whereabouts.

The legal troubles of male pop singer Nazril (Ariel) Irham, who was charged with violating the 2008 Information and Electronic Transaction Law for appearing in sexually explicit videos that were widely circulated online, held the attention of many Indonesians in late 2010 and 2011. The reason for the high degree of interest was that it revealed many levels of hypocrisy in society's views of sex and morality, and more broadly because it tested the limits of openness and personal freedoms in the new democracy. Arrested in mid-2010, Ariel was tried in January 2011 in a Bandung court, where 1,000 police officers were deployed to maintain security and order. He was sentenced to three and a half years in prison and a fine equivalent to US$27,500; an appeal was rejected in April. The case was used by the conservative minister of the Department of Communications and Information, Tifatul Sembiring, to garner support for his efforts to force Internet providers to filter out pornographic content. Providers complained that filtering would cost them more than US$110 million to implement and was, in any case, ineffective technologically. Nevertheless, the government persisted, even pressing the Canadian company, Research in Motion, to block porn from its Blackberry service. The government also attempted to enforce more widely a 2008 law that criminalizes viewing, owning, downloading, and distributing pornography, with sentences of up to six years in jail and fines of up to US$115,000.

But, by April 2011, it was unclear whether Indonesia's efforts to control Internet usage and public morality in this way could be sustained. The government's attempts—not least those by Minister Tifatul himself—were widely ridiculed, and the department was forced to admit publicly both that filters did not work very well and that it had only 40 staff available to monitor the issue—a clearly inadequate number. Respected lawmaker Arifinto of the Prosperous Justice Party (PKS), which had strongly supported the 2008 antipornography law, was caught watching pornography during a legislative session; he promptly resigned, but columnists and others wondered aloud why an entertainer had gone to jail but a legislator had not been charged, and they mused that a high percentage of the Indonesian population was now in danger of being declared criminals.

In early 2011, the aforementioned Jakarta housewife, Prita Mulyasari, was partially vindicated by the Supreme Court, which overturned a 2010 ruling that, although she was declared not guilty in a criminal suit, she was liable in a civil suit that fined her more than US$20,000. In 2009 the Supreme Court had also denied the hospital's libel suit asking US$250,000 in damages, but in July 2011 it granted a prosecutor's request for an appeal and reversed its opinion, finding Prita guilty and sentencing her to six months in prison. Prita immediately filed for a case review, but there was such widespread condemnation of the decision and of the judicial system as a whole that some editorials foresaw that the case might eventually force both abandonment of the 2008 law and broad judicial reform.

There is evidence that views of the Suharto era are being modified in public memory and thinking about contemporary society. Calls for the promotion of Pancasila, which had become a hated feature of the

Suharto era, continue to surface, and the government has announced its intention to revitalize the philosophy, but without saying how it would do so. The humanist thinker Radhar Panca Dahara acknowledged that most Indonesians still do not understand Pancasila, but he cautioned that interpretation has to be individual rather than codified to be effective. A member of the government commission overseeing culture and education initiatives suggested that Pancasila could best be revived by encouraging exemplary behavior rather than endless discussion. Youth activist Melki Lakalena proposed that, rather than any sort of rigid indoctrination, popular music and other forms of mass culture could be used as vehicles for reawakening interest in Pancasila. He said his suggested approach was a more "relaxed" way of recognizing "the political role of culture in disseminating the value of the state ideology," a statement with an oddly back-to-the-future ring.

Another feature of both the Old Order and the New Order that, after a brief eclipse, showed signs of returning was the government's use of book banning as a tool of social control. Between 1998 and 2006, no books had been banned, although the Sukarno-era law sanctioning such action remained in force. But after 2006 the practice saw some revival. In December 2009, the attorney general invoked a 2004 law (which had replaced a 1969 law based on a 1963 presidential decree) that did not address "banning books" but rather "supervising the circulation of printed materials" to ban five books. Among them was the Indonesian translation of John Roosa's *Pretext for Mass Murder: The September 30th Movement and Suharto's Coup d'etat in Indonesia*, a publication that the Attorney General's Office deemed disturbing to public order, even though it had already been in circulation in Indonesia for nearly two years. By mid-2010, the Department of Justice and Human Rights was reviewing about 200 books considered potential "threats to the country's unity," 20 of them seriously. On October 13, 2010, however, in a case brought by a group of prominent authors, the Constitutional Court ruled against the original 1963 decree that gave the Attorney General's Office the authority to place bans on specific titles or on an author's entire oeuvre, declaring instead that any calls for bans had to be made through the court system. The government can still proscribe certain works under a 1966 anticommunist law, and under the 2008 antipornography law, but the practice of book banning now is far more limited than in most of the past half-century.

All of these developments suggest that Indonesians are busy adjusting—and often moderating—their views of the pre-1998 period, reconsidering some aspects and rejecting others. Perhaps the most surprising evidence of this process was the nomination, in mid-October 2011, of former President Suharto as a "national hero," one of 10 persons put forward by local officials. This suggestion, which was first made by a Jawa Tengah district head on the 1,000-day anniversary of Suharto's death, elicited a vigorous debate in which there was unexpectedly strong support for Suharto's rehabilitation and recognition. Public-opinion polls noted that, although the approval rating of Indonesia's new democracy had grown from 42 percent in 1999 to 70 percent by late 2010, and few expressed any desire to return to the New Order, Suharto now seemed to command growing respect. In a May 2011 survey, 41 percent named him "Indonesia's Best President." The government finessed the national-hero issue by choosing only two minority candidates connected in some way with Indonesia's struggle for independence, former cabinet minister Johannes Leimena, a Christian from Maluku, and military officer Johannes Abraham Dimara, a Christian from Papua.

The struggle against terrorism continues to occupy the government, both within the country and in cooperation with Asian neighbors. In March 2011, for example, Indonesian police representatives traveled to Pakistan with fingerprints and DNA samples to identify the recently arrested Umar Patek, a Jemaah Islamiyah member thought to be one of the masterminds behind the 2002 Bali bombings and suspected of connections to many other incidents, including an explosion in an Islamic boarding school in Bima, Nusa Tenggara Barat, on July 11, 2011. As of that date, however, Indonesia was still one of three countries vying to extradite him. The radical cleric Abu Bakar Ba'asyir (also known as Abu Bakar Bashir), who was accused of intellectual leadership of Jemaah Islamiyah, charged in the Bali bombings, and served two years in prison before his conviction was overturned by the Supreme Court, was again arrested in August 2010 and later charged with funding and coordinating a training program for a militant jihadist group in Aceh. He was tried in June 2011 and sentenced to 15 years in prison. Antiterrorist forces maintained pressure on other suspected networks and individuals, but were unable to prevent several local attacks, the most disturbing of which probably was the April 2011 suicide bombing in Cirebon, Jawa Tengah Province, where a young man purportedly angry at karaoke bars and unregistered places of Christian worship blew himself up and wounded many others in a mosque located in a police station. Because it occurred in a place of Muslim worship and during Friday prayers, this event is said to have particularly shocked public opinion.

News commentators and columnists agree that intolerance is on the rise. The hardline group Islamic Defenders' Front (FPI) appears increasingly in reports of intimidation and often violent vigilantism. Its members have involved themselves in local efforts to close down "immoral" businesses, enforce fasting during Ramadan, and protest against or close down political meetings and other activities suspected—often wildly erroneously—of being communist. Apparently spontaneous outbreaks of violence also have occurred, such as a February 2011 incident in Banten, Jawa Barat Province, in which a crowd of 1,500 people attacked and killed three members of the unorthodox Muslim group Ahmadiyah while police stood by. In the eventual trial, prosecutors charged 11 participants jointly with inciting violence and committing assault leading to death, but no individuals were charged with the actual killings. Such events pose a dilemma for both law-enforcement and justice officials, not only because, as Muslims, they often find it difficult to act against "protectors of Islam," but also because it is often difficult, in Indonesia's still relatively recently democratized society, to determine the proper boundary between freedom of expression and intolerance.

Public reaction to violent and oppressive behavior by religious zealots appears to be increasingly negative. Growing disapproval is most notable where efforts to implement sharia are concerned. In Aceh, where in 2010 more than 800 detentions were carried out by the sharia police and men were forced to marry and women to have virginity tests, public dissatisfaction arose, and activists complained of violations of human rights. In the Bekasi area near Jakarta, polls taken between April 2009 and March 2010 showed that individuals in favor of the local government implementing sharia dropped from 43 percent to 36 percent, and those who believed that thieves should have their hands cut off declined from 38 percent to 32 percent. This and other pieces of evidence may have encouraged police in some areas to take stronger stances with regard to civilian organizations such as the FPI. In July 2011, for example, the Jakarta police announced they would take firm steps to prevent such groups from attacking businesses and individuals who failed to observe government regulations on certain kinds of entertainment during Ramadan, emphasizing that only the police are permitted to take such action when warranted.

Concerns over rising intolerance and the violence it generates also brought Indonesia's most important Muslim associations to strengthen and better publicize their stands against radicalism. In its centennial year and with a membership of 29 million, Muhammadiyah (Followers of Muhammad) strongly affirmed the ideas of former leader Ahmad Syafii Maarif, who now promotes tolerance. Five years earlier, Muhammadiyah appeared to be turning in a more uncompromising direction. In July 2011, Muhammadiyah announced that it "conveys an Islam that says no to conflicts between civilizations, an Islam that fosters cooperation, dialog, a cosmopolitan Islam [that is] a golden bridge for a dialog between East and West." Barely a week later, Nahdlatul

Ulama (Council of Scholars), Indonesia's largest Muslim organization, with 80 million followers, celebrated its eighty-fifth anniversary by announcing that it would begin a campaign for a peaceful, tolerant Islam, and argued that "Democracy is the best tool to improve people's welfare and to keep the nation united." Nahdlatul Ulama's youth organization—Ansor (Helpers of Muhammad)—also announced that, in response to the Cirebon mosque bombing, it was forming a special antiterrorist unit called Detachment 99, after the antiterrorism branch of the national police, Detachment 88.

Neither unresolved social problems nor threats of turbulence seem to have affected economic performance. In 2010 Indonesia's economy grew 6.1 percent, foreign investment rose 52 percent to US$16.2 billion, the stock market rose 20 percent in the first half of the year, and the rupiah (Rp—see Glossary) appreciated nearly 5 percent against the U.S. dollar. In the first quarter of 2011, Moody's and Standard and Poor's raised the nation's sovereign debt rating to BB+, or just one level below investment grade. Strength within the Asian sphere was particularly marked. For example, the largest share of foreign investment came from member countries of the Association of Southeast Asian Nations (ASEAN—see Glossary), and, as of late 2010, Indonesia was poised to become the world's largest manufacturer of footwear, as more companies from Taiwan and South Korea relocated there.

Still, 15 percent of Indonesia's population lives below the poverty line of US$1 per day. In recognition of this disparity, President Yudhoyono began 2011 by outlining the government's "growth with equity" philosophy of planning. Then, in a powerful and well-received special address entitled "The Big Shift and the Imperative of 21st Century Globalism," delivered at the World Economic Forum in Davos, Switzerland, on January 27, 2011, he called for a new sense of globalism that is "open-minded, pragmatic, adaptive and innovative," a globalism in which regional groupings play a crucial role in supplying both dynamism and restraint. The world economy, he stated, should be managed "so that it functions to meet our needs rather than satisfying our greed," and he repeated Indonesia's own national goal of "growth with equity," implying that the world community could well aim for something similar. Indonesia took up the chair of ASEAN in 2011, and it was clear on the eve of the organization's annual meeting in late July 2011 that Indonesia would use that opportunity to emphasize the same themes and enhance its growing international reputation as a political and economic power to be reckoned with.

The United States has recognized the growing importance of Indonesia, as well as a deepening rivalry with China for influence there. In November 2010, the U.S. president, Barack Obama, visited Indonesia to underscore the significance of improved relations between the two countries, and to launch what was termed a U.S.–Indonesian Comprehensive Partnership, which, it was emphasized, should be a partnership of equals, covering, among other things, a much-expanded program of educational exchange, expanded cooperation in security issues, and efforts to improve trade. President Obama's twice-postponed visit, although brief, was special because he was returning to the place he had lived for four years as a boy. His speech at Universitas Indonesia included lofty ideas on development, democracy, and religious tolerance and was quickly compared to his inspiring "New Beginning" speech in Cairo in 2009. But what the majority of Indonesians seemed to notice and appreciate most was that when Obama spoke about the changes that had taken place in Indonesia since the late 1960s, he did so first-hand and in colorful detail. Above all, perhaps, it was noticed that he appeared to have a genuine attachment to the country and its people; when he said simply, "Indonesia is a part of me," a great many Indonesians, including press and television pundits, responded emotionally.

Indonesia continued to experience a high level of volcanic activity. In late August 2010, Mount Sinabung, near Karo, Sumatera Utara Province, erupted for the first time in 410 years, and in 2011 noteworthy eruptions occurred in Java and Sulawesi. The extended series of eruptions at Mount Merapi in late 2010 caused evacuations of more than 135,000 people and more than 300 deaths near Yogyakarta. In addition, there were earthquakes, the largest of which occurred in October 2010, when an underwater quake off the Mentawai Islands, Sumatera Barat Province, registered a magnitude of 7.7 and produced a tsunami estimated to have killed more than 300 people.

Finally, several important personalities who helped define modern Indonesia passed from the scene. Akhdiat Miharja, a key figure in literature during the 1940s and 1950s, died at age 99 on July 8, 2010. Iwan Tirta (also known as Nusyirwan Tirtaamijaya), who had revitalized batik design and brought Indonesia batik international recognition, died at the age of 75 on July 31, 2010. Des Alwi, one of the last figures of the revolutionary period (he was the adopted son of Mohammad Hatta and a close associate of Sutan Syahrir), and later diplomat and writer, died just before his eighty-third birthday on November 13, 2010. Rosihan Anwar, legendary reporter, columnist, and public intellectual, was 88 when he died on April 14, 2011. And Franky Sahilatua, who played an important role in popularizing voguish music of social criticism during the Suharto era, died at 57 on April 20, 2011.

August 2, 2011   William H. Frederick

Chapter 1. Historical Setting

Relief panel at Borobudur showing a trading ship, ca. AD 800

DEBATE ABOUT THE NATURE of Indonesia's past and its relationship to a national identity preceded by many decades the Republic's proclamation of independence in 1945, and it has continued in different forms and with varying degrees of intensity ever since. But beginning in the late 1990s, the polemic intensified, becoming more polarized and entangled in political conflict. Historical issues took on an immediacy and a moral character they had not earlier possessed, and historical answers to the questions, "What is Indonesia?" and "Who is an Indonesian?" became, for the first time, part of a period of widespread public introspection. Notably, too, this was a discussion in which foreign observers of Indonesian affairs had an important voice.

There are two main views in this debate. In one of them, contemporary Indonesia, both as an idea and as a reality, appears in some degree misconceived, and contemporary "official" readings of its history fundamentally wrong. In large part, this is a perspective originating with the political left, which seeks, among other things, to correct its brutal eclipse from national life since 1965. But it also has been, often for rather different reasons, a dominant perspective among Muslim intellectuals and foreign observers disenchanted with the military-dominated government of Suharto's New Order (1966–98) or disappointed with the perceived failures of Indonesian nationalism in general. The foreign observers, for example, increasingly emphasized to their audiences that "in the beginning there was no Indonesia," portraying it as "an unlikely nation," a "nation in waiting," or an "unfinished nation," suggesting that contemporary national unity was a unidimensional, neocolonial, New Order construction too fragile to long survive the fall of that government.

An alternative view, reflecting government-guided textbook versions of the national past, defines Indonesia primarily by its long anticolonial struggle and focuses on integrative, secular, and transcendent "mainstream" nationalist perspectives. In this epic, linear, and often hyperpatriotic conception of the past, Indonesia is the outcome of a singular, inevitable, and more or less self-evident historical process, into which internal difference and conflict have been absorbed, and on which the national character and unity depend. Some foreign writers, often without fully realizing it, are inclined to accept, without much questioning, the essentials of this story of the development of the nation and its historical identity.

Both of these views came into question in the first decade of the twenty-first century. On the one hand, Indonesia's persistence for more than 60 years as a unitary nation-state, and its ability to survive both the political, social, and economic upheavals and the natural disasters that followed the New Order, have driven many foreign specialists to try to account for this outcome. Both they and Indonesians themselves found reason to attempt a more nuanced reevaluation of such topics as the role of violence and the various forms of nationalism in contemporary society. On the other hand, a general recognition took hold that monolithic readings of Indonesia's (national) historical identity fit neither past facts nor contemporary sensibilities. In particular, Indonesian intellectuals' penchant for attempting to "straighten out history" (*menyelusuri sejarah*) began to be recognized largely as an exercise in replacing one singular perspective with another. Some younger historians have begun to question the nature and purpose of a unitary "national" history, and to search for ways to incorporate more diverse views into their approaches. Although it is still too early to determine where these realignments and efforts at reinterpretation will lead, it is clear that in contemporary Indonesia, history is recognized as a key to understanding the present and future nation, but it can no longer be approached in the monolithic and often ideological terms so common in the past.

Origins

Early Inhabitation

Indonesia consists of parts of the Sunda Shelf, extending from mainland Asia and forming the world's largest submerged continental shelf; a deep-water channel charting what is known as Wallace's Line roughly running between the islands of Kalimantan and Sulawesi, and between the islands of Bali and Lombok; and parts of the Sahul Shelf, an extension of Australia (see The Geographic Context, ch. 2). Despite arcs of frequent volcanic activity and patterns of rising and falling sea levels, this has been a favored region for modern humans and their hominid predecessors for nearly 2 million years. Today Indonesia is of crucial importance to the study of human origins and evolution. Sites in central Java, such as Sangiran and Ngandong, now account for about 75 percent of the world's examples of *homo erectus*, an early hominid type. Most recently, the 2004 announcement of discoveries on the island of Flores (between Bali and Timor) created international controversy because they suggested an entirely new, locally evolved, and distinctively smaller hominid form overlapping chronologically with both *homo erectus* and modern humans.

About 800,000 years ago, some early hominids of the archipelago made stone tools, constructed water craft sophisticated enough to cross 25 kilometers of rough sea channel, and may have used fire and language. About 600,000 years ago, a fairly sophisticated hominid culture was widely distributed throughout what is now Indonesia. The earliest modern humans cannot currently be firmly dated before about 40,000 years ago, but some specialists argue either that they appeared much earlier (as much as 90,000 years ago) in a rapid dispersal from Africa, or that they evolved independently in East or Southeast Asia from existing hominid stock. Whatever the case, Indonesia's earliest modern humans did not immediately or everywhere displace their hominid relatives but coexisted with them for tens of thousands of years. The earliest modes of their existence show little evidence of having deviated markedly from those of their predecessors. A pattern evolved of small hunting-fishing-foraging communities depending on tools made of shell, wood, bamboo, and stone, adapting to a wide variety of ecological niches and remaining in contact with neighboring peoples over land and sea.

One center of these societies was in the northern Maluku and Papua region, where between 20,000 and about 9,000 years ago there is evidence of long-distance trade (for example, in obsidian, used for making cutting tools), deliberate horticulture, and the transport of plants (bananas, taro, palms) and animals (wallabies, flying squirrels) used as food sources. Possibly these communities also used sails and outriggers on their boats.

Social and Cultural Developments

About 10,000 years ago, the last ice age began to recede and seas rose, eventually creating from the Sunda Shelf the archipelago we know today. The next six or seven millennia saw the development of cultural and social characteristics that have been of lasting significance down to the present. Examples include the use throughout the archipelago of languages belonging to the same family (Austronesian); the spread of rice agriculture and sedentary life, and of ceramic and (later) metal technologies; the expansion of long-distance seaborne travel and trade; and the persistence of diverse but interacting societies with widely varying levels of technological and cultural complexity.

There is no entirely secure understanding of how and why these changes took place. The most widely held view, based heavily on historical linguistics, argues that about 6,500 years ago peoples whom scholars identify linguistically and culturally as "Austronesians" dispersed out of present-day southern China and Taiwan. In a fairly rapid process, they spread throughout the archipelago from the

Philippines (which they reached by 3,000 BC) to Indonesia (2,000–500 BC), and then farther west as far as Madagascar and farther east throughout the Pacific Ocean. Prehistory expert Peter Bellwood has characterized this dispersal as "one of the most astonishing bouts of colonization ... in early human history." Recent genetic and paleoecological research has raised a number of challenges to this model, however, among them counterindicative DNA configurations in archipelagic and Pacific populations of both humans and pigs, and indications of forest clearing in Sumatra as early as 5,000 years ago. These challenges suggest a more "entangled" and complicated process of change in which old and new populations, as well as their traditions and technologies, interacted in many different ways over a long period of time.

Evidence regarding social transformations during this period is at best indirect (and for Java and Sumatra, virtually absent), but causative models from European and continental Asian prehistory seem rarely to apply to the archipelago. Neither knowledge of agriculture nor contact with outsiders always resulted in technological revolution, for example, or rapid alteration in patterns of settlement. Political and economic changes occurred unevenly, and societies—in all likelihood small, animist chieftainships—underwent no fundamental transformation. Thus the archipelago came to be marked by a pattern of broad linguistic and cultural affinities but, at the same time, intricate diversity. Virtually all of Indonesia's subsequent history has been played out against the background of this remarkable human web.

Expanding Networks

Many parts of the archipelago played a role in local and wider trading networks from early times, and some were further connected to interregional routes reaching much farther corners of the globe. Nearly 4,000 years ago, cloves—which until the seventeenth century grew nowhere else in the world except five small islands in Maluku—had made their way to kitchens in present-day Syria. By about the same time, items such as shells, pottery, marble, and other stones; ingots of tin, copper, and gold; and quantities of many food goods were traded over a wide area in Southeast Asia. As early as the fourth century BC, materials from South Asia, the Mediterranean world, and China—ceramics, glass and stone beads, and coins—began to show up in the archipelago. In the already well-developed regional trade, bronze vessels and other objects, such as the spectacular kettledrums produced first in Dong Son (northern Vietnam), circulated in the island world, appearing after the second century BC from Sumatra to Bali and from Kalimantan and Sulawesi to the eastern part of Maluku. Around 2,000 years ago, Javanese and Balinese were themselves producing elegant bronze ware, which was traded widely and has been found in Sumatra, Madura, and Maluku. In all of this trade, including that with the furthest destinations, peoples of the archipelago appear to have dominated, not only as producers and consumers or sellers and buyers, but as shipbuilders and owners, navigators, and crew. The principal dynamic originated in the archipelago. This is an important point, for historians have often mistakenly seen both the trade itself and the changes that stemmed from it in subsequent centuries as primarily the work of outsiders, leaving Indonesians with little historical agency, an error often repeated in assessing the origins and flow of change in more recent times as well.

By the middle of the first millennium BC, the expansion of wet-rice agriculture and, apparently more importantly, certain requirements of trade such as the control of local commodities, suggested new social and political possibilities, which were seized by some communities. For reasons not well understood, most—and all of those that endured—were located in the western archipelago. Already acquainted with a wider world, these Indonesians were open to, and indeed actively sought out, new ideas of political legitimation, social control, and religious and artistic expression. Their principal sources lay not in China, with which ancient Indonesians were certainly acquainted, but in South Asia, in present-day India and Sri Lanka, whose outlooks appear to have more nearly reflected their own. This process of adoption and adaptation, which scholars have somewhat misleadingly referred to as a rather singular "Hinduization" or "Indianization," is perhaps better understood as one of localization or "Indonesianization" of multiple South Asian traditions. It involved much local selection and accommodation (there were no Indian colonizations), and it undoubtedly began many centuries before its first fruits are clearly visible through the archaeological record. Early Indonesia did not become a mini-India. Artistic and religious borrowings were never exact replications, and many key Indic concepts, such as those of caste and the subordinate social position of women were not accepted. Selected ideas filled particular needs or appealed to particular sensibilities, yet at the same time they were anything but superficial; the remnants of their further elaboration are still very much in evidence today.

Early Hegemonies

The Earliest Historical Records

Although some Indonesian peoples probably began writing on perishable materials at an earlier date, the first stone inscriptions (in Sanskrit using an early Pallava script from southern India) date from the end of the fourth century AD (in the eastern Kalimantan locale of Kutai) and from the early or mid-fifth century AD (in the western Java polity known as Taruma). These inscriptions offer a glimpse of leaders newly envisioning themselves not as mere chiefs (*datu*) but as kings or over-lords (*raja, maharaja*), taking Indic names and employing first Brahmanical Hindu, then Buddhist, concepts and rituals to invent new traditions justifying their rule over newly conceived social and political hierarchies. In addition, Chinese records from about the same time provide scattered, although not always reliable, information about a number of other "kingdoms" on Sumatra, Java, southwestern Kalimantan, and southern Sulawesi, which, in the expanding trade opportunities of the early fifth century, had begun to compete with each other for advantage, but we know little else about them. Historians have commonly understood these very limited data to indicate the beginnings of the formation of "states," and later "empires" in the archipelago, but use of such terms is problematic. We understand that small and loosely organized communities consolidated and expanded their reach, some a great deal more successfully than others, but even in the best-known cases we do not have sufficient specific knowledge of how these entities actually worked to compare them confidently with, for example, the states and empires of the Mediterranean region during the same period or earlier. More generalized terms, such as "polities" or "hegemonies," are suggestive of social and political models that are more applicable.

Srivijaya and Mataram

Srivijaya

Two great hegemonies dominate the period from about the mid-sixth to eleventh centuries. The first is known as Srivijaya, a Buddhist trading kingship centered on the region of today's city of Palembang, on the Musi River in present-day Sumatera Selatan Province. At its zenith in the ninth and tenth centuries, Srivijaya extended its commercial sway from approximately the southern half of Sumatra and the Strait of Malacca to western Java and southern Kalimantan, and its influence as far away as locations on the Malay Peninsula, present-day southern Thailand, eastern Kalimantan, and southern Sulawesi (see fig. 2). It probably arose out of policies of war and alliance applied, perhaps rather suddenly, by one local entity to a number of trading partners and competitors. The process is thought to have coincided with newly important direct sea trade with China in the sixth century, and by the second half of the seventh century Srivijaya had become a wealthy and culturally important Asian power. The Chinese pilgrim Yijing (635–713), who briefly visited Srivijaya in 671 and 687 and then lived there from 687 to 695, recommended it as a world-class center of Buddhist studies. Inscriptions from the 680s, written in Pallava script and the indigenous Old Malay language (forerunner of contemporary Bahasa Indonesia— see Glossary), identified the realm and its ruler by name and demanded the loyalty of allies by pronouncing elaborate threats and curses.

Srivijaya's preeminence depended in part on exercising a degree of control over the burgeoning commerce moving through the Strait of Malacca. This it accomplished by mobilizing the policing capabilities of small communities of seafaring *orang laut* (Malay for sea people), providing facilities and protection in exchange for reasonable tax rates on maritime traders, and maintaining favorable relations with inland peoples who were the source of food and many of the trade goods on which commerce of the day was built. But Srivijaya also promoted itself as a commanding cultural center in which ideas from all over Buddhist Asia circulated and were redistributed as far as away Vietnam, Tibet, and Japan.

Mataram

The second great hegemony, known as Mataram, arose as Srivijaya began to flourish in the early eighth century, in south-central Java on the Kedu Plain and southern slopes of Mount Merapi (Gunung Merapi). Mataram's early formation is obscure and complicated by the rivalry of two interrelated lines of aspiring paramount rulers, one supporting Shivaist Hinduism (the Sanjaya) and the other supporting Mahayana Buddhism (the Sailendra, who had commercial and family connections with Srivijaya). At some point between 824 and 856, these lines were joined by marriage, probably as part of a process by which the leaders of local communities (*rakai* or *rakryan*) were incorporated into larger hierarchies with rulers, palaces, and court structures. In this process, the construction of elaborately carved stone structures (*candi*) connecting local powers with Buddhist or Hindu worldviews played an important role. The best known and most impressive of these are the Borobudur, the largest Buddhist edifice in the ancient world (constructed between about 770 and 820 and located northwest of present-day Yogyakarta) and the magnificent complex of Hindu structures at Prambanan, located east of Yogyakarta and completed a quarter-century later. These and hundreds of other monuments built over a comparatively short stretch of time in the eighth and ninth centuries suggest that Javanese and Indic (Buddhist and Hindu) ideas about power and spirituality

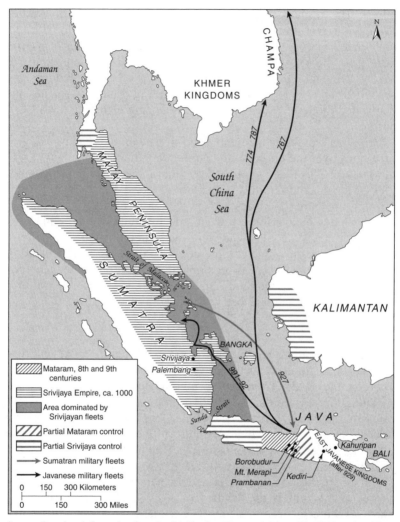

Source: Based on information from Jan M. Pluvier, *Historical Atlas of South-East Asia* (New
        York, 1995), Map 5; and Robert B. Cribb, *Historical Atlas of Indonesia* (Honolulu,
        2000), Map 3.5.

*Figure 2. Sumatra and Java from the Seventh Century to the Eleventh
Century*

both competed and intermingled in a dynamic political and religious
atmosphere.

Scholars have generally identified a highly productive irrigated
rice agriculture as the principal source of Mataram's power, seeing it
as a kind of inland, inward-looking antithesis to an outward-oriented,
maritime Srivijaya, but such a distinction is overdrawn. Central Java

was linked from a very early date to a larger world of commerce and culture, through connections with ports not far away on Java's north coast. Like Srivijaya, Chinese, Indian, and other students of Buddhist and Hindu thought visited Mataram, and Javanese ships traded and made war against competitors in the archipelago (including Srivijaya) and as far away as present-day Cambodia, Vietnam, and probably the Philippines. Mataram was certainly not isolated from the wider world, and in some respects its commercial life may have been more sophisticated than that of its Sumatran contemporary, as it made common use of gold and silver monetary units by the mid-ninth century, some 200 years earlier than Srivijaya. Politically, the two hegemonies were probably more alike than different. The rulers of both saw themselves and their courts (*kedatuan, keratuan,* or *kraton*) as central to a land or realm (*bhumi*), which, in turn, formed the core of a larger, borderless, but concentric and hierarchically organized arrangement of authority. In this greater mandala, an Indic-influenced representation of a sort of idealized, "galactic" order, a ruler emerged from constellations of local powers and ruled by virtue of neither inheritance nor divine descent, but rather through a combination of charisma (*semangat*), strategic family relationships, calculated manipulation of order and disorder, and the invocation of spiritual ideas and supernatural forces. The exercise of power was never absolute, and would-be rulers and (if they were to command loyalty) their supporters had to take seriously both the distribution of benefits (rather than merely the application of force or fear) and the provision of an "exemplary center" enhancing cultural and intellectual life. In Mataram, overlords and their courts do not, for example, appear to have controlled either irrigation systems or the system of weekly markets, which remained the purview of those who dominated local regions (*watak*) and their populations. This sort of political arrangement was at once fragile and remarkably supple, depending on the ruler and a host of surrounding circumstances.

Very little is known about social realities in Srivijaya and Mataram, and most of what is written is based on conjecture. With the exception of the religious structures on Java, these societies were constructed of perishable materials that have not survived the centuries of destructive climate and insects. There are no remains of either palaces or ordinary houses, for example, and we must rely on rare finds of jewelry and other fine metalworking (such as the famous Wonosobo hoard, found near Prambanan in 1991), and on the stone reliefs on the Borobudur and a handful of other structures, to attempt to guess what these societies may have been like. (The vast majority of these remains are Javanese.) A striking characteristic of both Srivijaya and Mataram in this period is that neither—and none of their smaller rivals—appear to have developed settlements recognizable as urban from either Western or Asian traditions. On the whole, despite evidence of socioeconomic well-being and cultural sophistication, institutionally Srivijaya and Mataram remained essentially webs of clanship and patronage, chieftainships carried to their highest and most expansive level.

The Rise and Fall of Majapahit

Successor Kingdoms of Java

During the first decades of the tenth century, Java's center of political gravity shifted decisively from the island's south-central portion to the lower valley and delta regions of eastern Java's Brantas River. The move reflected the Sanjaya line's long-term interest in eastward expansion, a reaction to increasingly frequent volcanic activity in central Java between the 880s and 920s, and economic rivalry with Srivijaya. Eastern Java was a rich rice-growing region and was also closer to the source of Malukan spices, which had become trade items of growing importance. By the early eleventh century, Srivijaya had been weakened by decades of warfare with Java and a devastating defeat in 1025 at the hands of the Cola, a Tamil (south Indian) maritime power. As Srivijaya's hegemony ebbed, a tide of Javanese paramountcy rose on the strength of a series of eastern Java kingdoms beginning with that of Airlangga (r. 1010–42), with its *kraton* at Kahuripan, not far from present-day Surabaya, Jawa Timur Province. A number of smaller realms followed, the best-known of which are Kediri (mid-eleventh to early thirteenth centuries) and Singhasari (thirteenth century), with their centers on the upper reaches of the Brantas River, on the west and east of the slopes of Mount Kawi (Gunung Kawi), respectively.

In this region, continued population growth, political and military rivalries, and economic expansion produced important changes in Javanese society. Taken together, these changes laid the groundwork for what has often been identified as Java's—and Indonesia's— "golden age" in the fourteenth century. In Kediri, for example, there developed a multilayered bureaucracy and a professional army. The ruler extended control over transportation and irrigation and cultivated the arts in order to enhance his own reputation and that of the court as a brilliant and unifying cultural hub. The Old Javanese literary tradition of the *kakawin* (long narrative poem) rapidly developed, moving away from the Sanskrit models of the previous era and producing many key works in the classical canon. Kediri's military and economic influence spread to parts of Kalimantan and Sulawesi.

Buddhist stupas on upper terrace of Borobudur, built ca. AD 800
Dieng Hindu temple complex, seventh and eighth centuries AD,
Jawa Tengah Province
Courtesy Jennifer Foley

In Singhasari, which defeated Kediri in 1222, there arose an aggressive system of state control, moving in new ways to incorporate local lords' rights and lands under royal control and fostering the growth of mystical Hindu-Buddhist state cults devoted to the powers of the ruler, who came to be accorded divine status.

Founding and Growth of Majapahit, 1268–1389

The greatest and most controversial of these kings was Kertanagara (r. 1268–92), the first Javanese ruler to be accorded the title of *dewaprabu* (literally, god-king). Largely by force or threat, Kertanagara brought most of eastern Java under his control and then carried his military campaigns overseas, notably to Srivijaya's successor, Melayu (then also known as Jambi), with a huge naval expedition in 1275, to Bali in 1282, and to areas in western Java, Madura, and the Malay Peninsula. These imperial ambitions proved difficult and expensive, however: the realm was perennially troubled by dissent at court and rebellion both at home and in the subjugated territories. Much farther afield, Kertanagara had provoked the new Mongol rulers of Yuan Dynasty (1279–1368) China to attempt to check his expansion, which they considered a threat to the region. But before their fleet of allegedly 1,000 ships and 100,000 men could land on Java, Kertanagara had been assassinated by a vengeful descendent of the Kediri kings, and in the convoluted events that followed, Kertanagara's son-in-law, Raden Wijaya, succeeded in defeating both his father-in-law's principal rival and the Mongol forces. In 1294 Wijaya ascended the throne as Kertarajasa, ruler of the new kingdom of Majapahit.

Majapahit is generally regarded as having been the largest premodern state in the archipelago, and perhaps the most extensive in all of Southeast Asia. At its zenith under the fourth ruler, Hayam Wuruk (known posthumously as Rajasanagara, r. 1350–89), and his chief minister, the former military officer Gajah Mada (in office 1331–64), Majapahit's authority appears to have extended over 20 eastern Java polities as direct royal domain; tributaries extending beyond those claimed by Singhasari on Java, Bali, Sumatra, Kalimantan, and the Malay Peninsula; and trading partners or allies in Maluku and Sulawesi, as well as present-day Thailand, Cambodia, Vietnam, and China. Majapahit's power was built in part on military might, which Gajah Mada used, for example, in campaigns against Melayu in 1340 and Bali in 1343. Its reach by force was limited, as in the failed campaign in 1357 against Sunda in western Java, however, making the kingdom's economic and cultural vigor perhaps more important factors. Majapahit's ships carried bulk goods, spices, and other exotic commodities throughout the region (cargoes of rice from eastern Java significantly altered the diet of Maluku at this time), spread the use of Malay (not Javanese) as a lingua franca, and brought news of the kingdom's urban center at Trowulan, which covered approximately 100 square kilometers and offered its inhabitants a remarkably high standard of living. Majapahit's writers continued the developments in literature and *wayang* (see Glossary) begun in the Kediri period. The best-known work today is Mpu Prapañca's *Desawarnaña*, often referred to as *Nāgarakertāgama*, composed in 1365, which provides us with an unusually detailed view of daily life in the kingdom's central provinces. Many other classic works also date from this period, including the famous Panji tales, popular romances based on the history of eastern Java that were loved and borrowed by storytellers as far away as Thailand and Cambodia. Many of Majapahit's administrative practices and laws governing trade were admired and later imitated elsewhere, even by fledgling powers seeking independence from Javanese imperial control.

The image of Majapahit as a glorious empire united under a powerful ruler has captured the imagination of many Indonesian nationalists since the 1920s. The modern national motto *Bhinneka Tunggal Ika* (roughly, "Unity in Diversity") was drawn from Mpu Tantular's poem "Sutasoma," written during Hayam Wuruk's reign; independent Indonesia's first university took Gajah Mada's name, and the contemporary nation's communication satellites are named Palapa, after the oath of abstinence Gajah Mada is said to have taken in order to achieve unity throughout the archipelago (*nusantara*). Construction of a "Majapahit Park" (*Taman Majapahit*) on the Trowulan site began in 2008, with the purpose of raising pride in the nation's past. (Some Indonesians interpret things rather differently and see the park as an unwelcome reminder of Javanese dominance over the rest of the archipelago, historically as well as in more recent times.)

Majapahit did not unify the archipelago in any modern sense, however, and its hegemony proved in practice to be fragile and short-lived. Beginning shortly after Hayam Wuruk's death, an agricultural crisis; civil wars of succession; the appearance of strong trading rivals, such as Pasai (in northern Sumatra) and Melaka (on the Malay Peninsula); and restive vassal rulers eager for independence all challenged the political-economic order from which Majapahit had drawn much of its legitimacy. Internally, the ideological order also began to falter as courtiers and others among the elite, perhaps following popular trends, abandoned Hindu-Buddhist cults centered on a supreme kingship in favor of ancestral cults and practices focused on salvation of the soul. In addition, new and often intertwined external forces also brought significant changes, some of which may have contributed to the dissolution of Majapahit's paramountcy.

Outside Influences

China

One of these external forces was the growing influence of China. After the Mongol incursions, the early Majapahitan state did not have official relations with China for a generation, but it did adopt Chinese copper and lead coins (*pisis* or *picis*) as official currency, which rapidly replaced local gold and silver coinage and played a role in the expansion of both internal and external trade. By the second half of the fourteenth century, Majapahit's growing appetite for Chinese luxury goods such as silk and ceramics, and China's demand for such items as pepper, nutmeg, cloves, and aromatic woods, fueled a burgeoning trade. China also became politically involved in Majapahit's relations with restless vassal powers (Palembang in 1377) and, before long, even internal disputes (the Paregreg War, 1401–5). At the time of the celebrated state-sponsored voyages of Chinese Grand Eunuch Zheng He between 1405 and 1433, there were large communities of Chinese traders in major trading ports on Java and Sumatra; their leaders, some appointed by the Ming Dynasty (1368–1644) court, often married into the local population and came to play key roles in its affairs.

Islam

Another external force of great importance was Islam, which had been known in the archipelago since the eighth century but does not appear to have begun to take hold until the beginning of the thirteenth century at the earliest. The first Indonesian Islamic ruler in the archipelago for whom we now have clear evidence was Sultan Sulaiman of Lamreh (northern Sumatra), who died in 1211; several other Sumatran kings, probably influenced by traders and intellectuals arriving from Gujarat and elsewhere in the Indian Ocean, became Muslims later in the thirteenth century. Javanese do not appear to have begun conversion until well into the fifteenth century, despite several centuries' presence there of foreign Muslims. Much of this story may not yet be clear to historians, however, for graves at Trowulan and Tralaya near the eastern Java heart of Hindu-Buddhist Majapahit strongly suggest that some members of that state's elite, perhaps even of the court, had converted to Islam as early as 1368, a time when Majapahit and its state orthodoxies were still very much in the ascendent. The small trading port states on the Pasisir—Java's north coast—many of which later broke away from Majapahit's control, do not appear to have begun to convert to Islam until at least the mid-fifteenth century. This probably developed from the influence of

1 *t Galgerild.* 2 *Vryborgers huyzen.* 3 *Compt Thuynhuysje.* 4 *Vryburgers huyzen.* 5 *de Markt.* 6 *Gouverneurs huys.* 7 *Niew Pakhuys.* 8 *Klede-markt.* 9 *t K*

Engraving from François Valentyn, Oud en nieuw Oost-Indiën
*(Old and New East Indies), Dordrecht, J. Van Braam, 1724–26,
showing the volcano and harbor at Ternate in the Maluku Islands,
with an inset outline view of the Dutch fort
Courtesy Library of Congress Prints and Photographs Division,
LC–USZ262–64526, digital ID cph 3b12115*

Chinese, Cham, and Chinese-Javanese Muslim merchants and later as
a result of the efforts of the so-called Nine Saints (*wali songo*), some
of whom were probably Chinese-Javanese and others connected with
Indian and Persian Islam. The conversion of the eastern archipelago
began with the king of Ternate in 1460, but that region was not
widely Islamized until the sixteenth and seventeenth centuries.

The spread of Islam in the archipelago is not well understood historically, and, especially regarding this early period, scholars continue to disagree on many fundamental points, such as the precise
sources and nature of Muslim influence and the attractions the new
religion held for those who eventually adopted it. It is not clear, for
example, whether individuals—rulers, elites, or commoners—converted for essentially practical considerations (such as the often very
real economic and political advantages of joining the *ummah*, or

community of believers), because of alienation from existing social and political values (in the Hindu-Buddhist kingdoms, for example), or out of an intrinsic interest in the new spiritual and cultural ideas Islam brought with it. Nor is it always obvious why some conversions appear to have been peaceful and others coercive and even violent, or why some indigenous histories emphasize "miraculous" or magical elements in conversions and others do not. Whatever the case, Islamization was not an event, or even a series of events, but rather a long, variegated, and evolutionary process best understood in terms of local, rather than universal, patterns.

Portugal

A third external force came into play with the arrival of the Portuguese in the archipelago. They reached the rich and expanding Melaka, on the Malay Peninsula, in 1509 and sought trading rights there. Some in Melaka's cosmopolitan trading community wanted to accept them (perhaps as a counterweight against Sultan Mahmud's controversial imperial policies), but others did not, heightening existing political tensions. When the Portuguese returned in 1511 commanded by the more demanding Alfonso de Albuquerque, they defeated Melaka militarily, soon establishing themselves in the trading ports of Banten (western Java) and Ternate (Maluku), and contacting the much reduced Majapahit kingdom at Kediri in eastern Java. These events do not, as is sometimes suggested, mark the beginning of Western colonial rule, or even European primacy, in Indonesia; that lay far in the future. Rather, the "Western intrusion" was at this stage merely one dynamic bound up, in often unpredictable ways, with many others. Thus, the final days of Majapahit, weakened by internal division, were determined by Trenggana, the half-Chinese Muslim ruler of its former vassal port Demak, who in 1527 conquered Kediri for reasons that had as much to do with economic and political rivalry (with Banten, the Portuguese, and Majapahit's remnants) as they did with religious struggle (with both Christianity and Hindu-Buddhist ideology).

The Early Modern Era

Commercial Developments

The period between the mid-fifteenth century and the end of the eighteenth century was a time of turbulence and profound change for the archipelago. Java lost much of its commanding position as new states, some great and some small, also raced to acquire wealth and exercise power. Urban populations grew rapidly, and with them the influence of expanding commercial elites. New technologies, for example in weaponry and ship design, changed the face of trade. And Islam extended its reach at the same time as a wide variety of influences diversified and secularized culture. It was also a time in which Europeans began to play a direct role in the archipelago's affairs, although they did not rule it, and Chinese merchants and laborers became more important. All of this took place in the context of a commercial boom that greatly expanded prosperity but also greatly heightened competition and exposed Indonesia directly to the swift and often dangerous currents of what might justifiably be called the "first globalization" (see fig. 3).

This early modern age of commerce was initially fueled by the buying and selling of Indonesian spices, the production of which was limited and the sources often remote. Nutmeg (and mace) come from the nut of the tree *Myristica fragrans*, which, until the late eighteenth century, grew almost exclusively on six tiny islands in the Banda Archipelago, some 300 kilometers west of the Papua coast. Cloves are the dried flower buds of the tree *Syzygium aromaticum*, the cultivation of which until the mid-seventeenth century was largely limited to a handful of small islands off the west coast of Halmahera in the Maluku Islands. These spices had long been distributed in modest quantities via the trade networks of the archipelago. After about 1450, however, demand and the ability to pay for them climbed rapidly in both China and Europe. In the century between the 1390s and the 1490s, for example, European imports of cloves rose nearly 1,000 percent, and of nutmeg nearly 2,000 percent, and continued to rise for the next 120 years. Another product, black pepper *(Piper nigrum)*, was grown more easily and widely (on Java, Sumatra, and Kalimantan), but it too became an object of steeply rising worldwide demand. These changing global market conditions lay at the bottom of fundamental developments, not only in systems of supply and distribution but in virtually all aspects of life in the archipelago.

Westerners and Indigenous Powers

Until the challenge of direct traders from Europe (first the Portuguese and Spanish at the beginning of the sixteenth century, then the Dutch, English, and others at the end of it) and renewed interest from the Chinese (after the Ming government relaxed prohibitions on private overseas trade in the mid-sixteenth century), Indonesians held virtually exclusive control of the spice trade, and decisive power in the extensive exchange of luxury and bulk goods that accompanied it. Over a period of about 250 years, however, they gradually lost their commercial primacy and, in some cases, much of their political

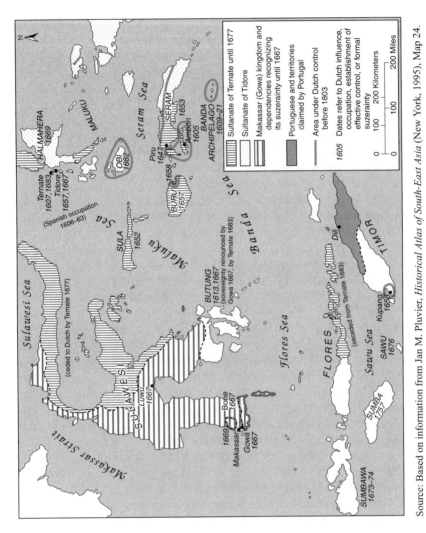

Source: Based on information from Jan M. Pluvier, *Historical Atlas of South-East Asia* (New York, 1995), Map 24.

Figure 3. The Eastern Archipelago in the Seventeenth and Eighteenth Centuries

independence. This crucial process was far too complex to be understood simply as a struggle between East and West, or Christianity and Islam, or "modern" and "traditional" technology. Europeans not only warred vigorously among themselves, but they routinely allied themselves with local powers, many of them Muslim, and became participants in local rivalries; they also frequently found that their weaponry did not give them obvious superiority over indigenous powers, who purchased both light and heavy firearms and sometimes, as in Java well into the eighteenth century, were able to manufacture serviceable copies of European models. Europeans found their position fluctuated as a result of a multitude of factors, some of them well beyond their control.

Some of these complexities can be glimpsed in a brief history of Ternate, Maluku, in the sixteenth and early seventeenth centuries. In 1512 seven Portuguese arrived in Ternate as the guests of Sultan Abu Lais (r. ?–1522), having been rescued by fishermen from a shipwreck of their locally built vessel (their original ship had become too unreliable to continue in service) loaded with spices purchased in Banda. The sultan sought an alliance with the Portuguese, of whom he had already heard, and was eager to exchange cloves for assistance against the rival sultanate of Tidore. When Spanish ships arrived in Maluku in 1521, Sultan Mansur of Tidore sealed a similar agreement with them, to which the Portuguese soon responded by building a large stone fortress on Ternate. This act touched off decades of warfare among Europeans and their local allies, in which political control, economic ascendancy, and religious identity all were contested. But it also brought change in Ternate itself, for the ruler there became essentially a prisoner of the Portuguese, whose increasingly arbitrary and oppressive interference in local affairs, including spice production and harvesting, eventually turned their former allies against them. Under the leadership of Sultan Babullah (r. 1570–83), Islam became a powerful tool with which to create alliances and gather widespread opposition to the Portuguese. After a siege in 1575 against the Ternate fort, he ousted the Portuguese forces. Babullah allowed a limited contingent of Portuguese merchants to continue trading in Ternate, but the fort became the royal residence, and the sultanate rapidly expanded its reach to key trading ports as far away as northern and southern Sulawesi until the arrival of the Dutch touched off new and even more complex struggles.

Elsewhere in the archipelago over the course of the seventeenth century, indigenous and outside powers engaged in a multifaceted struggle for control of maritime trade. Rapidly rising profits from this trade fueled the growth of ambitious states, the most important of which were Aceh (northern Sumatra), Banten (western Java),

Makassar (southern Sulawesi), and Mataram (central and eastern Java). The most important outside power was the Dutch-run United East Indies Company (VOC; for this and other acronyms, see table A). Each of the indigenous states experienced a slightly different trajectory during this period, but the essential contest was between a pattern of heavily state-controlled trade on the one hand and, on the other, a still tentatively oligarchical pattern, in which the so-called *orang kaya* or merchant elite, and often allied religious and traditional elites, played significant political and economic roles.

The best-known example is Aceh, which arose in the middle of the sixteenth century, partly as an effort to control dissension among northern Sumatran and Malay polities and partly to control the Malay trade, which had dispersed after 1511. (Although Aceh's rulers were often serious about promoting Islam, their major military efforts were over commercial rather than religious affairs, and were directed against Muslim as well as Christian rivals.) Aceh reached its apogee under Sultan Iskandar Muda (r. 1607–36). He pursued an aggressive military policy against neighboring powers, including Portuguese Melaka; he presided over a centralized and increasingly authoritarian state; he exercised arbitrary power, including attempting to establish royal monopolies, over the trading activities and even the private property of the *orang kaya*. He invested in huge, heavily armed seagoing ships—one, called *Terror of the Universe*, was more than 90 meters long and carried more than 700 men—of new design to compete with European and Chinese vessels. The sultan also practiced an assertive foreign policy, playing European and Asian powers against each other.

The ruthlessness of Iskandar Muda's regime made many enemies, however, and nearly caused a civil war. Its economic gains, rather than bringing about a permanent transformation of the political and economic structure of Aceh, proved ephemeral. The *orang kaya* reasserted themselves and sought ways to restrict royal power. Until the end of the seventeenth century, for example, they successfully sponsored a succession of female rulers, perhaps because they considered women to be either more moderate or more easily manipulated than men. But in the eighteenth and nineteenth centuries, both their influence and that of the court declined as that of hereditary district chiefs (*uleëbalang*) and Muslim leaders rose. The Acehnese state thus lost its imperial authority and much of its political coherence. Nevertheless—and unlike most of its contemporary regional states—Aceh remained an important local power and continued to be an economic force to be reckoned with, for example producing more than half the world's pepper supply as late as about 1820. Aceh did not hesitate to ally itself with Dutch forces in an attack on Portuguese Melaka in 1641, but in subsequent years it alone among the great nascent states of the early modern archipelago managed to avoid entanglement with the VOC, retaining its independence until the late nineteenth century.

The Role of the Dutch United East Indies Company, 1602–19

A common historical perspective on the seventeenth and eighteenth centuries is to portray the VOC as a uniquely powerful military and economic juggernaut that steadily and deliberately constructed the empire that came to be known as the Netherlands East Indies. In the twentieth century, such a view was frequently shared by Dutch colonial officials and Indonesian nationalists, who spoke of "350 years of Dutch rule" in the archipelago. The truth, however, was more modest. The VOC was neither the "first (modern) multinational corporation," as has sometimes been claimed, nor the instrument of a state policy of colonial expansion. It was founded in the Netherlands in 1602 as an effort to manage the competition and risk of the growing number of Dutch expeditions to the Indonesian archipelago (10 companies, 10 voyages, and 65 ships between 1595 and 1601), and to compete with the East India Company, formed by the English two years earlier, for control of the Asian trade. The VOC's initial charter established its sole right among Dutch enterprises to do business in Asia and gave it exceptional powers, such as those of keeping an army and using military force, making treaties with local rulers, building fortifications, and issuing coinage. In addition, it called for little government oversight and did not require the new company to pay dividends to investors at the end of each voyage (as had been the practice), allowing it to amass large sums of money over longer periods of time. The purpose of this state-supported enterprise was primarily to make a profit. At home the directors, known as the Heeren XVII (Seventeen Gentlemen), recognized that fighting wars, establishing colonies (rather than simple trading posts and fortifications), and becoming involved in local disputes diminished profits, and they generally warned against such activities.

Far away in the archipelago, VOC representatives, appointed after 1610 as governors general, tended to see the warring and political involvement as necessary and pursued them anyway, often vigorously. Even the more ambitious of their efforts, however, were restrained by certain realities. Above all, the VOC was never big enough or strong enough to dominate the entire archipelago and its people, and indeed the company found it impossible to enforce its will in local affairs without Indonesian allies, who frequently exacted a high price for their assistance and whose loyalty could never be taken for granted. It was also the case that even when it had its way—for example, by gaining control of specific trading ports or routes, or of the main areas in which particular spices were produced—interventions by the VOC often had unintended short- and long-term consequences that it could do little to control. Finally, of course, the VOC's fortunes were subject to the vagaries of a trading system that stretched far beyond the archipelago, including the rise and fall in world demand for spices and, later, for other products on which it came to depend, such as coffee. In the course of nearly two centuries, the company failed to control the spice trade and establish the stable conditions necessary for mercantile growth, and came to rule over only minute patches of territory, except for small areas in Maluku in the seventeenth century and Java in the eighteenth.

Nevertheless, the VOC had a shaping influence in the archipelago. In what today is eastern Indonesia, the company—with, it is important to reiterate, the help of indigenous allies—between 1610 and 1680 fundamentally altered the terms of the traditional spice trade by forcibly limiting the number of nutmeg and clove trees, ruthlessly controlling the populations that grew and prepared the spices for the market, and aggressively using treaties and military means to establish VOC hegemony in the trade. One result of these policies, exacerbated by the late-seventeenth-century fall in the global demand for spices, was an overall decline in regional trade, an economic weakening that affected the VOC itself as well as indigenous states, and in many areas occasioned a withdrawal from commercial activity. Others were the rise of authoritarian rulers dependent on VOC support and unrest among groups—traditional leaders, merchants, religious and military figures—who opposed one or the other or both. Among the most prominent examples are those found in the histories of Ternate in the time of Sultan Mandar (r. 1648–75) and the wars against Hitu and Hoamoal (1638–56), and of southern Sulawesi in the era of the ambitious Buginese (Bone) prince Arung Palakka (1634–96) and the wars against the Makassarese (Gowa) and others. By the end of the seventeenth century, the glories of the spice trade had faded, and the vitality of the large and small states of the post-Majapahit era had been sapped; the weight of affairs had again begun to shift west, to Java.

The Javanese and the VOC, 1619–1749

In 1619 the VOC had seized Jayakerta (Sunda Kelapa), a small but well-protected west Javanese port it had originally contracted from a disgruntled vassal of the sultanate of Banten, renaming it Batavia, forerunner of today's Jakarta. The resolute Governor General Jan

Copper coins used in Indonesian colonial trade: A Netherlands East Indies (VOC) one duit has on the obverse the crowned arms of Utrecht—where it was minted; the reverse shows the VOC monogram and the date 1790. This Chinese one cash reads Qianlong Tongbao *(Qianlong [the emperor] general treasury)—which dates the coin between 1736 and 1796—on the obverse, and the reverse has the Manchu-language inscription* chuanbao *for the Board of Revenue Mint in Beijing.*
Courtesy Robert L. Worden

Pieterszoon Coen (in office 1619–23 and 1627–29) had conceived of this port as a kind of fulcrum of the company's far-flung Asian enterprise, and he defended it vigorously against both Banten (allied briefly with England's East India Company) and, in 1628–29, the powerful land and sea forces of the expanding central Javanese state that had taken the name of Mataram, after the ninth-century kingdom. Mataram's ruler, Sultan Agung (r. 1613–46), was Java's greatest warrior king since Kertanagara nearly four centuries earlier. Using iron force and a keen sense of traditional diplomatic opportunities, Sultan Agung assembled a realm that consisted of all of Java and Madura (including the powerful kingdom of Surabaya) except Banten in the far west and the Hindu-Buddhist kingdom of Blambangan in the far east. Sukadana and Banjarmasin on Kalimantan also fell under his sway. He was not, however, able to dislodge the VOC, and after the failed campaign of 1628–29 he appears to have accepted the Dutch presence as a minor irritant. Contemporaneous Javanese historical works treated the company more as a potential ally than as a serious threat, a view that persisted among many in court circles for another century or more. And, indeed, at the time the VOC was neither interested in nor capable of tackling the full force of Mataram, which despite the destruction and political tensions wrought by nearly 40 years of expansion remained a formidable military power. The company saw itself as a maritime power, a rival for the control of produce and trade rather than territory, and it sought stable conditions for its activities rather than upheaval (see fig. 4).

Conditions began to change, however, during the disastrous reign of Sultan Agung's son, Amangkurat I (r. 1646–77), who lacked his father's talents but sought to further strengthen the realm by centralizing authority, monopolizing control of resources, and destroying all real or imagined opposition. His misguided efforts to control trade revenues by twice closing the ports of the Pasisir, and even destroying Javanese trading vessels and forbidding Javanese travel overseas, had the opposite effect, in addition to alienating the commercial community and damaging the wider economy of producers. His obsessive fear of opposition led him to kill more than 5,000 Muslim leaders and their families in a single, well-planned massacre, and to murder hundreds of court officials and members of the aristocracy, including his own family, actions that of course only increased the hatred and intrigues aimed at removing him. His attitude toward the VOC was ambivalent, for, on the one hand, he admired its apparent wealth and power and considered it a potential ally and protector, yet on the other hand he sought to bend it to his will and to extract all he could from its representatives in Batavia. Beginning in the early 1670s, rebellions began to rise, the most powerful of which was led by Raden Trunajaya (ca. 1649–80), a Madurese aristocrat conspiring with a disaffected son of Amangkurat I and allied with Makassarese and other forces. Trunajaya's armies won a decisive victory in 1676 and looted the capital the following year. Mataram was disintegrating.

In the course of this conflict, both sides requested assistance from the VOC, which now faced a momentous decision. The company sought political stability and a reliable supply of such key products as rice and teak, and it determined for the first time in more than a half-century that, in order to obtain them, intervention in Mataram's internal affairs was necessary. Company officials viewed Javanese kingship through a European lens as a relatively absolutist, centralized form of rule that legitimated succession by, if not strict primogeniture, then something very close to it. This was a misreading of Javanese (and, indeed, other Indonesian) cultural custom, but nonetheless the VOC gradually came to see itself as the upholder of order (tradition) and to justify its actions in terms of favoring continuity rather than change. It made its choices accordingly, often with the ironic result of creating rather than solving discord and of weakening rather than strengthening the sorts of order it hoped to achieve. In any case, the VOC decided in 1676 to back the forces of Amangkurat I, who died soon after having fled to VOC-controlled territory on the Pasisir, and then to support his rebellious son as successor, a project requiring five more years of warfare to complete. The company gained treaties promising, among other things, access to the products and trading rights it sought, as well as repayment of all its military costs. That these treaty obligations proved difficult to fulfill did not negate the fact that the VOC had now embarked on a course that slowly and expensively intertwined its own fate with that of Mataram. The dark legacy of Amangkurat's tyrannical misrule thus lay not only in 80 years of turbulence in Javanese life, punctuated by three destructive wars of succession, but also in the establishment of patterns of Dutch entanglement in indigenous affairs that were to outlive the VOC itself.

Decline of the VOC, 1749–1816

By the mid-eighteenth century, the VOC and the court of Mataram, at the same time rivals and allies, were exhausted by war. The dying ruler, Pakubuwana II (r. 1726–49), with his kingdom still threatened by rebellion from within and his court deeply divided over the proper course for the future, ceded Mataram to the company, perhaps thinking in this way to save it. The treaty was of little importance because it could not be enforced and the VOC was incapable of ruling Java, but it was followed in 1755 by the Treaty of Giyanti, which imposed a different solution. Mataram was to be ruled by two royal courts, one at Surakarta (also known as Solo) and one at Yogyakarta, out of which the junior courts of Mangkunegaran (1757) and Pakualaman (1812), respectively, later evolved by apportioning appanage rights among them. This division produced an extended period of peace lasting well into the nineteenth century, from which the Javanese populace benefited economically. The courts, particularly that of Yogyakarta, made use of their considerable autonomy and grew in prosperity and power, while the VOC consolidated its control over the Pasisir and pursued its commercial ventures. Although clearly recognized (and often resented) as the paramount power, the company interested itself in the courts' affairs and played a role in choosing

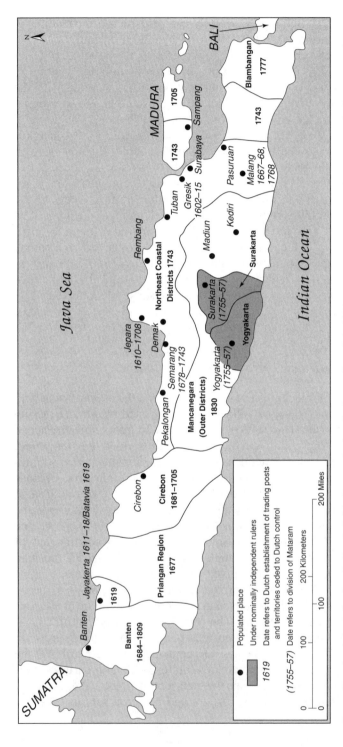

Source: Based on information from Robert B. Cribb, *Historical Atlas of Indonesia* (Honolulu, 2000), Maps 3.21, 3.25, 3.26, and 3.50; Jan M. Pluvier, *Historical Atlas of South-East Asia* (New York, 1995), Maps 22 and 23; and D. G. E. Hall, *A History of South-East Asia* (New York, 1981), 351.

Figure 4. Dutch Expansion in Java, 1619–1830

who reigned but refrained from meddling too deeply. It was a strange conquest.

The peace was in many respects also strange, for rather than settling Java into a calm "traditional" existence, it provided the setting for ongoing social and cultural ferment as Javanese reassessed not only their past but also their present. The literary reflections of this crisis have been insufficiently studied, but works ascribed to the Surakarta court poets Yasadipura I (1729–1803) and his son Yasadipura II (? –1844), for example, suggest that efforts to reexamine and revitalize old histories failed, not least because the ability to read them accurately had been lost, and that attempts to understand the Java—and, we might say, "Javaneseness"—of their own day led frequently to searing critiques of their own social hierarchy and customs, as well as those of foreigners and Islam. This sort of questioning and restlessness was not necessarily fatal, however, and might under different circumstances have permitted a continuation of the equilibrium already achieved or even conceivably have led to a kind of Javanese renaissance and a different, more advantageous relationship with the Dutch. But changes in the larger world determined otherwise.

In the early 1780s, the last in a series of wars with the British cost the Netherlands, including the VOC and its far-flung interests, dearly. Nearly half the company's ships were lost, and much of their valuable cargoes; enormous debts accumulated, which, despite state loans, could not be repaid. While the company certainly was burdened with other fiscal and administrative problems, among them a high level of corruption among its employees, the British war seems to have been the critical factor in its fiscal collapse. In 1796 the VOC was placed under the direction of a national committee until the end of 1799, when it was liquidated, its debts and possessions absorbed by the Dutch government.

By this time, however, the Napoleonic wars had brought the Netherlands under French control, and in rapid succession the former VOC territories fell under the direction of leaders appointed by France—the military officer Herman Willem Daendels from 1808 to 1811—and, after Napoleon's defeat, by Britain, which appointed an East India Company official, Thomas Stamford Raffles, for the period 1811–16. Daendels and Raffles saw themselves as liberal reformers, enemies of feudal privilege and practices such as forced labor and delivery of produce, proponents of the welfare of the common folk, and opponents of corruption and inefficiency. Raffles sought to "free" Javanese laborers by instituting a system of land rent, in which farmers grew cash crops and sold them in order to pay the government for the use of the land. But the sharpest break with VOC practice lay in the assumption by the new powers of sovereign rights over the Javanese courts, treating rulers and courtiers not as allies but as clear subordinates, and their representatives not as local lords but as mere bureaucratic officeholders. Both men interfered directly in court affairs. Daendels replaced Yogyakarta's ruler (on suspicion of rebellion) and annexed territory by force of arms. Raffles actually bombarded and looted the Yogyakarta court (for the same reason), establishing the Pakualaman from some of its appanage lands, and exiled an unruly Surakarta prince. These acts, and the attitudes behind them, foreshadowed nothing less than a new age for the archipelago, an age of Dutch colonial rule.

Development of European Colonial Rule

End of the Ancien Régime in Java, 1816–34

In 1816 the Netherlands regained responsibility for the East Indies—actually a welter of mostly coastal territories, some controlled directly and many others engaged through varying treaties—but the way forward was uncertain (see, for example, fig. 5). The growth of trade with Sulawesi and the establishment of plantation economies, especially those producing sugar (eastern and central Java) and coffee (western Java and western Sumatra) had begun to loosen customary ties and introduce elites to new sources of both riches and indebtedness. In Java, the general population increased and grew more prosperous but, on the other hand, fell victim to increasing crime, heavier taxation, and exploitation by local Chinese, especially in their roles of tax farmers, tollkeepers, and leasers of plantation lands. The legitimacy of ruling elites was questioned more widely. Both traditionalists and Muslims felt their ways of life threatened by changes they tended to identify with growing European influence. A Dutch decision in 1823 to end what it viewed as the abusive leasing of land and labor among central Java's aristocracy alienated many who had begun to adjust to the new circumstances and pushed them to support rebellion. The general atmosphere of restlessness in a time of change that few understood also became charged with superstition and millennial expectations in reaction to crop failures, outbreaks of disease, and, near Yogyakarta, a destructive eruption of the Mount Merapi volcano.

The struggle known as the Java War (1825–30) was led by a disaffected prince of the Yogyakarta court, Diponegoro (1785–1855). He was a complex figure who opposed rule by both the Dutch and the complicit Javanese ruler and aristocracy, and whose rebellion must therefore be seen as a Javanese civil war—although not one primarily concerned with questions of succession, as in the eighteenth century—at least as much as an anticolonial one. Despite his modern Indonesian status as a national hero, Diponegoro appears to have sought merely to have relations with the Dutch return to the form they had assumed in late VOC times, and certainly had no conception of a broader Indonesian nation.

Diponegoro was able to attract, for a time, the loyalty of those who felt the crumbling of the previous order in different ways and had a variety of social and moral expectations. He was seen variously as a protector of the general populace, as both a Muslim and a traditionalist messianic figure, a Ratu Adil (just king), and as an upholder of social hierarchy under a reformed or purified aristocracy. These alliances proved fragile, however. There were obvious internal tensions, for example, disagreements between those who had fought for religious reasons (responding to Diponegoro's declaration of a Muslim holy war, or jihad) and those, especially among the court elite, who had done so for essentially secular reasons. The difficulty of the war itself, for which the Dutch devised new military strategies and which spread destruction on a scale unseen in generations, was extreme: about two-thirds of Java was affected, a quarter of its cultivated land was laid waste; and approximately 200,000 Javanese and 15,000 government troops (8,000 of whom were Europeans) were killed. Backed initially by about half of Yogyakarta's ruling elite, by early 1830 Diponegoro had lost most of their support, as well as that of both his chief military commander and his most influential Muslim patron and his followers. Abandoned by all but a few loyal comrades, he attended a peace discussion with the Dutch commander of government forces at which he was arrested and sent into exile. He died imprisoned in the government fort in Makassar.

The conclusion of the Java War marked the end of Java's old social and political order. The government in Batavia sharply reduced the lands under the courts' control, and the fiction of Mataram finally gave way to what were now termed merely the *vorstenlanden* (principalities) and seen as comparatively minor vestigial powers. The Javanese elites acquiesced, although not without some resentment, in part because another war was inconceivable and in part because they calculated that acquiescence was necessary if they were to retain anything at all of their privileged socioeconomic status. At the same time, the end of the war made equally clear that a new era had begun—not only for Java, but for the broader archipelago—an era in which the government of the Netherlands assumed full sovereignty. It began to oversee its territories through the new Ministry of Colonies (established in 1834), and took a strikingly different attitude toward indigenous peoples. As J. C. Baud (1789–1859), the first governor general of the Netherlands East Indies with full executive authority (1834–36), stated succinctly, "We are the

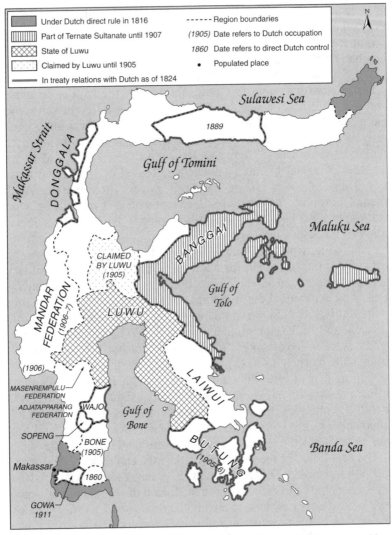

▣ Under Dutch direct rule in 1816	------ Region boundaries
▨ Part of Ternate Sultanate until 1907	*(1905)* Date refers to Dutch occupation
▨ State of Luwu	*1860* Date refers to direct Dutch control
▨ Claimed by Luwu until 1905	• Populated place
▬ In treaty relations with Dutch as of 1824	

N

Sulawesi Sea

1889

Gulf of Tomini

Makassar Strait

DONGGALA

Maluku Sea

BANGGAI

CLAIMED
BY LUWU
(1905)

*Gulf of
Tolo*

MANDAR
FEDERATION
(1906–7)

L U W U

(1906)

L A I W U I

MASENREMPULU–
FEDERATION

ADJATAPPARANG WAJO
FEDERATION

SOPENG

*Gulf of
Bone*

B U T U N G
(1905–6)

Banda Sea

BONE
(1905)

Makassar

1860

GOWA
1911

Source: Based on information from Jan M. Pluvier, *Historical Atlas of South-East Asia* (New
York, 1995), Map 40.

Figure 5. Sulawesi in the Nineteenth and Twentieth Centuries

rulers and they are the ruled." The resulting colonial state did not come
suddenly into existence, however, but developed in stages, from hybrid
arrangements of convenience to a modernizing administrative structure, over the course of more than a century.

Establishment of the Colonial State

The Dutch colonial state had its foundation in conquest. Unlike the violence used earlier by the VOC, the military expansion of the nineteenth century was deliberately territorial and penetrated far beyond the coastal areas. It generally had as its goal fundamental regime change and—although in truth this was often beyond Batavia's capability—the establishment of control by a centralized authority. Quite different from the eighteenth century, too, colonial forces enjoyed a degree of technological superiority over most of their adversaries, a result of the industrial revolution. And, whereas the VOC had fought with an assortment of indigenous allies, now the colonial state fought for its own interests, engaging indigenous men as soldiers. The colonial government's separate fighting force, known as the Royal Netherlands Indies Army (KNIL), was founded only a few weeks before Diponegoro's surrender in 1830. Although assigned the task of maintaining *rust en orde* (tranquillity and order) throughout the colonial state's territories, the KNIL became best known for its role in the colonial wars of expansion. Dominated by ethnic Dutch, and later Eurasian, officers, in the mid-nineteenth century about two-thirds of KNIL troops were Indonesians, predominantly Javanese and Ambonese, and the rest "European," a confusing category that included not only white Europeans but also a small number of black Africans and others.

Modern military intrusions began at about the same time as the Java War and lasted into the early twentieth century. Their circumstances varied. In some instances, such as that of the Padri Wars (1821–37) in Minangkabau in western Sumatra, the military assistance of the colonial government was sought by indigenous factions, in this case members of the aristocracy and some village clan leaders beleaguered by Wahhabi-influenced Muslim reformers. The reformers were defeated, but the aristocracy and clan leaders eventually surrendered their powers to the colonial state. In other examples, such as those of Banjarmasin (southern Kalimantan, 1857–59) and Palembang (southern Sumatra, 1823–49), the government imposed and then deposed rulers without invitation, but with similar results. The war against the great power of Aceh (northern Sumatra, 1873–1903) was the most extensive and costly of all these conflicts. The Dutch pursued it because of the imperial designs of other Western powers, commercial and military competition from the Acehnese, and the spread from Aceh of anti-Western, anticolonial Muslim movements. For a time, Batavia appeared to take up the cause of the *uleëbalang*, or traditional and more secular elite, as had been the case in Minangkabau, but this was a temporary tactic, and in any case the *uleëbalang* too ended up subservient to the colonial state, which finally annexed Aceh outright.

Among the last conflicts were those in Bali and Lombok, where the intervention of colonial forces after 1840 had been limited, in part by fierce Balinese resistance. After the mid-1880s, however, warfare and rebellion in a number of Balinese kingdoms, and Dutch interest in controlling the important, ongoing local trade in slaves and opium, led the colonial state to apply increasing military pressure. It conquered Lombok in 1894, and, between 1906 and 1908, the last independent Balinese rulers submitted. In the kingdoms of Badung, Tabanan, Klungkung, and others, the rajas and their families and followers sacrificed themselves in dramatic frontal assaults on the KNIL guns. These *puputan*, or ritual suicides, killed hundreds of men, women, and children, decimating the aristocracy and obliterating all meaningful further resistance to the expansion of colonial rule in Bali. With smaller campaigns to establish claims of colonial sovereignty in Timor and Flores between 1908 and 1910, the Netherlands East Indies reached, at least in outline, its final extent, including far-off territories such as the Kai Islands (in southeastern Maluku) and Papua (on the island of New Guinea).

The Cultivation System

A colonial state aimed at managing the territories and people acquired as a result of these conquests—or "pacifications," as some preferred to describe them—emerged gradually and piecemeal. It first began to take shape around the time of Diponegoro's defeat, with the inauguration in Java of policies that came to be known as the Cultivation System (Cultuurstelsel). This was the brainchild of Johannes van den Bosch, a military man and social reformer who became governor general (1830–34) and later minister of colonies (1834–39). He sought to solve the fiscal problems of Batavia and the Netherlands, both of which were on the brink of bankruptcy, as well as those of a populace devastated by warfare on Java. Van den Bosch believed that Java was a rich but underproductive land, primarily because Javanese farmers, even when their own prosperity was at stake, would not or could not produce beyond a subsistence level unless guided, even compelled, to do so. "Force," he wrote, "is everywhere the basis of industry ... where it does not exist there is neither industry nor civilization."

Van den Bosch's plan forced Java's farmers either to use existing agricultural lands or open new ones in order to cultivate crops for export, deliver them to the government at fixed prices, and utilize the income to offset or pay the government taxes on their land. The crops first targeted were sugar and indigo, but coffee and pepper were soon added, followed by newer crops, such as tea, tobacco, and

Dutch official's home in Surabaya, 1854
Courtesy Library of Congress Prints and Photographs Division,
LC–USZ62–105190, digital ID cph 3c05190

cinnamon. Unlike the system that Raffles had contemplated, van den Bosch proposed dealing with whole villages rather than individuals, and using government officials and local authorities (who received a percentage of revenues their areas generated) to regulate which crops would be grown, on which and how much land, with which and how much labor, and at what prices. Bringing the produce to the world market through the Netherlands became the monopoly of the Netherlands Trading Association (NHM), a private company in which the Dutch king was a major stockholder. Entrepreneurs in general were locked out of the state-run system. This approach, van den Bosch argued, would assure production and profits great enough not only to subsidize the colonial administration and contribute handsomely to the treasury of the Netherlands but also to substantially improve the well-being of the Javanese. Scholars and politicians alike have been arguing ever since over what exactly the results were.

There is little doubt that fiscally, and from a government perspective, the Cultivation System was an enormous success. Between 1830 and 1870, Java's exports increased more than tenfold, and profits nearly sevenfold; the colonial government regained solvency almost immediately and between 1832 and 1877 remitted a budgetary surplus (*batig slot*) totaling 823 million Dutch guilders to the treasury of the Netherlands, on average about 18 million guilders annually, about a third of the national budget. It is no exaggeration to say that nineteenth-century Dutch prosperity rested very largely upon these funds.

Whether the Javanese benefited from or were impoverished by the Cultivation System, however, is much less clear. Generalization about this question is made particularly difficult by the fact that the system as actually implemented was not very systematic and varied considerably according to time, place, and circumstance. In some regions, for example, 40 percent of the adult population labored for the system and in others, 100 percent; in some areas, less than 4 percent of agricultural land was used and in others, 15 percent. Abuses of the system's provisions, including official corruption, also varied sharply by locale. The principal criticisms were, and continue to be today, moral ones. The Cultivation System was portrayed as having been founded on greed and as being not only coercive and exploitative but also prone to a range of abuses, all of which produced, for the average villager, only impoverishment. This view was put forth most memorably in the 1860 Dutch novel *Max Havelaar* by Eduard Douwes Dekker (1820–77), an embittered former colonial official who wrote under the pseudonym Multatuli ("I have suffered much"). Douwes Dekker's account was widely understood, probably not entirely accurately, as a thoroughgoing indictment of colonial rule in general and the Cultivation System in particular, which he accused of having created a uniformly desperate, destitute peasantry. This, or something much like it, became the received view. Recent studies, however, based on rereadings of old evidence as well as on archival information that became available only in the mid-twentieth century, suggest a far more complex picture. While acknowledging that the burdens of the Cultivation System fell on the laboring Javanese populace, they also argue that the majority probably saw at least limited economic improvement and took advantage of new economic opportunities, although at the cost of a more regimented and government-controlled existence, and with the added risk of dependency on world markets. This was a form of circumscribed change that shaped Java's village world far into the future.

The Cultivation System had not required an elaborate state apparatus. It was deliberately a form of indirect rule using an existing hierarchy of the Javanese *priyayi* (see Glossary) elite, especially the upper ranks of traditional local officeholders known as the *pangreh praja* (rulers of the realm) and village heads. As late as the mid-1850s, European officials and regional supervisors numbered fewer than 300 for an indigenous population of more than 10 million. A

Rubber plantation workers, Java, between 1900 and 1923
Courtesy Library of Congress Prints and Photographs Division, Frank and
Frances Carpenter Collection, LC–USZ62–100045, digital ID cph 3c00045

small number of freelance European engineers and locally requisitioned laborers undertook the construction of roads and irrigation works needed for the new plantations. This began to change, however, as the system grew, underwent reform, and then, especially after the Sugar Act and Agrarian Act of 1870, gradually gave way to private enterprise. The responsibilities of the colonial government burgeoned, and in order to meet them, it expanded *pangreh praja* ranks by dividing and standardizing their administrative territories and tightened control, by rescinding their traditional rights to symbols of status and access to villagers' labor and services, tying them to government salaries and procedures. Alongside the *pangreh praja* now served a growing parallel hierarchy of European officials— ostensibly functioning as advisers or "elder brothers" of their native counterparts but increasingly directing them—whose reach, by 1882, extended as far down as the subdistrict level, just above the village head. In addition, more specialized government offices came into being: a Bureau of Public Works (with its own corps of engineers and an irrigation division), as well as departments of agriculture, education, finance, justice, and religion, all with their own structures and technical staffs.

The Ethical Policy

In 1901 Queen Wilhelmina of the Netherlands announced the government's acceptance of the idea that it owed a "debt of honor" to the East Indies because of the profits generated by the Cultivation System, and its intention of henceforth basing its colonial policies on a "moral duty" to them. This new direction, commonly referred to by historians as the Ethical Policy, called for new and extensive government initiatives to expand public schooling, improve health care, modernize infrastructure (communications, transportation, and irrigation), and reduce poverty. The administrative system was to be overhauled in favor of a more modern, efficient structure. Colonial authorities began decentralizing fiscal and administrative responsibilities (in 1903 and 1922, respectively), forming local and colony-wide semirepresentative political bodies (among them the Peoples' Council, or Volksraad, in 1918), and ending, or at least modifying, the dualism inherent in the interior administrative service with its parallel lines of European and indigenous officials. In addition, for the first time, the colonial state attempted to simplify and standardize the administrative features of its rule in the Outer Islands (see Glossary), using what was being done on Java (and Madura and Bali) as a rough template.

Although Ethicists, as supporters of the policy were called, may sometimes have been seen as arguing for a weakening of colonial rule and lessening of European influence, this was not the case. They aimed at modernizing the imperial state, which also meant Europeanizing, or at least Westernizing, it. It is fair to say that in technical matters the Ethicists were more successful than with social and political questions: food production generally kept pace with population growth, and distribution improved; efforts to combat the plague and other diseases were moderately effective; and irrigation and transportation facilities (roads, railroads, and shipping lines) grew rapidly. The problem of administrative dualism could not be resolved, however, largely because European officialdom was unwilling to surrender its position. Political decentralization and the introduction of some form of representation for Europeans and indigenes educated in Europe were limited by, among other things, the central government's reluctance to surrender its ultimate control of budgetary and legal affairs. Likewise, legal standardization foundered on the increasingly heated debate over whether non-Europeans should be subject to Western law or to other legal principles such as those of local unwritten custom (*adat*) or the sharia (see Glossary), Islamic law, called *syariah* in Bahasa Indonesia.

The Racial Issue

The unresolved issue of greatest importance was that of racial classification, which the modern Dutch historian Cees Fasseur has identified as both the "cornerstone and stumbling block" of the colonial state. Under the VOC, people were classified mainly on the basis of religion rather than race, Christianized indigenes generally falling under the same laws as Protestant Europeans. In the early nineteenth century, however, "enlightened" ideas began to emphasize—often on "humanitarian" grounds that sought protection of indigenous peoples—a separation between native and European rights, and the Cultivation System, with its clear distinction between rulers and ruled, emphasized that divide. In practice, if not yet in law, non-Europeans were treated very differently from Europeans in judicial and penal matters, and in 1848 legal and commercial codes appeared that were applicable to Europeans only. Statutes of 1854 made a formal (but not very specific) distinction between Europeans and natives (*inlanders*), at the same time as offering them "equal" protection. Everyday understanding and practice, however, was that "equal" did not mean "the same," and that, in particular, Europeans and Asians occupied separate legal spheres. Almost immediately, however, there were difficulties. The category of Asians was further divided into "natives" and "foreign orientals," among whom the Chinese, ostensibly for business reasons, in 1885 were determined to fall under European commercial law. The category "European" did not distinguish between full-blooded Europeans—the so-called *totok* Dutch—and those of mixed European and indigenous parentage—the Eurasians, or so-called Indos. In 1899, for political reasons, the Japanese were accorded European public and private legal status, and in 1925 the same was done for those whose country of origin adopted Western family laws, such as Turkey and Siam (after 1939, Thailand). "Natives" remained a separate, and lower, category.

One might think that these circumstances would soon have led to the abandonment of all racial or national distinctions and a unification of colonial law and policy in general, but instead a fundamental dualism—native and European—remained. This outcome is all the more remarkable because it was at odds with important realities in colonial life. In the early twentieth century, Europeans increasingly married across racial categories. In 1905 about 15 percent were in interracial marriages, rising to 27.5 percent by 1925. And, although by the mid-1920s the older mix of dress and sensibilities known as "Indies" (*Indische*) culture was rapidly giving way to more modern, urbanized, European- and American-influenced forms, numerous memoirs of Europeans, Eurasians, Chinese, and Indonesians make it clear that, despite obvious racial tensions and divisions, a new sort of Dutch-speaking, racially mixed, and culturally modern society was coming into being, mostly in the largest cities and mostly among the upper and upper-middle economic classes.

A powerful countercurrent was also developing, however. In part, this was the result of the stubborn refusal of the colonial state either to surrender the formal dualism on which it had been built, or to face squarely the many anomalies created by its insistence on legal classification. Especially as the specters of nationalism and communism came into focus after 1918, the idea of emancipation for all simply could not be accepted, either in the abstract or for practical reasons. Other factors included the greater numbers of newcomer, full-blooded Europeans, including women, arriving in the colony, most of whom had the notion that colonial life there should adjust itself to their standards, not the other way around. The resentment that resulted among Eurasians and indigenes, already chafing against the effects of both formal and informal discrimination, the Great Depression of the 1930s, and the approach of World War II (1939–45) in different ways deepened existing fears. After 1930, racism became more visible in all corners of colonial society. To all of this the colonial government remained strangely cold, taking merely an attitude of watchfulness and determination to "keep the peace." When, in 1940, the governor general appointed the Visman Commission to determine what the public really thought about issues connected with the constitutional development of the colony, the clearest finding was that discrimination was universally considered a serious problem, and that all other groups wished to hold legal equality with Europeans. The commission's own suggestions for solving the problem by replacing racial criteria with education, financial, and other measures were unworkable, and in any case time had run out. On December 7, 1941, two days after the commission submitted its report, Japan attacked the United States naval base at Pearl Harbor.

Modernism and Nationalism in the Colonial Age

The Rise of Education and Student Associations, 1900–1920

At the dawn of the twentieth century, the young daughter of a Javanese *pangreh praja*, Raden Ajeng (R. A.) Kartini (1879–1904), expressed in letters to Dutch friends her enthusiasm for the "Spirit of the Age ... [before which] solid ancient structures tottered," and her joy at witnessing the "transition from old to new" that was going on around her. Her main concern, however, was how her own people, whom she described as "grown-up children," might progress—not precisely on a European model, but certainly with Dutch assistance— and concluded that the only way forward was through Dutch education. Kartini was only in part echoing ideas close to the hearts of the Ethicists who befriended and later lionized her and her efforts to promote modern education for women as splendid examples of their cause; it is clear that she rebelled against her traditional environment early on, and also did not always agree with her Ethicist friends. She was not alone. At roughly the same time, young male contemporaries from the Javanese privileged classes who attended government schools were coming to similar conclusions, and were in a better position to take more public, activist positions. Like Minke, the hero of the 1980 novel set in Kartini's day by Pramudya Ananta Tur (1925–2006) in his *Bumi Manusia* (This Earth of Mankind), they were alienated from their parents' generation, saw no future in aristocratic status or careers as *pangreh praja*, and felt drawn to all that was new, scientific, and modern. They did not yet have the idea of a nation in mind, but they were busy trying to imagine a modern society of their own, and how to make it a reality. In the process, they began to coalesce as a new *priyayi* class—a class based on achievement rather than birth, devotion to modernity rather than tradition—that would determine the course of their country's history for the remainder of the century.

That was not, of course, exactly what the Ethicists had in mind when they promoted Western education. They had hoped to create a broad new *priyayi* class, which, thanks to a modern Western education, would take a cooperative, associationist path. Such was the goal behind the extensive education reforms that, beginning in 1900, overhauled the limited training available for medical personnel, vernacular primary school teachers, and prospective *pangreh praja*. The most important institutions to appear were the School for Training Native Government Officials (OSVIA) and the School for Training Native Doctors (STOVIA), both established in 1900, and the Dutch–Native Schools (HIS), established in 1914, which were Dutch-language primary schools for the upper classes. There was also a significant expansion of vernacular primary village schools (*sekolah desa*).

Looking at the colony as a whole, these advances may seem negligible. As late as 1930, about 10,000 *sekolah desa* enrolled roughly 1.6 million students, or 2.8 percent of a population estimated at 60 million. Dutch-language education enrolled far fewer indigenous students: about 85,000 or roughly 0.14 percent of the total population. General literacy was estimated at 7.5 percent and in Dutch, about 0.3 percent. The Dutch-language schools with Western-style curricula created a small but motivated group, however, who emerged with a changed outlook. The schools were located principally on Java, where they gathered together students from all over the archipelago and gave them a shared experience. More convinced than ever of the power of Western education, they also grew dissatisfied. Although Dutch-language schools above the HIS enrolled Europeans as well as indigenes, the latter were a comparatively small minority, and they often felt the sting of prejudice, both real and perceived. Equal in education, indigenous students began to chafe under obvious inequalities: legal, economic, and social. They also quickly became aware of what a tiny minority they were in their own society, and that the demand for Dutch-language education, widely seen as key to social and economic advancement, was far beyond the colonial government's ability or willingness to provide. Rather than generations of grateful and subservient graduates, the colonial schools quickly produced a significant number of malcontents, whose most common message was not that the colonial state was modernizing indigenous society too quickly, but precisely the opposite. They believed they could, and had the duty to, do better.

Students from Dutch-language schools founded the first indigenous groups organized along Western-influenced lines and aimed at modernization and education. Probably the first person to do this was the *pangreh praja* son, ex-STOVIA student, and pioneer journalist Raden Mas Tirtoadisuryo (1880–1918), who in 1906 established the Serikat Priyayi (Priyayi Association), aimed at convincing the colonial authorities to expand educational opportunities for *priyayi*. The best-known and officially recognized organization, however, was Budi Utomo (Noble Endeavor), founded in 1908 by Wahidin Sudirohusodo (1857–1917), also a *pangreh praja* son, graduate of a STOVIA predecessor school, and journalist. Wahidin's goal was to organize financial support that would allow more *priyayi* to attend Dutch-medium schools; he discovered his most enthusiastic supporters were found among STOVIA students, who formed the core of Budi Utomo. In 1909 a Surakarta batik merchant, Samanhudi (1868–1956), asked Tirtoadisuryo to organize native businessmen, apparently in response to Chinese competition in the trade. The result was the Sarekat Dagang Islam (Islamic Trade Association), which in 1912 became the Sarekat Islam (Islamic Association). Now under the leadership of Haji Umar Said (H. U. S.) Cokroaminoto (1882–1934), an OSVIA graduate who had left government service, the Sarekat Islam had as one of its major goals the expansion of education of, especially, lower *priyayi*, and as a result the colonial government initially reacted approvingly, as it had done with Budi Utomo.

Cokroaminoto's personal charisma, and his ability to use religion to attract wide public interest, helped the organization expand rapidly—perhaps to 2 million members in 1919—and this mass base in turn attracted those with quite different political interests. Founded in 1913 by the Dutch radical socialist Hendrik Sneevliet (1883–1942), the Indies Social-Democratic Association (ISDV), a small leftist party that had at first sought an audience in Eurasian groups and among laborers in modern industries, turned to Sarekat Islam. The young Javanese railway worker Semaun (1899–1971) and the Minangkabau journalist Abdul Muis (1890–1959) propagated radical Marxist ideas among followers of Sarekat Islam, which eventually split over political issues. The ISDV in 1920 became the Communist Association of the Indies (PKH), which after 1924 was known as the Indonesian Communist Party (PKI—see Glossary). The Muslim organization Muhammadiyah (Followers of Muhammad) was founded in Yogyakarta in 1912 by Kiyai Haji Muhammad Dahlan (1869–1933), a reforming "modernist" who had joined Budi Utomo three years earlier and had been encouraged by its members to establish modern Muslim schools. Muhammadiyah, and its "traditionalist" counterpart Nahdlatul Ulama, founded in Surabaya in 1926 by Kiyai Haji Hasyim Asyari (1871–1947), became very large and important associations, but their focus was primarily on educational and social affairs.

Formation of Political Parties, 1911–27

All of these organizations, and the myriad student groups that sprang up after 1915 under names such as Young Java (Jong Java), the Young Sumatrans' Association (Jong Sumatranen Bond), and Minahasa Students' Association (Studerende Vereniging Minahasa), had similar Western-oriented, upper-class, younger-generation, new *priyayi* outlooks and expressed similar dissatisfactions with—and sought one or another degree of emancipation from—the colonial state. Initially none of them articulated a national idea. Then one organization ventured down that path: the Indies Party (Indische Partij), founded in 1911 by the radical Eurasian E. F. E. Douwes Dekker (1879–1950), grandson of Multatuli's brother Jan. The younger Douwes Dekker was later joined by two Javanese, Cipto Mangunkusumo (1886–1943), a STOVIA graduate and charter member of Budi Utomo, and Raden Mas Suwardi Suryaningrat (1889–1959), an aristocrat of the Pakualaman, STOVIA student, and journalist. After 1922, under the name Ki Hajar Dewantara, Suwardi became an important leader in the field of education by establishing the private Taman Siswa (Student Garden) schools.

Douwes Dekker and the Indies Party not only called for independence of the colony but argued, using Austria-Hungary, Switzerland, and the United States as supporting examples, that all those who called the archipelago home should be citizens regardless of race. He called for a nation and nationalism that were modern and multiethnic. In 1913 Suwardi published an article entitled "Als ik eens een Nederlander was" (If I were a Dutchman), which, with famously acid humor, suggested that, if he were a Dutch person celebrating the centennial of liberation from Napoleonic rule in that year, he would not let the natives of the colony know about it, as they might get ideas about freedom, too. This was too much for the colonial government, which promptly banned the party and exiled its three leaders to the Netherlands for six years.

It was precisely there and at that time, however, that the idea of Indonesia (from the Greek *indos*—for India—and *nesos*—for island) was taking shape. The term was coined by mid-nineteenth-century English observers, who meant it in a general ethnographic or geographic sense. Europeans, including the Dutch, found the word descriptively handy, and it was used in learned circles in the early twentieth century. That is when the small number of indigenous students who came from the Netherlands Indies encountered it. Australian historian Robert E. Elson reports that the first recorded uses of the words "Indonesia" and "Indonesians" by an indigenous speaker were in 1917 public talks by the musicologist Raden Mas Sonder

Suryaputra in The Hague and Baginda Dahlan Abdullah in Leiden. They used the phrase "we Indonesians" and spoke of the right of Indonesians "to share in the government of the country." In 1922 the organization of Indonesian students in the Netherlands changed its name from the Indies Association (Indische Vereniging) to Indonesian Association (Indonesische Vereniging), the first organization to use the word "Indonesia" (in Dutch) in its name. When Suwardi gave a speech at Leiden University using the term a few months later, it was clear that both the idea and name of Indonesia had taken hold, and the struggle to give it intellectual and practical meaning had truly begun.

It has become customary to describe Indonesia's formative nationalist discourse in terms of three distinct streams of thought (*aliran*), and to emphasize the discord among the "secular" or "territorial," Marxist, and Muslim streams; a further division sometimes referred to is between "radical" and "moderate" followers. This sort of categorization is not entirely beside the point, for it indeed reflects many of the tensions and debates that filled the air. The colonial state, which founded the Political Intelligence Service (PID) in 1916 in an effort to understand the burgeoning political activity among Indonesians, borrowed these categories from the writings and speeches of those whom they watched and used them to organize their reports. The separation, however, was in some respects artificial. For one thing, Indonesians began rather early to speak of the movement (*pergerakan*), by which they meant all efforts that aimed at or presupposed obtaining freedom (*merdeka, kemerdekaan*) from Dutch rule. Among both sophisticates and more ordinary folk, membership in two or more organizations that straddled categories was not uncommon, and leaders made a variety of attempts to bridge them, for example Muslim and Marxist ideas by the Javanese "Red Haji," Mohamad Misbach (?–1926), or Marxist and nationalist principles by the Minangkabau Tan Malaka (1897–1949). Still, there was something thrilling about both the discord and the struggle to find a way out of it, something that suggested not just an intellectual world in motion but physical action.

Already, in 1919 bloody uprisings in Tolitoli, Manado (northern Sulawesi), and Cimareme, Garut (western Java), Sarekat Islam had been implicated and the specter of a radical, activist Islam raised. The colonial state moved in quickly with investigations and arrests. In 1925 PKI labor organizers led strikes in the principalities and in the cities of Semarang and Surabaya, and in 1926 and 1927 local PKI leaders prompted sabotage and rebellion in western Java and western Sumatra, respectively. The colonial state responded by arresting more than 13,000 people, of whom 4,500 were given prison sentences, and nearly one-third of these were sent to a newly con-structed prison camp in remote Boven Digul known as Tanah Merah (Red Earth), in Papua.

The Rise of Sukarno, 1921–26

At the same time as the colonial government was repressing Mus-lim- and Marxist-tinted movements, the "secular" stream was under-going significant change. This was principally the work of Sukarno (1901–70), son of a Javanese lower *priyayi* school teacher and a middle-class Balinese woman. He attended Dutch-language schools in Surabaya, where he boarded in the home of Cokroaminoto, and in Bandung, western Java, where he graduated as an architect from the new Technical College, one of the best and most expensive schools in the colony. Well-read and acquainted with many of the most prominent Indonesian political figures of the day, Sukarno first established a political study club on the model begun in Surabaya by the early Budi Utomo leader Dr. Sutomo (1888–1938), an ophthal-mologist, and then, in 1927, a political group which a year later became known as the Indonesian Nationalist Party (PNI). The funda-mental idea that Sukarno invested in the PNI was that achieving the nation—acquiring independence from Dutch rule—came before and above everything else, which meant in turn that unity was necessary. Quarrels about the role of Islam or Marxist ideas or even democracy in an eventual Indonesia were at the moment beside the point. Social class was beside the point. All differences dissolved before the need for unity in reaching the goal of *merdeka*.

In 1921 Sukarno had fashioned the idea of *marhaen*, the "ordinary person" representing all Indonesians, as a substitute for the Marxist concept of proletariat, which he found too divisive, and argued that developing a mass following among ordinary folk was the key to defeating colonial rule. And in 1926 he published a long essay enti-tled "Nationalism, Islam, and Marxism," in which he laid the foun-dation for a new nationalism, one that was neither Muslim nor Marxist but comprised its own—national—ideology, largely by sug-gesting that significant differences could not exist among those who were serious about struggling for freedom. This extravagant inclu-siveness did not, however, extend to race. Sukarno pitched the strug-gle as between us (Indonesians) and others, *sini* or *sana* (literally, here or there), a "brown front" against a "white front." With respect to the colonial state, one was either *ko* or non-*ko* (cooperative or not). Sukarno specified in the PNI statutes that non-Indonesians—Eurasians, Chinese, whites—could aspire only to associate member-ship at best. In his 1930 defense oration when on trial by the colonial authorities, entitled "Indonesia Menggugat!" (Indonesia Accuses!), Sukarno also depicted the Indonesian nation as not merely an invention of the present but rather a reality of the historical past now being revived. It was a glorious (racial) past leading through a dark present to a bright and shining future.

These ideas, delivered in Sukarno's famously charismatic style, were both radical and seductive. Part of their attraction was that they stirred deep emotions; in part, too, they permitted, even encouraged, the denial of genuine differences among Indonesians, and the highlighting of those between Indonesians and others. Not everyone agreed with the PNI program, even among those who joined. Mohammad Hatta (1902–80) and Sutan Syahrir (1909–66), Sumatrans who were among Sukarno's closest associates and later served him as vice president and prime minister, respectively, both had misgivings about the "mass action" approach and warned as early as 1929 against demagoguery and the growth of an intellectually shallow nationalism. Syahrir also was scathing about the *sini* or *sana* concept, especially for the way it implied an unbridgeable gap between East and West, a concept Syahrir thought both mythical and dangerous. Hatta was perhaps more equivocal, for in the Netherlands in 1926, as president of the Perhimpunan Indonesia (Indonesian Association), which had succeeded the Indonesische Vereniging, he had specifically prohibited Eurasians from membership.

The encompassing, driving sense of national unity and the defiant stand against colonial rule were, nevertheless, widely appealing and influenced Indonesians everywhere. They were clearly an inspiration behind the decisions of the Second Youth Congress in 1928, which adopted the red-and-white flag and the anthem "Indonesia Raya" (Great Indonesia) as official national icons, and on October 28, 1928, passed the resolution known as the Youth Pledge (Sumpah Pemuda), which proclaimed loyalty to "one birthplace/fatherland *(bertumpah darah satu, tanah air)*: Indonesia; one people/nation *(satu bangsa)*: Indonesia; and one unifying language *(bahasa persatuan)*: Indonesian." Little matter that, for example, the Malay language on which this new "Indonesian" was to be based was at the time little spoken among the Dutch-educated students who proclaimed it the national language; they would learn and develop it as they developed the nation itself.

Colonial Government Reactions, 1927–40

The colonial government found this new Indonesian nationalism at least as revolutionary, and at least as frightening, as it had the prospects of Muslim or Marxist revolution. In 1927–28 Hatta and several other Perhimpunan Indonesia members were arrested in the Netherlands and charged with fomenting armed rebellion, but acquitted. In the East Indies, after his arrest and trial in 1929–30, Sukarno served two years in prison. Taken into custody again in 1933, he was held under house arrest, first in remote Ende, Flores, then in Bengkulu, western Sumatra, until the Japanese occupation (see The Japanese Occupation, 1942–45, this ch.). Hatta and Syahrir were arrested in 1934 and sent to Boven Digul, and two years later to Banda Neira, Maluku, also for the remainder of Dutch rule. These and other arrests of leaders, along with ever-tighter political surveillance, crippled noncooperating parties and curbed public anticolonial expression but did not halt the spread of nationalist sentiment.

In 1932 the government, convinced—with some justification—that privately run Indonesian schools (for example, Ki Hajar Dewantara's Taman Siswa schools and schools supported by Muhammadiyah and by various political parties like the PNI) were nationalist breeding grounds, attempted to subject them to strict state control in a so-called Wild Schools Ordinance. The outcry was so loud and so unequivocal, even among the most cooperative groups, that the ordinance had to be modified, and in the following decade the number of Indonesian-run and -financed private schools grew rapidly. Far more Indonesians, particularly those from an expanding urban middle class, sought a modern education than the colonial government was able or willing to satisfy; the Indonesian intelligentsia took the initiative themselves, and effectively used the opportunity to further a nationalist agenda. History lessons, for example, did not follow the colonial curriculum but emphasized the glories of Majapahit and made national heroes of all those who had fought Dutch forces, such as Diponegoro. These schools had a significant impact. By the end of the 1930s in the city of Surabaya, for instance, they enrolled four times as many students as the government schools.

The attempts of the colonial government during the 1930s to repress Indonesian nationalism were associated particularly with Governor General B. C. de Jonge (in office 1931–36), infamous for his remark that the Dutch had already ruled the Indies for 350 years and were going to do so for 350 years more. Not everyone in the European community agreed with these hardline views, and some supported greater autonomy from The Hague so that they could run the Indies as they wished. Some voted in favor of the Sutarjo Petition of 1936, which modestly sought approval for a conference to consider dominion status for the Netherlands East Indies in 10 years' time (it was later rejected by the Dutch government); others complained aloud that the East Indies had become a police state. But the approaching war made the thought of change even less, not more,

Royal Netherlands Indies Army soldiers in training during World War II
Courtesy Library of Congress Prints and Photographs Division, U.S. Office of War Information Collection, LC–USE613–D–010623, digital ID fsa 8b13123

likely. The Netherlands fell to Hitler's forces on May 10, 1940, leaving the colony more or less to its own devices. Six months later, the colonial government made it clear that it was unalterably opposed to *Indonesia merdeka*—a free Indonesia—and therefore to the Indonesian national idea as it had developed to that time; no real accommodation was possible. Little wonder that by that time a great many thoughtful Indonesians, even the most moderate, had concluded that only the shock and dislocation of war in the archipelago might—possibly—bring about changes favorable to them.

War and Early Independence

The Japanese Occupation, 1942–45

Japan's decision to occupy the Netherlands East Indies was based primarily on the need for raw materials, especially oil from Sumatra and Kalimantan. Shortly after the attack on Pearl Harbor, Japanese forces moved into Southeast Asia. The occupation of the archipelago took place in stages, beginning in the east with landings in Tarakan, northeastern Kalimantan, and Kendari, southeastern Sulawesi, in early January 1942, and Ambon, Maluku, at the end of that month. At the beginning of February, Japanese forces invaded Sumatra from the north, and at the end of the month, the Battle of the Java Sea cleared the way for landings near Bantam, Cirebon, and Tuban, on Java, on March 1; Japanese forces met with little resistance, and the KNIL announced its surrender on March 8, 1942.

The occupation was to last for 42 months, from March 1942 until mid-August 1945, and this period properly belongs to Indonesia's colonial era. Indonesians who had cautiously welcomed the idea of a Japanese victory because it might advance a nationalist agenda were disappointed by Japan's initial actions. The idea that the colony might form a national unit did not appeal to the new power, which divided the territory administratively between the Japanese Imperial Army and the Japanese Imperial Navy, with the Sixteenth Army in Java, the Twenty-fifth Army in Sumatra (but headquartered until 1943 in Singapore, afterwards in Bukittinggi, western Sumatra), and the navy in the eastern archipelago. As late as May 1943, these areas were—unlike the Philippines and Burma—slated to remain permanent imperial possessions, colonial territories rather than autonomous states, within the Greater East Asia Co-Prosperity Sphere. Some Japanese pan-Asianists and national idealists did have notions that Japan's true duty was to bring independence to Indonesia, but they had little real influence on imperial policy. And less than two weeks after the Dutch surrender, the Japanese military government on Java not only banned all political organizations but prohibited the use of the red-and-white flag and the anthem "Indonesia Raya." Similar restrictions were enforced even more stringently in the other administrative areas.

Generalizing about Indonesia during the 1942–45 occupation period is extraordinarily difficult, not only because of varying policies and conditions in the separate administrative divisions, but also because circumstances changed rapidly over time, particularly as the war turned against Japan, and because Indonesians' experience varied widely according to, among other things, their social status and economic position.

The occupation is remembered as a harsh time. Japanese military rule was severe, and fear of arrest by the Kenpeitai (military police) and of the torture and execution of those who defied or were suspected of defying the Japanese was widespread. Particularly after mid-1943, economic conditions worsened markedly as a result of the wartime disruption of transportation and commerce, as well as misguided economic policies. Most urban populations were protected from extremes by government rationing of necessities, but severe food shortages and malnutrition developed in some areas, and cloth and clothing became so scarce by 1944 that villagers in some regions were reduced to wearing crude coverings made of old sacking or sheets of latex. The unrelenting mobilization of laborers—generally lumped under the infamous Japanese term *rōmusha* (literally, manual workers but in Indonesia always taken to mean forced labor)— came to represent in both official and public Indonesian memory the cruelty and repression of Japanese rule. Exact numbers are impossible to determine, but the Japanese drafted several million Javanese for varying lengths of time, mostly for local projects. As many as 300,000 may have been sent outside of Java, nearly half of them to

Sumatra and others as far away as Thailand. It is not known how many actually returned at the end of the war, although about 70,000 are recorded as being repatriated from places other than Sumatra by Dutch services; nor is it clear how many *rōmusha* died, were injured, or fell ill. But the casualties were undoubtedly very high, for in most cases the conditions were extremely grim.

The new *priyayi* and the urban middle classes, however, were often shielded from these extremes and often took a more equivocal attitude toward Japanese rule. They filled many of the positions left vacant by Dutch civil servants interned by the Japanese, and also vied for *pangreh praja* positions dominated by members of the traditional elite or those who had attended government schools. They also applauded the Japanese policies that ended dualism in education and the courts, and were receptive to Japanese pan-Asian East-versus-West sensibilities ("Asia for the Asians" as opposed to white supremacy, and "Asian values" as opposed to "Western materialism"). The *priyayi* and the middle classes also recognized the enormous advantages nationalist leaders had, however much the Japanese sought to control them, when they appeared before huge crowds and were featured in the newspapers or on the radio. Few expected much from the obviously propagandistic Japanese efforts to mobilize public support through a series of mass organizations, such as the Center of the People's Power (Putera) and the Jawa Hōkōkai (Java Service Association), or from the "political participation" promised through advisory groups formed at several administrative levels, including the Chūō Sangi-In (Central Advisory Council) for Java. Observers began to notice, however, that Sukarno and Hatta, both of whom had been released from Dutch internment by the Japanese in 1942, managed to slip nationalist language into their speeches, and the formation of the volunteer army known as Defenders of the Fatherland (Peta) in late 1943 was seen as an enormous step in furthering nationalist goals, one that of course could never have taken place under the Dutch.

Both Sukarno and Hatta agreed to cooperate with the Japanese in the belief that Tokyo was serious about leading Indonesia toward independence; they were, in any case, convinced that outright refusal was too dangerous. (Syahrir declined to play a public role.) Their cooperation was a dangerous game, which later earned both leaders criticism, especially from the Dutch and the Indonesian political left, for having been "collaborators." Sukarno's role in recruiting *rōmusha* became a particularly sore issue, although he later stubbornly defended his actions as necessary to the national struggle. Some Muhammadiyah and Nahdlatul Ulama leaders followed Sukarno's cooperative lead, seeing no reason why, if the Japanese were trying to use them to mobilize Muslim support, they should not use the Japanese to advance Muslims' agenda. They saw some advantage in the formation of the Consultative Council of Indonesian Muslims (Masyumi), which brought modernist and traditionalist Muslim leaders together, and of its military wing, the Barisan Hisbullah (Army of God), intended as a kind of Muslim version of Peta. But on the whole, Muslim enthusiasm for cooperation with the Japanese did not match Sukarno's.

Another group that was initially enthusiastic about the Japanese victory was made up of somewhat younger (mostly under 30), less established, but educated, urban, and mostly male, individuals. Many had been jailed or under surveillance in the late Dutch period for their political activism. They were courted by the Japanese and filled positions in news agencies, publishing, and the production of propaganda. Referred to loosely as *pemuda* (young men), they rapidly developed nationalist sentiments, eventually turning bitterly against Japanese tutelage and coming to play an important role in events after the occupation.

In April 1944, U.S. forces occupied the town of Hollandia (now called Jayapura) in Papua, and in mid-September Australian troops landed on Morotai, Halmahera (Maluku); toward the end of the month, Allied planes bombed Jakarta (as Batavia had been renamed) for the first time. Mindful of this new, critical stage of the conflict, Japan's new prime minister, Koiso Kuniaki, announced on September 7, 1944, that the Indies (which he did not define) would be prepared for independence "in the near future," a statement that appeared at last to vindicate Sukarno's cooperative policies. Occupation authorities were instructed to further encourage nationalist sentiments in order to calm public restlessness and to retain the loyalty of cooperating nationalist leaders and their followers. Their response was comparatively slow, but spurred perhaps by evidence of growing anti-Japanese sentiment—in mid-February 1945, for example, a Peta unit in Blitar (eastern Java) revolted—the authorities on Java announced on March 1, 1945, their intention to form the Commission to Investigate Preparatory Measures for Independence (BPUPK); the term "Indonesia" was initially not used. Its membership—54 Indonesians, four Chinese, one Arab, and one Eurasian, plus eight Japanese "special members"—was announced on April 29. Meetings began on May 28.

The BPUPK took up questions such as the philosophy, territory, and structure of the state. Sukarno's speech on June 1 laid out what he called the Pancasila (see Glossary) or Five Principles, which were acclaimed as the philosophical basis of an independent Indonesia. In the original formulation, true to Sukarno's prewar thinking, national unity came first, and while religion ("belief in a One and Supreme

God") was recognized in the fifth principle, one religion was pointedly not favored over another, and the state would be neither secular nor theocratic in nature. Thirty-nine of 60 voting members of the BPUPK voted to define the new state as comprising the former Netherlands East Indies as well as Portuguese Timor, New Guinea, and British territories on Borneo and the Malay Peninsula. Spirited debate on the structure of the state led finally to the acceptance of a unitary republic. An informal subcommittee, in a decision subsequently dubbed the Piagam Jakarta (Jakarta Charter), suggested that Muslim concerns about the role of Islam in the new state be addressed by placing Sukarno's last principle first, requiring that the head of state be a Muslim, and adding a phrase requiring all Muslim citizens to follow the sharia. This declaration was to be the source of continuing misunderstanding.

The United States dropped atomic bombs on Hiroshima and Nagasaki, respectively, on August 6 and 8, 1945, and the Japanese rushed to prepare Indonesian independence. Vetoing the "Greater Indonesia" idea, military authorities required that the new state be limited to the former Netherlands East Indies and called for the establishment of an Indonesian Independence Preparatory Committee (PPKI) with Sukarno as chairman. This group was established on August 12, 1945, but Japan surrendered three days later, before it had an opportunity to meet. The established Indonesian leadership, led by Sukarno and Hatta, greeted the surrender with initial disbelief and caution, but some *pemuda*, many of them followers of Sutan Syahrir, took a more radical stance, kidnapping Sukarno and Hatta on the night of August 15–16 in an effort to force them to declare independence immediately and without Japanese permission. Their efforts may actually have delayed matters slightly, as Hatta later accused, but in any case, in a simple ceremony held before a small group in the front yard of his home at 10:00 AM on August 17, 1945, Sukarno, after a brief speech, delivered a two-sentence statement officially proclaiming independence and noting that "details concerning the transfer of authority, etc., would be worked out as quickly and thoroughly as possible."

The next day, the PPKI met for the first time to adopt a constitution. Some key stipulations of the Jakarta Charter were cancelled, with the suggestion that such issues be revisited later, but the version of Pancasila that now became the official creed of the Republic of Indonesia began with the principle of "belief in [one supreme] God," followed by humanitarianism, national unity, popular sovereignty arrived at through deliberation and representative or consultative democracy, and social justice. Such was the idealistic vision of a national civic society with which Indonesia began its independent life.

The National Revolution, 1945–49

The struggle that followed the proclamation of independence on August 17, 1945, and lasted until the Dutch recognition of Indonesian sovereignty on December 27, 1949, is generally referred to as Indonesia's National Revolution. It remains the modern nation's central event, and its world significance, although often underappreciated, is real. The National Revolution was the first and most immediately effective of the violent postwar struggles with European colonial powers, bringing political independence and, under the circumstances, a remarkable degree of unity to a diverse and far-flung nation of then 70 million people and geographically the most fragmented of the former colonies in Asia and Africa. Furthermore, the Revolution accomplished this in the comparatively short period of slightly more than four years and at a human cost estimated at about 250,000 lives, far fewer than the several million suffered by India or Vietnam, for example. Representatives of the Republic of Indonesia were the first former colonial subjects to successfully use the United Nations (UN) and world opinion as decisive tools in achieving independence, and they carried on a sophisticated and often deft diplomacy to advance their cause. At home, it can certainly be argued that Republican forces fought a well-armed, determined European power to a standstill, and to the realization that further colonial mastery could not be achieved. Finally, although this point is much debated, it can be argued that the National Revolution generated irreversible currents of social and economic change marking the final disappearance of the colonial world and—for better or worse—serving as the foundation for crucial national developments over the next several generations. These were no mean achievements.

The new Republic's prospects were at best uncertain, however. The war had ended very suddenly, and the Dutch—themselves only recently freed from Nazi rule—were unable to reestablish colonial authority, a task that in Sumatra and Java fell to British and British Indian troops, the first of which did not arrive until September 29, 1945. In the interval of nearly six weeks, the Republic of Indonesia was able to disarm a great many Japanese troops and form a government with Sukarno as president and Hatta as vice president. The Central National Committee (KNIP) was established as the principal decision-making body. It had regional and local subcommittees, based largely on the structure and personnel of the Jawa Hōkōkai. A comparatively smooth transition to an Indonesian-controlled bureaucracy and civil service took place in most areas, especially of Java. Australian troops continued occupying the eastern archipelago in late 1944 and, in 1945, accompanied by Dutch military and civilian

Street scene with a military truck and walls with slogans,
during the Indonesia war for independence in 1945
Courtesy Library of Congress Prints and Photographs Division,
Lot 9033, LC–USZ62–43524, digital ID cph 3a42771

personnel of the Netherlands Indies Civil Administration (NICA),
which had formed in Australia during the war.

At the same time, however, tensions arising in part from conflict
with Japanese troops, now charged by Allied commander Earl Louis
Mountbatten (1900–79) with keeping the peace until his own troops
could arrive, and in part from the release of Europeans who had been
imprisoned by the Japanese and now sought to resume their lives,
exploded. Radical *pemuda* initiated, and encouraged others to take
part in, violence against all those—not only Dutch and Eurasians but
also Chinese and fellow Indonesians—who might be suspected of
opposing independence. Sukarno's government was powerless to
stop this bloodletting, which by the end of September was well
underway on Java. It grew in intensity and spread to deadly attacks
on local elites as Allied troops moved to secure the main cities of
Java and Sumatra. This sort of violence did not endear the Revolution to the outside world or, for that matter, to many Indonesians, but
at the same time it was clear that closely allied to it was a fierce
determination to defend independence. When Allied troops landed in
Surabaya in late October 1945, their plans to occupy the city were
thwarted by tens of thousands of armed Indonesians and crowds of
city residents mobilized by *pemuda*, resulting in the death of the
British commander and hundreds of his men. The ferocious British
counterattack that began on November 10, enshrined in Indonesian

nationalist history as Heroes' Day, is estimated to have killed 6,000 Indonesians and others, a terrible defeat that nevertheless convinced the British that they must plan for eventual withdrawal. A year later, the British turned military affairs over to the Dutch, who were determined to restore their rule throughout the archipelago.

In general, the Dutch view in late 1945 had been that the Republic of Indonesia was a sham, controlled largely by those who had collaborated with the Japanese, with no legitimacy whatsoever. A year later, this outlook had been modified somewhat, but only to concede that nationalist sentiment was more widespread than they had at first allowed; the complaint grew that, whatever its nature, the Republic could not control its violent supporters (especially *pemuda* and communists), making it unfit to rule. Attempts to broker a peaceful settlement of this postcolonial conflict were unsuccessful. The first, the Linggajati Agreement of November 12, 1946, acknowledged Republican control on Sumatra, Java, and Madura, as well as a federation of states under the Dutch crown in the eastern archipelago. The agreement also called for the formation, by January 1, 1949, of a federated state comprising the entire former Netherlands Indies, a Netherlands–Indonesian Union, or the so-called United States of Indonesia, which was also to be part of a larger commonwealth (including Suriname and the Dutch Antilles) under the Dutch crown. The Linggajati Agreement was not popular on either side and was not ratified until months later. Among many Indonesian nationalists of various political stripes, the agreement was seen as a capitulation by the Republican government. *Pemuda* of both left and right championed the idea of "100 percent Independence" (*Seratus Persen Merdeka*), and the communist-nationalist Tan Malaka coupled this with accusations that both Sukarno and Hatta had betrayed the nation once with their collaboration with the Japanese, and were doing so once again by compromising with the Dutch. Tan Malaka formed a united front known as the Struggle Coalition (Persatuan Perjuangan), which used the idea of total opposition to the Dutch to gather support for his own political agenda.

Less than two months after the KNIP had, following bitter debate and maneuvering, approved the agreement, Dutch forces launched what they euphemistically called a "police action" against the Republic, claiming it had violated or allowed violations of the Linggajati Agreement. They secured most of the large cities and valuable plantation areas of Sumatra and Java and arbitrarily established boundaries between their territories and the Republic, known as the Van Mook Line, after Lieutenant Governor General H. J. van Mook. The Republican military, the Indonesian National Army (TNI), and its affiliated militia (*laskar*) were humiliated, and yet greater criticism of the government arose, now even from within the military itself and from Muslim leaders.

The Republic had from the start of the Revolution pursued a vigorous if informal diplomacy to win other powers to its side, efforts that now bore fruit. The UN listened sympathetically to Prime Minister Syahrir's account of the situation in mid-August 1947, and a month later announced the establishment of a Committee of Good Offices, with members from Australia, Belgium, and the United States, to assist in reaching a settlement. The result was the Renville Agreement, named for the U.S. Navy ship—considered neutral territory—on which it was negotiated and signed between January 17 and 19, 1948. But this accord proved even less popular in the Republic than its predecessor, as it appeared to accept both the Van Mook Line, which in fact left numbers of TNI troops inside Dutch-claimed territories, requiring their withdrawal, and the Dutch notion of a federation rather than a unitary state pending eventual plebiscites. Republican leaders reluctantly signed it because they believed it was essential to retaining international goodwill, especially that of the United States. In the long run, they may have been correct, but the short-term costs were enormous.

Internally the Republic was threatening to disintegrate. Public confidence in the Republic began to erode because of the worsening economic situation, caused in part by the Dutch blockade of sea trade and seizure of principal revenue-producing plantation regions, as well as by a confused monetary situation in which Dutch, Republican, and sometimes locally issued currencies competed. Conflict became more frequent between the TNI and *laskar* and among *laskar*, as they competed for territory and resources or argued over tactics and political affiliation. The KNIP initiated a reorganization and rationalization program in December 1947, seeking to reduce regular and irregular armed forces drastically in order the better to supply, train, and control them. To patriots as well as those with other motives, this move seemed no better than treason, and the result was chaos. In addition, tensions mounted rapidly and at all levels between Muslims and both the government and leftist forces. Local clashes were reported in eastern and western Java after early 1948, but the most immediate challenge to the Republic was the movement led by S. M. Kartosuwiryo (1905–62), a foster son of H. U. S. Cokroaminoto, who had supported the 1928 Youth Pledge and *pemuda* nationalists in 1945 but later felt betrayed by the Renville Agreement and took up arms against the Republic, with himself at the head of an Islamic Army of Indonesia (TII). In the Garut-Tasikmalaya region of western Java in May 1948, Kartosuwiryo declared a separately administrated area, Darul Islam (Abode of Islam), which in 1949 he called the Islamic State of Indonesia (NII). He was captured and executed in 1962 by units of the armed forces.

Most serious of all, however, was the upheaval precipitated in September 1948 by the return from the Soviet Union of the prewar communist leader Muso (1897–1948), and his efforts to propel the PKI to a position of leadership in the Revolution. He berated the Sukarno–Hatta leadership for compromising with the Dutch and called for, among other things, an agrarian revolution. Driven by these new tensions, and animosities generated by the reorganization of the TNI, fighting broke out in Surakarta, central Java, between forces sympathetic to the PKI and the Republic. On September 18, PKI-affiliated *laskar* took over the eastern Java city of Madiun, where they murdered civil and military figures, announced a National Front government, and asked for popular support. The Republic responded immediately with a dramatic radio speech by Sukarno calling on the masses to choose between him—and the nation—or Muso. The TNI, especially western Java's Siliwangi Division under Abdul Haris Nasution (1918–2001), mounted a brutally successful campaign against the rebel forces. Muso and other PKI leaders were killed, and all told approximately 30,000 people lost their lives on both sides in the conflict.

The Madiun Affair remains controversial today, but its outcome strengthened the Republican government's efforts to control those who opposed it and changed the way in which Sukarno and the Republic were seen overseas, especially in the United States, where in the Cold War paradigm Indonesia now appeared as an anticommunist power. In the months after Madiun, the Dutch grew increasingly frustrated. Their negative portrayal of the Republic had lost international credibility, and on the ground their military position was deteriorating. Intelligence indicated as many as 12,000 Indonesian troops operating inside the Van Mook Line. On December 19, 1948, Dutch forces launched an attack—styled a second "police action"—designed to destroy the Republic, occupying its capital of Yogyakarta and capturing and imprisoning Sukarno, Hatta, five other cabinet members, and Syahrir (then an adviser). In response to this outright defiance, the UN Security Council demanded the reinstatement of the Republican government, and a full transfer of sovereignty to Indonesia no later than July 1, 1950. International pressure, which included a U.S. threat to withdraw Marshall Plan aid from the Netherlands, was too great for The Hague to withstand. At the same time, the Republic had initiated a guerrilla war (*gerilya*) against Dutch forces immediately after the

People's Security Forces machine gunner, 1946
Courtesy Library of Congress Prints and Photographs Division,
LC–USZ62–137192, digital ID cph 3c37192

fall of Yogyakarta. The significance of this *gerilya* has been generally underestimated, largely because it involved TNI struggles against armed internal opposition (for example, by the NII in western Java and by those loyal to Tan Malaka, who was captured and killed in eastern Java in February 1949) as well as Dutch forces. But Indonesian resistance was sufficiently effective to convince Dutch commanders that this was a war that could not be won on the ground.

After two efforts at cease-fires between May and August 1949, the Round Table Conference met in The Hague from August 23 to November 2 to reach the final terms of a settlement. The Round Table Agreement provided that the Republic and 15 federated territories established by the Dutch would be merged into a Federal Republic of Indonesia (RIS). The Dutch recognized the sovereignty of Indonesia on December 27, 1949. Because of widespread fear by nationalists in the Republic and in some of the federated territories that the structural arrangements of the RIS would favor pro-Dutch control, and because the TNI also found it unthinkable that they should be required to merge with the very army and police forces they had been fighting against, there was considerable sentiment in favor of scrapping the federal arrangement. This, and often heavy-handed pressure from within the Republican civilian bureaucracy and army, produced within five months a dissolution of the RIS into a new, unitary Republic of Indonesia, which was officially declared on the symbolic date of August 17, 1950. Only the breakaway Republic of South Maluku (RMS) resisted this incorporation. TNI forces opposed and largely defeated the RMS in the second half of 1950, but about 12,000 of its supporters were relocated to the Netherlands, and there and in Maluku itself separatist voices were heard for the next half-century.

The Road to Guided Democracy, 1950–65

Recovery

Developments during the first 15 years of Indonesia's independent history have been comparatively little studied in recent years and tend to be explained in rather simple, dichotomous terms of, for example, a struggle between "liberal democracy" and "primordial authoritarianism," between pragmatic "problem solvers" and idealistic "solidarity builders," or between political left and right. These analyses are not entirely wrong, for Indonesia was indeed polarized during these years, but they tend to oversimplify the poles, and to ignore other parts of the story, such as the remarkable flourishing of literature and painting that drew on the sense of personal and cultural liberation produced by the National Revolution. The new government also had extraordinary success, despite a lack of funds and expertise, in the field of education: in 1930 adult literacy stood at less than 7.5 percent, whereas in 1961 about 47 percent of those over the age of 10 were literate. It was a considerable achievement, too, that Indonesia in 1955 held honest, well-organized, and largely peaceful elections for an eligible voting public of nearly 38 million people scattered throughout the archipelago, more than 91 percent of whom cast a ballot. Still, it is fair to characterize the period as one of heavy disillusion as well, in which the enormously high expectations that leaders and the public had for independence could not be met, and in which the search for solutions was both intense and fragmented. While it may be true, as historian Anthony Reid has suggested, that the Revolution succeeded in "the creation of a united nation," in 1950 that nation was still no more than a vision, and it remained to be seen whether the same ideas that had brought it to life could also be used to give it substance.

Perhaps the greatest expectation of independence, shared by middle and lower classes, rural as well as urban dwellers, was that it would bring dramatic economic improvement. This hope had been embedded in the nationalist message since at least the 1920s, which

had played heavily on the exploitative nature of the colonial economy and implied that removal of colonial rule would also remove
obstacles to economic improvement and modernization. But the conditions Indonesia inherited from the eras of occupation and Revolution were grim, far grimmer than those of neighboring Burma or the
Philippines, for example, despite the fact that unlike them it had not
been a wartime battlefield. The Japanese had left the economy weak
and in disarray, but the Revolution had laid waste, through fighting
and scorched-earth tactics, much of what remained. In 1950 both
gross domestic product (GDP—see Glossary) and rice production
were well below 1939 levels, and estimated foreign reserves were
equivalent to about one month's imports (and only about three times
what they had been in 1945). In addition, provisions in the Round
Table Agreement had burdened Indonesia with a debt to the Netherlands of US$1.125 billion dollars and saddled it with the costs of
integrating thousands of colonial administrative and military personnel. (No other ex-colony in the postwar era was faced with such a
debt, 80 percent of which Indonesia had paid when it abrogated the
agreement in 1956.)

Economic Pressures

In the early 1950s, Indonesia's economy experienced a boomlet,
principally as a result of Korean War (1950–53) trade, especially in
oil and rubber; taxes on this trade supplied nearly 70 percent of the
government's revenues. Between 1950 and 1955, the gross national
product (GNP—see Glossary) is thought to have grown at an annual
rate of about 5.5 percent, and it increased 23 percent between
1953—when real GDP again reached the 1938 level—and 1957. In
retrospect, economists seem agreed that, against heavy odds, the
immediate postcolonial economy was not hopeless. Nevertheless,
what most Indonesians saw and felt did not seem like economic
progress at all: wages rose, but prices rose faster, and the growing
ranks of urban workers and government employees were especially
vulnerable to the resulting squeeze. The government also was
squeezed between falling trade-tax revenues and rising expenses,
especially those required to support a bureaucracy that nearly doubled in size between 1950 and 1960. Infrastructure, badly needing
rehabilitation, was neglected, adversely affecting production and
trade. Corruption and crime spread. In 1956 rice made up 13 percent
of Indonesia's imports, compared to self-sufficiency in 1938; by
1960 only 10 percent of the national income derived from manufacturing, compared to 12 percent in 1938. In economists' terms this
was "structural regression," but in everyday experience it meant that

the economy was not modernizing, and it was increasingly unable to provide for a population estimated to have grown from 77 million in 1950 to 97 million a decade later.

In order to solve these problems, the government at first embarked on plans—many of which had been initiated by the Dutch in the late 1930s and again in territories they held in the immediate postwar years—for large- and small-scale industrialization, import-substitution manufacturing, and private and foreign capitalization. It was not long, however, before policies more familiar to the prewar generation of nationalists, now firmly in power, took precedence. These were already visible in the Benteng (Fortress) Program (1950–57), one aspect of which was discrimination against ethnic Chinese and Dutch entrepreneurs in order to foster an indigenous class of businessmen.

The Benteng Program failed, leading instead to more corruption, but the call for "Indonesianization" of the economy was very strong. Policies increasingly favored a high degree of centralization, government development of state enterprises, discouragement of foreign investment, and, at least for a time, the encouragement of village cooperatives, all of which harkened back to provisions of the 1945 constitution and had been pursued in a limited fashion during the National Revolution. Gradual nationalization of some Dutch enterprises, the central bank, the rail and postal services, and air and sea transport firms began in the early 1950s, but the pace quickened after 1955 because of the continuing dispute over West New Guinea, control of which had not been settled in 1949. In 1957 and 1958, nearly 1,000 Dutch companies were nationalized and seized by the armed forces or, less frequently, by labor groups; in a corresponding exodus, nearly 90 percent of remaining Dutch citizens voluntarily repatriated. A year later, a decree banning "foreign nationals" resulted in 100,000 Chinese repatriating to mainland China. A victory from a nationalist perspective, this was from an economic standpoint—not least of all because Indonesia lacked capital and credit, as well as modern management and entrepreneurial skills—a setback from which recovery would be difficult.

Political Developments and Divisiveness

Independence had also brought with it expectations of a modern political framework for the nation. The Republic's founders had rejected colonialism, of course, and monarchy, settling on a vaguely defined democracy that leaned heavily on presidential authority. The constitution of the RIS and a third (provisional) constitution adopted in 1950 by the unitary state called for a prime ministerial, multiparty, parliamentary democracy and free elections. When voters went to the polls in September 1955, there was considerable hope that such a system would provide solutions to the political divisiveness that, freed from the limitations of the common anticolonial struggle, had begun to spread well beyond the mostly urbanized educated elite.

In the event, however, the national elections proved disappointing. The four major winners among the 28 parties obtaining parliamentary seats were the secular nationalist PNI (22 percent, with 86 percent of that from Java), the modernist Muslim Masyumi (21 percent, with 51 percent from Java), the traditional Muslim Nahdlatul Ulama (18 percent, with 86 percent from Java), and the PKI (16 percent, with 89 percent from Java). After the PKI, the next most successful party, the Indonesian Islamic Union Party (PSII), received less than 3 percent of the vote, and 18 of 28 parties received less than 1 percent of the vote. Both Nahdlatul Ulama and the PKI, which had especially strong followings in central and eastern Java, dramatically increased their representation compared with what they had held in the provisional parliament (8 to 45 seats, and 17 to 39 seats, respectively). In eastern Java, the vote was split almost evenly among the PNI, PKI, and Nahdlatul Ulama. The elections thus exposed and sharpened existing divides between Java and the other islands, raising fears of domination by Jakarta, and between the rapidly rising PKI and, particularly, Muslim parties, raising fears of communist (interpreted as antireligious) and populist ascendancy.

To make matters worse, there was a general perception that in the 30-month run-up to the elections, the political process had polarized villages as parties sought votes. There were many reports of villagers being pressured and even threatened to vote for one or another party, and of clashes between Muslim and communist adherents. More-educated voters tended to take hardened ideological positions. On the eve of the elections, Sukarno had declared that anyone who "tried to put obstacles in the way of holding them ... is a traitor to the Revolution." Barely six months later, he was urging the new parliament to avoid "50 percent + 1 democracy," and in October spoke of "burying" the political parties and of his desire to see Guided Democracy (*demokrasi terpimpin*, a term Sukarno had been using since 1954) in Indonesia.

Military Involvement and Rebellion

Into this deteriorating situation, the military increasingly inserted itself. During the Revolution, the armed forces had developed a strong distrust for—indeed, taken up arms against—both communist and Muslim movements that had opposed the central government.

The military had also itself exhibited a resistance to control by the central government and, especially after the second "police action" and subsequent *gerilya*, a high level of disapproval of civilian politics and politicians in general. Further, the armed forces had never been united, even on these issues, which made for extremely complex struggles in which military leaders often ended up opposing each other. These tensions surfaced, for example, when a dispute over demobilization plans resulted in a dangerous confrontation between some army commanders and parliament in Jakarta on October 17, 1952.

In 1956, in reaction to Jakarta's continued efforts to curb TNI-supported smuggling of oil, rubber, copra, and other export products, commanders in Sumatra and Sulawesi bolted from both government and central TNI control, arguing that their regions were producing more than their share of exports but receiving too little in return from the central government. The army was also growing increasingly concerned about the PKI's rise to power. PKI membership had leapt from about 100,000 in 1952 to a purported 1 million at the end of 1955, and, more successfully than any other party, it had cultivated village interests with community projects and support, particularly on Java. At the end of 1956, a dissident TNI commander, Zulkifli Lubis (1923–94?), wrote that Sukarno himself, recently returned from a visit to the People's Republic of China, had chosen that country as a political model. On February 21, 1957, Sukarno, supported by army chief Nasution, proposed instituting a system of Guided Democracy, which he now conceptualized as based on a politics of mutual cooperation (*gotong royong*) and deliberation with consensus (*musyawarah mufakat*) among functional groups (*golongan karya*) rather than political parties, which he believed was more in keeping with the national character. This seemed to many dissidents to signal both the end of any hope of improving regional prospects, and the beginning of, at the very least, a communist-tinted authoritarian rule.

In early March 1957, the TNI commander of East Indonesia announced Universal Struggle (Permesta) and declared martial law in his region, claiming a goal of completing the National Revolution. Nasution then proposed that Sukarno declare martial law for all of Indonesia, which he did on March 14. In the repression of suspected dissidents in Java, especially of Masyumi leaders, who had vigorously opposed the institution of Guided Democracy, a number of these prominent figures fled to Sumatra. They included the former prime minister from 1950–51, Mohammad Natsir (1908–93); former central bank president Syafruddin Prawiranegara (1911–89); and former minister of finance Sumitro Joyohadikusumo (1917–2001), who joined army dissidents in Sumatra, eventually declaring, in mid-February

1958, the Revolutionary Government of the Republic of Indonesia (PRRI). They were immediately joined by the Permesta rebels, and also attracted the clandestine support of the United States (revealed in May when an American pilot was shot down during a rebel attack on government forces). The central government acted swiftly, and TNI forces broke the rebellion in no more than two months, although sporadic guerrilla fighting continued until the early 1960s.

It has been pointed out many times that the PRRI did not represent a true separatist movement and sought instead what today would be termed "regime change." Be that as it may, the revolt was a watershed of some importance. Official figures estimate that at least 30,000 people lost their lives in the fighting, and Indonesian political life, far from being improved and stabilized as so fondly hoped, was instead gripped by regional, religious, and ideological turmoil and bitterness made worse by economic decay.

Political Paralysis

Symbolic of the paralysis that gripped political life at the time, the Constituent Assembly (Konstituante), which had been elected in late 1955 and began meeting a year later, by mid-1959 had failed to reach agreement on major issues that had troubled the BPUPK and PPKI a decade earlier: whether the form of the state should be federative or unitary and whether the state should be based on Islam or Pancasila. In May, Jakarta granted the northern Sumatra province of Aceh semiautonomous status (and thus the freedom to establish government by Islamic law) as the price of at last ending the struggle there with Darul Islam forces. The way seemed open for a dissolution of the unitary state. Sukarno's response on July 5, 1959, was unilaterally to dismiss the Constituent Assembly and to declare that the nation would return to the constitution of August 18, 1945, pointedly without the Jakarta Charter and its Islamic provisions. Illegal although it may have been, this was not an entirely unwelcome move. Many, although by no means all, Indonesians believed that their nation had lost its way, and a return to first principles and sentiments—now rather romantically misimagined—sounded in many ways attractive.

What followed, however, was the rapid development of an authoritarian state in which tensions were not reduced but greatly exacerbated. On August 17, 1959, Sukarno attempted to give Guided Democracy some precise content by announcing his Political Manifesto (Manipol), which included the ideas of "returning to the rails of the Revolution" and "retooling" in the name of unity and progress. Manipol was supplemented with the announcement of a kind of second Pancasila describing the foundations of the new state: the 1945 constitution,

Indonesian Socialism, Guided Democracy, Guided Economy, and Indonesian Identity, expressed in the acronym USDEK. These two formulations were followed in mid-1960 with a third, known by the contraction Nasakom, in which Sukarno returned to his 1920s attempts to work out a synthesis of nationalism (*nasionalisme*), religion (*agama*), and communism (*komunisme*). These ideas formed the basis of what was increasingly seen as a state ideology, printed up in fat, red-covered books to be used in obligatory indoctrination sessions for civil servants and students, and expressed in a rising rhetoric that excoriated the nation's internal and external enemies.

What was once Sukarno's gift for effecting conciliation and workable synthesis now turned sour, and, even to many of its earlier supporters, the promise of Guided Democracy seemed empty. The economy worsened and fell into a spiral of uncontrolled inflation of more than 100 percent annually. The army, after 1962 part of a combined Armed Forces of the Republic of Indonesia (ABRI), and the PKI confronted each other increasingly aggressively for control of state and society. Sukarno, although casting himself as the great mediator and attempting to balance all ideological forces, appeared to grow more radically inclined, drawing closer to the PKI and its leader, D. N. Aidit (1923–65), and away from Nasution's army. Widespread arrests of dissidents, censorship of media, and prohibition of "unhealthy" Western cultural influences (for example, dancing the Twist and listening to the Beatles) darkened Indonesia's social and intellectual world.

Worldview

Indonesian nationalists had the strong expectation that independence would also bring Indonesia international recognition and a place in the family of nations. Admission to the UN in September 1950 was a first step, and Indonesia quickly adopted an "independent and active" foreign policy, first articulated in 1948 by then Vice President Mohammad Hatta, who wished to steer a course between the Cold War powers but to do so in a way that was not merely "neutral." The first fruit of this outlook was the Asia–Africa Conference held in Bandung, Jawa Barat Province, in April 1955. This gathering of 29 new nations sought to avoid entanglement in the Cold War and to promote peace and cooperation; to many it represented the sudden coming of age of the formerly colonized world. It is generally considered the beginning of the Nonaligned Movement (see Glossary), although the movement itself was not formalized until 1961.

Sukarno was in his element at Bandung, speaking eloquently about ex-colonial peoples "awakening from slumber" and propos-

Sukarno, president of Indonesia from 1945 to 1967.
This photograph was taken during his trip to Washington, DC, on May 16, 1956.
Courtesy Library of Congress Prints and Photographs Division,
U.S. News and World Review Collection, digital ID cph 3c34160

ing—true to his homegrown pattern—an ideology of neither capitalism nor communism but one that merged the nationalism, religion,
and humanism of Asia and Africa. As at home, however, this grand
attempt at balance and synthesis did not hold. The failure of Indonesian nonalignment policies during the Cold War came about in part
because of the unwillingness of the superpowers, perhaps especially
the United States, to view the decolonized world in anything but
friend-or-foe terms. Sukarno's willingness to use Cold War rivalries
for what he viewed as Indonesia's national interests, which was not
precisely in the spirit of Bandung, also led to the abandonment of
neutrality.

In the ongoing dispute with the Dutch over West New Guinea, for
example, Sukarno had tentatively used the support of the Soviet Union
and China, and of the PKI at home, to encourage the United States to
pressure the Dutch to abandon the territory, implicitly in hopes of
forestalling an Indonesian slide toward the communist bloc. A U.S.-
and UN-brokered agreement turned over control to Indonesia in May
1963, which was confirmed in the much-disputed Act of Free Choice
in 1969. In the issues that arose over the formation of Malaysia—an

idea that had surfaced in 1961 as a solution to British decolonization problems involving Malaya, Singapore, and British Borneo, but which appeared in Jakarta's eyes to be a neocolonial plot against the republic and its ongoing revolution—Sukarno at first merely meddled and then, when the new state was formed in 1963, declared Confrontation (see Glossary), or Konfrontasi as it was called in Indonesian, a step that led the nation to the brink of war. Confrontation had support from both China and the Soviet Union (by then themselves estranged) as well as the PKI but was opposed by Britain and the United States, and, surreptitiously, by elements of ABRI. Sukarno was now faced with increasing isolation from the Western powers, and the deepening unpredictability of interlocking power struggles on both international and domestic fronts. This was not the "joining the world" for which most nationalists had hoped.

Years of Crisis

These tensions had escalated by late 1964, to the point that government was paralyzed and the nation seethed with fears and rumors of an impending explosion. In the countryside, especially in Java and Bali, the "unilateral actions" the PKI began a year earlier to forcefully redistribute village agricultural lands had resulted in the outbreak of violence along both religious and economic class lines. Especially in Jawa Timur Province, Nahdlatul Ulama mobilized its youth wing, known as Ansor (Helpers of Muhammad), and deadly fighting began to spread between and within now thoroughly polarized villages. ABRI increasingly revealed divisions among pro-PKI, anti-PKI, and pro-Sukarno officers, some of whom reportedly began to involve themselves in rural conflicts. In the big cities, demonstrations against the West reached fever pitch, spilling over into intellectual and cultural affairs as poets and artists confronted each other with diametrically opposed views on the nature and proper social role of the arts. The domestic economic crisis deepened as the price of rice soared beyond the means of most urban residents, especially those of the middle classes on government salaries, and the black-market rate of exchange exceeded the official rate by 2,000 percent.

Sukarno was furious that the newly formed Malaysia had been granted a temporary seat on the United Nations Security Council, and on January 1, 1965, he withdrew Indonesia from the UN, and later from other world bodies such as the International Monetary Fund (IMF) and the World Bank. In April, China announced that it supported the idea, proposed earlier by Aidit, of arming a "fifth force" of peasants and workers under PKI leadership to balance the power of ABRI's four armed services, and that it could supply 100,000 small arms for the purpose. Then on August 17, 1965, Sukarno, who two weeks earlier had collapsed during a public appearance and was thought to be gravely ill, delivered an Independence Day speech, which addressed joining a "Jakarta–Phnom Penh–Beijing–Hanoi–Pyongyang Axis" and creating an armed fifth force in order to complete Indonesia's revolution. It seemed to many that the PKI was poised to seize power, at the same time that the whole constellation of competing forces swirling around Sukarno was about to implode, with consequences that could only be guessed. On September 27, the army chief of staff, Ahmad Yani (1922–65), who was close to Sukarno and shared his anti-neo-imperialist outlook, nevertheless informed him that he and Nasution unequivocally refused to accept a "fifth force," a stand that brought them in direct opposition to the PKI, Sukarno, and even some ABRI officers. Air Force Vice Marshal Omar Dhani (1924–2009), for example, had begun to offer paramilitary training to groups of PKI civilians, apparently at Sukarno's urging. The balancing act was over.

The "Coup" and Its Aftermath, 1965–66

In the early morning hours of October 1, 1965, troops from four ABRI companies, including one from the Cakrabirawa Presidential Guard, deployed in air force motor vehicles through the streets of Jakarta to the homes of Nasution, Yani, and five other generals known to be opposed to the PKI. Three were killed resisting capture, and three were later murdered at the nearby Halim Perdanakusuma Military Air Base, where, it was later learned, their bodies were thrown into an abandoned well in an area known as Lubang Buaya (Crocodile Hole). The remaining general, then-Minister of Defense Nasution, narrowly escaped, but his adjutant was captured instead and also murdered at Lubang Buaya, and Nasution's daughter was injured in the intrusion and later died. Not long thereafter, Jakartans awoke to a radio announcement that the September 30 Movement (Gerakan September Tiga Puluh, later referred to by the acronym Gestapu by opponents) had acted to protect Sukarno and the nation from corrupt military officers, members of a Council of Generals that secretly planned, with U.S. Central Intelligence Agency (CIA) help, to take over the government. The announcement stressed that the action was an internal ABRI affair. At noon a Decree No. 1 was broadcast, announcing the formation of a Revolutionary Council as the source of all authority in the Republic of Indonesia.

Faced with the news of this apparent coup attempt, the commander of the Army Strategic Reserve Command (Kostrad), General Suharto (1921–2008), who had not been on the list of those to be captured, moved swiftly, and, less than 24 hours after events began, a radio broadcast announced that Suharto had taken temporary leadership of ABRI, controlled central Jakarta, and would crush what he described as a counterrevolutionary movement that had kidnapped six generals of the republic. (Their bodies were not discovered until October 3.) When the communist daily *Harian Rakjat* published an editorial supportive of the Revolutionary Council on October 2, 1965, it was already too late. In Jakarta, the coup attempt had been broken, and anti-PKI, anti-Sukarno commanders of ABRI were in charge. Within a few days, the same was true of the few areas outside of the capital where Gestapu had raised its head.

These momentous events, which triggered not only a regime change but also the destruction of the largest communist party outside the Soviet Union and China, hundreds of thousands of deaths, and a generation of military rule in what was then the world's fifth (now fourth) most populous country, have long eluded satisfactory explanation by scholars. Debate over many points, both in and outside of Indonesia, continues to be stubborn, polarized, and dominated by intricate and often improbable tales of intrigue. The circumstances and available data are such that a wide variety of explanations are equally plausible. Scholarly opinion has been especially skeptical of the conclusion drawn almost immediately by Suharto (and later the government he headed) and the CIA, that the PKI was to blame for Gestapu. Experts have offered numerous scenarios instead, suggesting that the (anti-PKI) military, and perhaps even Suharto himself, were in fact the real masterminds.

More recently, however, a view that has gained credence (originally posited in an early CIA report and raised by captured PKI leaders) is that Gestapu was in fact the result of highly secret planning—secret even within the PKI leadership structure—by party head D. N. Aidit and his close friend since *pemuda* days in 1945, "Syam" Kamaruzaman (ca. 1924–86), head of the party's supersecret Special Bureau. For reasons that are not entirely clear but were probably connected with Aidit's fears that Sukarno was near death and that without his protection the party could not survive, Syam was given responsibility for constructing a plot to neutralize army opposition. It is generally acknowledged that the plans were ill-conceived and so poorly executed that investigators often found comparatively simple errors unbelievable, taking them instead as clues to hidden conspiracies. The movement collapsed almost instantaneously, more from its own weaknesses than as a result of any brilliance or preparation that might be ascribed to Suharto's response.

Whether or not the Aidit–Syam thesis is accepted, there remains the very important question of who, or what factors, should bear responsibility for the mass killings that took place, mostly between October 1965 and March 1966 and then in occasional outbursts for several years thereafter. Although there are no satisfactory data on which reliable national calculations can be made, and Indonesian government estimates have varied from 78,500 to 1 million killed, a figure of approximately 500,000 deaths was accepted in the mid-1970s by the head of the Operational Command for the Restoration of Security and Order (Kopkamtib) and is widely used in Western sources. As many as 250,000 persons may have been imprisoned as well. As to who carried out these killings, the available evidence is meager and mostly anecdotal and suggests a complex picture. In some areas, clearly Muslim (in central and eastern Java, predominantly Nahdlatul Ulama) vigilantes began the murders spontaneously and, in a few places, even had to be reined in by army units. In others, army contacts either acquiesced to or encouraged such actions, and in a number of these there was a clear coordination of efforts. In what seems to have been a smaller number of places, army units alone were responsible. People participated in the killings, or looked the other way, for a wide variety of reasons, personal, community-related, and ideological.

Whatever the case, the mass killings amounted to a cataclysmic ideological cleansing in which not only communists but also suspected communists (and in some areas miscellaneous other perceived enemies, including Chinese) lost their lives. Violence of this type and on this scale, although perhaps foretold in episodes of the National Revolution, was new to Indonesia. It is perhaps true, as historian Robert B. Cribb has suggested, that after the disillusionment of the struggle for independence, and the deprivations and hostilities of Guided Democracy, Indonesians were "ready for a culprit," but the fury unleashed seems too intense and too broad to be explained in this way alone. Similar questions about the origins of extreme violence in Indonesia were to arise a generation later, at the end of the regime that in 1965–66 was just beginning to take hold.

The abrupt narrative break of the violent events that immediately followed Gestapu gives the impression that the transition from the Old Order to the New Order (as they came to be called, first by anti-PKI, anti-Sukarno student protesters) was swift. In reality, Sukarno's power and Guided Democracy policies dissolved more slowly, despite fierce opposition in some circles to his continued defense of the PKI and his refusal to concede that Guided Democracy had failed. Suharto and his supporters were aware that Sukarno continued to have loyal followers, and they did not wish to risk more upheaval, much less a backlash against the army. Military tribunals began holding well-managed trials of PKI figures, and a gradual removal began of ABRI officers and troops thought to be strong PKI or Sukarno loyalists.

In early 1966, Sukarno, still the acknowledged president, was pressured into signing the Letter of Instruction of March 11 (Surat Perintah Sebelas Maret, later known by the acronym Supersemar—see Glossary), turning over to Suharto his executive authority, for among other reasons, to keep law and order and to safeguard the Revolution. The next day, the PKI was officially banned and its surviving leaders, as well as prominent pro-Sukarno figures, arrested and imprisoned. Over the next few months, the new government largely dismantled Sukarno's foreign policy as Jakarta broke its ties with Beijing, abandoned confrontation with Malaysia, rejoined the UN and other international bodies, and made overtures to the West, especially for economic assistance. The Inter-Governmental Group on Indonesia (IGGI—see Glossary) was formed to coordinate this aid. In mid-1966, the Provisional People's Consultative Assembly (MPR(S)) demanded that Sukarno account for his behavior regarding Gestapu, but he stubbornly refused; only early the next year did he directly claim that he had known nothing in advance of those events. But by then, even many of his supporters had lost patience. On March 12, 1967, the MPR(S) formally removed Sukarno from power and appointed Suharto acting president in his stead. The New Order thus officially began as the Old Order withered away. Alone and bitter, Sukarno lived under virtual house arrest in the presidential palace in Bogor, Jawa Barat Province, until his death in 1970, and he was buried far from the nation's capital in his home town of Blitar in Jawa Timur Province.

Contemporary Indonesia

Rise of the New Order, 1966–85

On the surface, and particularly through a Cold War lens, the New Order appeared to be the antithesis of the Old Order: anticommunist as opposed to communist-leaning, pro-Western as opposed to anti-Western, procapitalist rather than anticapitalist, and so on. As new head of state, Suharto seemed to reflect these differences by being, as historian Theodore Friend put it, "cold and reclusive where Sukarno had been hot and expansive." And certainly many Indonesians saw the change of regime as representing a great deal more than a mere shift or transition. Separated from the Old Order by a national trauma, the New Order was unabashedly dominated by the military, focused on economic development (*pembangunan*), and determined to create stability. The promoters of the New Order saw themselves as pragmatic and realistic, generally apolitical and opposed to all ideologies, characteristics that, in the wake of the Guided Democracy years, were by no means unpopular even among those who were nervous about the prospects of military rule.

It became obvious in time, however, that alongside the differences there were a number of important similarities between the two regimes. For example, both Sukarno and Suharto developed into authoritarian rulers, compared by critics to ancient Javanese kings and seen as unique and uniquely potent figures—the sole *dalang* (puppet master)—on whom everything depended. Both men believed in a strong, highly centralized, and religiously neutral state, and both found established political parties and organized public opposition difficult to tolerate. Both searched for and hoped to define an appropriate national identity, looking back to Indonesia's beginnings as an independent nation for inspiration in so doing. Both men overestimated their own powers and were in the end forced from office and publicly disgraced in ways and for reasons they could not grasp. The two "orders," like the two individuals who epitomized them, are best viewed not in either/or terms, but in the light of nuance and an awareness of similarities and differences, changes and continuities.

It was still far from clear in 1966, either to Suharto himself or to his civilian and military supporters, what the New Order was actually going to look like. At a seminar entitled "In Search of a New Path" held at Jakarta's Universitas Indonesia in May that year, students and intellectuals grappled primarily with problems associated with the economy, focusing on the role that could be played by those with specialized training in economic development and finance, so-called technocrats. Three months later, the armed forces, under Suharto's leadership, held their own seminar in Bandung, entitled "Broad Policy Outlines and Implementation Plans for Political and Economic Stability." There was extended discussion, with civilian leaders in attendance, of the appropriate role of the military in rebuilding Indonesia. They settled on "safeguarding the Revolution," and exercising *dwifungsi* (dual function) of national defense and participation in the nation's political and social affairs, twin responsibilities said to be rooted in the army's experience during the struggle for independence (see Suharto's New Order, 1965–98, ch. 5).

There were vague references at this time to elections, but it was reasonably clear that there would be no return to the open party politics of the early 1950s, which military, and many civilian, leaders considered divisive because they either tapped into "primordial" loyalties and identities or created such loyalties on the basis of inappropriate ideologies. On the other hand, Sukarno's Guided Democracy had proven unworkable. The New Order solution was to attempt an apolitical, nonideological, quasi- or pseudo-democratic system that would promote unity, prevent both internal conflict and the obstruction of economic development, and satisfy some of the basic requirements of world opinion.

Political Structure

What came to be called Pancasila Democracy appears to have been constructed principally by Ali Murtopo (1924–84), a long-time army associate of Suharto. Of modest social and educational background, Ali Murtopo rose to prominence in the military, primarily as an "operator" with strategic sense and a "can do" attitude. His role as a leading military intelligence officer earned him a reputation as an unscrupulous and rather mysterious manipulator, but in some respects he mirrored views held far beyond a small group of military leaders and shared among the civilian middle classes, and his activities were widely known. His plan had three key elements. First, government control of the parliamentary process would be achieved by stipulating that a certain percentage of the membership of the chief legislative body, the People's Representative Council (DPR), and the chief representative body, the People's Consultative Assembly (MPR), were to be government civilian appointees, with an additional group of appointed members from the armed forces. Second, control of the electoral process would come by limiting the number of political parties and prying them away from ethnic, religious, regional, or personal identities, as well as by establishing a government-backed parliamentary representative group (pointedly not a "political party") of government employees and other groups, such as Golkar (see Glossary), an organization of functional groups, to participate in elections. Third, control over the majority of the voting public would result from limiting the periods of political campaigning and restricting such activities to the district level. The inhabitants of villages and small towns—the majority of Indonesians—were to be "freed" from mass political mobilization, manipulation, and polarization, becoming instead a more or less depoliticized "floating mass." They would be encouraged to vote for whichever party or group they thought might best answer their needs at the moment, but not to make their choices on the basis of "primordial" or personal identifiers.

An additional component, designed initially under the direction of Ruslan Abdulgani (1914–2005), who had served as Sukarno's chief ideological adviser a decade earlier, was a national indoctrination program intended to give Pancasila clarity and application, and to ensure that all Indonesians uniformly understood and accepted it. The

*Suharto, president of
Indonesia from 1967 to 1998
Courtesy Embassy of
Indonesia, Washington, DC*

military, the extraconstitutional Kopkamtib, and the civilian National Intelligence Coordinating Board (Bakin) all exerted degrees of watchfulness and enforcement.

These arrangements, which came to characterize the New Order, did not emerge suddenly and fully formed but rather were the product of gradual change and, generally, pragmatic adjustment. The consolidation of political parties, for example, did not take place until 1973, two years after the first elections (in which Golkar won nearly 63 percent of the vote). Government strategists seem to have thought consolidation might be preferable to the direct but clumsy manipulation of party leadership attempted before the elections. A strong fear persisted that, even with communism outlawed, potential threats to order remained in the form of religiously identified parties and the former followers of Sukarno. Islamic parties had to combine, for this reason, in a government-created Development Unity Party (PPP), and other parties, including Sukarno's old PNI, amalgamated in the Indonesian Democracy Party (PDI). Where Pancasila was concerned, the government attempted to introduce draft bills on the subject in 1969 and 1973, but nothing came of them. It was only in 1978 that moral instructions, the so-called Guide to Realizing and Experiencing the Pancasila (P4), took shape, and Pancasila education began to enter school curricula and civil service training in earnest. Not until 1985 did all organizations, including political groups, have to adopt the Pancasila as their *asas tunggal* (underlying principle).

Particularly after its first decade and down until its final years, the New Order's political design gave the impression that it had produced a tight, highly centralized, and closely managed system, and one that depended to an extraordinary degree on the political genius of one individual, Suharto. Scholars and others, especially those who opposed the rise of the New Order, struggled to find an appropriate term with which to describe it—autocratic, militarist, neofeudal, patrimonial, paternalist, neofascist, corporatist, military-bureaucratic, developmentalist, or command-pragmatist—and periodically announced that its demise was imminent. None of the terms proved altogether satisfactory, but even so the New Order lasted for 32 years.

The continuity of the New Order was not achieved solely, or perhaps even largely, by force or the threat of force. For one thing, Indonesia was far too large and too diverse to be ruled entirely uniformly by a single institution, much less a single person. As political scientist Donald K. Emmerson noted in 1999, "'Suharto's Indonesia' had never been more than a metaphor." Further, the military itself was neither monolithic nor a caste apart from civilian society. The actual practice of *dwifungsi*, which by 1969 had, for example, placed military men as governors in nearly 70 percent of the nation's provinces and as mayors and district heads in more than half of all cities and districts, did more to "civilianize" the military than to militarize civil society. And it was under "military rule" that the civilian bureaucracy ballooned, between 1975 and 1988 more than doubling to 3.5 million. It is also true that the New Order was founded, and continued to depend upon, a rough and largely unspoken consensus among the middle classes, military as well as civilian, that economic development came before everything else. The New Order government had a great deal of leeway as long as it could make good on promises of economic growth.

None of this meant, however, that government policies and actions went unopposed. Indeed, the period of greatest political structural change and economic expansion saw serious outbursts of dissent: the 1974 Malari riots over big business and the burgeoning Japanese economic presence were followed in 1976 by the Sawito Affair accusing Suharto and the government of corruption. In 1980 came the Petition of 50 in which notables, many of them former ABRI officers and close allies of Suharto, protested that the New Order had misinterpreted Pancasila and misunderstood the proper mission of the armed services, and in 1984 the Tanjung Priok riots protested corruption and ABRI's handling of Islam. These upheavals were handled in coarse, often coercive, ways. But they could be weathered because a broad public feared unrest and had made a certain peace with the supposition, long nursed in both military and some civilian circles, that potential enemies to national order included not only communism and Islam but also unfettered Western-style liberal democracy.

Economic Growth

The New Order's primary goal and justification was rapid economic growth, to be achieved not by a thorough-going reversal from Guided Democracy's state-centered socialist ideals to liberal capitalism, but by finding a realistic, flexible way to deliver results without entirely abandoning those ideals. This was a formidable task. Economic historian Pierre van der Eng has estimated that at the start of the New Order, Indonesia's per capita GDP was below what it had been in 1940, and probably below the level of 1913. The country was also saddled with an enormous foreign debt and crippling inflation (see The Role of Government, ch. 3). The strategy drawn up and managed by a team of Western-educated economists headed by Wijoyo Nitisastro (1927–2005) was ambitious but fiscally cautious and uninterested in economic nationalism or dogma. Beginning in 1969, Repelita (see Glossary)—five-year plans that were really more guidelines than economic plans—laid out broad priorities but left much room for policy maneuvering and adjustment to changing conditions. The focus was squarely on alleviating poverty, and in the simplest terms the approach was to improve agricultural productivity and rural incomes. Successes there would then provide the dynamic for industrialization, which would in turn bring the nation to a point of "takeoff" to full and self-sustaining modernization.

Remarkably, and despite widespread skepticism, the New Order did succeed in bringing about a rapid transformation of Indonesia's economy. During the roughly 30-year period, for example, Indonesia averaged a real GDP growth of roughly 5 percent. and real per capita GDP trebled. Average caloric intake increased by 70 percent, average life expectancy rose from about 47 to 67 years, and the manufacturing and industrial sectors' combined share of GDP rose from 19 percent to roughly 65 percent while agriculture's share dropped from 53 percent to 19 percent. The incidence of poverty dropped from 61 percent to 10 percent on Java, and from 52 percent to 7 percent elsewhere in the country. In 1993 the World Bank placed Indonesia among the highest-performing developing economies and pointed to its success in achieving both rapid growth and improved equity.

This was an astounding performance, and understanding it has occasioned heated and continuing academic debate. Some scholars point out that Indonesia's accomplishments must be evaluated in a broader, comparative context. Surpassing Nigeria in virtually all macroindicators, and India and China in some of them, Indonesia nevertheless lagged behind neighboring Malaysia, Thailand, and the Philippines in others. Especially considering the point from which it began, Indonesia performed remarkably well, but on a world scale in a long generation of economic improvement, it is important to identify both comparative strengths (sustained growth rate, structural change) and weaknesses (inflation, terms of trade, and debt service).

Other writers have questioned the accuracy of the statistical data used to support many of the findings about New Order economic development, suggesting among other things that the ways poverty was measured were flawed and that methods of gauging inequality simply did not match up with either observation or public commentary. Between the early 1970s and the mid-1990s, for example, there was a common assumption that the gap between rich and poor in Indonesia grew fairly rapidly, although during the same period the nation's Gini index (see Glossary), based on household expenditure, remained relatively steady at about 0.34, well below Thailand (0.45), the Philippines (0.48), and Malaysia (0.50). It seems likely, however, that the divergence is best explained not by flawed methods of measurement, but by changing perceptions. New Order Indonesians were the first to acquire wealth in significant numbers, and to a vastly better-informed society with rising expectations it appeared that the rich were getting richer and the poor poorer even though this was not statistically the case.

Some critics have also characterized Indonesia's economic progress during the New Order as ephemeral because it was dependent on foreign aid, state investment (and control), and/or the exploitation of nonrenewable resources, especially oil and gas. Such arguments are difficult to support with real data. Oil revenues, for instance, supplied much of Indonesia's budgetary income during the boom years between 1973 and 1981, but agriculture did so before that time, and by the end of the New Order, non-oil revenues, bolstered largely by industrial and manufacturing growth, accounted for nearly 70 percent of the budget. Oil and oil prices did not determine growth throughout the period, and the New Order is widely credited among economists for managing the oil windfall more wisely than other newly oil-rich nations, such as Nigeria and Venezuela, in order to head off dependency on that source.

Economic development during the New Order was more than a mere façade or, as one of Indonesia's most prominent public intellectuals, Gunawan Mohammad, once characterized it, an "epic illusion." The gains were real and widely shared, and there can be no doubt that the average Indonesian was economically better off toward the end of the New Order than at its start. (Nor were these gains entirely erased by the economic crisis of the late 1990s, as some predicted.) Several problems, however, rooted as much in the development program's successes as in its failures, were of great long-term significance. The most obvious was corruption, the scale of which burgeoned as the economy grew. A notorious harbinger of things to come was the fiscal scandal surrounding Colonel Ibnu Sutowo (1914–2001), head of the State Oil and Natural Gas Mining Company (Pertamina), who by 1975 had sunk the corporation into enormous international debt while personally enjoying a luxurious lifestyle that reportedly included a US$1 million wedding for his daughter. By the early 1990s, the financial dealings of Suharto's own children, particularly his eldest daughter, Siti Hardiyanti Rukmana, better known as Tutut (born 1949), and youngest son, Hutomo Mandala Putra, nicknamed Tommy (born 1962), attracted widespread attention because of their scale and their family conglomerates' dependence on privilege. And, well beyond financial circles, corruption extended far into the bureaucracy, the courts, and the police. Despite numerous campaigns proposing to deal with corruption in various corners of society, government task forces and investigations made little headway; corruption ate corrosively at the New Order from the inside.

Other difficulties were less straightforward. For example, New Order technocrats had sought to address the economic imbalance between Java and the Outer Islands, whose natural resources had contributed disproportionately to the national income, a source of rebellion in the 1950s and early 1960s. New Order industrialization policies, depending heavily on the relatively cheap labor available in densely populated Java, changed this. By the mid-1990s, Java produced 40 percent of the country's exports, double the figure of only a decade earlier and, for the first time since independence, contributed a portion of the national economic output—roughly 60 percent—equivalent to its share of the population. But this shift produced its own imbalance as the economy of the Outer Islands slipped comparatively and some regions began to see widening poverty, a new source of heightened tension between the regions and Jakarta. A similar irony can be seen in the changing role of the private sector of the economy, a goal sanctioned by the New Order government and pushed especially hard by the IMF and World Bank. During the first four Repelita (1969–88), private investment, foreign as well as domestic, provided a very modest percentage of national investment funding, but by the end of Repelita V in 1993, it made up more than 70 percent of the total, a rapid shift. The change was particularly significant, however, because it went unaccompanied by appropriate reforms in fiscal regulation. The economy became increasingly driven by the market, and, among other things, private entrepreneurs began to make decisions not always in the best interests of the national economy, for example by greatly increasing risky borrowing from overseas sources and from loosely regulated domestic banks, factors that contributed in a major way to the economic crisis of 1997–98.

Challenges to the State

Underlying these New Order initiatives for political and economic change was an important but largely undiscussed continuity in some fundamental ideas about the nature of both the nation and the state. Consistent with the ideas of the founders of independent Indonesia, New Order architects viewed the state as necessarily unitary and powerful, having little patience with notions of federalism or decentralization of powers. Indeed, civilian and military leaders alike appear to have assumed that only this highly centric form of state authority could bring about the political stability and economic growth they sought. The same leaders also inherited assumptions about the extent and unity of a national territory generally accepted as comprising the former Netherlands East Indies and did not find other suggestions tolerable.

These convictions led among other things to raising an enlarged, more centralized bureaucratic structure for the New Order state, and requiring administrative authorities to apply centrally developed policies on matters ranging from taxes to traditional performances, education to elections, firmly and uniformly throughout the nation. Seen from the government perspective, the effort represented a rational, modern approach, while to critics it often appeared narrow, oppressive, and self-serving. Resentment and debate, as well as legal and physical struggles, over such issues were a regular feature of life under New Order governance.

Inherited sensitivity to potential challenges to national unity also led to military involvement—and long-term enmities—in several corners of the archipelago. The first of these took place in West New Guinea (later called Irian Jaya, now the provinces of Papua and Papua Barat). During the 1949 Round Table Conference, the Dutch had refused to discuss the status of this territory, which, upon recognition of Indonesian independence, was still unresolved. Conflict over the issue escalated during the early 1960s, as the Dutch prepared to declare a separate state, and Sukarno responded with a military campaign. In August 1962, the Dutch were pressed by world opinion to turn over West New Guinea to the UN, which permitted Indonesia to administer the territory for a five-year period until an unspecified "Act of Free Choice" could be held (see Local Government, ch. 4).

Thus it fell to the New Order to complete a project begun by the Old Order. Ali Murtopo—with the military support of troops commanded by Sarwo Edhie Wibowo (1927–89)—arranged the campaign that, in mid-1969, produced a consensus among more than 1,000 designated local leaders in favor of integration with the Indonesian state. This decision was soon approved by the UN, and the territory became Indonesia's twenty-sixth province before the end of the year.

The integration process did not go unopposed, however. Initial bitterness came from Papuans who had stood to benefit from a Dutch-sponsored independence and who formed the Free Papua Organization (OPM) in 1965. But resentment soon spread because of Jakarta's placement of thousands of troops and officials in the territory, exploitation of natural resources (for example, by signing contracts for mining rights with the U.S. corporation Freeport-McMoRan Copper and Gold in 1967), encouragement of settlers from Java and elsewhere, and interference with local traditions such as dress and religious beliefs. OPM leaders declared Papua's secession in 1971 and began a guerrilla resistance. Despite internal splits, OPM resistance continued throughout the New Order era, peaking in the mid-1980s and again in the mid-1990s, attracting a significant ABRI presence.

In Aceh, northern Sumatra, resistance to Jakarta's extension of authority arose in the mid-1970s. This area, known for its 30-year struggle against Dutch rule in the nineteenth century, had also found it necessary to fight for its autonomy after independence, in a movement led by the Muslim political figure Muhammad Daud Beureueh (1899–1987) and affiliated with Darul Islam. Aceh won status as a separate province in 1957 and as a semiautonomous special territory with greater local control of religious matters in 1959. In the early 1970s, however, the discovery of natural gas in Lhokseumawe, Aceh, and the fact that this location could be more readily developed than other deposits found in eastern Kalimantan and the Natuna Islands, meant that for Jakarta Acehnese autonomy was now less tolerable. By 1976 armed resistance to the central government began under the banner of a Free Aceh Movement (GAM), led by Hasan di Tiro (1925–2010), a former Darul Islam leader who claimed descent from a hero of the 1873–1903 Aceh war against the Dutch. Jakarta responded with limited military force that crushed the small movement, but a decade later, when GAM reappeared with greater local support and funding from Libya and Iran, both the movement and the Jakarta response were far more extensive and brutal: estimates were of between 2,000 and 10,000 deaths, mostly civilian. In the mid-1990s, Jakarta claimed to have defeated GAM's guerrilla forces, but resentment ran deep, and thousands of government troops remained posted in Aceh.

The military involvement of greatest significance during the New Order, however, was that in East Timor. The status of this small imperial remnant changed when a radically new, democratic government came to power in Lisbon in 1974, and Portugal soon decided to shed its colonial holdings. Local political parties quickly formed in favor of different visions of the future, the most prominent being the leftist Revolutionary Front for an Independent East Timor (Fretilin—see Glossary) and the Timorese Popular Democratic Association (Apodeti), which sought integration with Indonesia as a semi-autonomous province. By mid-1975, it appeared that Fretilin would be the likely winner in an upcoming general election, a prospect that brought internal political violence as well as escalating concern in Jakarta that a "communist" government (a designation generally considered inaccurate) might plant itself in the midst of the Indonesian nation. On November 28, 1975, Fretilin announced the independence of the Democratic Republic of East Timor (as of 2002, the Democratic Republic of Timor-Leste), which it controlled. Driven by ideological fears rather than a desire for national expansion, Jakarta reversed its earlier avowed policy of noninterference and, with the implicit consent of Australia and the United States, on December 7 launched an assault on East Timor and soon began a brutal "pacification" requiring more than 30,000 ABRI troops. On July 15, 1976, East Timor, as Timor Timur, became the twenty-seventh province of Indonesia, and Jakarta began both exploiting the limited natural resources—coffee, sandalwood, marble, and prospects for vanilla and oil—and undertaking rebuilding and development programs.

In the late 1980s, the province opened to foreign observers, and in 1990 ABRI finally captured the charismatic Fretilin leader José Alexandre "Xanana" Gusmão (born 1946), but widespread resentment of the occupation festered. Then, in November 1991, Indonesian soldiers fired on a crowd of demonstrators at the Santa Cruz Cemetery in Dili, the capital, and dramatic video footage of this event, in which between 50 and 250 civilians were killed, was distributed worldwide. The majority of Indonesians knew and cared little about East Timor and had not basically disagreed with New Order policies there, but the outside world felt very differently. Indonesia found itself increasingly pressured—for example, by the United States, the European Union (EU), the Roman Catholic Church, and the UN—to change course. Indonesia resisted, and, indeed, military pressures in East Timor tightened, and Muslim migration, especially from Java, increased rapidly in this largely Catholic and animist area. Not surprisingly, indigenous opposition increased, especially among a younger generation born in the 1970s. Jakarta did not recognize this response as either legitimate protest or nascent nationalism, which it had unwittingly done much to foster.

Decline and Fall of the New Order, 1985–98

The New Order probably reached the peak of its powers in the mid- to late 1980s. The clear success of its agricultural strategy, achieving self-sufficiency in rice in 1985, and its policies in such difficult fields as family planning—Indonesia's birthrate dropped exceptionally rapidly from 5.5 percent to 3.3 percent annually between 1967 and 1987—earned it international admiration. Economic progress for the middle and lower classes had seemed to balance any domestic discontent. In retrospect, however, signs of serious weakness were discernible by about the same time. Although there had always been a certain level of public and private dissension under New Order rule, by the early 1990s it had grown stronger, and the government appeared increasingly unable to finesse this opposition with force (veiled or otherwise) or cooptation. In addition, intense international disapproval, particularly over East Timor, proved increasingly difficult to deflect.

Several important shifts had taken place, which in turn altered the New Order in fundamental ways. One was international: the collapse of the Soviet Union in 1991 and the end of the Cold War both provided New Order leaders with frightening examples of political upheaval and religious and ethnic conflict following in the wake of a relaxation of centralized power, and these events also left Indonesia more vulnerable to pressures from the West. An important result was a new uncertainty in domestic policy, for example, toward public criticism, Islam, and ethnic and religious conflict. In the military, opinions grew more varied, many of them frankly disapproving of certain government policies, including those toward the armed services. A second important change took place as the advice of "technocrats" responsible for the successfully cautious economic strategizing of the 1970s and 1980s began to give way to that of "technicians" such as Suharto protégé Bacharuddin J. (B. J.) Habibie (born 1936), who became a technology czar favoring huge, risky expenditures in high-technology research and production, for example by attempting to construct an indigenous aeronautics industry.

Some observers detected a third area of change in the attitude of Suharto himself. He grew more fearful of opposition and less tolerant of criticism, careless in regard to the multiplying financial excesses of associates and his own children, and increasingly insensitive to pressures to arrange a peaceful transition of power to new leadership. And, by the late 1990s, he seemed to lose the sense of propriety he had professed earlier. Circumventing all normal procedures, Suharto had himself appointed a five-star general, a rank previously accorded only the great revolutionary leader Sudirman (1916–50) and his successor, Nasution. Further, he not only ignored his own earlier advice against running for a seventh term but also placed daughter Tutut, son-in-law General Prabowo Subianto (born 1952, and married at the time to Suharto's second daughter, Siti Hediati Hariyadi—known as Titiek, born 1959), and a host of individuals close to the family in important civilian and military positions. These and other transgressions lost Suharto and many of those around him the trust of even his most loyal supporters, civilian as well as military.

The changes of greatest long-term significance, however, may have been social and cultural. New Order architects had planned on controlling the nation's politics and transforming its economy, but they had given comparatively little consideration to how, if they succeeded, society—their own generation's and their children's—might change as a result. If economic improvement expanded the middle classes and produced an improved standard of living, for example, would these Indonesians begin to acquire new outlooks and expectations, new values? What might be the cultural results of much greater openness to the outside, especially the Western, world? Although the New Order became infamous for efforts to inculcate a conservative, nationalist Pancasila social ideology, and to promote a homogenized, vaguely national culture, these endeavors were far from successful. Despite a penchant for banning the works of those considered to be influenced by communism (author Pramudya Ananta Tur became the world-famous example) and an undisguised distaste for "low," popular culture (a high government official once disparaged *dangdut*, a new and wildly popular music style blending modern Western, Indian, Islamic, and indigenous influences, as "dog-shit" music), the New Order's leaders turned a comparatively blind eye to cultural developments and seemingly had little idea what such changes might reflect of shifting social values.

Indonesianist Barbara Hatley has pointed to "a vigorous process of reinterpretation" of tradition during the New Order period, as well as new reflections of the present. For example, in a series of four novels about the lives of young, urban, middle-class Indonesians in the late 1970s and early 1980s, Yudhistira Ardhi Nugraha (born 1954) satirized the world of their pompous, hypocritical parents, civilian as well as military. Playwright Nobertus "Nano" Riantiarno (born 1949) used mocking language and absurdist humor to make fun of the world of politicians and government bureaucrats in his 1985 *Cockroach Opera*, which was finally banned five years later. By the late 1980s, many of the older generation had begun to question the implicit bargain they had struck with the New Order; their children, who had little or no memory of the Sukarno period or the dark days of the mid-1960s, merely saw the limitations and injustices around them and resisted, often with humor and cynicism.

More openly and widely challenged than ever before, the New Order was in 1997 confronted with economic collapse in the wake of a wider Asian financial crisis. The government's response was slow and inadequate, pleasing neither liberals nor nationalist conservatives. Over an eight-month period, the value of the rupiah (see Glossary) fell 70 percent. Over the course of a year, the economy as a whole shrank nearly 14 percent, 40 percent of the nation's businesses went bankrupt, per capita income fell an estimated 40 percent, and the number of people living in poverty catapulted, by some accounts, to as much as 40 percent of the population. By March 1998, when Suharto and his chosen running mate, Habibie, became president and vice president, respectively, it was clear that a line had been crossed. Public calls for reform turned angry, and within weeks bitterly anti-government, anti-Suharto student demonstrations spilled out of campuses across the nation. On May 12, at Trisakti University in Jakarta, members of the police force, then under ABRI command, fired on demonstrating students, killing four (and two bystanders) and wounding at least 20 others. This event, which created instant martyrs and removed any lingering hesitancy for a broad spectrum of Indonesians, launched several days of horrific violence, which ABRI could not or would not control. In Indonesia as a whole, an estimated 2,400 people are said to have died; as much as US$1 billion in property was damaged; and tens of thousands of foreign residents and Indonesian Chinese fled the country. The government that had come to power promising stability and economic growth now demonstrably could deliver neither, and its leader was precipitously abandoned by even his closest associates. In a simple ceremony held on May 21 at 9:00 a.m., Suharto resigned, bringing a symbolic end to the now jaded and discredited New Order leadership.

Reformasi and the Post–New Order Era, 1998–2009

Suharto's departure, however, brought neither relief nor calm to Indonesia, instead ushering in an extended period of upheaval and escalating violence. This took many forms—interethnic, interreligious, political, both neighborhood and military-organized vigilantism, and even bizarre mob attacks on "ninjas" and sorcerers—and was spread throughout the country, most notably in Kalimantan, Maluku, central Sulawesi, and eastern Java. Everywhere sensational examples of savagery were recorded in the media: piles of human heads in Kalimantan, suspected sorcerers dragged through the streets by motorcycles in eastern Java, petty thieves beaten and burned alive in many places, and killers in Kalimantan and Ambon reportedly drinking their victims' blood and eating their organs. As many as 20,000 people may have been killed between 1998 and 2001 and more than 200,000 displaced from their homes. There was vigorous debate over the causes of the violence, and widespread talk of revolution, civil war, and the disintegration of the nation as it descended into a surreal and barbarous chaos (see Violence, Vengeance, and Law, ch. 2).

These paroxysms did not deter, and remarkably indeed may have done much to propel, movement in the direction of dismantling the political structure built by the New Order. Even before it began, the post-Suharto era had been called a time of *reformasi* (see Glossary) by a broad spectrum of activists, and the name stuck despite uncertainty over exactly what it might mean. Perhaps the greatest surprise in the early days of this *reformasi* proved to be Habibie, Suharto's constitutional successor and by virtually all sides considered politically suspect, incompetent, or both. During his brief interim presidency (May 1998 to October 1999), however, Habibie oversaw the start of fundamental change in Indonesia's political and economic structure and attempted conciliatory solutions to the conflicts in Papua, Aceh, and most notably East Timor, to which he offered the option of voting for independence. He reduced many powers of ABRI (which was separated from the police in April 1999 and became known again as the TNI); began decentralizing civilian government; and countermanded discriminatory laws aimed at Chinese Indonesians (see Political Dynamics, ch. 4).

None of these fundamental changes was completed without difficulty. East Timor, for example, passed through an agony of civil conflict and military-backed violence after voting to separate from Indonesia in August 1999; independence as Timor-Leste finally came in May 2002 after a long and difficult transition under UN auspices. Genuine reform measures had been launched, however, and, for the most part, the nation responded positively to them. The scheduled general elections from June to October 1999 occurred amidst conflict, but under the circumstances it was remarkable that they could be held at all. In the end, a politically intricate but reasonably peaceful transition was made to the presidency of Nahdlatul Ulama leader and prominent intellectual figure Abdurrahman Wahid (1940–2009), who

*B. J. Habibie, president of
Indonesia, 1998–99
Courtesy Embassy of Indonesia,
Washington, DC*

maneuvered to have his main opponent, Sukarno's daughter Megawati Sukarnoputri (born 1948), selected as his vice president.

During the interelection period 1999–2004, Indonesia seemed in danger of losing its way as the pace of *reformasi* slackened and new problems arose. Wahid, known familiarly as Gus Dur, was the darling of many liberal Muslims and, particularly, Western Indonesia-watchers, many of whom knew him personally and saw him as an exponent of liberal democracy, pluralism, openness, and informality, the antithesis of everything they had despised about New Order government. To some degree, he was all those things, but both he and those around him proved managerially and politically inept, unable to satisfy a diverse following. Many conservative Muslims had expected him to further their agenda of an Islamic state, and were appalled by Wahid's insistence on religious tolerance and visiting Israel. Military leaders were shocked to discover that he intended to follow through on plans to hold them accountable for violence the armed forces had sponsored in East Timor, and they joined with some Muslim politicians in bitter opposition to his effort to open the long-silenced trauma of 1965–66 to public scrutiny and reconciliation. In July 2001, a special session of the MPR voted Wahid out of office and recognized Megawati as his successor.

This second interim presidency in three years suggested to many that, whatever *reformasi* was going to amount to would be limited and slow in coming. Some declared it dead altogether, for not only did Megawati lack her father's charisma (which might have been harnessed to promote change), she possessed—irony of ironies—more of a New Order outlook than many of her supporters suspected, and was little inclined to challenge the status quo. She was also much influenced by conservative military leaders who argued that revived separatist movements of the OPM and GAM could successfully be met with force. Jakarta declared martial law in Aceh and deployed 50,000 troops, which predictably only served to alienate more Acehnese than ever before. The economy began to recover (with an annual growth rate of more than 7 percent), but corruption flourished, and many of the financial practices and business networks continued to operate as before, at least in part because the tainted judicial system remained unchanged.

During this period, however, two fundamental reforms quietly took hold. The first was a Decentralization Law that went into effect in early January 2001. This sweeping legislation (with some revisions in 2004) made the Indonesian state system one of the world's most decentralized, with budgetary and most other bureaucratic and electoral matters being turned over to local authorities down to the district level. This dramatic change carried risks, as it left plenty of room for misuse, but it represented real movement toward transparency and away from the accumulation of centralized power. The second important reform, a major overhaul of the nation's constitution undertaken in four stages between 1999 and 2002, called for, among other things, the direct election of the president and vice president; a limitation of the president to two terms in office; free and secret elections of regional legislatures and a two-house MPR consisting entirely of elected members; establishment of the Constitutional Court; and a much expanded delineation of human rights (see The Structure of Government, ch. 4). Only slightly more than 10 percent of the original constitution of 1945, the cornerstone of New Order legal thought, remained unchanged. Together, these developments laid the groundwork for a thorough refashioning of the way the Indonesian state functioned.

One issue not directly addressed by the *reformasi* movement concerned the rise of Islamic politics and, increasingly since 1998, of the use of violence by extremist Muslims, some of them seeking to recreate Indonesia as an Islamic state. The best-known group was Jemaah Islamiyah (Congregation of Islam), one of whose founders appears to have been the Javanese cleric Abu Bakar Ba'asyir (born 1938), believed to have ties to Al Qaeda and other terrorist organizations. Between 2000 and 2005, members of Jemaah Islamiyah were responsible for a number of bombings, the most infamous being the October 12, 2002, explosions in Bali, which killed 202 people and injured more than 300, including many foreign visitors. Attacks in Jakarta (2003, 2004, and 2009) and Bali (2005) killed 49 people and wounded 458, mostly Indonesians (see Terrorism, ch. 5). In part because of what was perceived as hype and hatred behind the American "global war on terrorism" after the September 11, 2001, attacks in the United States, and in part because of a reluctance to criticize fellow Muslims professing to act on behalf of their religion, most Indonesians initially refused to believe that Islamist terror had come to their nation or that it might be of any genuine political importance. Many subscribed to fantastic conspiracy theories to explain events, and some public figures, including Megawati's vice president, Hamzah Haz (born 1940), attempted to make political use of such ideas. As a proliferation of Islamist parties jostled for position in the more open political arena, many worried that the new democratization might end up benefiting precisely those who, intolerant of religious diversity, sought to curtail it.

The complex electoral contest of 2004, in which more than 145 million voters cast ballots for tens of thousands of local and national candidates and then returned to the polls twice more in the largest direct presidential election in world history, was widely viewed as a critical test for both *reformasi* and the future of Islamist politics. Although local contests generated some violence, the election process itself went far more smoothly than generally predicted, and the results did much to suggest that *reformasi* had indeed brought Indonesia to the threshold of a sustainable, moderate, democratic polity, the world's third largest. Against all expectations, the presidential winner, with 61 percent of the vote, was Susilo Bambang Yudhoyono (born 1949), a retired general who abandoned Suharto after the 1998 Trisakti University shootings, later refused then-President Wahid's order to declare a state of emergency in order to forestall his impeachment, and went on to form the small, independent Democrat Party (PD). This victory was part of a pattern suggesting to pollsters that, given both chance and choice, Indonesian voters were more inclined to vote individualistically than along familiar party or ideological lines. The outcome also suggested that in this Muslim-majority nation, most voters had little real interest in parties or candidates that identified themselves primarily with Islamic aims rather than national or local goals such as development and reform. Some close observers in the West, who only two years earlier had seen a bleak sociopolitical future for Indonesia, now gushed about the country's transformation with the advent of a robust democracy.

It soon became clear, however, that after the momentous 2004 elections, Indonesia passed into a post–New Order, post-*reformasi* era, the character and direction of which were still uncertain. On the one hand, concern that the nation was still very fragile proved in many respects unfounded. The new administration was able, with international assistance, to cope reasonably competently and transparently with the December 2004 tsunami, thought to be the most destructive ever recorded and responsible in Indonesia alone for at least 166,561 deaths and 203,817 displaced persons, mostly in Aceh, as well as untold devastation. A combination of skill and goodwill also made it possible for Jakarta to turn the catastrophe to some good account by negotiating a peace settlement with GAM the next year. The new government also proved itself unexpectedly determined and adept in bringing to justice those responsible for various terrorist activities. In

November 2008, it proceeded with the execution of the three men responsible for the 2002 Bali bombings, who had been held since their capture and conviction in 2003. The administration also showed it could make difficult economic decisions when it announced dramatic cuts to subsidies on gasoline and cooking fuel in order to save a troubled budget; significantly, this move did not result in angry protests and demonstrations. And despite a much curtailed presidential authority, far more circumscribed military powers, and rapid turnover in local governance (between 2004 and 2008, voters removed nearly 40 percent of all governors, mayors, and district heads), Indonesians showed that they could function in a less authoritarian, less predictable structure than New Order leaders had supposed was necessary.

Disquieting questions remained, on the other hand, about the role of Islam in Indonesian society. The opening of politics in the post–New Order era had, along with world developments, served to intensify and complicate the struggle between radical conservative Islam and progressive liberal Islam in Indonesia. This contest has taken many different forms and has come to inform a wide and varied discourse throughout the nation. Radical conservative groups have proliferated. They have used print and electronic media to give voice to their ideas and in some areas have been effective in using local elections to get approval for instituting the sharia in local government. (More than a dozen provinces are said to have considered or adopted such laws, but in many cases the laws have either been quickly rescinded or gone unenforced.) In a long debate over a so-called pornography law, proposed in 2005 and finally passed in late 2008, radical conservative Muslim parties and supporting groups framed their arguments in ways to gather support from secularist nationalist groups, who found it difficult politically not to support such legislation—who could be seen as being "for" pornography?—even though it threatened pluralism and had been opposed by a range of human-rights and feminist groups.

It is important to realize that this is not a contest between Muslims and non- or merely nominal Muslims, but among Muslims. Some radical conservative groups have gone so far as to declare death fatwas on their moderate opponents, who in turn have publically denounced such acts as "stupid." And radical conservative groups have taken very loud public stands against government messages about the plurality of Islam in Indonesia and against progressive Muslim publications, such as a Paramadina Foundation book arguing the values of a pluralist understanding of modern Islam (even supporting interfaith marriage and inheritance rights). What these disputes will mean for the nation is as yet far from obvious.

It can be argued that even the controversies over Islam have been carried out very much in the public view (not possible a decade before), and neither the nation nor national society has been torn apart, as some have feared. In many respects, Indonesian society appears to have settled on new and calmer middle ground, relatively comfortable with new freedoms and also with the debate and even conflicts that come with them (see Islam, ch. 2). On the whole, Indonesians of the younger generation seem more at ease than their parents with plurality and individuality, and less in need of old-fashioned nationalism, ideological guidance, or state leadership. Some of these attitudes are reflected in the enormously popular 2005 novel *Laskar Pelangi* (Rainbow Warriors) by Andrea Hirata, who refuses to reveal his age but is a child of the New Order era; a film version appeared in 2008. Hirata's work is autobiographical and traces his childhood and education in a poor Muslim community and a run-down Muhammadiyah school on the tin-mining island of Belitung. It is essentially a personal success story of overcoming poverty, making the most of schooling under difficult conditions, and (we learn in three later volumes) becoming a modern Indonesian who is also a citizen of the world. Government, bureaucracy, and hierarchy are of little relevance; neither, in the end, are ethnicity, gender, and religion. What matters is understanding that all people have talent, and that individual determination, education, and the bonds of common humanity can develop it. Anyone can succeed, and success is not necessarily defined by wealth or power or social status. Some commentators have seen this novel as a key to the new values of the post-Suharto, post-*reformasi* generation; others have gone much further, suggesting that it shows clearly for the first time that Indonesian hopes for the future are, in fact, universal and not merely national ones, and that Indonesians, after 65 years of independence, are at last joining the world.

*   *   *

The literature on Indonesian history is quite large, and includes materials in many languages. This bibliographic essay mentions only works in English. The most satisfactory summaries of Indonesian history are Colin Brown's *A Short History of Indonesia: The Unlikely Nation?* and the short but sophisticated chapter by Robert B. Cribb, "Nation: Making Indonesia." The basic reference works any serious student of Indonesian history will find indispensable are Cribb's and Audrey R. Kahin's *Historical Dictionary of Indonesia*, Cribb's *Historical Atlas of Indonesia*, and the relevant portions of Jan M. Pluvier's *Historical Atlas of South-East Asia*.

The most comprehensive guide to pre- and proto-history is still Peter Bellwood's *Prehistory of the Indo-Malaysian Archipelago*, but this is a field that changes very rapidly, and the best information is contained in articles in specialist journals. The volume *Ancient History* (edited by John N. Miksic) in the Indonesian Heritage Series is a wonderful summary and is superbly illustrated. It can be supplemented with the more comprehensive and academic work by Paul Michel Munoz, *Early Kingdoms of the Indonesian Archipelago and the Malay Peninsula*.

For a general guide to the period after 1200, the standard work is Merle C. Ricklefs's *A History of Modern Indonesia Since c. 1200*. A detailed guide to the following few centuries is the *Early Modern History* volume, edited by Anthony J. S. Reid, in the Indonesian Heritage Series. Reid's *Southeast Asia in the Age of Commerce, 1450–1680* and *Charting the Shape of Early Modern Southeast Asia* contain very helpful information on Indonesia, as well as challenging interpretations. Merle C. Ricklefs's works on Java in the seventeenth through nineteenth centuries, beginning with *War, Culture, and Economy in Java, 1677–1726*, set high standards of scholarship in that difficult field.

The literature on Dutch expansion and the Netherlands East Indies is extensive. The most comprehensive work on the Cultivation System is perhaps Robert E. Elson's *Village Java under the Cultivation System*. The 1860 novel *Max Havelaar: Or the Coffee Auctions of the Dutch Trading Company* by Multatuli, penname of Eduard Douwes Dekker, is still captivating reading. *A History of Modern Indonesia* by Adrian Vickers begins its coverage with the late nineteenth century, and the collection of papers edited by Robert B. Cribb in *The Late Colonial State in Indonesia* is very useful. The subjects of nationalism and modernism are woven together in Robert E. Elson's valuable consideration of *The Idea of Indonesia: A History* and can also be studied through the lens of biography in, among many available works, John D. Legge's *Sukarno: A Political Biography* and Rudolf Mrázek's *Sjahrir: Politics and Exile in Indonesia*. The periods of Japanese occupation and revolution are the subject of a great many publications, but few attempt a comprehensive view. The essays by Ken'ichi Gotō in *Tensions of Empire: Japan and Southeast Asia in the Colonial and Postcolonial World* are mostly about Indonesia, and, coupled with Remco Raben's volume entitled *Representing the Japanese Occupation of Indonesia*, are good places to begin. Peter Post's *The Encyclopedia of Indonesia in the Pacific War* is a valuable new resource on the World War II period. On the years 1945–50, Anthony Reid's brief but comprehensive *The Indonesian National Revolution, 1945–1950* is still the best overall treatment.

There is no entirely satisfactory general history covering the entire post–1945 period, beyond the excellent relevant chapters in Ricklefs and in Vickers, mentioned above, but Robert B. Cribb and Colin Brown's *Modern Indonesia. A History Since 1945* packs a great deal of information and analysis in a very short book, and Theodore Friend's colorful *Indonesian Destinies* offers an intimate view. A number of works illuminate aspects of each of the political periods of Liberal Democracy, Guided Democracy, the New Order, and *reformasi*, but none of these periods yet has found a comprehensive treatment.

Scholarly articles in English on various aspects of Indonesian history can be found in specialized journals such as *Bijdragen tot Taal-, Land- en Volkenkunde* (Leiden, Netherlands) (http://www.kitlv-journals.nl); Cornell University's *Indonesia* (http://cip.cornell.edu/Indonesia); *Journal of Southeast Asian Studies* (Singapore) (http://journals.cambridge.org/action/displayJournal?jid=SEA); and *South East Asia Research* (London) (http://www.ingentaconnect.com/content/0967-828X).

There are numerous useful Web sites on various aspects of the Indonesian past, many of them in the Dutch and Indonesian languages. A well-known English-language site offering a detailed, and sometimes annotated chronology (up to 2004) is Charles A. Gimon's *Sejarah Indonesia: An Online Timeline of Indonesian History* (http://www.gimonca.com/sejarah). A useful collection of relevant Web sites is maintained by the International Institute of Social History (http://www.iisg.nl/w3vlindonesia/). (For further information and complete citations, see Bibliography.)

Chapter 2. The Society and Its Environment

Papuan pontoon boat

INDONESIA'S SOCIAL AND GEOGRAPHIC ENVIRONMENT is one of the most complex and varied in the world. By one count, at least 731 distinct languages and more than 1,100 different dialects are spoken in the archipelago. The nation encompasses some 17,508 islands; the landscape ranges from rain forests and steaming mangrove swamps to arid plains and snowcapped mountains. Major world religions—Islam, Christianity, Buddhism, and Hinduism—are represented, as well as many varieties of animistic practices and ancestor worship. Systems of local political authority vary from the ornate sultans' courts of central Java to the egalitarian communities of hunter-gatherers in the jungles of Kalimantan. A variety of economic patterns also can be found within Indonesia's borders, from rudimentary slash-and-burn agriculture to highly sophisticated computer microchip industries. Some Indonesian communities rely on traditional feasting systems and marriage exchange for economic distribution, while others act as sophisticated brokers in international trading networks operating throughout the world. Indonesians also have a variety of living arrangements. Some go home at night to extended families living in isolated bamboo longhouses; others return to hamlets of tiny houses clustered around a mosque; still others go home to nuclear families in urban high-rise apartment complexes.

There are, however, striking similarities among the nation's diverse groups. Besides citizenship in a common nation-state, the single most unifying cultural characteristic is a shared linguistic heritage. Almost all of the nation's estimated 240 million people speak at least one of several Austronesian languages, which, although often not mutually intelligible, share many vocabulary items and have similar sentence patterns. Most important, an estimated 83 percent of the population can speak Bahasa Indonesia (see Glossary), the official national language. Used in government, schools, print and electronic media, and multiethnic cities, this Malay-derived language is both an important unifying symbol and a vehicle of national integration.

The national average population density, according to the 2000 census, was 109 persons per square kilometer. However, in 2007 some 50 percent of Indonesians lived in cities, defined by the government's Central Statistical Office (BPS; for this and other acronyms, see table A) as areas with population densities greater than 5,000 persons per square kilometer or where fewer than 25 percent of households are employed in the agricultural sector. The percentage of Indonesians who live in rural areas, and who are closely associated with agriculture, stockbreeding, forestry, or fishing, has been declining steadily. For example, about 53 percent of the workforce was employed in agriculture, hunting, forestry, and fishing as recently as the mid-1980s; by 2005 that figure had decreased to 44 percent. As the Indonesian population has grown, become more educated, and moved increasingly toward urban centers, small-scale agriculture and trading have played decreasing roles in defining people's lifestyles. The rapid expansion of the manufacturing, retail, and service industries has led to ways of living defined more by social, cultural, and economic interests than by geographic and environmental forces.

The mobility, educational achievement, and urbanization of the Indonesian population have increased overall since the mid-1990s. Indonesians have become increasingly exposed to the variety of their nation's cultures through television, the Internet, newspapers, schools, and cultural activities. Links to indigenous geographic regions and sociocultural heritage have weakened, and the contexts for the expression of those links have narrowed. Ethnicity is a means of identification in certain situations but not in others. For example, during Ramadan, the Islamic month of fasting, peasants from Java might emphasize their Islamic faith and affiliation, whereas in other settings they emphasize their membership in the national state by attending school, participating in family-planning programs, and belonging to village cooperatives, and by invoking the Pancasila (five principles; see Glossary), the state ideology, as a moral justification for personal and family choices. In a similar way, isolated hill tribes living in the interior of islands such as Sulawesi, Seram, or Timor might express devotion to ancestral spirits through animal sacrifice at home but swear loyalty to the Indonesian state in school or at the polls. A person's identity as an Indonesian is richly interwoven with familial, regional, and ethnic heritage.

The Geographic Context

Indonesia's variations in culture have been shaped by centuries of complex interactions with the physical environment. Although Indonesians in general are now less vulnerable to the vicissitudes of nature as a result of improved technology and social programs, it is still possible to discern ways in which cultural variations are linked to traditional patterns of adjustment to their physical circumstances.

Geographic Regions

Indonesia is a vast archipelagic country extending 5,120 kilometers from east to west and 1,760 kilometers from north to south. According to the Indonesian Naval Hydro-Oceanographic Office, the country encompasses 17,508 islands, about 6,000 of which are inhabited. There are five main islands (Sumatra, Java, Kalimantan, Sulawesi, and Papua), two major archipelagos (Nusa Tenggara—also known as the Lesser Sunda Islands—and the Maluku Islands—also called the Moluccas), and 60 smaller archipelagos. Three of the islands are shared with other nations: Kalimantan, the world's third-largest island—also known as Borneo—is shared with Malaysia and Brunei; Papua and Papua Barat provinces (two provinces carved from what was formerly called West New Guinea or, later, Irian Jaya) share the island of New Guinea with the nation of Papua New Guinea; and the island of Timor is divided between Timor-Leste (former East Timor) and Indonesia's Nusa Tenggara Timur Province (see fig. 6). Indonesia's total land area is 1,811,569 square kilometers. Included in the nation's total territory are another 93,000 square kilometers of inland waters (straits, bays, and other bodies). These areas, plus the seas and oceans immediately surrounding Indonesia, bring the country's generally recognized territory (land and water) to about 5 million square kilometers. The government, however, also claims a 200-nautical-mile exclusive economic zone (see Glossary) that brings the total to about 7.9 million square kilometers.

Geographers have conventionally labeled Sumatra, Java (and Madura, a small island near Java's northeast coast), Kalimantan, and Sulawesi collectively as the Greater Sunda Islands. These islands, except for Sulawesi, lie on the Sunda Shelf, an extension of the Malay Peninsula and the Southeast Asian mainland. Far to the east are Papua and Papua Barat provinces, which take up the western half of the world's second-largest island, New Guinea, which lies on the Sahul Shelf. Sea depths on the Sunda and Sahul shelves average 200 meters or less. Between these two shelves lie Sulawesi, Nusa Tenggara, and the Maluku Islands, whose adjacent seas are 4,500 meters deep in some places. The term Outer Islands (see Glossary) is used inconsistently by various writers but is usually taken to mean those islands other than Java, Bali, and Madura.

Volcanoes and Earthquakes

The islands that make up Indonesia are highly unstable tectonically, and although the resultant volcanic ash has provided the basis for fertile soils, it makes agricultural conditions unpredictable in some areas. The nation has numerous mountains and some 400 volcanoes, about 25 percent of which are active. Well-known examples are Mount Merapi (Gunung Merapi), in Jawa Tengah Province, which last erupted in 2007, and Soputan, in Sulawesi Utara Province, which last erupted in 2008. Between 2000 and 2009 alone, 110 new or continuous volcanic

Figure 6. Topography and Drainage

eruptions were recorded in Indonesia, mostly in Java. The most violent geologic events in modern times have occurred in Indonesia: In 1815 the explosion of Mount Tambora (Gunung Tambora), a massive volcano in Nusa Tenggara Barat Province on the island of Sumbawa, reportedly killed an estimated 60,000 people. It last erupted in 1967. Krakatau, a volcano situated on an island between Java and Sumatra, erupted in 1883, and more than 36,000 died in the resulting tsunamis, which were felt as far away as the Arabian Peninsula, and changes in the water level were reported as far away as Wales. Krakatau is still active, having erupted as recently as March 2009. The Lumpur Sidoarjo (Lusi) mud volcano in Jawa Timur Province, which began in late May 2006 coincident with natural gas exploration drilling and, as some believe, an offshore earthquake, is an eruption of hydrogen sulphide gas and hot mud rather than a traditional volcano with its explosive ejections and flows of lava.

Earthquakes also frequently shake Indonesia. Thirty-eight major earthquakes, measuring between 6.5 and 9.1 magnitude—26 of them greater than 7.0—hit throughout most of the archipelago between 2000 and 2009. On the morning of December 26, 2004, an offshore earthquake registering 9.1 magnitude created a massive tsunami that hit the northwestern coast of Sumatra, primarily the Special Region of Aceh (called Nanggroe Aceh Darussalam, 1999–2009), killing 166,561 people and displacing another 203,817. Other tsunamis caused by this earthquake also devastated coastal and island areas of the Indian Ocean as far west as the east coast of Africa and as far north as Burma. Overall, the earthquake and tsunamis killed more than 227,898 persons and displaced more than 1.7 million in Indonesia and 13 other countries. On March 28, 2005, another devastating earthquake, registering a magnitude of 8.6, struck the island of Nias and nearby islands in Sumatera Utara Province. It killed more than 1,300 persons and displaced 40,000. More than 5,700 people were killed, 38,000 injured, and 600,000 left homeless when a 6.3 earthquake hit offshore of the coast of the Special Region of Yogyakarta, on May 27, 2006. Then, on September 2, 2009, a 7.0 magnitude earthquake struck Jawa Barat Province, causing severe damage and 72 deaths, and was felt widely on Java. Several weeks later, on September 30, 2009, a 7.6 magnitude earthquake hit Padang, Sumatera Barat Province, and was felt throughout Sumatra and Java, as well as in Malaysia, Singapore, and Thailand. It caused at least 1,100 deaths, more than 2,180 were injured, and thousands were missing amid the severe structural damage.

Climate

The main variable in Indonesia's climate is not temperature or air pressure but rainfall. The almost uniformly warm waters that make up 81 percent of Indonesia's area ensure that temperatures on land remain fairly constant. Traversed by the equator, the archipelago is almost entirely tropical in climate. Temperatures average 28° C on the coastal plains, 26° C in inland and mountain areas, and 23° C in the higher mountain regions. Winds are moderate and generally predictable; monsoons usually blow in from the south and east between June and September and from the northwest between December and March. Typhoons and other large storms pose little hazard to mariners in Indonesia's waters; the primary danger comes from swift currents in channels such as the Lombok, Sape, and Sunda straits.

Extreme variations in rainfall are linked with the monsoons. There is a dry season (June to September), influenced by the Australian continental air masses, and a rainy season (December to March) that is influenced by air masses from mainland Asia and the Pacific Ocean. Local conditions in Indonesia, however, can greatly modify these patterns, especially in the central islands of the Maluku group. This oscillating seasonal pattern of wind and rain is related to Indonesia's geographic location as an archipelago between two continents and astride the equator. During the dry monsoon, high pressure over the Australian deserts moves winds from Australia toward the northwest. As the winds reach the equator, the Earth's rotation causes them to veer off their original course in a northeasterly direction toward the Southeast Asian mainland. During the wet monsoon, a corresponding high-pressure system over the Asian mainland causes the pattern to reverse. The resultant monsoon is augmented by humid breezes from the Indian Ocean, producing significant amounts of rain throughout many parts of the archipelago.

Prevailing wind patterns interact with local topographic conditions to produce significant variations in rainfall throughout the archipelago. In general, the western and northern parts of Indonesia experience the most precipitation because the northward- and westward-moving monsoon clouds are heavy with moisture by the time they reach these more distant regions. The average annual rainfall for Indonesia is around 3,175 millimeters. Western Sumatra, Java, Bali, and the interiors of Kalimantan, Sulawesi, and Papua are the most consistently damp regions of Indonesia, with rainfall measuring more than 2,000 millimeters per year. In part, this moisture originates on certain high mountain peaks that, because of their location, trap damp air and experience more than 6,000 millimeters of rain a year. The city of Bogor, near Jakarta, has a high rainfall rate of 3,500

Small fishing boats with view of Manado Tua volcano,
Sulawesi Utara Province
Courtesy Anastasia Riehl

to 4,000 millimeters annually. On the other hand, the areas closest to Australia—including Nusa Tenggara and the eastern tip of Java—tend to be dry, with some areas experiencing less than 1,000 millimeters of rainfall per year. Some of the islands of southern Maluku experience highly unpredictable rainfall patterns, depending on local wind currents.

The air temperature changes little from season to season or from one region to the next, but cooler temperatures prevail at higher elevations. In general, temperatures drop approximately 1° C per 90 meters of increase in elevation from sea level; night frosts occur in some high interior mountain regions. The highest mountain ranges in Papua are permanently capped with snow.

Located on the equator, the archipelago experiences relatively little change in the length of daylight hours from one season to the next; the difference between the longest day of the year and the shortest is only 48 minutes. The archipelago stretches across three time zones: Western Indonesian Time—seven hours in advance of Greenwich Mean Time (GMT)—applies to Sumatra, Java, and west and central Kalimantan; Central Indonesian Time—eight hours ahead of GMT—is observed in Bali, Nusa Tenggara, south and east

Kalimantan, and Sulawesi; clocks are set to Eastern Indonesian Time—nine hours ahead of GMT—in the Malukus and Papua. The boundary between the western and central time zones—established in 1988—is a line running north between Java and Bali through the center of Kalimantan. The border between the central and eastern time zones runs north from the eastern tip of Timor to the eastern tip of Sulawesi. Indonesia does not operate daylight-saving time in the summer.

Environmental Concerns

Centuries-old patterns of resource exploitation in Indonesia began to change very rapidly in the late twentieth and early twenty-first centuries. The rice-growing peasantry is shrinking as a result of mechanization, fertilizer use, and intensification of agriculture; the coastal commercial sector has been transformed by overfishing and new technology for interisland commerce; and traditional swidden farming communities of the upland forest have been increasingly crowded out by industrial logging.

The cumulative effects of rising population density, urbanization, agricultural intensification, resource extraction, and manufacturing have had a significant impact on the Indonesian environment in recent decades. Home to the world's largest reef system, one of its largest expanses of rain forest, and some of its richest areas of biodiversity, Indonesia is now experiencing serious environmental deterioration. Air pollution, caused by rapidly rising levels of motor-vehicle emissions (90 percent of vehicles still use leaded fuel) and by forest fires linked to palm-oil plantation development, have given rise to respiratory problems that have become the country's sixth most common cause of death. Forest fires in Kalimantan during 1997–98 produced a thick, smoky haze that covered much of Southeast Asia, resulting in closed schools and businesses as well as deaths and illnesses related to respiratory disorders. The fires also drew worldwide attention to the uncertain future of the region's forest resources.

Indonesia has some of the worst water pollution in Asia. The shortage of sewerage facilities is an especially serious problem. For example, because less than 3 percent of Jakarta's population is connected to a sewerage system, the city's waste is typically discharged either into private septic tanks or directly into rivers or canals. Sewage disposal into such bodies of water is linked in particular with repeated epidemics of gastrointestinal infection. In rural areas, runoff from increased use of pesticides and fertilizers has resulted in raised levels of toxicity in the water supply, excessive accumulation of algae in riverbeds, and the consequent destruction of marine life. The coastal commercial sector suffers from environmental pressures originating in the highland interiors of the islands. Soil erosion from upland deforestation exacerbates the problem of silting downstream and into the sea. Silt deposits cover and kill once-lively coral reefs, creating mangrove thickets and making harbor access increasingly difficult, if not impossible, without massive and expensive dredging operations.

National Territory: Rights, Responsibilities, and Challenges

The legal rights to, and responsibility for, Indonesia's territorial environment are a matter of controversy. Among the continuing concerns are the exact boundaries between Indonesia and Timor-Leste; another issue of concern between the two states is sovereignty over a tiny uninhabited island off the coast of Timor that is called Pulau Batek by Indonesia but known locally as Fatu Sinai. Differences over the precise maritime boundaries between Australia and Indonesia in the Timor Gap remain an area in need of reconciliation. In another dispute, the International Court of Justice ruled in favor of Malaysia in 2002 regarding jurisdiction over the Sipadan and Ligitan islands (off northeastern Kalimantan). However, Indonesia continues to assert a claim to the outer islands of the Ligitan group and has established a presence on them. In 2005 tensions flared again between Indonesia and Malaysia concerning Ambalat Island, located in the Sulawesi Sea (Celebes Sea) on the boundary between the two states, off the northeast corner of Kalimantan Timur Province. Basing its claim on a doctrine of the political and security unity of archipelagic land and waters (*wawasan nusantara*), the Indonesian government has asserted its rights to marine and geologic resources within a coastal zone of 200 nautical miles. Indonesia, Malaysia, and Singapore each consider the Strait of Malacca (Selat Malaka in Bahasa Indonesia), one of the most heavily traveled sea-lanes in the world, to be their primary responsibility. At a conference in Singapore in 2004, the United States recognized the right of the three countries to organize security as they saw fit, while at the same time offering assistance for their efforts.

Since the late 1990s, Indonesia has experienced major challenges to its territorial integrity. The most profound resulted from a United Nations (UN)–monitored referendum in August 1999 in East Timor on whether to accept special autonomy within Indonesia or to separate from Indonesia and declare independence. After 78.5 percent of East Timorese voted for independence, pro-Indonesia and pro-independence forces fought each other, and thousands died or fled to West Timor (Nusa Tenggara Timur Province) to avoid the fighting. The violence began shortly after President Bacharuddin J. (B. J.) Habibie announced the referendum and continued until well after the vote. On October 25, 1999, the UN Transitional Administration in East Timor (UNTAET) was established, and on May 20, 2002, East Timor, as the Democratic Republic of Timor-Leste, became fully independent of Indonesia. Most of the estimated 200,000 refugees who went to West Timor had returned by 2003 (see Relations with Neighboring Nations, ch. 4; East Timor, ch. 5).

Two other regional struggles in recent times were in the Special Region of Aceh, in northwestern Sumatra, and in Papua. In Aceh, the long-standing conflict between the Free Aceh Movement (GAM—see Glossary) and the Indonesian military intensified into an open secessionist effort. The struggle escalated in 1998, but two years later secret negotiations held in Geneva led to a Cessation of Hostilities Agreement signed on December 9, 2002.

The parties had agreed to a dialogue leading to democratic elections and a cessation of hostilities. Within six months, however, the agreement had broken down, and martial law was declared in the province until May 2004. Following the December 2004 earthquake and tsunami, a much more comprehensive peace agreement, brokered by former Finnish president Martti Ahtisaari, was officially signed in Helsinki on August 15, 2005, by chief Indonesian negotiator Hamid Awaluddin and GAM leader Malik Mahmud. The Indonesian government agreed to facilitate the establishment of Aceh-based political parties and to allow 70 percent of the income from local natural resources to stay within Aceh. On December 27, 2005, GAM leaders announced that they had disbanded their military wing and GAM itself was dissolved the next month (see Separatist Rebellions, ch. 5).

Another important challenge to Indonesia's sovereignty comes from the Free Papua Organization (OPM). After years of sabotage, secret meetings, and public demonstrations, OPM gained considerable international attention in January 1996 when members of the group kidnapped 14 members of a multinational World Wildlife Fund for Nature scientific expedition. All except two hostages were freed following negotiations; later a rescue operation was conducted in which six OPM members and the two remaining Indonesian hostages were killed. Although in 2001 local leaders were granted more financial and political autonomy and had been permitted a year earlier to change the name of their province from Irian Jaya to the locally more acceptable Papua, tension persists. (In 2003 Papua was subdivided into Papua and Irian Jaya Barat provinces; the latter was renamed Papua Barat in 2007.) Amnesty International reported grave concern about acts of torture and prisoner abuse in 2000 by the Indonesian military. Demonstrations for Papuan independence intensified in 2006 in the wake of revelations of pollution caused by the Grasberg mine, a source of copper, gold, and silver operated by Phoenix, Arizona–based Freeport-McMoRan Copper and Gold. In 2008 Indonesian police arrested separatist leader Buchtar Tabuni as he was about to attend a massive rally in Jayapura, the capital of Papua, to show support for an international legislative caucus for Papua Barat.

Even as Indonesia defended its claims to various territories, international environmental groups were pressing Jakarta to accept environmental responsibility for those territories. Indonesia was encouraged to monitor pollution in its national territorial waters and to take legal action to prevent the destruction of its rain forests. Since the late 1960s, the government has addressed increasing environmental problems by establishing resource-management programs, conducting environmental-impact analyses, developing better policy enforcement, and enacting appropriate laws to give government officials proper authority. Despite these efforts, corruption, overlapping competencies among government departments, and legal uncertainties about departmental jurisdictions have slowed progress against environmental degradation.

Emerging Dynamics of Indonesian Communities

Population

Indonesia's population was estimated by U.S. government sources at 240,271,522 in July 2009. (The next Indonesian census was scheduled for 2010.) This marked an increase of 37.6 million since 2000. The annual growth rate had changed slightly, from 1.3 percent in 2000 to an estimated 1.1 percent in 2009, with a birthrate estimated at 18.8 per 1,000 population. Life expectancy at birth for the total population stood at an estimated 70.8 years (versus 67.9 years in 2000), with males projected to live 68.3 years and females 73.4 years. Fertility rates for women, based on births per woman, decreased slightly, from 2.6 in 2000 to an estimated 2.3 in 2009, and the infant mortality rate improved from 40.9 deaths per 1,000 live births in 2000 to an estimated 29.9 deaths per 1,000 in 2009. The overall death rate was estimated in 2009 at 6.2 deaths per 1,000 of the population.

Indonesia is a young nation. In 2008 it was estimated that the median age was 27.6 years for the total population (males, 27.1; females, 28.1). The overall age structure was such that 28 percent of

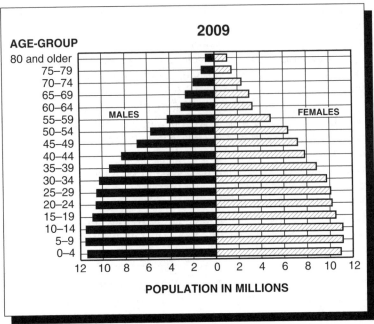

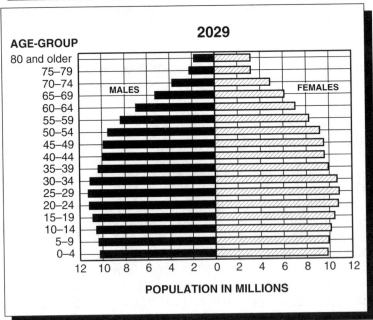

Source: Based on information from United States, Department of Commerce, Census Bureau, International Programs Center, *International Data Base Population Pyramids (Indonesia)* (Washington, DC, 2008), http://www.census.gov/ipc/www/idb.

Figure 7. Age-Sex Ratio, 2009, and Projected Ratio, 2029

the population was age 14 or younger, 66 percent was 15–64 years old, and 6 percent was 65 or older. Based on estimates for 2009, Indonesians aged nine or younger represent the largest age cohort, totaling some 44.9 million, or nearly 19 percent of the population (see fig. 7). Indonesia's gender ratio is fairly balanced, and comparable to that of its regional neighbors: the 2009 estimate was 1.05 males born for every female born, the same as for Australia, Brunei, Papua New Guinea, the Philippines, and Timor-Leste. Malaysia's gender ratio stood at 1.07:1 and Singapore's at 1.08:1.

Family

The structure, size, and function of the Indonesian family exhibit considerable variation in the country's hundreds of different ethnolinguistic groups. Enshrined in official rhetoric and documents as a model for the nation as a whole, the family is regarded as the foundation of morality, justice, and duty concerning public behavior. Although Indonesians in different parts of the archipelago have different traditional notions about inheritance, marriage, and filial rights and responsibilities, certain commonalities are beginning to emerge, in part as a result of the influence of national laws, institutions, and policies, as well as the increasing integration of the population into a national economy.

One of the most striking and far-reaching changes since the mid-1970s has been the continued decline in fertility. As a result of improved education, an effective family-planning program, and reduced child mortality, the average number of children born per Indonesian woman has steadily declined, from approximately 5.0 in 1970 to an estimated 2.3 in 2009. The decline has been steepest in Java and Bali. Despite the reduction in family size, the archipelago is increasingly overcrowded, with an estimated population density of 131 persons per square kilometer in 2009 (compared with 33.8 per square kilometer in the United States). In Java, Madura, and Bali, population densities are more than 900 per square kilometer.

Since the early 1990s, Indonesian women have tended to bear fewer children as infant mortality has decreased. In 1991 the estimated infant mortality rate was 59 deaths per 1,000 live births. By 1995 that figure had declined to 48 deaths; it then dipped to 40.9 by 2000. In 2009 the infant mortality rate was estimated at 29.9 deaths per 1,000 live births. Strikingly, even as the number of births per woman has declined in Indonesia, there has been no evidence of a preference for sons in the number of children born or who survive as infants. Another factor influencing Indonesian families is a general trend toward equality in inheritance patterns and allocation of family resources. The gap between the amounts inherited by sons and daughters appears to have shrunk over the course of the 1980s and 1990s, and by 2009 it had probably nearly closed.

The mobility of working-age adults has increased greatly, meaning that households have become more dynamic in the early twenty-first century. The structure and size of households fluctuate more rapidly than in the past. This trend is both a cause and a consequence of the economic, social, and demographic changes that have occurred, as well as the result of transportation improvements (see Migration, this ch.).

Despite these forces of rapid change, Indonesian marriages continue to exhibit a typical pattern in which wives exert control over household finances and overall management of children and household affairs while husbands and unmarried young adults are responsible for discretionary spending and ties to the larger community. Polygamy is permitted but relatively rare. The law states that men and women are equal, and that both are responsible for maintaining the home and caring for the children. The rate of participation of women in the workforce has remained more or less stable, and, overall, Indonesian marriages have experienced a decline in the divorce rate to less than 40 percent. This contrasts with the 1960s, when the rate peaked at nearly 60 percent. The reasons for this decline are controversial, but financial, political, and social insecurity, combined with growing religious conservatism, may be factors in keeping marriages together. The actual divorce process exhibits considerable variation in different parts of the archipelago, but in general a divorce is relatively easy to obtain in Islamic courts by either a man or a woman. Judicial divorces are harder to get.

National, Religious, and Local Authority

Most Indonesians have a strong sense of citizenship in the larger Indonesian state and its various levels of government in addition to feeling attached to their family and household. Three generations of schoolchildren have worn similar uniforms, sung common songs, learned a common language, and recited similar facts of history, civics, and the Pancasila ideology. The red and white Indonesian flag is a common sight throughout the archipelago. Uniformed state employees and ordinary citizens alike have all grown accustomed to carrying their *kartu tanda penduduk*, or national identification card.

In 1998, however, after nearly 32 years of gradual centralization of power and authority under Suharto (1967–98), the relationship of ordinary Indonesians to their vast nation-state began to change rapidly (see The Political Process, ch. 4). One of the most noticeable changes was a trend toward challenging central authority occurring at the same time as a move toward decentralization. Assertions of local control and authority became more frequent in the early twenty-first century. In some cases, such assertions took the form of vigilante violence and protests, as local citizens bypassed the courts and took the search for justice into their own hands. As protests and unrest increased, citizens began monitoring calls for change (generally dubbed *reformasi*—see Glossary) in newly uncensored newspapers and Internet sources; print circulation and Internet subscriptions both increased rapidly.

These challenges often took the form of assertions of religious rather than secular authority, as the leadership of Islamic groups, long suppressed during the New Order government of Suharto, began to find its voice. One striking trend was visible in Java among young women, who, in increasing numbers, began to wear the *jilbab*, the traditional Islamic women's head covering. Anthropologist Suzanne Brenner has argued, based on extensive interviews with Javanese women, that this was less a statement of submission to an ideology of male-dominated tradition than an assertion of independence from a perceived status quo of secular authoritarianism. Young women, in other words, were employing the veil or head covering as a way of making a statement about their feelings toward what they regarded as the moral laxity and corruption of the state, and of society more generally. It did not necessarily signal a stance in favor of an Islamic state.

Urbanization and Decentralization

One of the most significant trends in Indonesia since the 1970s has been toward urbanization. The segment of the population living in urban areas grew from 17 percent in 1971, to 31 percent in 1990, and to 46 percent in 2003. In 2006 Indonesia's Urban and Regional Development Institute projected that the nation's urban population could reach more than 50 percent by 2010 and 60 percent by 2025. Surveys showed that the movement toward urban areas, particularly those in Jawa Barat Province, southwestern Sulawesi, and Kalimantan, among other areas, stemmed not from the innate lure of the cities but from the lack of employment in the countryside. Migrants seemed to view the pollution, crime, anonymity, and grinding poverty of the city as short-term discomforts that would eventually give way to a better life. For high school and college graduates with no prospects for employment in the rural areas, this may in fact have been a correct assumption. But for those migrants without capital or qualifications, the main hope for employment was in the so-called informal sector, which offered work such as street vending, scavenging, and short-term day labor (see Employment and Income, ch. 3). Many migrants also cultivated tiny but nutritionally important gardens.

Much urban growth has been in mid-sized cities. Jakarta's population (8.5 million, with a population density of nearly 12,900 persons per square kilometer in 2009) has experienced a rate of increase of about 1 percent a year, but there were signs of decentralizing trends in the early twenty-first century. For example, much growth has occurred in the greater Jakarta metropolitan area, known as Jabodetabek (for Jakarta–Bogor–Depok–Tangerang–Bekasi), home to an estimated 24.3 million in 2007, rather than in Jakarta proper. While the capital enjoyed a disproportionate amount of the nation's resources in technology, health care, wealth, and political power during the Suharto era, after 1998 provincial governments began to demand a larger share. On January 1, 2001, a rapid decentralization program began that placed more authority at the level of the regency (*kabupaten*, a subprovincial but nonmunicipal unit of government) and municipality (*kota*) (see Local Government, ch. 4). This process reportedly was going well in the mid-2000s.

The transformation of a well-established pattern of urbanization may have been possible because, as anthropologist Pauline D. Milone observed in the mid-1960s, Jakarta has never been a true primate city in terms of being the only center for economic, political, administrative, higher education, and technical functions in the way that, for example, Bangkok has been for Thailand. In Java, Surabaya has always been a major import-export center and has long been home to an important naval station, and Bandung has been a center for transportation, higher education, and industry. Nonetheless, in terms of population growth and as a symbol of the centralization of power in the nation, Jakarta has grown steadily in size and importance.

Migration

Indonesians, particularly Javanese, are sometimes stereotyped as highly immobile, rarely venturing beyond the confines of their village environment, but this image may be due to a lack of clear data and an extraordinarily complex pattern of movement in the population. By the early 1990s, out-migration had become a common response to overcrowded conditions caused by population growth. Some of these resettlements resulted in conflicts with the indigenous populations, and by the late 1990s, many transmigrants were fleeing conflicts in Aceh, Kalimantan, Maluku, Sulawesi, and Timor. As a result, by 2000 the government's long-standing Transmigration Program (see Glossary) was discontinued.

Many communities, particularly in Sumatra, have a long tradition of sending young adult males on *merantau* (cyclical out-migration) as a means for them to gain experience and income and reduce

*Javanese dancer at the Exposition universelle in Paris, 1889
Courtesy Library of Congress Prints and Photographs Division, Lot 6634, LC–USZ62–109527, digital ID cph 3c09527*

household expenses. Since the 1970s, however, interprovincial migration has increased dramatically for all regions. In addition, the financial crisis of 1997–98 resulted in a major increase in migration overseas in search of work, and the violence in Aceh, Kalimantan, Maluku, Sulawesi, and Timor has resulted in some 1.2 million internally displaced persons, about half of whom are living in refugee camps. According to the 2000 census, some 7.1 million of all Indonesian males living in urban areas (16.6 percent of this population category) were migrants. Among individual localities, Jakarta led with 42.6 percent of its male population being migrant, followed closely by Kalimantan Timur Province, with 41.3 percent, and Papua and Riau, each with 39.0 percent. The proportion in rural areas was much less; overall, only 6.1 percent of males in these areas nationwide were emigrants. Kalimantan Timur and the province of Riau had the greatest proportions, with 30.7 percent and 28.2 percent, respectively.

Indonesians were also engaging in what demographers call circular migration and other kinds of commuting in greater numbers than ever before. This trend was linked in part to the steep increase in the number of motor vehicles, from 3.0 per 1,000 population in the 1960s to 26.2 in 1980, 46.3 in 1990, 78.1 in 2000, and 132 in 2007. With the widespread availability of public bus transportation connecting cities and villages, many workers commute 50 kilometers or more daily to work. Others live away from their homes for several days at a time in order to work. The World Bank has estimated that 25 percent of rural households have at least one family member working for part of the year in an urban area.

In part because of increasing migration, Indonesians of different ethnic backgrounds and occupations are increasingly intermingling. They more frequently find themselves in circumstances in which they cannot rely on kin and village networks for social support, and so they look to government services for help, particularly in the areas of education and health care (see Education; Health, this ch.).

Social Class

The experience of population mobility in the archipelago has not necessarily resulted in social mobility in terms of social class. Indeed, recent studies underscore the continuing importance of social stratification in Indonesia, as least as measured by regional inequalities in income and consumption. However, scholars and policy analysts continue to debate the degree to which social classes can be defined in ethnic, economic, religious, or political terms. While it is clear that Indonesia is a highly stratified society, and that sensitivity to prestige or status (*gengsi*) is widespread, it is nonetheless difficult to identify an upper class. Hereditary ruling classes and traditional elites reinforced by their positions in the Dutch colonial bureaucracy no longer possess unchallenged access to political power and wealth (see Modernism and Nationalism in the Colonial Age, ch. 1). Indeed, they cannot even claim to form an elite. The real power holders—generals, politicians, and wealthy capitalists of the postindependence period—are newcomers to their positions, and, apart from extravagant conspicuous consumption and cosmopolitanism, they demonstrate few clear institutional and cultural patterns that suggest they constitute a unitary group.

Defining a lower class in Indonesia is equally difficult. Even before the banning of the Indonesian Communist Party (PKI—see Glossary) in 1966, Indonesia's poor formed alliances that had less to do with class than with economics, religion, and community ties. In some cases, the poor peasantry identified across class lines with orthodox Muslim landowners on the basis of their common religious ideologies or *aliran kepercayaan* (streams of belief). This alliance was particularly evident in lowland Jawa Timur Province. In other cases, small landowners united against both the Islamic right wing and Chinese entrepreneurs. There also were divisions between the indigenous, or long-settled, peoples (*pribumi*—see Glossary) and later Chinese and Arab immigrants. The oil boom of the 1970s affected society and income distribution in ways that benefited the landed peasantry and the urban middle class. However, no independent social group based on lower-class affiliations emerged as a major political force.

Income disparities between the Outer Islands and the rest of the country and between rural and urban areas remain a major cause of concern, although the productivity gap between Java and the Outer Islands has narrowed. While the urban areas of Indonesia, especially Java and Bali, grew disproportionately wealthy in relation to their counterparts in more rural areas and the Outer Islands through much of the 1990s, they were also hit particularly hard by the 1997–98 financial crisis. By 2000, income and consumption inequalities were back to levels experienced in the 1980s. United Nations Development Programme data based on the Gini index (see Glossary) indicate that Indonesia stands comparatively well regarding income inequality. For example, the Gini index for Indonesia in 2008 was estimated at 0.34, significantly lower than the indexes for several neighboring countries: Singapore (0.42), the Philippines (0.44), Malaysia (0.49), and Papua New Guinea (0.51).

Between the nation's poor and privileged classes lies a complex mosaic of groups forming what might loosely be called a middle class. Not characterized by a common political vision, a set of economic interests, ethnic identification, or even income levels, the notion of a middle class in Indonesia is invoked by outsiders and analysts but rarely defined, especially by Indonesians themselves. While middle-income Indonesians appear to share some consumption patterns—the purchase and exclusive use of consumer durables such as televisions, motorcycles, newspapers, cell phones, and DVD players—the decentralization of power after 1998 does not seem to have resulted in an empowered middle class. As Richard Robison and Vedi Hadiz argued in 2004, the Indonesian oligarchy adapted to the collapse of the New Order and the financial crisis in some new ways but continues to use state power for private interests.

Civil Society

Although the family, the community, and the government are important sources of authority in Indonesia, nongovernmental organizations (*lembaga swadaya masyarakat*, or LSM, or also sometimes *organisasi nonpemerintah,* or *ornop),* such as foundations or charitable organizations (*yayasan),* associations (*perserikatan),* and movements (*gerakan),* play an increasingly important role in defining and shaping social life. While some *yayasan,* for example, provide complex but significant financial loopholes for businesses, since the 1980s, environmental, legal aid, and women's groups have played an increasingly important public role.

The increasingly free news media are an important means of expression for Indonesian civil society. Immediately preceding the fall of Suharto in 1998, Indonesians began to enjoy expanded access to print and electronic news sources. Although not completely unfettered, the news media were vibrant and played an increasingly important role in informing public debate. Immediately upon Suharto's departure, however, the media were openly reporting on strikes, popular demonstrations, and other expressions of opposition to government authority. Intimidation by officials and private interests remained a serious problem, but journalists reported and advocated positions at odds with those of the government, sometimes at their peril. Media observers, such as Krishna Sen and David T. Hill, believe that the Internet may also have played a role in this new openness, as the freedom it offered during the waning days of the Suharto era became a constant reminder of the absence of openness and freedom in other media.

Islamic civic organizations constitute another important manifestation of civil society in Indonesia. In the period following the 1997–98 economic crisis and the downfall of Suharto, these organizations played an important role in filling the vacuum of authority. Well before the term civil society became widespread in the 1980s, Islamic organizations in Indonesia participated in activities that mediated between the state and the family. For instance, Muhammadiyah (Followers of Muhammad) is one of the two most important, modern Islamic social-religious organizations in Indonesia. Established in 1912, it has played an increasingly important role in social and cultural spheres of Indonesian life, such as education, finance, socioeconomic development, health care, and care for indigent people and orphans. After the collapse of the New Order in 1998, when new political parties were being established across the archipelago, Muhammadiyah had the opportunity to transform itself from a social and cultural organization into a political party. However, the membership rejected this change, and in 2008 no official link existed between Muhammadiyah and any political party.

Indonesia's other first-rank Muslim organization, the Nahdlatul Ulama (literally, "revival of the religious teachers," but often translated as Council of Scholars), was founded in 1926 as a religious voluntary organization by traditional Muslim religious scholars. It is the largest Muslim organization in Indonesia, with a membership of approximately 35 million. Unlike Muhammadiyah, the more orthodox Sunni (see Glossary) Nahdlatul Ulama in the 1950s was also a political party, but it now is strongly oriented toward civic and social activities. Its base is rural and traditional, practicing forms of Islam strongly linked to legal, theological, and mystical traditions that are nurtured in traditional boarding schools (*pondok pesantren*). Nahdlatul Ulama emphasizes tolerance in its view of society. In 1983 it decided to accept the Indonesian state ideology, Pancasila, as the foundation of its social programs, and to work for a just society for all Indonesians, not just Muslims. In 1998 Nahdlatul Ulama unofficially backed the formation of the National Awakening Party (PKB), and its leader, Abdurrahman Wahid, was elected president by the People's Representative Council (DPR) in 1999. However, the PKB's moderate stance, and opposition to an Islamic state, led more conservative members to leave the party. Although Wahid was ousted from power in 2001, he and Nahdlatul Ulama continued (until Wahid's death in 2009) to be voices for tolerance, secular government, and democracy.

As in many other societies, civil-society organizations in Indonesia ideally promote peace, justice, and social tolerance, but that is not always the reality. For instance, on October 12, 2002, terrorists associated with the radical group Jemaah Islamiyah (Congregation of Islam) blew up two Bali nightclubs, killing 202 people. On August 5, 2003, individuals allegedly linked to the same group struck the Jakarta JW Marriott Hotel, killing 14. Nonetheless, a national poll in 2003 suggested that politically militant Islam was not on the rise. Fully 85 percent of the respondents indicated that they did not support the idea of an Islamic state or rollbacks of democratic freedoms. In spite of high-publicity attacks by militant Muslim groups, Muslim conservatives play a far smaller role in national politics than they did in the 1950s (see Islamic Political Culture, ch. 4; Terrorism, ch. 5).

Violence, Vengeance, and Law

Indonesia experienced a high level of civil violence from about 1996 to 2003. Instances included ethnic conflict in Sumba (Nusa Tenggara Timur); apparently ethnic and religious strife in Kalimantan, Sulawesi, Ambon, and Halmahera (in the Malukus); sectarian rioting in the cities of Situbondo (Jawa Timur) and Tasikmalaya (Jawa Barat); race rioting in Jakarta; gang warfare in Timor; and government repression of student protests at Trisakti University in

Jakarta on May 12, 1998. The cumulative casualty toll was in the thousands, and the number of displaced persons rose to more than 500,000, according to the U.S. Committee for Refugees.

The predominant theme to this unrest, according to some analysts, was not religion, ethnicity, or politics, but rather a tendency to use extralegal means to exact vengeance and retaliate against enemies. As the Suharto administration began to assume power, it was involved in a bloody retaliation against alleged communist actions during 1965–66; for the next 30 years, vigilante neighborhood watch groups consisting of young men routinely captured and killed alleged thieves without legal process but with the implicit approval of the government. Because the court system was viewed as corrupt and susceptible to bribery, and many law enforcement agencies were nearly bankrupt because of the financial crisis, many Indonesians came to believe that violence was the only route to justice. The violence of 1996–2003 represented a continuation and intensification of these patterns.

Religion and Worldview

Religion in Indonesia is a complex and volatile issue, not easily analyzed in terms of social class, region, or ethnic group. Long discouraged by the New Order government (1966–98) from political participation, Islam, Christianity, Hinduism, Buddhism, and other religions were increasingly influential frameworks for defining social participation after 1998. The state guaranteed tolerance of certain religions (*agama*) regarded as monotheistic by the government, but popular violence between Christians and Muslims in Java, Sulawesi, Kalimantan, Ambon, and Halmahera made those guarantees difficult to honor. In some cases, the police and army were on different sides of clashes defined in religious terms.

Islam

Islam is the dominant religion by far in Indonesia, with the greatest number of adherents: around 86.1 percent of the population according to the 2000 census; in 2009 this would have been about 207 million people. No other country in the world has more Muslims than Indonesia.

The main strand of Islamic practice in Indonesia by far is Sunni, with only a very small number of Shia (also Shiite—see Glossary). Differing understandings of the role of the clergy are a key distinction between Sunni and Shia. Emphasizing predestination and predetermination by Allah, Sunni clerics interpret the sunna within limits

*Cows being readied for slaughter for the Muslim holiday Idul Adha
(Feast of Sacrifice at the end of Hajj), in front of al Istiqlal Mosque,
Manado, Sulawesi Utara Province
Courtesy Anastasia Riehl*

imposed by centuries of learning and scholarship. Shia clerics emphasize free will and the infallibility of divinely inspired imams to interpret ancient texts. Cutting across the difference between Sunni and Shia groups, a small minority of Indonesians can be characterized in terms of what Australian scholar Greg Fealy calls radical Islam, although even mainstream Muslims sympathize with some aspects of their teachings, if not their practices. Among these radical groups in Indonesia are Darul Islam (House of Islam), Jemaah Islamiyah (internationally regarded as a terrorist organization), Majelis Mujahidin Indonesia (Indonesian Islamic Warriors' Council), and Front Pembela Islam (Islamic Defenders' Front). These groups share a sense that the West (that is, Christians and Jews) has used economic and military power to enfeeble Islam; their solution is to call for a return to the pure Islam of the righteous ancestors (*as-salaf as-salih*), or Salafism. Varieties of Salafism include Wahhabism, the official form of Islam in Saudi Arabia.

According to orthodox practice, Islam is a strictly monotheistic religion in which God (Allah, or, in Indonesian, Tuhan, which is also used to refer to the Christian God and other gods) is both a pervasive presence and a somewhat distant figure. The Prophet Muhammad is not deified but rather is regarded as a human who was selected by God to spread the word to others through the Quran, Islam's holy book, the revealed word of God. Islam is a religion based on high moral principles, and an important part of being a Muslim is commitment to these principles. Islamic law (sharia, or *syariah* in Indonesian) is based on the Quran; the sunna, which includes the hadith (*hadis* in Indonesian), the actions and sayings of Muhammad; *ijma*, the consensus of local Islamic jurisprudence and, sometimes, the whole Muslim community; and *qiyas*, or reasoning through analogy. Islam is universalist, and in theory there are no national, racial, or ethnic criteria for conversion.

Over the course of the mostly peaceful introduction of Islam to Indonesia beginning in the ninth century AD, tensions periodically arose between orthodox Muslims and practitioners of more syncretistic, locally based religions. These tensions are still evident in the early twenty-first century. In Java, for instance, they are expressed in the contrast between a *santri* (see Glossary), a pious Muslim, and an *abangan* (see Glossary), an adherent to a syncretistic blend of indigenous, Hindu-Buddhist beliefs with Islamic practices, sometimes called *kejawen* (Javanism), *agama Jawa* (Javanese religion), or *kebatinan* (mysticism—see Glossary). In Java, *santri* not only refers to a person who is consciously and exclusively Muslim, but also describes persons who have removed themselves from the secular world to concentrate on devotional activities in Islamic schools called *pesantren*—literally, the place of the *santri*, but meaning Islamic school. Although these religious boarding schools, typically headed by a charismatic *kiai* (Muslim religious scholar), provide education for only a minority of Indonesian children (less than 10 percent), they remain an important symbol of Muslim piety, particularly in rural areas.

There is also a long history of religious practice associated with more mystical and often highly syncretistic beliefs. Drawing variously on Hindu-Buddhist ideas about self-control and intellectual contemplation, as well as more animistically inclined ideas about the spiritual character of nature, and often based on miraculous revelations, various kinds of hybrid Islamic beliefs flourished in Java until a presidential decree in 1965 urged consolidation under the rubric of the main scriptural religions (*agama*), including Islam, Christianity, Buddhism, Hinduism, and Confucianism. Several of the more mystical varieties of Islam continued to flourish under the Suharto regime, and some continued to struggle for autonomy and recognition by the government, eventually receiving recognition in 1973 as *keper-*

cayaan (faiths), albeit under the umbrella of one of the scriptural *agama*. Among the more prominent of these faiths was *kebatinan*. Only nominally Muslim, *kebatinan* is an amalgam of animist, Hindu-Buddhist, and Muslim, mostly Sufi (see Glossary), spiritual practices concerned with harmonizing the inner self with the outer material world. Spirits are believed to inhabit natural objects, human beings, artifacts, and grave sites of important *wali* (Muslim saints). Illness and other misfortunes are traced to such spirits, and if sacrifices or pilgrimages fail to placate angry deities, the advice of a *dukun*, or healer, is sought. While it connotes a turning away from the militant universalism of orthodox Islam, *kebatinan* moves toward a more internalized universalism. In this way, it seeks to eliminate distinctions between the universal and the local, the communal and the individual.

Another important tension dividing Indonesian Muslims is that between traditionalism and modernism. The nature of this antipathy is complex and a matter of considerable debate. One key issue concerns the self-sufficiency of scripture and the moral responsibility of the individual. Modernists emphasize the absolute and transparent authority of the Quran and the responsibility of individuals to follow its teachings; traditionalists contend that Quranic texts can be ambiguous, and that it is wiser to trust in the collective wisdom of past teaching. While traditionalists accept a variety of ritual forms, they underscore the responsibility of believers to the community, and are less concerned with individual responsibility to interpret scripture. Specifically, traditionalists are suspicious of modernists' support of the urban madrassa (*madrasah* in Bahasa Indonesia), a reformist school that includes the teaching of secular topics. The modernists' goal of taking Islam and carrying it more directly to the people has been opposed by traditionalists because it threatens to undermine the authority of the *kiai*. On the other hand, some modernists accuse traditionalists of escapist tendencies and of failing to directly confront the individual responsibility to make sense of a changing world. One point of agreement is that both modernists and traditionalists have sought, unsuccessfully, to add a clause to the first tenet of the Indonesian constitution requiring that, in effect, all Muslims adhere to the sharia. In fact, some even hint that modernist and traditionalist *santri* harbor greater loyalty toward the *ummah* (community of believers) of Islam than to the Indonesian state.

Christianity

Christianity—Roman Catholicism and Protestantism—is the most rapidly growing religion in Indonesia, although Christians are modest in number compared to adherents to Islam (8.7 percent of the population versus 86.1 percent according to the 2000 census). Christianity has a long history in the islands, with Portuguese Jesuits and Dominicans operating in Maluku, southern Sulawesi, and Timor since the sixteenth century. When the Dutch defeated Portuguese forces in 1605 and began what was to be more than 350 years of Dutch presence in the Indonesian archipelago, however, the Catholic missionaries were expelled, and the Dutch Reformed Church, a Calvinist denomination, became the dominant Christian presence in the region, as it would be until Indonesia became independent (see The National Revolution, 1945–49, ch. 1). Because the United East Indies Company (VOC) was a secular enterprise, and Calvinism was a strict and intellectually uncompromising interpretation of Christianity that demanded a thorough understanding of what, for Indonesians, were foreign scriptures, Christianity advanced little in Indonesia until the nineteenth century. Only a few small communities endured, in Java, Maluku, northern Sulawesi, and Nusa Tenggara (primarily on the islands of Roti and Timor). After the dissolution of the VOC in 1799, and the adoption of a more comprehensive view of their mission in the archipelago, the Dutch permitted Christian proselytizing in the territory. This evangelical freedom was put to use by the more tolerant German Lutherans, who began work in Sumatra among the Toba Batak in 1861, and by the Dutch Rhenish Mission in central Kalimantan in 1845. In addition, Jesuits established successful Catholic missions, schools, and hospitals throughout the islands of Flores, Timor, and Alor in the late nineteenth century.

The twentieth century witnessed the influx of many new Protestant missionary groups, as well as the continued growth of Catholicism and of large regional and reformed Lutheran churches. Following the 1965 coup attempt, all nonreligious persons were labeled atheists and hence were vulnerable to accusations of harboring communist sympathies (see The "Coup" and Its Aftermath, ch. 1). At that time, Christian churches of all varieties experienced explosive growth in membership, particularly among people who felt uncomfortable with the political aspirations of Islamic parties.

Most Christians in Indonesia are Protestants (about 19 million in 2009) of one denomination or another, with particularly large concentrations located in the provinces of Sumatera Utara, Papua, Papua Barat, Maluku, Kalimantan Tengah, Sulawesi Tengah, Sulawesi Utara, and Nusa Tenggara Timur. Large concentrations of Roman Catholics (a total of about 8 million in 2009) live in Jawa Tengah, Kalimantan Barat, Papua, Papua Barat, and Nusa Tenggara Timur. In addition, a substantial number of ethnic Chinese Indonesians are Roman Catho-

Nativity scene in front of a Roman Catholic Church on Sulawesi
Courtesy Anastasia Riehl

lic. Catholic congregations grew less rapidly in the 1980s and 1990s, in part because of the church's heavy reliance on European personnel. These Europeans experienced increasing restrictions on their missionary activities imposed by the Muslim-dominated Department of Religion (later called the Department of Religious Affairs).

Hinduism

Indonesian Hinduism, an amalgam of related traditions and cults that explains the nature of the universe in terms of interactions among numerous gods, is strongly associated with Bali. In 1953, in response to the central government's exclusion of Balinese Hinduism from its list of officially recognized religions, religious leaders on that island sought official recognition of Agama Hindu Bali (Hindu Balinese Religion) as a creed equivalent to Islam, Catholicism, and Protestantism. Led by Pandit Shastri, various Hindu reform organizations on Bali agreed in 1958 on the Hindu Dharma (Principles of Hinduism), which emphasized the *Catur Veda* (religious poems), the *Upanishads* (treatises of Brahmanic knowledge), and the *Bhagavad Gita,* as well as two Old Javanese texts (*Sarasamuccaya* and *Sanghyang Kamahayanikan*). Together, these works came to form the holy canon of Balinese Hinduism. Other Hindu sacred texts, such as the *Puranas*

(Sanskrit cosmogonic histories), were relegated to a minor position. In addition, a daily prayer called the *trisandhya* was devised by Pandit Shastri to correspond to the five daily prayers of Muslims. These reforms were accepted by Sukarno in 1959, and Balinese Hinduism gained full recognition in 1963.

Arriving in the archipelago before the second century AD with traders and missionaries from India, Hindu beliefs were greatly modified when adapted to Indonesian society. The central concept of ritual purity, maintained through a division of society into occupational groups, or castes (*varna*, literally color), was never rigidly applied in Indonesia. The categories of Brahman (priests; *brahmana* in Indonesian), Kshatriya (ruler-warrior; *satria* in Indonesian), Vaishya (merchant-farmer; *waisya* in Indonesian), and Shudra (commoner-servant; *sudra* in Indonesian) do exist in Bali; besides the category of Brahman, however, they appear to have little influence over occupational choices, or even over social status and marital opportunities. Two Hindu epics, the *Mahabharata* (Great Battle of the Descendants of Bharata) and the *Ramayana* (The Travels of Rama), have become classics among Indonesians, both Hindu believers and others, especially in Java, and are rendered in *wayang* (see Glossary) and dance performances.

Indonesian Hindu believers are relatively few outside Bali, where they make up more than 93 percent of the population. Others are scattered throughout the other 32 provinces and special regions, where diverse, and largely indigenous, religious practices have sought and gained recognition as Hindu by the Department of Religious Affairs. On a nationwide basis, only about 1.8 percent of the population was Hindu according to the 2000 census, although the U.S. Department of State reported 10 million adherents in 2009. Because lacking an official *agama* was associated with communism during the New Order, and being communist was a crime punishable by death or exile, some of Indonesia's heterogeneous animist, ancestor worship, and syncretic cults sought refuge under the tolerant Hindu aegis. Among these non-Balinese communities, one finds, for example, the adherents of the Kaharingan religion in Kalimantan Tengah, where government statistics generally have counted them among Hindus as 7.8 percent of the local population. In addition, there are significant communities labeled Hindu among the Toraja in Sulawesi Tengah and Sulawesi Selatan provinces, among the Karo Batak in northern Sumatra, and in Jawa Tengah and Jawa Timur provinces, most notably among the Tenggerese.

Anthropologist Robert Hefner has noted that significant changes in state policy occurred with respect to Javanese Hinduism in the late 1980s and early 1990s. During the early phases of the New Order,

Ruins of a Hindu temple in Yogyakarta
Courtesy Library of Congress Prints and Photographs Division,
Lot 11356, LC–USZ62–95443, digital ID cph 3b41593

syncretically and mystically inclined Javanese previously affiliated loosely with Islam had converted to Hinduism. While there was government support initially for such groups, including the *kebatinan*, pressure from conservative Muslim groups on the one hand and government leadership on the other resulted in an increasingly poor fit between the syncretic practice of Javanese Hinduism and the official Hindu dharma.

Buddhism

Introduced before the second century AD by the same waves of traders and scholars who brought Hinduism, Indonesian Buddhism is now overwhelmingly associated with the ethnic Chinese and is an unstable product of complex accommodations among religious ideology, Chinese ethnic identification, and a gradually more tolerant policy by the central government. Traditionally, Chinese Daoism, Confucianism (*agama Konghucu*), and Buddhism, as well as the mass Buddhist organization Perhimpunan Buddhis Indonesia (Perbuddhi), founded in 1958, all had adherents in the ethnic Chinese community. Following the events of 1965, with any deviation from the monotheistic tenets of the Pancasila regarded as treason, the founder of Perbuddhi, Bhikku Ashin Jinarakkhita, proposed that there was a single supreme deity, Sang Hyang Adi Buddha. He successfully sought confirmation for this striking innovation to Buddhist beliefs in ancient Javanese texts, and even in the shape of the Borobudur temple in Jawa Tengah Province. After 1965 the number of Buddhists swelled; some 90 new monasteries were built, mostly supported by Indonesia's Chinese population, but also drawing significant numbers from syncretistically oriented Javanese disaffected by the increasingly strict emphasis on doctrinaire forms of Islam. By 1987 there were seven schools of Buddhism affiliated with the Perwakilan Umat Buddha Indonesia (Walubi): Theravada, Buddhayana, Mahayana, Tridharma, Kasogatan, Maitreya, and Nichiren. In 2009 Buddhism had an estimated 2 million followers in Indonesia (less than 1 percent of the population), with a growing presence in Kalimantan Barat Province, home to large numbers of ethnic Chinese.

Confucianism and Daoism

The New Order administration officially tolerated Confucianism. However, because it was regarded as a system of ethical relations rather than a religion per se, it was not represented in the Department of Religion. Daoism, which is practiced both as a philosophy and a religion, is recognized by the department as an official religion.

The Emerging National Culture

Living Environments

The government of Indonesia saw itself as having a responsibility to advance a national culture throughout most of the New Order period, a project that was linked to requirements of national development and political integration. Government mandates aside, however, as more and more of the Indonesian population sought employment in large, poorly integrated cities consisting of diverse ethnic groups, the concept of a national culture had great appeal as a way of regulating these changing urban environments. Although the central government attempted to guide the formation of this culture through educational curricula, celebrations of national holidays, and careful control of the national media (popular art, television, and print media), this emerging culture came about only partly through central planning. Evidence of an emerging national culture also appeared in the far less controlled layout and social organization of cities; routines of social interaction using the official national language, Bahasa Indonesia; patterns of eating and preparing food; the viewing of team

Altar in a Buddhist temple, Tomohon, Sulawesi Utara Province
Courtesy Anastasia Riehl

sports, such as soccer, badminton, and volleyball; movies and television programming; and material displays of wealth.

In smaller Indonesian cities, the heart of urban culture before the mid-twentieth century was a commercial sector surrounding a central square. The Dutch left a legacy of a basic civil architecture and street plans for large cities and towns in Java, Sumatra, and Bali, but after World War II most failed to experience a level of improved urban design and services commensurate with their tremendous population growth. Many cities, as a result, had minimal or makeshift services, with very simple sanitation, transportation facilities, and fire protection.

Indonesian cities are internally segmented in complex, overlapping ways that differentiate ethnic groups, income levels, and professional specializations. Some older neighborhoods tend to house well-to-do business owners and high-level government officials, whereas other newer areas tend to be home to migrant communities from the rural areas. Some of these areas retain their system of close-knit social networks and are distinguished by the label *kampung* (village). However, the boundaries between one area and another are often unclear.

Language

The major languages of Indonesia belong to the Austronesian family, a group of agglutinative languages spoken in the area bounded by Madagascar in the western Indian Ocean and Easter Island in the eastern Pacific Ocean. There is a considerable diversity in the languages used in Indonesia. No fewer than 731 languages—the vast majority Austronesian, the rest Papuan and used in parts of Timor, Papua, and Halmahera—existed in the early twenty-first century.

Based on reports of ethnic self-identification in the 2000 census, the primary languages spoken by 2 million or more people were Javanese (83 million), Sundanese (30 million), Malay/Indonesian (17 million), Madurese (6.7 million), Batak (6.1 million), Minangkabau (5.4 million), Buginese (5.1 million), Balinese (3 million), and Acehnese (2.2 million). In addition, some 2 million inhabitants spoke one of several dialects of Chinese. Arabic and languages of India and Europe also are used.

The central and most successful feature of the Indonesian national culture is probably the Indonesian language. Malay was used for centuries as a lingua franca in many parts of the archipelago. The term Bahasa Indonesia, which refers to a modified form of Malay, was coined by Indonesian nationalists in 1928 and became a symbol of national unity during the struggle for independence. Bahasa Indonesia is spoken in more than 90 percent of households in Jakarta. Outside the capital, only 10 to 15 percent of the population speaks the language at home, but this number appears to be on the rise. In Javanese areas, only 1 percent to 5 percent of the people speak Bahasa Indonesia in the home. Nationwide, some 17 million Indonesians use Bahasa Indonesia as a primary language, while more than 150 million to 180 million others use it as a second language. It is now indisputably the language of government, schools, national print and electronic media, and interethnic communication. In many provinces, it is the primary language of communication between ethnic Chinese shopkeepers and their non-Chinese patrons.

Bahasa Indonesia is infused with highly distinctive accents, vocabularies, and styles in some regions (particularly Maluku, parts of Nusa Tenggara, and Jakarta), but there are many similarities in patterns of use across the archipelago. For example, it is common to vary the use of address forms depending on the rank or status of the individual to whom one is speaking. This variation is not as complex as in the elaborately hierarchical Javanese language, but it is nonetheless important. For instance, in Bahasa Indonesia respected elders are typically addressed in kinship terms—*bapak* (father or elder) or *ibu* (mother). The use of second-person pronouns in direct address is generally avoided in favor of more indirect references unless speaker and listeners are on intimate terms. In casual contexts, however, such as when one is speaking to taxicab drivers, street peddlers, and close friends, formal textbook Indonesian often gives way to the more ironic, sly, and earthy urban forms of address and reference.

Food, Clothing, and Popular Culture

Although Indonesia has a varied environment, and many different ethnic cuisines, rice is a national staple, even in areas such as eastern Indonesia, where the main source of starch is corn, cassava, taro, or sago. On ceremonial occasions such as funerals, modern weddings, and state functions, foods such as *sate* (small pieces of meat roasted on a skewer), *krupuk* (fried chips made with rice flour and flavored with fish or fried shrimp), and highly spiced curries of chicken and goat are commonly served. At public events, these foods are often placed on a table from which guests serve themselves buffet style. Rice is placed in the center of the plate, with meats or other condiments around the edges. Food is eaten—usually quite rapidly and without speaking—with the fingertips or with a spoon and fork. Water is generally drunk only after the meal, when men (rarely women) smoke their distinctive clove-scented *kretek* cigarettes.

On many formal national occasions, men wear untucked batik shirts with no tie. Head wear usually consists of a *peci*, a black felt cap once associated with Muslims or Malays but which acquired a more secular, national meaning during the struggle for independence. Indonesian men generally wear sarongs only at home or on informal occasions. Women wear sarongs on formal occasions, along with the *kebaya*, a tight-fitting, low-cut, long-sleeved blouse. On these occasions, women often tie their hair into a bun, sometimes adding a hairpiece. In addition, they often carry a *selendang*, a long, narrow cloth draped over the shoulder, which on less formal occasions is used to carry babies or objects. Increasing numbers of young women have adopted traditional Islamic clothing such as the *jilbab* (head scarf) or other head covering.

Urban Indonesian nightlife centers on night markets, where people shop in *toko* (stores) and *warung* (food stalls). Also popular are forms of the performing arts such as pop music concerts, puppet shows, and the cinema. American and Indian films are popular, while Indonesian motion pictures selectively emphasize certain aspects of Indonesian life. Indonesian-made films are set in cities—even though the population has traditionally been largely rural—and most films employ Bahasa Indonesia even though most viewers are Javanese. There is rarely mention of religion or ethnicity, even though most of the population has a religious affiliation (see Religion and

Worldview, this ch.). Anthropologist Karl Heider has observed that Westerners in general are unambiguously presented as modern and having no tradition whatsoever. Western women are presented as having few constraints on their sexuality. The audiences for films consist almost entirely of teenagers and young adults and are more male than female.

Television use in Indonesian households increased dramatically in the late twentieth and early twenty-first centuries, as did the variety of broadcast stations and programming, especially after the end of the New Order in 1998. Public and private radio stations also bring a range of popular culture programs to people throughout the archipelago (see Post and Telecommunications, ch. 3).

Popular programs include *sinetron* (television dramas), which are serialized, Indonesian-language dramas about everyday life. In addition, variety news and entertainment shows are available, such as *Selamat Pagi Indonesia* (Good Morning Indonesia) and the "soft news" program *Seputar Indonesia* (Around Indonesia). Popular foreign dramatic serials from Australia, India, Japan, and the United States also appear in dubbed, subtitled, or original-language versions. Most programming is in Bahasa Indonesia, although some local arts programs are presented in regional languages. Nielsen Indonesia regularly conducts rating surveys of the Indonesian television market, and the results are influential in determining programming. Recent figures suggest that Indonesia is one of the fastest-growing markets for television advertising as well as for burgeoning private and commercial television networks (see Media, ch. 4).

Sources of Local Identification

Tradition and Multiethnicity

Indonesian society comprises numerous ethnic groups. The Javanese are the largest, at 41.0 percent of the total population. Sundanese make up 15.0 percent, followed by Malays (3.4 percent) and Madurese (3.3 percent). More than 14 percent of the population consists of numerous small ethnic groups or minorities. The precise extent of this diversity is unknown, however, because the Indonesian census stopped reporting data on ethnicity in 1930, under the Dutch, and only started again in 2000. In that year's census, nine categories of ethnicity were reported (by age-group and province): Jawa, Sunda and Priangan, Madura, Minangkabau, Betawi, Bugis and Ugi, Banten, Banjar and Melayu Banjar, and *lainnya* (other).

As this increasingly mobile, multiethnic nation moves into its seventh decade of independence, Indonesians are becoming aware—

through education, television, cinema, print media, and national parks—of the diversity of their own society. When Indonesians talk about their cultural differences with one another, one of the key words they use is *adat*. The term is roughly translated as "custom" or "tradition," but its meaning has undergone a number of transformations in Indonesia. In some circumstances, for instance, *adat* has a kind of legal status—certain *adat* laws (*hukum adat*) are recognized by the government as legitimate. These ancestral guidelines may pertain to a wide range of activities: agricultural production, religious practices, marriage arrangements, legal practices, political succession, or artistic expression.

Even though the vast majority of them are Muslims, Indonesians maintain very different systems of social identification. For example, when Javanese try to explain the behavior of a Sundanese or a Balinese counterpart, they might say "because it is his *adat*." Differences in the ways ethnic groups practice Islam are often ascribed to *adat*. Each group may have different patterns of observing religious holidays, attending the mosque, expressing respect, or burying the dead.

Adat in the sense of "custom" is often viewed as one of the deepest—even sacred—sources of consensus within an ethnic group, however, the word itself is from Arabic. Through centuries of contact with outsiders, Indonesians have a long history of contrasting themselves and their traditions with those of others, and their notions of who they are as a people have been shaped in basic ways by these encounters. On some of the more isolated islands in eastern Indonesia, for instance, one finds ethnic groups that have no word equivalent to *adat* because they have had very little contact with outsiders.

Early in the New Order, the notion of *adat* came to take on a national significance in touristic settings such as Balinese artistic performances and museum displays. Taman Mini, a kind of ethnographic theme park on the outskirts of Jakarta, seeks to display and interpret the cultural diversity of Indonesia. This 100-hectare park is landscaped to look like the Indonesian archipelago in miniature when viewed from an overhead tramway. There is a house for each province, to represent vernacular architecture. The park sells distinctive local hand weapons, textiles, and books explaining the customs of the province. One powerful message of the park is that *adat* is contained in objective, material culture, which is aesthetically pleasing and indeed marketable, but which is more or less distinct from everyday social life. Furthermore, the exhibits convey the impression to some observers that ethnicity is a simple aesthetic matter of regional and spatial variations rather than an issue of deep emotional or political attachments. However, the park provides visitors with a vivid and attractive (if not always convincing) model for how the Indonesian national motto, *Bhinneka Tunggal Ika* (Unity in Diversity, a Javanese slogan dating to fourteenth-century Kediri poet Mpu Tantular's poem "Sutasoma") might be understood.

When Indonesians talk about their society in inclusive terms, they are more likely to use a word such as *budaya* (culture) than *adat*. One speaks of *kebudayaan Indonesia*, the "culture of Indonesia," as something grand, that refers to traditions of refinement and high civilization. The dances, music, and literature of Java and Bali and the great monuments associated with these islands' religion are often described as examples of "culture" or "civilization" but not "custom" (or *adat)*. However, as the following descriptions show, the variety of sources of local identification underscore the diversity rather than the unity of the Indonesian population.

Javanese

There are approximately 83 million Javanese, the majority of whom live in Jawa Timur and Jawa Tengah provinces; most of the rest live in Jawa Barat Province and on Sumatra, Kalimantan, Sulawesi, and other islands. (Altogether, some 110 million people live on Java.) Although many Javanese express pride at the grand achievements of the illustrious courts of Surakarta and Yogyakarta and admire the traditional arts associated with them, most Javanese tend to identify not with that elite tradition, or even with a lineage or clan, but with their own village of residence or origin. These villages, or *desa*, are typically situated on the edge of rice fields, surrounding a mosque, or strung along a road.

Most Javanese villages are divided into smaller administrative units, each known as either a *rukun kampung* (village mutual assistance association) or *rukun tetangga* (neighborhood association). *Rukun* is an important Javanese word of Arabic origin describing both "state of being and a mode of action .... a state in which all parties are at least overtly at social peace with one another," according to anthropologist Robert Jay; it is "a process of sharing through collective action." Anthropologist Mary Hawkins has argued that while modern forms of contract labor and technology may have eroded the rural communalism implied in earlier senses of *rukun*, the term remains important as an ideological construct for representing valued aspects of collective life. Australian anthropologist Patrick Guinness has written that the neighborhood is the "largest social grouping, whose members participate in household rituals, gather for rituals, organize working bees, whose youth band together for sports teams and organizations, who maintain *arisan* (rotating credit associations) and who hold certain property such as funeral equipment." In rural areas, these groups also sometimes collaborate on harvesting their rice. The *rukun* associations were rooted in the ideals of the family but became official administrative units during the Japanese occupation in World War II. Many of these local communities organized security arrangements called *ronda malam* (night watches). Neighbors watched closely for any suspicious activity and participated vigorously in the apprehension of thieves, even exacting immediate justice on their own. The heads of these organizations were elected or appointed officials and were considered representatives of the government.

Differences in social class are less elaborate and less pronounced in Javanese rural villages than in urban areas. In villages where land is relatively evenly distributed, some form of mutual labor exchange is common; in villages where there are large numbers of landless peasants, however, there also are relationships of a clear client–patron nature with landowners, who themselves rarely own more than two hectares. In urban centers, the distinctions among a refined, traditional elite, an intermediate-level bourgeoisie sharing patterns of consumption, and a more collectivist peasantry are more pronounced.

Leaders are usually male, in both the village and the urban neighborhood. Although some are political appointees, these leaders are theoretically chosen by popular consensus. This consensus system proceeds—ideally—through a discussion of different points of view, after which a senior-level participant makes a final decision. Although there is increasing acceptance of competitive elections, in many decision-making contexts it is not uncommon to make use of a process referred to as *musyawarah mufakat* (deliberation with consensus).

Javanese kinship ties are reckoned through the mother and father equally. The nuclear family of mother, father, and children is more or less independent; formal obligations between kin groups are not much greater than in Western societies. The reduced occurrence of divorce—rates were as high as 60 percent in some areas in the 1960s—has made the shifting of responsibility for children—particularly among the mother's kin—less likely in recent years. This three-decade trend toward more stable marriages is attributed to rises in the level of educational attainment, age at first marriage, and income level. Migrations during the 1997–98 financial crisis took a toll on marriages, but stricter laws and a more conservative religious ethos have mitigated some of those effects. Javanese have no clans, lineages, or other kin-based social groupings that, among some other ethnic groups, form the basis of corporate entities such as family businesses. Sons tend to treat their fathers with great formality and deference. Although the mother is the focus of the family in many respects—she usually handles the finances—she is often depicted as suffering the most when the family experiences any loss. She is usually the one who disciplines the children, while the father is mostly occupied outside the home.

The Javanese view childhood as a series of shocks from which children must be protected. Although the youngest children are much indulged, major transitions can be sharp and radical. The process of weaning, for instance, is traditionally a rapid one in which the mother simply leaves the child with a relative and then returns a few days later. Overall, however, a baby's general contentment and resistance to disease and misfortune are viewed as dependent on the child's being protected from any form of emotional upset. Babies are constantly held and nursed on demand; babies must not be disappointed. Once weaned, they are often released into the care of an older sibling or relative who indulges and protects them.

Children become increasingly capable of withstanding the shocks and stresses of life as they grow older, in part because they have become more aware of the rules defining social interaction. The rules of etiquette help a child learn self-control. For example, children must learn to address their father respectfully, using refined speech. Failure to comply properly with the rules will result in a sharp reprimand. For Javanese, learning the proper degree of shame, according to anthropologist Ward Keeler, is a matter of becoming aware of one's vulnerability in interaction. Children learn that dealing with others in a face-to-face encounter always poses a threat to one's sense of self.

Many of the rules of etiquette center on the proper use of language, which is more problematic in Javanese than in most other languages. When addressing someone, Javanese speakers must choose from several different levels of politeness. These "speech levels" comprise words that have the same meaning but are stylistically different. For instance, among the Javanese variations of the word "now," *saiki* is the least refined, while *saniki* is a little fancier, and *samenika* is the most elegant. Javanese has many such triads—so many that people cannot speak for long in the language without having to decide whether the situation is formal or informal and what the relations among the participants are.

People generally use the highest level of language to speak to high-status people in formal situations and the lower levels to speak to people of lower rank or with whom they are most intimate. Although children learn to speak at the lowest level first, they gradually are socialized to speak to some of their more distant kin and respected strangers in higher-level forms of Javanese. This formality

Javanese gamelan player
Javanese New Year festival, Ponorogo, Jawa Timur Province
Courtesy Embassy of Indonesia, Washington, DC

is particularly common in cities, where there are marked distinctions in status. However, there is evidence that these practices are slowly changing. Many children who go elsewhere in Indonesia for work or school or who live overseas refuse to write letters home to their elders in Javanese because of their fear of making a glaring error. Increasingly, in formal situations, they use Bahasa Indonesia because they are no longer sure of the social situation at home. Although Bahasa Indonesia possesses a relatively simple system for indicating status distinctions, it is regarded as a foreign idiom among many Javanese.

An expectation that women would use the higher levels more than men would be valid within the domestic environment—and primarily for the purpose of showing deference among their relatives. Men use more politeness levels in public than women do. Moreover, in the public sphere, the use of Javanese politeness levels is not so much associated with humility as it is with efforts to raise oneself above another. Men are more likely to see the use of politeness levels as a strategy for negotiating status.

There is great diversity among Javanese religious practices. Although most Javanese are Muslims, the wide variations in Islamic beliefs and practices are associated with complex factors such as regional history and social class. The most pious, and recognizably Muslim, varieties of Javanese religion are associated with the *santri* tradition, nurtured by traditional Muslim schools. *Santri* hold more tightly to the moralistic tone of Islam and express the fundamental universalism of its teachings. They may make a pilgrimage (*hajj* in Indonesian) to Mecca, teach their children the Quran, and work for the social, spiritual, and even political advancement of the *ummah*. In contrast to the *santri* tradition, varieties of *kejawen* ("Javanist") religious practice variously incorporate pre-Islamic, animistic, and aesthetic forms of spirituality. Although some observers have distinguished between elite and common varieties of *kejawen* practice, many now see the traditional aristocracy and peasantry losing their distinctiveness in this regard. Religiosity is expressed through fasts, trances, visits to graves, and performance genres such as *wayang kulit* (a form of shadow theater employing flat leather puppets), concerts by gamelans (Javanese orchestras featuring percussive instruments), dance, and other arts of the courtly tradition, which are widely appreciated by the Javanese community as a whole.

Most observers of Javanese religion agree that the core Javanese religious ritual is a brief feast known as the *slametan*. Neighbors, relatives, and coworkers may be invited to attend on the occasion of a birth, marriage, death, or change in status. The host typically gives a speech in high Javanese explaining the purpose of the event to the guests, after which some incense is burned, a prayer is recited in Arabic, and the special festive food is consumed, at least in part. Then, what is left is divided among the guests and taken home. Believers seek to protect themselves against harmful spirits by making offerings, enlisting the aid of a *dukun* (healer), or engaging in spiritual acts of self-control and right thinking.

Balinese

There is probably no group in Indonesia more conscious of its own ethnic identity than the nearly 3 million Balinese. Inhabitants of the islands of Bali and Lombok and the western half of Sumbawa, Balinese are often portrayed as a graceful, poised, and aesthetically inclined people. Although such descriptions date back six centuries or more and are at least partially based on legend, this characterization is also partly based on the realities in contemporary Indonesia. Virtually no part of Bali has escaped the gaze of tourists, who come in increasing numbers each year to enjoy the island's beautiful beaches and stately temples and to seek out an "authentic" experience of its "traditional" culture. The market for "traditional" carvings, dance performances, and paintings has boomed, and many Balinese successfully reinvest their earnings in further development of these highly profitable art forms.

Balinese have a long history of contrasting themselves profitably with outsiders. The contemporary distinctive Hindu religious practices of the Balinese date back at least to the fifteenth and sixteenth centuries, when Javanese princes from Majapahit fled the advances of Islam and sought refuge in Bali, where they were absorbed into the local culture. Since that time, Balinese, with the exception of a minority of Muslims in the north, have maintained great pride in their own distinctiveness from the surrounding Muslim cultures. Since the terrorist bombing of two nightclubs in the Balinese beach town of Kuta in 2002 by Muslim extremists, tensions between Balinese and non-Balinese Muslims have increased.

Balinese society is stratified, as with the Javanese. In Balinese society, however, the social hierarchy is described in distinctly Hindu terms: there is a small hereditary Brahman class, as well as small groups of Vaishya and Kshatriya classes. However, the Balinese caste system involves no occupational specializations or ideas about ritual contamination between the ranks. It does not prohibit marriage between ranks but does forbid women to marry beneath their class. The vast majority of Balinese, including many wealthy entrepreneurs and prominent politicians, belong to the Shudra (commoner-servant) class.

Unlike most Javanese, Balinese participate enthusiastically in several interlocking corporate groups beyond the immediate family. One of the most important of these is the *dadia*, or patrilineal descent group. This is a group of people who claim descent through the male line from a common ancestor. The group maintains a temple to that ancestor, a treasury to support rituals associated with it, and certain chosen leaders. The prestige of a *dadia* depends in part on how widespread and powerful its members are. However, most of these organized groups tend to be localized, because it is easier to maintain local support for their activities and temple. Balinese prefer to draw spouses from within this group. These corporate kin groups can also be the basis for organizing important economic activities, such as carving cooperatives, gold- and silversmithing cooperatives, painting studios, and dance troupes.

Another important affiliation for Balinese is with the *banjar*, or village compound, which overlaps with, but is not identical to, the *dadia*. The *banjar* and the *dadia* share responsibility for security, economic cooperation in the tourist trade, and the formation of inter-village alliances. The *banjar* is a council of household heads and oversees marriage, divorce, and inheritance transactions. In addition, it is the unit for mobilizing resources and labor for the spectacular cremations for which Bali has become increasingly well known. Each *banjar* may have individual orchestra, dance, and weaving clubs.

Yet another important corporate group is the agricultural society, or *subak*, each of which corresponds to a section of wet-rice paddies. Each *subak* is not only a congregation of members who are jointly responsible for sacrificing at a temple placed in the center of their particular group of paddies, but also a unit that organizes the flow of water, planting, and harvesting. Because 50 or more societies sometimes tap into a common stream of water for the irrigation of their land, complex coordination of planting and harvesting schedules is required. This complexity arises because each *subak* is independent. Although the government has attempted periodically to take control of the irrigation schedule, these efforts have produced mixed results, leading to a successful movement in the early 1990s to return the authority for the agricultural schedule to the traditional and highly successful interlocking *subak* arrangement.

The very complexity of Balinese social organization has provided it with the flexibility to adapt to the pressures of modern life and its requirements for the accumulation, distribution, and mobilization of capital and technological resources. Although the Balinese remain self-consciously "traditional," they have been neither rigid in that tradition nor resistant to change.

Peoples of Sumatra

The large island of Sumatra forms the southwestern shore of the Strait of Malacca. Although nearly all of the approximately 20 ethnolinguistic groups of Sumatra are devout practitioners of Islam, they nonetheless differ strikingly from one another, particularly in their family structures.

Acehnese

Residing in the Special Region of Aceh, Sumatra's northernmost provincial-level jurisdiction, the more than 2 million Acehnese are most famous throughout the archipelago for their devotion to Islam, their militant resistance to colonial and republican rule, and their tragic experience as victims of the tsunami that struck Aceh's western coast on December 26, 2004. Although the Acehnese were renowned throughout the nineteenth century for their pepper plantations, most are now rice growers in the coastal regions.

Acehnese do not have large descent groups; the nuclear family consisting of mother, father, and children is the central social unit. Unlike that of the Javanese or Balinese, the Acehnese family system shows marked separation of men's and women's spheres of activity. Traditionally, males are directed outward toward the world of trade. In the practice of *merantau*—going away from one's birthplace in order to return later—young adult males seek fortune, experience, and commercial repute. This may involve travel to another village, province, or island. This maturation process among males is viewed as growing out of the domestic female-dominated world of sensory indulgence and into the male world of reasoned rationality, the practice of which is expressed through trade. One model of Acehnese family life is that a woman sends a man out of the house to trade and welcomes him back when he brings home money. When he has exhausted his money, she sends him out again. Meanwhile, women and their kin are responsible for working the fields and keeping the gardens and rice fields productive. This oscillating pattern of migration encountered some difficulties in the 1980s and 1990s as increasing numbers of men failed to return to the Acehnese homeland, instead remaining and marrying in remote locations, such as Jakarta or Kalimantan. In addition, many Acehnese felt pressure from the continuing influx of temporary workers seeking employment in the natural gas and timber industries, and the conflict between the Indonesian army and Acehnese separatists.

The August 16, 2005, peace agreement between the Free Aceh Movement (GAM) and the Indonesian central government was propelled by the desire on both sides to smooth the flow of aid to victims of the December 2004 tsunami. The rebels dropped their secession demands, and the government agreed to give them some form of political representation. Since 2006 ex-GAM members have been elected as governor and to many lower-level posts in Aceh, and by 2009 the remnants of GAM had splintered into several parties.

Batak

The term "Batak" designates any one of several groups inhabiting the interior of Sumatera Utara Province, south of Aceh: the Angkola, Karo, Mandailing, Pakpak, Simalungun, Toba, and others. The Batak number around 6 million and are mostly Christian, with some Muslim groups in the south and east. Historically isolated from Hindu-Buddhist and Muslim influence, they bear closer resemblance culturally to highland swidden cultivators elsewhere in Southeast Asia, even though most practice wet-rice farming. Unlike the Balinese, who have several different traditional group affiliations at once, or the Javanese, who affiliate with their village or neighborhood, the Batak traditionally orient themselves primarily to the *marga*, a landowning patrilineal descent group. Traditionally, each *marga* is a wife-giving and wife-taking unit. Whereas a young man takes a wife from his mother's clan (men must seek wives outside their own *marga*), a young woman marries into a clan within which her paternal aunts live.

The *marga* has proved to be a flexible social unit in contemporary Indonesian society. Batak who resettle in urban areas, such as Medan or Jakarta, draw on *marga* affiliations for financial support and political alliances. While many of the corporate aspects of the *marga* have undergone major changes, Batak migrants to other areas of Indonesia retain pride in their ethnic identity. Batak have shown themselves to be creative in drawing on modern media to codify, express, and preserve their "traditional" *adat*. Anthropologist Susan Rodgers has shown how audiotaped cassette dramas with some soap-opera elements circulated widely in the 1980s and 1990s in the Batak region to dramatize the moral and cultural dilemmas of one's kinship obligations in a rapidly changing world. In addition, Batak have been prodigious producers of written handbooks designed to show young, urbanized, and secular lineage members how to navigate the complexities of their marriage and funeral customs.

Minangkabau

The Minangkabau—who predominate in the coastal areas of Sumatera Utara Province, Sumatera Barat Province, the interior of Riau Province, and northern Bengkulu Province—number more than

5.4 million. Like the Batak, they have large corporate descent groups, but unlike the Batak, the Minangkabau traditionally reckon descent matrilineally. A young boy, for instance, has his primary responsibility to his mother's and sisters' clans. It is considered "customary" and ideal for married sisters to remain in their parental home, with their husbands having a sort of visiting status. Not everyone lives up to this ideal, however. In the 1990s, anthropologist Evelyn Blackwood studied a relatively conservative village in Sumatera Barat where only about 22 percent of the households were "matrihouses," consisting of a mother and a married daughter or daughters. Nonetheless, there is a shared ideal among Minangkabau in which sisters and unmarried lineage members try to live close to one another or even in the same house.

Landholding is one of the crucial functions of the *suku* (female lineage unit). Because Minangkabau men, like Acehnese men, often migrate to seek experience, wealth, and commercial success, the women's kin group is responsible for maintaining the continuity of the family and the distribution and cultivation of the land. These family groups, however, are typically led by a *penghulu* (headman), elected by groups of lineage leaders. With the agrarian base of the Minangkabau economy in decline, the *suku*—as a landholding unit—has also been declining somewhat in importance, especially in urban areas. Indeed, the position of *penghulu* is not always filled after the death of the incumbent, particularly if lineage members are not willing to bear the expense of the ceremony required to install a new *penghulu*.

The traditions of sharia—in which inheritance laws favor males—and indigenous female-oriented *adat* are often depicted as conflicting forces in Minangkabau society. The male-oriented sharia appears to offer young men something of a balance against the dominance of law in local villages, which forces a young man to wait passively for a marriage proposal from some young woman's family. By acquiring property and education through *merantau* experience, a young man can attempt to influence his own destiny in positive ways.

Increasingly, married couples go off on *merantau*; in such situations, the woman's role tends to change. When married couples reside in urban areas or outside the Minangkabau region, women lose some of their social and economic rights in property. One apparent consequence is an increased likelihood of divorce.

Minangkabau were prominent among the intellectual figures in the Indonesian independence movement. Not only were they strongly Islamic, they spoke a language closely related to Bahasa Indonesia, which was considerably freer of hierarchical connotations than Javanese. Partly because of their tradition of *merantau*,

Minangkabau developed a cosmopolitan bourgeoisie that readily adopted and promoted the ideas of an emerging nation-state.

Ethnic Minorities

In Indonesia, the concept of ethnic minorities is often discussed not in numerical but in religious terms. Although the major ethnic groups claim adherence to one of the major world religions (*agama*) recognized by the Department of Religious Affairs—Islam, Christianity, Hinduism, Buddhism, and Daoism—millions of other Indonesians engage in religious or cultural practices that fall outside these categories. These practices are sometimes labeled animist or *kafir* (pagan). In general, these Indonesians inhabit the more remote, sparsely populated islands of the archipelago. Following the massacre of tens of thousands associated with the alleged 1965 coup attempt by "atheist" communists, mandatory religious affiliation became an even more intense political issue among minority groups. The groups described in the following sections represent a broad sample, chosen for their geographic and cultural diversity.

Toraja

The Toraja of Sulawesi Selatan, Sulawesi Barat, and Sulawesi Tengah provinces are one minority group that has been successful in gaining national and international attention. This group became prominent in the 1980s, largely because of the tourist industry, which was attracted to the region because of the picturesque villages and the group's spectacular mortuary rites involving the slaughter of water buffalo.

Inhabiting the wet, rugged mountains of the interior of southern Sulawesi, the Toraja grow rice for subsistence and coffee for cash. Traditionally, they lived in fortified hilltop villages with from two to 40 houses featuring large, dramatically sweeping roofs resembling buffalo horns. Until the late 1960s, many of these villages were politically and economically self-sufficient. This autonomy developed in the late nineteenth and early twentieth centuries partly as protection against the depredations of the slave trade and partly as a result of intervillage feuding associated with headhunting.

The Toraja have strong emotional, economic, and political ties to a number of different kinds of corporate groups. The most basic tie is that of the *rarabuku*, which might be translated as "family." Toraja view this grouping as encompassing relations of "blood and bone," that is, relations between parents and children—the nuclear family. Since Toraja reckon kinship bilaterally, through both mother and father, the possibilities for extending the concept of *rarabuku* in several different directions are many. Another important kind of group with which Toraja have close affiliations is the *tongkonan* (ancestral house), which contrasts with the *banua* (ordinary house). The *tongkonan* is a group of people who reckon descent from an original ancestor. The physical structures belonging to the *tongkonan* are periodically renewed by replacing their distinctively shaped roofs. This ritual is attended by members of the social group and accompanied by trancelike dances in which the spirits are asked to visit. A third important kind of affiliation is the *saroan*, or village work group, originally probably an agricultural work group based in a particular hamlet. Beginning as a medium for labor and credit exchange, the *saroan* has since evolved into a unit of cooperation in ritual activities as well. When sacrifices and funerals take place, groups of *saroan* exchange meat and other foods.

The flexibility of these affiliations is partly responsible for the intensity of the mortuary performances. Because there is some ambiguity about one's affiliation (that is, one's claims to descent are not only based on blood relationships but also on social recognition of the relationship through public acts), Toraja may attempt to demonstrate the importance of a relationship through elaborate contributions to a funeral, which provides an opportunity not only to show devotion to a deceased parent but also to claim a share of that parent's land. The amount of land an individual inherits from the deceased might depend on the number of buffalo sacrificed at that person's funeral. Sometimes people even pawn land to get buffalo to kill at a funeral so that they can claim the land of the deceased. Thus, feasting at funerals is highly competitive.

With the oil boom in the 1960s and 1970s, there was massive out-migration among young upland Sulawesi men looking for jobs in northeastern Kalimantan. During this period, many of these youths became Christians. Although proselytization began among Toraja in the nineteenth century, mass conversions were provoked after the abortive 1965 coup and mass labor migrations in the 1970s and 1980s, a move that implied a rejection of many Toraja beliefs and practices. But when these migrants returned to their villages as wealthy men, they often wanted to hold large status displays in the form of funerals, causing what anthropologist Toby Alice Volkman has called "ritual inflation" as well as intense debates about the authenticity of their conversion to Christianity. Because of the successful efforts of highly placed Toraja officials in the central government, Toraja feasting practices have been granted official status, loosely described as *agama* Hindu.

Dayak

Another group of ethnic minorities struggling for recognition are the peoples of southern, central, and eastern Kalimantan. From an outsider's perspective, most of the scattered ethnolinguistic groups inhabiting the interior of the vast island have been referred to as Dayak. The word is a collective term used by outsiders since 1836 to indicate the indigenous peoples of Kalimantan. Among the people labeled as Dayak, however, one finds Ngaju Dayak, Maanyan, and Lawangan, among others. Although they reside in longhouses that traditionally served as a means of protection against slave raiding and intervillage conflict, the Dayak are not communalistic. They have bilateral kinship, and the basic unit of ownership and social organization is the nuclear family. The various Dayak peoples have typically made a living through swidden agriculture. In regard to religion, they tend to practice either Protestantism or Kaharingan, a form of indigenous religious practice blending animism and ancestor worship classified by the government as Hindu. The Dayak perform elaborate death ceremonies in which the bones are disinterred for secondary reburial.

Through its healing performances, Kaharingan serves to mold the scattered agricultural residences into a community, and it is at times of ritual that the Dayak peoples coalesce as a group. There is no set ritual leader, nor is there a fixed ritual presentation. Specific ceremonies may be held in the home of the sponsor. Shamanic curing, or *balian*, is one of the core features of these ritual practices. Because illness is thought to result in a loss of the soul, the ritual healing practices are devoted to its spiritual and ceremonial retrieval. In general, religious practices focus on the body, and on the health of the body politic more broadly. Sickness results from giving offense to one of the many spirits inhabiting the earth and fields, usually from a failure to sacrifice to them. The goal of the *balian* is to call back the wayward soul and restore the health of the community through trance, dance, and possession.

Following the fall of Suharto in 1998, reassertions of ethnic identity and land claims caused tensions leading to violence with Muslim migrants. Violent clashes between Dayaks and migrants had started even earlier, in December 1996, when a Madurese migrant accused of raping a Dayak woman was killed, and province-wide rioting occurred. In the following months, violence escalated, troops were flown in, a crackdown took place, and the cycle of violence continued with schools, homes, and businesses burned by Dayaks and migrants in retaliation against one another. Hundreds died in these clashes, and thousands were displaced or reported missing.

Couple in wedding garb,
Nusa Tenggara Timur
Courtesy Embassy of
Indonesia, Washington, DC

Long-simmering feuds between Dayaks and mostly Madurese Muslim migrants erupted again over issues of land and economic competition in mid-2001, causing massive displacements of population. Angry Dayaks, dressed in traditional clothing, sometimes flamboyantly displayed symbols of their headhunting tradition in gestures of defiance toward what they perceived as a flood of migrants and toward the central government as a whole.

Weyewa

The Weyewa inhabit the western highlands of Sumba and Nusa Tenggara Timur Province, where they cultivate rice, corn, and cassava using both slash-and-burn methods and continuous irrigation of paddy fields. They supplement this income through the sale of livestock, coffee, vanilla, cloves, and their distinctive brightly colored textiles.

There were few challenges to Weyewa notions of political and religious identity until the 1970s. Because Sumba is a rather dry and infertile island, located away from the ports of call of the spice trade, it was comparatively insulated from the Hindu-Buddhist, Muslim, and later Dutch influences, each of which helped shape the character of Indonesia's cultures. Each Weyewa belongs to a *kabizu*, a patrilineal clan whose founding ancestors are spirits requiring frequent ritual propitiation, gifts, and respect in exchange for continued prosperity among the descendants. Each clan is headquartered in a fortified hilltop *wanno kalada* (ancestral village); the most traditional villages are characterized by houses with spectacular high-pointed thatch roofs. Young people are supposed to seek spouses outside their clan, and clan members assist with the often substantial marriage payments that are required.

The Weyewa system of ritual production and exchange began to undergo major technological development and an economic shift in the 1970s and 1980s that resulted in a gradual weakening of the authority of lineages. With greater amounts of arable land available as a result of improved irrigation techniques and more crops produced because of the use of faster-growing and higher-yielding varieties of rice, the legal and cultural rights to these new resources came to be assigned to individuals rather than to clans. Younger farmers were increasingly reluctant to invest in costly, large-scale ritual feasts honoring the spirits. Meanwhile, government officials put further pressure on traditional leaders to give up ritual feasting practices as "wasteful" and "backward." Furthermore, as with the Kaharingan adherents of Kalimantan, failure to affiliate with an approved religion was regarded as potentially treasonous. Unlike the Toraja and others, however, the Weyewa were not politically organized for the preservation of their indigenous religion. Most people simply converted to Christianity as a symbolic gesture of participation in the nation-state. Indeed, whole villages in the late 1980s and early 1990s conducted feasts in which residents settled their debts with ancestral spirits and became Christians. The number of Weyewa professing affiliation with the Christian religion (either Roman Catholic or Calvinist Protestant) jumped from approximately 20 percent in 1978 to more than 90 percent in 2005.

Sumba did not escape violence during the post-Suharto reform period, but the rioting took on distinctive forms. Because the central government was generally perceived in eastern Indonesia as a bountiful—if inequitable—source of funds for education, development, and jobs, the collapse of central authority resulted in open disputes. In November 1998, conflict broke out along ethnic lines as Weyewa men sought to defend the reputation of an ethnic Weyewa government official accused of corruption. The ensuing riots left at least 20 people dead and more than 600 homes destroyed. The public performance of peace rituals in 1999 began a slow, painful process of rebuilding trust between aggrieved parties.

Asmat

The approximately 65,000 Asmat people of the south-central alluvial swamps of Papua Province are of a Papuan genetic heritage. They live in villages with populations that vary in size from 35 to 2,000 inhabitants. Until the 1950s, warfare, headhunting, and cannibalism were constant features of Asmat social life. The people would build their houses along river bends so that an enemy attack could be seen in advance. Houses in coastal areas still are generally built on pilings two or more meters high, to protect residents from daily flooding by the surging tides of the brackish rivers. In the foothills of the Jayawijaya Mountains, Asmat live in tree houses that are five to 25 meters off the ground. In some areas, they also build arboreal watchtowers as much as 30 meters above the ground.

The Asmat are primarily hunters and foragers who subsist by gathering and processing the starchy pulp of the sago palm, finding grubs, and hunting down the occasional wild pig, cassowary, or crocodile. Although the Asmat population has steadily increased since coming into contact with missionaries and government health workers, the forest continues to yield an adequate supply and variety of food. According to anthropologist Tobias Schneebaum, "Some Asmat have learned to grow small patches of vegetables, such as string beans, and a few raise the descendants of recently imported chickens. The introduction of a limited cash economy through the sale of logs to timber companies and carvings to outsiders has led many Asmat to consider as necessities such foods as rice and tinned fish; most have also become accustomed to wearing Western-style clothing and using metal tools."

Many Asmat have converted to Christianity, although a large number continue to practice the religion of their ancestors. For example, many believe that all deaths—except those of the very old and very young—come about through acts of malevolence, either by magic or actual physical force. Ancestral spirits demand vengeance for these deaths. The ancestors to whom they feel obligated are represented in shields, in large, spectacular wood carvings of canoes, and in ancestor poles consisting of human figurines. Until the late 1980s, the preferred way for a young man to fulfill his obligations to his kin and his ancestors and prove his sexual prowess was to take the head of an enemy and offer the body for cannibalistic consumption by other members of the village.

The first Dutch colonial government post was not established in Asmat territory until 1938, and a Catholic mission began its work there only in 1958, but the pace of change in this once remote region greatly increased after the 1960s. Beginning in the early 1990s, many Asmat enrolled their children in Indonesian schools, and many converted to Christianity. As large timber, oil, and mining companies expanded their operations in the region, the fragile, low-lying mangrove forests that were home to many Asmat came under threat from industrial waste and soil erosion. The Asmat appear to be gaining some national and international recognition for their artwork; however, this fame has not resulted in their acquiring any significant political input into decisions of the Indonesian government affecting the use of land in traditional Asmat territory. Although there is currently little evidence of Free Papua Organization (OPM) activity among the Asmat, there has been a history of resistance to logging companies and other outside intruders, often in the form of cargo cults and other ritual activity.

Chinese

Identifying someone in Indonesia as a member of the Chinese (Tionghoa) ethnic group is not an easy matter, because the physical characteristics, languages, names, areas of residence, and lifestyles of Chinese Indonesians are not always distinct from those of the rest of the population. The national census does not record the Chinese as a special group, and there are no simple racial criteria for membership in this group. There are some people who consider themselves Chinese but who, as a result of intermarriage with the local population, are less than one-quarter Chinese in ancestry. On the other hand, there are some people who by ancestry could be considered half-Chinese or more but who regard themselves as fully Indonesian. Furthermore, many people who identify themselves as Chinese Indonesians cannot read or write the Chinese language.

The policy of the Indonesian government by the early 1990s strongly advocated the assimilation of the Chinese population into the communities in which they lived, but the Chinese had a long history of enforced separation from their non-Chinese neighbors. For nearly a century prior to 1919, Chinese were forced to live in separate urban neighborhoods and could travel out of them only with government permits. Most Chinese continued to settle in urban areas of Indonesia even after this "quarter system" was discontinued in 1919. In some areas, such as the city of Pontianak in Kalimantan Barat and Bagansiapiapi in Riau Province, Chinese even came to form a majority of the population. They began to settle in rural areas of Java in the 1920s and 1930s, but in the 1960s the government again prohibited the Chinese from exercising free choice of residence, requiring them to live in cities and towns.

The Chinese who immigrated to Indonesia were not linguistically homogeneous. The dominant languages among these immigrants were Hokkien, Hakka, and Cantonese. There was great occupational

Papuan men,
Papua Province
Courtesy Embassy of
Indonesia, Washington, DC

diversity among the Chinese in the late nineteenth and early twentieth centuries, but Dutch colonial policies channeled them into trade, mining, or skilled artisanship. In the twenty-first century, Chinese continue to dominate the Indonesian economy's private sector, despite central government policies designed to promote non-Chinese entrepreneurs. Nonetheless, Chinese are not a monolithic group. Not all are rich and urban. They seldom share a common language besides Indonesian or Javanese. One of the historical distinctions among Indonesian Chinese in the 1960s and 1970s—between the *peranakan* (local-born Chinese with some Indonesian ancestry) and *totok* (full-blooded Chinese, usually foreign-born)—has begun to fade as fewer foreign-born Chinese immigrate to Indonesia. Although the distinctiveness and social significance of this division vary considerably from place to place in the archipelago, ties to the Chinese homeland are weaker within the *peranakan* community, and there is stronger evidence of Indonesian influence. Unlike the more strictly male-dominated *totok*, *peranakan* families recognize descent along both female and male lines. *Peranakan* are more likely to have converted to Christianity (although some became Muslims) and to have assimilated in other ways to the norms of Indonesian culture. They typically speak Bahasa Indonesia as their first language.

The Suharto government's program of assimilation for the Chinese began to be phased out in 1998. Long-discouraged symbols of Chinese identity such as Chinese-language newspapers, schools, and public rituals, and the use of Chinese names, are no longer subject to strict regulation. During the Suharto years, nearly all Chinese Indonesians obtained Indonesian citizenship, often at high cost and as a result of considerable government pressure.

Popular resentment persisted toward Chinese economic success, however, and nurtured a perception of Chinese complicity in the Suharto regime's corruption. In May 1998, riots broke out in which hundreds of Chinese stores were burned and Chinese women were raped and murdered. When many Chinese Indonesians fled the violence, the subsequent capital flight resulted in further economic hardship in a country already suffering a financial crisis. By 2005 many had returned, but the economic and social confidence of many Chinese in the country was badly shaken by the experience.

Education

The character of Indonesia's education system reflects the country's diverse religious heritage, its struggle for a national identity, and the challenge of resource allocation in a poor but developing archipelagic nation with a population that is young (median age 27.6 years) and growing (at an estimated annual rate of about 1.1 percent) in 2009. Tremendous progress has been made toward the goal of universal education since 1973, when nearly 20 percent of youth were illiterate. At that time, then-President Suharto issued an order to set aside portions of oil revenues for the construction of new primary schools. This act resulted in the construction or repair of nearly 40,000 primary-school facilities by the late 1980s, and literacy rates improved significantly nationwide. During 1997–98, the financial crisis affected the poorest families the most, resulting in their selectively cutting back on their education expenditures. Government funding struggled to keep up with rising costs during this period, but by 2002, according to the World Bank, only 2 percent of those between the ages of 15 and 24 could not read, and by 2009, the adult literacy rate was 90.4 percent.

Primary and Secondary Education

Indonesians are required to attend nine years of school. They can choose between state-run, nonsectarian public schools supervised by the Department of National Education (Depdiknas) or private or semi-private religious (usually Islamic) schools supervised and financed by the Department of Religious Affairs. However, although 86.1 percent of the Indonesian population is registered as Muslim, according to the 2000 census only 15 percent of school-age individuals attended religious schools. Overall enrollment figures are slightly higher for girls than boys and much higher in Java than the rest of Indonesia.

A central goal of the national education system is not merely to impart secular wisdom about the world but also to instruct children in the principles of participation in the modern nation-state, its bureaucracies, and its moral and ideological foundations. Beginning under Guided Democracy (1959–65) and strengthened in the New Order after 1975, a key feature of the national curriculum—as was the case for other national institutions—has been instruction in the Pancasila. Children age six and older learned by rote its five principles—belief in one God, humanitarianism, national unity, democracy, and social justice—and were instructed daily to apply the meanings of this key national symbol to their lives. But with the end of the New Order in 1998 and the beginning of the campaign to decentralize the national government, provincial and district-level administrators obtained increasing autonomy in determining the content of schooling, and Pancasila began to play a diminishing role in the curriculum.

A style of pedagogy prevails inside public-school classrooms that emphasizes rote learning and deference to the authority of the teacher. Although the youngest children are sometimes allowed to use the local language, by the third year of primary school nearly all instruction is conducted in Bahasa Indonesia. Teachers customarily do not ask questions of individual students; rather, a standard teaching technique is to narrate a historical event or to describe a mathematical problem, pausing at key junctures to allow the students to call out responses that "fill in the blanks." By not identifying individual problems of students and retaining an emotionally distanced demeanor, teachers are said to show themselves to be *sabar* (patient), which is considered admirable behavior.

After completion of the six-year primary-school program, three years of junior secondary school may be followed by three years of senior secondary school; or students can choose among a variety of vocational and pre-professional junior and senior secondary schools, each level of which requires three years of study. After secondary school, students may choose either three years of postsecondary vocational and pre-professional schools or three years of high school. There are academic and vocational junior high schools that lead to senior-level diplomas. There are also "domestic science" junior high schools for girls. At the senior high school level, three-year agricultural, veterinary, and forestry schools are open to students who have graduated from an academic junior high school. Special schools at the junior and senior levels teach hotel management, legal clerking, plastic arts, and music.

The completion rate for Indonesian primary schools is excellent. Indeed, 100 percent of the relevant age-group had completed primary education as of 2003, according to World Bank data. The gross enrollment rate for primary schools was 100 percent, but it decreased to 62 percent for secondary schools and 16 percent for postsecondary schools. There were nearly equal numbers of girls and boys in primary and secondary schools; in the late 2000s, the ratio was 96.7 girls to 100 boys. Depdiknas reported that in school year 2007–8 there were 63,444 kindergartens, with a total enrollment of 2.8 million pupils and 176,061 teachers. Later statistics are available for primary and secondary levels for school year 2008–9. They indicate that there were 144,228 primary schools, with a total enrollment of 26.9 million students and 1.5 million teachers; 28,777 junior secondary schools, with a total enrollment of 8.9 million students and 629,036 teachers; 10,762 general senior secondary schools, with a total enrollment of 3.8 million students and 314,389 teachers; and 7,592 vocational senior secondary schools, with a total enrollment of 3 million students and 246,018 teachers. Additionally, there were 1,686 special education schools from kindergarten to senior secondary levels, with a total enrollment of 73,322 and 18,047 teachers.

Teacher-training programs are varied and gradually being upgraded. For example, in the 1950s anyone completing a teacher-training program at the junior high school level could obtain a teacher's certificate. Since the 1970s, however, primary-school teachers have been required to have graduated from a senior high school for teachers, and teachers of higher grades have been required to have completed a university-level education course. Remuneration for primary- and secondary-school teachers, although low, compares favorably with that in other Asian countries such as Malaysia, India, and Thailand. Student–teacher ratios also compare satisfactorily with those in many Asian nations: They were 23.4 to 1 and 18.8 to 1, respectively, for primary and secondary schools in 2004; that same year, the overall averages for Asia-Pacific countries were 22 to 1 and 18 to 1, respectively.

By 2008 the staff shortage in Indonesia's schools was no longer as acute as in the 1980s, but serious difficulties remain, particularly in the areas of teacher salaries, teacher certification, and finding qualified personnel. In many remote areas of the Outer Islands, in particular, there is a severe shortage of qualified teachers, and some villages have school buildings but no teachers, books, or supplies. Providing

Elementary school children on Madura, Jawa Timur Province
Courtesy Florence Lamoureux, used with permission
© Center for Southeast Asian Studies, University of Hawai'i

textbooks and other school equipment to Indonesia's 37 million schoolchildren throughout the far-flung archipelago continues to be a significant problem as well, especially in more remote areas.

Islamic Schools

The secular and nationalist emphasis in public schools has been resisted by some of the Muslim majority. A distinct and vocal minority of these Muslims prefer to place their children in a *pesantren*, or Islamic school. Usually located in rural areas and directed by a Muslim scholar, *pesantren* are attended by young people seeking a detailed understanding of the Quran, the Arabic language, the sharia, and Muslim traditions and history, as well as more modern subjects such as English, mathematics, and geography. Students can enter and leave the *pesantren* any time of the year, and the studies are not organized as a progression of courses leading to graduation. Although the chief aim of *pesantren* is to produce good Muslims, they do not share a single stance toward Islam or a position on secularism. Some *pesantren* emphasize the autonomy of modern students to think for themselves and to interpret scripture and modern knowledge in a way that is consistent with the teachings of Islam. Others are more traditional and stress the importance of following the wisdom of elders, including their teachings on science, religion, and family life. Although the terrorist bombings in Kuta, Bali, in 2002 raised suspicions about whether *pesantren* promote extremist views, the majority of these schools in Indonesia are theologically moderate, reflecting the views of the Indonesian population as a whole. For those who opt for a *pesantren* education, a sixth-grade equivalency certificate is available after successful completion of a state test.

In order for students to adapt to life in the modern nation-state, in the 1970s the Muslim-dominated Department of Religion (now the Department of Religious Affairs) advocated the spread of a newer variety of Muslim school, the madrassa. This kind of school integrates religious subjects from the *pesantren* with secular subjects from the Western-style public-education system. Although in general the public believes that Islamic schools offer lower-quality education, among Islamic schools a madrassa is ranked lower than a *pesantren*.

Higher Education

Indonesia's institutions of higher education have experienced dramatic growth since independence. In 1950 there were 10 institutions of higher learning with a total of about 6,500 students. In 1970, 450 private and state institutions enrolled about 237,000 students, and by 1990 there were 900 institutions with about 141,000 teachers and nearly 1.5 million students. By 2009 there were 2,975 institutions of higher education and more than 4.2 million students. Of these institutions, 3 percent were public, with 57.1 percent of the student enrollment, and 97 percent were private, with 42.9 of the student enrollment. Even though government subsidies finance approximately 80 to 90 percent of state-university budgets, universities have considerably more autonomy in curriculum and internal structure than primary and secondary schools. Whereas tuition in such state institutions is more affordable for average students than private-university tuition, faculty salaries are low by international standards. Lecturers often have other jobs outside the university to supplement their wages.

Private universities are generally operated by foundations. Unlike state universities, private institutions have budgets that are almost entirely tuition-driven. A onetime registration fee (which can be quite high) is determined at the time of entry. If a university has a religious affiliation, it can cover some of its costs with donations or grants from international religious organizations. The government provides only limited scholarship support for students wishing to attend private universities.

Muslim girls in school uniforms, Madura, Jawa Timur Province
Courtesy Florence Lamoureux, used with permission
© Center for Southeast Asian Studies, University of Hawai'i

Indonesian institutions of higher education offer a wide range of programs. However, about 52 percent of all non-teacher-training students enrolled in higher education were social sciences majors in the 2008–9 academic year, while only 3 percent majored in laboratory-intensive fields of study, largely because universities prefer to offer social science courses that do not require expensive laboratories and equipment. The major academic degree programs are the *sarjana* (literally "scholar," roughly corresponding to a bachelor's degree) and the *pasca sarjana* (master's or doctoral degree). Professional schools offer "diploma" and "specialist" degrees, the latter graded either "SP1" or "SP2," depending on the level of advancement. From 2001 to 2004, the number of students completing their *sarjana* degrees grew dramatically from about 308,000 in 2001 to nearly 683,000 in 2004, a 122-percent increase. This level stood at 652,364 graduates at the end of academic year 2008–9.

Discussion about how to improve Indonesian higher education focuses on the issues of teacher salaries, laboratory and research facilities, and professors' qualifications. Only 7 percent of university faculty overall held a Ph.D. in the mid-2000s, although the proportion was greater (11 percent) in state institutions. Because doctoral programs are few in Indonesia and there is little money to support education overseas, this situation is improving only slowly. Despite these difficulties, most institutions of higher education receive large numbers of applications; in state institutions, less than one in four applications was accepted in 2004; in private institutions, the acceptance rate was nearly two out of three. One of the most serious problems for graduates with advanced degrees, however, is finding employment suited to their newly acquired education. In 2003 the unemployment rate for college graduates with the *sarjana* degree was approximately 20 percent, and 10 percent for graduates of professional schools.

The Republic of Indonesia Institute for Higher Education (BPTRI) was founded in Jakarta shortly after independence was declared in 1945. When the Dutch returned in force, BPTRI dispersed its various schools to other parts of Java. The Dutch established Nood Universiteit (Emergency University) in Jakarta in 1946, and the following year changed its name to Universiteit van Indonesië (UVI), or University of Indonesia. On February 2, 1950, in the wake of the war for independence, the government established a state university in Jakarta called Universiteit Indonesia. It was composed of units of BPTRI and UVI; the name Universiteit Indonesia was later changed to Universitas Indonesia. This institution enrolls about 37,000 students per year. Universitas Gadjah Mada lays claim to being the oldest Indonesian university. It was founded in Yogyakarta on December 9, 1949, but was giving its first lectures in early 1946 (when Yogyakarta was the Republican capital). State-owned Gadjah Mada has an annual enrollment of about 54,000 students. Other major universities include Catholic University and the Institut Teknologi Bandung, both in Bandung; and the Institut Pertanian Bogor, in Bogor. There also are important regional universities in Sulawesi Selatan, Sumatera Utara, Jawa Barat, and Papua. Approximately 15 percent of Indonesia's students of higher education attend a public or private Islamic university, institute, academy, or polytechnic institute. Among these is the State Muslim University (UIN)—formerly called the State Institute for Islamic Religion (IAIN)—which has been an important venue for progressive debates about Islam.

Health

Services and Infrastructure

As access to education has improved throughout the archipelago, use of modern forms of health care also has increased. For example, in 2003 the United Nations Children's Fund (UNICEF) reported that 68 percent of births in Indonesia were attended by a trained midwife or other health specialist. Recent studies show a correlation between the rise of education levels and the increased use of hospitals, physicians, and other health resources. Indeed, since the 1980s, health in Indonesia has shown overall improvement. Life expectancy was estimated at 70.8 years in 2009, a substantial increase since 1980, when it stood at 52.9 years. However, the distribution of improvements, like the distribution of resources for health maintenance and improvement, has been unequal. In 2003 life expectancy was 72 years in Jakarta and Yogyakarta but only 63 years in Nusa Tenggara Barat Province. Whereas infant mortality nationwide decreased from an average of 105.0 deaths per 1,000 live births in 1980 to 75.2 in 1990, to 36.0 in 2000, and to an estimated 29.9 in 2009, local rates varied dramatically. The poor, rural, and less-educated classes generally suffered much higher mortality rates than their educated urban counterparts.

Community and preventive health programs form another component of Indonesia's health system. Established in 1969 as part of the first Repelita (see Glossary), the government's five-year economic development plan, community health services are organized in a three-tier system with *puskesmas* (community health centers) at the top. Usually staffed by a physician, these centers provide maternal and child health care, general outpatient curative and preventive health care, pre- and postnatal care, immunization, and communicable disease–control programs. Specialized clinic services are periodically available at some of the larger clinics.

Second-level community health centers include *subpuskesmas* (community health subcenters) consisting of small clinics and maternal and child health centers staffed with one to three nurses and visited weekly or monthly by a physician. Toward the middle of the first decade of the twenty-first century, the World Health Organization (WHO) reported that there were 3.6 health centers per 100,000 population. Since the early 1990s, the Department of Health planned to have three to four subcenters per health center, depending on the region, and this plan has been largely realized in the twenty-first century. The third level of community health services consists of village-level *posyandu* (integrated service posts). These posts are not permanently staffed facilities but rather monthly clinics on rented premises, in which a visiting team from the regional health center supports local health volunteers.

The distribution of Indonesian health-care workers is also highly uneven. To alleviate the problem of physician maldistribution, the government requires two to five years of public service by all graduates of medical schools, whether public or private. In order to be admitted for specialist training, physicians first have to complete this service, which is normally fulfilled by staffing *puskesmas*. Only two years of public service are required for those physicians working in remote areas such as the provinces of Nusa Tenggara Timur, Sulawesi Tenggara, Kalimantan Timur, Maluku, Papua, and Papua Barat, whereas three to five years of service are required for a posting in Java, Bali, or Sumatra. Despite such requirements, it is difficult to attract medical-school graduates to these remote, understaffed regions, particularly without additional cash incentives. With an average of only about 0.1 physicians, 0.8 nurses or midwives, and 0.6 hospital beds per 1,000 population, Indonesia compares unfavorably with all of its Southeast Asian neighbors.

Government Support

One of the most notable features of Indonesia's health-care system, in comparison with those of other Southeast Asian nations, is the low level of government support. For example, in 2006 the Philippines expended 3.3 percent of its gross domestic product (GDP—see Glossary) on health care, Malaysia 4.3 percent, Singapore 3.4 percent, and Timor-Leste 16.4 percent. That same year, only 2.2 percent of the GDP of Indonesia was devoted to health care, far less than the 5 percent recommended by the WHO. Of these percentages, however, as of 2006, the Indonesian government provided 50.4 percent of the total national expenditure on health care. This compares favorably with Malaysia's 45.2 percent, Philippines' 39.6 percent, and Singapore's 33.6 percent but not with Timor-Leste's 88.8 percent.

The modern health-care system continues the Dutch colonial pattern of low levels of investment in health care. The Dutch did relatively little in the field of public health prior to 1910, with the exception of giving smallpox vaccinations. In the 1930s, however, the government devoted increased attention to health education and disease prevention, particularly in rural areas. An elaborate public-health infrastructure had developed by 1939, including a particularly sophisticated model program in Purwokerto in central Java. But this public-health system collapsed after the Japanese invasion in 1942. During World War II, the mortality rate rose dramatically, and the general health situation of the country deteriorated.

In the postwar period, a network of maternal and child health centers was established, but resources were extremely limited, with just one physician for every 100,000 people. The first dramatic improvements resulted from the establishment of the network of community health centers in 1969. Although at first the general population strongly resisted using these facilities, by the time of the 1980 census, 40 percent of people reporting illness in the prior week had sought treatment at one. By 2005 the community health centers catered largely to the rural and urban poor, and most urban residents who could afford to do so sought health care from private physicians and clinics.

Traditional and Modern Health Practices

Dukun—traditional healers—continue to play an important role in health care, particularly in rural areas. Often, the services of a *dukun* are used in conjunction with Western-style medicine. In some rural areas, these healers represent a treatment option of first resort, especially when there is no community health center nearby, or if the only modern health care available is expensive, or the facility is understaffed. Ideas about healing differ greatly among the hundreds of ethnic groups, but often healers use extensive knowledge of herbal medicines and invoke supernatural legitimacy for their practice.

Following childbirth, women in many parts of the archipelago engage in "roasting." Although different ethnic groups have different explanations for the practice, it usually involves the seclusion of the mother and her child for a period following childbirth—from a few weeks to months—so that she might submit herself to prolonged exposure to the warmth of a hearth or other source of heat. In general, it is believed that this speeds the process of recovery, but many believe it helps replace a woman's lost blood, returns her body to a trim and fit shape, and helps "dry her out."

Major Health Problems

The major cause of death in Indonesia is from communicable diseases, mainly resulting from a lack of clean water. Tuberculosis is the second-leading cause of death and the first among infectious diseases. Malaria also is a major public-health problem, as are seasonal episodes of dengue hemorrhagic fever in both urban and rural areas, according to the WHO.

Human immunodeficiency virus/acquired immune deficiency syndrome (HIV/AIDS) poses a major public-health threat in Indonesia. Although in an April 1992 report the Department of Health reported only 47 documented cases of individuals whose blood tested positive for HIV, by 2007 there were an estimated 270,000 people living with HIV/AIDS, the highest rate among its neighbors and third highest in Southeast Asia. Indonesia's estimated 8,700 deaths from HIV/AIDS by 2007 also placed it far above the figures for any of its neighbors and fourth highest in Southeast Asia. The rate of infection is particularly high in Papua. The Ford Foundation and the U.S. Agency for International Development have funded HIV/AIDS prevention and awareness programs in Bali and Papua, and Family Health International was operating a program, Aksi Stop AIDS (ASA), in many parts of the archipelago in 2009.

Two other important public-health concerns are avian influenza and polio. The first outbreak of H5N1 avian influenza in Indonesia occurred in 2004, when cases in poultry were reported in 11 provinces. In 2005 the Department of Health reported that a 38-year-old man who had died on July 12 was the country's first laboratory-confirmed positive human case of H5N1 avian influenza. By the end of the year, 19 more cases had been confirmed. By January 2009, Indonesia had confirmed 140 cases of avian influenza in humans in various parts of the country. The Department of Health, working with the WHO, presents seminars and workshops with the goal of strengthening surveillance of influenza-like illness, outbreak investigation, and appropriate isolation and barrier nursing. The National Committee for Avian Influenza Control and Pandemic Influenza Preparedness (Komnas FPBI) coordinates the Indonesian government response to the H5N1 avian influenza virus. Stockpiling of personal protective equipment to protect the health of veterinary workers, as well as the general health, and procurement of antivirals for treatment and prophylaxis, as appropriate, are continuing. Prevention guidelines for the general Indonesian community emphasize practices such as frequent hand washing, avoidance of contact with sick animals, and safe and hygienic handling and cooking of poultry. Although some mass cullings have taken place in Indonesia, they have not been as extensive as in other countries. Although there were more than 1,800 deaths in Southeast Asia as a result of the 2009 pandemic influenza H1N1, Indonesia was largely spared. Only a few fatal cases were reported in Kalimantan by the end of 2009. To confront the threat of the H1N1 pandemic, Komnas FPBI established an H1N1 Command Post at the Office of the Coordinating Minister of People's Welfare. As of July 2005, there were 122 polio cases confirmed in Indonesia, primarily in Jawa Barat and Jawa Tengah, and in Sumatra. Two emergency vaccination campaigns were conducted by the government in May and June 2005.

Pharmaceuticals

Indonesia achieved self-sufficiency in basic pharmaceutical production by the early 1990s, but as the twenty-first century began, Indonesians still had one of the lowest per capita expenditures for modern drugs among the members of the Association of Southeast Asian Nations (ASEAN—see Glossary). According to one estimate in 2000, Indonesia's annual consumption of medicine was US$4 per capita, compared to US$6 in the Philippines and US$11 in Thailand and Malaysia. Many Indonesians continue to rely at least partially on traditional herbal medicines, in part because modern pharmaceuticals are expensive. When modern medicines are used, ongoing problems include overprescription of antibiotics, overuse of injections, poor patient compliance, use of unlabeled drugs, and inattention to drug interactions. By 2005 Indonesia had about 200 pharmaceutical companies and nearly 1,000 pharmaceutical wholesalers. Most were located on Java.

Public Sanitation

In 2008 about 89 percent of the urban population in Indonesia had access to clean water, and about 60 percent had access to piped water, mostly from a shared faucet. The number of urban dwellers with a household connection rose between 1990 and 2008, from 28 percent to 37 percent. In rural areas, the proportions were smaller: approximately 71 percent had access to an improved water source, and about 8 percent had a household connection in 2008. Many middle- and lower-class Indonesians continue to rely on the country's frequently polluted streams, canals, and water catchment areas. In many coastal cities, the freshwater table is being threatened by the drilling of private wells, which become contaminated by leaking septic tanks. This situation has given rise to the popularity of commercially purified water sold in sealed plastic containers.

According to the WHO, 82 percent of urban residents and 54 percent of rural residents had access to modern sanitation facilities in 2007, but only 67 percent and 36 percent, respectively, used these improved facilities in 2008. Even in urban areas, the WHO estimated that 16 percent of residents were without proper sanitation. Many commercial and residential areas are served by a waterborne sewerage system of open drainage canals discharging raw wastes directly into rivers or the sea. In the slum areas of Jakarta, residents are subjected to frequent flooding and the outbreak of waterborne diseases resulting from clogged sewers.

Society's Prospects

As the world's largest archipelago, and fourth most populous country, the diverse nation of Indonesia faces environmental and social challenges of breathtaking scope. While improved access to education has resulted in lower birthrates, rising incomes, better health, and greater levels of political participation, it has also come at a severe cost to the environment. The preservation of the country's rich ethnic, linguistic, and ecological diversity must increasingly be negotiated in relation to the homogenizing influences of the ever more integrated and interconnected national and international economies. Achieving a sustainable balance among these interests will be one of the central challenges facing Indonesia in the coming decades.

* * *

Several sources give a broad, useful perspective on the cultures of Indonesia. *The Potent Dead: Ancestors, Saints and Heroes in Contemporary Indonesia*, edited by Henri Chambert-Loir and Anthony Reid, has several good articles on the role of religion in Indonesia. Andrew Beatty's *Varieties of Javanese Religion: An Anthropological Account* provides a useful analysis of varieties of Muslim practice in Java. Martin Ramstedt's volume, *Hinduism in Modern Indonesia: A Minority Religion Between Local, National, and Global Interests*, contains several useful essays, particularly his introductory article. The contributors to *Chinese Indonesians: State Policy, Monoculture, and Multiculturalism*, edited by Leo A. Suryadinata, discuss the evolution of state policies toward the religion and culture of Chinese Indonesians. A good survey of history, beliefs, and practices associated with sex and gender in Indonesia can be found in *Fantasizing the Feminine in Indonesia*, edited by Laurie Sears. Diane Wolf's *Factory Daughters: Gender, Household Dynamics, and Rural Industrialization in Java* provides a particularly useful analysis of a significant aspect of economic growth in Indonesia. Freek Colombijn and J. Thomas Lindblad place Indonesia's unrest in historical and cultural context in *Roots of Violence in Indonesia: Contemporary Violence in Historical Perspective*. James N. Sneddon's *The Indonesian Language* provides a survey of its subject's history and role in contemporary society. Christopher Bjork's *Indonesian Education* provides a contemporary picture of the struggle among teachers, schools, and the central educational bureaucracy. A particularly useful compilation of current essays pertaining to recent violence, political and religious developments, and environmental problems is contained in John McDougall's *Indonesia Publications: Online University Course*.

For a description of the history behind current environmental debates, *Environmental Challenges in South-east Asia*, edited by Victor King, is the best source. A demographic perspective on population growth, health, labor, and migration is the focus of *The Demographic Dimension in Indonesian Development*, by Graeme Hugo et al. (For further information and complete citations, see Bibliography.)

Chapter 3. The Economy

Perahu pinisi—*indigenous trading vessels—moored in Jakarta's old harbor of Sunda Kelepa*

THE INDONESIAN ECONOMY, BY MANY MEASURES, prospered during the New Order government of President Suharto, whose long tenure, from 1966 to 1998, both began and ended in political and social upheaval. Rapid growth of Indonesia's gross domestic product (GDP—see Glossary) endured over a long period of time, significantly raising the standard of living. Social achievements under the New Order are widely considered to have been far less impressive, however. The most urgent challenge facing Suharto's four immediate successors, who took office between 1998 and 2004, was to reignite the fast-paced economic expansion of the New Order years.

The role of government has been absolutely crucial in the shaping of economic development in Indonesia since the 1960s. The main themes of government economic policy during the latter part of the Suharto period were liberalization and deregulation, which in the 1980s and 1990s radically changed the economic landscape as well as the relationship between private capital and political power. The financial crisis that started in Thailand in the summer of 1997 soon reached Indonesia—and other Asian nations—and crisis management with international assistance became the most pressing topic of economic policy in Jakarta over the next several years. In the early years of the new century, the government started putting economic reforms in place. Among other new policies, these reforms included a far-reaching decentralization of economic authority and policy making. Central government finance and the execution of monetary and exchange-rate policies now drew special attention. A resumption of economic growth, though not at the same torrid pace experienced prior to the 1997 crisis, accompanied the implementation of the reforms.

Three trends characterize the changes that have occurred in the Indonesian economy since the late 1960s: increasing integration with the world economy, profound structural change, and intense diversification. These trends are highlighted in discussions about major aspects of the Indonesian economy, such as international trade, aid, and payments; employment and income development; and the main sectors of economic activity. The economy has experienced a fundamental reorientation from agriculture to industry, and within the industrial sector itself, from oil and gas production to other branches of manufacturing, both labor-intensive (for example, textiles and food processing) and capital-intensive (for example, chemicals and electrical and electronic goods). Modernization has enabled the services sector and the transportation and communication infrastructures to make a greater contribution to economic growth. In the early twenty-first century, the national economy no longer depends only on natural resources such as oil and gas.

The Role of Government

The government pursued policies to support *pribumi* (see Glossary) businessmen in the early years of nation building, from independence in 1945 to 1957. These included subsidized credit from the state-owned Indonesian People's Bank (BRI—for this and other acronyms, see table A), and positive discrimination in favor of indigenous traders in the allocation of scarce foreign exchange for imports. The first five-year development plan (1956–60) proposed a realistic level of government investment in physical infrastructure but offered little regulation or overall guidance to the private sector. This plan was superseded by dramatic developments in the political and economic sphere, in particular the takeover of virtually all remaining Dutch-owned private enterprises in December 1957, which led to nationalization and state control of key sectors of the economy. Indonesian civil servants and military officers, most of whom had little managerial experience, replaced Dutch management personnel.

The expansion of the state's role in the economy was sustained by general policy shifts. The Guided Economy of President Sukarno (in office 1945–67) was initiated in a new eight-year development plan begun in 1959, which entailed a twelvefold increase in spending on government projects without a clear indication of sources of finance. By the mid-1960s, credit from Bank Indonesia—the central bank—accounted for half of government expenditures. This situation led to budget deficits and a mounting foreign debt, as well as galloping inflation, which peaked at an annual rate of 900 percent in 1966. In spite of a highly visible public building campaign, the economy stagnated, and by 1965 per capita GDP was back at its 1957 level.

Following the downfall of Sukarno in 1967, the New Order regime under Suharto drew upon financial assistance from the International Monetary Fund (IMF) in the pursuit of a variety of emergency stabilization measures. During the late 1960s, a team of five economists from the Faculty of Economics at the Universitas Indonesia (University of Indonesia) in Jakarta became influential presidential advisers, even gaining cabinet-level posts. Because three of the advisers were graduates of the University of California at Berkeley, the group, led by Widjoyo Nitisastro, who headed the National Development Planning Board (Bappenas), became colloquially known as the Berkeley Mafia. Foremost among this group's recommended reforms was a balanced budget, although foreign borrowing and aid counted as sources of revenue. In a radical break from the socialist tenor of Sukarno's Guided Economy, Suharto's New Order heralded a return to private-market development.

The New Order remained committed to a stable economic environment encouraged by responsible fiscal and monetary policy, but concerns over foreign economic dominance, the limited national industrial base, and the need for *pribumi* economic development mandated increased government regulation during the 1970s. The economy continued to prosper throughout that decade, with GDP growing at an average rate of 8 percent annually. In the early 1980s, a precipitous drop in the growth rate pointed to limits in the industrialization strategy, and a new generation of reformers advocated a more limited role for the government. When the oil market collapsed in 1986, the balance was tipped in favor of these advocates of "free-fight" economic competition.

The Political Economy of Reform

Two main forces of influence within the New Order government battled to shape economic policy: the technocrats, favoring market reform and little intervention by the government; and the economic nationalists, arguing that trade protection and direct government control and regulation were necessary. The leaders of the technocrats were the original members of the Berkeley Mafia. After Nitisastro, the most influential technocrat was Ali Wardhana, initially minister of finance and later coordinating minister of economics, finance, and industry. Although retired by 1988, both men remained influential behind-the-scenes advisers until the early 1990s. Beneficiaries of the tutelage of Sumitro Joyohadikusumo, former cabinet member and founding dean of the Faculty of Economics at the Universitas Indonesia, these Western-trained economists were advocates of economic liberalism.

The economic nationalists included prominent officials in the Department of Industry, which was headed by Hartarto; Bacharuddin J. (B. J.) Habibie, minister of research and technology, who since childhood had enjoyed Suharto's special protection; and officers on the Capital Investment Coordinating Board (BKPM). The balance of power between the technocrats and the economic nationalists was for several decades mediated by Suharto, but around 1993 the nationalists gained a decisive influence over economic policy and increasingly pushed the technocrats into the background. This change reflected Suharto's rising confidence that he was capable of managing economic development without much advice from others, his great trust in Habibie's capacity to stage major economic advances, and the rise of his children's business empires in the 1980s and 1990s.

The technocrats had initially gained a great deal of credibility by curbing rampant inflation and restoring financial stability after the New Order government came to power in 1966. As oil revenues increased, starting in 1974, government agencies responsible for trade and industrial policy sought to extend Indonesia's domestic industrial base by investing in basic industries, especially steel manufacturing, and by erecting trade barriers to protect domestic producers from foreign competition. Government regulations proliferated, and oil taxes fueled investment in development projects and state enterprises.

The private sector became dominated by large conglomerates, often owned by Indonesians of Chinese descent who had sufficient wealth and know-how to assist the government with large-scale modernization projects. During the 1970s, Chinese Indonesian conglomerates were estimated to account for 75 percent of private-sector investment. Around 1990, the top 200 conglomerates accounted for sales that taken together corresponded to 25 percent of GDP. Turnover of the five largest, including the Salim and Astra International groups, amounted to Rp16 trillion (US$6.8 billion; for value of the rupiah—Rp—see Glossary), and 18 of the 22 largest conglomerates were owned by Indonesians of Chinese descent. Among them, the top 200 conglomerates controlled almost 45,000 individual firms. The growth of the conglomerates throughout the 1970s and 1980s was in most cases highly dependent on political patronage. In exchange for monopoly privileges related to production and imports of key industrial products, conglomerates would undertake large-scale investment projects that helped the government reach its industrialization goals.

By the mid-1980s, about 1,500 items representing 35 percent of the value of imports were either imported by licensed importers or controlled through a quota system. Nontariff barriers affected virtually all manufactured imports but were a particular impediment to foreign-made textiles, paper and paper products, and chemical products. As a result, domestic firms in these lines of production were effectively protected from foreign competition or were able to sell their products at a higher cost. Firms that obtained import licenses were also highly profitable, but costs were borne by the entire economy because imports were often key inputs for other manufacturers. Popular resentment grew as gains from the restrictions enriched a privileged minority and added to a long-standing public sensitivity toward the prominent economic position of the Indonesian Chinese minority.

In the 1980s, Suharto's six children came of age and quickly became the most visible beneficiaries of direct access to the apex of political power. Each of them was connected with one or more conglomerates that based their business success at least partly on lucrative government contracts. For example, the Bimantara Citra Group, run by Suharto's second son, Bambang Trihatmojo, started out by selling allocations of imported oil to Pertamina (the State Oil and Natural Gas Mining Company, sometimes translated as State Oil Company). Around 1990, the business groups of Suharto's children were among the foremost non-Chinese conglomerates in Indonesia.

Examples from two vital industries illustrate the symbiotic relationship between government and business in Indonesia. In 1984 Suharto's long-time personal friend Liem Sioe Liong, founder of the Salim Group, agreed to invest US$800 million to expand the operations of a government-owned company, Krakatau Steel, in Cilegon, Banten Province, by adding production of cold-rolled sheet steel. In return, a company partly owned by Liem received a monopoly on imports of cold-rolled steel. Once domestic production was underway, Liem's imports were restricted to ensure demand for the Krakatau product. In a similar way, imports of plastic raw materials were monopolized through a government license issued to Panca Holding, which had two Suharto sons, Bambang Trihatmojo and Sigit Harjoyudanto, on its board of directors. In each case, the price of an important commodity for Indonesian users—either steel products or plastics—was artificially and significantly raised.

Oil prices fell from US$25 to US$13 per barrel in 1986, which resulted in a 5-percent decline in national income. Suddenly, there was a great need to promote non-oil exports. Meanwhile, dissatisfaction had been growing over the Suharto administration's trade and industrial policies; in particular, local chambers of commerce and industry voiced criticism of the "high-cost" economy. Some reforms had been in preparation before 1986, but without provisions that would directly affect trade restrictions. Major trade deregulation began in 1986 but left the main import monopolies untouched until 1988. This very gradual approach to reform became characteristic of the later years of the Suharto regime. The first sector to experience reform in the 1980s was finance and banking.

Financial Reform

The Suharto administration inherited a system dominated by large state banks in which private banking had virtually ceased to exist. The New Order government immediately revived the legal foundation for commercial banking, and by 1983 Indonesia had 81 private banks, including 11 foreign or joint-venture institutions. Nevertheless, the banking sector remained highly regulated until the early 1980s, when the technocrats spearheaded a return to market-led development. Their sweeping reforms were aimed at transforming Indonesia's financial sector into a competitive source of credit at market-determined interest rates, with a much greater role for private banks and a growing stock exchange. By the 1990s, critics complained that deregulation had gone too far, introducing excessive risk.

So-called liquidity credits extended by Bank Indonesia at very low interest rates subsidized state bank lending during the 1980s. In 1983 such credits represented more than half of all state bank lending, which in turn made up three-quarters of all bank lending in Indonesia. Lending by private commercial banks had been severely curtailed, even though such institutions offered better service and competitive interest rates on deposits. In addition, Bank Indonesia imposed credit quotas on all banks, ostensibly to reduce inflationary pressures. In June 1983, credit quotas were lifted, and state banks began to offer market-determined interest rates on deposits. Important restrictions remained, however, and by 1988 state banks still accounted for almost 70 percent of total bank credit, with liquidity credits still constituting one-third of total state bank credit. In October 1988, further financial deregulation eliminated the remaining restrictions on bank competition.

The number of banks increased as limitations on licenses lifted. In 1990 there were 103 private banks, including 12 new foreign joint-venture banks. The expansion accelerated in the early and mid-1990s, and by 1997 Indonesia counted 237 banks, more than Japan. These institutions included 203 private commercial banks, 43 of which were foreign or joint-venture banks and 34 state banks, including 27 that were run by provincial governments.

Two spectacular bank scandals demonstrated that professional, uncorrupted regulation and oversight were sorely needed. In 1990 Bank Duta, Indonesia's second-largest private bank, had to be bailed out after losing more than US$400 million in foreign-exchange dealings. Bank Indonesia organized a rescue operation with the money raised from the shareholders of Bank Duta, including several foundations chaired by Suharto. In late 1992, Bank Summa found itself in a similar predicament, but the government did not come to the rescue, possibly because of the honorable public image of the bank's owner, William Suryajaya (Tjia Kian Liong), founder of Astra International, who had consistently declined to enter into dubious deals with government agencies. Liquidation of assets for the recovery of losses at Bank Summa in fact paved the way for a takeover of Astra International by a group of Suharto cronies, including Liem Sioe Liong.

A few idiosyncrasies of Indonesian banking deserve special mention. One is the option for banks to offer deposits denominated in foreign currency, usually U.S. dollars. This gave rise to the so-called

Rush-hour traffic in Jakarta
Courtesy Embassy of Indonesia, Washington, DC

Jakarta dollar market, and in 1990 Bank Indonesia determined that a bank's net foreign position (the difference between foreign assets and foreign liabilities) could correspond to as much as 25 percent of the bank's total outstanding capital. Also characteristic was the close link between banks and conglomerates. Prior to the reforms of 1988, it was often the case that a private bank was virtually the financial arm of a large conglomerate and only lent money to firms connected with the bank's owners. The reforms constrained such loans, although they remained difficult to control. In addition, starting in 1990 the government requested that banks lend 20 percent of their loan portfolios to small businesses. This policy reflected a growing concern that the public might perceive the benefits of economic growth as accruing only to the well-connected, wealthy few.

The Jakarta Stock Exchange, which operated for several years as a small and ineffective institution, experienced a spectacular expansion once various restrictions were lifted in the 1980s. The number of listed firms rose from 24 in 1988 to 125 in 1991, and market capitalization (total market value of issued stocks) climbed above Rp12 billion (about US$6.2 million). Although market capitalization corresponded to less than 15 percent of total bank credit to private firms, the stock market promised to become an important source of finance. However, the early 1990s saw extreme swings between euphoric expansion and virtual collapse, and at one point in 1991 one stock brokerage firm was even charged with swindling other

171

brokers by issuing bad checks. The Jakarta Stock Exchange settled into a more stable existence in the mid-1990s as the public and brokers grew more familiar with procedures. (The Jakarta Stock Exchange merged with the Surabaya Stock Exchange in 2007 to form the new Indonesia Stock Exchange.)

Deregulation and liberalization of the financial sector led to a very rapid enlargement of credit in Indonesia. Total outstanding credit by 1997 reached Rp306 trillion (US$105 billion), 80 percent of which was denominated in rupiah. Interest rates at domestic banks remained high, at around 15 to 16 percent on deposits, which made borrowing from foreign banks all the more attractive.

Industrial and Trade Reform

Indonesia's industrialization during the 1970s and 1980s occurred with many trade restrictions and government regulations that made private businesses hostage to government approval or protection. As a consequence, almost all of Indonesia's industrial production was sold in the domestic market, leaving exports to be dominated by oil and agricultural products. Trade policy reforms in the mid-1980s proved successful in promoting the growth of new export industries, but the large conglomerates were in the best position to benefit from the more competitive business environment. The uneven distribution of gains from economic growth caused mounting popular dissatisfaction by the mid-1990s.

The Indonesian government favored a strategy of import-substitution industrialization that did not expose domestic manufacturing to competition in world markets (see Industry, this ch.). This strategy was supported by a great variety of barriers to imports: almost 1,500 nontariff restrictions and tariffs ranging up to 200 percent of the value of imported goods. Inefficiencies plagued the import-substitution approach, and it offered generous opportunities for corruption. Case studies of import substitution in manufacturing showed that it generated only 25 percent of the jobs export-oriented production would have provided.

The government initiated trade reforms in May 1986, when duty refunds compensated for tariffs paid on goods imported by domestic producers that exported a substantial share of their output. A major trade reform in November 1988 began the dismantling of the elaborate nontariff barriers and the simplification and reduction of tariffs. The reforms reduced the share of domestic manufacturing protected by nontariff barriers from 50 percent in 1986 to 35 percent in 1988. By 1990, some 60 percent of nontariff barriers had been abolished, and import tariffs had a maximum rate of 40 percent.

There were important exceptions to the credo of economic liberalism that accompanied the series of deregulation packages introduced between the mid-1980s and mid-1990s. Strict government control remained in key sectors, notably natural-resource exploitation, technology, and the sensitive area of *pribumi* entrepreneurship.

The exploitation of oil and natural gas (marketed in the form of liquefied natural gas, or LNG) remained tightly controlled by the government through contractual agreements between Pertamina and foreign oil companies (see Petroleum and Natural Gas, this ch.). In the early 1980s, restrictions also increasingly restricted the logging industry, culminating in a total ban on log exports in 1985. This strategy, aimed at fostering a domestic plywood and sawmill industry, proved successful and was later extended to exports of sawn timber in order to bolster wood furniture manufacturing.

Ten state-owned enterprises entrusted with the strategic task of raising the level of Indonesia's technological sophistication benefited from special protection. They included Krakatau Steel and the embryonic Archipelago Aircraft Industry (IPTN) and were under the direct supervision of the powerful minister of research and technology, Habibie, a talented aircraft engineer. The strategic industries enjoyed extrabudgetary funding and were accountable only to the president himself.

In order to counter resentment of the privileges of the conglomerates, President Suharto urged large corporations to divest part of their equity to employee-owned cooperatives on credit supplied by the employer and also to sponsor smaller *pribumi* firms that could serve as subcontractors. None of these actions were legally mandated, but Suharto made it clear to the Chinese Indonesian tycoons that he expected them to comply if they were to continue getting priority access to lucrative government contracts. A survey of the Suharto family's corporate wealth, published in the Hong Kong–based *Far Eastern Economic Review* in 1992, demonstrated that public resentment of the ruling elite was growing, although government officials and businessmen still declined to voice criticism openly.

Corruption scandals involving members of the Suharto family proliferated in the mid-1990s, and there were frequent public outcries of indignation. Some of the most notorious cases concerned the president's youngest son, Tommy Suharto (Hutomo Mandala Putra). In blatant contradiction of the prevailing general policies of deregulation, he was granted monopoly rights to purchase and distribute cloves needed by Indonesia's cigarette industry, and before long his agency obtained large credits from state banks, despite outstanding debts to Bank Indonesia. Even more infamous was his involvement with the national car industry, set up as a joint venture with the automobile manufacturer Kia of the Republic of Korea (South Korea). In 1996 Tommy Suharto's company, National Son Timor (TPN), was exempted from payment of import tariffs when importing South Korean–made sedans that were subsequently marketed as a domestic product called the Timor. Because of this flagrant violation of its own trade legislation, the Indonesian government was brought before the World Trade Organization (WTO—see Glossary) by Japanese, U.S., and European car manufacturers operating in Indonesia. The Indonesian government predictably lost the case, adding to the considerable damage already done to its prestige, both internationally and at home.

In *The East Asian Miracle*, a well-known analysis of spectacular economic success in East Asia published in 1993, the World Bank classified Indonesia as a "high-performing Asian economy," along with Hong Kong, Japan, Malaysia, Singapore, South Korea, Taiwan, and Thailand. Indonesia's GDP growth had indeed been impressive, averaging 5.5 percent annually during the preceding decade (1984–93). A growth acceleration occurred in the mid-1990s, with the annual average approaching 8 percent over the years 1994–96. Exports grew by 8 percent per year, and growth figures were higher still in finance, construction, utilities, and various branches of manufacturing. As late as May 1997, only a few months before the Asian financial crisis spread to Indonesia, the World Bank, in its annual assessment, expressed confidence in the growth prospects and macroeconomic fundamentals of the Indonesian economy.

Crisis Management

No one foresaw that when Bank Indonesia floated the rupiah on August 14, 1997, this would be the starting point of a severe financial crisis with profound social and political ramifications. The downward adjustment in the value of the currency turned into a free fall of the exchange rate, a near collapse of the stock market, massive capital flight, an abrupt end to growth in almost all sectors of the economy, mass layoffs, galloping inflation, and a rapidly increasing incidence of poverty. In May 1998, riots and political upheaval culminated in the downfall of Suharto. The key issues surrounding the financial crisis that struck Indonesia relate to the reasons why the crisis became so severe and the ways in which crisis management was executed.

There is general agreement among scholars that high rates of growth and apparently healthy macroeconomic indicators, notably a balanced budget and moderate rates of inflation, masked structural weaknesses that made Indonesia highly vulnerable to a financial cri-

The headquarters of Bank Indonesia, Jakarta
Courtesy Yadi Jasin

sis imported from abroad. Such weaknesses included rapidly increasing private debt, a quasi-fixed exchange rate despite large inflows of mobile short-run capital, a poorly supervised banking system that left much room for reckless lending and widespread collusion, and corruption in the allocation of government contracts. Private external debt grew from US$7.5 billion in 1991 to nearly US$58 billion in 1997, an almost eightfold increase. Much of this debt was short-term and lacked hedging in the form of safeguards against fluctuations in the exchange rate. Banks and conglomerates tacitly assumed that the government would step in and bail them out if they were unable to meet their foreign obligations. Such behavior, commonly regarded as constituting a "moral hazard," was a characteristic feature of the Asian crisis in general, but in the case of Indonesia it was more strongly linked than elsewhere to the political economy, in particular the nexus between private economic interests and the apex of political power. Corruption and poor governance did not cause the financial crisis in Indonesia, but these factors did make the crisis worse.

Predicaments in the financial sector became acute because short-run loans from foreign creditors had to be repaid in international currency, whereas revenues were generated from long-run investment and denominated in domestic currency. The sharp depreciation of the rupiah led to an instant increase in the number of nonperforming loans. The government had little choice but to turn to the IMF for assistance. From late October 1997 until December 2002, crisis management and postcrisis recovery policies were determined by the interplay between the IMF and the Indonesian government.

The rescue package envisaged a huge standby assistance fund of US$38 billion, at the time the largest sum of this kind ever offered by the IMF to an individual nation, with disbursement conditional on the implementation of specific reforms. The IMF concluded no fewer than four consecutive agreements with Indonesia, on October 31, 1997, and January 15, April 10, and July 29, 1998. The agreements required the establishment of facilities for bank and debt restructuring, prudence in fiscal and monetary policies, and the pursuit of deregulation with greater vigor than in the past. However, action following the first IMF agreement backfired as the closure of 16 ailing banks triggered large-scale capital flight that put the rupiah under even greater strain than before. Doubts arose about Suharto's commitment to reform, especially after one of the shuttered institutions, Bank Andromeda, owned by his second son, Bambang Trihatmojo, reopened under a new name. It took a telephone call from U.S. president William J. Clinton in January 1998 to persuade Suharto to sign a second agreement with the IMF, which more forcefully committed the Indonesian government to reform and, in particular, did away with monopoly privileges such as those enjoyed by Tommy Suharto's national car project and B. J. Habibie's aircraft company. The IMF also permitted the government to run a deficit, corresponding to 1 percent of GDP, to allow for aid to the large numbers of people now struck by poverty.

Lack of cooperation on the part of the central authorities continued into the first half of 1998, Indonesia's worst year of economic crisis, when GDP contracted by an unprecedented 13.7 percent, more than during the entire depression of the 1930s. Suharto's selection of Habibie as vice president, and the appointment of well-known cronies and his own daughter as cabinet ministers, eroded confidence in the long-serving president's ability to deliver Indonesia from crisis. The IMF grew alarmed by Suharto's toying with the idea of a currency board that would operate on the basis of a fixed rate of exchange. This arrangement would have been in direct violation of the reform agreements, but the rumor was that it would allow the Suharto family to get assets out of the country without serious damage to their value.

The third IMF agreement (April 10, 1998) reiterated the commitments made in the two previous agreements but raised the permitted deficit on the budget to 3.5 percent of GDP and pressed anew for determined action by the Indonesian government. By that time, even Suharto's most ardent supporters were realizing that the aging president was part of the problem rather than the means for its solution. The fourth and final IMF agreement (July 29, 1998) followed Habibie's installation as Suharto's successor. The extreme increase in poverty necessitated a far larger budget deficit; in fiscal year (FY—see Glossary) 1999, it would correspond to 8.5 percent of GDP and would be financed with a loan provided by an international aid consortium, the Consultative Group on Indonesia (CGI—see Glossary; see Government Finance, this ch.).

Precious time was lost between the onset of the financial crisis in August 1997 and the fourth IMF agreement in July 1998. The main reason was the Suharto administration's inability to confront the fundamental problems of the crisis. This delay understandably caused serious doubts on the part of the IMF, which deferred disbursement of the pledged assistance. By July 1998, only a small proportion of the huge rescue package had actually been paid out. Cooperation with the IMF improved significantly under President Habibie and his two immediate successors, Abdurrahman Wahid and Megawati Sukarnoputri. Two key members of the Megawati cabinet, Minister of Finance Budiono and Coordinating Minister for the Economy Dorojatun Kuncoro-Yakti, were both Western-trained and highly responsive to IMF recommendations. The IMF also displayed an increasing sensitivity to the demands of the specific crisis in Indonesia, notably by abandoning the priority of a balanced budget in fiscal policy and by recognizing the need for social safety-net programs to protect the most vulnerable groups in society from the effects of the crisis.

Postcrisis Reform

The most pressing problems of structural reform in the wake of the financial crisis fell to two newly established institutions, the Indonesian Bank Restructuring Agency (BPPN, also IBRA) and the Indonesian Debt Restructuring Agency (Indra), established in January and July 1998, respectively. The BPPN had the task of taking over assets of bankrupt banks and arranging recapitalization of ailing banks. Indra focused on corporate debts but was superseded by another agency, the so-called Jakarta Initiative, set up jointly by the government and the World Bank in September 1998, which smoothed debt settlement through bilateral negotiations and debt–equity swapping. As a result, the government acquired substantial holdings of assets that were to be sold off gradually so as to retroactively finance the debt settlements. Privatization became a key strategy of economic policy.

The BPPN took over 10 private banks in 1998 and 1999, closed down another 66, and merged four troubled state banks into one new institution, Bank Mandiri, which became the single largest bank in Indonesia. In May 1999, the total cost of bailing out and recapitalizing troubled banks was estimated at Rp406 trillion (US$51.4 billion).

By 2002 the total amount needed for bailout and recapitalization had reached Rp660 trillion (US$70.8 billion). The country then had 179 banks remaining, 93 of which were scheduled for restructuring, including 31 state-owned, 57 joint ventures, and 5 privately owned. Progress was slow, however, especially in terms of divesting the assets that had been taken over from these institutions. By the time the BPPN was dissolved in February 2004, it had recovered 28 percent of the nominal value of loans it had taken over but had been able to return only 25 percent of the value of the bonds the government had issued to pay the banks' creditors. Remaining assets, carrying a book value of US$8.3 billion, came directly under the auspices of the Department of Finance. Assessments of BPPN's performance pointed out that it would have been unrealistic to expect the agency to get more for assets that had been grossly overvalued in the first place.

Bank and debt restructuring in the period from 1998 to 2004 suffered from two problems beyond the strict confines of financial policy and management. One problem was in the legal sphere and concerned bankruptcy. A 1998 bankruptcy law finally replaced one dating from Dutch colonial times, but it still proved very difficult to get debt-ridden firms declared bankrupt. Creditors won very few cases, in a judicial system widely known to be rife with corruption. The other problem concerned the divestment of seized corporate assets. When assets were sold off, there was a real risk that the BPPN would come across former owners trying to buy back their assets at low prices, possibly under other names. Whenever foreign buyers were involved, political opposition was likely in the legislature or through pressure groups. In 2001 nationalist opposition in Sumatera Barat Province successfully blocked the sale of a majority equity share in a state-owned cement factory to the Mexican cement giant CEMEX (formerly Cementos Mexicanos). Eventually, CEMEX bought 25 percent of the shares, but it expressed a wish to pull out in 2006.

Good governance became a top priority of postcrisis reform, and recent administrations have, in varying degrees, pledged to combat corruption and enhance democracy and the transparency of government affairs. One of the most sweeping reforms entailed a far-reaching delegation of authority to subnational levels of government (see Decentralization, this ch.). Although implementation was quick and complete, with maximum involvement of democratic institutions, success was limited, largely because of great variation in the capacity of local governments to exercise their authority in taxation and fiscal policy. Even though he supported democratic reforms, including arrangement of Indonesia's first fully free general elections since 1955, Habibie enjoyed little credibility, as he himself was the product of a corrupt and despised system. A scandal in September 1999 involving secret money transfers from the private Bank Bali to the ruling political party erased any remaining faith in Habibie's commitment to genuine reform.

Elected to the presidency by the People's Consultative Assembly (MPR) in October 1999, Abdurrahman Wahid initially profited from much goodwill both at home and abroad, but this support vanished as a result of his erratic style of government and lack of tangible accomplishments (see The Political Process, ch. 4). Direct adminis-trative intervention by the president frequently had unfortunate results. For example, in April 2000 Wahid dismissed Laksamana Sukardi as minister for investment and state enterprises development without offering any clear explanation. Sukardi had an undisputed image of integrity and was in fact the first cabinet-level minister to expose the way Suharto had abused his power in order to give signif-icant favors to his business associates. Shortly afterward, Wahid also had the governor of Bank Indonesia, Syahril Sabirin, placed under detention out of displeasure with the central bank's independent action. Wahid's successor, his vice president, Megawati Sukarnopu-tri, had the good fortune of being surrounded by some very capable economic advisers. During her presidency, economic recovery pro-ceeded reasonably smoothly, but strikingly little was achieved in combating corruption, including that in the judicial system.

Two institutions in particular had a mandate to combat corruption, the Corruption Eradication Commission (KPK) and the Corruption Crimes Court (Tipikor), both established in 2002 on the recommen-dation of the IMF. After a relatively slow start, they became more active in 2005. In that year alone, 450 corruption cases were prose-cuted, compared with only about 200 during the three years of Mega-wati's presidency (2001–4). This increase seemed to reflect a genuine commitment on the part of Megawati's successor, Susilo Bambang Yudhoyono (known colloquially by his initials, SBY), to weed out corrupt practices from public administration in Indonesia. Signifi-cantly, by early 2006 Yudhoyono had allowed corruption charges to be levied against 52 high-ranking government officials at the provin-cial and district levels, as well as against seven governors, nine may-ors, and 36 district heads.

The Yudhoyono administration also sought to improve the invest-ment climate in Indonesia by presenting a reform package in Febru-ary 2006 that included a new investment law, tax incentives, facilities for training personnel, and financial aid to small-scale busi-ness enterprises. The reform package also proposed the establish-ment of eight new special economic zones for export production. At mid-decade, economic reform policies pursued by the Indonesian government seemed to have a new momentum. By 2008, however, there was again mounting disappointment with the slow pace of reform, especially in local governments, state-owned enterprises, and some central government departments.

Government Finance

Central Government Budget

Five-year development plans (Repelita—see Glossary) were an important tool in economic planning beginning in the 1960s. These plans offered broad guidelines and set general priorities. The emphasis was on rehabilitation in Repelita I (1969–73), but it then shifted to increasing productivity in agriculture and improving infrastructure in particular during the 1970s. After the drop in oil prices in the early and mid-1980s, consecutive Repelitas stressed industrialization and export promotion. By the time of Repelita V (1989–93), the main objectives included continued export diversification and reduced reliance on foreign aid. The 1980s and early 1990s also saw increasing attention given to social development issues, such as education, health, and family planning. Repelita VI (1994–98) stressed the expansion of manufacturing and set growth targets that were overtaken by actual developments on the eve of the 1997–98 financial crisis. The government abandoned conventional Repelitas in the wake of the crisis and thereafter replaced them with national medium-term development plans (NMDPs), also set out in five-year increments. The main objectives of the 2004–9 NMDP included a sharp reduction in poverty and registered unemployment and an average annual rate of growth of 6.6 percent.

The Repelitas served as general indicators of the direction of government policy rather than concrete priorities (the latter being provided by the annual budget of the central government). Indonesia traditionally had a fiscal year that ran from April 1 to March 31, with the national government's draft budget for a particular year usually submitted to the People's Representative Council (DPR) in January, only months before the budget was to become effective (see Legislative Bodies, ch. 4). Beginning in 2000, the fiscal year coincided with the calendar year, with the budget now sent to the DPR at mid-year. As a consequence, the budget for 2000 covered only nine months. Public spending historically was divided into two broad categories, routine and development expenditures. Routine expenditures included the salaries of civil servants and most spending on materials, operations, and maintenance, whereas development expenditures consisted of project-related spending in areas such as investment, research, and training. Over time, however, the line dividing the two categories became somewhat arbitrary in practice. Starting with the FY 2005 budget, the distinction between routine and development expenditure was abandoned entirely and replaced by a classification system recommended by the IMF that differentiated more carefully between current and capital outlays and among levels of government authority. The distinction between spending by the central government and that by regional governments has become ever more important since the decentralization reforms that followed the collapse of the New Order government.

Since the 1980s, the total government budget has been rather stable, about or slightly less than 20 percent of GDP. In 2003 total government expenditures amounted to Rp371 trillion (US$43.2 billion), or 19.1 percent of GDP, against a total revenue of Rp336 trillion (US$39.2 billion), or 17.3 percent of GDP. The resulting deficit corresponded to 1.8 percent of GDP. The 2009 budget envisaged government revenue at 21.2 percent of GDP and government expenditure at 23.4 percent of GDP. Deficit spending has been the exception rather than the rule in Indonesian government finance since the late 1960s. Fiscal prudence and rapid economic growth resulted in balanced budgets throughout the 1980s and early and mid-1990s. Even the initial draft budget for the crisis year 1998–99, prepared in mid-1997, included projection of a small surplus, which proved entirely unrealistic. Combating crisis and staging economic recovery necessitated deficit spending by the central government starting in 1998. The budget deficit rose to 6.8 percent of GDP in FY 1999 (12 months) and was 5 percent of GDP in FY 2000 (nine months). It then fell gradually, reaching 2.5 percent in FY 2002 and creeping below 1 percent in FY 2005 and FY 2006. The budget for FY 2008 displayed a deficit of Rp73 trillion (US$8.1 billion) corresponding to 1.7 percent of GDP, whereas the one agreed for FY 2009 showed a slightly higher deficit at 2.2 percent of GDP.

A bottleneck in central government finance in Indonesia occurs because of the heavy reliance on sources of revenue based in the oil and gas sector. Taxes paid by foreign oil companies burgeoned during the oil boom of the 1970s, raising oil's contribution to total government revenue from one-third in 1974 to more than two-thirds by 1979. Even in the early 1980s, at least half of government income came from oil-related taxes. A major tax reform in 1984 introduced a value-added tax (VAT) on consumer goods and a moderately progressive income tax. Although 85 percent of households did not earn enough to be subject to the income tax, the contribution of non-oil tax revenue did increase significantly, climbing from less than Rp10 trillion (about US$9 billion) annually in the mid-1980s to almost Rp60 trillion (about US$26 billion) by the mid-1990s. As a consequence, revenues from oil and gas dropped to 20 percent of total domestic revenue, but the downward trend was reversed by the steep decline in incomes during the Asian financial crisis. The contribution of oil and gas revenues again rose to about 30 percent of total government revenue and oscillated around that level in the years immediately following the turn of the century, even rising somewhat as a result of high oil prices on the world market in 2005 and 2006. Oil and gas contributed 20 percent of total government revenue in the agreed budget for FY 2008.

The tax-revenue bottleneck has been reflected in a high dependence on foreign aid and borrowing abroad. Foreign public debt increased sharply in the 1980s, approaching US$50 billion by that decade's end. In the early 1990s, the government shifted from its traditional reliance on long-term public debt to allowing more private and short-run lending. The stock of foreign debt declined from about 80 percent of GDP to less than 60 percent as a result, and also because of simultaneous rapid economic growth. On the eve of crisis in 1997, Indonesia's public debt amounted to US$58 billion. This downward trend was reversed by the crisis, which saw another sharp increase in foreign indebtedness, up to more than 100 percent of GDP. Foreign funding was vital to finance two-thirds of the deficit on the FY 1999 (April 1999–March 2000) budget and half of the deficit on the budget for FY 2000 (April–December 2000); the Indonesian government had little choice. Tax revenues were constrained by the real decline in GDP, proceeds from the sale of seized corporate assets were slow in coming, and it was next to impossible to cut expenditures in the midst of a severe economic crisis. Prior to the crisis, routine expenditures usually made up about two-thirds of total public spending, but this proportion rose to 85 percent at the time of the crisis. The traditional expenditure ratio of roughly two-thirds routine and one-third development was restored around 2000, but the allocation now needed for debt servicing represented a far heavier burden than before. The distribution between routine and development expenditures stabilized at 75 percent for the former and 25 percent for the latter during the 2002–4 period, preceding the change in the system of budgetary classification.

The budget for FY 2002, in part designed by ministers Budiono and Dorojatun of the newly inaugurated Megawati cabinet, may serve to illustrate some typical features of public finance in Indonesia that held true for the most part in subsequent years. Tax revenue was expected to contribute 73 percent of total government income, corresponding to less than 13 percent of GDP, which was low by international standards. Most other government revenue was projected to derive from the exploitation of oil and natural gas resources, an assumption that implied a continued dependence on strong world oil prices in government financial planning. Expenditures, corresponding to 20 percent of GDP, were divided between routine and development purposes at a ratio of 78 percent to 22 percent. The central government assumed responsibility for 72 percent and regional governments for 28 percent of total outlays, a ratio that testifies to the strong start of the decentralization reforms. Total development spending at the central level was set at Rp50 trillion (about US$5.3 billion), about 25 percent of which was designated for education and culture but only 10 percent for health and welfare. The scope for expenditure on social-development projects remained severely constrained. Interest payments would make up more than 25 percent of central government outlays in the FY 2002 budget, whereas around 12 percent would go to subsidies on consumption, in particular fuel use. Neither expenditure lent itself to easy reduction. The interest payments were a legacy of the crisis management of the late 1990s, which entailed the buildup of a large public debt, and the subsidies were politically untouchable because no administration in search of popular support would tamper with a benefit enjoyed by large segments of the population. The subsidies on fuel consumption were substantially reduced in October 2005 after many years when the change was motivated—and justified—by the finding that 80 percent of this entitlement represented a generous handout to those in the top 60 percent of income distribution. Fuel subsidies increased again in early 2009, arguably with an eye to the upcoming presidential elections.

Decentralization

Under Suharto's administration, Indonesia had one of the most centralized governments among developing nations. Spending at the regional level was highly dependent on transfers of funds from the top level of government through a complex system of direct grants from both the routine and development budgets, complemented by special allocations made at the direction of the president. One legacy of the short-lived Habibie administration in the late 1990s was the transformation of this arrangement into its virtual opposite, one of the most decentralized public-finance systems among the major nations of the world. The basis for this far-reaching reform was laid down in two laws promulgated in 1999—Law 22, on regional government, and Law 25, on the financial balance between the center and the regions. Law 22 did away with the hierarchical relationship between the central government and the provinces and regencies. The most striking feature of the new system, which took effect in January 2001, is that it granted considerable discretionary authority in public finance to the regencies and municipalities, which by that time numbered 353. The provincial level was virtually bypassed. Law 25 enumerates categories of revenue for activities under the direct responsibility of the district government. They include the district's own sources of income through local taxation; so-called equalization grants, which replaced transfers from Jakarta; and borrowing at home and abroad. The equalization grants contain a general fund allocation, a special fund allocation, and provisions for revenue sharing in the exploitation of natural resources within the borders of the district. This revenue sharing ranges from 15 percent of revenues for oil exploitation and 30 percent for natural gas, up to 80 percent for logging, fisheries, and non-oil, non-gas mining. This provision meant that certain districts located in resource-rich jurisdictions such as the Special Region of Aceh (called Nanggroe Aceh Darussalam, 1999–2009) and the provinces of Kalimantan Timur and Papua quickly started to receive substantially more income than previously.

The decentralization reform enjoyed considerable popular support from the outset. It was generally regarded as having gotten off to a strong start, but the authorities were criticized for proceeding too hastily. Rules for allocating funding preceded a precise definition of tasks under district responsibility, and the distinctions among the various levels of government remained blurred by liberal use of the term region (*daerah*) in legislation and official instructions. One direct consequence of the reform was the reassignment of 1.9 million civil servants from the central government to local authorities, without these individuals actually having to move physically. The transfer affected almost 50 percent of all civil servants in Indonesia, including large numbers of teachers and health-care workers. By 2005 two out of three civil servants in Indonesia were working for a local government.

The overall allocation of budgetary expenditures to the central and local governments stabilized at a ratio of 70 percent to 30 percent during the five years immediately following the decentralization reform. This division implies that as much as 6 to 7 percent of GDP was actually being transferred annually by the central government to be spent by a local authority. Intergovernmental transfers form the chief source of income for local governments, accounting for an average of 76 percent of disposable funds at the local level. Moreover, bypassing the provincial level of government, in accordance with the 1999 legislation, led to the expenditure of 75 percent of decentralized revenue

Rambutan fruit seller, Jakarta
Courtesy of Anastasia Riehl

according to the priorities of district administrative heads or regents (*bupati*) in rural regencies and mayors in the municipalities. The direct link between budget authority and locally elected officials can have a positive impact in terms of enhancing democracy, but it may equally well offer enlarged opportunities for corruption. Subsequent revisions to decentralization legislation restored some authority to provincial governments.

Monetary and Exchange-Rate Policy

Bank Indonesia, the nation's central bank, was founded in 1953 as the successor to the Java Bank, which had been nationalized two years earlier. Bank Indonesia has since then been supervised by a monetary board chaired by the minister of finance, which has made it difficult for the central bank to pursue monetary policies independently of the current administration. Although this arrangement remained unchanged in 2008, legislation in 1999 had strengthened the position of the governor of Bank Indonesia vis-à-vis the government, notably by precluding dismissal unless criminal charges were raised. The bank's major tasks are regulating the money supply, setting the exchange-rate policy, and supervising the financial sector. A chief instrument for monetary policy was established in 1984 when Bank Indonesia started issuing its own debt in the form of certificates, Sertifikat Bank Indonesia (SBIs). Because commercial banks have been encouraged to invest short-term funds in SBIs, Bank Indonesia has been able to influence the volume of bank reserves by buying and selling SBIs. Bank Indonesia also has supported the development of other privately issued short-term debt instruments. A sophisticated market in short-term securities has offered banks a tool for more flexible management of their total assets and has encouraged them to hold short-term funds in rupiah rather than in international currency deposits, which had become the practice in the 1970s and early 1980s. Because the Indonesian government maintained a balanced budget, no securities were made available until crisis management required financing by means of large-scale issuing of government bonds.

Very high inflation was a major problem during the final years of the Sukarno administration, when budget deficits were increasingly financed by Bank Indonesia in compliance with instructions from the monetary board but in flagrant violation of the bank's own charter, which limited central bank credit to 20 percent of gold and foreign-exchange reserves. The Suharto government curbed inflation, reducing it from about 900 percent in 1966 to 9 percent by 1970. When oil revenues surged in 1974, the central bank found itself, in essence, printing rupiah currency in exchange for oil revenues denominated in U.S. dollars. Bank credit increased precipitously once the currency was deposited in domestic banks. Inflation shot to more than 40 percent annually, and Bank Indonesia responded by imposing direct controls on the volume of credit issued by individual banks, a policy that made it harder for private banks to compete with the favored state banks. By 1978 inflation had come down to less than 10 percent per year, but four years of double-digit increases had seriously undermined the competitiveness of Indonesia's exports.

The liberalization of the financial sector was accompanied by measures to contain inflationary pressures, such as imposing high rates of interest on domestic bank credit. Bank Indonesia also intervened directly by controlling the availability of SBIs. On two occasions, in late 1987 and early 1991, the central bank required state-owned corporations to withdraw large sums from their deposits, Rp800 billion (about US$486 million) in 1987 and Rp8 trillion (about US$4.1 billion) in 1991, to purchase SBIs, which deprived banks of a major source of funds to be used for speculative purposes. As a result, inflation in Indonesia continued at an average of about 14 percent per year throughout the 1980s, which was low by the standards of many developing countries but above that of many of Indonesia's industrialized trading partners. Rapid growth in the early and mid-1990s reintroduced inflationary pressures, but cautious monetary policies resulted in a relatively moderate rate of inflation averaging 9 percent per year during the 1991–96 period.

The immediate inflationary impact of the Asian financial crisis severely eroded purchasing power, bringing whole segments of the economy to a virtual standstill and pushing millions of people from just above to below the poverty line (see Employment and Income, this ch.). Controlling inflation became a top priority during the subsequent economic recovery. In 2002 the IMF assumed that 9 to 11 percent per year would be a manageable rate of inflation. In budgetary planning for 2001–3, the government projected a lower rate, 8 to 9 percent, which was generally sustained despite a spike to 15 percent in early 2002. By 2004 restrictive monetary policies had reduced the rate of inflation to 5 percent annually, and in its planning for 2005 and 2006 the government chose less-than-ambitious targets in the range of 6 to 8 percent. Actual inflation in 2007 amounted to 6.6 percent, and, for 2008, the central bank targeted 4 to 6 percent inflation.

Bank Indonesia also managed the exchange rate between the rupiah and foreign currencies, a responsibility that sometimes conflicted with its tasks of regulating the volume of bank credit and the size of the base money supply. After floating the rupiah from 1966 to 1971, Bank Indonesia pegged the exchange rate at Rp415 per US$1. To maintain this exchange rate, the central bank had to buy or sell as much foreign currency as necessary at the predetermined rate. Three major devaluations occurred in the following years. Bank Indonesia set new rates of exchange at, respectively, Rp625 per dollar in 1978, Rp970 per dollar in 1983, and Rp1,641 per dollar in 1986. The main objective was to address the eroding competitiveness of non-oil exports resulting from Indonesia's rate of inflation being higher than the rate in the home countries of important buyers of Indonesian manufactured products. The exchange-rate strategy became an important instrument supporting the industrialization policy to reduce dependence on oil and natural gas.

From the late 1980s onward, the rupiah was effectively, if not officially, pegged to the U.S. dollar in such a way that it was allowed to depreciate in a smooth but highly predictable manner at a rate slightly above 5 percent per year. The nominal value of the rupiah fell by 37 percent against the dollar, from Rp1,840 per dollar in 1990 to Rp2,900 per dollar in mid-1997. Then came the financial crisis, and with it the urgent need to control the free fall of the rupiah and mitigate the extreme short-run fluctuations in the exchange rate. By agreement with the IMF, Indonesia became committed to a floating exchange rate under which the value of the currency would be determined exclusively by market forces. This commitment was retained even after direct involvement by the IMF in Indonesian economic policy came to a conclusion, thus precluding pursuit of an active exchange-rate policy by Bank Indonesia. Assumptions underlying the central government budget during the period of economic recovery in the first years of the twenty-first century stayed within a narrow range, from Rp8,600 per dollar in 2004 to Rp9,900 per dollar in 2006. The value of the currency averaged Rp8,875 per dollar during the period 2002–4, stabilized at Rp9,250 per dollar in August 2007, but increased to Rp12,000 during the emerging world economic crisis in 2008.

Market interventions with SBIs served to secure a stable increase in the base money supply of about 7 percent per year, which was, incidentally, also the target that the IMF had recommended in the wake of the financial crisis. Continuous monetary expansion was accompanied by an increase in credits made available by commercial banks. In 2000 total outstanding commercial credit reached Rp720 trillion (US$86 billion), 140 percent above the level of March 1997, and by 2004 it amounted to Rp965 trillion (US$110 billion). The annual increase during the intervening period had been 8.5 percent, which may be contrasted with the 26.0 percent increase in banking credit in FY 1996 alone. Stability returned to monetary and exchange-rate developments as soon as the recovery from the crisis gained momentum.

Indonesia in the Global Economy

The Changing Nature of Trade and Aid

Indonesia is highly integrated into the global economy, and exports are vital to its economic development. By the 1980s, exports accounted for about 25 percent of GDP, and this proportion has stayed remarkably stable over time. In 2004 total foreign exports amounted to Rp625,295 trillion (US$71.6 billion), corresponding to 27 percent of GDP, and in 2007 the total value of exports approached Rp1,100,000 trillion (US$114 billion), or about 31 percent of GDP. Expressed in current market prices, export revenues rose threefold between 1980 and 2004. During the next several years, 2004–7, exports increased by an average of 17 percent per year. The traditional range of exports, consisting almost exclusively of oil, natural gas, and other primary products, has broadened to include manufactured goods. The most vital distinction in the structure of exports refers to the division between oil and natural gas on the one hand and all other products on the other. The share of oil and natural gas reached nearly 80 percent around 1980 but fell to about 50 percent in the late 1980s, 32 percent in the early 1990s, and 22 percent by 1997. After the 1990s, scarcely more than 20 percent of Indonesia's export revenues originated from deliveries of oil and natural gas.

The export sector's traditional reliance on the country's rich natural resources made the economy vulnerable to the vicissitudes of changing world prices for these products. The need to shift to manufactured exports became especially urgent when world oil prices fell sharply in the mid-1980s. This shift having been successfully accomplished, Indonesia now faces increasingly stiff competition from other low-cost producers of manufactured goods, especially China. Initially, plywood was the most important manufactured export, its production having been facilitated by a total ban on log exports in the early 1980s. However, by the late 1990s plywood accounted for only 10 percent of manufacturing exports, and textiles, in particular garments, and electrical appliances were both of greater importance, whereas paper products, footwear, and chemical goods each equaled plywood among manufactured exports. In 2007 the total value of manufactured exports amounted to US$76 billion, with three categories of products accounting for 28 percent of this total: textiles at 13 percent and electrical goods and wood products at 7 and 8 percent each. Although manufactured exports have come to dominate Indonesian deliveries to the world market, the emphasis has remained on labor-intensive production. An estimate from just before the 1997–98 financial crisis suggested that only 15 percent of Indonesia's manufactured exports originated from industries characterized by an intensive use of technology and know-how. Access to local raw materials and cheap labor have remained the main sources of competitiveness for Indonesian manufactured exports in world markets.

Steady growth in non-oil exports has helped Indonesia to finance imports, in particular inputs needed for manufacturing production for exports. During the 1980s and early 1990s, imports increased more rapidly than exports, but this trend reversed radically during the financial crisis as the depreciated Indonesian currency effectively reduced the volume of purchases from abroad. As a result, the surplus on the commodity balance of trade improved from about 20 percent of total export earnings in the first half of the 1990s to 47 percent in 1999, only to stabilize at a slightly lower level in the first years of the twenty-first century. On the eve of the crisis, imports consisted of about 71 percent raw materials and intermediate goods, 22 percent capital goods, and only 7 percent consumer goods. This pattern has remained unchanged, reflecting an increasing dependence for export production on foreign imports as well as far-reaching import substitution.

The positive trade balance notwithstanding, Indonesia has often suffered from a deficit on the current account because of increasing service costs and interest payments on outstanding foreign debt. The deficit on the current account worsened from scarcely more than US$1 billion in 1989 to almost US$8 billion in 1996. Driven by rapidly declining imports, the huge improvement in the balance of trade during the financial crisis turned the deficit on the current account into a surplus. The surplus on the current account grew to US$5.9 billion in 2000 and stayed at that level until 2003, when outflows began to increase as a result of economic recovery. One consequence of the crisis for the surplus on the current account was that international reserves were not depleted but actually increased between 1996 and 2000. A key factor in the state of Indonesia's capital account has been the inflows and outflows of foreign direct investment.

Export growth has also contributed to Indonesia's ability to borrow from world financial markets and to obtain foreign aid. Public debt grew in particular during the 1980s, whereas private debt expanded dramatically during the 1990s, providing a major cause of the financial crisis that struck Indonesia in 1997–98. Increasing foreign indebtedness as a means of combating the crisis and staging an economic recovery implied a heavy burden on the government budget in the early twenty-first century. Successive repayments reduced the total outstanding foreign debt from almost US$150 billion in 2001 to US$113 billion by 2004. The reduction applied fully to private indebtedness, whereas the public foreign debt increased from US$69 billion in 2001 to US$80 billion in 2004. These trends reversed after 2004, as private debt increased by US$35 billion in the face of a decline in public debt to US$69 billion. As a result, Indonesia's total foreign indebtedness amounted to US$137 billion in December 2007.

Multilateral aid to Indonesia has traditionally been an area of international interest, particularly on the part of the Netherlands, Indonesia's former colonial ruler. Starting in 1967, the bulk of Indonesia's multilateral aid was coordinated by a consortium of foreign governments and international financial organizations, the Inter-Governmental Group on Indonesia (IGGI—see Glossary). The IGGI met annually under Dutch leadership, although aid from the Netherlands accounted for an ever-smaller proportion of the total. The Netherlands suspended aid to Indonesia following the shootings by the Indonesian army of between 50 and 270 demonstrators in Dili, Timor Timur Province, in November 1991; in turn, in March 1992 the Indonesian government said it would henceforth refuse all Dutch aid. The IGGI was replaced by the Consultative Group on Indonesia (CGI), formed on the initiative of the World Bank and chaired by Japan, Indonesia's single largest aid donor. The CGI was instrumental in facilitating international debt restructuring during the Asian financial crisis. The volume of annual commitments of assistance declined gradually from a peak of US$8 billion during the crisis to a stable level of US$3 billion during the period 2002–4. An additional US$5.1 billion for tsunami relief reached Indonesia in 2005 (see Volcanos and Earthquakes, ch. 2).

Principal Trade Relationships

Indonesia's trading partners have traditionally included numerous countries throughout the world. At the end of the twentieth century, most imports came from just three places: the European Union (EU; 26 percent), Japan (18 percent), and the United States (18 percent). Member countries of the Association of Southeast Asian Nations (ASEAN—see Glossary) supplied only 10 percent. In the twenty-first century, China has also emerged as a major supplier of imports to Indonesia. The growth in Indonesia's production of manufactured products has contributed to a diversification of export markets, especially in Asia. In 2006 more than 50 percent of all exports went to Asian trading partners, in particular to Japan, the ASEAN states, China and India, whereas the United States and the EU between them purchased 27 percent of all Indonesian exports. Oil and liquefied natural gas (LNG), however, continued to be supplied to a rather limited number of customers. In the late 1990s, Japan bought one-third of Indonesia's oil and two-thirds of its LNG; South Korea and Taiwan also figured prominently among customers for Indonesian LNG. Five leading trading partners, China, Japan, Malaysia, Singapore, and the United States, accounted for more than 50 percent of all non-oil and natural gas exports in 2004. The United States and Japan became key markets as the development of manufacturing export production in Indonesia gained momentum, while Singapore retained its traditional role as an intermediary in trade with third countries. Rapid increases in non-oil, non-gas exports to China and ASEAN neighbors such as Malaysia signified new trends in Indonesian trade.

Diplomatic relations with China were reestablished in 1991, and exports to that country doubled over the next six years (see Relations with East Asia, ch. 4). Bilateral trade declined during the 1997–98 crisis but recovered by 2000. Indonesian imports from China increased by more than 60 percent in the year 2000 alone, reflecting a tendency among Indonesian importers to replace expensive imports from Japan with cheaper goods from China. Bilateral trade experienced a rapid expansion starting in 2002, and already by 2005 the value of Indonesian exports to China was 150 percent above the 1997 level. The expansion of Indonesian imports from China was even more spectacular. In 2005 their level was almost four times that of 1997. The shift from a trading relationship based on Indonesian exports to one based on Indonesian imports in bilateral trade with China testified to the dynamic nature of international commerce in the region.

ASEAN was founded in 1967 to promote regional stability, economic development, and cultural exchange in Southeast Asia. Its original members were Indonesia, Malaysia, the Philippines, Singapore, and Thailand; starting in the mid-1980s, Brunei, Burma (Myanmar), Cambodia, Laos, and Vietnam also joined. Not until the late 1970s did the ASEAN states give serious attention to matters of economic integration, such as the establishment of joint industrial projects. In January 1993, preparations began for an ASEAN Free Trade Area (AFTA). Originally scheduled for 2008, implementation was moved forward to 2002, and by 2006 most import tariffs in intra-ASEAN trade were 2 percent or less. Intra-ASEAN exports doubled between 2002 and 2006, rising from US$ 9.9 billion to US$ 18.5 billion. Four priority areas were designated for further rapid expansion: electronics, agro-processing, rubber-based products, and transport vehicles, all of which were important branches of manufacturing for Indonesia. In 2003 Bank Indonesia predicted that full implementation of AFTA would increase competition and reduce prices in the domestic market while offering new opportunities for Indonesian exporters. Confidence in the growth potential of both large and small enterprises was also voiced in 2006 by then ASEAN secretary general Ong Keng Yong. The association's stated ultimate goal is to establish an ASEAN Economic Community by 2015.

Employment and Income

The world's fourth most populous nation, Indonesia had an estimated 240.3 million inhabitants in 2009, 60 percent of whom lived in Java, 21 percent in Sumatra, and another 12 percent in Kalimantan and Sulawesi taken together. The increase in population over the preceding 18 years alone amounted to almost 50 million people. At least 60 percent of all persons 15 years of age and older were gainfully employed. The labor force grew from 75 million in 1988 to 86 million in 1993 and 106 million in 2006, or 117 million when including those who were economically active but not at work. The rapid growth reflected both the increase in the working-age population, estimated at 2.7 percent per year, and an increasing rate of economic participation by women. It has been a major challenge for the Indonesian economy to offer employment to such large numbers of people entering the labor market each year.

Structural change in the Indonesian economy has had fundamental repercussions for employment patterns and especially the composition of national income. In 1985 agriculture contributed only 25 percent of GDP but provided employment for 53 percent of the labor force. In addition to the agricultural employment in the 1980s, 11 percent of the labor force worked in manufacturing, 18 percent in trading, 14 percent in finance and other services, and 4 percent in construction. A milestone was reached around 1990 when agriculture's share of employment fell below 50 percent, and Indonesia was no longer a predominantly agrarian economy. Further expansion of employment outside agriculture, particularly in services, reduced the agricultural proportion of the labor force to 43 percent by 1997. Modernization of employment patterns came to a halt in the wake of the 1997–98 financial crisis; for instance, the share of the workforce in agriculture was 44 percent in 2005, up a point from 1997. There has been a tendency for the labor force in the primary sector, comprising agriculture, forestry, and fisheries, to increase somewhat in relative terms at the expense of manufacturing and services. The interruption of the trend toward restructuring of the economy away from the traditional predominance of the primary sector in employment patterns is one of the most serious consequences of the financial crisis.

In a developing country such as Indonesia, official open unemployment is a statistic with much less meaning than in an industrial economy. Registration as being unemployed carries no benefits, and those laid off from jobs in the formal sector are likely to work fewer hours or resort to some kind of pursuit in the informal sector. Open unemployment was registered at only 3 percent of the labor force around 1990, but this figure ignored much underemployment. Official unemployment increased only marginally even during the worst year of the financial crisis, from 4.7 percent in 1997 to 5.5 percent in 1998. Supplementary data offer a different impression. During the first crisis year alone, the number of workers declined 15 percent in medium-sized and large manufacturing enterprises and 20 percent in small manufacturing firms and cottage industries. More than 300,000 workers in the textiles and garment industry had already lost their jobs by March 1998. The International Labour Organization (ILO) estimated conservatively that 7 percent of the Indonesian labor force would be out of work by the end of 1998. The informal sector in rural areas had to absorb more than 3 million workers who had been laid off in the cities.

In 2001 the Central Statistical Office (BPS) tried to obtain a better representation of actual unemployment by applying a wider definition that included discouraged workers. As a result, the official unemployment figures, 5.8 percent in 2000 and 6.5 percent in 2004, were adjusted upward to 8.1 percent and 10.1 percent, respectively. The rate of unemployment stayed at a stubbornly high level after the initial recovery from the financial crisis, and in late 2004 the newly installed administration of Susilo Bambang Yudhoyono pledged to reduce official open unemployment by half by 2009. However, in 2007 officially registered unemployment was still as high as 9.1 percent.

The introduction of minimum-wage legislation in 1992 appeared contradictory to the prevailing mode of deregulation at the time. The Indonesian government took this measure partly in response to criticism from the ILO and the American Federation of Labor about poor working conditions in Indonesian manufacturing. Implementation of this policy led to considerable regional differences in nominal daily wage rates, which ranged in 1995 from Rp3,100 (about US$1.38) in Sulawesi Selatan Province to Rp4,600 (about US$2.04) in Jawa Barat Province. Real wage rates, after correction for inflation, increased by more than 200 percent in Jawa Barat and Jawa Tengah provinces but by less than 100 percent in the capital, Jakarta, and in Sumatera Utara Province. Earnings outside the industrial sector were typically lower, with the exception of services such as finance and banking.

The financial crisis, with its concomitant rapid inflation, brought a sharp dip in real minimum wages in 1998 and 1999; only in 2001 was the pre-crisis level of the real minimum-wage rate restored. Yet, this was the outcome of political and administrative change rather than a sign of economic recovery. The decentralization reform that became effective in January 2001 vested the power to set minimum-wage rates with provincial authorities, which caused an immediate increase in the minimum-wage rate in many provinces. Jakarta led the way with a wage hike of 38 percent, followed by adjacent districts in Jawa Barat Province. Other centers of labor-intensive manufacturing industry limited increases to 20 percent. After 2001 real minimum-wage rates also continued to rise, but the pace of increase remained smooth and moderate. In 2004 the highest nominal wages were paid in the greater Jakarta metropolitan area—then known as Jabotabek (for the four adjacent population centers of Jakarta, Bogor, Tangerang, and Bekasi), now known as Jabodetabek to include Depok—where rates were on average 72 percent higher than in the city of Surabaya in Jawa Timur Province, or 144 percent higher than in the Special Region of Yogyakarta in central Java. Workers in non-oil mining were likely to earn three times as much as employees in highly labor-intensive lines of manufacturing production such as textiles.

Chili vendors, Karambosan market, Sulawesi Utara Province
Courtesy Anastasia Riehl

Effective enforcement of minimum-wage rates was difficult from the start. Attempts by employers to circumvent the legislation had already become a frequent cause of labor unrest in the mid-1990s. The problem of enforcement survived the collapse of the Suharto regime. Statistics for 2000 show that only 43 percent of surveyed employees actually received more than the minimum wage. The score was especially bad for female workers, 75 percent of whom received less than the minimum wage. Rural workers were also disadvantaged, and wages in manufacturing were found to be seriously lagging behind those in the services sector.

Labor unrest increased significantly in the 1990s, although there was only one officially sanctioned trade organization, the All-Indonesian Workers' Union (SPSI), which was converted in 1995 into the All-Indonesian Workers' Union Federation (FSPSI). Activism was furthered by the rise of two rival independent unions. One, the Indonesian Prosperous Workers' Union (SBSI), was founded in 1992 and run by Muchtar Pakpahan, who was exceptionally outspoken in his criticism of the government. Confrontations between the Suharto administration and the SBSI culminated in a rising number of strikes during the mid-1990s, and the imprisonment of Pakpahan. Frequent violent strikes accompanied the financial crisis and other events leading up to the change of government during 1997–98. Labor unrest subsided somewhat in 1999 but flared up again in 2000. That year there were 173 major strikes—compared with 125 in 1999—involving more than 60,000 workers. Demands for higher wages were the main reason for trade-union action, but other grievances, such as dismissals, meager food provisions, the cost of transportation, and failure to pay out accrued social-security benefits, were other causes. Most strikes were in the labor-intensive branches of manufacturing. Trade unionism grew in the more liberal political climate prevailing immediately after the fall of the Suharto regime. In 2001 some 36 trade unions were operating on a national level, but many more restricted themselves to individual regions or even districts. Several unions, including the SBSI and FSPSI, maintained close links with political parties, which had also mushroomed in the wake of reformism after 1998. Some trade unions expressed a strong Muslim identity. These developments signified a belated ideological awakening within organized labor in Indonesia.

Observers saw an impressive increase in per-capita income in Indonesia up to 1997. The nominal average income increased 120 percent between 1991 and 1996. But the financial crisis had a severe impact on incomes, reducing the real per-capita level 13 percent between 1997 and 1999 alone, and it was well into the first years of the twenty-first century before Indonesians' per-capita GDP returned to the 1997 level. However, doubts have frequently been voiced about the unequal distribution of income, especially in light of the conspicuous consumption by wealthy Chinese Indonesians and members of the Suharto family. Studies have shown the Gini coefficient, which measures the degree of inequality in income distribution, to have remained stubbornly constant over time. The coefficient fell slightly during the first two decades of the Suharto era, from 0.35 in the mid-1960s to 0.32 in the late 1980s, but rose to 0.34 in the mid-1990s and

0.37 during the financial crisis. Indonesia's long-run stability on the Gini index (see Glossary) may be interpreted both as an achievement by government policies, in the sense that inequality did not get worse, and as a failure, in the sense that rapid growth should have resulted in relatively more gains accruing to low-income groups rather than sustaining existing discrepancies in income levels.

Reduction of poverty was invariably listed as one of the major achievements of the Suharto government. The BPS defined an official poverty line on the basis of the expenditure needed to maintain a daily intake of 2,100 calories and to meet other basic needs. The proportion of Indonesians living below that line declined from 40 percent in 1976 to 17 percent in 1987 and to 11 percent by 1996. However, it must be noted that the official criteria were set at far lower levels than in neighboring countries in Southeast Asia, and that considerable regional differences were concealed by the nationwide averages. The incidence of poverty was higher in rural areas than in cities, and the 11 percent registered as poor in 1996 corresponded to more than 22 million people. The full onslaught of the economic crisis in 1998 occasioned a number of projections about the resulting increase in poverty. In August and September 1998, a team from the ILO and the United Nations Development Programme (UNDP) predicted that a staggering 48 percent of the Indonesian population, 94 million people, would be counted as poor by the end of the year, and that this number was likely to continue to increase in 1999. A few months later, in December 1998, revised estimates by BPS produced a figure of about 20 percent, still high in that it corresponded to 40 million people, but nonetheless closer to reality than the alarming ILO–UNDP forecast.

The recovery of the Indonesian economy in the early years of the twenty-first century was slow and at best partial. As a result, the incidence of poverty declined slowly, from 18.4 percent in 2001 to 16.7 percent in 2004. These figures again conceal much differentiation by region. Rural areas were especially severely struck by poverty. There the incidence by official measure averaged 20 percent in 2004, against 12 percent for cities. In 2006 the government and observers were alarmed by an unexpected increase in the incidence of poverty in the face of resumed economic growth. Pockets of poverty existed in a number of regions where the economic recovery failed to generate jobs. The poverty rate climbed to 17.8 percent but again reduced, touching 16.6 per cent by 2007.

Agriculture

Indonesia has followed a well-recognized trend among developing nations, in which agriculture's share of GDP has declined over time, even though the sector still provides employment for a large proportion of the labor force. The agricultural sector in Indonesia has remained vital for several reasons. A significant segment of the population lives and works in rural areas, and rice, the chief food crop, is the staple nutrient for most households, urban and rural alike. Adequate supplies of affordable rice are deemed essential to preventing political instability.

The share of agriculture in GDP oscillated around 25 percent throughout the 1970s and early 1980s but then fell sharply, reaching 16 percent by 1995. This trend was temporarily reversed with the financial crisis, with agriculture's contribution reaching almost 20 percent of GDP in 1999. Economic recovery reduced the share of agriculture again; the average remained stable around 16 percent during the first years of the twenty-first century and by U.S. government estimates was about 14.4 percent in 2008—as compared with the Central Statistical Office figure for 2007, of 13.8 percent. Meanwhile, the share of agriculture in the total labor force dropped, too, from more than 50 percent to a little above 40 percent. Within agriculture, food crops have always accounted for the predominant share of output, leaving considerably smaller proportions to tree-crop cultivation, fisheries, and forestry.

Food Crops

A total land area of about 42 million hectares was being cultivated for agricultural purposes in Indonesia around the turn of the twenty-first century. Slightly more than 50 percent was dedicated to food-crop cultivation, both intensive *sawah* (irrigated or wetland) cultivation in Java (8.5 million hectares) and *ladang* (not irrigated) cultivation on other islands (16.0 million hectares; see fig. 8). Estates (large state-owned or private units of production with a high degree of specialization of tasks) accounted for 25 percent of the land in use. Since around 1960, expansion of output in food-crop cultivation has been attained through intensified land use and application of high-yield seed varieties. By 2000 total rice output exceeded 50 million tons per year, largely realized in *sawah* cultivation. *Ladang* cultivation was responsible for most of the non-rice food-crop output, in particular the production of cassava and corn, which together accounted for an annual yield of more than 25 million tons by 2000.

In the 1980s, rice cultivation covered a total of around 10 million hectares, primarily on *sawah* land. About 60 percent was irrigated, which was crucial to the productivity of land when planted with high-yield seed varieties. Output grew at a spectacular rate of 7 percent annually from 1977 to 1982, and by 1985, Indonesia, once the world's single largest importer of rice, was self-sufficient in its most important foodstuff. Annual production grew from about 25 million tons in the late 1970s to some 50 million tons in the mid-1990s, and it then continued at about that level thereafter. The government was intensely involved, both in stabilizing prices for urban consumers and expanding domestic output to achieve national self-sufficiency in rice production. Various government policies included the dissemination of high-yield seed varieties through the government-sponsored Mass Guidance System (Bimas) in agriculture, which also subsidized the use of fertilizer and pesticides and provided rural credit. Moreover, government intervention included control of the domestic rice price through the National Logistical Supply Organization (Bulog). Government investment in irrigation also made a significant contribution. Between 1970 and 1990, about 2.5 million hectares of existing irrigated land were rehabilitated, and irrigation was extended to another 1.2 million hectares.

Expansion of food-crop cultivation slowed in the late 1980s and early 1990s as a result of ecological constraints on the intensification of cropping ratios and lower government investment in irrigation.

Also, markets for agricultural commodities were depressed. Poor harvests in the mid-1990s necessitated a temporary return to rice imports, and the situation during the crisis was aggravated by repeated droughts during 1997–98 caused by El Niño. By the early years of the twenty-first century, it was apparent that the Green Revolution, started in the late 1960s, had run its course in Indonesia, but also that it had had a lasting impact on productivity in food-crop agriculture.

Although rice is by far the most important food crop, cassava and corn have remained major sources of calories for large groups of Indonesians. Corn cultivation is concentrated in Java and Madura, usually on rain-fed land (*tegalan*), and much of the output is generally consumed as a staple food. Both corn and cassava have increased in importance as major supplements to rice. Between 2000 and 2005, production of these two crops increased by 15 and 20 percent, respectively.

Export Crops

Indonesia has a strong tradition of export crops cultivated by estates and smallholders. Java was once the world's third-largest producer of sugarcane, and rubber from Sumatra and Kalimantan provided important non-oil export revenues during the 1950s and 1960s. Sugar no longer is an export crop; in fact, Indonesia now imports sugar. Rubber lost its strong position in the world market to synthetic rubber, and palm oil overtook agricultural exports. By the

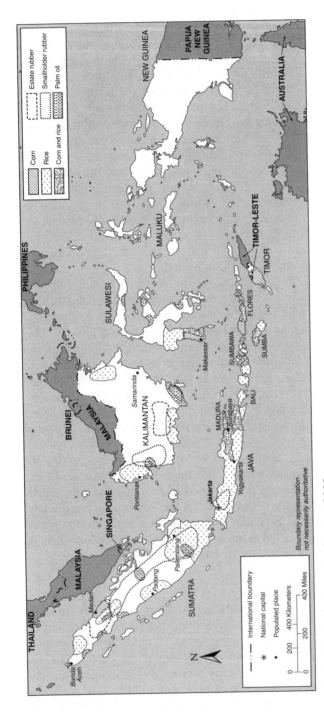

Figure 8. Major Crop Production, 2009

beginning of the twenty-first century, rubber and palm oil accounted for more than 5 million hectares of arable land, with production by smallholders as well as by government-owned estates appropriated in the nationalization of Dutch properties in the late 1950s. Rubber is cultivated on 3 million hectares, of which about 80 percent is land owned by smallholders with holdings of two hectares or less. Smallholder cultivation is concentrated in Sumatra.

Palm-oil estates, primarily in Kalimantan and Sumatra, expanded rapidly, covering 2.2 million hectares by the mid-1990s. The estates represented major investments by leading domestic conglomerates and also increasing investment by estate companies based in Malaysia. In 2005 Indonesia was the world's second-largest producer of palm oil, behind Malaysia, accounting for more than one-third of world output. Palm-oil production in Indonesia climbed from 6.5 million tons in 2000 to 10.3 million tons in 2004, an impressive 58 percent increase. Estates provided the largest part of production, but the contribution of smallholders increased at a faster rate, exceeding one-third by 2004. In 2006 total output amounted to 16 million tons.

Government efforts to transfer new technologies and increase productivity in export-crop cultivation were less successful than they were with food crops. The Nucleus People's Estate (PIR) program, which provided small plots of high-yield tree crops to participating farmers in predetermined locations, was the main government undertaking. One anticipated advantage was the sharing of benefits from centralized technological and managerial assistance. However, only a few cultivators participated, and little success was achieved, especially in rubber cultivation by smallholders. The centralization of facilities, which in turn remained seriously understaffed, allegedly stifled individual initiative.

Other export crops, notably cocoa, coconuts, coffee, and tea, cover far smaller planted areas and contribute only marginally to the aggregate earnings of the overall Indonesian economy. Coconuts are cultivated almost exclusively by smallholders, with production centered in Sulawesi. High prices on the world market secured rising incomes for some local producers even in the midst of the 1997–98 financial crisis. The main source of Indonesian coffee beans has traditionally been the southern Sumatran province of Lampung, where smallholders strongly dominate production. The predominance of smallholders has increased since the late 1990s; in the early twenty-first century, they accounted for at least 95 percent of output. A temporary decline in smallholder production in 2001 was followed by an impressive recovery during 2002. Annual coffee production by smallholders has since remained rather stable, averaging about 660,000 tons. Nevertheless,

Indonesian output has not increased as fast as that of chief rivals in the world market. By 2005 Indonesia not only ranked behind Brazil, Colombia, and Mexico but also had been overtaken by Vietnam.

Livestock

Smallholders own nearly all the livestock in Indonesia; these animals are sources of draft power, manure, meat for home consumption, and, if sold, revenue. The livestock population in Indonesia in the first years of the twenty-first century included 35 million ducks, 21 million goats and sheep, 11 million cows, 7 million pigs, 2.5 million buffalo, and 500,000 horses. Numbering in the hundreds of millions, chickens were the fastest-growing type of commercial livestock, notwithstanding the spread of avian influenza in Indonesia since 2004. Government-sponsored programs to increase productivity through extension services to livestock farmers and the expansion of ranching began operation in the Outer Islands (see Glossary) in the early 1990s.

Fishing and Forestry

Fishing

Fish has traditionally been a main source of animal protein in the average Indonesian diet, being generally far more available than meat. The fishing industry engages more than 2 million households working in Indonesia's large archipelagic sea area, about 50 percent of them in Java and 25 percent in Sumatra (see Geographic Regions, ch. 2). The industry is divided into two widely different branches, marine and inland, of which the latter includes harvesting from open water as well as ponds and aquatic cages. Productivity is far greater in marine fisheries, which employ only 25 percent of the producer households but operate 75 percent of all fishing boats and account for almost 80 percent of total output. Total annual production of fish in Indonesian waters oscillated between 2 million and 3 million tons during the 1980s, reached 4.5 million tons in 1996, and continued to increase, albeit slowly, during the years of crisis. The annual total surpassed 5.6 million tons by 2003. Foreign-owned fishing enterprises, which must be licensed, operate on a much smaller scale than the domestic industry. Fish exports consist primarily of shrimp and tuna for the Japanese market.

Enormous changes have taken place in Indonesian fisheries since around 1980, when the physical possibility of extending catch areas began to be exhausted. The government designated offshore waters as exclusive economic zones closed to fishing, and it banned trawling in the waters surrounding Java and Bali. The frontier of expansion was thus literally closing, and output could increase only by

Planting rice, Banyumas, Jawa Tengah Province
Courtesy Eric Stein
A fishing boat under construction, Madura, Jawa Tengah Province
Courtesy Florence Lamoureux, used with permission
©Center for Southeast Asian Studies, University of Hawai'i

intensification and overfishing. By the mid-1990s, the trawling ban had ceased to be effective, having resulted in numerous incidents in which small-scale Indonesian fishers took matters into their own hands, attacking intruding Thai and Taiwanese trawlers. Mangrove forests all along the eastern coastline of Sumatra have been transformed into shrimp ponds; large fish-catching stakes tended by teenage boys have been put into operation in Sumatran estuaries; and coral reefs off Papua have been severely damaged by the use of cyanide poisoning and fish blasting as harvesting practices. With the biodiversity of Indonesian waters seriously threatened, the government doubled its efforts between 1999 and 2006 to reduce foreign fishing in order to at least reserve the scarce resources for the large domestic industry.

Forestry

Forests cover 110 million hectares, or 57 percent, of Indonesia's land area; two-thirds of the forested area is tropical rain forest in Kalimantan and Papua. Estimates of the rate of depletion reached 1 million hectares per year during the mid-1980s, while targets for reforestation and afforestation were set at 95,000 and 250,000 hectares, respectively. The government revised these targets significantly downward in the late 1980s but increased them again during the 1990s, reaching a combined level of nearly 200,000 hectares by the late 1990s. Official logging output fell by two-thirds during the period 1998–2002, but targets for rehabilitation of forests were reduced even further, being restored to 250,000 hectares in 2003, 339,000 hectares in 2004, and as little as 27,000 hectares by 2005. In 1999 estimates put the extent of endangered forest land at 23.2 million hectares, of which only 1.2 million hectares, or about 5 percent, had been rehabilitated four years later. Forest Watch Indonesia, the Indonesian Forum for Environment, and the Department of Forestry estimated that the rate of deforestation rose to a staggering 4 million hectares per year in 2003. Replenishment of forest resources in Indonesia clearly was lagging far behind both ecological and commercial needs and official targets.

Uncontrolled expansion of logging operations, both legal and illegal, has magnified the ecological issues in Indonesian forestry. The 1970s witnessed a boom in logging concessions, both large-scale and small-scale, whereas a ban on log exports put in place by the government in 1983 fostered the emergence of timber conglomerates. The expansion was fueled by liberal regulation of concessions, extremely low taxation, lax enforcement of reforestation obligations, and widespread corruption. During the 1980s alone, large business groups acquired concessions covering millions of hectares, and the production capacity of Indonesia's 100 or so plywood plants rose eightfold. Together with Malaysia, Indonesia then supplied more than 90 percent of the world's tropical plywood exports. Government promotion of the domestic timber-processing industry was seen as the most immediate threat to Indonesia's forests, but in the long run, settlement by migrants under government-sponsored transmigration programs may have had an even greater impact.

In the 1990s, the gap between total demand from the plywood industry and officially authorized logging output widened, giving a new impetus to illegal logging. In 2001 the total timber harvest in Indonesia amounted to 60 million cubic meters, 50 million of which may have been obtained illegally. Possibly 10 million cubic meters was smuggled abroad, mostly to Malaysia. The Indonesian press and politicians generally have put the blame for illegal logging and timber smuggling on small-scale loggers and Malaysian and ethnic Chinese traders. In the early twenty-first century, they were also held responsible for the haze of smoke that regularly emanated from forests burning in Sumatra and Kalimantan, causing both health hazards and irritation in neighboring countries. Yet such viewpoints easily overlook the far-reaching involvement of Indonesian conglomerates in large-scale logging and plywood production and also divert attention from a long history of forest mismanagement dating back to the boom of the 1970s. This history entered a new phase with the decentralization of responsibility for forest policies in 2001. The delegation of authority had the potential to enhance local involvement in the terms of implementation, but it could equally well prove conducive to further corruption at the local level.

Industry

Indonesia was a late starter in industrialization, lagging behind regional neighbors such as Malaysia and Thailand by at least a decade. This delay may be attributed to the generous revenues from exploiting natural resources that effectively postponed a sense of urgency regarding rapid industrialization. The first phase of import substitution relied on labor-intensive production with a low level of technological sophistication and took place in the 1970s, but its impact on the economy was limited. By the early 1980s, manufacturing not related to oil and gas still accounted for only 11 percent of GDP, and production catered almost exclusively to the domestic market. In the 1980s, a second phase of import substitution shifted the focus to selected key upstream industries with a relatively high level of technological sophistication, including heavy industries such as petroleum refining, steel, and cement, in which state-owned enterprises often dominated.

The next shift in industrial policy favored private investment and an export orientation. Between 1987 and 1997, a rapid industrialization took place that caused a surge in manufacturing exports while raising the share of non-oil and gas manufacturing to 25 percent of GDP, a level sustained into the twenty-first century.

A detailed study by Australian economist Hal Hill of the industrial structure in Indonesia in the 1980s underscored the continuing predominance of oil and natural gas processing and showed the second major industrial activity to be the production of *kretek* cigarettes, a popular Indonesian product made from tobacco blended with cloves. Most of the 13,000 firms Hill surveyed were privately owned, and generally much smaller than the joint ventures with either the government or foreign investors, which employed, on average, six times as many people. Government enterprises controlled all processing of oil and natural gas and were important in other heavy industries, such as basic metals, cement, paper products, fertilizer, and transportation equipment. The growing industries manufacturing for export offered far more employment opportunities than the capital-intensive heavy industries dominated by government and joint ventures with foreign capital.

As the twenty-first century began, the three leading industries outside the oil and gas sector contributed 18 percent of GDP. They were, in descending order of size, food (including beverages and tobacco), transportation equipment (including electrical appliances), and chemical products (including fertilizer and rubber goods). By 2005 there were 20,700 individual large and medium-size manufacturing enterprises employing a total work force of 4.3 million people.

Industrial development has been unevenly distributed across the archipelago (see fig. 9). Significant oil and LNG production occurs mainly in the Special Region of Aceh and in the provinces of Sumatera Selatan, Riau, Jawa Tengah, Kalimantan Timur, and Papua Barat. In western Java, manufacturing outside the oil and gas sector centers on Jabodetabek, and in and around Surabaya, Indonesia's second-largest city, in Jawa Timur Province. Regional forms of specialization in industrial production include batik printing and furniture making in the Special Region of Yogyakarta and in Jepara, as well as *kretek* cigarette manufacturing in Kudus, the latter two in Jawa Tengah Province.

Foreign Inputs

Foreign direct investment (FDI) has particularly targeted the industrial sector since the beginning of Suharto's New Order in 1966. There have been several marked shifts in the climate for FDI over time. The launch of new FDI legislation by the Suharto government in 1967 initiated a liberal period of seven years, after which came 20 years of restrictive policies prompted by nationalist riots during the visit of Japan's prime minister to Jakarta in January 1974. Regulations in effect from 1974 to 1994 precluded majority equity ownership in a firm by a foreign investor in the long run and urged gradual divestment of such holdings. Although these regulations produced a slowdown in investment, the new opportunities for export-oriented manufacturing that opened up in the late 1980s proved highly attractive to foreign investors. A deregulation package announced in June 1994 radically liberalized foreign investment. Foreign majority control of equity again became legal, and divestment rules relaxed. An immediate surge in FDI followed that even persisted far into the 1997–98 financial crisis.

Total realized FDI from 1991 to 2005 exceeded US$75 billion, US$31 billion of which dated to the five years from 1996 to 2000, which included the worst of the financial crisis years. This total can be compared to the aggregate for realized domestic investment during the 1991–2005 period, which was closer to US$215 billion. The United States remained the chief investor in the oil and natural gas sector but played only a marginal role in other branches of industry (see Other Minerals, this ch.). Japan traditionally was the first-ranking foreign investor outside the oil and natural gas industry, but investment from the newly industrializing economies of Hong Kong, Singapore, South Korea, and Taiwan became equally important during the rapid enlargement of incoming FDI in the 1990s. Investors from the EU made only a belated entry, or in some cases reentry, into the Indonesian capital market on the eve of the 1997–98 crisis. It took some time before FDI inflows were restored after the 1997–98 crisis. Total approved FDI rose from US$14 billion in 2003 to US$40 billion by 2007.

Foreign investment has often been crucial to the development of capital-intensive heavy industries. A prime example is the Asahan Hydroelectric and Aluminum Project, a government joint venture with a consortium of Japanese companies. Investment in an aluminum smelter and two hydroelectric power stations, located in Sumatera Utara Province, was worth a total of US$2.2 billion, a welcome change from the relative stagnation that characterized Japanese investment in Indonesia from the mid-1970s to the mid-1990s. In another type of project, the development of special economic zones on the Riau Archipelago islands of Batam, Bintan, and Karimun was entrusted to a consortium consisting of a state-owned Singapore company and two private Indonesian firms, in an agreement signed June 28, 2006. About 80 percent of Indonesia's oil-equipment industry is located on Batam

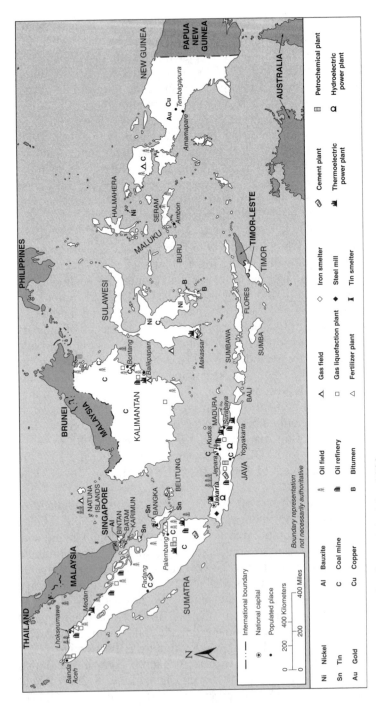

Figure 9. Selected Industrial Activity, 2009

Island, and the project will likely lead to further development of these facilities as well as others involving electronics, chemicals, precision equipment, garments, and other manufactures.

In many industries, foreign firms have supplied technical assistance and arranged for domestic production under licensing agreements without direct equity participation in the domestic firm. For example, domestic Indonesian plants have produced automobiles for about 20 international car makers, foremost among them Toyota, some of whose vehicles are built in Indonesia by Astra International, the country's largest auto manufacturer. Other Japanese companies, as well as South Korean, European, and American firms, assemble their vehicles in Indonesia. The Indonesian automotive industry has grown amid heavily protected markets.

Foreign inputs of a different nature have been applied in high-technology enterprises, particularly ones headed by B. J. Habibie, first as minister of research and technology and later as president. IPTN, established in 1976, assembled helicopters and small fixed-wing aircraft under licenses from French, German, and Spanish firms aided by imported personnel and know-how. Many people considered IPTN a premature leap into advanced technology. Extra-budgetary support and credit privileges stopped at the request of the IMF in January 1998, and operations at IPTN all but ceased subsequently.

Small-Scale Industry

The modern sector of large and medium-sized firms is the main focus of government policy, but small-scale factories employing fewer than 20 workers and cottage industries with up to five workers are far more numerous and crucial in terms of providing employment. Small-scale establishments engage in a wide range of activities from traditional bamboo weaving to metal and leather working. Many of these industries offer part-time employment to rural workers during off-peak seasons. In 1986 small-scale industries employed 3.9 million workers, corresponding to 67 percent of total industrial employment, twice as many as in large and medium-sized firms. Still, this figure reflected a significant decline from the 1970s, when small-scale industry accounted for 86 percent of total industrial employment. By 2004 the number of small-scale enterprises was around 250,000, and together they employed 1.8 million workers, 16 percent of the industrial labor force. The foremost branches were food and beverages, including tobacco, with about 33 percent of these workers, followed by wood and textiles, including footwear, each of which accounted for slightly more than 20 percent. Labor productivity has remained relatively low in small-scale industry. In

2004 value-added contributions in this sector amounted to only Rp12 million (about US$1,342) per worker, as compared with Rp77 million (about US$8,614) in large and medium-sized firms. Fostering small-scale manufacturing is especially important in terms of generating employment, whereas a successive upgrading of technology is more easily achieved by stimulating large and medium-sized units of production.

The considerable productivity gap compared to larger industrial enterprises has slowed in the development of small-scale industry. Differentials of 1:10, or even more, have been reported, with few signs of improvement. The New Order policy of supporting small-scale industry through sponsorship or partnership relationships with bigger firms evolved in the early 1990s and officially launched in 1996, but it had little effect when the financial crisis caused priorities to be shifted elsewhere.

Minerals

Indonesia is the leading producer of petroleum in Southeast Asia and has the world's tenth-largest proven natural gas reserves, 70 percent of which are offshore. It exported 16 percent of the world's total volume of LNG in 2005, but more recent reports indicate that the share is diminishing. It also has significant reserves of other valuable minerals, such as bauxite, coal, copper, gold, nickel, and tin. Much of the nation's industrial development, however, is based on the processing of oil and natural gas. Most mineral production, after some degree of domestic processing, is exported to industrial nations, especially Japan. Some of Indonesia's own mineral-intensive industries, notably, steel and aluminum, rely on imports of raw materials. On balance, however, Indonesia is a net exporter of minerals, in large part because of large-scale exports of LNG.

Petroleum and Natural Gas

Between 1962 and 2009, Indonesia's oil production was formally governed by a quota allocation from the Organization of the Petroleum Exporting Countries (OPEC—see Glossary). In 2005 Indonesian output of crude oil amounted to about 1.1 million barrels per day, corresponding to 3.5 percent of OPEC's total production. This was about 20 percent less than the level of crude output in 1999 and also failed to meet the allocated OPEC quota of 1.4 million barrels per day. In 2006 the crude oil output fell below 1 million barrels per day. Experts attribute the decline in output to a slowdown in investment and declining productivity. With oil exports governed at least in part by long-run contractual agreements and domestic fuel consumption increasing rapidly as Indonesia shook off the effects of the Asian financial crisis, oil imports into the country in the early twenty-first century were rising at a rate considered alarming by outside observers. The increase from 2004 to 2005 amounted to 30 percent, and purchases of foreign oil, in both crude and refined forms, corresponded to 22 percent of total expenditures on imports in the latter year. Exports looked likely to increase with production commencing from the Cepu oil field in Jawa Tengah Province.

Indonesia's oil industry is one of the oldest in the world. The two pioneering oil firms in the then-Dutch colony, Royal Dutch and the British company Shell, exploited reserves in eastern Kalimantan and northern Sumatra starting in the late 1890s. The firms, which in 1907 forged an alliance, Royal Dutch Shell, virtually monopolized the oil sector through joint subsidiaries for production and distribution for several decades in the twentieth century. Two American rivals, Standard-Vacuum Oil Company (Stanvac) and California Texas Oil Company (Caltex), gained prominence shortly after independence in 1945 and survived into the Suharto era; Royal Dutch Shell withdrew from Indonesia in 1965. By the 1990s, five of the six largest foreign oil companies operating in Indonesia were American-owned. For decades, exploitation of Indonesia's oil and gas reserves has taken place under a production-sharing arrangement between the government and foreign oil companies, by which the state-owned enterprise Pertamina disburses the bulk of output, retaining for itself the proceeds from sales in international markets. A smaller part of output serves to recover the costs of investment and operations incurred by the foreign firms. Initially the ratio was 65:35, but the Suharto government negotiated a shift to 85:15. Contract terms for Indonesian oil have been considered among the toughest in the world.

Annual oil production expanded quickly in response to rising world prices during the 1970s, reaching a peak of almost 1.7 million barrels per day in 1977. Prices continued to soar until 1982, when a gradual decline set in, culminating in the sharp drop in world oil prices of 1986. Total production in the late 1980s amounted to around 1.2 million barrels per day. Production then increased, averaging 1.35 million barrels per day over the 1991–99 period. A gradual decline followed, to slightly more than 1 million barrels per day by 2003–5, dropping below that benchmark in early 2006. It seemed probable that Indonesia might become a net importer of crude oil, which indeed occurred temporarily in 2008, and since January 2009 Indonesia has suspended its membership in OPEC.

By the 1990s, Pertamina was operating eight large oil refineries, in Sumatra, Kalimantan, and Java. Major investments negotiated in the first years of the twenty-first century involved the new exploitation of offshore oil reserves in Jawa Timur and Kalimantan Timur, as well as the construction of long pipelines connecting southern Sumatra, Java, and eastern Kalimantan. The Indonesian government continues to subsidize domestic fuel prices at well below international market prices.

Natural gas fields exist in the Special Region of Aceh, the Natuna Islands in Kepulauan Riau Province, and in Kalimantan Timur and Papua Barat provinces. After conversion to LNG—a refrigeration process that reduces it to 1/600th of its volume—the gas is exported primarily to Japan, South Korea, and Taiwan, and increasingly to China. Conversion facilities were constructed in the late 1970s at Lhokseumawe (in Aceh) and Bontang (in Kalimantan Timur) and, in the late 2000s, in Bintuni Bay (in Papua Barat). The total capacity of these plants reached 23 million tons by 1990. Continued expansion brought the total to a peak of 32 million tons in 1999, and by the beginning of the twenty-first century the level of output had stabilized at an annual average of 27.5 million tons. Indonesia supplies as much as 15 percent of the natural gas produced by OPEC members.

Most output goes to liquefying plants for export, although a growing proportion is needed for domestic consumption, especially of fertilizer, the production of which requires that natural gas be processed into ammonia and urea. Growing domestic and export demand have encouraged the development of the gas field in the Natuna Islands in the South China Sea and the Tangguh gas field in Bintuni Bay.

Other Minerals

The New Order government made efforts to rejuvenate the coal industry, mainly located in the provinces of Sumatera Barat, Sumatera Selatan, and Kalimantan Timur, so as to encourage coal use by, for example, cement and electric-power plants. Joint ventures between the state and foreign investors have resulted in a steady increase in production. Output exceeded 50 million tons in 1997 and climbed to more than 100 million tons in 2002.

Another extractive industry dating from the colonial period is tin mining, based on the islands of Bangka and Belitung (Bangka-Belitung Province) in the Java Sea off the southeastern coast of Sumatra. Along with Malaysia and Bolivia, Indonesia is one of the world's top-three producers of tin. Production was fully controlled by the government starting in the late 1950s, but it stagnated in the early Suharto period,

Freeport-McMoRan's Grasberg copper and gold mine, Papua Province
A bulk carrier ship at Timika, upriver from the seaport of Amamapare
Courtesy Freeport-McMoRan

with output falling below 30 million tons annually throughout most of the 1980s. A gradual increase followed in the 1990s as a result of new investment in production capacity, and by 2000 Indonesia was producing 50 million tons per year. Rising tin prices on the world market caused a further increase by 2006 to a level in excess of 81 million tons.

Another postindependence development in the mineral industry was nickel mining in Sulawesi Tenggara Province, where a Canadian investor entered into a joint venture with the government. In the 1980s, Indonesia emerged as one of the world's top-five producers of nickel. Capacity increased to 2.5 million tons per year in the early 1990s and substantially enlarged during the first couple of years of the twenty-first century, nearing a level of 4.4 million tons by 2003.

One of the world's most spectacular mines is the huge P. T. Freeport-Indonesia copper and gold mine, located atop Ertsberg Mountain near Tembagapura, Papua Province. Since the beginning of the Suharto period, the mine has been run by a joint venture with the U.S.-based Freeport-McMoRan Copper and Gold. The ore is transported by pipeline 96 kilometers down the mountain slopes and through the rain forest to Freeport's port of Amamapare for export. A second mine, on nearby Grasberg Mountain, came online in the early 1990s. Both Ertsberg and Grasberg are north of the city of Tembagapura. Much attention has been given in the news media to the environmental degradation resulting from this kind of open-cast mining and also to confrontations between the American enterprise—protected by the Indonesian military—and the local Papua population concerning land use and the exploitation of the region's natural resources. Given its participation in the equity of the Freeport subsidiary, the Indonesian government has always had high profits at stake. Total copper production has risen rapidly, climbing to more than 1 million tons in 1994, reaching 2.5 million tons per year in the late 1990s, and approaching 4 million tons per year by 2002. In 2007, however, total output fell below 3 million tons.

Other Indonesian mineral products also are important. They include gold, mainly extracted as a by-product at the Freeport copper mines, and bauxite found on Bintan Island in Kepulauan Riau Province, used in the domestic production of aluminum.

Services and Infrastructure

In the first years of the twenty-first century, service industries provided jobs for about 40 million Indonesians, corresponding to 39 percent of the total labor force, a proportion that had risen only marginally since the 1990s. About 50 percent of these jobs were in trading, hotels, and restaurants; 33 percent were in a variety of community, social, and personal services; and the remainder, approximately 17 percent, were mostly in the transportation, communications, and storage sectors. Jobs in finance accounted for less than 2 percent of total employment in the services sector. Indonesia also had about 4 million civil servants at all levels of government. A large proportion of work in the services sector, about 70 percent, consisted of informal employment. Petty traders made up the majority of the informal sector, and unincorporated establishments accounted for as much as 90 percent of employment in commerce. Ubiquitous self-employed small-scale traders plied their wares in village markets and on urban streets.

The government's attitude toward the informal sector has often been ambivalent. On the one hand, its importance as a source of employment required support as part of the overall effort to promote *pribumi* entrepreneurship. On the other hand, policies often thwarted informal-sector activities. For example, the once common *becak* (pedicab) was restricted to small side streets in many urban areas and phased out altogether in Jakarta.

Transportation

An elaborate upgrade of the long-neglected transportation infrastructure began in the 1970s. The physical infrastructure, such as roads, railroads, ports, and airports, was significantly expanded and improved with the aid of burgeoning revenues from oil exports. This process slowed in the 1990s and came to a complete halt during the financial crisis and subsequent recovery. In 2005 attention focused on reconstruction in the Special Region of Aceh after the damage caused by the December 26, 2004, tsunami. Outlays for infrastructure alone in 2005 were estimated at US$660 million. In early 2006, the government announced a new package for infrastructure development at a total cost of US$48 billion during the subsequent five-year period.

Roads

Indonesia had some 437,760 kilometers of roads by 2008, of which 59 percent were paved, and about 60 percent were located in Java, Madura, Bali, and Sumatra (see fig. 10). There are less extensive networks of roads in Sulawesi and Kalimantan, while smaller islands often have just a few roads within or connecting major settlements. About 40,000 kilometers of roads administered by the national and provincial governments were considered to be in good condition; another 35,000 kilometers were in varying stages of repair. About 32 percent of the nation's roads are classified as highways.

The nation's roads and highways are used annually by some 5.5 million passengers cars, 1.2 million buses, 2.9 million trucks, and 28.5 million motorcycles. Motor vehicles increasingly dominate urban transit, and in major cities the policy is to increase the role of larger public buses over that of privately owned, smaller-capacity vehicles such as the nine-seat Opelet microbus and the six-seat Bemo. The formerly ubiquitous *becak* has been largely replaced in the major cities by the *bajaj*, a three-wheeled, multipassenger motorcycle, which itself is losing ground to minibuses and automobiles. In Jakarta the increased use of private vehicles contributes to urban sprawl, ever-greater traffic congestion, and air pollution.

Vehicular congestion and automotive emissions are increasing, particularly in urban areas. Some new toll roads were constructed in the 1990s, such as the one between Jakarta city center and Sukarno-Hatta International Airport to the west and the industrial areas around Cikarang and Cikampek to the east. However, such developments fell far short of keeping up with rapidly expanding demand, and new projects were shelved altogether when the financial crisis struck in 1997, resuming only after several years of recovery. A toll road opened in 2005 significantly reduced travel time between Jakarta and Bandung, the nearest major city to the capital. Newly constructed toll roads connect Semarang and Surakarta (also known as Solo) in Jawa Tengah Province and improve access to Pasuruan in Jawa Timur. Investment in a mass public-transport system in Jakarta lagged behind developments in other Southeast Asian capitals such as Bangkok, Kuala Lumpur, Manila, and Singapore. A system of priority bus lanes introduced in 2005 has offered a temporary solution. In 2004 construction started on an elevated, two-line monorail serving Jakarta's central business district and suburban areas east and west of the city. Completion of the monorail, scheduled for 2007, was delayed with construction barely underway in 2008, and little progress was made thereafter. Administrative hurdles and disputes over land generally are cited as factors that severely slow down investment in the transportation infrastructure in Indonesia.

Railroads

In 2008 Indonesia had 8,529 kilometers of railroad track, all of it owned by the government and operated by the Department of Transport, a gain of more than 30 percent since 2006. About 75 percent of railroad track is located in Java. In 2006 most of the track (5,961 kilometers) was 1.067-meter narrow gauge, 125 kilometers of which was electrified in 2006; the rest (497 kilometers) was 0.750-meter gauge. Although trains are used mostly for passenger transportation, freight haulage has made significant advances, having increased to more than 17 million tons by 2005, a gain of 50 percent over the level of the early 1990s. Rail transportation is especially suited to hauling bulk items such as fertilizer, cement, and coal, and freight has proved more profitable than passenger service. Sumatra accounts for 75 percent of freight handling. In 2007 railroads carried about 175 million passengers, 97 percent of whom boarded trains in Java.

Shipping

Maritime transportation experienced major investments and various reforms in the 1980s after growing increasingly restrictive and bureaucratic during preceding decades. The Indonesian National Shipping Company (Pelni) had been established in 1952 but gained the upper hand in interisland shipping only after the nationalization of the Dutch-owned shipping company in 1959. By 1965 Pelni accounted for 50 percent of tonnage in interisland shipping, but its market share declined sharply despite a virtual monopoly on passenger travel. In 1982 a "gateway policy" was introduced in order to discourage transshipment via Singapore and direct Indonesia's nonbulk exports through four designated deep-sea ports: Tanjung Priok (Jakarta), Tanjung Perak (Surabaya, Jawa Timur Province), Belawan (Medan, Sumatera Utara Province), and Makassar (formerly Ujungpandang, in Sulawesi Selatan Province). The protectionist measures were accompanied by a US$4 billion investment plan launched in 1983 that in particular favored upgrading facilities at the four gateway ports. However, such a gateway policy became irrelevant as exports were increasingly handled by container shipping. By 1987 Indonesia's trade with North America and Europe moved almost exclusively via transshipment in Singapore. In fact, the closing of Indonesian ports to feeder vessels denied Indonesian shippers the benefits of lower freight rates made possible by the cargo consolidation at Singapore. By the late 1980s, the gateway policy had been abandoned.

Total freight volume handled by some 95 commercial Indonesian ports reached a total of 1.2 billion tons by 2004, 75 percent of which went to foreign destinations. The greatest volume passed through ports adjacent to oil refineries: 30 million tons at Dumai, Riau Province, and 22 million tons at Balikpapan, Kalimantan Timur Province. By contrast, the four main ports in Java—Tanjung Priok (Jakarta), Tanjung Perak (Surabaya), Semarang, and Cilacap—were together responsible for just 30 million tons. In addition to major ports, there are more than 30 other significant ports supporting interisland maritime trade throughout the archipelago.

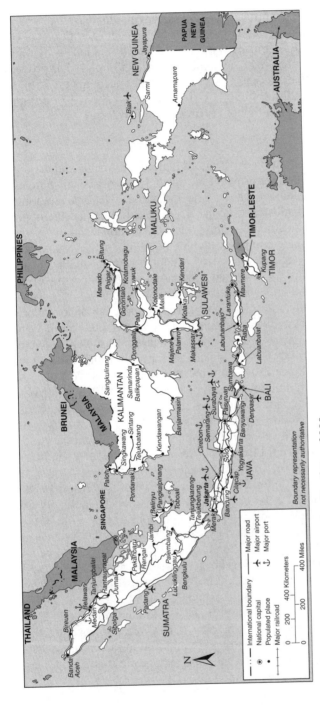

Figure 10. Major Transportation Facilities, 2009

Civil Aviation

Although passenger transportation by sea still exceeded domestic air travel in 2002, with 17 million passengers compared to 12 million, by 2007 civil aviation had become of far greater importance. In that year, 31 million passengers boarded an airplane compared with only 6 million using sea transport. The phenomenal increase in domestic air travel in the early twenty-first century was caused by a proliferation of private budget airlines linking all parts of the archipelago and making air travel affordable for large groups of new customers. By comparison, international arrivals by air increased from 4.3 million passengers in 2000 to 5.3 million in 2004 and then declined to 4.5 million by 2007. Civil aviation is handled by the state-owned national carrier, Garuda Indonesia, which dates from 1949; its subsidiary, Merpati Nusantara Airlines; and a host of private budget airlines, which expanded from three in 2000 to 29 by 2005.

The enlargement of physical infrastructure in the late 1970s and early 1980s included construction of airports throughout the archipelago so that every provincial capital was within hours of Jakarta. The hub, Sukarno-Hatta International Airport at Jakarta, opened in 1985 and was followed by international airports in Denpasar, Bali (Ngurah Rai), Surabaya, Jawa Timur (Juanda), and Medan, Sumatera Utara (Polonia). In 2009 Indonesia had 683 airfields, 164 of which were full-fledged airports, including at least 22 designated as international. There also were 36 heliports. The largest numbers of passengers disembarked at Jakarta, Surabaya, Medan, and Denpasar. Runways at least 3,000 meters long were available in Medan, Padang, Jakarta, Surabaya, Denpasar, and Biak (Papua Barat Province). Besides these major airports, Indonesia is well served by 35 or more significant airports. In this regard, Papua is particularly well served.

Post and Telecommunications

The national postal system is the most important means of communication for the majority of citizens. Postal services are available in all subdistricts, and, by the first years of the twenty-first century, the total number of post offices had increased to 7,000 from fewer than 3,000 in 1980. Having invested early in satellite communications, since the 1980s Indonesia has possessed a sophisticated telecommunications infrastructure. It is supported by the Palapa system of satellites (the name signifies unity). The first two Palapa-A satellites were launched in 1976; they were successfully replaced by Palapa-B satellites in 1987. The first Palapa-C was launched in January 1996, and a second in May 1996, providing coverage not only for the Indonesian archipelago but also for Malaysia, the Philippines, and Singapore. Formerly government-owned, the Palapa system was acquired by a private-sector company, Satelindo, established in 1993. The system includes international direct-dialing facilities and a fully integrated national telephone system. By 2007 there were 17.8 million main telephone lines in use, and the number of mobile phones had reached 81.8 million. Although there are more than 200,000 telephone kiosks, many located in remote areas, recent expansion has almost entirely been in mobile-phone connections. The number of mobile-phone subscribers more than doubled between 2004 and 2007, whereas only 12 million inhabitants, less than 6 percent of the total population, had access to a fixed telephone line. Privatization of the telecommunications sector has facilitated competition and reduced costs for the consumer.

Television and radio traditionally have been dominated by government networks, but private commercial channels have been emerging since the introduction of Hawk Television Indonesia (RCTI) in the Jakarta area in 1988. By early in the new century, the improved communications system had brought television signals to every village in the country, and most Indonesians could choose from 11 channels. In addition to the state-owned Television of the Republic of Indonesia (TVRI), there were 10 national private channels in 2009. The best known are Indosiar, RCTI, Sun Television (SCTV), Metro TV, and Trans 7. Some channels have a specific orientation, for instance, Global TV, which initially offered broadcasts from MTV Indonesia, and Indonesian Educational Television (TPI), which originally carried only educational programming but expanded into quiz programs, sports, reality shows, and other popular entertainment. There also were 54 local television stations in 2009, such as Bali TV in Bali, Jak TV in Jakarta, and Pacific TV in Manado. There were about 3,000 live radio stations throughout Indonesia, but only a few broadcast nationally. Examples include Jakarta News, Sonara, and Prambors in the nation's capital; JJFM, Radio DJ, and Radio Istra in Surabaya; Swaragama in Yogyakarta; and Global FM Bali in Denpasar.

Internet usage has surged since 2000, when there were 2 million users. In 2009 there were nearly 30 million users, a 1,500-percent increase since the start of the twenty-first century. Indonesia has the most Internet users among all other Southeast Asian nations.

Electric Power

As it had been for many years, the government-owned National Electric Company (PLN) was virtually the sole source of electricity for domestic consumption in the early twenty-first century. Capacity had been growing at a rate of 15 percent per year since the 1970s and was especially enhanced by the addition of large coal-fired generating facilities at Paiton, Jawa Timur Province, in the late 1990s. Industry tended to use almost 50 percent of domestically generated power. By 2004 total installed capacity amounted to 22,000 megawatts, and PLN had more than 40,000 employees. There was a slowdown in the expansion of capacity and production during the Asian financial crisis, but starting in 2000 production growth again achieved annual increases of 10 percent or more.

Economic Prospects

The big challenge for Indonesia in the early twenty-first century is to resume rapid economic growth while retaining the achievements of reform and democratization won since the collapse of the New Order government in 1998. This is no easy task. Short-run prospects for major macroeconomic variables looked quite favorable at the end of the first decade of the twenty-first century. Production capacity was being enlarged as a result of new investment, the current account in the balance of payments was improving, the exchange rate had reached a stable level, inflation was slowing, and the government budget deficit had been significantly reduced. An average annual growth rate in the 6 to 6.5 percent range appeared possible, with 6.2 percent specified as the target for 2010. That would be sufficient to reduce poverty and official unemployment to the levels laid down in the long-run economic plans. But such positive prospects were offset by external and internal uncertainties. Continued high oil prices in the world economy could have an adverse effect on the prices of imports in general and put an additional strain on foreign-exchange earnings if Indonesia were indeed to stay a net importer of fuels. Another external source of uncertainty was the excessive dependence of the Indonesian capital market on short-run foreign portfolio investments with an inclination toward high sensitivity to sudden fluctuations in expectations. The most crucial internal source of uncertainty concerned the government's capability to create sound business conditions. Progress was urgently needed in combating corruption and guaranteeing legal security for both foreign and domestic firms. The administration of President Susilo Bambang Yudhoyono, who took office in 2004 and was reelected in 2009, initially enjoyed considerable credit for its determination to tackle these huge problems, but signs of disappointment with the slow pace of progress have been mounting.

The three chief trends in Indonesian economic development since the late 1960s—increasing integration with the world economy, profound structural change, and intense diversification—remain relevant to an assessment of long-term prospects in the twenty-first century. Further integration with the world economy is expected to be strengthened, in particular, following the accelerated implementation of AFTA, which was moved up from 2008 to 2002. Already by 2006 the average tariff rate on imports in the five original ASEAN member states (plus Brunei) for goods covered by the AFTA agreement had declined to less than 2 percent from 12 percent in the early 1990s. The successful reduction of tariffs prompted the formulation of a single market, the ASEAN Economic Community, as an official target to be achieved by 2015. Structural change, notably the shift of resources from the primary to the secondary sector, was temporarily halted by the 1997–98 financial crisis and its aftermath but is likely to gain momentum as rapid economic growth resumes. Further diversification of the economy is likely to occur and may be reinforced when economic effects materialize from the far-reaching decentralization of government authority that became effective in 2001. In the process, however, regional disparities may be widened. It will be a major challenge for the central government to give substance to its motto "Unity in diversity," which has so often been applied to the Indonesian society and economy.

*   *   *

The quality of statistics on the Indonesian economy has improved substantially, and a wide range of publications, often in bilingual format, are available from the BPS Web site in Jakarta (http://www.bps.go.id/). The annual reports issued by the central bank, Bank Indonesia, contain a wealth of information on current economic conditions. In addition, the World Bank prepares an elaborate analysis of the nation's economic prospects each year. The *Far Eastern Economic Review* (Hong Kong, formerly published weekly and now monthly) and daily *Asian Wall Street Journal* (Hong Kong) offer less scholarly but more up-to-date information. Most informative journals published in Indonesia are in the Indonesian language.

The most accessible and up-to-date source in the secondary literature is the *Bulletin of Indonesian Economic Studies*, published by the Indonesia Project at the Australian National University in Canberra. Each issue opens with a "Survey of Recent Developments," a tradition sustained since the journal was founded in the 1960s that provides a succinct overview of the most current data and issues. The Indonesia Project also organizes an annual conference on various aspects of the Indonesian polity and economy, the "Indonesia Update," which has resulted in a series of conference proceedings published under the title "Indonesia Assessment" until 2001 and thereafter as "Indonesia Update Series," available at http://rspas.anu.edu.au/economics/ip/publications.php.

Authoritative surveys of Indonesian economic history include one written by Anne Booth, *The Indonesian Economy in the Nineteenth and Twentieth Centuries: A History of Missed Opportunities*, and another by an international team of scholars, Howard Dick, Vincent J. H. Houben, J. Thomas Lindblad, and Thee Kian Wie, *The Emergence of a National Economy: An Economic History of Indonesia, 1800–2000*. Anne Booth's *The Oil Boom and After: Indonesian Economic Policy and Performance in the Soeharto Era* is a comprehensive summary of economic developments. It replaced an earlier version coedited with Peter McCawley, *The Indonesian Economy During the Soeharto Era*, but was itself superseded by a full-fledged monograph, Hal Hill's *The Indonesian Economy*. The vast literature on the Asian financial crisis includes numerous publications on Indonesia. An early and especially useful summary was offered by Hal Hill in *The Indonesian Economy in Crisis*. Two other monographs on more specific topics were of particular importance to this chapter, one on political economy, Richard Robison's *Indonesia: The Rise of Capital*, and the other on labor relations by Chris Manning, *Indonesian Labour in Transition: An East Asian Success Story*.

Authoritative and durable Web sites posted in Indonesia include those of the Central Statistical Office (http://www.bps.go.id), the National Development Planning Board (http://www.bappenas.go.id), Bank Indonesia (http://www.bi.go.id), and the Capital Investment Coordinating Board (http://www.bkpm.go.id). A highly useful nongovernmental documentation center is the Centre for Strategic and International Studies in Jakarta (http://www.csis.or.id); the best university collection of materials is found at the Web site of the Universitas Indonesia in Jakarta (http://www.ui.ac.id). Several international organizations maintain Web sites offering a wealth of information on Indonesia. Two leading examples are the ASEAN secretariat in Jakarta (http://www.aseansecr.org) and the Asian Development Bank in Manila (http://www.adb.org). (For further information and complete citations, see Bibliography.)

Chapter 4. Government and Politics

A precolonial Javanese jong

PRESIDENT SUHARTO RESIGNED IN 1998, and Indonesia began a transition to democracy, a process that has had the country struggling to establish a new political identity. This struggle has taken place on four fronts: executive–legislative relations, center–region relations, religion–state relations, and interethnic relations. A slow but eventually successful process of constitutional reforms from 1999 to 2002 addressed the first three fronts. Political elites in the People's Consultative Assembly (MPR; for this and other acronyms, see table A) established a strongly presidential system with directly elected national and local chief executives, stronger legislatures, and an independent judiciary, as well as a decentralized political system with significant local autonomy. They also maintained Indonesia's identity as a plural, tolerant, and moderate Muslim-majority society with significant non-Muslim minorities, but not an Islamic state. This vision was sorely tested by the passage in some districts of local regulations implementing parts of Islamic law—sharia, or *syariah* in Bahasa Indonesia (see Glossary)—and by the Al Qaeda–linked terrorist attacks in Bali and Jakarta from 2002 to 2009. Indonesian citizens heartily endorsed these changes through their broad, enthusiastic, and largely nonviolent participation in the 1999, 2004, and 2009 electoral processes. The constitutional reform process indicated little on the fourth front, interethnic relations, except that Indonesia was still to be a state based on Pancasila (see Glossary), the five-point pan-religious, pan-ethnic state ideology created by the first president, Sukarno (in office 1945–67). Indonesians have struggled to overcome deadly communal strife in Maluku, Sulawesi, and Kalimantan, among other places, but by 2009 much of this violence had receded.

Consolidation of the new democracy remains a significant challenge. By the end of the first decade of the twenty-first century, reforms in the national-security sector were only partial at best. The military and police remained neutral in elections between 1999 and 2009, and they were stripped of their appointed seats in legislatures at all levels. The system of secondment of military officers to the civilian bureaucracy was also abolished. However, the roots of the military's political influence—the territorial system, business ventures, and the lack of democratic civilian oversight—only began to be addressed under the leadership of President Susilo Bambang Yudhoyono, who took office in 2004. The police were organizationally separated from the military in 1999 and have done a respectable job of addressing the threat of terrorism, but for most Indonesian citizens, daily interactions with the police have not been reformed: overall, corruption and ineffectiveness remain widespread. The implementation of decentralization, including revised autonomy laws passed in 2004 and the direct election of regional chief executives (governors, mayors, and district administrative heads or regents—*bupatis*) beginning in 2005, created its own problems, as corruption also has been decentralized, and the national government is confronted with a host of local regulations that are inconsistent with national laws and the constitution. Executive–legislative relations are frequently contentious, as the president and the legislative branch establish a working relationship within the new constitutional parameters and the legislature itself adjusts to the presence of a new upper house, the Regional Representative Council (DPD), established in 2004. Internal reform of these entities, to unclog the process of enacting laws and strengthen institutional capacity, is a pressing need.

Corruption has tainted every branch and level of the state: the civilian bureaucracy, the military and police, the legislatures, and the judiciary. Efforts to root out corruption, including the passage of new laws and regulations and the establishment of an array of commissions, have been only partially effective. Nonetheless, for ordinary citizens, fighting corruption remains a matter of primary concern, particularly the corruption they experience on a day-to-day basis at the village or ward offices, schools, government offices, courts, and police stations. Private investors, both domestic and foreign, are reluctant to commit their capital to Indonesia because of the high cost of doing business and the lack of consistent contract enforcement by a clean and impartial judiciary.

The new political system that President Yudhoyono inherited has made dealing with these pressing issues more complex than previously. Legislatures are more independent of the executive branch, and there are now two legislative bodies at the national level. Provincial and district governments are more powerful and have greater autonomy vis-à-vis the central government. The judicial system is no longer under the administrative and political control of the executive branch. The military retains significant latent political influence. Nonetheless, the success of the 2004 electoral process gave the new system broad legitimacy, and, again in 2009, Yudhoyono enjoyed a strong popular mandate from voters to move the country forward.

Foreign policy is frequently a significant issue in domestic politics, particularly when it concerns relations with the United States, Australia, or the complex tangle of problems in the Middle East. Yudhoyono has had to navigate these political minefields, given his ties to the United States from his prior military career and his cultivation of a profile as a secular nationalist rather than an Islamist politician (although he is personally pious). When Indonesia cooperates with the United States and Australia on counterterrorism measures, the Yudhoyono administration has to be careful not to be labeled as an agent of a perceived Western "war on Islam." Indonesia has also had to balance maintaining good relations with the West with supporting the Palestinian cause and opposing the U.S.–led war in Iraq. Indonesia has contributed troops, including Yudhoyono's elder son, to the United Nations (UN) peacekeeping force in Lebanon, while simultaneously preventing private citizens from volunteering to fight beside Hezbollah in the 2006 war with Israel.

When Indonesia's international treaty obligations have come into conflict with expressing solidarity with a fellow Muslim nation—for example, its March 2007 vote to approve UN Security Council Resolution 1747 on Iran's nuclear-weapons program—the government has been harshly criticized at home as a tool of Western interests. The legislature has also attempted to force the president to face questioning regarding this vote. In the late New Order period under President Suharto (in office 1967–98), Indonesia had begun to project a more assertive presence in the international arena, corresponding to its large population, strategic location, abundant natural resources, economic success, and growing nationalism. After a setback of a decade of focusing inward to solve its political and economic crisis, by 2008 Indonesia began to reassert itself on the global stage as a generally constructive force, offering to help solve conflicts ranging from the Korean Peninsula to Iran, from Burma (Myanmar) to Iraq. Indonesia's good relations with independent Timor-Leste (East Timor, formerly Timor Timur Province of Indonesia), and its implementation of a peace agreement in the Special Region of Aceh, have helped bolster its case to play this role, largely free of criticism over its own nagging human-rights issues.

The Political Debate

Indonesia has been a magnet for students of comparative politics as well as foreign diplomats and policy makers ever since independence from the Netherlands was declared in 1945. Fascination with Indonesia stems in part from its large population (estimated at more than 240 million people in 2009), strategic location, economic potential, great cultural and ethnic diversity, and fragmented archipelagic geography confounding centralized administration. Equally compelling is Indonesia's tumultuous political history, from Indianization and Islamization to Dutch colonialism and an often violent decolonization process.

Contemporary Indonesian political history can be divided into four periods, each defined by a central issue. First, during the 1950s, there was the question of the political integrity of the state itself, beset as it was by religious, regionalist, and ethnic revolts and rebellions. Second, and of great concern to U.S. policy makers, was the drift that became a rush to the left and the Indonesian Communist Party (PKI—see Glossary) during the period of Sukarno's Guided Democracy (1959–65). Third, from 1966 to 1998, there was the developmentalist authoritarianism of Suharto's army-dominated New Order. Finally, since 1998, the year Suharto left the presidency, the successful transition to and ongoing consolidation of liberal democracy has provided inspiration for reformers and democrats in other Muslim-majority societies.

The political transition in Indonesia has produced a requisite change among academic observers of Indonesian politics: Indonesia has become a "normal" country that can be examined with all of the standard theoretical and methodological tools available. As before, some continue to debate the basic nature of the Indonesian state. Others, however, adopt a more micro-analytical approach, examining trends in various policy areas, public opinion, etc., an approach that had been greatly hampered under the previous authoritarian regime. In addition to providing more varied empirical fodder for research, democratization in Indonesia has also resulted in much greater freedom for researchers to conduct their studies. One conclusion on which most observers have agreed is that the complexity, number, and interdependence of various social, cultural, economic, and political factors are so great that no single theory suffices.

Harking back to previous debates regarding the basic nature of the Indonesian state, one of the broadest current discussions concerns whether the still-fragile democratic order can be consolidated and sustained. Some scholars argue that the relatively nonviolent and gradual nature of the transition bodes well for the future of Indonesian democracy. As positive signs in this regard, they point to the success of the national elections in 1999, 2004, and 2009; the acquiescence (however grudging) of the security forces to the establishment of democracy; and the consensual process and broad scope of the constitutional reforms passed between 1999 and 2002. Others posit that it is precisely the lack of a cleaner and deeper break with the past that has created internal contradictions that may doom the new democracy. For instance, a substantial level of continuity in the political, military, bureaucratic, and economic elite has meant that old habits have been adapted to the new institutions and retained their strength, ensuring the superficiality of institutional change. There has been little accountability, especially at the highest levels, for the political and economic sins of the New Order, fostering simmering resentments that could one day be tapped as a reservoir of opposition to democracy itself. Most importantly, despite a number of successful high-level prosecutions, rampant bureaucratic, military, legislative, and judicial corruption remains the most significant factor keeping private foreign investors on the sidelines. Their absence lowers economic growth rates, which in turn hampers the performance legitimacy of the new democratic regime. Whatever approach is used to describe and analyze Indonesian government and politics, it requires an understanding of the legal basis and institutional structures of the system.

The Constitutional Framework

The legal basis of the Indonesian state is the 1945 constitution, promulgated the day after the August 17, 1945, proclamation of independence from the Netherlands and amended four times between 1999 and 2002. The original constitution was essentially a temporary instrument hurriedly crafted by the Independence Preparatory Committee in the last months before the Japanese surrender (see The Japanese Occupation, ch. 1). According to George McTurnan Kahin, whose 1952 book *Nationalism and Revolution in Indonesia* was the pioneering study of modern Indonesian politics, the constitution was considered "definitely provisional." Provisional or not, the constitution provided structural continuity in a period of political discontinuity after 1998. Beginning with the preamble, which invokes the principles of the Pancasila, the 37 articles of the constitution set forth the boundaries of both Sukarno's Old Order and Suharto's New Order. Amendment of the 1945 constitution was one of the principal demands of the student movement that forced Suharto to resign in 1998, and as of 2009 was one of the few of those demands that had been largely fulfilled. Four amendments eliminated many ambiguities and transformed the constitution into a more democratic framework, with extensive separation of powers and checks and balances.

The Japanese efforts to establish an independent Indonesian state encouraged the writing of the 1945 constitution, which was very soon temporarily put aside and had not been fully implemented when the transfer of sovereignty from the Netherlands took place on December 27, 1949. The 1949 agreement called for the establishment of the Federal Republic of Indonesia (RIS). Subsequently, a provisional constitution adopted in February 1950 provided for the election of a constituent assembly to write a permanent constitution (see The National Revolution, 1945–49, ch. 1). A rising tide of more radical nationalism, driven partly by perceptions that the RIS was a Dutch scheme to divide and reconquer their former colony, rapidly moved political leaders in the direction of a unitary republic. The Committee for the Preparation of the Constitution of the Unitary State was established on May 19, 1950, and on August 14 a new constitution (technically an amendment to the RIS constitution) was ratified, to be in force until an elected constituent assembly completed its work. The new, interim constitution provided for a parliamentary system of government, in which the cabinet and the prime minister were responsible to a unicameral legislature. The president was to be head of state but without real executive power except as a catalyst in forming a cabinet.

As the political parties wrestled ineffectually in the parliamentary forum, dissident ethnic politicians and army officers joined in resisting central authority and even engaged in armed rebellions in various provinces between 1949 and 1962 (see The Road to Guided Democracy, 1950–65, ch. 1). Sukarno assumed an extra-constitutional position from which he wielded paramount authority in imposing his more defined concept of Guided Democracy in 1959. This move was backed by the senior military leaders whose revolutionary experiences had already made them suspicious, even contemptuous, of civilian politicians, and who were now dismayed by the disintegrative forces at work in the nation. The military moved to the political forefront, where it remained until 1998.

Sukarno sought to legitimize his authority by returning to the 1945 constitution. He would have preferred to accomplish this goal constitutionally by having the 402-member Constituent Assembly formally adopt the 1945 constitution. However, the Constituent Assembly, elected in 1955 and divided along secular and religious lines, could not muster the required two-thirds majority necessary to approve new constitutional provisions. According to political scientist Daniel S. Lev, the body deadlocked on two fundamental issues: the role of Islam in the state and the question of federalism. Furthermore, division on these issues meant that ideological consensus among the anticommunist parties could not be translated into effective political cooperation. As long as the Constituent Assembly failed to agree on a new constitutional form, the interim constitution with its weak presidency continued in force. Backed by the Indonesian National Armed Forces (TNI—see Glossary) and a large part of the public, which was impatient with the political impasse and the government's failure to implement the promises of independence, on July 5, 1959, Sukarno decreed the dissolution of the Constituent Assembly and a return to the 1945 constitution. Martial law had already been proclaimed on March 14, 1957, and Sukarno claimed that under martial law his legal authority stemmed from his position as supreme commander of the TNI.

The national coat of arms of Indonesia depicts the Garuda—an ancient mythical bird—which symbolizes creative energy, the greatness of the nation, and nature. The 8 feathers on the tail, 17 on each wing, and 45 on the neck stand for the date of Indonesia's independence (August 17, 1945). The shield symbolizes self-defense and protection in struggle. The five symbols on the shield represent the state philosophy of Pancasila (see Glossary). The motto "Bhinneka Tunggal Ika" ("Unity in Diversity") on the banner signifies the unity of the Indonesian people despite their diverse ethnic and cultural backgrounds.
Courtesy of Embassy of Indonesia, Washington, DC

The original 1945 constitution proved to be extremely elastic as a provisional legal framework for a modern state, subject to broad interpretation depending upon the constellation of political forces in control at any given time. Other than outlining the major state structures, the document contained few specifics about relations between citizens and the government and left open basic questions about rights and responsibilities of citizen and state. For example, Article 28 states that "The freedom to associate and to assemble, to express written and oral opinions, etc., shall be established by law." Subsequent laws, however, did not fully recognize the fundamental rights of the individual citizen stipulated by the constitution. These rights have now been enshrined and further delineated in a new chapter on human rights immediately following the original Article 28—Articles 28A to 28J, approved in 2000. However, the 1945 document also is an expression of revolutionary expectations about social and economic justice. The original Article 33 states that the economy shall be organized cooperatively, that important branches of production affecting the lives of most people shall be controlled by the state, and that the state shall control natural resources for exploitation for the general welfare of the people. An additional clause introduced in 2002 now states that the national "economic democracy" shall be organized on the basis of such principles as togetherness, efficiency, justice, sustainability, environmental perspectives, self-sufficiency, and balance.

The political struggle from 1945 to 1959 over the constitutional framework of the state stemmed not from the ambiguities of the 1945 document nor its heavy weighting of executive power, but over deep disagreements about the nature of the state itself, particularly the issues of federalism and the role of Islam. Once the common battle against Dutch imperialism had been won, the passionate differences dividing various nationalist groups about the future of Indonesia surfaced. The possibility of a federation of loosely knit regions was denied by the use of force, first in crushing the Republic of South Maluku (RMS) in 1950, then in suppressing the Darul Islam insurgencies in Jawa Barat, Aceh, and Sulawesi Selatan between 1949 and 1962, and finally in defeating the Revolutionary Government of the Republic of Indonesia (PRRI) and the Universal Struggle Charter (Permesta) regional rebellions of 1957 to 1961. In subsequent decades, the central government was always sensitive to the issue of separatism, and the existence of a unitary republic, expressed through a primary "Indonesian" national identity, seemed secure. The difficulty of integrating an Islamic political identity with the Indonesian Pancasila identity was no longer of primary importance by the late 1990s and, although hotly debated at times, was never a major stumbling block in the constitutional-amendment process from 1999 to 2002 (see Pancasila: The State Ideology, this ch.).

The Structure of Government

The original 1945 constitution established a presidential system with significant parliamentary characteristics, whereas the amended constitution establishes a pure presidential system with extensive separation of powers and checks and balances. Sovereignty in Indonesia is vested in the people, who exercise their will through six organs of state of roughly equal stature. The president and vice president lead the executive branch and are chosen as a team through direct, popular elections; the president is both head of state and head of government (see fig. 11). Legislative power is vested in the People's Representative Council (DPR) and the new but less powerful upper house, the Regional Representative Council (DPD). Although the People's Consultative Assembly (MPR) is now no more than a joint sitting of the DPR and DPD, it retains separate powers that have been restricted to swearing in the president and vice president, amending the constitution, and having final say in the impeachment process. At the apex of the judicial system are the Supreme Court and the new Constitutional Court, whose powers include reviewing the constitutionality of laws, reaching a verdict on articles of impeachment, resolving disputes among state institutions, dissolving political parties, and resolving electoral disputes. Significant decentralization of power to subnational authorities has also been enshrined and delineated in the amended constitution.

Legislative Bodies

People's Representative Council

Primary legislative authority is constitutionally vested in the People's Representative Council (DPR; often referred to as the House of Representatives), which had 500 members in 1999, 550 members in 2004, and 560 members in 2009. Members are elected for a five-year term from multimember districts under an open-list system of proportional representation. These electoral districts consist either of whole provinces (*propinsi*) or of several municipalities (*kota*) and regencies (*kabupaten*) within the same province (see Elections, this ch.). Parties must win at least 2.5 percent of the national vote in order to win DPR seats. Thirty-eight national parties contested the 2009 elections, and nine of those parties won seats in the DPR. Since 2004 the military and police no longer have appointed seats in any legislative body. Active members of these security forces were still disenfranchised in 2009 but may be allowed to vote beginning in 2014.

The DPR is led by a speaker and four deputy speakers elected by and from the membership, and each has a policy portfolio. Work is organized through 11 permanent commissions (like U.S. congressional committees), each with specific functional areas of governmental affairs corresponding to one or more ministries, and a budget committee. The DPR also has other bodies that specialize in interparliamentary cooperation, the legislative agenda, ethics violations, and internal financial and administrative management. The DPR secretariat includes a small research unit designed to provide nonpartisan information to members. Individual members have only one or two staff members, who primarily handle administrative tasks. Commissions also have a limited number of staff, mainly for administration. Party blocs have a handful of professional staff supported by the DPR budget. The DPR's budget remains inadequate to support a professional legislature, and employees of the secretariat are still technically civil servants in the Department of Home Affairs.

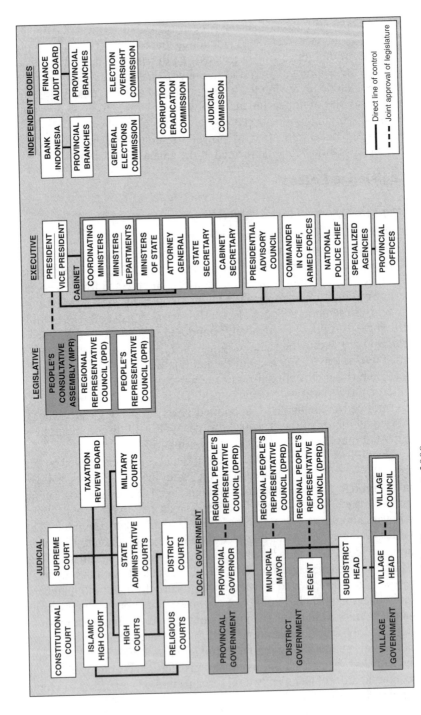

Figure 11. Structure of the Government, 2009

The legislative process in Indonesia has an extraordinary provision in Article 20(2) of the amended 1945 constitution, which requires bills to achieve the "joint approval" of the DPR and the president in order to become law. The unique twist is that approval by the president takes place as part of the legislative committee deliberations, not when the bill is sent to the president for signature. Bills may be initiated by either the executive or the DPR; most still originate in the executive branch. The president must issue a separate "presidential mandate" for each bill to the relevant cabinet minister to represent the executive branch in legislative deliberations. Issuance of this mandate is normally not a problem when the government initiates a bill but can be when the DPR is the initiating branch. Withholding this mandate in essence gives the president a veto that cannot be overridden by the DPR, which cannot deliberate on a bill without executive-branch participation.

Legislative deliberations generally follow a four-step process. The first two of the four steps are a reading of the bill in a plenary session by a representative of the initiating branch, followed by a formal response from the other branch. In the third step, the bill is referred for further discussion and amendment to one of the permanent commissions, or often instead to a working committee (*panitia kerja* or *panja*) or special committee (*panitia khusus* or *pansus*) formed on an ad hoc basis for the purpose of addressing that bill. This step is the locus of the achievement of joint approval, and the executive branch participates directly in these committee deliberations in the person of the relevant minister or department officials. This step is also the second source of the president's untrammeled veto power; if the president withholds approval of the bill, it cannot move forward. In the fourth step, when a bill has achieved joint approval in committee, it goes back to the plenary session for a final vote. The approved bill then goes to the president for signature; Article 20(5) of the constitution ensures that this is a formality, for any bill not signed by the president within 30 days of its approval by the DPR automatically becomes law. (The president cannot exercise a veto at this point, as there is not a third option of rejecting the bill and sending it back to the DPR.) Occasionally, circumstances compel the president to issue emergency regulations rather than wait for this lengthy legislative process to run its course. In this case, during the legislative session immediately following the issuance of such regulations, the DPR must approve them; lacking such approval, they must be revoked.

DPR deliberations are designed to produce consensus. It is the political preference of the leadership to avoid overt expressions of opposition or less than complete support. This practice is justified by a cultural predisposition to avoid, if possible, votes in which majority–

minority opposing positions are recorded. If votes are necessary, however, a quorum requires a two-thirds majority. On issues of nomination and appointment, voting is by secret ballot; on all other matters, it is by a show of hands.

The DPR also has an important role in various nonlegislative matters under the amended constitution. The DPR begins the impeachment process by approving an indictment that is sent to the Constitutional Court for trial. The DPR must approve declarations of war and peace, treaties, and other international agreements initiated by the president. It also must approve the president's appointment and dismissal of the commander in chief of the armed forces, the national police chief, and members of the Judicial Commission. The DPR selects members of the Finance Audit Board (BPK) and three of the nine members of the Constitutional Court; it also approves the Judicial Commission's nominations for Supreme Court justices. Finally, the president must consider the DPR's views regarding Indonesia's ambassadors to other countries, foreign ambassadors in Indonesia, and the granting of amnesties and pardons. In one of the few remaining vestiges of the parliamentary characteristics of the political system under the original 1945 constitution, the DPR has the right of interpellation, the power to summon the president before the legislature to answer questions. In practice, however, the DPR has found this power difficult to enforce.

The legislature has become a more vibrant, vocal branch of government with increasing pluralism and freedom and the expansion of the DPR's constitutional authority. Nonetheless, most legislation still originates in the executive branch. The DPR continues to lack sufficient professional research staff—whether attached to individual members, party blocs, commissions, or the legislature as a whole—and its constituency-outreach efforts remain limited as well. The legislative process itself remains slow, and the DPR suffers from a backlog of proposed bills waiting to enter the process. However, approximately 65 percent of the members elected in 2009 were new to the DPR, and even among those reelected there is a group interested in reforming the institution, revising the standing orders to streamline the legislative process, and expanding the DPR budget to give it the resources to begin to study policy issues and draft legislation on its own.

Regional Representative Council

The DPR's less-powerful partner in the legislative process is a body established in October 2004 to represent regional interests at the national level: the Regional Representative Council (DPD; sometimes referred to colloquially as the Senate). This 132-member body

Main assembly building of Indonesia's legislature, with the legislative office
complex to the right
Part of Indonesia's legislative complex, including staff offices and meeting
rooms for the MPR, DPR, and DPD
Courtesy Yadi Jasin

meets on the same calendar as the DPR, which is required by the constitution to hold sessions at least once every year. Four members from each province are elected directly by voters for the same five-year term as the DPR. To be eligible for nomination for the 2004 election, candidates could not be affiliated with political parties, must have collected 1,000 to 5,000 signatures from verified registered voters (depending on the size of the province), and must have resided in the province for five years. The DPR tried to strip the nonpartisan and residency requirements for the 2009 elections. However, the DPD petitioned the Constitutional Court to overturn this decision as inconsistent with the constitutional intent for the DPD; the court sided with the DPD and restored the provincial-residency requirement but ruled that it was constitutional to allow for partisan DPD candidates. Candidates' photographs appear on the ballot paper, and voters are eligible to vote for one candidate; the four candidates with the highest vote totals win.

The DPD is led by a speaker and two deputy speakers; one of each of the three leaders represents western, central, and eastern Indonesia. The DPD has divided itself into four committees, each of which deals with a set of policy areas. Its role in the legislative process is more indirect than and subordinate to the DPR's. The DPD can propose bills to the DPR in the areas of regional autonomy; center–region relations; the formation, division, and merger of regions; the management of natural resources and other economic resources; and the financial balance between the center and the regions. The constitution also specifies that the DPD may participate in the deliberations regarding bills in these areas, but it does not indicate how this should happen, leaving that up to the two bodies to negotiate. The DPD must also provide its opinion to the DPR on the state budget and on bills regarding taxation, education, and religion. Finally, the DPD has oversight authority related to all of these policy areas; however, it cannot take action on the results of its inquiries, which go to the DPR for further action.

One of the first acts of the DPD after its establishment was to begin work on a constitutional amendment to increase its powers. Passage of any amendments requires the support of a substantial portion of the DPR, and it is not likely that the DPR would support an amendment that would require it to share legislative power. In the 2004 term, the proposal failed to garner sufficient support, but a commission has been established to study the issue, and it was likely the DPD would try again in the 2009 term.

People's Consultative Assembly

No longer the highest constitutional body, the People's Consultative Assembly (MPR) nonetheless retains important roles in the political process. The MPR inaugurates the president and vice president, has the final say in the impeachment process, and remains the only body permitted to amend the constitution. The "Broad Outlines of State Policy," a document that theoretically established policy guidelines for the next five years and was subject to MPR approval during the Suharto years, has been abolished because competing presidential candidates are expected to present their policy platforms to the public during the campaign. The MPR now consists solely of the members of the DPR and DPD, having dropped the vague "functional group delegates" as part of the constitutional reform process. The MPR is led by a speaker (who also must be a DPR member) and four deputy speakers, two each from the DPR and the DPD.

The Executive

President and Vice President

Indonesia's government is a strong presidential system with, since 2004, significant checks and balances by the legislative and judicial branches as well as by local authorities. The president and vice president are directly elected as a ticket for a five-year term in a two-round system; if no ticket wins a simple majority in the first round, the two tickets that received the most votes advance to the second round. The winning presidential ticket must gain at least 20 percent of the vote in half of the provinces. A president is limited to two terms in office. The only qualifications for office provided in the constitution are that the president be a native-born Indonesian citizen, never have acquired another citizenship, never have committed treason, and be "spiritually and physically capable" of the office. Although the DPR is vested with primary legislative power, the president has de facto veto power over any legislation, with no possibility of override by the DPR. The president serves as the supreme commander of the armed forces. The president appoints cabinet members, with no requirement for legislative confirmation.

Between 1945 and 2009, Indonesia had six presidents: Sukarno (1945–67), Suharto (1967–98), Bacharuddin J. (B. J.) Habibie (1998–99), Abdurrahman Wahid (1999–2001; also known as Gus Dur), Megawati Sukarnoputri (2001–4; Sukarnoputri means "daughter of Sukarno"; it is not a family name), and Susilo Bambang Yudhoyono (since 2004; often referred to as SBY). When Suharto was forced to resign on May 21, 1998, Vice President Habibie became president and immediately announced a package of political reforms that included new legislative elections in June 1999. Although Megawati's Indonesian Democracy Party–Struggle (PDI–P) won a plurality in those elections, she was defeated in the MPR vote for president in October 1999 by Wahid when Habibie withdrew his candidacy following a vote of no confidence. The MPR then elected Megawati as Wahid's vice president. Two years later, the MPR removed Wahid from office following allegations of corruption and incompetence, and Megawati became president. Yudhoyono and vice presidential candidate Muhammad Yusuf Kalla defeated Megawati and three other tickets in Indonesia's first direct presidential elections in July and September 2004. Yudhoyono was reelected, this time running with Bank Indonesia governor Budiono, in one round in July 2009.

Although the vice president is elected on a ticket with the president, the question of their relationship is a political issue. This is in part because the level of political pluralism forces parties and candidates to form coalitions: in 2004 Yudhoyono, from the Democrat Party (PD), chose Kalla to obtain support from the much larger, better organized, and wealthier Golkar Party. This dynamic became even more pronounced two months after they were inaugurated, when Kalla was elected Golkar chairman at its party congress. During their administration, Kalla was wont on occasion to take a different stance than Yudhoyono on certain issues. Although privately Yudhoyono sometimes admonished Kalla for this behavior, in public he insisted that they remained a solid team. Nonetheless, in early 2009 Yudhoyono began to distance himself from Kalla, signaling his intention to choose a different running mate. Following the April 2009 legislative elections, Yudhoyono surprised many by bucking the logic of party coalitions when he chose the technocratic, nonpartisan central banker Budiono as his vice presidential candidate; nonetheless, they were easily elected with 60.8 percent of the vote. Kalla was unsuccessful in forming a ticket with Megawati, and instead ran with retired General Wiranto, coming in a distant third place with 12 percent. Megawati and retired Lieutenant General Prabowo Subianto, Suharto's former son-in-law, placed second with 27 percent.

The Cabinet

The president appoints and is assisted by a cabinet of ministers. In October 2009, Yudhoyono named his second "United Indonesia" cabinet, with 34 ministers representing six parties (the five that formed the nominating coalition for his presidential ticket plus Golkar). Twenty departments were headed by ministers, and these departments were grouped under three coordinating ministers: political, legal, and security affairs; economic affairs; and people's welfare. The state secretary, who supports the president's role as head of state, also was a minister. There were 10 ministers of state, that is, ministers with portfolios but without full departments. Yudhoyono also revived the use of vice ministers, a practice allowed by law since 2008, appointing 11 to ministries with particularly heavy workloads. Most of these vice ministers were career bureaucrats rather than partisan or retired military appointees. In addition to the ministers, two high-ranking state officials were accorded cabinet rank: the attorney general and the cabinet secretary.

Specialized Agencies

Specialized agencies and boards at the central government level are numerous and diverse. They include the National Development Planning Board (Bappenas), the National Family Planning Coordinating Agency (BKKBN), the Capital Investment Coordinating Board (BKPM), and the Agency for the Study and Application of Technology (BPPT). At lower levels there are regional planning agencies, investment boards, and development banks under the aegis of the central government.

Presidential Advisory Council

Article 16 of the amended constitution authorizes the president to establish an advisory council, and a law passed in 2006 further specifies this provision. Yudhoyono established the nine-member Presidential Advisory Council in 2007, but in 2009 this body was still trying to determine what its role would be in relation to the cabinet and the advisers in the office of the president. The larger Supreme Advisory Council was abolished in 2002 by the Fourth Amendment.

The Security Forces

Article 30 of the constitution establishes the existence of the Indonesian National Armed Forces (TNI) and the National Police of Indonesia (Polri). The constitution further specifies that the role of the military is national defense, and the role of the police is public order and domestic security. However, the constitution does not explicitly establish the principle of civilian control of the security forces, leaving this matter to the laws on the military and police. Both of these institutions report directly to the president rather than through a cabinet minister, such as (for the military) the minister of defense or (for the police) the minister of home affairs or the minister of justice and human rights (see The Armed Forces in National Life; The National Police, ch. 5).

The Judiciary

The Indonesian legal system is extraordinarily complex, the independent state having inherited three sources of law: customary or *adat* law, traditionally the basis for resolving interpersonal disputes in the village environment; Islamic law (sharia), often applied to disputes between Muslims; and Dutch colonial law. *Adat* courts were abolished in 1951, although customary means of dispute resolution are still in use in villages. The return to the 1945 constitution in 1959 meant that Dutch laws remained in force except as subsequently altered or found to be inconsistent with the constitution. A criminal code enacted in 1981 expanded the legal rights of criminal defendants. The government in 2009 was still reviewing its legacy of Dutch civil and commercial laws in an effort to codify them in Indonesian terms. The types of law recognized in MPR Decree No. 3 of 1999 include the constitution, MPR decrees, statutes passed by the DPR and ratified by the president, government regulations promulgated by the president to implement a statute, presidential decisions to implement the constitution or government regulations, other implementing regulations such as ministerial regulations and instructions, and local (provincial and district) regulations. Obviously, the executive enjoys enormous discretion in determining what is law.

Article 24 of the amended constitution states that judicial power shall be vested in the Supreme Court, the Constitutional Court, and subordinate courts established by law, and that the organization and competence of courts shall be established by law. In Sukarno's Guided Democracy, the justice system became a tool of the revolution, and any pretense of an independent judiciary was abandoned. Although in theory one of the goals of the New Order was to restore the rule of law, in practice the judiciary remained both corrupt and a means for suppressing political dissent. Judicial reform was thus a key demand of the 1998 student movement and remains one of the most important items on the political-reform agenda. Important steps were taken in this regard as part of the 1999–2002 constitutional-amendment process. A new body, the Constitutional Court, was established to review the constitutionality of laws, resolve disputes among the various branches and levels of government, have final say in the dissolution of political parties, and decide disputes over election results. The Constitutional Court also plays a role in the presidential-impeachment process by issuing a verdict on an indictment made by the DPR. The court has nine justices, three each nominated by the Supreme Court, the DPR, and the president. Justices must be knowledgeable about the constitution and may not be state officials. The Constitutional Court chief justice and deputy chief justices are chosen by and from among the justices.

The judicial branch stands coequal with the executive and legislative branches. Justices of the Supreme Court are nominated by the independent Judicial Commission for approval by the DPR and formal appointment by the president. The chief justice and deputy chief justice are elected by and from among the justices. Members of the Judicial Commission must have a legal background or experience and are appointed and dismissed by the president with the approval of the DPR. The Supreme Court has exclusive jurisdiction in disputes between courts of the different court systems and between courts located in different regions. It can annul decisions of high (appellate) courts on points of law, not fact. On request, it can give advisory opinions to the government and guidance to lower courts. However, its powers of judicial review are limited to decisions on whether administrative regulations and local regulations conform to the laws as passed by the DPR. Another reform to strengthen the system of checks and balances was the 2004 shift of administrative and financial control over the lower courts from the Department of Justice (now called the Department of Justice and Human Rights) to the Supreme Court.

Four different court systems operate below the Supreme Court. First, there are courts of general civil and criminal jurisdiction. District courts are the courts of first instance. High courts (at the provincial level) are appellate courts. Following the Dutch legal system, cases are decided by panels of judges rather than juries. Sources of law on which parties to a dispute may base their claims include: international law (to date rarely used); modern Indonesian civil law, which has replaced but is often rooted in colonial-era Roman-Dutch civil law; and *adat* (customary) law, which differs widely among ethnic groups (see Tradition and Multiethnicity, ch. 2). The court system remains highly corrupt, with verdicts in both civil and criminal cases influenced by bribery by both plaintiffs and defendants. Although judicial reform is key to consolidating democracy and establishing a more favorable investment climate, efforts at judicial reform have so far been half-hearted and largely ineffective.

Second, religious courts exist throughout Indonesia to resolve disputes between Muslims in matters of marriage, divorce, inheritance, and gifts. These district-level courts base their decisions on Islamic law. As in the secular court system, religious high courts are appellate courts at the provincial level. One of the persistent tensions between Muslims and the state arises from efforts to expand the jurisdiction of the religious courts.

Third, the state administrative court system resolves matters pertaining to the decisions of government officials. In addition, the Taxation

Review Board adjudicates taxation disputes. Other administrative courts were eliminated as part of the government's effort to simplify and standardize the court system.

Fourth, military courts have jurisdiction over TNI members. After the 1965 coup attempt, temporary special military courts were given authority to try military personnel and civilians alleged to be involved in the abortive coup (see The Coup and Its Aftermath, 1965–66, ch. 1). Hundreds of sentences ranging from 20 years' imprisonment to death were meted out by the special military courts, with executions occurring more than two decades after the event. The DPR has included a provision in a draft military law that would require all military personnel accused of nonmilitary crimes to be investigated by civilian prosecutors and tried by the civil court system. The military leadership opposed this provision, and it is still being debated.

Another court, the Corruption Crimes Court (Tipikor Court), was established in 2003 to confront widespread corruption in Indonesia, especially in cases of financial loss to the state and as a deterrent to future corruption. In 2006, however, the Constitutional Court ruled that the Tipikor had no legal basis and gave the DPR and the government until December 2009 to pass a law to justify the court's continued existence. Tipikor was allowed to continue to function during this period, and in September 2009 the DPR complied with appropriate enabling legislation, thus ensuring the court's constitutionality.

Independent Bodies

The Finance Audit Board is specified in Chapter VIIIA of the constitution as an independent body existing at both the national and provincial levels to conduct official examinations of the government's finances. The board reports to the DPR and DPD, which approve the national budget, and to each Regional People's Representative Council (DPRD), the legislative body that approves the budget at the provincial, municipality, or regency level of government. The board's members are chosen by the DPR with nonbinding input by the DPD.

The constitution established a number of independent bodies besides the Finance Audit Board and the Judicial Commission. In Article 22E(5), the constitution requires that elections shall be managed by an independent commission. The electoral law established the General Elections Commission (KPU), whose members are nominated by the president and chosen by the DPR following a hearing and confirmation process called in Indonesia a "fit and proper test." One weakness of this system, as with the selection process for many other bodies in Indonesia, is that the president nominates multiple candidates for each position on the commission, from which the DPR is free to select. Nominating multiple rather than single candidates makes the process much more vulnerable to favoritism and corruption, and in fact the DPR was widely criticized for choosing inexperienced over much more qualified candidates in its selections of KPU commissioners in 2007. In Article 23D, the constitution also established a central bank, known as Bank Indonesia (see Monetary and Exchange-Rate Policy, ch. 3). The constitution only establishes the existence of the bank, leaving all of the details on its composition, status, authority, accountability and independence to the central bank law.

Local Government

Government administration operates through descending levels of administrative subunits. Indonesia is made up of 33 provinces and special regions (each led by a governor), up from 27 at the end of the New Order in 1998, as some provinces were subdivided, a process that may yet continue. There are two special regions (*daerah istimewa*; Aceh and Yogyakarta) and one special capital-city region (*daerah khusus*; Jakarta). The 30 provinces (*propinsi*), in turn, are subdivided into districts, called municipalities (*kota*, led by a mayor) in urban areas and regencies (*kabupaten*, led by a regent or *bupati*) in rural areas, and below that into subdistricts (*kecamatan*, led by a *camat*). At the lowest tier of the administrative hierarchy is the village (*desa*). According to the Department of Home Affairs, Indonesia in 2009 had 348 regencies, 91 municipalities, 5,263 subdistricts, and 66,979 villages.

The New Order was a highly centralized system, but subnational governance has undergone significant change since 1999. In that year, the Habibie administration introduced two new laws collectively known as "regional autonomy policy," one on regional governance and the other on the financial relationship between the center and the regions. This policy was further codified between 1999 and 2002 in amendments to Chapter VI of the 1945 constitution. In 2004 revised regional autonomy laws replaced the 1999 laws. This entire legal framework remains based on Indonesia as a unitary state. Since the Dutch-imposed RIS in 1949–50, federalism has been anathema to Indonesian politicians and the public. At the end of the 1945–49 war, as part of the negotiations over the terms of independence, the Dutch insisted that the nationalist Republic of Indonesia join with the various puppet states they had established around the archipelago to form the RIS. Nationalists saw this action as an attempt to maintain indirect Dutch control over Indonesia, and Sukarno ended the federal experiment only eight months later. One of the initial agreements in 1999, at the outset of the constitutional amendment process, was to maintain Indonesia as a unitary state, as it has been since 1950.

Indonesia, nonetheless, now enjoys a level of political decentralization greater even than some federal systems. Regional autonomy reserves six policy areas to the central government: foreign relations, national defense, internal security, justice, monetary policy, and religion. All other policy areas are primarily handled by provincial and district governments, with the central government's role limited to interregional coordination, setting service-delivery standards, and providing block grants. The 1999 laws bypassed the provincial governments and made district governments the primary locus of decentralized authority. This was because, at the time, the overriding concern was that the unfolding democratic transition might lead to the breakup of the nation, as had happened in Yugoslavia and the Soviet Union. The assumption was that districts would not have the size, resources, or distinctive ethnic identity sufficient to mount a separatist challenge to the center. This concern had receded significantly by the 2004 legal reforms, and provincial governments regained some measure of authority.

Service design, planning, and delivery are concentrated at the provincial and district levels, although these subnational authorities do not have the power to raise much revenue on their own. Taxation remains primarily the prerogative of the central government, which then provides block grants to local authorities. The size of these grants for each province or district is determined by a complex formula that takes into account the geographic size, population, and natural resource base of each unit. Although provinces and districts rich in natural resources cannot keep all of the revenues associated with those resources, they receive a much higher share than under the New Order.

Another reform introduced in the revised regional autonomy laws of 2004 is that governors, mayors, and *bupatis* are now directly elected for the first time in Indonesia's history. Under the New Order, they had been appointed by the central government, and beginning in 1999 they were elected by the local assembly. Since 2005, as the terms of these local chief executives expired, elections for their replacements for five-year terms have occurred on a rolling basis. Despite fears of administrative chaos, fraud, or violence, these local elections have generally proceeded smoothly, as was the case with the national elections of 1999, 2004, and 2009.

Parallel to their chief executives, each province, municipality, and regency also has a local assembly, similar to the DPR, called the Regional People's Representative Council (DPRD). These councils range in size from 20 to 100 members, depending on the administrative level and the population of the region. They are elected at the same time as the DPR and for the same five-year term, which means that the terms of the regional assemblies and their corresponding regional chief executives are never the same. The DPRDs have powers similar to the

Political grafitti, "We are forced
to cultivate on the moon,"
Yogyakarta, 2002
Courtesy Eric Stein

DPR: approving the regional government budget, passing regional statutes, and providing oversight of the regional government.

Five provincial-level units have special status, in addition to the devolution of power to all provinces under regional autonomy. Aceh and Papua (which was divided in two in 2005), the two remaining provincial-level units with active separatist movements once East Timor separated from Indonesia in 1999, were granted "special autonomy." Jakarta and Yogyakarta have "special-region" status, although in practice they are not much different from other provinces. The main difference in Jakarta is that its five municipalities, while they have mayors, do not have corresponding assemblies (the only assembly is at the provincial level). In Yogyakarta the primary difference is that the sultan of the larger of the two palaces or *kratons* (in 2009, Sultan Hamengkubuwono X) automatically becomes governor.

Indonesia's experience in East Timor (Timor Timur Province)—in the course of which President Habibie offered the province a referendum on special autonomy, Timorese voters defeated that referendum, and Indonesia was forced to acknowledge its independence—raised concerns for the government that this would set an example for other provinces. This fear has turned out to be largely unjustified, however, as no significant new separatist movements appeared in any provinces where they did not already exist prior to 1999. The main domestic impact of Timor-Leste's independence was to somewhat exacerbate existing separatist sentiments in Aceh and Papua. In Aceh in particular, a student-led group called the Aceh Referendum Information Center (SIRA) sprang up not long after Habibie's offer to East Timor and posted banners in the province calling for a referendum. Nonetheless, Aceh subsequently turned its focus to special autonomy and various peace negotiations (see Separatist Rebellions, ch. 5). In Papua the idea of a UN-administered referendum reminded many of the region's own decolonization process in the 1960s, the legitimacy of which is still questioned by many Papuans. As in Aceh, however, the focus in Papua then turned to a debate over special autonomy.

Aceh

The Special Region of Aceh (called Nanggroe Aceh Darussalam, meaning the State of Aceh, Abode of Peace, from 1999 to 2009), in northwestern Sumatra, is the area of Indonesia where the Islamic character of the population is the most pronounced. The Acehnese demand for autonomy, expressed in support for the 1950s Darul Islam rebellion, was partially met by the central government's acceptance of a "special-region" status for the province in 1959, allowing a higher-than-usual official Indonesian respect for Islamic law and custom. This special-region status, together with growing prosperity, brought Aceh into the Indonesian mainstream. Nevertheless, in the early twenty-first century the idea of an independent state was kept alive by the Free Aceh Movement (GAM). Thought to have been crushed in the mid-1970s, the guerrilla campaign of the insurgents, under the leadership of Swedish-based Hasan di Tiro and with Libyan support, renewed its hit-and-run warfare in the late 1980s, hoping to build on economic and social grievances. The military reacted with crushing force but never was able to defeat the separatists fully.

President Habibie's offer in 1999 to revive the railroad from Medan in Sumatera Utara Province to Aceh's capital, Banda Aceh, and other economic-development projects in exchange for Acehnese loyalty to Jakarta was seen as a continuation of the patronizing, centralistic politics of the New Order. Habibie's policy on East Timor led to growing calls among Acehnese civilians for a similar referendum. In response, the central government hurriedly passed a new law updating Aceh's "special-autonomy" status, including particularly the right to incorporate elements of Islamic law into local legal codes, which had not actually been a demand of most Acehnese. President Wahid involved international participants in resolution of the conflict for the first time by inviting the Geneva-based Henri Dunant Centre for Humanitarian Dialogue to help mediate a Cessation of Hostilities Agreement (COHA). Although Vice President Megawati was not particularly supportive of this policy, she allowed the process to continue after she became president in July 2001, and the COHA was signed in December 2002. Nonetheless, by May 2003 the agreement had broken down. President Megawati declared martial law in Aceh and unleashed the military once again.

The military had much more success than previously in breaking up GAM cells, but it still could not achieve final victory. Following her party's defeat in the legislative elections of April 2004, Megawati lifted martial law in May. In December 2004, a massive earthquake and tsunami struck Aceh, following which both the government under newly elected President Yudhoyono and the rebels returned to the negotiating table, this time with facilitation by former Finnish president Martti Ahtisaari through his nongovernmental organization Crisis Management Initiative. A memorandum of understanding detailing the peace agreement was signed in August 2005 and began to be implemented in September. A joint civilian effort between the European Union (EU) and the Association of Southeast Asian Nations (ASEAN), called the Aceh Monitoring Mission, monitored the entire process. Ahtisaari was awarded the Nobel Peace Prize in 2008, in part for his efforts in Aceh.

For its part, GAM relinquished the goal of independence, and its fighters were demobilized and their arms destroyed in public ceremonies between September and December 2005. The central government withdrew some military forces and paramilitary police units from the province. Funds were set up to provide cash or land (or both) to various categories of demobilized GAM ex-combatants and supporters, as well as (in a controversial move) pro-Indonesian militias, and training programs were established to provide job skills. A new law on governance in Aceh replaced the special-autonomy law, and direct elections for governor, mayors, and *bupatis* occurred in December 2006. GAM formally dissolved itself in January 2006, but remnants may remain. A GAM-affiliated ticket running as independents, Irwandi Yusuf and Muhammad Nazar (the former leader of SIRA), were elected as governor and vice governor, respectively, and GAM-affiliated candidates also won in 11 of the 19 districts holding elections (in two of the 21 districts the *bupati's* term had not yet expired). Acehnese were also allowed to form local political parties, unlike in the remainder of the country, to contest the 2009 special-region and district legislative elections. Although the Aceh–Nias Rehabilitation and Reconstruction Agency (BRR), set up in the wake of the tsunami, was dissolved in early 2009, the central government and international donors remain heavily invested in reinforcing the peace process and supporting reconstruction in Aceh.

Papua

Papua—formerly called at various times Irian Jaya, West Irian, West Papua, Dutch New Guinea, and West New Guinea—remained under Dutch control after Indonesian independence in 1949. A combination of Indonesian political and military pressure and international efforts led to an October 1962 Dutch transfer of sovereignty to the UN Temporary Executive Authority, which was supported by a military observation force that oversaw the cease-fire. In May 1963, the UN gave Indonesia full administrative control. After a controversial 1969 "Act of Free Choice," the territory, which the Indonesians called Irian Barat (West Irian) until 1972, was integrated into the republic as Indonesia's twenty-sixth province and later renamed Irian Jaya (Victorious Irian). In 2000, in a vain attempt to dampen separatist sentiments, President Wahid renamed the province Papua. In a move widely perceived in Papua as an effort to divide and conquer, President Megawati in 2003 set in motion a tortuous three-year process by which the northwestern portion was split off to form the new province of Irian Jaya Barat (West Irian Jaya), with the eastern two-thirds retaining the name Papua. (Irian Jaya Barat was renamed Papua Barat in 2007.) Further division of the rump Papua was blocked at the time, although various proposals for as many as four new provinces remain in circulation. Rich in natural resources, this is Indonesia's least densely populated region. The central government's efforts to exploit these resources and to assimilate indigenous Papuans, who are racially Melanesian, into the national administration and culture have met with sporadic armed resistance from the Free Papua Organization (OPM) and have aroused international concerns.

Although the OPM is a marginal domestic actor, more visible as an international symbol, the fact of its existence has been used by the central government to justify suspicions about Papuan loyalties and an intimidating Indonesian military presence in the region, leading to human-rights abuses. Cultural differences between Indonesians and the indigenous population, and complaints about the "Indonesianization" of Papua, have exacerbated tensions. The cultural conflict is aggravated by resentment of racially Malay in-migrants (Javanese, Buginese, Bataks, and other groups) from other parts of Indonesia, who dominate the state bureaucracy and urban economies. Despite human-rights abuses and ethnic tensions, charges by some international activists that the central government is waging genocide in Papua are overblown.

As in Aceh, the central government has responded to unrest in Papua with both repression and a new "special-autonomy" law. This law, passed in December 2002, provided for a much greater share of Papua's natural resource wealth to return to the region as block grants and specifies that these funds should prioritize the infrastructure, education, and health sectors. The law also provided for the establishment of a special upper house of the local legislature, the Papuan People's

Council (MRP). This body consists of representatives of religious leaders, traditional (*adat*) leaders, and women. The MRP is involved in all decisions regarding special autonomy, in any proposals to subdivide Papua, and in vetting candidates for governor, mayor, and *bupati* to ensure that they are native Papuans. Implementation of this law has been slow and partial. The enhanced fiscal resources began to flow to the region immediately, but without local-government capacity to use these funds properly, much has been wasted in corruption or inappropriate projects. The MRP did not form until November 2005 and was immediately thrust into the uncomfortable position of having to rule on the formation of the new province of Irian Jaya Barat and gubernatorial candidates in both provinces. In February 2006, the first direct elections for governor proceeded in both Irian Jaya Barat and Papua, despite continued controversy regarding the sheer existence of the new province. At first the provincial government of Irian Jaya Barat did not receive special-autonomy funds (instead relying for its existence solely on support provided by the central government), but in July 2008 the DPR passed a law mandating that special autonomy also be implemented fully in the renamed Papua Barat.

Problems in Papua have implications for Indonesia's foreign relations as well, particularly with neighboring Papua New Guinea and Australia. The border crossing with Papua New Guinea on the north coast near Jayapura reopened in late 2005, but relations with Australia soured after it granted 42 Papuan boat people temporary protection visas in March 2006. Despite resolution of the separatist conflicts in East Timor and Aceh, albeit via very different outcomes, it is likely that problems in Papua will continue to fester for many years, as the central government does not yet seem serious about addressing issues there in a systematic manner.

Political Culture

Following the constitutional amendments of 1999 to 2002, the reformed Indonesian political system is characterized by a set of institutions labeled a "difficult combination" in many other countries: a powerful presidency and multiparty politics. There is a fixed term for the president as well as separate popular elections, and thus roughly equal democratic legitimacy, for the president and the national legislature. Some of the dangers inherent in this system are divided government, in which the presidency and the legislature are controlled by different political parties, and the possibility of electing as president a political outsider who has no experience forging political compromises in the legislature. These dangers are exacerbated in a multiparty polity, in which the likelihood of a single party controlling the legislature is much lower than in a two-party system. Under this difficult combination of institutions, deadlock can occur between the president and the legislature, leading one or both to be tempted to use extra-constitutional means to break the deadlock. When that occurs, democracy itself can be threatened.

The strong presidential system tends to be associated with much more of a "winner-take-all" political culture than has been evident in Indonesia since 1999. One of the hallmarks of the new Indonesian democracy is that although its institutions are strongly presidential, many of its practices are much more common in multiparty parliamentary government, including numerous possible inclusionary coalitions as well as consensus-based decision making. These inclusionary and consensual practices have contributed positively to making the blending of a strong presidency with multiparty politics function fairly well so far in Indonesia. This style of governance can be linked to other political cultures in Indonesia, particularly Javanese and Islamic, as well as to the cultural roots of Pancasila.

Inclusionary Coalitions

The Indonesian political party system is as highly fragmented after the 2009 elections as it was in the 1950s. According to the Laakso-Taagepera Index (see Glossary), there are 6.1 "effective" political parties in the 2009 DPR versus 6.4 in the legislature following the 1955 elections. Nonetheless, all of the major parties (and even most of the minor ones) cluster around the middle of the political spectrum. Thus, although the contemporary party system is equally fragmented, it is less polarized than in the 1950s. At that time, on the right end of the spectrum, both of the two major Muslim-based parties—Nahdlatul Ulama and the Consultative Council of Indonesian Muslims (Masyumi)—were Islamist, favoring the implementation of Islamic law. Now, of the four major Muslim-based parties, only two are Islamist, and only one of these as a matter of principle, the other out of political expediency. The other two parties take a much more moderate stance (see Muslim Parties, this ch.). On the left end of the spectrum, in the 1950s the Indonesian Communist Party (PKI) was the most organized and grassroots-based of all the major parties, and was the largest communist party outside of the Soviet bloc and China. There is no radical leftist equivalent in the contemporary Indonesian party system. In 1999 the Democratic People's Party (PRD), which was the only party to include a hammer and sickle in its symbol, won barely 0.1 percent of the national vote, and its founder, Budiman Sujatmiko, joined the national leadership board of, and in 2009 was elected to, the DPR from Megawati's PDI–P.

The consequence of this clustering around the middle in the contemporary party system is that parties mainly compete for political spoils rather than act on a programmatic basis. Coalition-building is thus a key element in determining political prosperity and even survival. High fragmentation means that in order to build even a significant bloc of votes (much less an outright majority), the coalition often must include several partners. Low polarization means that all three major and six smaller parties are potential coalition partners with each other. Both of these rules have proven to hold in Indonesia. With decentralization and the inauguration of direct election of governors, mayors, and *bupatis* beginning in 2005, there are now hundreds of examples from around the nation of numerous, shifting coalitions being formed based on parties' local strength, even if these local coalitions often do not match the parties' political positions at the national level. The two parties that are farthest apart on the political spectrum—the strongly secular PDI–P and the fervently Islamist Prosperous Justice Party (PKS)—have even formed local coalitions when it suited their needs.

The coalition pattern at the national level has set the tone for these local alliances. The presidential election process in the MPR in 1999 saw intense jockeying among most of the parties other than the PDI–P in a successful effort to deny front-runner Megawati the presidency. The newly elected president, Abdurrahman Wahid, then surprised some of these erstwhile supporters by reaching out to Megawati and supporting her nomination for vice president, which she accepted. Their first cabinet included ministers from all five major parties, and this pattern was maintained throughout subsequent reshuffles and Megawati's rise to the presidency in 2001. Prior to the 2004 legislative elections, most parties did not reveal their preferred presidential candidate in order to maximize their coalitional possibilities in the first round of the direct presidential elections later in the year. That election included some strange bedfellows, such as former military commander General Wiranto, accused by many of human-rights abuses in the 1998 transition and the 1999 East Timor referendum, gaining support from former President Wahid (a long-time human-rights activist) once the latter was disqualified from becoming a candidate himself. Wahid's brother Salahuddin Wahid even resigned from the National Human Rights Commission to be Wiranto's running mate. The coalitions shifted again for the second round, with the parties behind the three losing tickets having to support either Megawati or Susilo Bambang Yudhoyono. The inclusionary pattern broke down briefly following Yudhoyono's election, when Golkar, the PDI–P, the National Awakening Party (PKB), and the Reform Star Party (PBR) formed the National

Front and took all DPR leadership positions for themselves. The exception proved the rule, however, as this maneuver was perceived as inappropriate, and within weeks the committee leaderships had been reshuffled to include all parties. In addition, Yudhoyono's first cabinet even included some figures affiliated with some of the National Front parties, creating links "across the aisle," even if these people tended to be marginal within their parties and were not officially representing their parties in the cabinet. Yudhoyono also worked assiduously to bring more and more of those parties over into his camp, leaving the PDI–P as the only steadfast opposition to his administration.

This inclusionary political culture was less prominent during the 2009 presidential elections but, after those elections, once again returned to the fore. Despite Golkar's position as the second-largest party after Yudhoyono's Democrat Party (PD), Yudhoyono decided to jettison Muhammad Yusuf Kalla as his running mate for reelection. Following the logic of the inclusionary political culture, all of Yudhoyono's presidential coalition partners expected him to choose one of their leaders as his new running mate. Instead, Yudhoyono chose the nonpartisan, technocratic economist Budiono, who had served as his coordinating minister for economic policy before becoming governor of Bank Indonesia. Kalla and Megawati failed to form a coalition of the second- and third-largest parties, instead settling for coalitions with Wiranto of the People's Conscience Party (Hanura Party) and Prabowo Subianto of the Great Indonesia Movement Party (Gerindra Party), respectively. Nonetheless, after Yudhoyono won the presidential election with exactly the same large majority as in 2004 (60.8 percent), he still turned to Kalla and Megawati to negotiate an inclusionary cabinet. Megawati rebuffed him, and so the cabinet formed in October 2009 did not include representatives from the PDI–P, the Hanura Party, or the Gerindra Party, but it did include representatives from Golkar as well as the five parties that nominated the Yudhoyono-Budiono ticket: the PD, PKS, National Mandate Party (PAN), Development Unity Party (PPP), and PKB.

Consensus-Based Decision Making

One of the ironies of Indonesian political culture is that while Suharto's New Order paid lip service to the achievement of consensus through deliberation as being an integral part of "Pancasila Democracy," in reality the system was then highly centralized, autocratic, and nonparticipatory, and instead it is the new democracy that has actually adopted consultative consensus. The preference for deliberation and consensus is partly driven by the exigencies of shifting inclusionary coalitions described above. However, even in situations in which a strong majority coalition already exists, Indonesian political elites have preferred to continue to work to achieve consensus where practical.

This cultural predilection was strongly evident in the MPR debates over constitutional reforms from 1999 to 2002 and is one of the main reasons those reforms took three years to achieve rather than one, as originally planned. In this case, the achievement of consensus also has an instrumental rationale: because the constitution is the source of the basic rules of politics, the wider the acceptance of those rules, the more likely they are to be followed in practice, contributing to democratic stability. Nevertheless, this predilection has also manifested itself even when an instrumental rationale is lacking, such as in the DPR. The DPR has continued the New Order practice of dividing all leadership positions—from speaker down to deputy committee chair—among all parties proportional to each party's share of seats, rather than just a majority coalition. There is no need to form an all-party coalition in support of the speaker or the president; rather, this practice is rooted in a desire to give every party a voice in the legislative process. Legislators have also seen voting by majority rule as a last resort, preferring to achieve consensus on legislation among all party blocs, even if this means extended deliberations and compromises. This practice has been one of the factors contributing to the DPR's very low legislative output.

Traditional Political Culture

Public tolerance of President Yudhoyono's careful, deliberative decision-making style and of the slow, consensus-based legislative process is partly due to the way these political practices reflect shared cultural values and expectations about leadership. In a nation as ethnically diverse as Indonesia—from Melanesian tribes in Papua to Chinese-Indonesian billionaires in Jakarta—and with its population differentially incorporated into the modern political economy, it is difficult to identify a political culture shared by all Indonesians (see Sources of Local Identification, ch. 2). Nevertheless, there are major cultural forces at work that do influence the political judgments of large groups of Indonesians.

There are numerous traditional political cultures in Indonesia, but many aspects of modern Indonesian government and bureaucracy reflect Javanese cultural underpinnings. Even though Indonesia is a cultural mosaic, the Javanese, with about 41 percent of the total population, are by far the largest single ethnic group. Moreover, they fill—to a degree somewhat greater than their population ratio—the most important roles in government and the military. Javanese cultural predispositions therefore influence the way the government appeals to and interacts with the population. Although the Javanese kingship model was particularly appropriate for understanding Suharto and the authoritarian New Order, it continues to have relevance in democratic Indonesia (see Javanese, ch. 2).

Political power on Java historically was deployed through a patrimonial bureaucratic state in which proximity to the ruler was the key to command and rewards. This power can be described in terms of a patron–client relationship in which the patron is the *bapak* (father or elder). The terms of deference and obedience to the ruler are conceived in the Javanese *gusti–kawula* (lord–subject) formulation, which describes man's relationship to God as well as the subject's relationship to his ruler. The reciprocal trait for obedience is benevolence. In other words, benefits flow from the center to the obedient. By extension, government's developmental activities are a boon to the loyal. Bureaucratically, Javanese culture is suffused with an attitude of obedience—respect for those more senior, conformity to hierarchical authority, and avoidance of confrontation—characteristics of the preindependence *priyayi* (see Glossary) class whose roots go back to the traditional Javanese courts.

Javanism (*kejawen*) also has a mystical, magical dimension in its religiously syncretic belief system, which integrates pre-Indian, Indian, and Islamic beliefs. Its practices include animistic beliefs, which invest sacred heirlooms (*pusaka*) with animating spirits, and rites of passage whose antecedents are pre-Islamic. Javanism also encompasses the introspective ascetic practices of *kebatinan* (see Glossary), mysticism as related to one's inner self, that seek to connect the microcosms of the self to the macrocosms of the universe (see Islam, ch. 2). The politics of Javanism have been defensive, seeking to preserve its particular heterogeneous practices from demands for Islamic orthodoxy.

Islamic Political Culture

According to the 2000 census, 86.1 percent of the population (in 2009 an estimated 240.3 million people) identified themselves as Muslim, making Indonesia the largest Muslim nation in the world, united with the universal Islamic community (*ummah*) in the profession and practice of the faith (see Religion and Worldview, ch. 2). The appeal of Islam did not weaken when modern secular nationalism became the predominant basis for the independent Indonesian state. In fact, given the prominence of Islamic proselytization and reinvigoration, the people's desire to maintain Islamic institutions and moral values arguably is at an all-time high in Indonesia. There is, however, a distinction between Islam as a cultural value system and Islam as a political movement.

Islam in Indonesia is not monolithic. Indonesia's nominal or statistical Muslims, referred to as *abangan* (see Glossary), are mostly, with varying degrees of self-awareness, believers in *kebatinan*. It is notoriously difficult to parse out the percentage of Indonesian Muslims who are *abangan* and those who are *santri* (see Glossary), the term for orthodox believers. What is clear is that the latter have been gaining ground since the 1970s and are probably now a majority of the population as a whole. The vote totals of Muslim and Islamist political parties, about 37 percent in both 1999 and 2004 and about 26 percent in 2009, are not a very good measurement of the appeal of orthodox Islam, as many *santri* are personally pious but believe that religion should be kept out of politics and thus support secular nationalist parties (see Muslim Parties, this ch.). Furthermore, the orthodox are themselves divided into traditionalists and modernists, and each of these streams then subdivides into extremist, conservative, moderate, and liberal camps (see Political Dynamics, this ch.).

The principal organization reflecting the traditionalist outlook is Nahdlatul Ulama (literally, "revival of the religious teachers"), founded in 1926. Nahdlatul Ulama has its roots in the traditional rural Islamic schools (*pesantren*) of central and eastern Java. Claiming more than 40 million members, Nahdlatul Ulama is the largest Muslim organization in the world. Modernist, or reformist, Islam in Indonesia is best exemplified by the Muhammadiyah (Followers of Muhammad), which claims 30 million members. The latter organization was founded in 1912, when the spirit of the Islamic reform movement born in Egypt in the late nineteenth century reached Southeast Asia. In addition to their reform agenda, modernists sought to purify (critics argue Arabize) Indonesian Islam.

Both *santri* streams found formal political expression in the postindependence multiparty system. Masyumi was the main political vehicle for the modernists. However, its apparent support for the PRRI–Permesta regional rebellions between 1957 and 1961 led to constraints on its activities, and the party was banned in 1959. Nahdlatul Ulama directly competed as a party in the politics of the 1950s and, seeking to capitalize on Masyumi's banning, collaborated with Sukarno in the hope of winning patronage and followers. Nahdlatul Ulama also hoped to stop the seemingly inexorable advance of the secular left under the leadership of the PKI. Islamic political parties were prohibited from advancing an explicitly Islamist message in the New Order, but traditional systems of communication within the community of believers, including instruction in Islamic schools and mosque sermons, passed judgments on politics and politicians—the so-called "hard" *dakwah* (vigorous promotion of Islam).

The followers of the hard *dakwah* form a minority, albeit a vocal one. Some Islamists might be disaffected with the state; however, the goal of urban, middle-class Muslims, who share in the benefits of government economic policies and are relatively untouched by the preaching of rural Muslim teachers, is not to overthrow democracy. They want to transform the government from within to make its acts conform more with Islamic values, a focus not on the state itself but on reforming policies and practices that are offensive. The issues that energize middle-class Muslims include not just the persistent Muslim complaints about secularization, Christianization, and moral decline, but also contemporary political grievances about the inequitable distribution of income, corruption, and concentration of wealth and power in the hands of Chinese Indonesians to the detriment of indigenous (*pribumi*—see Glossary) entrepreneurship. These kinds of issues cut across religious boundaries and unite moderate middle-class Muslims with more secular members of the middle class.

Pancasila: The State Ideology

The government undertook at independence the major effort of subsuming all of Indonesia's political cultures, with their different and often incompatible criteria for legitimacy, into a national political culture based on the values set forth in the Pancasila. The preamble of the 1945 constitution establishes the Pancasila as the embodiment of basic principles of an independent Indonesian state. These five principles were announced by Sukarno in a speech on June 1, 1945. In brief, and in the order given in the constitution, the Pancasila principles are belief in one supreme God, humanitarianism, nationalism expressed in the unity of Indonesia, representative democracy, and social justice. Sukarno's statement of the Pancasila, while simple in form, resulted from a complex and sophisticated appreciation of the ideological needs of the new nation. In contrast to Muslim nationalists who insisted on an Islamic identity for the new state, the framers of the Pancasila insisted on a culturally neutral identity, compatible with democratic or Marxist ideologies, and overarching the vast cultural differences of the heterogeneous population. Like the national language, Bahasa Indonesia, which Sukarno also promoted, the Pancasila did not come from any particular ethnic group and was intended to define the basic values for a national political culture.

The Pancasila has its modern aspects, although Sukarno presented it in terms of a traditional Indonesian society in which the nation parallels an idealized village: society is egalitarian, the economy is organized on the basis of mutual cooperation (*gotong royong*), and decision making is by deliberation (*musyawarah*) leading to consensus (*mufakat*). In Sukarno's version of the Pancasila—further defined by Suharto—political and social dissidence constituted deviant behavior.

One reason why both Sukarno and Suharto were successful in using the Pancasila to support their authority, despite their very different policy orientations, is the generalized nature of the principles of the Pancasila. The Pancasila has been less successful as a unifying concept when leadership has tried to give it policy content. Suharto greatly expanded a national indoctrination program established by Sukarno to inculcate a regime-justifying interpretation of the Pancasila in all citizens, especially schoolchildren and civil servants. The Pancasila was thus transformed from an abstract statement of national goals into an instrument of social and political control. To oppose the government was to oppose the Pancasila. To oppose the Pancasila was to oppose the foundation of the state. The effort to enforce conformity to the government's interpretation of Pancasila ideological correctness was not without controversy. The issue that persistently tested the limits of the government's tolerance of alternative or even competitive systems of political thought was the position of religion, especially Islam.

Islam and the Indonesian state had a tense political relationship from the very outset of independence. The Pancasila's promotion of monotheism is a religiously neutral and tolerant statement that equates Islam with the other religious systems: Christianity, Buddhism, and Hindu-Balinese beliefs. However, Muslim political forces had felt betrayed since signing the June 1945 Jakarta Charter, under which they accepted a pluralist republic in return for agreement that the state would be based upon belief in one God "with Muslims obligated to follow the sharia." The decision two months later to remove this seven-word phrase from the preamble of the 1945 constitution, to keep predominantly Christian areas of eastern Indonesia from breaking away from the nationalist movement and declaring their own independence, set the agenda for future Islamic politics. At the extreme were the Darul Islam rebellions of the 1950s, which sought to establish a Muslim theocracy.

Orthodox Muslim groups saw the New Order's emphasis on the Pancasila as an effort to subordinate Islam to a secular state ideology, even a "civil religion" manipulated by a regime inherently biased against the full expression of Muslim life. By the 1980s, however, within the legal and politically acceptable boundaries of Muslim involvement, the state had become a major promoter of Islamic institutions. The government even subsidized numerous Muslim community activities. Within the overall value structure of the Pancasila, Islamic moral teaching and personal codes of conduct balanced the materialism inherent in secular economic development. By wooing Islamic leaders and teachers, the state won broad support for its developmental policies. There is no question but that Islam was a state-favored religion in Indonesia, but it was not a state religion. That reality defined the most critical political issue for many orthodox Muslims. The so-called "hard" *dakwah*, departing from sermons and texts tightly confined to matters of faith and Islamic law, was uncompromisingly antigovernment. The Islamists called for people to die as martyrs in a "struggle until Islam rules." This call, for the government, was incitement to "extremism of the right," subversion, and terrorism. The government reaction to radical Islamic provocations was unyielding: arrest and jail.

The democratic transition has entirely dismantled the New Order structures that institutionalized politicization of the Pancasila. Although the Pancasila is still taught in schools, the national indoctrination program for adults and the agency charged with managing it have both been abolished. Most importantly, political parties and social organizations are no longer required to adopt the Pancasila as their underlying ideological principle (*asas tunggal*). Prominent Muslim organizations in particular immediately took advantage of this change. For instance, the Development Unity Party (PPP) reestablished Islam as its ideological basis and returned to its pre-1984 party symbol, the Kaaba in Mecca. Secular nationalist parties and organizations, however, have retained the Pancasila as their ideological basis. In the early twenty-first century, the Pancasila thus remains alive in Indonesian political discourse in two ways. Harkening back to the pattern in the 1940s and early 1950s, it is one among several ideological strands underpinning political conflicts that have many other dimensions as well: economic, social, regional, and ethnic. On occasion, however, it is still used as a unifying force that can tie all Indonesians together within a national political culture. For example, President Yudhoyono has made several major speeches extolling the Pancasila's virtues in this regard. While generally still aimed at countering the influence of Islamist discourse, this latter usage elevates the Pancasila above the fray of mundane political squabbles.

The Political Process

Many political parties representing all parts of the Indonesian sociocultural spectrum contest national and local elections. Smaller parties disappear, and larger parties split and recombine, no longer because of government interference, but rather, simply, because of the harsh sink-or-swim logic of the free political marketplace: election results and the internal dynamics of these parties. In other words, although Indonesian democracy is not yet fully consolidated and faces many challenges, it is well on its way to becoming "the only game in town."

The Multiparty System: Significant Pluralism

Indonesian voters have clearly rejected the controlled party politics of Guided Democracy and the New Order. Since 1998 hundreds of parties have been founded; 48 qualified to take part in the 1999 elections, 24 for the 2004 elections, and 38 for the 2009 elections (the latter not including the six local parties that contested only in Aceh). Of the 38 national parties, nine won seats in the 2009 DPR. The level of political pluralism (as measured by the Laakso-Taagepera Index of effective political parties) increased from 4.7 in 1999 to 7.1 in 2004 (compared to 6.4 in 1955). Efforts to engineer the electoral framework in order to consolidate the party system, by reducing district magnitude and instituting an electoral threshold of 2.5 percent, were successful: the level of pluralism in 2009 dropped to 6.1 effective political parties. This remains, however, a comparatively high level of pluralism for a presidential system. Party registration criteria in essence prohibit regional parties and force parties to be national in scope. The first and so far only exception to this rule was made as a concession to GAM in the Aceh peace negotiations. Ex-GAM supporters used this exception to form numerous parties, and six qualified to contest the 2009 provincial and district legislative elections.

The largest political parties are secular nationalist parties, which espouse Pancasila as their ideological foundation and have developed platforms that appeal to all Indonesians regardless of religion. Given an overwhelming Muslim-majority population, most of these parties' supporters are Muslim by faith, but they do not believe in mixing faith and politics. These parties include the Golkar Party (the New Order ruling party), the Indonesian Democracy Party–Struggle (PDI–P), and the Democrat Party (PD). Muslim parties draw their support primarily through informal linkages with mass-based Muslim social organizations such as Nahdlatul Ulama and Muhammadiyah, but they are secular nationalist in ideology and platform. These parties include the National Awakening Party (PKB), associated with Nahdlatul Ulama, and the National Mandate Party (PAN), associated with Muhammadiyah. Islamist parties are those that proclaim Islam as their ideological foundation and base their platforms on Islam, including support for Islamic law. This category includes the Development Unity Party (PPP) and the Prosperous Justice Party (PKS).

Although links can be made between these contemporary parties and their predecessors from the 1950s, two differences stand out.

First, the Muslim/Islamist end of the spectrum is much more divided and moderate. Second, there is no direct heir to the Indonesian Communist Party (PKI), and in fact parties professing Marxism-Leninism continued to be outlawed until the Constitutional Court declared this ban unconstitutional in 2005. Despite this decision, it is not likely the PKI will be revived any time soon because of the strong emotions it engenders among many Indonesians and because its former constituency has found a home within several parties, particularly Golkar, the PDI–P, the PD, and the PKB. Most of the major parties draw their strength from association with one or another of Indonesia's socioreligious streams of belief (*aliran kepercayaan*) and a popular individual leader. The parties tend to be highly centralized and riven with internal factionalism. It is very common for factions that lose out in internal party leadership elections to leave to form a rival party. However, few of these splinter parties have fared well in national elections.

Secular Nationalist Parties

Golkar Party

The Golkar Party is the revamped, democratic version of the New Order authoritarian ruling party Golongan Karya (Golkar), the military-backed organization of "functional groups." The longer original name has been dropped, and now the party is simply known as Golkar. Its traditionally very close ties to the military and civil service no longer exist, although many officers and bureaucrats have chosen to continue to support the party rather than join another. However, this support is now personal and private, as the election laws prohibit the use of state resources to support any party, and individual military officers and government officials must resign their positions in order to stand as political candidates. Despite these new restrictions on Golkar's ability to tap its traditional constituencies, the party enjoys advantages over its rivals as a result of its national network, which extends to every village; its experienced politicians; and its strong fund-raising capabilities. The party no longer commands the electoral majorities of 60 to 70 percent that it engineered under the New Order, but it still makes a strong showing, winning 22.4 percent of the vote (120 of 500 DPR seats) to come in second to the PDI–P in the 1999 legislative elections, the largest share of the votes in 2004 (21.6 percent, 128 of 550 DPR seats), and in 2009 the second-largest share (14.5 percent of the vote, 106 of 560 DPR seats). Golkar has also won some of the direct elections for governor, mayor, and *bupati*, and the party's chair, Muhammad Yusuf Kalla, held the vice presidency from 2004 to 2009.

A Yogyakarta storefront display, in June 2000, of portraits of Abdurrahman Wahid (Indonesia's third president, 1999–2001), Sukarno (Indonesia's first president, 1945–66), and Megawati Sukarnoputri (Wahid's vice president, 1999–2001, Indonesia's fourth president, 2001–4,and daughter of Sukarno) Courtesy Florence Lamoureux, © Center for Southeast Asian Studies, University of Hawai'i

Golkar had its roots in Sukarno's Guided Democracy as an army-sponsored coalition of nearly 100 anticommunist organizations and Sukarno's Indonesian Nationalist Party (PNI) to balance the weight of the PKI. After 1966 it was reorganized by Suharto as an ostensibly nonpartisan civilian constituency for the New Order's authority. Its core membership was the military, police, civil service, and employees of state-owned enterprises. Over the course of the New Order, the balance of power in the party slowly shifted to civilians, particularly those such as future party chairman Akbar Tanjung who cut their organizational teeth in the Islamic University Student Association (HMI) and later the Indonesian Muslim Intellectuals' Association (ICMI). As chair from 1983 to 1988, Sudharmono, who served as vice president of Indonesia from 1988 to 1993, attempted to make Golkar a more effective political instrument by shifting from a "functional group" basis to individual cadre membership. As a mass-mobilizing, cadre party loyal to Suharto, Golkar emerged as an autonomous political force in society, no longer fully responsive to the military.

Following Suharto's resignation in May 1998, at a special party congress in July, Golkar took its first major step toward transforming

265

itself into a more dynamic and viable democratic party by choosing Akbar Tanjung over Lieutenant General (retired) Edi Sudrajat as its new chair. Akbar retained control over the party, installing many of his HMI/ICMI faction colleagues in leadership positions and steering the party successfully through the political minefields of the 1999 and 2004 elections, until losing the chairmanship to newly elected Vice President Kalla at the party congress in December 2004. With Kalla's political fortunes declining in 2009, Golkar's election of outgoing Coordinating Minister for People's Welfare Aburizal Bakrie as its new chairman in October 2009, just weeks before the announcement of the new cabinet, was an attempt by the party to retain some national political power. Golkar is generally stronger outside Java and Bali, as reflected by two of its most recent chairs: Akbar is from Sumatera Utara, and Kalla is from Sulawesi Selatan. Kalla and Bakrie also represent an important constituency within Golkar: wealthy *pribumi* (see Glossary) private businesspeople whose family fortunes are largely a product of Sukarno's protectionist economic policies and Suharto's patronage politics.

Indonesian Democracy Party–Struggle

The PDI–P is the successor party to one of the two other parties besides Golkar allowed to exist by the New Order: the Indonesian Democracy Party (PDI). The PDI emerged in 1973 from a fusion of two Christian parties: the Indonesian Christian Party (Parkindo) and the Catholic Party (Partai Katolik); and three secular parties: the Indonesian Nationalist Party (PNI), the League of the Supporters of Indonesian Independence (IPKI), and the Party of the Masses (Partai Murba). With no common ideological link among these constituent parties other than a commitment to Pancasila, the PDI was highly factionalized, torn by personality disputes, and held together only by direct government intervention into its internal affairs. For example, the IPKI had been strongly anti-PKI in the Old Order in contrast to the once-leftist Partai Murba. The PNI, strongest in Jawa Timur and Jawa Tengah, was the largest of the five parties and the legatee of the late President Sukarno. With Sukarno's gradual public rehabilitation as an "Independence Proclamation Hero" and the father of Pancasila, the PDI was not reluctant to trade upon the Sukarnoist heritage of the PNI, including recruiting several of Sukarno's children as candidates and campaigners. Most prominent among them was his eldest daughter, Megawati Sukarnoputri, whose presence helped expand the PDI's vote total in the 1992 elections. After she was elected party chair in 1993, Suharto began to see her as a greater threat and tried to have her removed, but she stood her ground. In 1996 the government backed a rival faction to forcibly eject Megawati and her supporters from party offices. She responded by founding the PDI–P to distinguish it from the New Order–backed PDI, which garnered only 3 percent of the vote in the 1997 elections. Because the PDI–P was not allowed to run in those elections, Megawati instructed her supporters to punish the rump PDI by voting for the PPP, which grew enormously as a result.

Both the PDI–P and the rump PDI competed in the 1999 elections, but with vastly different results. The PDI–P won the largest share with 33.7 percent (153 DPR seats), while the PDI languished with only 0.6 percent (two seats). Megawati became the frontrunner for the October 1999 presidential selection process in the MPR but lost to Abdurrahman Wahid, who then helped her get selected as vice president. When Wahid was removed from office in 2001, she became president until 2004, when she was defeated in direct elections by Susilo Bambang Yudhoyono. The PDI–P's vote in the 2004 legislative elections suffered as well, losing almost half of its support to fall to 18.5 percent (109 DPR seats), as a result of public disappointment with her performance as president, her husband Taufik Kiemas's reputation for corruption, and the party as a whole. Despite these setbacks, Megawati was reelected party chair at the 2005 congress, prompting some disaffected leaders led by Laksamana Sukardi to bolt and found the Democracy Renewal Party (PDP). In the 2009 legislative elections, the PDI–P's support dropped further to 14 percent (94 DPR seats) as a result of competition from the Democrat, Gerindra, and Hanura parties. Megawati, this time running with Prabowo Subianto, was defeated in a rematch with Yudhoyono in the 2009 presidential election.

Democrat Party

The Democrat Party (PD) was founded by then-Coordinating Minister of Politics and Security Susilo Bambang Yudhoyono in 2001 to be his political vehicle. He broke with the usual pattern in Indonesia, however, and did not become the party's chairman. The bulk of the party's initial cadres were mostly mid-level ex-Golkar and former military leaders. Although the party's local branch structure remained weak at the time of the April 2004 legislative elections, the PD still managed to capture 7.5 percent of the vote (57 DPR seats), and thus become one of the seven largest parties, largely on the strength of Yudhoyono's personal popularity. Between 2004 and 2009, the success of the party and Yudhoyono's presidential bid attracted new cadres, who expanded the party's structure into a truly national presence. This expansion, combined with Yudhoyono's continuing popularity, gave the PD the most votes in the April 2009 legislative elections, with 20.9 percent of the vote (148 of 560 DPR seats). The party's prospects in 2014 and beyond remain unclear, however, with Yudhoyono no longer eligible to run for reelection at that time.

Gerindra and Hanura Parties

The two smallest of the nine parties to win DPR seats in the 2009 elections were new parties both founded by retired army generals with highly tainted human-rights records. The Great Indonesia Movement Party (Gerindra Party) is the political vehicle for retired Lieutenant General Prabowo Subianto, the son of famed economist and finance minister Sumitro Joyohadikusumo and the former son-in-law of Suharto. Prabowo has a particularly cruel reputation from his career in the Army Special Forces Command (Kopassus) and has been implicated in severe human-rights abuses in East Timor, the temporary or permanent disappearance and death of 23 prodemocracy activists in 1997 and 1998, and the Jakarta riots, as well as a coup attempt against newly installed President Habibie, in May 1998. Despite this record, Prabowo was able to convince three of the activists he is alleged to have kidnapped and tortured to run under the Gerindra Party banner, and the party won 4.5 percent of the vote and 26 DPR seats. Prabowo ran as Megawati's vice presidential candidate, but they placed a distant second to Yudhoyono.

The People's Conscience Party (Hanura Party) was founded by retired General Wiranto, who helped force Suharto from power, quash Prabowo's attempted coup, and begin military reforms. He also was in command during the Indonesian army–backed militia rampage in East Timor in September 1999 as well as during several bloody incidents with demonstrators in Jakarta. In 2009 the Hanura Party won 3.8 percent of the vote and 17 DPR seats. Wiranto ran as Kalla's vice presidential candidate, but the ticket won only 12 percent of the vote to place third.

Muslim Parties

National Awakening Party

Founded by Abdurrahman Wahid in 1998 as the heir to the Nahdlatul Ulama political party from the 1950s, the National Awakening Party (PKB) is the most successful of the Muslim parties that have tried to draw on Nahdlatul Ulama's vast organizational strength. Although formally Nahdlatul Ulama is not associated with any of these parties, it is the backbone of them all, including the PKB. Nonetheless, the PKB certainly does not have a monopoly on the political loyalties of Nahdlatul Ulama supporters, who are scattered

Supporters of the Indonesian Democracy Party–Struggle (PDI–P)
march in a campaign parade, Sulawesi Utara Province, 2004.
The banner, shown here in reverse, touts the No. 12 candidate on the ballot
for the Regional Representative Council (DPD).
Courtesy Anastasia Riehl

among nearly all the major and some minor parties. Following the geographic pattern of Nahdlatul Ulama's organizational depth and Wahid's personal cachet, the PKB's electoral strength is concentrated in Jawa Timur and Jawa Tengah.

The PKB does not support the rigid implementation of Islamic law and is an open party with support in parts of Indonesia with significant Christian populations, such as in Sulawesi Utara, Kalimantan Barat, and Papua. Because of Wahid's personal control over the PKB, his and the party's fortunes moved more or less in tandem. He used the PKB's performance in the 1999 legislative elections (third-largest party with 12.6 percent of the vote and 51 DPR seats) as a springboard to build a coalition behind his successful presidential bid that year in the MPR voting. Wahid's erratic administration reflected poorly on the PKB as well, and the party lost some of its public support, as well as access to patronage and the bully pulpit, when he was removed from office in July 2001. As a result, in 2004 the PKB lost two percentage points of its 1999 vote share, dropping to 10.6 percent in 2004. (Nonetheless, because all five of the major parties from 1999 lost support in 2004, the PKB retained the third-largest party share of the popular vote.) After Wahid lost the presidency, the party began to splinter, and the 2004 election results caused a major split, with both pro- and anti-Wahid factions claiming the PKB's mantle. At the outset of the new administration, the party took an independent stance vis-à-vis President Yudhoyono, sometimes supporting and sometimes opposing his policies. However, by 2007 the PKB had swung around much more solidly in support of the administration because of Yudhoyono's success and Wahid's complete loss of control over the party. As a result of party splintering, reduced support overall for Muslim and Islamist parties, and greater competition from secular nationalist parties, the PKB vote share was more than halved in 2009 to 4.9 percent (28 DPR seats).

National Mandate Party

Paralleling the PKB's relationship with Nahdlatul Ulama and Wahid, the National Mandate Party (PAN) is strongly associated with Muhammadiyah and political-science professor Amien Rais from Yogyakarta. Beginning in the early 1990s, Rais became a thorn in Suharto's side, calling for presidential succession and highlighting cases of corruption and other malfeasance. Despite (or perhaps because of) this vocal opposition, he was elected chair of Muhammadiyah in 1995. In 1998 he became the most prominent adult face of the student-led *reformasi* (see Glossary) movement, which succeeded in forcing Suharto's resignation. (Wahid had had a stroke in January 1998, and Megawati remained on the sidelines.) Following the founding of the PAN in August 1998, Rais had to step down as Muhammadiyah's chair. Although founded as an open party, with Christians and ethnic Chinese prominent among its leadership, the PAN also has a significant hardline Islamist wing. As that wing gained ascendancy within the party, many of the PAN's initial secular and Christian leaders began to abandon it. While few of these leaders were linked to mass-based organizations that could deliver votes, they were among the key intellectual capital in the party, and their departure also fostered the perception of a party in trouble.

In the 1999 elections, the PAN fared worse than had been expected, given Rais's prominence in opposing Suharto, winning only 7.1 percent of the popular vote (34 DPR seats). Although this result dashed his presidential ambitions, it was enough, combined with clever political maneuvering, for Rais to be elected speaker of the MPR. From this position, Rais chose to involve himself more in politicking against presidents Wahid and Megawati than in the constitutional-reform process being undertaken by the MPR. This strategy may have hurt the PAN, for it reinforced the public perception of Rais as strident, divisive, and having abandoned the *reformasi* movement for sheer power politics. In addition, the PAN's poor showing weakened Rais's position within the party, enhancing the ascendancy of the Islamist wing and leading to further defections by members of the secular/Christian wing.

The Islamist wing's hypothesis that a more focused albeit more narrowly based party would attract more voters than a less focused, but broader-based, party was proven wrong in the 2004 elections, in which the PAN's share of the popular vote shrank to 6.4 percent (52 DPR seats), making it the smallest of the seven major parties. (The PAN's support in 2004 was more evenly spread around the country than in 1999, and so its share of DPR seats actually increased from 7.4 percent to 9.5 percent.) Although Rais tried his hand in the first direct presidential election, he lost in the first round and subsequently left the political scene after completing his term as MPR speaker in October 2004. He was replaced as PAN chair by a much less well-known figure, Sutrisno Bachir, and returned to his former life as an academic at Universitas Gadjah Mada in Yogyakarta. With several of its leaders holding cabinet posts in the Yudhoyono administration, the PAN mostly supported the administration, although it has reserved the right to criticize on occasion. In 2009 the PAN's support declined to 6.0 percent of the vote (46 DPR seats), because of waning overall support for Muslim and Islamist parties as well as greater competition from the DP, Gerindra, and Hanura parties.

Islamist Parties

Development Unity Party

The Development Unity Party (PPP; often erroneously referred to as the United Development Party) was the umbrella grouping formed when the government compelled four Muslim parties to merge in the 1973 restructuring of the party system. The four components were Nahdlatul Ulama, the Muslim Party of Indonesia (PMI), the Islamic Association Party of Indonesia (PSII), and the Islamic Educational Movement (Perti). The PPP's constituent parties neither submerged their identities nor merged their programs. As a result, no single PPP leader emerged with a platform acceptable to all the sectarian and regional interests represented by the PPP. Despite their manifest differences representing divergent *santri* streams, however, the PPP's parties had the common bond of Islam, and it was this that gained them the government's close attention.

The dominant partners were Nahdlatul Ulama and the PMI; the latter was a resurrected but emasculated version of Masyumi, which had been banned in the Sukarno era and continued to be proscribed under Suharto. The return of modernist Islamic interests (represented by the PMI) to mainstream politics was stage-managed by the government, which apparently favored the PMI within the PPP to counterbalance the appeal of Nahdlatul Ulama. In 1984 the government forced the PPP to adopt Pancasila (as opposed to Islam) as its basic ideological principle. The decline in Nahdlatul Ulama's influence in the PPP, together with constraints on the Islamic content of the PPP's message, confirmed the traditionalists' perception that Nahdlatul Ulama should withdraw from the political process and concentrate on its religious, social, and educational activities. The theme of Nahdlatul Ulama's 1984 congress was "Back to Nahdlatul Ulama's Original Program of Action of 1926." While constitutionally accepting Pancasila as its sole ideological principle, Nahdlatul Ulama opted out of the Pancasila political competition by holding that political party membership was a personal decision and that individual Nahdlatul Ulama members had no obligation to support the PPP.

Nahdlatul Ulama's withdrawal from the PPP combined with Megawati's rise in the PDI to shift some of the opposition votes from the PPP to the PDI in the 1987 and 1992 elections. In the 1997 elections, after her forcible ejection from the PDI offices in 1996, Megawati instructed her supporters to vote for the PPP. This was called the "Mega-Bintang" campaign (*bintang* means "star," the party symbol for the PPP, which after 1984 was no longer allowed to use the Kaaba in Mecca as its symbol), and it greatly weakened the PDI, to the PPP's benefit. One consequence of these election results was that in late 1998 and early 1999, as the DPR debated the package of laws for the 1999 democratic elections, the PPP positioned itself as the voice of the *reformasi* movement within the legislature and forced several important changes to those laws. For instance, Golkar proposed an electoral system it called "proportional plus" that would in essence have established single-member districts in many parts of the country. Given Golkar's overwhelming resource advantage at the time, it could have swept many of these seats and possibly maintained its grip on power. Instead, the PPP was able to use its position in the DPR to mobilize public opposition to this proposal, which was dropped in favor of retaining proportional representation in order to encourage political pluralism. In light of the founding of rival parties such as the PKB and the PAN, this tactic helped save the PPP from fading into political obscurity as has the PDI.

In 1999 the PPP was allowed to restore Islam as its ideological basis and the Kaaba as its symbol, and it won 10.7 percent of the popular vote (58 DPR seats) to become the fourth-largest party. The PPP supported Wahid for president and was rewarded with several cabinet positions. During the constitutional-reform process following those elections, the party supported the reinsertion of language calling for Islamic law to be established for Indonesian Muslims, in part to protect its right flank from smaller but harder-line Islamist parties. This is one of the markers that distinguishes "Muslim" from "Islamist" parties: the PKB and the PAN opposed this proposal, which eventually was soundly defeated. Party leadership rivalries caused a faction to break off and form the Reform Star Party (PBR). The PBR proved to be one of the few splinter parties to gain any significant share of votes in the 2004 legislative elections, winning 2.4 percent (13 DPR seats). The split, combined with voter disappointment with the performance of all the major parties, caused the PPP's vote share to drop to 8.2 percent (58 DPR seats), but it still maintained its position as the fourth-largest party by popular vote. The PPP supported a rival ticket in the first round of the 2004 presidential election, although it threw its weight behind Yudhoyono and Kalla in the second round and again garnered several cabinet seats as a result. In 2009, although the PBR won only 1.2 percent of the vote and no DPR seats because of the electoral threshold, the PPP vote share slid to 5.3 percent (38 DPR seats) as a result of overall voter dissatisfaction with Muslim and Islamist parties.

Prosperous Justice Party

The Prosperous Justice Party (PKS) contested the 1999 elections as the Justice Party (PK), founded in 1998. Because the PK won only 1.4 percent of the popular vote in 1999 (seven DPR seats), the law required it to change its name in order to contest the 2004 elections. The PK drew on networks of university campus-based Quranic study groups as its organizational backbone. Nearly all of its leaders had advanced degrees, mostly from universities in the Middle East and the United States. The party's emphasis on Islamic law limited its appeal in 1999. The PK spoke frequently of its vision for managing religious pluralism in Indonesia as being based on the Medina Charter, promulgated in AD 622 by the Prophet Muhammad, who guaranteed protection for Christian and Jewish communities. Many non-Muslims in Indonesia, however, interpreted this as a form of second-class citizenship under Islamist rule. Despite the party's low vote total, President Wahid appointed its leader, Nur Mahmudi Isma'il, minister of forestry. Nur Mahmudi set an unusual precedent in Indonesian politics by stepping down from the party presidency upon entering the government, in order to concentrate on his role as a minister. The PK also enhanced its influence by joining the PAN to form the Reformasi Bloc in the DPR and the MPR.

The party also set about expanding its base as part of its transformation from the PK to the PKS. The PKS is unusual in that it is the only true cadre party in Indonesia. It requires prospective members to study party doctrine and regulations and to take an oath of loyalty to those principles. The party has disciplined or expelled members for violating these principles. Party members may also attend regular training programs. The party's support base remains more heavily urban and more highly educated than the general voting population, but it has begun to make inroads in rural areas.

The PKS quintupled the PK's 1999 share of the vote in 2004 to 7.3 percent of the popular vote (45 DPR seats), largely by emphasizing themes of anticorruption and good governance in its campaign and de-emphasizing Islamic law. Although all the parties campaigned on fighting corruption, the PKS came across as the most credible in this regard, for two reasons. First, the party exploited its reputation for religiosity as a source of morally based and clean governance, and some voters differentiated between this and the establishment of Islamic law. Second, PK leaders and legislators had developed a track record in the 1999–2004 term. Minister of Forestry Nur Mahmudi attempted to purge the industry of some of its most unsavory practices and business partners. Although he did not last long in office, and his efforts met with only limited success, they helped burnish the PKS's reformist credentials. Provincial and district legislators across the country had continued the New Order practice of voting themselves large allowances, often ostensibly for official vehicles or uniforms. PK legislators made a point of very publicly returning these questionable allowances to the local treasury or donating them to a mosque or community group. The party used the newspaper clippings describing these actions in its 2004 campaign. The PKS also developed a reputation for conducting peaceful and orderly campaign rallies, and for cleaning up after its followers when the rallies were over. These actions made the party especially popular in Jakarta, where it won the largest share of votes in the 2004 legislative elections.

The party's success landed its president, Hidayat Nur Wahid, the position of MPR speaker for the 2004 term. Following party regulations, he stepped down from his leadership role upon accepting this government position. In 2005 Nur Mahmudi Isma'il was directly elected mayor of Depok, the city on the western outskirts of Jakarta that is home to Universitas Indonesia. The party intended to use these positions to demonstrate its commitment to clean governance, setting its sights on eventually winning the presidency. The party had to contend, however, with widespread voter suspicion, among both non-Muslims and moderate Muslims, that the PKS's de-emphasis of Islamic law was simply a tactical rather than a truly strategic shift. The party's stated support for such radical figures as Jemaah Islamiyah spiritual leader Abu Bakar Ba'asyir reinforced these concerns. These limits on the party's appeal were vividly demonstrated in 2007, when it failed to win the governor's race in Jakarta despite its 2004 plurality victory in the city's legislative elections.

The PKS has won more positions in various levels of government, inevitably finding that it has to make hard choices and compromises, and its appeal to its more puritanical core constituency has begun to suffer. The PKS no longer enjoys the same level of credibility in fighting corruption, and thus it has lost its uniqueness and increasingly come to be viewed as just one more party on the spectrum. Although in 2009 it bucked the overall trend of major parties losing voter support, its gains were hardly as spectacular as in 2004. In 2009 its vote share rose slightly to 7.9 percent (57 DPR seats), making the PKS Indonesia's fourth-largest party.

Elections

Indonesia has now held three sets of democratic national elections, in 1999, 2004, and 2009, following decades of stage-managed elections under the New Order. The 1999 elections were the first democratic national elections since 1955. Local direct elections for governor, mayor, and *bupati* have been held on a rolling basis in all parts of the country since 2005. The political maturity of Indonesian voters, combined with extensive monitoring by civil-society groups, helped make all of these elections largely free of violence and fraud, despite great concerns beforehand to the contrary.

To be eligible to participate in 1999, parties had to be national in scope, with party branches established in at least one-third of the provinces and one-half of the administrative districts within those provinces. A reconstituted General Elections Commission (KPU) administered the elections. It consisted of 48 representatives of the parties and five "government" representatives. (To avoid perceptions of continuity with the authoritarian management of elections under the New Order, the Habibie government chose to fill these positions with members of civil society and academia.) Although this structure functioned well to signal a clean break with the past and a level playing field for all parties, it broke down both in the run-up to the elections (when many of the party representatives were off campaigning) and following the elections (when most of the 48 parties won few votes or seats and began making unfounded allegations of fraud and boycotting KPU meetings).

Since 2002 the KPU has consisted of nine nonpartisan commissioners selected by the DPR from a longer list of candidates nominated by the president from civil society and academia. The 1999 elections continued the New Order practice of a closed-list proportional-representation system with the provinces as the electoral districts for the DPR; thus, the districts ranged in size from four seats (in former Timor Timur Province, now independent Timor-Leste) to 82 seats (Jawa Barat). These were simultaneous elections for the national DPR and the provincial and local DPRDs; each voter used a nail to punch a hole in one of the 48 party symbols on each of the three ballots. These legislative elections were followed by the presidential selection process within the MPR in October. Governors, mayors, and *bupatis* were selected by their respective DPRD.

The 2004 and 2009 elections were more complicated than those in 1999. There were three electoral processes: legislative elections in early April, the first round of the presidential election in early July, and the second round in September (necessary in 2004 but not in 2009). The vote for the legislative entities consisted of four separate and simultaneous elections, not just three as in 1999 and throughout the New Order. In addition to the DPR and the provincial and district DPRDs, voters now also elected representatives to the new upper house of the national legislature, the Regional Representative Council (DPD).

Two reforms addressed the complaint that representatives in the DPR and DPRDs had been too detached from their constituents. First, electoral districts were limited to between three and 10 seats (for 2009; in 2004 the upper limit was 12 seats). In the 19 least populated provinces, this rule meant that the province remained the electoral district. The other 14 provinces were divided along municipality and regency boundaries into between two and 11 electoral districts in order to fall into the mandated seat range. (All of these electoral districts consisted of more than one administrative district; in no case was an electoral district made up of a single administrative district.) The average DPR district across the 77 electoral districts nationwide had approximately seven representatives. Second, voters could choose a candidate from anywhere on the party's list rather than just voting for a party. This open-list proportional-representation system is designed to make representatives more beholden to voters than to party leaders for their seats, and, in fact, nearly 20 percent of DPR members in 2009 (104 of 560) were chosen by voters from lower positions on the candidate lists. This method does make election logistics incredibly compli-

SURAT SUARA PEMILIHAN UMUM
ANGGOTA DEWAN PERWAKILAN RAKYAT (DPR)

2004

DAERAH PEMILIHAN :

Ballot with party logos for 2004 elections
Courtesy Embassy of Indonesia, Washington, DC

cated; ballots look like newspapers, and each electoral district has to have a separate ballot listing its candidates.

A further complication for voters was that the election system for the DPD was entirely different from that for the DPR and DPRDs. DPD candidates, who represented entire provinces, campaigned more as individuals, even if they were affiliated with a political party. (DPD candidates had to have been residing in the province they represented and obtain thousands of signatures of registered voters in order to be nominated. For the 2004 elections, candidates were not allowed to have a political-party affiliation, but for the 2009 elections, candidates could be—but did not have to be—partisan.) Candidates' names and photographs appeared on the ballot. Each voter marked one candidate, and the four candidates with the most votes were elected.

The DPR elections served as a sort of primary for the presidential election. Parties or coalitions thereof with at least 20 percent of DPR seats, or 25 percent of the national DPR vote, were eligible to nominate presidential and vice-presidential tickets (this threshold was only 3 percent of DPR seats in 2004). In 2004 five tickets were nominated:

277

Susilo Bambang Yudhoyono and Muhammad Yusuf Kalla (winning 33.6 percent of the vote in the first round) by the PD, Indonesian Justice and Unity Party (PKPI), and Star and Moon Party (PBB); Megawati Sukarnoputri and Hasyim Muzadi (26.2 percent) by the PDI–P; Wiranto and Salahuddin Wahid (22.2 percent) by Golkar; Amien Rais and Siswono Yudohusodo (14.9 percent) by the PAN, PKS, and several smaller parties; and Hamzah Haz and Agum Gumelar (3.1 percent) by the PPP. The PKB did not nominate a ticket because its presidential candidate, former President Wahid, was declared physically unfit for the position (a new criterion instituted in reaction to his administration). Because no ticket won more than 50 percent in the first round, a second round occurred in which Yudhoyono and Kalla soundly defeated Megawati and Hasyim, 60.9 percent to 39.1 percent, respectively. Three tickets were nominated in 2009: Yudhoyono and Budiono by the PD, PKS, PAN, PPP, and PKB (winning 60.8 percent of the vote in the first round); Megawati and Prabowo Subianto by the PDI–P and Gerindra (26.8 percent); and Kalla and Wiranto by Golkar and Hanura (12.4 percent). Because Yudhoyono and Budiono won more than 50 percent in the first round, a second round was not necessary.

The huge rallies of motorcycles, automobiles, and trucks cruising around cities, hallmarks of previous Indonesian campaigning, were banned beginning in 2004. Mass rallies in stadiums and other venues were still one of the most popular campaign techniques, although the open-list system for the DPR and the DPD elections did prompt more frequent door-to-door campaigning than had been the case previously. Television proved to be a significant campaign medium in the presidential election, and Yudhoyono used it particularly effectively in 2004 to overtake other, better-known candidates. Other candidates were busy lining up endorsements from political parties and political elites, but Yudhoyono tried to get coverage of his campaign rallies on the news every evening. In this way, he turned a nominating coalition that together had won only 11.4 percent of the vote in the legislative elections in April into convincing victories in both rounds of the presidential election.

Political finance continues to be problematic in Indonesia. Both parties and candidates fund raise for executive and legislative elections. Election laws include limits on donations, although these regulations are poorly enforced, and spending is not limited. Most parties require legislative candidates to donate to party coffers in exchange for a place on the list; as a general rule, the higher the financial donation, the closer a candidate is placed to the top of the list. Even in an open-list system, placement near the top is advantageous. Similarly, most parties require local executive candidates to donate in exchange for nomination, a situation that creates incentives for elected candidates to engage in corruption in order to recoup these payments and begin amassing funds for future elections. The process has been overseen, in all the national and local elections since 1999, by an official Election Oversight Committee (Panwaslu) system. However, the law has granted this system few real powers except to be a repository for complaints; any serious matters must still be handled by the police and the judicial system. The system is also underfunded, hampering its efficiency. More effective monitoring and observation of the elections since 1999 have been conducted by political parties, domestic civil-society groups, the media, and international organizations. The parties and domestic groups in particular have mobilized and trained hundreds of thousands of volunteers to monitor the process and report election results.

Political Dynamics

Political Opposition

President Yudhoyono's first term in office was marked by repeated natural and other environmental disasters. These included the Aceh earthquake and tsunami in December 2004, the Yogyakarta earthquake in May 2006, the Lumpur Sidoarjo (Lusi) mud volcano in Jawa Timur beginning in May 2006, the Pangandaran earthquake and tsunami in July 2006, forest fires in Sumatra and Kalimantan that caused choking haze in Malaysia and Singapore in October 2006 and 2007, massive floods in Jakarta in February 2007, and the Tasikmalaya and Padang earthquakes in September 2009. Despite these and other challenges, Yudhoyono remained quite popular; public-opinion polls generally gave him an approval rating between 40 and 60 percent. His continued popularity created problems for the formation of a sustained opposition, and he exploited this situation to shore up his legislative support. Having only Megawati as a strong challenger, he was easily reelected in 2009.

The Yudhoyono-Kalla administration's consolidation of its political position began within months of taking office. Golkar, the PDI–P, the PKB, and the PBR had formed the National Front in opposition to the new administration and had swept all DPR leadership positions. At Golkar's December 2004 congress, however, Kalla was elected to be the new party chairman just days before the Aceh tsunami. This broke up the National Front and brought the largest party solidly behind the vice president (if not always the president himself).

Yudhoyono also managed to neutralize the PKB, PAN, and PPP so that even though these parties were not solid supporters, neither were they strident opponents. The PKB has suffered from internal rivalries between pro- and anti-Wahid factions, both of which have claimed control of the party. Wahid remained a frequent critic of the president, although even his own faction in the party leadership drew closer to the administration in order to sideline their opponents within the party. Wahid himself suffered further health problems and died in December 2009. PAN leaders had held several seats in the cabinet since the beginning of the Yudhoyono administration, but the party remained at arm's length from the president until its founder, one-time presidential rival and frequent critic Amien Rais, stepped down as chair and retired from active engagement in politics at the party congress in 2005. A similar dynamic occurred within the PPP, led until the party congress in 2007 by former Vice President Hamzah Haz, another of Yudhoyono's rivals in the 2004 election. The party elected then-Minister for Cooperatives and Small and Medium Enterprises Suryadharma Ali to be its new chairman over Arief Mudatsir Mandan, a DPR member supported by Haz. This left the PDI–P as the only one of the seven major parties remaining as a consistent member of the opposition. Following the 2009 elections, the PDI–P was joined in opposition only by the two smallest parties in the DPR, Gerindra and Hanura.

Islam

The *reformasi* period has witnessed a great debate among four camps within Islam in Indonesia: extremists, conservatives, moderates, and liberals. These camps exist within both the traditionalist and modernist streams of Islam in Indonesia. The smaller and more marginalized of these camps are the extremists and the liberals on the right and left fringes of the debate, respectively; the bulk of the debate is thus in the center of this spectrum between the conservatives and the moderates.

The extremists are the groups and individuals that have been involved in acts of terrorism, communal violence, and small-scale thuggery and extortion; what sets them apart from the other three camps is their use of violence. These groups and individuals participate in the debate mainly through actions rather than words; surprisingly, their information campaigns have been limited. Terrorism has mainly been associated with Jemaah Islamiyah, Al Qaeda's Southeast Asian affiliate, whose spiritual leader is Abu Bakar Ba'asyir. Jemaah Islamiyah has been associated with the five most prominent terrorist bombings in Indonesia in recent years: in the Kuta tourist district in southern Bali in October 2002 and October 2005, the JW Marriott Hotel in Jakarta in August 2003, the Australian Embassy in

Jakarta in September 2004, and the JW Marriott and Ritz-Carlton hotels in Jakarta in July 2009.

Communal violence has been associated mainly with organizations such as Laskar Jihad, a Java-based group that involved itself in the conflicts in Maluku and Sulawesi Tengah. These organizations often justified their actions by claiming that they intervened to defend Muslims from physical attack by Christians. In all of these communal conflicts, however, while religious affiliations were used to mobilize people on all sides, the roots of the conflicts were much deeper and more complex; religion was and continues to be layered with ethnic, economic, political, and personal rivalries. The involvement of these organizations thus simply served to polarize and extend the conflict even further.

Thuggery and extortion are the realm of groups such as the Islamic Defenders' Front (FPI), which consists of criminal gangs posing as social organizations in a very similar manner to New Order–era groups such as Pancasila Youth (Pemuda Pancasila). The main difference is that the FPI uses Islamic rather than nationalist symbols and slogans to mobilize supporters and neutralize critics. The FPI and similar groups have raided bars and discos, held violent demonstrations at the offices of the Indonesian edition of *Playboy*, and so forth. These groups likely have numerous motives for their actions, including both religious convictions and the desire for protection money in exchange for leaving such businesses alone.

Conservatives have concentrated their efforts on incorporating Islamic law into Indonesian daily life in various ways. Their initial efforts focused on reinserting the phrase from the Jakarta Charter ("with Muslims obligated to follow the sharia") into the 1945 constitution as part of the amendment process from 1999–2002. This proposal, most strongly supported by the PK and the PBB, but also by the PPP to cover its right flank from these two smaller parties, was soundly defeated in the MPR in 2002. The conservatives then took advantage of decentralization to win approval by various district and municipality assemblies of local regulations implementing several aspects of Islamic law, especially those commonly used to regulate women's dress and behavior. These regulations may be unconstitutional, as religion is one of the six major policy areas reserved for the central government under decentralization; however, as of 2009 none of these regulations had been challenged before the Constitutional Court.

Local implementation of Islamic law became institutionalized in the special-autonomy law for Aceh, despite the fact that this was not a primary Acehnese demand. Resulting developments include a religious police force for Aceh and the drafting of regional regulations, such as a punishment for theft that involves cutting off the perpetrator's hand.

Aceh governor Irwandi Yusuf, a former rebel leader, has vowed not to enforce such regulations even if they are approved.

Moderates still represent the vast majority of Indonesian Muslims. Although large organizations such as Nahdlatul Ulama and Muhammadiyah are internally diverse, including conservatives, moderates, and liberals among their members, they remain dominated by moderates. Of the two, however, Muhammadiyah has tended to be more conservative than Nahdlatul Ulama. As the dominant majority faced with rising extremism and a newly resurgent conservative minority, moderates have been put on the defensive. They have often struggled to make their voices heard without being labeled lackeys of the West or apostates. The main distinction between conservatives and moderates is that the former want Islamic law codified and enforced as part of Indonesian law, whereas the latter see it more as a set of rules for personal behavior, enforced only by one's faith and self-discipline. Moderates are also much more likely to engage with non-Muslims in interfaith initiatives and to speak publicly of tolerance of differences and the equality of believers of all faiths.

There is a small but highly visible group of mostly young intellectuals and activists from both the traditionalist and modernist streams that can be characterized as liberals, pushing the envelope of *ijtihad* (exegesis) with innovative and often highly controversial ideas. Consistent with this cutting-edge profile, the most prominent organizational home for this group is virtual, the Liberal Islam Network (JIL), an online discussion forum. The JIL's physical headquarters is in the Utan Kayu complex in East Jakarta. This complex was established in the late New Order period by Gunawan Mohammad (the leading intellectual and journalist who helped found the news magazine *Tempo*) as an incubator for a wide range of creative, opposition-minded young people. Many conservatives and extremists have a visceral negative reaction to the liberals and have demonstrated at the Utan Kayu complex, threatening to expel and shut down the JIL and calling for the death of JIL leader Ulil Abshar Abdalla, who temporarily fled the country for his own safety.

The Military

More than a decade after the beginning of the democratic transition, the Indonesian National Armed Forces (TNI) retains the potential for significant political influence. This latent influence is rarely used in public, however, and may not even be that effective behind the scenes. Nonetheless, it exists. The sources of this influence are twofold: institutional and cultural. Although the military has been stripped of many of the direct powers it enjoyed under the New

Order, the institutional core of its power—the army's territorial system and the network of off-budget companies, foundations, and cooperatives supported by that system—remains intact (see Administrative and Command Structure, ch. 5). The Yudhoyono administration has made an inventory of these military enterprises, with the aim of transferring them all to civilian state control for privatization or closure, a process not complete in 2009. No serious proposals have been made to dismantle the territorial system as part of the effort to reorient the military to focus on external defense. It is important not to overstate the power of this system, which is more effective as a subtle threat than in actual use. In fact, the military is small relative to the population as a whole, and the territorial system is staffed by the more poorly trained and equipped half of the army, limiting its ability to move in more than a few cities simultaneously. These limitations were clearly evident in 1998 in the face of a nationwide, grassroots student movement, and that was a time when the military still enjoyed its more direct levers of power.

The cultural source of the military's latent political influence is the public's perception, rightly or wrongly, of officers as firm decision makers who consider the national interest in those decisions, as opposed to the stereotype of bickering civilian politicians who take only their parochial interests into consideration. This perception also has its limitations, for the public does not prefer just any officer. When given a choice, voters have clearly expressed their preference for those with less baggage in terms of human-rights violations or corruption. Thus, while it is a sign of this source of influence that someone with retired General Wiranto's dismal human-rights record could gain 22.2 percent of the vote in the first round of the 2004 presidential election, missing moving forward into the second round by only four percentage points, he was soundly defeated by a candidate with many fewer allegations of human-rights violations and much greater credibility in fighting corruption, retired Lieutenant General Susilo Bambang Yudhoyono. This pattern repeated itself in 2009, when Wiranto and Prabowo Subianto, who has an even worse human-rights record, were unable to help their presidential tickets against Yudhoyono. At the subnational level, there are now many fewer governors, mayors, and *bupatis* with a military background than in the New Order. Furthermore, these individuals (like presidential and legislative candidates) have had to retire from the armed forces in order to become involved in politics, and their election does not seem to have directly benefited the military as an institution.

Despite the limitations on the military's institutional and cultural sources of political influence, this latent power could be called upon were Indonesia to have a populist demagogue leader, somewhat along the lines of Venezuela's Hugo Chávez. Under the right circumstances (such as economic stagnation), such a leader could offer the Indonesian public relief from their economic woes at the cost of a rollback of democratic freedoms. Recent commanders have made significant progress in instilling a culture of professionalism and political neutrality in the military. However, more reforms will be necessary to ensure that less scrupulous leaders could no longer use the military as a tool of political repression.

Communal Violence

One of the greatest fears among the political elite in 1998 was that Indonesia would break apart into smaller countries, as had happened in the Soviet Union and Yugoslavia. This did not happen, but in various parts of the archipelago other developments did begin to mirror events in Yugoslavia in the 1990s. Communities that had previously coexisted in relative harmony rapidly spiraled into conflict, although in Indonesia none of these tensions ever approached the scale of communal violence in the former Yugoslavia.

Sporadic incidents had already begun in 1996 when the New Order still appeared quite solid, with church burnings in such places as Pasuruan (in Jawa Timur) and Tasikmalaya (in Jawa Barat). The scale and geographic spread of violence ramped up significantly, however, following Suharto's resignation, as the national government became preoccupied with the political transition and security forces could no longer repress long-simmering local grievances. In January 1999, following the expulsion of Ambonese gangs from Jakarta to Ambon, as well as the breakdown of informal ethnic power-sharing agreements in Maluku Province, a minor traffic accident in Ambon exploded into terrible and sustained violence between Muslims and Christians in that city. Over the next three years, several thousand members of both communities were killed, and parts of the city became no-go zones for one group or the other. Extremist Muslim groups such as Laskar Jihad—allegedly supported by like-minded senior military officers— flocked to Ambon and played a major role in the dramatic expansion of violence in that city. The violence that erupted in Kalimantan Barat was even more horrific, as indigenous (Christian) Dayaks in rural Sambas District went on a rampage against Muslim Madurese in-migrants who had taken a prominent role in local commerce and agriculture. Hundreds were killed, some of their severed heads left on poles as a warning to others, and many houses burned to the ground. Sustained violence also erupted between Muslims and Christians in Sulawesi Tengah around the cities of Poso and Tentena, where Laskar

Jihad and the more sinister Jemaah Islamiyah terrorist group had established a training camp. At the end of the first decade of the twenty-first century, this conflict continues to fester, with sporadic incidents of violence by one community on the other.

Many of these conflicts appear, on the surface, to be between ethnic or religious communities, particularly Muslims and Christians. However, deeper analysis reveals that very localized struggles over political and economic power are the underlying cause. Unfortunately, these political and economic struggles have often been framed by conflict entrepreneurs as being rooted in ethnic or religious cleavages, making it easier to mobilize communities against one another. External forces have also exacerbated such conflicts. In Ambon, security forces were perceived as taking sides, the army with Muslim communities and police mobile brigades with Christian communities.

Yusuf Kalla gained greater political prominence when, as coordinating minister of public welfare in President Megawati's cabinet, he helped mediate negotiations to resolve the longer-running of these conflicts in Poso and Ambon. The resulting agreements were called Malino I (for Poso) and Malino II (for Ambon), after the location of the negotiations. Malino II has largely held, but peace has not yet fully returned to Poso. Kalla trumpeted his role in these accords in helping Yudhoyono win the 2004 presidential election and drew on these experiences in dealings with Aceh as vice president.

Civil Society

Indonesia's post–New Order democracy has a civil society that is vibrant but that also has fairly shallow roots in the broader citizenry, with certain important exceptions. Most Indonesian nongovernmental organizations (NGOs) are small urban organizations founded and staffed by a handful of former student activists (see Civil Society, ch. 2). They tend to claim to speak on behalf of "the people" (*rakyat*) broadly or of certain communities, but often they have not bothered to reach out to, educate, or mobilize those communities. Many of these organizations fail to attract significant support and are short-lived; those with larger budgets are often dependent on foreign-donor funding. This leaves them open to charges by conservative nationalists that they are puppets of foreign governmental interests.

The proliferation of NGOs since the late 1970s is an indicator of the increased diversity of society, the growth of a modern middle class, and the penetration of the political culture by issues of global concern. These organizations raise issues ranging from human rights and the rule of law to corruption and environmental degradation. Despite the fact that most NGOs are small grassroots organizations that focus on economic development and social-welfare issues, many of the more prominent NGOs are aggressively intervening in areas of agrarian or other fundamental human rights. In the 1990s, these organizations also provided a new outlet for student activism, confined since the 1970s to nonpolitical behavior. University students found both a cause and a vehicle for renewed social involvement. This repoliticization and organizing experience laid the groundwork for the student movement of 1998 that toppled Suharto.

Religious organizations of all denominations are the primary exceptions to the rule regarding the shallow nature of Indonesian civil society. These organizations, most prominently the two largest Muslim associations, Nahdlatul Ulama and Muhammadiyah, had been the most successful at resisting New Order control. It is not a coincidence that two of the most prominent leaders of the *reformasi* movement, Abdurrahman Wahid and Amien Rais, were the national chairs of Nahdlatul Ulama and Muhammadiyah, respectively. In the 1980s and 1990s, religious organizations also had spawned dozens of affiliated NGOs, as younger leaders wanted to translate their faith into social activism but found that the parent organizations were not nimble enough to do so. However, the parent organizations' national networks and penetration down to the village level became a valuable resource during the transition to democracy, as they played a prominent role in such activities as civic and voter education as well as election monitoring. This involvement demonstrated to both Indonesian citizens and the world at large that religion (particularly Islam) and democracy are not incompatible.

The legal framework supporting a healthy civil society is much stronger than during the Suharto era. President Habibie scrapped the rule forcing all organizations to adopt Pancasila as their sole ideological basis. The new chapter in the constitution on human rights contains unequivocal statements guaranteeing the freedoms of speech and assembly. Equally important, these clauses do not just exist on paper but also are being enforced. For instance, in two separate landmark rulings in 2006 and 2007, the Constitutional Court struck down the sections of the criminal code that outlawed defamation of the president and other political leaders and criticism of the state. These sections derived from Dutch colonial laws designed to muzzle nationalist leaders, and authoritarian and democratic leaders alike had used them against government critics.

The Media

Indonesia's new-found freedoms have been felt most strongly by the media. Long suppressed and harassed by the New Order, the Indonesian press is now among the freest and liveliest in Asia. The trend toward somewhat greater pluralism and openness had begun in the late New Order, when the regime allowed the founding of a number of new television and radio stations. (The television stations all had to be Jakarta-based at first.) Many of the new television stations enjoyed penetration rates of around 70 to 80 percent of the population within a few years. Although the television licenses were all given to various Suharto family members, cronies, and other wealthy conglomerates, competition for advertising revenue and a large potential national audience meant that some of these stations were tempted to push the boundaries, especially regarding the ban on news programs other than those produced by the state-run Television of the Republic of Indonesia (TVRI). These stations were very lucrative, so it became difficult for the regime to punish its own cronies by shutting down a station if it crossed the line by broadcasting independently produced news. Sun Television (SCTV) and Hawk Television Indonesia (RCTI) news programs, in particular, were very popular with viewers across the country as an alternative, albeit still relatively tame, to the stultifying TVRI (see Post and Telecommunications, ch. 3). Broadcasting is regulated by the government through the Directorate General of Radio, Television, and Film.

Thousands of new print publications and radio stations have started up across the country, and more television broadcasters, including regional stations, have licenses since the transition to democracy. The government cannot revoke these publishing and broadcasting licenses based on what the outlets write and say. President Wahid further weakened the government's ability to control the media when he abolished the Department of Information at the outset of his administration. The censorship board for motion pictures remained in existence, however, mainly to police "public morality" (nudity, sexuality) rather than political statements, and President Megawati reestablished the Department of Information on her ascension to power. In the absence of significant government repression, spurious defamation lawsuits by private individuals have become the principal means of stifling media scrutiny. The most prominent of these cases involved businessman Tomy Winata, who sued *Tempo* editor in chief Bambang Harymurti. Harymurti was convicted and given a one-year prison sentence, which the Supreme Court overturned.

More than 50 principal daily newspapers are published throughout the archipelago, the majority in Java. Those with the largest readership are *Kompas* (Jakarta), circulation of 523,000; *Suara Merdeka* (Semarang), circulation of 200,000; *Berita Buana* (Jakarta), circulation of 150,000; *Pikiran Rakyat* (Bandung), circulation of 150,000;

and *Sinar Indonesia Baru* (Medan), also with a circulation of 150,000. The largest English-language dailies, both published in Jakarta with print runs of 40,000, are the *Jakarta Post* and the *Jakarta Globe*. The principal weekly news magazines are *Tempo*, which also produces an English-language edition, and *Gatra*. All of these newspapers and magazines have online editions as well.

Foreign Policy

Political Considerations

The internal dynamics of Indonesian politics since independence have been linked to an external environment perceived as inherently dangerous. Indonesian foreign policy has had as its most important goals security of the state and territorial integrity. The jurisdictional boundaries of the state were greatly expanded with the incorporation of the "archipelago principle" into the new international law of the sea, a new regime codified as the UN Convention on the Law of the Sea in 1982. The archipelago principle effectively territorialized all ocean space inside straight baselines drawn from the farthest points of the most distant islands of Indonesia, thus giving new sanction to the Indonesian doctrine of the political and security unity of archipelagic land and sea space (*wawasan nusantara*), first promulgated in the 1950s (see National Territory: Rights, Responsibilities, and Challenges, ch. 2).

Sukarno's response to challenge was to attack the status quo, to "live dangerously," to cite his 1964 Independence Day address, "A Year of Living Dangerously." Beginning with Suharto, the approach of subsequent governments has been one of cooperation and accommodation in order to gain international support for Indonesia's political stability and economic development while, at the same time, maintaining its freedom of action. Nonetheless, Indonesia's level of engagement with the rest of the world has fluctuated, mainly dependent on domestic developments: it was high under Sukarno, in the latter half of Suharto's three decades in power, and again in the early twenty-first century, but low in the first half of the New Order and in the transitional period after the 1997–98 Asian financial crisis.

Sukarno relished leading the "new emerging forces" against the "old established forces," whereas subsequent governments have turned to the Western developed economies for assistance. From 1967 to 1991, countries aiding Indonesia organized as a consortium in the Inter-Governmental Group on Indonesia (IGGI—see Glossary), subsequently reorganized in 1992 without the Netherlands—and with Japan as chair—as the Consultative Group on Indonesia

(CGI—see Glossary). These countries, along with the World Bank and the Asian Development Bank (see Glossary), gave massive economic assistance, amounting in the 2006 budget to more than US$5.4 billion in loans and grants. Even after the Indonesian government disbanded the CGI in 2007, foreign assistance continues on a bilateral basis. The pragmatic, low-profile style of post-Sukarno administrations has been a far cry from the radical internationalism and confrontational anti-imperialism of his foreign policy, although there has been some continuity in a nationalism that colored Indonesia's perceptions of its role in the region. The promotion of Islamic international political interests has not been high on the Indonesian foreign-policy agenda, despite Indonesia's having the world's largest Muslim population. Indonesia is a member of the Organization of the Islamic Conference (OIC), but, unlike Malaysia, has not aspired to a major role in that organization.

Following two decades of New Order "low-profile" foreign policy, by Suharto's fourth term (1983–88) a more assertive Indonesian voice on foreign policy was heard, as Jakarta began to reaffirm its claim to a leadership position, both regionally and worldwide, corresponding to its geographic vastness, resource endowment, population, and political stability. After an international rehabilitative period, Indonesia rejoined the community of nations, broke the Jakarta–Phnom Penh–Hanoi–Beijing–Pyongyang axis, ended the Indonesian–Malaysian Confrontation (Konfrontasi—see Glossary), worked to strengthen ASEAN, forged cooperative nonthreatening links with its neighbors, and became a moderating voice in developing world forums. By the early 1990s, Indonesia, which American scholar Donald K. Emmerson could still describe as "invisible" in 1987, had become apparent both as a regional power and a major developing world voice in the global political and economic arenas. In 1992 Indonesian foreign policy reflected a proud national identity and what British scholar Michael Leifer called its "sense of regional entitlement."

Indonesia's full reemergence on the world stage was highlighted in September 1992 when it hosted the Nonaligned Movement summit, an acknowledgment of its credentials to speak authoritatively in the developing world. Indonesia had hosted the Asia–Africa Conference in Bandung in 1955 and was a founding member of the Nonaligned Movement in 1961. Its adherence to and promotion of the ideals of nonalignment had been one of the few consistencies between the foreign policies of the Old Order and New Order governments. At the same time, Indonesia was the only founding member that had not hosted a Nonaligned Movement summit, as a result of the unpopularity in the developing world of some of its policy positions: its domestic anticommunism, cold relations with China, incorporation of East Timor as Timor Timur Province, and solidarity with ASEAN on the Cambodian issue. Suharto used the summit to begin the effort of shifting the Nonaligned Movement agenda from its traditional concerns to the economic and social issues confronting the developing world. The Jakarta Message, the summit's final communiqué, reflected Suharto's call in his opening speech for a constructive dialog between the developed and developing nations, warning that North–South polarization loomed as "the central unresolved issue of our time." In an expression of Indonesia's pride in its own development, Suharto offered technical assistance to countries with food and population problems. As chairman of the Nonaligned Movement, Suharto brought the Jakarta Message to the 1992 session of the UN General Assembly.

All of this new-found constructive activism ended in 1997–98 as the economy collapsed under the weight of the Asian financial crisis, and Suharto was forced to resign. With the exception of President Habibie's engagement with the UN on a referendum for East Timor, Indonesia once again slipped into the shadows of the world stage as it sorted out its economic woes and domestic political transition. This shroud of invisibility only began to lift—for all the wrong reasons—in October 2002, with the first Bali bombing and the subsequent roughly annual terrorist attacks in Jakarta and Bali from 2003 to 2005, which contributed to making Southeast Asia the "second front" in President George W. Bush's "global war on terrorism." Only under President Yudhoyono has Indonesia once again returned to a constructively activist foreign policy profile. This shift has been most evident in Indonesia's contribution of troops, including Yudhoyono's elder son, Agus Harimurti, a junior army officer, to the UN peacekeeping force in Lebanon after the 2006 war between Israel and Hezbollah. Indonesian military or police contingents also were deployed in Congo and Sudan. The shift has also been reflected in Yudhoyono's offers to assist with resolution of conflicts in Iraq, Iran, the Korean Peninsula, and Burma.

Participation in ASEAN

Since its founding on August 8, 1967, ASEAN has been a major focus of Indonesia's regional international relations, and Jakarta is the site of ASEAN's general secretariat. Founding members Indonesia, Malaysia, the Philippines, Singapore, and Thailand helped construct a regional multinational framework to facilitate economic cooperation, diminish intra-ASEAN conflict, and formulate ASEAN positions regarding potential external threats. Brunei joined in 1984, and ASEAN further expanded in the late 1990s with the accession of Vietnam (1995), Laos and Burma (1997), and Cambodia (1999). In

Susilo Bambang Yudhoyono,
president of Indonesia since 2004
Courtesy Embassy of Indonesia,
Washington, DC

2009 the organization was considering Timor-Leste's application for membership.

These countries were not always so cooperative with one another. In 1963 the Philippines and Indonesia both tried to prevent or delay the formation of the Federation of Malaysia, the Philippines because it had its own claim to Sabah (formerly North Borneo) and Indonesia because it suspected a British imperialist plot. Indonesia soon turned to political and military confrontation, an attempt to undermine the new state of Malaysia. Sukarno's radical anti-Western rhetoric, combined with the growing strength of the PKI, marked Indonesia as a disturber of the regional international order rather than a cooperative, peaceful contributor to it.

By 1967 Indonesia's disruptive stance had changed. ASEAN provided a framework for the termination of the Confrontation, allowing Indonesia to rejoin the regional community of nations in a nonthreatening setting. Furthermore, the five founding members of ASEAN now shared common policies of domestic anticommunism. The ASEAN process of decision making by consensus allowed Indonesia to dictate the pace of change within the organization. Some observers asserted that ASEAN moved only at the pace of its slowest member, which often was Indonesia. With ASEAN increasingly seen as a symbol of regional peace and stability, its strength became an end in itself in Indonesian foreign policy. Suharto became ASEAN's elder statesman by the time of ASEAN's Fourth Summit, held in Singapore January 27–29, 1992. He was the only head of government at ASEAN's 1967 establishment to attend the ASEAN

First Summit, held in Bali, February 23–24, 1976, who was still head of government in the early 1990s. In the meantime, Indonesia had played a key role in resolving the Cambodian conflict, setting the stage for ASEAN's expansion to encompass nearly all of the region by the end of the millennium.

Indonesia, ASEAN, and the Cambodian Conflict

The official ASEAN response, formulated by Indonesia, to Vietnam's December 1978 invasion of Cambodia, was to deplore the invasion and call for the withdrawal of foreign forces from Cambodia. Indonesia and other ASEAN members immediately placed the issue on the agenda of the UN Security Council. However, deep differences soon arose between Indonesia and Thailand. Although compelled to make a show of solidarity with Thailand by its interest in sustaining ASEAN, Indonesia began to see the prolongation of the war in Cambodia, the "bleeding Vietnam white" strategy, as not being in its or the region's interests. Although never retreating from ASEAN's central demands of Vietnamese withdrawal from Cambodia and Khmer self-determination, Indonesia actively sought to engage the Khmers and Vietnamese and their external sponsors in a search of a settlement that would recognize legitimate interests on all sides. Indonesia opened what came to be called "dual-track" diplomacy, in which it pursued bilateral political communication with Vietnam while maintaining its commitment to the ASEAN formula. By 1986 ASEAN had accepted Indonesia as its official "interlocutor" with Vietnam. From 1982 to the signing of the Final Act of the Paris International Conference on Cambodia on October 23, 1991, Indonesian diplomacy played a central role in peace negotiations that led to the deployment of forces of the UN Transitional Authority in Cambodia (UNTAC).

Indonesia's sense of achievement and pride in its role in bringing peace to Indochina was reflected in three events. On November 12, 1990, Suharto arrived in Hanoi for the first meeting between an ASEAN head of government and a Vietnamese counterpart since Premier Pham Van Dong visited Thailand's Prime Minister Kriangsak Chomanan in 1977. On March 15, 1992, Japan's Akashi Yasushi, the UN undersecretary general for disarmament and newly appointed head of UNTAC, arrived in Phnom Penh to be greeted by a color guard of Indonesian troops who were part of the first full battalion-sized contingent of UNTAC peacekeepers dispatched to Cambodia. At the peak deployment of foreign peacekeeping forces in late 1992, Indonesia had the largest force in Cambodia with nearly 2,000 military and police personnel, representing 10 percent of the total. Finally, in mid-1991, fresh from diplomatic success in helping to end the Cambodian civil war, Indonesia took the initiative in seeking to open multilateral negotiations on competitive South China Sea claims, especially those claims involving jurisdictional disputes over the Spratly Islands. Indonesia's gradually assertive role in the Cambodian peace effort demonstrated that Jakarta was not entirely willing to place its commitment to ASEAN solidarity above its own national interests. According to leading Indonesian academic Dewi Fortuna Anwar, the "challenge for Indonesian foreign policy in the future is how to maintain a balance between an ASEAN policy which requires goodwill and trust of the other members, and satisfying some of the internationalist aspirations of a growing number of the Indonesian political elite."

Reorienting ASEAN in a Post–Cold War Context

The resolution of the Cambodian conflict, combined with the dramatically altered balance of power in the region, raised the question of what new political cement might hold ASEAN together in the post–Cold War environment throughout the 1990s and 2000s. Competitive claims by the nations involved in the jurisdictional competition in the South China Sea had the potential for conflict but did not pose a direct threat to ASEAN's collective security interest, as had the Vietnamese invasion and occupation of Cambodia (see Relations with East Asia, this ch.). The answer has come in the nature of the post–Cold War environment itself: global unipolarity combined with regional multipolarity. The end of the global bipolarity of the Cold War has resulted in the hegemony of the United States and ended the ability of Southeast Asian states to play off one superpower against the other. Regional solidarity has come to be seen as the appropriate response to counterbalance a global hegemon. The importance of regional solidarity has been enhanced by the political, military, and economic rise since the 1980s of China and more recently of India, joining longtime powers Russia, Japan, and Australia in increasing Asia's geostrategic complexity. Indonesia has decided that only as part of a regional bloc can it (and Southeast Asia as a whole) fend for itself in this increasingly competitive environment.

Indonesia has been solidly supportive of ASEAN's response, which has been first to expand to encompass nearly all of Southeast Asia (in the 1990s) and then to deepen both its internal cooperation as well as its relationships with regional and global powers (in the twenty-first century). To facilitate internal cooperation, the member states in 2003 streamlined the organization's various efforts into three pillars: the ASEAN Security Community, building on the 1971 Zone of Peace, Freedom, and Neutrality (ZOPFAN), the 1976 Treaty of Amity and

Cooperation in Southeast Asia (TAC), and the 1997 Treaty on the Southeast Asia Nuclear Weapon-Free Zone; the ASEAN Economic Community Blueprint; and the ASEAN Socio-Cultural Community. This legal and institutional framework was further strengthened with the adoption of the ASEAN Charter, which came into force on December 15, 2008. External relationships include: since 1987 allowing non-Southeast Asian states to accede to the TAC (those that have done so include Australia, Britain, China, France, India, Japan, Mongolia, New Zealand, Democratic People's Republic of Korea (North Korea), Pakistan, Papua New Guinea, Russia, Republic of Korea (South Korea), Sri Lanka, Timor-Leste, and the United States); establishing the ASEAN Regional Forum (ARF) in 1994; and inaugurating ASEAN Plus Three (China, Japan, and South Korea) in 1999.

Indonesia's support for the internal and external expansion of ASEAN's reach represented an important shift in its strategic thinking; in ASEAN's first three decades, Indonesia was reluctant to cede any significant authority to the supranational organization or to tie other powers too closely to it; for example, Indonesia had previously resisted the urging of some ASEAN members that the organization formally adopt a more explicit common political-security identity. Indonesia successfully opposed Singapore's proposal at the ASEAN Fourth Summit in 1992 that would have invited the UN Security Council's five permanent members to accede to the TAC. In part, Indonesian ambivalence about an ASEAN security role, together with its reluctance to mesh its economy with an ASEAN regional economy, had arisen from Indonesia's desire to keep its options open as it pursued its interests, not just as an ASEAN member, but as an increasingly important Asia–Pacific regional power.

The economic and political turmoil generated by the 1997–98 Asian financial crisis sidetracked Indonesia's efforts to enhance its status as an important middle power for about a decade. In the aftermath of that crisis, as well as in the context of post–Cold War global and regional power structures, Indonesia has concluded that its own political and economic security interests are best served by strengthening ASEAN. To avoid a repeat of the financial crisis, within the organization Indonesia has supported the Roadmap for Financial and Monetary Integration of ASEAN (a part of the ASEAN Economic Community), and externally the ASEAN Plus Three forum has launched the Chiang Mai Initiative to address regional financial stability.

Indonesia's fundamental interests have not changed substantially, and Indonesian nationalism retains a xenophobic streak. One of the country's most consistent foreign-policy goals has been to reduce regional dependence on external military powers. It has also worked assiduously to dampen or end regional conflicts that often have created openings for greater external meddling in the region's affairs. What has changed is Indonesia's perception of the most effective means to serve these interests. As a valuable instrument for wielding noncoercive regional influence and gaining attention in the wider international arena, ASEAN has become one of the platforms from which Indonesia can enhance its profile as a middle power with international aspirations.

Relations with Neighboring Nations

Fears on the part of Indonesia's neighbors in previous decades that its desire to play a larger international role would also carry with it an inclination to become a regional hegemon have been much reduced in the twenty-first century. Indonesia's abandonment of support for the East Timorese pro-integration militias after their forcible ejection into West Timor (Nusa Tenggara Timur Province) in late 1999 by the UN-mandated International Force in East Timor (INTERFET, 1999–2000), its positive response to the independent government of Timor-Leste's proffer of peace, and its efforts to convince Burma's junta to pursue meaningful national reconciliation have helped erase the memories of Sukarno's and Suharto's more expansive foreign policies.

Timor-Leste

Timor-Leste, the former Portuguese Timor and then East Timor, was incorporated into the Republic of Indonesia in 1976 as Timor Timur Province, although Portugal never recognized what it saw as forcible annexation. The status of East Timor also remained on the UN agenda. Indonesia had invaded in December 1975 in reaction to a chaotic decolonization process that had led to civil war. The human cost of the civil war, Indonesian military actions, and the famine that followed was heavy. Estimates of Timorese deaths between 1975 and 1999 because of the conflict range from 100,000 to 250,000, out of a total population of less than 1 million. The ability of the Revolutionary Front for an Independent East Timor (Fretilin—see Glossary) to mount a low-intensity resistance, the draconian countermeasures adopted by Indonesian military forces against suspected Fretilin sympathizers, and charges of Indonesian aggression combined to make the status of East Timor a continuing foreign-policy problem for Indonesia through the late 1990s.

When President Habibie took over in May 1998, his advisers suggested bold initiatives to address the problem. In early 1999, Habibie announced that Indonesia would allow the UN to administer a referendum in the province on August 30. Although formally the question posed to the East Timorese was whether or not they supported having special autonomous status within Indonesia, it was understood that a "No" vote meant support for independence. The referendum offer was apparently based on faulty intelligence that claimed majority support in the province for integration. Instead of emphasizing the benefits of remaining a province of Indonesia, the military and intelligence apparatus supported pro-integration militia forces that used threats and force in an attempt to frighten the populace into a pro-Indonesia vote. The use of cellular phones, camcorders, and the Internet brought scenes of violence and intimidation to the outside world and caused a storm of criticism against Indonesia's government and its armed forces. Despite the intimidation, the referendum itself proceeded smoothly, with 98.6 percent turnout and 78.5 percent voting against integration. Within days of the referendum, as these results became increasingly clear, the pro-integration militias went on a rampage, implementing a well-planned scorched-earth campaign. Although initial reports of mass killings later turned out to be exaggerated, hundreds of thousands of Timorese were internally displaced or became refugees streaming across the land border into West Timor. Army and militia forces destroyed much of East Timor's infrastructure in the process. The situation only stabilized when INTERFET, led by Australia, arrived to restore order. The UN then established a civilian administration, the UN Transitional Administration in East Timor (UNTAET), to run the country and prepare it for independence, which came on May 20, 2002.

Despite the brutal history shared by Indonesia and Timor-Leste, the two nations' relations since 2002 have been surprisingly cordial. Given Timor-Leste's small size, geographic isolation, and dependence on Indonesia for imports of foodstuffs, fuel, and other vital commodities, it has not wished to antagonize its much more powerful neighbor. Indonesia, to its credit, since September 1999 has not attempted further military or militia interference in Timor-Leste and has welcomed the latter's offer of reconciliation as a way to counter criticism by international human-rights groups, block attempts to set up an international criminal tribunal, and burnish its reputation on the world stage. However, Indonesia has not been cooperative in the various efforts regarding truth, justice, and accountability for the serious crimes against humanity that took place in the province between 1975 and 1999 (see East Timor, ch. 5).

Papua New Guinea

In 1975 Papua New Guinea gained independence from an Australian-administered UN trusteeship. Since then the 760-kilometer-long border it shares with Indonesia's Papua Province has been a focus of mutual suspicion. Indonesia has sought through diplomacy and intimidation to prevent Papua New Guinea from becoming a cross-border sanctuary for Free Papua Organization (OPM) separatists. Port Moresby's policy on the border situation was conditioned by fears of Indonesian expansionism and sympathy for West Papuan efforts to defend their cultural identity against Indonesianization. The Papua New Guinea government was also keenly aware of the military imbalance between the two countries.

Talks to draw up a new agreement to regulate relations and define rights and obligations along the border culminated in the signing on October 27, 1986, of the Treaty of Mutual Respect, Cooperation, and Friendship. The treaty was, in effect, a bilateral nonaggression pact in which the two sides agreed to "avoid, reduce and contain disputes or conflicts between their nations and settle any differences that may arise only by peaceful means" (Article 2), and promised that they "shall not threaten or use force against each other" (Article 7). The treaty also provided a basis for building a lasting framework of peace and cooperation. The structure for peace was enhanced by the 1987 ASEAN decision to allow Papua New Guinea to become the first non-ASEAN country to accede to the TAC. Indonesia has continued, however, to block Papua New Guinea's promotion from observer status to full ASEAN membership.

The 1986 treaty left many issues unresolved. It did not solve, for example, the problem of Indonesian Papuan refugees in Papua New Guinea. Furthermore, Papua New Guinea did not agree to joint security operations in the border regions, and Indonesia did not give categorical assurance that its military, in all circumstances, would not cross the border. Criticism of Jakarta's policies in Papua persisted in Port Moresby. In addition, Indonesia was accused of covert intervention in Papua New Guinea's domestic politics. Nevertheless, the tension and threat-filled atmosphere that clouded the first decade of bilateral relations dissipated considerably. In 1990 the two countries signed a new 10-year border agreement. In January 1992, in the course of a state visit by Papua New Guinea's prime minister, Rabbie Namaliu, the defense ministers of the two countries signed a "status of forces" agreement regulating rights and obligations when on each other's territory. Although the two parties denied that the agreement provided for joint security operations, the possibility of rights for Indonesian "hot pursuit" seemed to exist. At that time, Namaliu, reviewing the course of relations since the 1986 treaty, said, "ties have never been better."

Further improvement in the bilateral relationship was marked by Vice President Megawati's state visit to celebrate the twenty-fifth anniversary of Papua New Guinea's independence on September 16, 2000, at which time the two countries signed a trade agreement.

Indonesia and Papua New Guinea also established a joint commission to improve bilateral communications; the first meeting took place on June 6–8, 2004. At the same time, the two foreign ministers agreed to the establishment of a mechanism for occasional joint cabinet meetings. Nonetheless, despite Papua New Guinea's status as one of only three countries with which Indonesia shares a land border, Indonesia places a much higher priority on its relationships with its other neighbors, such as Singapore, Malaysia, and Australia.

Singapore and Malaysia

Singapore, ASEAN's own ethnic Chinese financial and economic powerhouse, is geostrategically locked in the often suspicious embrace of its Indonesian and Malaysian neighbors. More than 40 years after the end of Confrontation, a racially tinged, jealous Indonesian ambivalence toward Singapore remains strong. On the one hand, Jakarta has sought to link Singapore's capital, technology, and managerial expertise to its own abundant natural resources, land, and labor in an economically integrative process. On the other hand, when the relationship has been perceived as imbalanced or harmful, old suspicions have been revived. For instance, the Indonesian government has welcomed Singaporean investment in its telecommunications sector. However, because those investments issue from Singaporean government-owned firms and have involved purchases of shares of the two leading Indonesian telecommunications firms, Indosat and Telkomsel, the investments have come under the scrutiny of Indonesia's Commission for the Oversight of Business Competition (KPPU). Former MPR speaker, 2004 presidential candidate, and PAN chair Amien Rais, well-known as a sometimes virulent economic nationalist, has publicly supported the KPPU's scrutiny of the investments. There is also great resentment in Indonesia that Singapore has served as the most prominent offshore haven for Indonesian crony capital flight, exacerbating the 1997–98 financial crisis, and for harboring the fleeing cronies themselves. In April 2007, the two countries signed an extradition treaty, which was warmly welcomed in Indonesia as a means of helping bring to justice some of the worst offenders in the financial crisis. However, a streak of nationalism surfaced again in the DPR, where enough members objected to certain provisions of a parallel defense arrangement that the DPR refused to approve the treaty.

This pattern of ambivalence has been replicated at the subnational level over the now largely stalled development of the SIJORI growth triangle, which includes Singapore, Malaysia's state of Johor, and Indonesia's Riau Province (see Industry, ch. 3). Through the 1990s, Indonesia continued to perceive the growth triangle in terms of functional interdependence in joint economic development at the maritime core of ASEAN, and local and regionalized economic cooperation strengthened a common interest in good relations. Since the turn of the century, however, Indonesia has viewed aggressive Singapore private and state capital as taking on exploitative characteristics, threatening to turn Indonesian cheap labor, land, and water into a colonial-style dependency. Jakarta has thus banned any further exports of sand that had been feeding Singapore's unquenchable construction appetite.

New interdependencies between Indonesia and Singapore have also been forged in the unlikely area of security cooperation, although these have demonstrated their limits as well. An unprecedented degree of military cooperation through personnel exchanges, joint military exercises, and a joint air-combat range has allowed Singapore to demonstrate its value as an ally in a South China Sea security environment (see Branches of Service, ch. 5). Influential nongovernmental Indonesian voices openly promoted military trilateralism among Indonesia, Singapore, and Malaysia. In 1995 Indonesia and Singapore signed a treaty allowing the use of Indonesian airspace and territorial waters for training by Singapore's air force and navy. Negotiations began in 2005 to extend this treaty into a broader bilateral defense cooperation agreement, which was bundled into a package with the extradition treaty. Nonetheless, the new defense treaty, signed with much fanfare in April 2007, was set aside in October because of objections raised by the DPR during the ratification process that it only benefited Singapore. The treaty was still pending at the decade's end.

In the years after the end of Confrontation, Indonesian–Malaysian relations improved as both governments became committed to development and cooperation in ASEAN. This new warmth was reinforced by the natural affinities of race, religion, culture, and language. Although intensive and extensive bilateral ties have generally promoted good relations, these have been tested by irritants such as Indonesian concerns about Malaysia's handling of illegal Indonesian temporary workers, and Malaysian (and Singapore) concerns about chronic haze during the dry season produced by Indonesian plantation owners setting fires to clear the land for planting. The more conciliatory tone set by Malaysian prime minister Abdullah Badawi helped in overcoming these irritants.

Australia

The most problematic of Indonesia's neighborly relations are those with Australia. The tension inherent in the population differential between the two countries in such close geostrategic proximity is exacerbated by their very different political cultures. Criticism of

Indonesia under Suharto in the 1980s and 1990s by the Australian press, academics, and politicians provoked angry retorts from Jakarta. More recently, East Timor and Papua have been the primary irritants in the bilateral relationship. Since 1975 Australia had served as one of the primary locations for the East Timorese diaspora, and many Indonesians suspected Australia of wanting to break up the country by supporting East Timor's independence movement, including during the 1999 referendum. For many Indonesians, these suspicions were confirmed when Australian troops were the first to arrive in Dili in September 1999 and made up the largest contingent within INTER-FET, which was commanded by an Australian. Indonesian fears that Australian attention had turned to Papua once Timor-Leste achieved independence were heightened when Australia granted temporary protection visas to 43 Papuan asylum seekers who landed on Cape York Peninsula in northeastern Australia in January 2006, a decision denounced by Jakarta in harsh terms.

The victimization of Australians in the first Bali bombing in 2002 and the Australian Embassy bombing in Jakarta in 2004 did not elicit substantial Indonesian public sympathy, although the Indonesian government did allow for significant assistance by Australian crime investigators. Bilateral relations were particularly poor under Prime Minister John Howard because of his close relationship with President George W. Bush, illustrated by Howard's strong support for the war in Iraq and the persistent misperception that he had once stated that Australia was America's "deputy sheriff" in Asia. The implicit long-term Indonesian "threat," as it appeared in Australia's defense-planning documents, underlined a latent suspicion in Jakarta that Australian policy toward Indonesia was based on fear, not friendship. This perception had to be constantly allayed by official Australian visits to Jakarta, and it was the driving force behind the signing of a bilateral security pact in 2006 (see Foreign Military Relations, ch. 5).

The Philippines

The Philippines is a contiguous state and an ASEAN partner, yet Indonesia's relations with it are more distant than with its other immediate neighbors. The Philippines' aligned status with the United States and its territorial dispute with Malaysia over the sovereignty of Sabah inhibit a close relationship with Indonesia and other ASEAN members.

Nonetheless, when President Ferdinand Marcos resigned in 1986, Jakarta joined other ASEAN states in welcoming a peaceful transfer of power to Corazon Aquino. Jakarta was the first capital visited by the Philippines' new president, unprecedentedly even before Washington, and Suharto took the opportunity to press the urgency of defeating the communist New People's Army in the Philippines. To show support for Aquino's government, Suharto insisted that the 1987 ASEAN Manila Summit meeting go forward despite apprehensions in other ASEAN capitals about the security situation. Jakarta was not displeased that Aquino was succeeded in 1992 by Fidel Ramos, who, as chief of staff of the Armed Forces of the Philippines and later secretary of national defense, was well known to the Indonesian military's senior leadership. In more recent years, Indonesia has been concerned about chronic political instability in the Philippines under presidents Joseph Estrada and Gloria Macapagal-Arroyo.

Most worrisome for Jakarta is the seeming inability of the Philippines to put an end to its internal wars. Indonesia viewed the growth of the New People's Army as destabilizing for the region. Moreover, the Muslim insurrection in the south of the Philippines has had implications for global terrorism, regional territorial integrity, and Indonesian Muslim politics. Post–September 11, 2001, revelations that Indonesian terrorists had trained in camps in Mindanao and regularly traveled between the Philippines and Indonesia have prompted greater security cooperation between the two countries, although Indonesia was uncomfortable with the George W. Bush administration's designation of Southeast Asia as the "second front in the global war on terrorism" and with the U.S. military's significant engagement in Mindanao as a result.

Relations with East Asia

China

Bilateral relations between Indonesia and China have warmed considerably since the resumption of diplomatic ties in 1990, although residual suspicion remains about China's ultimate security and economic goals in the region. Trade that once had to be transshipped through Singapore or Hong Kong has become direct and has increased exponentially. China has become an important market for Indonesia's natural gas and minerals. There have even been efforts to improve bilateral defense and security cooperation through direct military-to-military ties. Nonetheless, Indonesia has largely preferred to contain China's regional expansionism via ASEAN rather than bilaterally, by establishing forums such as ASEAN Plus Three in 1997 and supporting China's accession to the TAC in 2003.

Indonesia's diplomatic relations with China were suspended in 1967 in the aftermath of the 1965 attempted coup d'état. Beijing was suspected of complicity with the PKI in planning the coup and was viewed by the new military-dominated government as a threat through its possible support of a resurgent underground PKI, both directly and through a "fifth column" of Chinese Indonesians. Jakarta repeatedly demanded an explicit disavowal by Beijing of support for communist insurgents in Southeast Asia as its sine qua non for a normalization process. Underlying the Indonesian policy was unease about China's long-range goals in Southeast Asia. The break in relations persisted until 1990, when, in the face of shifting global and regional realities as well as renewed mutual confidence, the two countries resumed their formal ties. An exchange of visits by Chinese premier Li Peng to Jakarta in August 1990 and by Suharto to Beijing in November 1990 symbolized the dramatic alteration that had taken place. In particular, normalization was driven by four factors: China's market reforms had made it less threatening ideologically and more formidable as an economic force; the end of the Cold War had weakened the Soviet Union and thus strengthened China's regional position; Indonesia's deep involvement in the Cambodian peace process was hampered by a lack of direct relations with the Khmer Rouge's main sponsor; and Indonesia's desire to mediate the South China Sea disputes was similarly hampered in the absence of direct relations with the largest party to the disputes.

Japan

The quality of Indonesia–Japan relations is best measured by statistics on trade, investment, and the flow of assistance. In 2008 Japan was the single-largest destination of Indonesia's exports, the second-largest source (after China) of its imports, the single-largest foreign investor, and by far the most important donor of development assistance (see The Changing Nature of Trade and Aid, ch. 3). In return, as the dominant foreign economic presence in Indonesia, Japan is subject to all the expectations and resentments attendant on that status, for example, Indonesia has sought greater technology transfer as part of Japanese investment. The association of Japanese firms with politically well-connected Indonesians has led to charges of exploitation. With their memories of World War II and the anti-Japanese demonstrations during Prime Minister Tanaka Kakuei's 1974 visit, the Indonesian leadership was keenly sensitive to the possibility of a disruptive anti-Japanese backlash (see Rise of the New Order, 1966–98, ch. 1). However, the issues of Japan's version of World War II history and of comfort women, so critical to its relations with China and South Korea, do not weigh as heavily in the relationship with Indonesia.

In the long term, the critical issue for Indonesia in the early twenty-first century is access to Japan's markets for manufactured goods. Yet, Indonesia shares the ASEAN-wide concern about the implications for Southeast Asia of Japanese remilitarization and was ambivalent about Japanese military participation in UN peacekeeping operations in Cambodia. From Tokyo's point of view, there is only an indirect linkage between Japan's economic presence and the political relationship between the two countries, but Japan is aware of Indonesia's geostrategic straddling of the main commercial routes to the Middle East and Europe. In addition, Japan struggles in Indonesia, as elsewhere in the region and the world, to compete with a resurgent China.

Relations with the United States

Indonesian relations with the United States are in some respects the warmest they have ever been. Ironically, this rapport came at a time when Southeast Asia as a whole, including Indonesia, had dropped significantly in terms of U.S. global priorities. The fundamental underpinning of the warm relations is Indonesia's successful transition to democracy. Not only do the two countries now share a political system and political values, but also human-rights violations and restrictions on bilateral military ties have become a much less prominent impediment to good relations. It has certainly also helped that President Yudhoyono spent several stints in his military career obtaining training and education in the United States, including at Fort Benning in 1975 and 1982 and at Fort Leavenworth in 1990–91, during which time he earned a master's degree in management from Webster University, which has a campus at Fort Leavenworth. The 2008 election as president of Barack H. Obama, who lived in Jakarta for several years as a child, has dramatically raised expectations of even closer ties with the United States. The importance of these ties to the Obama Administration was signaled in February 2009 by Secretary of State Hillary Clinton's addition of Indonesia to the Northeast Asian itinerary of her first overseas trip.

To the extent Indonesia was a priority for the United States under the George W. Bush administration, it was primarily through a security lens. This focus included counterterrorism, maritime security, Indonesia's utility as a voice for moderation in the Muslim world, and nontraditional security threats such as avian influenza. The 2002–5 bombings in Jakarta and Bali drove home for both Indonesia and the United States that international terrorism is a significant problem in Southeast Asia. Indonesian security forces, particularly the police, provided unprecedented access to American investigators and trainers, resulting in the killing or capture and conviction of hundreds of militants. Maritime security mainly focuses on the Strait of Malacca, where the emphasis is on piracy and international shipping, and on the Sulawesi–Sulu corridor, where the focus is on counterterrorism. The United

States also appreciated Indonesian support in March 2007 for UN Security Council Resolution 1747 on Iran's nuclear-weapons program.

Indonesia, for its part, resented the narrow focus of American interest in it. Indonesia certainly shares many of these security concerns, but its interests in the bilateral relationship are much broader, including reviving military ties, increasing trade and investment, addressing climate change, and expanding access to American educational institutions for Indonesian postsecondary students. Under rules known as the Leahy Amendment, the U.S. Congress totally cut off bilateral military sales and assistance following the violence accompanying the East Timor referendum in 1999. This cutoff expanded restrictions put in place after the 1991 Santa Cruz Massacre in Dili. Indonesia has made the case that these sanctions are anachronistic given its transition to democracy. The George W. Bush administration began to reestablish the military relationship, but the U.S. Congress continues to back some restrictions in response to pressure from human-rights groups (see Post–Suharto Reforms, ch. 5). Indonesia's interests in a broader bilateral relationship were given concrete form in President Yudhoyono's proposal for a "comprehensive partnership" in a November 2008 speech at the United States–Indonesia Society (USINDO) in Washington, DC. The emphasis of this partnership would not be on U.S. assistance to Indonesia, which would nonetheless continue, but rather on global and regional issues that the two countries could help solve together. The Obama administration, while maintaining the significant levels of security cooperation established under the Bush administration, welcomed this initiative by proposing that, in addition to existing security concerns, the partnership should focus on energy, the environment, and climate change; economic, trade, and investment cooperation; democracy and good governance; education; and health.

The United States is the second-largest destination (after Japan) of Indonesia's exports, and the third-largest source (after China and Japan) of its imports. American investment in Indonesia's oil, gas, and mining sectors is significant but remains quite low in other sectors as a result of American companies' concerns about corruption, low labor productivity, an inflexible labor law, and uncertain contract enforcement. Indonesia has assumed global leadership on environmental issues by hosting the UN Climate Change Conference in Bali in December 2007 and has continued to press the United States on this issue. Finally, after the September 11, 2001, terrorist attacks on the United States, Washington tightened its visa policies, making it much harder for foreign students wishing to study in America, particularly from Muslim-majority countries such as Indonesia. This change, combined with the slow decline over several decades in

American scholarships for foreign students, has made it much more difficult for Indonesians to access U.S. institutions of higher learning. Indonesia places a high priority on education as a means to spur its development, and the United States remains a favorite destination for Indonesian students. All of these issues are important to resolve in further improving the bilateral relationship, but none has yet been a serious impediment to the increasingly warm connection.

Consolidating Democracy, Contributing to Global Peace

Indonesia has made substantial progress toward democratization since 1998. It has successfully navigated a transition to democracy, minimizing the military's direct political influence, amending the constitution, holding multiple credible elections, and embarking on an unprecedented decentralization of power. It is also making significant progress in consolidating this new democracy, and the 2009 election cycle was another significant milestone in this regard. Addressing corruption, improving economic performance, strengthening local governance, and fixing the judicial system will also contribute to democratic consolidation. Indonesia has rebounded from the depths of the 1997–98 Asian financial crisis, but its growth rates need to be higher in order to reduce poverty and make the leap to the next level of development. A stable democracy and a prosperous economy would provide Indonesia with strong foundations for its dream of playing a middle-power role regionally and even globally in some interest areas. Its peacekeeping role in Lebanon in 2007, as well as its offers to help address conflicts in the Korean Peninsula, Burma, Iran, and Iraq, are emblematic of the constructive role Indonesia envisions for itself in a post–Cold War, post–September 11 world.

*   *   *

Useful general surveys of contemporary Indonesian politics include Ross H. McLeod and Andrew MacIntyre's *Indonesia: Democracy and the Promise of Good Governance*; John Bresnan's *Indonesia: The Great Transition*; and Donald K. Emmerson's *Indonesia Beyond Suharto: Polity, Economy, Society, Transition*. Blair A. King analyzes constitutional reform in "Empowering the Presidency: Interests and Perceptions in Indonesia's Constitutional Reforms, 1999–2002." Military reform is addressed in John B. Haseman and Eduardo Lachica's two works: *Toward a Stronger U.S.–Indonesia Security Relationship* and *The U.S.–Indonesia Security Relationship: The Next Steps* as well as in Marcus Mietzner's *The Politics of Military Reform in Post-Suharto Indonesia: Elite Conflict, Nationalism, and Institutional Resistance* and Dewi Fortuna Anwar's *Negotiating and Consolidating Democratic Civilian Control of the Indonesian Military*. Andrew MacIntyre's *The Power of Institutions: Political Architecture and Governance* offers contemporary analyses of Indonesia's political economy, as does Chris Manning and Peter Van Diermen's *Indonesia in Transition: Social Aspects of Reformasi and Crisis*.

Decentralization is the subject of many studies, such as Henk Schulte Nordholt and Gerry van Klinken's *Renegotiating Boundaries: Local Politics in Post-Suharto Indonesia*. East Timor's achievement of independence is analyzed by Richard Tanter, Gerry van Klinken, and Desmond Ball in *Masters of Terror: Indonesia's Military and Violence in East Timor*. Edward Aspinall studies the Aceh peace process in *Helsinki Agreement: A More Promising Basis for Peace in Aceh?* Blair A. King's *Peace in Papua: Widening a Window of Opportunity* addresses the challenges of resolving separatism and poor governance in Papua. The communal violence that has plagued Indonesia is the subject of Jacques Bertrand's *Nationalism and Ethnic Conflict in Indonesia* and Gerry van Klinken's *Communal Violence and Democratization in Indonesia: Small Town Wars*.

Political Islam is also the subject of numerous studies, such as Bahtiar Effendy's *Islam and the State in Indonesia*, Robert W. Hefner's *Civil Islam: Muslims and Democratization in Indonesia*, Zachary Abuza's *Political Islam and Violence in Indonesia*, and Azyumardi Azra's *Indonesia, Islam, and Democracy: Dynamics in a Global Context*. R. William Liddle gives a succinct overview of Indonesian political culture in *Politics and Culture in Indonesia*. Mikaela Nyman considers contemporary developments in Indonesian civil society in *Democratising Indonesia: The Challenges of Civil Society in the Era of Reformasi*.

Indonesian foreign policy and regional implications are analyzed in Dewi Fortuna Anwar and Harold A. Crouch's *Indonesia: Foreign Policy and Domestic Politics*, Angel Rabasa and Peter Chalk's *Indonesia's Transformation and the Stability of Southeast Asia*, and Anthony L. Smith's *Strategic Centrality: Indonesia's Changing Role in ASEAN*.

Gerald L. Houseman's *Researching Indonesia: A Guide to Political Analysis* is an overall guide to the analysis of Indonesian politics. Annual surveys of Indonesian political events can be found in the January–February issue of *Asian Survey* and the annual *Southeast Asian Affairs* (Singapore). For current politics, the *Asian Wall Street Journal* (Hong Kong) and the *Far Eastern Economic Review* (Hong Kong) are extremely useful. The Indonesian government also offers a variety of Web sites, many of which are listed on http://indonesia.go.id/en. (For further information and complete citations, see Bibliography.)

Chapter 5. National Security

PC–40 type fast patrol craft underway

INDONESIA'S MILITARY AND NATIONAL POLICE have undergone important changes since the Suharto era ended in 1998; however, they retain a role in national society that is perhaps unique in the world. Historically, the Indonesian military has been involved in many affairs of state that elsewhere are not normally associated with the armed forces. Since the Netherlands recognized Indonesian sovereignty in 1949, the military has been the dominant political institution in Indonesia. In comparison with the armed forces of nations of comparable background and state of development, the Indonesian military is cautious in its exercise of traditional military authority over society. However, until discarded in 1999, its doctrine of *dwifungsi* (dual function) gave the military a role in virtually every aspect of civil society, from village-level politics through the full spectrum of security and intelligence missions. This legacy has been a major factor in the military's effort to define its role in the course of the nation's transition from autocracy to democracy in the post-Suharto era.

From Suharto's assumption of power in 1966 to his forced retirement 32 years later, the armed forces accepted and supported the rationale behind his regime, namely, that economic and social development was the nation's first priority and that social and political stability was absolutely essential if that goal were to be achieved. Regime protection and maintenance of internal stability were the primary missions of the Indonesian National Armed Forces (see Glossary). The armed forces are currently called Tentara Nasional Indonesia (TNI but earlier ABRI; for these and other acronyms, see Table A). They were eminently successful in this regard, leading the nation out of a period of political and social upheaval in the mid-1960s into a period of relatively long-lasting domestic order and unprecedented economic growth. The price paid by society was tight control of the citizenry, intolerance of criticism or other forms of opposition to the regime, and heavy censorship of the news media.

Suharto's resignation from the presidency in May 1998 came amid a combination of regional economic recession and popular discontent. The long-serving president's removal gathered even greater impetus from his inattentiveness to outbreaks of violence concentrated mainly in Jakarta, and from the popular perception that he and his family were involved in corrupt activities. The armed forces establishment, Suharto's primary instrument of political control for more than three decades, was also a crucial element in his fall from power. The military leadership declined to take control of the government to keep Suharto in office and acted with restraint while overseeing a constitutional transfer of leadership to his vice president, Bacharuddin J. (B. J.) Habibie. Many analysts felt at the time that the ambitious commander in chief of the armed forces, General Wiranto, believed that Habibie would resign along with Suharto and that he himself would be asked to take the presidency in a move eerily similar to Suharto's own accession to power in 1966. In many subsequent public interviews, Wiranto said that he had been asked twice by Suharto to take power but had declined to do so. Wiranto subsequently was credited with supporting the constitutional change of leadership.

The fall of Suharto prompted a reconsideration of the military's role in government and society over the long period of his rule. A free press and a newly empowered national legislature—the People's Consultative Assembly (MPR)—focused on abuses by the military during the Suharto years. Revelations of human-rights abuses, improper use of power, corruption, economic intimidation, and other unprofessional conduct caused the military acute embarrassment and loss of prestige. But the years immediately following Suharto's fall brought disorganized civilian government, widening corruption, and, in a number of different parts of the country, religious and ethnic violence on a scale not seen for a generation. The apparent inability of the civilian administration to impose order on society, combined with widespread yearning for the stability that had characterized most of the Suharto era, resulted in popular demands for a more effective and decisive government. By assuming a lower profile and engaging in a series of reforms, the military regained much of its lost stature. Furthermore, it remained the most organized and disciplined element of Indonesian society.

Throughout the Suharto years, the central government had provided insufficient funding for the military, with only about one-third of its administrative and operational costs covered by the defense budget. The rest of the military's financial requirements were met by receipts from its extensive business empire or diversions from other government institutions. But the 1997–98 financial crisis, compounded by arms embargoes imposed by Indonesia's traditional military suppliers, had an immediate effect on force readiness. Within a few years, the armed forces' primary weapons systems had deteriorated as a result of lack of maintenance and an inability to purchase spare parts for major systems. International reaction to human-rights violations perpetrated during the 1990s in East Timor (Timor Timur Province; since May 20, 2002, the independent Democratic Republic of Timor-Leste) had particularly severe consequences, prompting the United States and other nations to embargo arms sales and military training. Indonesia consequently turned to nontraditional suppliers, primarily in Eastern Europe and Asia, to upgrade its aging ground, air, and naval systems. Even so, the deterioration of the TNI's capabilities was demonstrated by the military's deficient performance in the aftermath of the December 26, 2004, tsunami that devastated the coast of the Special Region of Aceh (called Nanggroe Aceh Darussalam, 1999–2000, in an effort to assuage separatist sentiment in the region). Although the TNI's personnel performed very well on the ground, where the large military presence turned largely from combat to recovery efforts and other forms of civic action, its air-transport systems were woefully unprepared to confront such a massive natural disaster. That outcome, along with the visible deterioration of the TNI's capabilities, figured heavily in the U.S. decision to reestablish military ties with Indonesia.

The inauguration in October 2004 of Susilo Bambang Yudhoyono as Indonesia's sixth president, and the fourth since the fall of Suharto, came at an important juncture for Indonesia's national-security posture. The election of a retired general by a majority of more than 60 percent of the votes cast reflected not only respect for him as a leader perceived to be free of corruption, but also a yearning for a more focused and active government. President Yudhoyono benefited from his reputation as a "thinking general," who supported reform of the military and whose independence from preceding administrations appealed to an electorate weary of continued corruption, inefficiency, and generally uninspired government.

The biggest challenge facing Yudhoyono as he began his administration may have been to meet excessive popular expectations while showing competence with the practical matters of government. The national leadership would have to address the issues of economic growth and political change in a security environment made more tenuous by the threat of international and domestic terrorism, as well as by long-standing separatist rebellions at its eastern and western extremes, Papua Province and the Special Region of Aceh. With its transition to democracy reinforced by peaceful and honest legislative and presidential elections, Indonesia still had to address the significant domestic security issues of separatism; sectarian and ethnic violence and its causes; and Islamic extremism, the effect of which was to help sustain international terrorism.

Historical Context

Independence and the Sukarno Period, 1945–65

The Indonesian armed forces grew out of the diverse experience of the Dutch colonial period (the early seventeenth through the early twentieth centuries), the Japanese occupation (1942–45) during World War II, and the struggle for independence (1945–49). During the colonial period, a small number of Indonesians were recruited into the Royal Netherlands Indies Army (KNIL). Subsequently, Japanese occupation forces recruited Indonesians, often former KNIL soldiers, for use as military auxiliaries (*heiho*) and as supply and support personnel attached to the Japanese army. These Indonesian enlisted personnel frequently were sent to the front in the Pacific, the Philippines, and other war zones, such as Burma. The deteriorating military situation in 1943 led the Japanese occupation authorities to organize an indigenous volunteer self-defense force called the Defenders of the Fatherland (Peta). In Java some 37,000 Peta recruits, including officers, received training in combat tactics. The number of such troops trained in Sumatra, where the forces were usually known by their Japanese name—Giyūgun (volunteer army)—is unknown, but knowledgeable sources estimate about one-third of the number trained for Java's Peta.

Along with former *heiho* and KNIL troops, Peta provided the emergent Indonesian state with a ready source of trained military personnel following Japan's defeat in 1945. This force was supplemented by large numbers of young people with experience in various paramilitary youth corps that had been organized by the Japanese; they mobilized the population and provided a recruiting base for Peta.

An embryonic military organization, with these elements as its nucleus, the People's Security Forces (BKR), was formed on August 22, 1945. Just five days earlier, on August 17, Sukarno and Mohammad Hatta had proclaimed Indonesian independence. Thousands of members of various local militias (*laskar*) also joined the newly consolidated national armed forces. From the beginning, the Western ideal of a politically neutral military had few proponents. Many of those who joined the new force, called the Indonesian National Armed Forces (TNI) from 1947 to 1962 (also APRIS—Armed Forces of the Federal Republic of Indonesia—from 1949 to 1950 and APRI—Armed Forces of the Republic of Indonesia—in 1950), were nationalists who sought both military victory and political change for their nation.

The disparate forces fought a largely guerrilla-style war against the returning Dutch troops. Commanded by the young and charismatic

Circa 1923 image of the bodyguard of the sultan of Yogyakarta
Courtesy Library of Congress Prints and Photographs Division, LC–USZ62–106137, digital ID cph 3c06137

General Sudirman, the newly formed army avoided entrapment and fought on even after the Dutch forces captured Sukarno and the civilian government at Yogyakarta. Sudirman, Indonesia's youngest-ever general, was the first commander in chief of Indonesia's armed forces. He led the army in battle from 1945 to 1949 even though he suffered from tuberculosis and had to be carried from place to place in a modified palanquin. He remained in command until his death in January 1950 at the age of 35. Sudirman has been honored as the founding father of the Indonesian military ever since, a national hero whose spirit and nationalism are invoked as key ingredients of the Indonesian military ethos.

Experiences during the armed struggle against the Dutch strengthened the military's political involvement in national affairs. Faced with better-trained and better-equipped Dutch forces, the Indonesians conducted a guerrilla war in which fighters had to rely heavily on the support of the local population. This tie to the populace reinforced the concept of *perjuangan* (the struggle), which stressed reliance on the people for support, intelligence, and succor against both external threats and internal divisiveness. This concept was at the heart of army chief of staff and former KNIL soldier General Abdul Haris Nasution's ideas about guerrilla warfare or total people's war. *Dwifungsi*, later used by Suharto to justify his use of the armed forces as the primary pillar of support of his lengthy rule, referred to the military's right, drawn from the revolutionary experience, to fill both military and civilian political and civil roles in society.

An attempt by the Indonesian Communist Party (PKI) to seize power at Madiun, East Java, in September 1948 turned the military against the communist movement. Considered a treasonous and treacherous betrayal because it occurred during the independence struggle against the Dutch, the incident—commonly called the Madiun Affair—caused a deep and permanent suspicion within the military, not only of communism but of leftist movements in general.

At the end of the independence war in 1949, the government had as many as 500,000 armed fighters potentially at its disposal. Demobilization reduced this number to 200,000 by mid-1950, when the military was officially designated the Armed Forces of the Republic of Indonesia (APRI). The first priority of the military leadership was to form some semblance of a unified structure from numerous disparate elements—many of them loyal to local leaders and regional power holders—and to establish central control over these elements. General Nasution made progress in this direction, overseeing the restructuring of operational units in all three military services, in accordance with organizational charts borrowed from Western armed forces, and instituting formal training programs. Similar changes occurred in the structure of the National Police of Indonesia (Polri).

After 1955, Nasution initiated a series of personnel transfers and instituted several reforms to gain control over local commanders. Between 1950 and 1958, several opponents of Nasution's policies joined local rebellions in the Outer Islands (see Glossary; The Road to Guided Democracy, 1957– 65, ch. 1). Any one of these disparate movements, such as the Universal Struggle (Permesta) rebellion in central and western Sumatra and Sulawesi, the Darul Islam (House of Islam) rebellion in western Java, and the establishment of the short-lived Republic of South Maluku (RMS), could have fatally splintered the young republic, had it succeeded. Deploying to the rebellious regions, the army overcame these various uprisings, its members often fighting against former comrades. These operations were another national success cited by the armed forces in justifying a leadership role in national affairs.

The armed forces' position in the government became institutionalized during the period of Sukarno's Guided Democracy (1957–65). Vowing that it would neither be a "dead tool of the government" nor assume total control of the nation, the military took what General Nasution referred to as the "middle way," working cooperatively with the civilian leadership through its representation in the cabinet, the MPR, and the civil service. The services became, along with the PKI, a "junior partner" to Sukarno in ruling the nation. Uniformed personnel held positions throughout the nation down to the village level, in both the administration of martial law and the management of economic enterprises (mostly nationalized former Dutch properties), and in the deployment of regional cadre units assigned to mobilize local resistance in the event of a threat to national security.

To support the activist foreign policy of the Guided Democracy period, especially the 1962 campaign against Dutch forces in West New Guinea (also called West Irian or Irian Barat, and renamed Irian Jaya—Victorious Irian—in 1972 by the national government; now called Papua and Papua Barat) and the 1963–66 armed Confrontation (see Glossary), or Konfrontasi, with Malaysia, Sukarno rapidly enlarged the armed forces (see Relations with Neighboring Nations, ch. 4). Most affected were the formerly tiny air force and navy, which greatly expanded and acquired advanced arms and equipment by means of military credits from the Soviet Union and the Soviet-bloc states of Eastern Europe. By the mid-1960s, Indonesia had one of the largest and best-equipped armed forces in Southeast Asia.

Trying to contain the army's expanding political influence in the early 1960s, Sukarno encouraged the air force, navy, and police (the latter was a fourth branch of the armed forces until 1999) to act independently of the army. The army leadership became alarmed by the resulting divisions among the services, the growing influence of the PKI in all four branches, and Sukarno's increasing support for the PKI. Tension within the armed forces increased following proposals by the PKI in early 1965 to place political advisers in each military unit (as in the Chinese and Soviet systems) and to establish a "fifth force" of armed peasants and workers outside the control of the existing armed services.

Suharto's New Order, 1966–98

An attempted coup d'état on the last day of September 1965 by alleged communist sympathizers in the military—the September 30 Movement (Gestapu)—was the seminal event in the evolution of the modern Indonesian armed forces. The details of the event remain clouded and controversial even as post-Suharto research continues. The accepted government version is that General Suharto, at the time not widely regarded as part of the most powerful senior military elite, organized quick and effective resistance to a PKI-organized attempted coup. The precise nature and significance of his role in this crucial affair remain matters of considerable debate, but whatever the truth, Suharto rose rapidly to a position of paramount national power. Sukarno was obliged to relinquish de facto authority to Suharto in March 1966, and Suharto was appointed acting president one year later. Along with unrestrained violence, in which hundreds of thousands of civilians died, and a subsequent wave of arrests, the coup attempt led to the suppression of the PKI. The expansionist military doctrine of the Sukarno era was ended, and national expenditures began to be focused on economic development.

The military establishment, led by the army, has been the country's premier institution since 1966, when, in its own view, it answered the summons of the people and moved to center stage. Comprising the three military services and the police, the armed forces operated according to the *dwifungsi* doctrine, enacted into law in 1982, which gave the military a dual role—traditional responsibility as defenders of the nation, plus duty as a sociopolitical force promoting stability, order, and national development. Under this very broad charter, active-duty and retired military personnel were assigned throughout the government to posts filled in most other countries by civil servants or politically appointed civilians. Military personnel most frequently received postings as provincial governors, district heads, members of legislative bodies, functionaries in a variety of civilian governmental departments, and ambassadors. The armed forces became a dominant factor in the social—including even sports and entertainment—and political life of the country and acted as a major executive agent of government policies.

To understand fully the role of the armed forces in contemporary Indonesian society, one must understand the absolute priority the government and the military leadership gave to internal security and national stability during the New Order (1966–98). Having experienced attempted coups in 1948 and 1965, which they identified as communist-inspired, as well as a number of regional separatist struggles and instability created by radical religious movements, the New Order government had little tolerance for public disorder.

The Suharto government brought the nation unprecedented stability, remaining in firm control and without serious challenge from 1966 to 1998. The leadership remained alert to real or potential subversive threats, maintaining surveillance—and sometimes control—over the activities and programs of a wide range of groups and institutions. The government was acutely sensitive to any signs of opposition to its policies. In general, it seemed to label as subversive anything not supportive of the national ideology, the Pancasila (see Glossary; Pancasila: The State Ideology, ch. 4). The extent of change in the years after the fall of Suharto can be fully realized only by comparing that environment of close control of society and repression of dissent with the openness experienced in the period after 1998, with its robust free news media and aggressive debate in the national legislature.

Separatist insurgencies have long been the most serious threat to national security. The Suharto government referred to such insurgent activity as a Security Disturbance Movement (GPK). Three such movements, the Revolutionary Front for an Independent East Timor

(Fretilin—see Glossary) in Timor Timur Province, the Free Aceh Movement (GAM) in Aceh, and the Free Papua Organization (OPM) in Papua Province, have important roles in the nation's modern security history (see Post-Suharto Reforms, this ch.).

Groups advocating the establishment of an Islamic state, either over the whole national territory or over discrete areas, were an occasional security threat in the 1970s and 1980s. Such organizations as Darul Islam, Bangsa Islam Indonesia (Indonesian Nation of Islam), and Komando Jihad (Commando Jihad) carried out insurgency and terrorist operations against the secular state. Komando Jihad was held responsible for bombings of churches and theaters in 1976 and 1977, attacks on police stations in 1980 and 1981, and the 1981 hijacking to Bangkok of a Garuda Indonesia domestic flight.

During the 1980s, Indonesia's rapid economic development—with annual growth rates approaching 9 percent—caused social pressures on society that brought new domestic tensions. These changes, including improved educational opportunities, rising expectations, industrialization, unemployment, and crowded cities, were blamed for generating urban crime, student and political activism, and labor strikes. One example of government action to address these issues occurred in the early 1980s, when an alarming rise in violent crime in Jakarta and other large cities on Java prompted the notorious undercover "Petrus" (*penembakan misterius*—mysterious shootings—or *pembunuhan misterius*—mysterious killings) campaign, in which known criminals were killed by handpicked execution squads and their bodies dumped in public places as a warning. Despite the number of killings, which human-rights groups estimated at 6,000 to 8,000 nationwide, most of the public expressed cautious approval of the Petrus campaign, usually accompanied by criticism of the police for being unable to stop the rise in crime.

Government operations had driven extremist groups underground by the early 1990s. Interestingly, some of these groups had eked out an existence for decades, undercover and largely through family connections and generational transfers, before reemerging in the late 1990s as a recruiting base for resurgent domestic and international terrorist organizations (see Terrorism, this ch.).

Violent ethnic disputes generally were kept to a minimum during the Suharto years because of the assurance of a quick and brutal response by security forces. Most such outbreaks were directed against Indonesians of Chinese descent. The nation's ethnic Chinese minority, estimated at 4 million or more in the early twenty-first century, has evoked popular resentment since the colonial era, when Chinese individuals often served as business intermediaries between the Dutch elite and the indigenous population (see Ethnic Minorities, ch. 2). In the modern period, resentment has continued over Chinese Indonesians' wealth and domination of the economy, including their roles as intermediaries for foreign investors and as advisers and silent partners for senior armed forces personnel and civilian government leaders with business interests. These ethnic Chinese businesspeople, known as *cukong* (see Glossary), were particularly important in the Suharto family's increasingly rapacious commercial arrangements.

Anti-Chinese feeling surfaced violently in the turmoil immediately preceding Suharto's May 1998 resignation, when large numbers of ethnic Chinese homes and businesses were destroyed, and dozens of ethnic Chinese women were raped by mobs of rioters. The violence caused a major flight of ethnic Chinese capital from Indonesia, which worsened the economic depression that started in 1997. The continued slow repatriation of that capital remains an important reason for Indonesia's delayed economic recovery (see Postcrisis Reform, ch. 3).

The absence of a perceived external threat has been widely credited with allowing Indonesia to concentrate on its internal defense and national development priorities. Successive armed forces commanders stressed military readiness and training even as economic realities constrained new equipment purchases. Until 2007, when new armored personnel carriers were purchased from France to support Indonesia's United Nations (UN) deployment to Lebanon, the only major acquisition for the ground forces was the 1981 purchase, through the U.S. Foreign Military Sales (FMS) program, of new 105-millimeter towed howitzers. New acquisitions for the other services during the late 1970s and early 1980s included F–5 fighter and A–4 ground-attack aircraft for the air force and used, but still serviceable, ships for the navy. Twelve F–16 fighters, also purchased from the United States, were not delivered until 1989. Over the years, the armed forces had been seriously weakened by national spending priorities that stressed economic development and relegated defense spending to a much lower priority than in most developing nations. The low priority given to defense spending continued into the early years of the twenty-first century. This situation has compromised the military's readiness posture even further, because income from the military business empire is far less than in the past, as a result of the 1990s regional recession, corruption, and inept management (see Participation in the Economy, this ch.). In 2008, for example, the lower house of the national legislature, the People's Representative Council (DPR), provided the TNI and Department of Defense (Dephan) with less than one-third of the funding requested.

Suharto deliberately underfunded the military for several reasons. First, national development claimed first priority for funding. Second, there was, realistically, no external threat to Indonesia's security and thus no need for top-of-the-line military arms. Third, by requiring the military to rely on its extensive business empire for an estimated two-thirds of its operational and administrative requirements, Suharto encouraged off-budget income and expenditures and accepted the inevitable corruption as a way to ensure the loyalty of the military through financial gain. The major disadvantage of this system was that it loosened the central government's control over the armed forces. A military that obtains two-thirds of its funding from its own resources is far less responsive to government control than a military establishment fully funded by the central government. It is for this reason that proponents of military reform focused on the need to gain civilian governmental control over the military business empire (see Defense Spending and the Defense Industry, this ch.).

Post-Suharto Reforms

The military establishment was pilloried by both the press and the populace over a series of revelations of human-rights abuses that came out after the fall of Suharto in May 1998. Furthermore, the armed forces leadership had become disillusioned by years of demands by Suharto for unprofessional conduct, such as intervention in most aspects of civil society and tight control over every aspect of political activity. Indonesia's military leaders responded to these developments by embarking on a process of change. The armed forces assumed a lower political profile and began a revision of doctrine to meet some—but by no means all—of the calls for reform. This process of change was a major part of national *reformasi* (see Glossary), and both the process and the pace of change became subjects of analysis and criticism (see The Political Process, ch. 4).

The military introduced reforms in an attempt to meet the new demands of a democratic society. The National Police, which had been a coequal branch of the armed forces since 1960, was separated from the military in 1999 and placed under the president. The name of the military establishment was changed from Armed Forces of the Republic of Indonesia (ABRI) to Indonesian National Armed Forces (TNI). The name change signaled a change in focus by which the National Police took the country's internal security as its primary responsibility. The Department of Defense and Security (Hankam) was redesignated simply the Department of Defense (Dephan), a move that underscored how the military's primary mission had changed (see fig. 12).

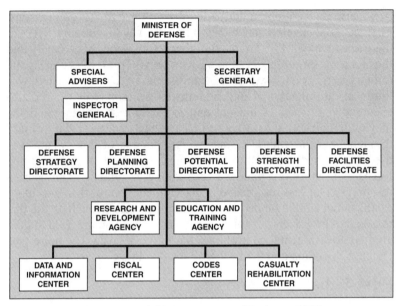

Figure 12. Organization of the Department of Defense, 2009

The TNI leadership discarded *dwifungsi* and replaced it with a doctrine called the New Paradigm (Paradigma Baru), which emphasized "leading from behind" rather than domination of the political process. Constitutional reforms eliminated the TNI's blocs of reserved seats in the national and local legislatures. The TNI redirected its primary mission from internal security to external defense, although the DPR's passage of a new military law in 2004 granted the armed forces significant responsibilities for counterterrorism and counterinsurgency, because of the inability of the understaffed and poorly trained police to meet these intense challenges to domestic security.

In 1999 Indonesia took one of the initial steps toward democratic civilian control of the military when, for the first time since the 1950s, President B. J. Habibie appointed a civilian academic—Yuwono Sudarsono—as minister of defense. Other civilians followed him in that post during the presidencies of Abdurrahman Wahid and Megawati Sukarnoputri. In 2004 President Susilo Bambang Yudhoyono appointed Sudarsono as minister of defense a second time. Despite starting a trend of civilian ministers of defense, however, the TNI commander retained full command authority and remained directly responsible to the president. The DPR recognized the concept of civilian leadership of the armed forces, however, and it included this principle in the 2004 military law but did not specify when, or how, it would be implemented. Military officers now must resign from the armed forces before taking civilian government positions. The military withdrew from day-to-day politics and remained neutral in the legislative and presidential elections of 1999, 2004, and 2009.

East Timor

East Timor was a colony of Portugal for more than 350 years. The Portuguese first came to the island of Timor in the sixteenth century, finding sandalwood in considerable quantity. The colony was later made profitable by the introduction of coffee, which remains the island's principal crop. Portuguese traders, backed by small detachments of soldiers, quickly conquered or established relations with a number of small Timorese kingdoms. The Dutch arrived on the island in the early seventeenth century, and surrogates of the governments of Portugal and the Netherlands competed for power and influence for 200 years. The partition of the island of Timor into Dutch and Portuguese colonies in 1859 laid the basis for economic and social hardship that lasted into the early twenty-first century.

In 1974, after a liberal military coup d'état in Lisbon, the Portuguese government withdrew from its overseas colonial empire. Concerned after the fall of Vietnam, Cambodia, and Laos to communist armies, Indonesia—as well as some other regional and international powers, especially Australia and the United States—feared that East Timor's leftist Fretilin, the dominant political power in East Timor, might provide a haven for communist infiltration. Indonesia consequently engineered a formal request by four of the five East Timorese political parties for integration into Indonesia, known as the Balibo Declaration. On November 28, 1975, Fretilin declared East Timor's independence from Portugal; nine days later, Indonesia's armed forces launched a full-scale invasion, and East Timor was incorporated as Indonesia's twenty-seventh province. ABRI treated its military campaign against Fretilin guerrillas as an internal security operation, and the province was closed to the news media and foreign observers until 1988.

The UN never recognized Indonesian sovereignty over the territory, and Australia was the only country to formally recognize the integration of East Timor into Indonesia. The United States took a middle position that accepted the integration of East Timor into Indonesia but held that the Balibo Declaration and a subsequent "referendum" were not legitimate. This political issue dogged Indonesia for years. Fretilin forces withdrew to the rugged mountains of the interior and waged guerrilla warfare against the Indonesian army. During the next 20 years, at least 100,000 and possibly as many as 250,000 East Timorese died in combat or from disease and privation.

The majority of East Timorese did not support integration. It quickly became apparent that discontent was far more widespread than the Indonesian government and armed forces acknowledged publicly. Although Indonesian military operations reduced Fretilin's strength to only several hundred armed partisans, the resistance movement was supported by what the armed forces termed the *klandestin*, a large clandestine apparatus that provided intelligence, shelter, food, and supplies. The Indonesian army was unable to subdue the military force, even though over the years it killed or captured a succession of Fretilin military and political leaders. ABRI was never able to win the hearts and minds of the East Timorese people because of mutual mistrust and misunderstanding, and the persistent use of the military to force the civilian populace into submission. A series of major human-rights abuses and atrocities kept an international focus on East Timor. Western criticism increased as improved communications and access to the province revealed the extent of the army's violence against civilians.

In November 1991, Indonesian soldiers killed between 50 and 250 civilians and wounded others participating in a funeral procession at the Santa Cruz Cemetery in Dili, East Timor's capital. This incident proved to be the turning point that focused international opposition to Indonesian military operations in East Timor. In an effort to address the problem, the army implemented for the first time the principle of command responsibility. The respected armed forces commander in chief, General Edi Sudrajat, disciplined five levels in the military chain of command involved in the incident, including two generals— the highest ranking in the East Timor operations—and a number of field-grade officers. The platoon leaders involved were court martialed and imprisoned. But both the military and the civilian government, apparently obeying orders from Suharto himself, persistently failed to give a full accounting of the number of civilians killed or the disposition of the remains of the dead. The attack at Santa Cruz Cemetery, and the government's refusal to reveal the true number of civilians killed in the incident, led to a dramatic decline in military-to-military relations between the United States and Indonesia, including an end to the International Military Education and Training (IMET) Program for Indonesia.

In January 1999, President Habibie proposed an expansive local autonomy package for East Timor. He added controversy to the issue by promising "separation" of East Timor if the people voted against his proposal. There followed a campaign of vicious intimidation by pro-Indonesian militia groups, supported by elements of the Indonesian army, intended to persuade the populace to approve the autonomy package. Despite the intense intimidation, however, on August 30, 1999, the East Timorese voted against autonomy by a margin of 78.5 percent to 21.5 percent, and thus began a process of transition toward independence.

The violence worsened following the vote against autonomy. As they withdrew, pro-Indonesia militia forces, in many cases assisted by Indonesian troops, systematically destroyed most of the town centers and infrastructure of East Timor. Estimates vary, but militias and soldiers may have killed more than 1,300 civilians and forced more than 200,000 people across the border into Indonesian West Timor (Nusa Tenggara Timur Province). Violence was so widespread, and the Indonesian security forces so deeply involved, that worldwide pressure compelled Indonesia to accept the entry of an international body of armed peacekeepers. The International Force in East Timor (INTERFET), led by Australian troops and recognized by the UN—although it was not designated as a UN force—restored order in East Timor. In October 1999, the MPR formally detached East Timor from Indonesia. The next month, INTERFET turned over control to the UN Transitional Administration in East Timor (UNTAET), which, along with the advisory Timorese National Council, ran the territory until independence—as the Democratic Republic of Timor-Leste—on May 20, 2002.

The egregious behavior of army-backed militias, and the unwillingness of armed forces commander in chief General Wiranto to accept any responsibility for it or to discipline those involved, caused Australia, Britain, the United States, and other nations to further limit military relations with Indonesia. The United States suspended arms sales, halted the few remaining education and training programs, and imposed political conditions on the restoration of military-to-military relations. Only after the December 2004 tsunami struck Aceh did the United States restore Indonesia's eligibility for IMET funding and allow the sale of spare parts for transport aircraft under Foreign Military Financing (FMF) beneficial pricing.

Separatist Rebellions

The primary threat to Indonesia's national security has been posed by separatist guerrilla insurgencies in East Timor, Aceh, and, to a lesser extent, Papua and by extremist and terrorist organizations. The separation of East Timor in 1999 removed what Indonesia's former foreign minister Ali Alatas once injudiciously described as "a pebble in Indonesia's shoe." The peaceful political settlement of the Aceh separatist insurgency ended a major security threat as well. Indonesia's primary security threat is now posed by Islamic extremist and terrorist organizations opposed to the moderate secular government system in Indonesia. Jemaah Islamiyah (Congregation of Islam), a regional terrorist organization with links to Al Qaeda, whose goal is to create a Muslim state in Southeast Asia, has conducted several terrorist attacks around the country and has been deeply involved in communal violence in Maluku and Sulawesi Tengah provinces.

Aceh

Aceh, on the northern end of the island of Sumatra, was for decades the most troubled and insecure province of Indonesia, with a history of opposition to outside rule from its time as an independent sultanate. Acehnese maintained a broad range of grievances against the central government that included a desire to keep a greater percentage of the revenue from the rich natural resources in the province, resentment over brutal tactics by police and military forces, and a desire for more native Acehnese to be employed in the lucrative natural resources sector.

A small minority of Acehnese have demanded independence. The separatist Free Aceh Movement (GAM) began guerrilla warfare in Aceh in the mid-1970s. Its political and military wings were distinct. A succession of GAM military commanders had given allegiance to the GAM's political leader, Hasan di Tiro, a longtime refugee in Sweden. However, years of separation and the resentment caused by the relative safety of political leaders in Europe while GAM personnel in Aceh faced daily danger, led to a split that persists to this day. Attacks on public facilities and transportation, reprisal operations by both sides, and a lack of skill in combating insurgency on the part of the military and the police contributed to a high level of noncombatant casualties and insecurity throughout the province. By 2000 the GAM had made extensive advances in the countryside and was providing government services in several areas of the province.

The first three post-Suharto administrations attempted to negotiate a political settlement with the GAM. In early 2002, President Megawati Sukarnoputri authorized negotiations for a political settlement while maintaining military pressure on the GAM. In December 2002, the two sides signed the Cessation of Hostilities Agreement. The situation on the ground was fragile from the start, and the agreement collapsed in May 2003 over the basic issue of the future of Aceh—whether it should be a province of Indonesia or an independent state.

In May 2003, after the collapse of the agreement, the central government implemented a year of martial law in Aceh, and combat operations resumed immediately. The subsequent joint military–

Antiterrorism sign, Sulawesi
Courtesy Anastasia Riehl

police action was the largest security operation since Indonesia's 1975 invasion of East Timor, with an estimated 30,000 military personnel and 20,000 police deployed against the GAM. Security operations resulted in the death, capture, or surrender of thousands of alleged GAM cadre and supporters and drove armed GAM bands into remote areas of the province. Human-rights organizations charged that many of the casualties were innocent civilians. Because of heavy casualties, the GAM reverted to classic guerrilla warfare tactics. Nonetheless, it remained a potent military adversary and political force.

When the devastating earthquake and tsunami struck Aceh in 2004, more than 166,000 people died. The tragedy struck both sides of the insurgency, with heavy casualties among both guerrillas and government security forces and their families. The sheer magnitude of the tragedy created the conditions conducive to a comprehensive political settlement. As a result of the tragedy and the relief operations that followed, Aceh finally reached the beginning of a comprehensive solution to the long-running insurgency. After secret talks between representatives of the Indonesian government and the GAM, by mutual agreement between Indonesian President Yudhoyono and the GAM leadership, representatives of the two sides met in Helsinki, Finland, under the auspices of Crisis Management Initiative (CMI), a nongovernmental organization, led by the former Finnish president, Martti Ahtisaari.

Both sides made significant concessions: The GAM agreed to accept the principle of autonomy and dropped its demand for complete independence, while the Indonesian government agreed to allow GAM members to run for elective office. The two sides signed a peace agreement on August 15, 2005. Disarmament of GAM forces and removal of police and military forces went smoothly, with decommissioning and demobilization completed on schedule by December 27, 2005. The GAM formally dissolved itself in January 2006, although it is possible that remnants continue to exist. Indonesia's legislature passed a revised local autonomy law for Aceh in June 2006, which contained many of the provisions in the Helsinki agreement. Acehnese political leaders vowed to continue to strive for additional legislative concessions in the future.

Successful province-wide elections took place in December 2006, in which former GAM figures competed for office with existing political parties. The election for governor resulted in a resounding victory for a former GAM spokesman, who defeated seven other candidates and won almost 40 percent of the total votes cast. His closest competitor received only 17 percent. The election was significant for several reasons. First, it was peaceful, with virtually no violence during the campaign and vote. Second, the victor was a "local GAM"— one who stayed in Aceh during the insurgency—who defeated candidates representing the long-exiled international GAM leadership. Third, the winner defeated candidates supported by the existing political parties in Aceh. And fourth, there was no challenge to his victory, and national leaders and legislators in Jakarta pledged support for his tenure in office. District-level elections held at the same time brought many former GAM fighters into political office as well (see Elections, ch. 4). By 2009 Aceh's government and administration functioned much as those in other provinces, although disputes over the application and enforcement of Islamic law or sharia (see Glossary) were here more strident than anywhere else in the nation.

Papua

Indonesia no longer faces a significant secessionist movement in its easternmost provinces of Papua and Papua Barat. Rather, the rapid changes at the start of the twenty-first century have exacerbated the preexisting problems of poverty, high unemployment, environmental degradation, and the poor quality of many government services. The greatest threat to security is posed not by secessionist violence but by increased social, ethnic, and religious tensions between the indigenous Papuan population and the swelling tide of non-Papuans from elsewhere in Indonesia, drawn by opportunities in the commercial, agricultural, and extractive industries in the two provinces.

The remaining small secessionist movement in Papua is remote and fragmented. The Free Papua Organization (OPM) formed in 1969 and has been conducting a low-level armed insurgency since then. The OPM is fragmented into several factions whose goals range from independence to a merger with neighboring Papua New Guinea, autonomy, or better treatment by the central government. The influx of new residents resettled under the government's now-defunct Transmigration Program (see Glossary) caused resentment among the indigenous population and brought new recruits into both the OPM's political and military structures. However, since the early 2000s that resentment has manifested itself in mostly urban political demonstrations, and the OPM has steadily lost strength. Indonesian military operations in Papua have claimed many lives over the years, and nonviolent pro-independence OPM spokespersons have been jailed on charges of subversion.

The fight between the OPM and the security forces pits a rudimentary force against a high-technology police and military. The remaining OPM guerrilla bands were concentrated in the hinterlands of Jayapura, Merauke, Mimika, and Paniai by late 2008. The guerrillas coordinate few, if any, of their operations; instead, they select and strike at targets as resources and opportunities become available. OPM targets include small police and military posts and patrols and unarmed, nonmilitary groups, such as civilian timber workers. The last significant attack by the OPM occurred in 2002, when a force led by admitted OPM guerrillas attacked a group of mostly American teachers near Tembagapura, site of a huge open-face mine operated by Freeport-McMoRan Copper and Gold—known locally as P. T. Freeport-Indonesia—and protected by Indonesian military and police, who are paid by Freeport. Two Americans and one Indonesian were killed, and eight Americans and Indonesians were wounded. By 2006 the leaders of the attack had been captured, tried, and convicted of assault and murder. There were other attacks, also near the Freeport mine in 2009.

The OPM is believed to have fewer than 1,000 armed guerrillas. Many of its unarmed supporters have turned their attention to peaceful urban demonstrations to express grievances. Active, full-time OPM activity is limited to those guerrillas living in the jungles fighting with spears, bows, arrows, bush knives, and stolen and captured guns, mostly of military and police origin. The OPM is viewed as a political movement with an extremely limited military capability that poses no threat to Jakarta. However, it is another centripetal force encouraging the fragmentation of Indonesia. The central government maintains approximately 10,000 military and police in Papua. The missions of these forces include the destruction of OPM military units, general law and order and security, and protection of the designated strategic industry locations that include the Freeport mine at

Tembagapura and the growing development of the BP Tangguh natural gas field around Bintuni Bay, in Papua Barat Province.

Ethnic and Religious Conflict

A key characteristic of Suharto's New Order regime was the prevalence of security and order throughout the nation. Any outbreak of violence between ethnic or religious groups was quickly and sternly repressed. Tensions simmered below the surface, however, and after Suharto's fall in 1998, ethnic and religious conflict erupted in several regions. Security forces were initially ineffective in regaining control because the police, poorly trained, poorly equipped, and understaffed, were ill prepared to handle large-scale unrest. The TNI, stung by accusations of human-rights abuses, and resentful of the change in mission responsibility, was reluctant to intervene without a formal request for assistance from local authorities.

In Kalimantan Barat Province, the relative harmony that had prevailed among native Malays, ethnic Chinese, and Dayaks for generations was upset by the influx of hundreds of thousands of Madurese under the Transmigration Program in the 1970s and 1980s. Communal violence in the 1990s was triggered by Dayak discontent with the Madurese community's hold on the economic balance of power in the region, and by a perception that the Madurese were illegally taking Dayak land. Hundreds of settlers were killed in the Sambas area of Kalimantan Barat in early 1999 and the Sampit area of Kalimantan Tengah Province in February 2001. By April 2001, almost 100,000 Madurese, many of whom had resided in Kalimantan for several generations, had been evacuated to Madura and Java. Dayak leaders and government officials conducted reconciliation talks, but the return of the Madurese was slow to occur.

Conflict broke out in Maluku Province in 1999 after a seemingly minor clash between a bus driver and a passenger who refused to pay his fare exploded into wide-ranging Muslim–Christian violence in Ambon that quickly expanded throughout the Maluku Islands. More than 5,000 people were killed between 1999 and 2002. Islamic militants in Jakarta called for jihad to support their coreligionists on the islands. Similar Muslim–Christian violence flared around the Sulawesi Tengah city of Poso during the same period. Hard-line civilian and military sympathizers, who wanted to destabilize the regime of then-President Abdurrahman Wahid, collaborated to organize, train, equip, and arm the Laskar Jihad (Jihad Militia) and arranged the unimpeded transfer of several thousand members of the militia to both Ambon and Poso. This caused a major escalation of the conflict. The government declared a civil emergency, one step short of martial law. In February

2002, leaders of the Christian and Muslim communities in Poso and Maluku Province signed two separate peace agreements aimed at ending three years of sectarian fighting. Both agreements were brokered by Muhammad Yusuf Kalla, who, two years later, was elected vice president of Indonesia. The level of conflict quickly fell, but sporadic violence remained endemic to the entire region.

Terrorism

Religious extremism has disturbed Indonesia's domestic security as far back as the 1950s and 1960s, when organizations such as Darul Islam and Bangsa Islam Indonesia fought for the establishment of an Islamic state. It was not until the early twenty-first century that terrorism, both domestic and international, was recognized as a major internal threat. In 2000 dozens of people died in a series of urban terrorist attacks on the Jakarta Stock Exchange and on churches and shopping malls on Sumatra and Java. In Singapore and Malaysia, authorities uncovered plots by the regional terrorist organization Jemaah Islamiyah. Suspects arrested in Singapore revealed the existence of Jemaah Islamiyah cells in Indonesia.

Indonesian authorities initially ignored intelligence warnings about terrorists inside Indonesia. Then, on October 12, 2002, Jemaah Islamiyah terrorists bombed two nightclubs in Kuta, Bali, killing 202 people and injuring around 300, many of them foreign tourists. Subsequent Jemaah Islamiyah attacks in Jakarta in August 2003 and September 2004, as well as other bombings in Bali in October 2005, killed 49 more and injured 458, almost all Indonesians. These attacks finally led to recognition throughout Indonesia that Islamist terrorists were active in the country. Indonesian and international investigators tied earlier domestic terrorist attacks to Jemaah Islamiyah as well, and Indonesian leaders acknowledged the threat posed by international as well as domestic terrorists. In late 2004, the Yudhoyono government adopted a more confrontational policy against terrorism, which appeared likely to remain a significant threat to Indonesia's security.

Several security units have been specifically assigned a counterterrorism mission. The newest of these is the National Police counterterrorism unit, usually called Detachment 88, which was formed in 2002 with extensive funding, training, and equipment from the United States. It has both investigative and tactical-response capabilities (see The National Police, this ch.). Detachment 88 has been successful in tracking down and arresting scores of accused and suspected terrorists and support personnel. Several high-value terrorists were killed in armed shootouts. The Indonesian judicial system has convicted and imprisoned dozens of terrorists since 2005. The three men who planned the Bali bombings were executed in November 2008 after more than three years of investigation, trials, convictions, and legal appeals. Indonesian authorities have made important progress against both organized terrorist organizations, such as Jemaah Islamiyah, and affiliated splinter terrorist cells.

Each of the three branches of the TNI has at least one special operations unit with a counterterrorism mission. The largest of these, Unit 81, is part of the Army Special Forces Command (Komando Pasukan Khusus—Kopassus). There are also smaller counterterrorism units in the air force and navy. Unit 81 is highly trained in intelligence, detection, and tactical-assault counterterrorist tactics. The navy's "frogman" unit trains for counterterrorism raids against such maritime targets as offshore oil platforms, docks and harbor targets, and ships that have been seized by terrorists.

The Armed Forces in National Life

The armed forces did not initially seek to play a dominant political position, even though they played a role in the establishment of the republic, in the formative years of Indonesian parliamentary democracy. Circumstances, rather than deliberate planning, pressed the armed forces to gradually enlarge their role in national life. As it consolidated each stage of its growing political power, however, the military leadership grew protective of its gains. Suharto skillfully used the military as his primary instrument of power during his 32-year rule. In return, the military leadership was handsomely rewarded. The inculcation of Pancasila and the institutionalization of *dwifungsi* brought the military to its most powerful position in the early 1990s.

Some influential senior officers had, however, become concerned by the mid-1990s that the prestige and honor of the military were being compromised by excessive involvement in the day-to-day political and social affairs of the nation. Many moderate officers pressed for change, including former armed forces commander in chief General Edi Sudrajat, former National Defense Institute commandant Lieutenant General Sofian Effendi, the late Lieutenant General Agus Wirahadikusumah, and leading military intellectual Lieutenant General Agus Wijoyo. All four became leaders in the military reform movement after their retirement.

Suharto's forced resignation in May 1998 was discreetly facilitated by the military leadership, which refused to seize power to protect the president's position. From its earliest days, the Indonesian military had never contemplated a coup d'état in Indonesia; that tradition and the growing reformist element in the military played an important

*Training in the field
Courtesy U.S. Defense
Attaché's Office, Jakarta
Special forces troops in formation
Courtesy Indonesian
Department of Defense*

role in keeping the armed forces from taking power even though Suharto reportedly offered the presidency to General Wiranto, then the armed forces commander in chief. Since then, the armed forces have supported the transition to democracy, implemented a number of reforms, displayed a more moderate face to the populace, and maintained discipline and a leadership image in contrast to that of the often corrupt and hapless post-Suharto civilian officialdom. The TNI remains the most powerful element in Indonesian society and retains significant influence over the country's political life.

Political and Administrative Role

Indonesia's transition from autocracy to democracy has been lengthy and difficult, with various power centers vying for a role in the new political environment. Enlightened leadership by Admiral Widodo Adi Sucipto (appointed by President Abdurrahman Wahid as the first naval officer to head the armed forces) and General Endriartono Sutarto, whose tenure as TNI commander in chief spanned the presidencies of Megawati Sukarnoputri and the early months of the first Susilo Bambang Yudhoyono administration, confirmed the relatively restrained and more moderate role of the military at the beginning of the twenty-first century. The armed forces' perception of their political role has developed into that of a national institution above partisan interests and closely tied to the people, with a duty to foster conditions of order and security in which the habits of a stable and institutionalized political process can develop. This self-perception identifies a force far different from the one that fought for independence in the 1940s, evolved through the tumultuous political changes of the 1950s and 1960s, and subsequently engaged in a complex process of give-and-take with the autocratic Suharto during his long rule.

Participation in the Economy

The military has never been as dominant in the economic sphere as in the political sphere. Total military expenditures as a percentage of gross national product (GNP—see Glossary) began a steady decline in the 1960s, with the military share of the budget shrinking from 29 percent in 1970 to just over 1 percent by 2009.

The military's primary means of economic influence derives from operation of a business empire, comprising both legal and illicit enterprises, which had its beginnings in the struggle for independence. It expanded in December 1957, when Dutch enterprises and agricultural estates were taken over by local trade unions and immediately put under direct military supervision. December 1958 legislation led to the nationalization of these enterprises and estates during the first half of 1959. This involvement in commercial enterprises projected the military, especially the army, into a new sphere of activity, where it acquired entrepreneurial expertise, a vast patronage, and a source of enrichment for many of its personnel. By the 1990s, the military business empire may have provided as much as two-thirds of the total military budget. However, the region-wide economic crisis that began in 1997 had a significant adverse effect on the TNI's income from off-budget sources. While the policy of economic involvement continued through the 1990s and into the twenty-first century, it was estimated that the large military business empire, and diversions from other budgetary resources, had declined significantly in the first decade of the 2000s. Although no definitive information has ever been provided on the amount of funds received from the military's business enterprises, it was estimated to have shrunk to less than half of the total funding received by the TNI.

Engaged in enterprises such as air and highway transportation, shopping centers, and mines, many military-owned businesses operate in the open market much like any private company. In an effort to gain greater control over the military-run business empire, in 2004 the DPR mandated that such military businesses be civilianized by 2009, a process that was not 100- percent completed on schedule. The TNI will continue to operate military-supervised cooperatives (similar to the U.S. military's post-exchange and commissary systems).

Far more controversial than these legitimate enterprises are the illicit businesses run by both the military and the police. Accurate information on such activities is understandably difficult to obtain. Both the armed forces and the police allegedly are involved in illegal businesses ranging from extortion, gambling, and "security protection" rackets to more substantial enterprises such as illegal logging, support of renegade mining operations, and trafficking in marijuana. Subsequent to the separation of the police and the military in 1999, there have been occasional outbreaks of violence as personnel from the two institutions strive to protect "turf" and at the same time poach on the illegal enterprises of the other side.

Another kind of military enterprise was the service-owned factory, which had as its primary purpose the production of ordnance and equipment for the armed forces. By the mid-1980s, however, the government had taken over and managed as public-sector enterprises such major concerns as the navy's P. T. PAL shipyard in Surabaya, Jawa Timur Province, and the army's munitions factories.

While they cannot be singled out from other actors in the national economy, the armed forces of the early twenty-first century continue to face the problem of coping with a legacy of corruption. The military, though, is still viewed by Indonesian society as generally less corrupt than other sectors of the government. Nonetheless, the low salaries of military personnel require that they take up "constructive employment" to make ends meet.

Total People's Defense

Indonesia's military operations rely on a well-developed doctrine of national security called Total People's Defense (Hankamrata). Based on experiences during the struggle for independence, this doctrine proclaims that Indonesia can neither afford to maintain a large military apparatus nor compromise its hard-won independence by sacrificing its nonaligned status and depending on other nations to provide its defense. Instead, the nation will defend itself through a strategy of territorial guerrilla warfare in which the armed forces, deployed throughout the nation, serve as a cadre force to rally and lead the entire population in a people's war of defense. Military planners envision a three-stage war, comprising a short initial period in which an invader might defeat conventional Indonesian resistance and establish its own control, a long period of unconventional, regionally based fighting, and a final phase in which the invaders eventually are repelled.

The success of this strategy, according to the doctrine, requires that a close bond be maintained between citizen and soldier to encourage the support of the entire population and enable the military to manage all war-related resources. The people would provide logistical support, intelligence, and upkeep in this scenario, and, as resources permit, some civilians would be organized, trained, and armed to join the guerrilla struggle. To support these objectives, the TNI maintains the army's territorial organization, comprising 12 military regional commands (Komando Daerah Militer—Kodams) encompassing an estimated two-thirds of the army's strength. The territorial commands parallel the civilian governmental structure, with units at the province, district, and village level. Armed forces personnel also engage in large-scale civic-action projects involving community and rural development in order to draw closer to the people, ensure the continued support of the populace, and develop among army personnel a detailed knowledge of the region to which they are assigned. (Finally, and doctrine aside, the territorial structure provided the base upon which most of the army business empire flourished.)

Attention to potential external threats grew during the 1970s as planners became concerned with the growing military power of the

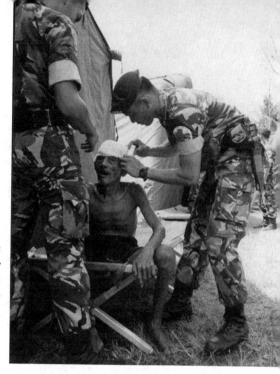

*Army medics on
civil-disaster duty
Courtesy Indonesian
Department of Defense*

newly unified Socialist Republic of Vietnam and its allies, including the Soviet Union. At the same time, China began publishing maps that made a claim to virtually all of the South China Sea, including the Natuna Islands, a chain off the western tip of Kalimantan. Indonesia responded with a major intraservice military exercise (Latihan Gabungan—LatGap—Joint Exercise) in the Natuna Islands. China soon withdrew the map, and relations between the two countries remained stable.

Political developments in the late 1980s and early 1990s subsequently relieved tensions in Southeast Asia. These developments included efforts to bring peace to Cambodia, during which Indonesia's three-battalion deployment was the largest military contribution to the UN Transitional Authority in Cambodia (UNTAC); the withdrawal of Vietnamese troops from Cambodia; and the reduced perception of a general threat from Vietnam and China. Nonetheless, the potential for regional conflict—for example, over territorial claims in the Spratly Islands in the South China Sea—continued to trouble strategic planners (see Foreign Policy, ch. 4). In the post–Cold War era, Indonesia has quietly continued to support the maintenance of a U.S. regional security presence to prevent a vacuum that could be filled by potentially less benevolent outsiders.

Defense Spending and the Defense Industry

Indonesia is unique among developing countries, and unusual among other Asian countries, in the relatively low priority given to defense spending. In 2009 there were some 302,000 personnel in Indonesia's active armed forces, and the military budget totaled US$3.4 billion, about the same military budget and force level as Thailand, a country with less than one-third of Indonesia's population, and Burma (Myanmar), which has only one-quarter of Indonesia's population. Singapore, with a population less than 2 percent of Indonesia's, has more than 72,000 active-duty military personnel—a force more than nine times larger than Indonesia's on a per-capita basis. The results of Indonesia's relatively limited commitment to the military are aged weapons systems, poor maintenance, and low levels of combat readiness. The TNI's readiness posture was also badly affected by the arms embargo imposed by the United States and other arms suppliers. Chronic poor maintenance was compounded by Indonesia's inability to purchase spare parts, which resulted in the inoperability of most of the air force C–130 transport fleet, most of the transport helicopter fleet, and many of the navy's logistics and transport ships. The effect of these shortcomings was sadly demonstrated in the TNI's inability to respond quickly to the devastation caused by the 2004 tsunami.

By the late 1970s, Indonesia had retired most of the Soviet-bloc military hardware left over from the Sukarno era. Between 1977 and 1982, national allocations to the Department of Defense and Security and armed forces doubled in absolute terms, and modest upgrades took place in all three military services. Ensuing years saw the military portion of the budget stabilize at between 6 and 7 percent of the overall state budget. However, with the military having to obtain as much as two-thirds of its total revenues from its own business empire, the official budget figures were misleading.

The last quarter of the twentieth century saw the purchase of matériel such as F–5 and F–16 fighter aircraft (in 1978 and 1988, respectively) and A–4 ground attack aircraft (in 1981); several used frigates and destroyers; and tanks, armored personnel carriers, and towed howitzers. The most controversial acquisition was the purchase, in the mid-1990s, of nearly the entire navy of the former Democratic Republic of Germany (East Germany—DDR). While the price for the 39 ships was relatively low, the costs to upgrade, acclimatize, and maintain these aging vessels soon became prohibitive. The purchase strained the defense budget for many years, and by the early twenty-first century most of the ships were no longer operational. This purchase was arranged by then-Minister of Research and Technology B. J. Habibie, thus straining his relationship with the military.

Many traditional military suppliers began to reduce the scope and breadth of military relations with Indonesia in the 1990s, to protest human-rights abuses in East Timor. The violence there in 1999 caused the United States, the European Union (EU), and Australia to cease arms sales entirely. As a result, Indonesia's military equipment deteriorated dramatically because of a lack of spare parts and maintenance. Only after the December 2004 tsunami disaster in Aceh did those countries resume progress toward normalization of their respective military-to-military relations. Because of that experience and to avoid the potential of any future military embargo, Indonesia has deliberately broadened its sources of military equipment and weapons systems. In the early twenty-first century, Indonesia completed agreements to acquire major weapons systems from Russia, China, several East European nations, the Republic of Korea (South Korea), and the Netherlands, among others.

Indonesia is far from self-sufficient in the production of weapons and defense-related matériel. Domestic facilities remain inadequate for the repair of certain complex weapons systems, and equipment inventories often represent considerable overstatements of what is actually in functioning order. Moreover, although defense guidelines favor the standardization of weaponry and other defense matériel, such as communications equipment and ground and air transport systems, the armed forces still possess and continue to procure equipment from a variety of sources. This situation has caused serious problems in obtaining and stocking spare parts and training technical maintenance personnel.

Major defense industries were transferred from the armed forces to civilian control in the 1980s. Under a new policy, these plants also served the commercial and civilian sectors. For example, when fully operational in the 1990s, the aircraft industry produced parts and equipment for commercial aviation. Although the aircraft industry was for decades the favorite project of Suharto and his minister for research and technology (and successor as president), B. J. Habibie, it was another money-wasting effort that cost hundreds of billions of dollars. After Suharto's 1998 resignation, the aircraft industry stagnated; and, by the early 2000s, it was producing very little, not even spare parts. The army's former munitions plants, by contrast, became very successful, manufacturing commercial explosives for the mining and petroleum industries as well as defense-related products. P. T. Pindad, another former army plant, now produces much of the TNI's small arms as well as several models of wheeled and armored vehicles. The P. T. PAL shipyard also manufactures commercial ships and maritime equipment, in addition to naval vessels.

Personnel

The size of the armed services—approximately 302,000 in 2009—is small in relation to Indonesia's large population. The military is also small in comparison to the forces of other nations of comparable population, and in comparison to the forces of other Asian countries. The army is by far the dominant branch of the Indonesian military, with approximately 233,000 personnel; the navy and marine corps total about 45,000 and the air force, about 24,000.

The Indonesian constitution states that every citizen has the right and obligation to defend the nation. Conscription is provided for by law, but in light of limited civilian-sector employment opportunities, the armed forces have been able to attract sufficient numbers to maintain mandated strength levels without resorting to a draft. By 2008 almost all service members were volunteers who had met the criteria set for conscription. However, officer specialists, such as physicians, are occasionally conscripted for short-term service. Most enlisted personnel are recruited in their own regions and generally train and serve most of their time in units near their homes. Each service has small women's units (see Women in the Armed Forces, this ch.).

The combined officer corps for the three services was estimated to total some 53,000 personnel in 2008. Until 2005 the mandatory retirement age for officers was 55, but a 2004 military act passed by the DPR provided for a gradual extension to age 60. Virtually all career noncommissioned officers (NCOs) serve 20 years and retire in their mid-forties, thereafter often going into private business. With personnel strength mandated to remain static, a steady balance between new officer accessions and losses (through death, attrition, and retirement) seems likely to be maintained.

For the first 20 years of independence, entry into the officer corps was very competitive. According to both patriotic and traditional values, a military education and military career were regarded as highly desirable. Since the late 1970s, however, the armed forces have experienced difficulty attracting a sufficient number of the best-qualified candidates to the Armed Forces Military Academy (Akmil), the national service academy at Magelang, Jawa Tengah Province. Field commanders have long complained of not getting enough high-quality young officers from Akmil. Improved job opportunities in Indonesia's advancing economy have persuaded many of the brightest and best-qualified high-school graduates to attend civilian degree-granting universities (Akmil does not grant academic degrees). In the late 1990s, the armed forces began to expand their source of officers by instituting a program similar to the U.S. Reserve Officers' Training Corps

(ROTC) and experimented with educating a small number of cadets in overseas civilian colleges.

The armed forces have maintained cohesion and a professional esprit de corps, in spite of problems with officer recruitment. Maturation through institutionalization, increased education, and an emphasis on national (rather than regional) loyalty have produced a military that is a far cry from the factionalized and ideologically diverse force that existed at the time of the 1965 coup attempt. Uniting the services under a strong central command and eliminating "warlordism" and regionalism by routine rotational assignments have contributed to this cohesion and minimized the impact of the occasional emergence of personality-driven cliques.

The senior officer corps reflects the ethnic composition of the national population. The TNI does not publish data on ethnicity in its personnel rosters, but a review of the names of 60 top officers in TNI headquarters and the three services suggested that in 2008 about 55 percent were from Java (ethnically Javanese, Sundanese, or Madurese), a proportion approximately reflective of the national population. There is a continued trend toward assignments based on ability rather than ethnic or religious considerations.

Organization and Equipment of the Armed Forces

Administrative and Command Structure

The TNI consists of three military services—the army, navy, and air force. The Department of Defense (Dephan) is responsible for planning, acquisition, and management tasks, but has no command or control of troop units (see fig. 13). As part of the post-Suharto reform program, each of Suharto's successors as president has appointed a civilian as minister of defense. However, each of these ministers has remained outside the military chain of command. A major goal of political reformers is to restructure the chain of command to place the TNI under genuine civilian control. This intent was reflected in the policy guidance contained in the military law passed by the DPR in 2004, but there was no time schedule for effecting such a major change. The TNI commander retains command and control of all armed forces, in the meantime, and continues by tradition to be the senior Indonesian military officer. Since the separation of the Department of Defense from the armed forces headquarters in 1985, the department's staff has been composed largely of active-duty and retired military personnel. The structure of Dephan consists of the offices of the minister of defense, a secretary general, an inspector

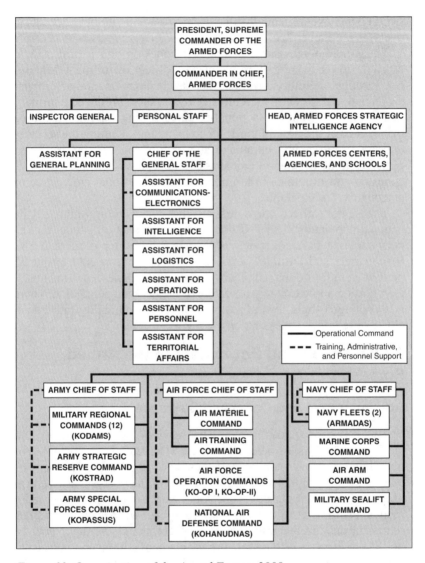

Figure 13. Organization of the Armed Forces, 2009

general, and five directors general, as well as several functional centers and institutes. In 2009 the minister of defense was a civilian, while the secretary general was an active-duty military officer. The inspector general and five directors general were a mix of active and retired senior military officers.

The role of the individual armed services has not changed since 1969, when the heads of the army, navy, and air force were reduced to chiefs of staff. At that time, operational control of almost all military units was vested in the armed forces commander in chief. The headquarters of each military service functions primarily as an administrative and support center.

The TNI staff and its functions remain directly subordinate to the commander in chief of the armed forces, who remains, in turn, directly responsible to the president, who holds the formal title of supreme commander of the armed forces. Directly under the TNI commander are the chief of the general staff (Kasum), the TNI's next most senior officer; the inspector general; the assistant for general planning; and the heads of a number of agencies and institutes. The TNI Kasum has assistants for communications and electronics, intelligence, logistics, operations, personnel, and territorial affairs. The TNI general staff supports the headquarters of each of the three services, and its personnel are drawn from all three services.

The army territorial structure focuses on the 12 military regional commands (Kodams), with the chain of command flowing directly from the armed forces commander in chief to the Kodam commanders, and from them to subordinate army territorial commands (see fig. 14). The senior operational air force commands are the National Air Defense Command (Kohanudnas) and the East Operations Command and West Operations Command (Komando Operasi—Ko-Ops). The navy has an Eastern Fleet and a Western Fleet (each called an Armada).

The armed forces commander in chief exercises control over most of the combat elements of the army, navy, and air force through the 12 army Kodams, the two air force Ko-Ops, and the two navy Armadas. The commander in chief also exercises operational control over the air force's Kohanudnas and the two army strike force commands—the Army Strategic Reserve Command (Kostrad) and the Army Special Forces Command (Kopassus).

Kostrad was formed in the early 1960s during the West Irian campaign. It was from his position as Kostrad commander that Suharto organized opposition to the 1965 coup attempt. The powerful post has been filled since then by officers considered particularly loyal to the president. In 2009 Kostrad had a strength of approximately 40,000 personnel. It consists of two divisions, each containing airborne and

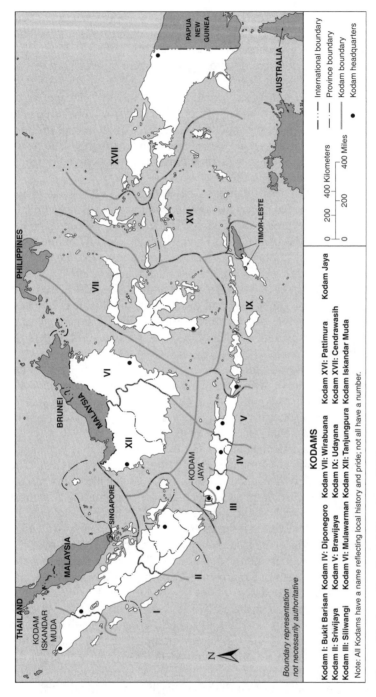

Figure 14. Army Territorial Structure, 2009

infantry brigades; a separate airborne brigade; one cavalry brigade; two field artillery regiments; and several combat support and service support units. In early 2005, the armed forces commander in chief announced plans to expand the independent brigade, based near Makassar, Sulawesi Selatan Province, into a third division to be based primarily in Papua.

Kopassus numbered some 5,000 military personnel in 2009, identifiable by their distinctive red berets. Organized into three operational groups, a counterterrorism unit, and a training center, Kopassus personnel receive training in intelligence gathering, special operations techniques, sabotage, and airborne and seaborne landings.

There are official and unofficial militia-style paramilitary formations throughout Indonesia in addition to the regular armed forces. Once a formidable force estimated between 70,000 and 100,000 strong, the official militia units have been largely disbanded or integrated into the army. The far more dangerous unofficial militia-style units act as surrogate forces, usually for Kopassus, and have a reputation for violence and intimidation. Many are little more than criminal gangs protecting their "turf," often around markets and shopping centers, where they collect "security and protection" money. They also have provided manpower for political demonstrations and intimidation. Militia units trained by army cadre were responsible for much of the wave of violence that swept East Timor in 1999.

Military Education

The TNI operates a central military academy headquarters charged with curriculum standardization, but the three service academies are under the control of their respective service chiefs of staff. Cadets begin a one-year training program at the Armed Forces Military Academy (Akmil) in Magelang, which is followed by three-year courses in the specialized branches of Akmil run by each service. The army branch, referred to simply as the Military Academy, is located in Magelang as well. The Air Force Academy is located in Yogyakarta and the Naval Academy, in Surabaya.

The TNI also maintains a joint headquarters for the Armed Forces Command and Staff School (Mako Sesko) and the three service command and staff schools, but control of the individual command and staff colleges is under the service chiefs of staff. Cohort ties formed at the service academies and at the command and staff school are strong unifying elements among officers. The joint TNI Command and Staff College (Sesko TNI) trains officers at the lieutenant colonel level, and the National Resiliency Institute (Lemhanas) provides training at the colonel and brigadier general levels. Half of each Lemhanas class is filled by senior civil servants and leaders of the business community. In 2009 Dephan established the Indonesian Defense University (Universitas Pertahanan Indonesia), modeled on the U.S. National Defense University in Washington, DC. It is the first military school in Indonesia to award academic degrees.

Branches of Service

Army

The Army of the Republic of Indonesia (TNI–AD) historically has been the dominant military service, headed by the army chief of staff, a four-star general. His staff includes a vice chief of staff, an inspector general, and assistant chiefs of staff for logistics, operations, personnel, planning and budget, security, and territorial affairs. Army strength in 2009 was approximately 233,000.

The chief of staff is responsible for personnel, training, administration, and logistical support of the army. Commanders and staff of each Kodam are responsible for administration, logistics, personnel, training, and the general welfare of assigned and attached combat units. Each Kodam is divided into successively smaller administrative units. These include the Military Resort, or Garrison, Command (Korem); Military District Command (Kodim); and Military Subdistrict Command (Koramil). At the bottom of the structure, noncommissioned officers (NCOs) are assigned to every village in the country, where they are known as the village NCO (*babinsa*).

Military operations are rarely, if ever, conducted in any formation larger than a battalion. Each Korem has control of at least one battalion, and one or more battalions come under the direct control of the Kodam. Army doctrine distinguishes between centrally controlled units and regionally controlled units. Centrally controlled units are found in Kostrad and Kopassus. Regionally controlled units by definition are those assigned to the 12 Kodams. The battalions have a planned strength of nearly 700 personnel, although many—those in the Kodams in particular—are under strength. Each Kodam has at least one designated quick-reaction force battalion; these are the best-trained and -equipped units in the territorial structure. Both types of battalions have experienced frequent temporary deployments to areas of insecurity, including East Timor (prior to 1999), Aceh (prior to 2005), and Papua.

The army has an aviation arm that performs liaison and limited transport duties. The unit operates several rotary-wing squadrons with helicopters of various national origins and one composite fixed-wing squadron composed mostly of light aircraft and small transports, such as the domestically produced CASA–235.

The army is equipped with a variety of weapons systems acquired from several European and Asian countries and the United States, as well as domestically manufactured items. Because of funding constraints, emphasis is placed on maintenance and rehabilitation of older equipment. The mainstays of the armored force are its French-built AMX–13 light tanks and the variant AMX–VCI reconditioned armored personnel carrier, mostly acquired in the late 1970s. Domestic industry supplies nearly all of the army's small-arms requirements, although a substantial number of M–16 rifles purchased from the United States in the 1980s remained in the inventory two decades later. Domestically produced arms include Belgian-licensed FNC rifles, submachine guns, and machine guns. Ammunition is in short supply.

Although army recruits receive their basic training in a local training facility located in each Kodam area, specialist corps training is provided at the appropriate national corps centers. NCOs must attend training courses and pass examinations in their specialized fields prior to promotion. The army maintains a large tactical training area at Baturaja, Sumatera Selatan Province, where selected units undergo small-unit training on a rotational basis.

Navy

The Navy of the Republic of Indonesia (TNI–AL) became a separate service in 1946, after the National Revolution began. Its vessels come from a variety of countries, including the United States. The fleet includes submarines from the Federal Republic of Germany, light frigates from the Netherlands and Britain, and fast-attack craft from South Korea. In 1992 the Indonesian government acquired 39 used ships of various types from the navy of the former Democratic Republic of Germany (East Germany). The acquisition proved to be a mistake of major proportions. The ships were in poor condition, not suited for operations in the tropics, and difficult to staff and maintain. By 2005 many of them had been mothballed. The Indonesian navy itself produces numerous small coastal craft in national shipyards.

In 2009 the fleet consisted of more than 90 ships and numerous smaller vessels. The newest warships are four Sigma-class corvettes from the Netherlands, three of which were delivered by 2008 and the fourth, by 2009. As newer warships and patrol craft entered the inventory, the navy decommissioned older vessels. Nevertheless, the navy was underequipped and under strength for its mission of protecting the nation's huge maritime expanse against piracy, poaching, and smuggling. Specifically, it needed a large infusion of fast-patrol craft to cover its wide internal seas and coastlines, as well as increased sealift capacity to move marine corps and army units and equipment to trouble spots across the archipelago.

Structurally, the navy comprises the headquarters staff at Jakarta under the overall command of the navy chief of staff, two fleet commands (the Eastern Fleet at Surabaya and the Western Fleet at Jakarta), the marine corps, a small air arm, and a military sealift command (see fig. 15). About 45,000 uniformed personnel were serving in the navy in 2009, including about 20,000 marines. The marines are organized into two divisions (formerly designated as brigades), one stationed in Jakarta and the other in Surabaya. A third independent brigade is planned to become the core of a third division, once funds and manpower become available. The marine corps is equipped with light tanks, armored personnel carriers, and antiaircraft guns. Most of the corps' heavy equipment consists of badly outdated former Soviet-origin armored vehicles.

The navy began maintaining a small air arm in 1958. Headquartered at Surabaya, it had about 1,000 personnel in 2009. It is equipped primarily for naval reconnaissance and coastal patrol duties, flying three squadrons of light airplanes, as well as several transports and helicopters. The military sealift command coordinates the navy's logistical support systems.

The navy's missions include providing strategic sealift for the army and marine corps and support for operations responding to natural disasters. Other responsibilities include patrolling the strategic straits through which a major portion of the world's shipping passes between the Pacific and Indian oceans, particularly the Strait of Malacca. That crucial waterway carries an estimated 80 percent of commercial and military traffic between the Pacific and Indian oceans. Formerly a haven for piracy, the Strait of Malacca is now patrolled by the cooperative efforts of Indonesia, Malaysia, and Singapore, and piracy incidents have declined. Another naval mission focuses on halting smuggling and illegal fishing, both of which are especially prevalent near the Natuna Islands and in the seas around Sulawesi and Maluku. In support of this latter mission, the navy announced plans in the late 1980s to construct a number of limited-role bases in isolated areas in the eastern and western sections of the national territory. Funding restrictions, however, have kept this project from fulfillment. Some new bases have been built, including Tual in the southeastern part of Maluku Province, and the naval stations on Biak and Manokwari in Papua Barat Province have been upgraded. Patrol activity in the Sulu Sea and Sulawesi Sea (Celebes Sea) has increased as part of operations to detect and interdict movement by terrorists and maritime criminal activities where the maritime borders of Indonesia, Malaysia, and the Philippines meet.

The P. T. PAL shipyard, operated since the 1980s by the civilian government, along with other facilities in Surabaya, continues to be the navy's primary training, repair, and industrial center. Smaller-craft construction facilities are located at shipyards in Jakarta, Semarang (Jawa Tengah Province), Manokwari (Papua Barat Province), and Ambon (Maluku Province). P. T. PAL also constructs commercial ships in a variety of sizes and types. The navy has begun an innovative acquisition program by which individual provincial governments fund the purchase of fast-patrol craft to be turned over to the navy. Those ships are used for maritime security, generally in the territorial waters bordering the donor province.

Air Force

The Air Force of the Republic of Indonesia (TNI–AU), like the navy, was established as a separate service in 1946. The influence and capability of the air force decreased sharply after the 1965 coup attempt. The service was heavily purged because of the alleged involvement of its chief of staff, General Omar Dhani, in the Indonesian Communist Party (PKI). Significant modernization did not get under way until the late 1970s, with acquisition of F–5 and A–4 aircraft from the United States, and in the 1980s, with the acquisition of F–16 fighters from the United States and Hawk fighters from Britain. The imposition in the late 1990s of arms embargoes by the United States and other countries in response to Indonesia's human-rights violations, particularly in East Timor, resulted in a very low readiness level in the air force. In the early 2000s, Indonesia began to seek nontraditional suppliers, purchasing Sukhoi jet fighters from Russia and obtaining jet trainers from Singapore (by donation) and South Korea (primarily through countertrade). The United States ended its arms embargo of Indonesia in 2005, and the air force began a high-priority program to restore the readiness of its C–130 transport fleet and the F–16 fighter force.

Air force strength was about 24,000 in 2009. Approximately 4,000 of these personnel formed four battalions of "quick-action" paratroopers. Structurally, the air force consists of a headquarters staff in Jakarta supporting the chief of staff; three operational commands: Ko-Op I/West, Ko-Op II/East, and the National Air Defense Command; and two support commands: the Air Matériel Command and the Air Training Command (see fig. 16). The Air Matériel Command is headquartered in Bandung, Jawa Barat Province, and the Air Training Command is in Surabaya, Jawa Timur Province. Air operations are covered by two area commands, with the boundary between Jawa Tengah and Jawa Timur provinces being the east–west dividing line. The largest of the operational commands is Ko-Op II, headquartered in Makassar,

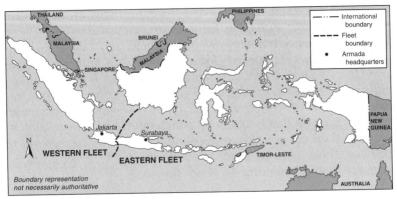

Figure 15. Navy Fleet Commands, 2009

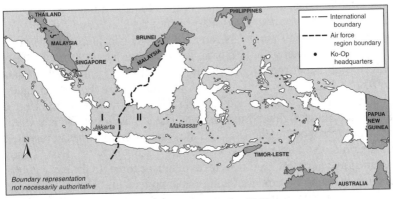

Figure 16. Air Force Operations Commands, 2009

Sulawesi Selatan Province. Ko-Op I is headquartered in Jakarta. The National Air Defense Command, also headquartered in Jakarta, has operational control over all fighter and counterinsurgency aircraft.

Most of the major weapons systems operated by the air force are manufactured in the United States. The C–130 Hercules, OV–10F Bronco, F–5E Tiger II, A–4E Skyhawk, and F–16 Fighting Falcon aircraft are all U.S.–made. Aircraft manufactured elsewhere include the British Hawk and Russian Sukhoi fighters. The air force also deploys several B–737 aircraft for maritime reconnaissance, a number of domestically produced small transports, and a fleet of helicopters. During the modernization period of the 1980s, the air force also purchased the Automated Logistics Management System (ALMS) from the United States to upgrade its ability to track and requisition spare parts and other materials.

In 1980 the air force enunciated a forward defense strategy that required it to build or upgrade air bases throughout Indonesia as well as main bases in Java. Most of those upgrades affected civilian airfields also used by the air force. A major upgrade at Ranai Air Base in the Natuna Islands provided a post for improved surveillance of the South China Sea. Iswahyudi Air Base in Jawa Timur Province was upgraded to enable it to handle modern jet fighter aircraft. Acquisition of the F–16 and Hawk systems resulted in further upgrades at Pekanbaru Air Base, Riau Province, and at Hasanuddin Air Base near Makassar, Sulawesi Selatan Province.

New pilots generally begin flight instruction in propeller-driven T–34 Turbo-Mentors. A squadron of British Aerospace T–53 Hawks is used for advanced training. Acquisition of the KT–1 Wongbee from South Korea, the SF260 SIAI Marchetti from Singapore, and training versions of the F–16 has significantly expanded the training base. However, competition with higher-paying civilian airlines has led to a chronic shortage of pilots and aviation support personnel.

Conditions of Service

Compensation of all TNI personnel is on a sliding scale according to rank and is uniform nationally and across the three services. Officers and enlisted personnel receive housing for married service members of appropriate rank, subsistence items and rations paid in kind, and a variety of allowances in addition to base pay. Especially at the lower ranks, compensation is so low that the need for supplementary income is a significant factor in service members' involvement in outside, often unsavory, employment.

The retirement age for officers was 55 until passage of the 2004 military laws, which raised the retirement age to 60 effective in 2009. Retirement at age 42 is mandatory for enlisted personnel. The president has the authority to grant an unlimited number of one-year extensions to active duty; these usually go to officers in key leadership posts. Officers are eligible for small pensions at age 48; those who have failed to gain promotion to lieutenant colonel are required to retire at that time. Two years before retirement, personnel can be placed on preretirement status, in which they draw full pay and allowances while beginning to develop civilian careers.

Women in the Armed Forces

Each branch of the TNI and the National Police has a women's component: the Women's Army Corps, the Navy Women's Corps, the Air Force Women's Corps, and the Women's Police Corps. According to official publications, women members of the armed forces are "set to work at places and in functions conform[ing] to their feminine disposition." More specifically, women are assigned to administrative work, intelligence work, English-language instruction, and activities to improve the health and social conditions of armed forces members and their families.They also specialize in the welfare of women and children. Despite the advance of women in the civilian workplace, including one former president, several cabinet members and legislators, and important business leaders, women do not advance to comparable rank in the armed forces. Women police officers are said to "play an important role in solving problems [of] drug addicts and juvenile delinquents." Some police commands in large cities also have rape/gender-based violence units staffed by female officers, but these are still rare.

Uniforms, Ranks, and Insignia

Grade and rank structure is standard throughout the three military services and corresponds to that common to most military systems. One title unique to Indonesia is *panglima*, a traditional heroic rank revived during the National Revolution. Although *panglima* is often translated as "commander," it has a stronger connotation of honor and power. In the 1980s, tradition evolved to limit the title *panglima* to the armed forces commander in chief and the Kostrad and Kodam commanders.

Uniforms of the three services are distinguished by color and style, with variations in headgear and other details distinguishing some elite troops, who wear berets of various colors. Army working and ceremonial uniforms are olive drab. Air force uniforms are medium blue, and navy uniforms are navy blue. Rank insignia are standardized among the services (see fig. 17; fig. 18). In ceremonial and service dress, officers wear rank insignia on the shoulder epaulet. Field-uniform insignia were moved in 1991 from the front of the fatigue shirt to the collar tip. Rank insignia are worn on the sleeves by NCOs and enlisted personnel.

Foreign Military Relations

Consistent with its foreign policy of nonalignment, Indonesia does not maintain defense pacts with other nations. It has security agreements with a broad range of countries (not including the United States), and it does participate in combined military exercises with several other countries. Over the years, Indonesia also has contributed troop contingents—some including either military or police personnel or both—to most UN peacekeeping forces deployed to global trouble

	LETNAN DUA	LETNAN SATU	KAPTEN	MAYOR	LETNAN KOLONEL	KOLONEL	BRIGADIR JENDERAL	MAYOR JENDERAL	LETNAN JENDERAL	JENDERAL
INDONESIAN RANK ARMY	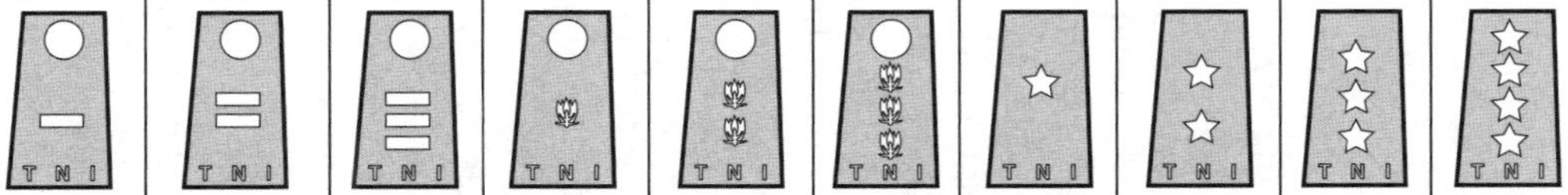									
U.S. RANK TITLE	2D LIEUTENANT	1ST LIEUTENANT	CAPTAIN	MAJOR	LIEUTENANT COLONEL	COLONEL	BRIGADIER GENERAL	MAJOR GENERAL	LIEUTENANT GENERAL	GENERAL
INDONESIAN RANK AIR FORCE	LETNAN DUA	LETNAN SATU	KAPTEN	MAYOR	LETNAN KOLONEL	KOLONEL	MARSEKAL PERTAMA	MARSEKAL MUDA	MARSEKAL MADYA	MARSEKAL
U.S. RANK TITLE	2D LIEUTENANT	1ST LIEUTENANT	CAPTAIN	MAJOR	LIEUTENANT COLONEL	COLONEL	BRIGADIER GENERAL	MAJOR GENERAL	LIEUTENANT GENERAL	GENERAL
INDONESIAN RANK NAVY*	LETNAN DUA	LETNAN SATU	KAPTEN	MAYOR	LETNAN KOLONEL	KOLONEL	LAKSAMANA PERTAMA	LAKSAMANA MUDA	LAKSAMANA MADYA	LAKSAMANA
U.S. RANK TITLE	ENSIGN	LIEUTENANT JUNIOR GRADE	LIEUTENANT	LIEUTENANT COMMANDER	COMMANDER	CAPTAIN	REAR ADMIRAL LOWER HALF	REAR ADMIRAL UPPER HALF	VICE ADMIRAL	ADMIRAL

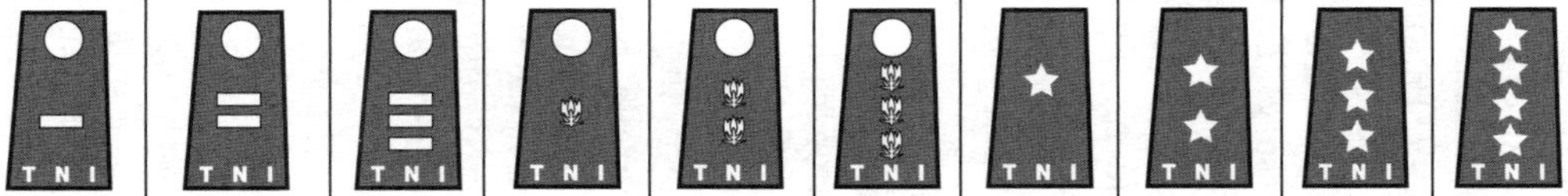

*Marine insignia are same as for navy personnel; marine rank titles are same as for army personnel.

Figure 17. Officer Ranks and Insignia, 2009

spots. Among other places, Indonesia has sent forces to the Suez Canal–Sinai Peninsula area (1957 and 1973–79), Democratic Republic of the Congo (1960–64), Iran–Iraq border (1988–90), Namibia (1989–90), Kuwait–Iraq border (1991), Somalia (1991), Cambodia (1991–93), Bosnia–Herzegovina (2000), and Lebanon (2006–8).

Indonesia was a founding member of the Association of Southeast Asian Nations (ASEAN—see Glossary), and although the organization was not established as a defense alliance, there is a history of military cooperation between Indonesia and its ASEAN partners. This cooperation is manifested both frequently and bilaterally and includes exchanges of military representatives at national defense institutions, periodic security consultations, and a series of joint military exercises with individual ASEAN states. ASEAN countries pledge their support for the security of each of the other ASEAN nations but stop short of discussing formation of a military alliance. The Indonesian government stresses that defense cooperation among ASEAN nations is a function of each nation's right to protect itself and that bilateral cooperation will not lead to any bilateral or ASEAN-wide defense pact. Indonesia plays a leading role in the ASEAN Regional Forum (ARF), a non-treaty security umbrella organization that includes nations and organizations as members—including the United States, China, the EU, and Russia—that are not ASEAN states.

Indonesia also conducts combined military exercises with non-ASEAN nations, including Australia, Britain, France, India, New Zealand, and the United States. During the 1980s, defense officials suggested that joint border patrols might be set up with Papua New Guinea, and the two countries signed a status-of-forces agreement in January 1992. Indonesian troops sometimes cross the border from Papua Province into Papua New Guinea in pursuit of armed insurgents.

Indonesia has maintained military-assistance agreements with several countries. It received funded security assistance from the United States every year between 1950 and 1992 except 1965 and 1966, when relations were at a low ebb. Most security-assistance programs were restored after 2005. Grant aid for military equipment, which ended in 1978, averaged US$13 million per year and was used mainly to procure logistics equipment, communications systems, and combat matériel for internal security. The United States also provided grant aid training under the International Military Education and Training (IMET) program from 1950 until 1992, when the U.S. Congress cut the aid in reaction to the human-rights situation in East Timor. In that 42-year period, more than 4,000 Indonesian military personnel received IMET training in the United States. The IMET program resumed in 2005. U.S. Foreign Military Sales (FMS) credits were

INDONESIAN RANK	PRAJURIT DUA	PRAJURIT SATU	PRAJURIT KEPALA	KOPRAL DUA	KOPRAL SATU	KOPRAL KEPALA	SERSAN DUA	SERSAN SATU	SERSAN KEPALA	SERSAN MAYOR	PEMBANTU LETNAN DUA	PEMBANTU LETNAN SATU
ARMY	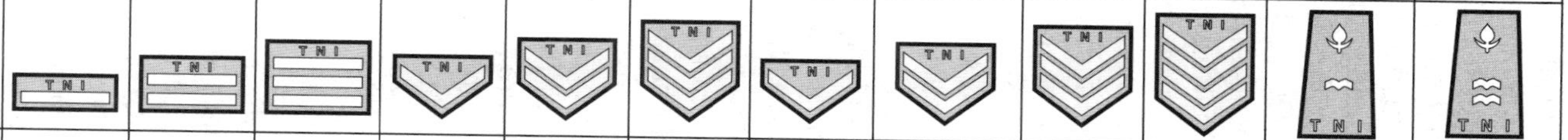											
U.S. RANK TITLE	PRIVATE (E-1)	PRIVATE (E-2)	PRIVATE 1ST CLASS	CORPORAL/ SPECIALIST	SERGEANT	STAFF SERGEANT	SERGEANT 1ST CLASS	MASTER SERGEANT/ FIRST SERGEANT	SERGEANT MAJOR/ COMMAND SERGEANT MAJOR		WARRANT OFFICER W-1	CHIEF WARRANT OFFICER W-2
INDONESIAN RANK	PRAJURIT DUA	PRAJURIT SATU	PRAJURIT KEPALA	KOPRAL DUA	KOPRAL SATU	KOPRAL KEPALA	SERSAN DUA	SERSAN SATU	SERSAN KEPALA	SERSAN MAYOR	PEMBANTU LETNAN DUA	PEMBANTU LETNAN SATU
AIR FORCE	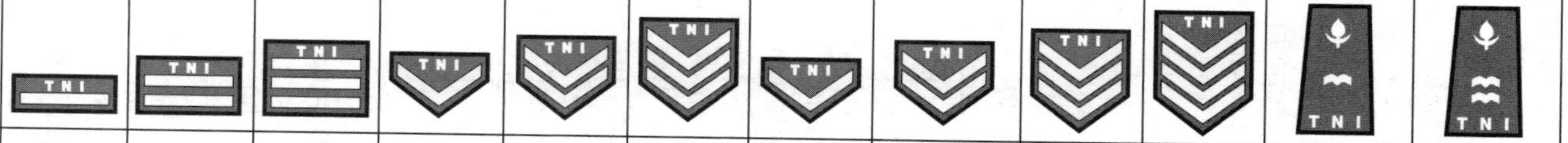											
U.S. RANK TITLE	AIRMAN BASIC	AIRMAN	AIRMAN 1ST CLASS	SENIOR AIRMAN	STAFF SERGEANT	TECHNICAL SERGEANT	MASTER SERGEANT	SENIOR MASTER SERGEANT	CHIEF MASTER SERGEANT		NO RANK	NO RANK
INDONESIAN RANK	KELASI DUA	KELASI SATU	KELASI KEPALA	KOPRAL DUA	KOPRAL SATU	KOPRAL KEPALA	SERSAN DUA	SERSAN SATU	SERSAN KEPALA	SERSAN MAYOR	PEMBANTU LETNAN DUA	PEMBANTU LETNAN SATU
NAVY*	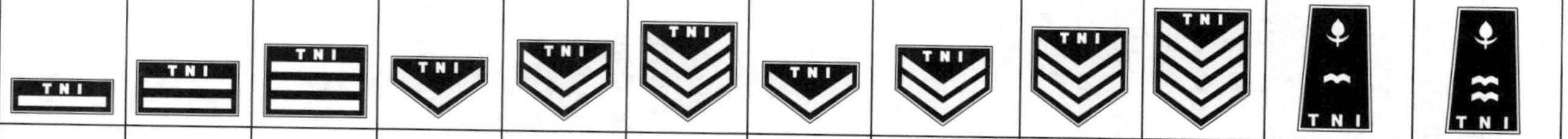											
U.S. RANK TITLE	SEAMAN RECRUIT	SEAMAN APPRENTICE	SEAMAN	PETTY OFFICER 3D CLASS	PETTY OFFICER 2D CLASS	PETTY OFFICER 1ST CLASS	CHIEF PETTY OFFICER	SENIOR CHIEF PETTY OFFICER	MASTER CHIEF PETTY OFFICER		WARRANT OFFICER W-1	CHIEF WARRANT OFFICER W-2

*Marine insignia are same as for navy personnel; marine rank titles are same as for army personnel.

Figure 18. Enlisted Ranks and Insignia, 2009

periodically made available to Indonesia starting in 1974 and have helped defray the cost of procuring U.S.-made military equipment. U.S. Foreign Military Financing (FMF) provides grants or loans for the acquisition of U.S. military articles, services, and training by Indonesia. Indonesia has also received military aid from Australia, Britain, France, Germany, the Netherlands, and Russia, among others. In the early 1960s, Indonesia acquired equipment from the Soviet Union, and though most of it was inoperative by the 1970s, Jakarta continued to make payments to the Russian government after the demise of the Soviet Union in 1991. Since the late 1990s, Russia has again become an important arms supplier for the Indonesian armed forces, including a US$1 billion loan that Indonesia is using to buy, among other items, attack and transport helicopters and jet fighters.

The military relationship with the United States went into decline starting in 1992 and worsened in 1999, when the United States suspended all military cooperation programs to protest the TNI's support of militia forces that rampaged across East Timor in the wake of that former province's vote for independence. Australia, Britain, and several other countries also reduced or suspended their military programs with Indonesia at the same time. However, the terrorist attacks against the United States on September 11, 2001, began the slow return of some cooperation programs because of the perceived need to enlist the support of the world's most populous Muslim nation in the global war against terrorism. The December 2004 earthquake and tsunami that devastated parts of Aceh prompted the U.S. government to reexamine its policy of isolating the TNI from training, education, and other aspects of the military-to-military relationship. In March 2005, the United States began FMS sales of nonlethal spare parts for transport aircraft. By 2008 Indonesia had regained eligibility to participate in most aspects of a military-to-military relationship with the United States.

Security and Intelligence Agencies

Only very general information has been made public regarding the organization and activities of Indonesia's intelligence and security bodies. In 2001 the name of the central intelligence-gathering institution was changed from the National Intelligence Coordinating Body (Bakin) to the National Intelligence Agency (BIN). Primarily cosmetic, the name change was designed to reflect the changes associated with the end of the Suharto era. BIN analyzes both domestic and foreign intelligence gathered by its own personnel as well as by the military services and the police. It is directly under the control of the president and maintains its own communications network outside the civilian and military administrations.

In 2004, after a series of devastating terrorist bombings in Indonesia, the president strengthened the authority of the BIN chief to coordinate all intelligence activities conducted by the military, police, and civilian intelligence agencies. In practice, such coordination has proved difficult to achieve because of inherent conflicts of interest and zealous protection of turf by the various agencies. BIN also was authorized to establish branch offices at the provincial level throughout Indonesia, and to direct all counterterrorism intelligence operations.

The TNI's agency for intelligence collection relating to external defense and internal security, processing, and operational functions is the Armed Forces Strategic Intelligence Body (Bais). Commanded by a major general, Bais is directly subordinate to the TNI commander.

The National Police

The National Police of Indonesia (Polri) has been financed, directed, and organized by the central government since 1945. Polri's main duties are to maintain public order and security. However, its personnel strength is far below the UN-prescribed police-to-populace ratio of 1:350 (the Indonesian ratio is approximately 1:630). For many decades, Polri was a fourth branch of the armed forces, then known as ABRI. In 1999, after the fall of Suharto, the police force was separated from the military and placed directly under the president. As part of this reorganization, the police did away with military ranks and titles and adopted standard international police nomenclature. In the 10 years since Polri ceased being part of the armed forces, it has enjoyed a resurgence in professionalism and an increase in strength. In 2009 Polri's estimated strength was around 280,000.

The national chief of police is the highest-ranking police officer in the nation. Like the TNI commander, he is appointed by the president and must be confirmed by the DPR. Assigned to Polri headquarters in Jakarta are a deputy police chief, extensive staff, and several separate administrative bodies that handle specialized police functions. Polri has its own territorial organization, with a police unit and police chief for each province (Regional Police—Polda). Each Polda unit is administratively subdivided at the district, subdistrict, and village levels. Polda Metrojaya, which has responsibility for metropolitan Jakarta, is subdivided into precincts, sections, and police posts.

Each province is assigned police units varying in strength and composition according to the needs dictated by the characteristics of the different areas within that province. These forces are organized as municipal police forces or rural units and are under the operational direction of the Polda commander, who in turn is directly responsible to Polri headquarters. All police elements are charged with supporting the local government in their respective areas.

Polri has maintained its centralized chain of command but has also been made responsive to the individual provincial governors since the rise of sustained democratic governance. Each governor is authorized to call on the police to respond to emergencies, for example, and both the police chief of an affected region and the governor may request military assistance if police resources prove insufficient.

Police forces are functionally organized into a number of specialized elements. The largest of these is the uniformed police, which includes both the general police, who perform conventional police duties relating to the control and prevention of crime and the protection of property, and the traffic police, who patrol the nation's roadways and supervise the licensing of drivers and the registration of motor vehicles. Also part of the uniformed force are the Women's Police Corps, which has been increasingly integrated into the Polri structure. Female police officers have been transformed from their old orientation, which was primarily directed toward the provision of social services, to a situation in which female police officers are involved in virtually every aspect of Polri missions, including counterterrorism and antiriot duties. The first female provincial police chief was appointed in 2007, in Banten Province. Elite units of special police enforce order in terrorist situations beyond the capability of the regular forces. These units had about 14,000 personnel in 2009, were better armed and more mobile than the general police, and lived in separate barracks under stricter discipline. The special police wear the same uniform as other police but are distinguished by special badges. Plainclothes police have the primary responsibility for criminal investigations, especially in complex cases or in cases involving several jurisdictions. They also handle forensics, intelligence, security, and the technical aspects of crime fighting, such as fingerprinting and identification.

A small unit, the Sea and Air Police, patrols the national waters and airspace, providing tactical aid to other elements by regulating traffic, guarding against smuggling and illegal fishing, and supplying personnel transport. The unit also participates in disaster relief. Its equipment includes a few helicopters and light airplanes and various small seacraft.

The Mobile Brigade, one of the oldest Polri units, was formed in late 1945. Its original tasks were disarming remnants of the Japanese Imperial Army and protecting the chief of state and the capital city. The brigade fought in the Revolution, and its troops took part in the military confrontation with Malaysia in the early 1960s and in the conflict in East Timor from the mid-1970s through 1999. The Explosive Ordnance Devices Unit, formed in 1981, is part of the Mobile Brigade.

The exigencies of fighting separatist insurgents in Aceh and Papua required the rapid expansion of the Mobile Brigade. Between 1998 and 2005, it grew from 7,500 to approximately 34,000 personnel. Such a rapid expansion brought problems in training and discipline, and the Mobile Brigade has come to be regarded by many observers as the least disciplined and most brutal of all forces deployed against insurgents. It is essentially a paramilitary organization trained and organized along military lines. The brigade is used primarily as a deployable combat force in emergencies, aiding in police operations requiring quick action. It also works in domestic security and defense operations and has special riot-control equipment. Elements of the force also are trained for airborne operations.

The need to forge a capable police counterterrorism unit in response to the spread of international terrorism resulted in the establishment in 2002 of another elite element, the National Police counterterrorism unit, better known as Detachment 88. This unit was largely funded and trained by the United States and graduated its first cadre in 2003. It has the capability to conduct counterterrorism and modern forensic investigations, and it includes a quick-reaction counterterrorist team. Detachment 88 has been particularly successful in its counterterrorist operations. Its personnel, supported by technical assistance and training from the United States and Australia in particular, have captured or killed many of the most-wanted terrorists in the country, including those responsible for bombings in Bali and Jakarta, terrorism in Sulawesi Tengah Province, and attacks against civilian targets elsewhere in Indonesia.

Rank-and-file police service is voluntary. Recruits must have at least a sixth-grade education and pass a competitive examination. Other qualifications include physical fitness and good moral character. After three years' service as ordinary police, personnel with only junior secondary-school diplomas can enter training to become NCOs. Those with three years' experience as NCOs are eligible for further training to enable them to become candidate officers and eventually enter the officer corps. The majority of the police officer corps enters the force as graduates of the National Police Academy, located near Sukabumi, Jawa Barat Province. The Polri working and ceremonial uniforms are dark brown.

Advanced training in vocational and technical subjects is available to regular police, NCOs, and officers. Promotions often are based on performance in advanced education. The Police Command and Staff School at Semarang, Jawa Tengah Province, offers advanced training in administration and logistics to police officers assigned to command units at the subdistrict, district, and Polda levels.

The Criminal Justice System

The nation's criminal jurisprudence and its institutions of criminal justice derive from Indonesia's experience as an independent state and from the Dutch colonial heritage. Dutch-based criminal law is one of three systems of law in operation in the nation since the nineteenth century, the other two being a system of European-derived commercial codes and civil law based on customary law (*adat*), which includes Islamic law or sharia (see Islam, ch. 2). Criminal law is the only one of these three systems that is essentially codified and applied uniformly throughout the national territory. Criminal justice is administered through a system that includes a hierarchy of trial and appellate courts with the Supreme Court at the top of the pyramid; a prosecutorial arm of the national government; and an independent bar. Indonesians and outside observers have long considered the criminal justice system one of the most corrupt branches of the Indonesian government.

Several factors limit the use of formal legal channels in dealing with activity defined as criminal. Owing in large part to a general shortage of trained legal personnel, the infrastructure of the criminal justice system is more extensive in urban locales and in Java than in rural or remote areas. In any case, the system's procedures often do not apply to military, security, and intelligence organizations, which in practice sometimes deal with both political and ordinary crime. Indonesians do not always resort to the formal legal system to resolve their conflicts, however, because many do not share Western views regarding the nature of individual rights and the efficacy of law and procedural justice but prefer to settle disputes by arbitration or accommodation. Retribution and revenge, moreover, are still common ways of settling disputes, especially away from the big cities and towns.

In rural areas, many conflicts, including some (mostly minor) criminal cases, are settled by village chiefs. Complaints often go unfiled with authorities, even in villages and cities, and cases frequently settle out of court in order to save time and money or to avoid attracting public or official attention. In criminal cases, such settlements typically entail accommodation between the accused and the police or prosecutors, whose roles in the criminal justice system are generally more critical than those of courts or judges. Wealth and status are apt to be important factors in the outcome.

Crime and Political Offenses

Indonesia, like many nations, has experienced a rising crime rate as a by-product of increased urbanization and the social and economic dislocations associated with national development. The scope of the crime problem is difficult to gauge, but conditions such as large numbers of unemployed or underemployed people in the cities, a lack of jobs for high school and university graduates, and a breakdown in traditional systems of social control often are cited as responsible for the increase in crime. By the start of the twenty-first century, the annual increase in crime was moderate. Both the authorities and the public, however, continued to be concerned about the increasingly violent nature of Indonesian society.

Certain categories of crime are handled under special statutes outside the penal code under Indonesian law. After the fall of Suharto, offenses such as bribery, the assessment of *pungli* (a contraction of *pungutan liar*—illegal levies), and the diversion of public funds for private use by business figures or officials were grouped in a special class of crimes under the jurisdiction of anticorruption courts and the Commission to Investigate Public Officials' Wealth. The transition to democracy also included abolition of an internal subversion act that had been used to jail critics of the Suharto government.

Criminal Law and Proceedings

The Indonesian criminal code in force at independence was basically the Netherlands Indies Criminal Code, adopted in 1918, plus certain amendments promulgated by the revolutionary government in 1946. Known as the Code of Criminal Law, since 1958 it has been applied uniformly throughout the national territory.

The Code of Criminal Law has three chapters. Chapter I defines the terms and procedures to be followed in criminal cases and specifies mitigating circumstances that may affect the severity of a sentence. Chapters II and III, respectively, define the categories of felonies and misdemeanors and prescribe the penalties for each type of offense. The distinction between felonies and misdemeanors generally conforms to that in Western countries. Several other statutes dealing with criminal offenses are also in force, the most significant of which are laws concerning economic offenses, subversive activities, and corruption.

Penalties for major offenses include death (infrequently imposed, for treason, drug trafficking, and—since 2002—terrorism, among other crimes), imprisonment for periods up to life, local detention, and fines. Total confiscation of property is not permitted. Penalties for minor crimes and misdemeanors include deprivation of specified rights, forfeiture of personal property, and publication of the sentence of the court. Punishments listed in the code are the maximum allowable; judges have discretionary authority to impose a lesser punishment.

New guidelines on criminal proceedings were promulgated on December 31, 1981. These new guidelines, known collectively as the Code of Criminal Procedures, replaced a 1941 code that was itself a revision of an 1848 Dutch colonial regulation that stipulated legal procedures to be used in both criminal and civil cases. Both national jurists and government officials had complained that statutory ambiguity in the old code and certain of its provisions in some cases had led to abuses of authority by law enforcement and judicial officials. Under the old system, several authorities, including the police, the regional military commands, and the public prosecutors, shared powers of arrest, detention, and interrogation—an often confusing situation that sometimes led plaintiffs to file complaints with the particular agency they believed would deal most favorably with their case. Individuals could be arrested and detained on suspicion alone, and there were broad limits on how long a suspect could be held before being charged or brought to trial. Moreover, the accused could request legal counsel only when that individual's case was submitted to a judge, and not during any pretrial proceedings.

The 1981 code represents a considerable step forward in the establishment of clear norms of procedural justice. Under it, criminal investigation powers lie almost entirely with the police. A suspect can be held only 24 hours before the investigating officials present their charges and obtain a detention order from a judge. Specific limits are established on how long a suspect can be held before a trial. The 1981 code expressly grants the accused the right to learn the charges against him or her, to be examined immediately by investigating officials, and to have the case referred to a prosecutor, submitted to a court, and tried before a judge. The accused also has the right to obtain legal counsel in all of the proceedings. Should it turn out that a person has been wrongly charged or detained under the 1981 code, that individual has the right to sue for compensation and for the restoration of rights and status.

Administration of Criminal Justice

The prosecutorial function rests with the attorney general, who holds the position of supreme public prosecutor. The president sometimes grants the attorney general cabinet-level status, and the attorney general has direct access to the president. The Attorney General's Office is separate from the Department of Justice and Human Rights.

The Attorney General's Office, Jakarta
Courtesy Yadi Jasin

The public prosecutor's principal functions are to examine charges of felonious conduct or misdemeanors brought by individuals or other parties, and then either to dismiss a charge or refer it for trial to the state court having jurisdiction. The prosecutor's office is also responsible for presenting the case against the accused in court and for executing the sentence of the court.

The Code of Criminal Procedures of 1981 made a clear division between the investigation function, solely the preserve of the police, and the prosecution function, which remained with the prosecutor's office. The only exception was in the case of "special crimes," a category that was not further defined but that was believed to be reserved for unusually sensitive cases such as espionage and subversion, in which the prosecutor could also take an investigatory role. Continuing tension between the prosecutor and the police was evident during debate over a new prosecution service law in 1991. The law as passed gave the attorney general the power to conduct limited investigations in cases that were determined to be incomplete. The 1991 law also established deputy and associate attorney general positions responsible for civil cases and administrative affairs.

The court system has four branches: general courts, religious courts, military courts, and administrative courts (see The Judiciary, ch. 4). All criminal cases are tried in the general courts. The Code of

Criminal Procedures set forth rules to determine the court in which a case must be tried, should military and general court jurisdiction combine or overlap. In 2004 the armed forces accepted Supreme Court jurisdiction over the military court system, and in 2007 the DPR introduced legislation stipulating that all crimes committed by military personnel outside of operational military duties will be prosecuted in the civil court system. The TNI has opposed this new law by claiming that the civilian court system neither understands the military justice system nor is capable of taking over responsibility for prosecution of military personnel accused of nonmilitary crimes. Service members remain subject solely to the military legal system for all crimes allegedly committed while in the pursuit of military duties.

Penal System

Indonesia's prisons are administered by the Department of Corrections within the Department of Justice and Human Rights and include three categories of prisons based mainly on the number of inmates they can hold. The nine largest prisons, designated Class I, hold prisoners sentenced to life imprisonment or death.

The U.S. Department of State's *Country Reports on Human Rights Practices for 2009* found prison conditions harsh throughout the Indonesian penal system. Poor food, unsanitary conditions, and inadequate medical care were common, as were mistreatment and corruption. "Money talks," and wealthy inmates were able to purchase better prison accommodations, food, and treatment. Overcrowding in ancient and inadequate facilities also occurred. The report indicated that those conditions had existed for a very long time and noted the need for better training of prison personnel and renovation of prison facilities.

Several specialized prisons for women and two for youths are located in Java. Where it is not possible to confine such prisoners in separate institutions, as is usually the case outside Java, efforts are made to segregate juvenile from adult offenders and females from males in separate sections of the same institution. Ordinarily, prisoners are permitted visits by family members and may receive limited amounts of food and other articles to supplement the minimal supplies they are issued. Under some circumstances, prisoners are permitted to spend their nights at home. Most prisons try to provide medical care of some kind, although it is generally regarded as insufficient.

Rehabilitation provisions include literacy classes, moral and religious training, and workshops to teach crafts and skills. Some prisons operate small industries or agricultural enterprises that sell their products on the local market. Proceeds are used to pay a small wage to the working inmates, to buy recreational equipment, and to maintain buildings and grounds. In some prisons, inmates work in fields outside the prison confines.

Narcotics and Counternarcotics Operations

Production of narcotics, particularly opiate-derived products from the "Golden Triangle" where Thailand, Burma, and Laos meet, substantially increased in the 1980s and 1990s. Despite its proximity, Indonesia is neither a major producer nor a major user of illicit drugs, although there is an increasingly broad niche for designer drugs, such as methylenedioxymethamphetamine (MDMA, or Ecstasy), among wealthy youth in the larger cities. There is, however, considerable concern on the part of the national leadership and police officials that Indonesia might become an important drug-trafficking center as major drug routes in mainland Southeast Asia shift to take advantage of Indonesia's relatively innocent reputation.

Bali, which has become a booming international tourist destination, provides a base for individual traffickers and transactions. Although there is no extradition treaty between the United States and Indonesia, Indonesian authorities are cooperative in deporting drug suspects, particularly if the International Criminal Police Organization (Interpol) is involved. During 1991, for example, a suspected American drug trafficker was deported to the United States with the cooperation of the U.S. Drug Enforcement Administration, the National Police of Indonesia, and Interpol. In addition, there have been periodic police campaigns in Aceh and Sumatera Utara Province, which are historically the country's leading producers of marijuana (some of which has long been used traditionally in the local cuisine).

Narcotics trafficking is a severe offense in Indonesia, as is the case in neighboring Singapore and Malaysia. A considerable number of traffickers—mostly foreigners—have received death sentences from the courts; most executions in Indonesia are for crimes involving narcotics trafficking.

National Security in the Contemporary Era

Indonesia has changed dramatically since the fall of Suharto in 1998, and the military and police forces have changed with the country. No longer an autocracy, Indonesia is now the world's third-largest democracy. The Indonesian military has implemented an impressive array of reforms that have removed the armed forces from an intrusive role in virtually every aspect of civil society and taken them out of day-to-day political involvement. At the same time, the military is still the most powerful institution in Indonesia and will likely remain so for some time. This is due both to the slow development of viable civilian institutions—repressed during the 32-year rule of Suharto—and the military's inherent power. Similarly, the National Police is evolving, thanks to extensive international assistance and a core of reform-minded police leaders determined to improve both the image of the police force and its professionalism in maintaining law and order.

Indonesia is the most populous Muslim-majority nation in the world, and its practice of Islam the world's most moderate. The dynamic changes since 1998 have shown that democracy and Islam can coexist peacefully in a multi-ethnic, multi-religious society. The world's fourth most populous country, Indonesia can play a major role in international and regional political, economic, and social affairs. By 2008 Indonesia had become a valued, long-standing participant in the war against international terrorism.

Neither the armed forces nor the police has implemented the full range of reforms called for by their most vocal critics. Vested interests remain in play, and resistance to change is as natural to the Indonesian security forces as to those of other countries. But a new president and minister of defense, a newly empowered MPR, Southeast Asia's most free press establishment, and a civilian society anxious to realize its potential have combined to make continued change in the security and military institutions inevitable. Greater civilian control over military and police forces, realizable only when much better budget control can be achieved, is a longer-term goal that might take as long as 10 to 20 years to attain.

Many challenges remain. The military and, to a lesser degree, the police have an ingrained culture of impunity that can be broken only by implementation of clear accountability for misdeeds, successful implementation of the rule of law, and reform of the national judicial system. These are system-wide reform objectives not achievable by the military and police alone.

*   *   *

Several works treat the development of the Indonesian armed forces before 1970, the most balanced and comprehensive being Ulf Sundhaussen's *The Road to Power: Indonesian Military Politics 1945–1967*. Ernst Utrecht's *The Indonesian Army: A Socio-Political Study of an Armed Privileged Group in the Developing Countries* offers a detailed and often critical view from the perspective of a former insider. Ruth T. McVey's two-part "The Post-Revolutionary Transformation of the Indonesian Army" focuses mainly on the military's shortcomings in its early years. *The Indonesian Tragedy*, by Brian May, and *The Army and Politics in Indonesia*, by Harold A. Crouch, are more concerned with the causes and effects of the 1965 coup attempt; they also evaluate the armed forces in a somewhat negative light. *The National Struggle and the Armed Forces in Indonesia*, a collection of essays by ABRI's former official historian, Nugroho Notosusanto, presents the viewpoint of the armed forces and the government regarding ABRI's historical development, its role, and its doctrine. The most comprehensive look at Indonesian military organization, the *dwifungsi* concept, and the role of the military in Indonesian society is Robert Lowry's 1986 work *The Armed Forces of Indonesia*.

A number of books examine recent developments. Kevin O'Rourke's *Reformasi: The Struggle for Power in Post-Suharto Indonesia* provides background on economic and political issues as well as details on the chaos surrounding Suharto's resignation. Adam Schwarz's *A Nation in Waiting: Indonesia in the 1990s* covers Indonesian political maneuvering during that decade. Two recent accounts of the issues facing the TNI in the transition to democracy are *The Military and Democracy in Indonesia: Challenges, Politics, and Power*, by Angel Rabasa and John B. Haseman, and *Toward a Stronger U.S.–Indonesia Security Relationship*, by John B. Haseman and Eduardo Lachica. Readers interested in detailed histories of the TNI's intelligence-gathering and special operations will find Kenneth J. Conboy's books of particular interest, including *Kopassus: Inside Indonesia's Special Forces*; *Intel: Inside Indonesia's Intelligence Services*; and *Elite: The Special Forces of Indonesia 1950–2008*. A particularly useful account of modern Indonesian history is *Indonesian Destinies*, by Theodore Friend.

Current reportage is available in the Indonesian chapter of *Jane's Sentinel Security Risk Assessments: Southeast Asia*, regularly updated and available on-line by subscription (http://sentinel.janes.com/) or in hard copy. *The Van Zorge Report*, published fortnightly in Jakarta, provides excellent reportage and analysis on all aspects of Indonesian political, economic, and security affairs. The periodically updated "Current Data on the Indonesian Military Elite," compiled in Cornell University's journal *Indonesia*, is helpful in keeping up with the most current assignments of senior military officers. The periodic reports on Indonesia published by the International Crisis Group are distinctive for their depth and accuracy of research and reporting. Data on the size and composition of the armed forces are collected by the International Institute for Strategic Studies in its annual publication, *The Military Balance*, and in an annual U.S. Department of Defense resource, the *Congressional Presentation Document*. Dephan offers a public Indonesian-language Web site (http://www.dephan.go.id), part of which includes its Defense Media Centre with an English-language option.

Annual reports by Amnesty International and Human Rights Watch examine the state of human rights practices in Indonesia, as do the annual *Country Reports on Human Rights Practices* prepared for the U.S. Congress by the Department of State. (For further information and complete citations, see Bibliography.)

Bibliography

Chapter 1

Andaya, Leonard Y. *The World of Maluku: Eastern Indonesia in the Early Modern Period*. Honolulu: University of Hawai'i Press, 1993.

Anderson, Benedict R. O'G. *Java in a Time of Revolution: Occupation and Resistance, 1944–1946*. Ithaca: Cornell University Press, 1972.

Association for Asian Studies. *Bibliography of Asian Studies*, 2009. http://quod.lib.umich.edu/b/bas/.

Aveling, Harry, ed. *The Development of Indonesian Society: From the Coming of Islam to the Present Day.* New York: St. Martin's Press, 1980.

Barrett Jones, Antoinette M. *Early Tenth Century Java from the Inscriptions*. Dordrecht, Netherlands: Foris, 1984.

Bellwood, Peter. *Prehistory of the Indo-Malaysian Archipelago*. Rev. ed. Honolulu: University of Hawai'i Press, 1997.

Benda, Harry J. "The Pattern of Administrative Reforms in the Closing Years of Dutch Rule in Indonesia." *Journal of Asian Studies* 25, no. 4 (August 1966): 589–605.

Bernet Kempers, August J. *Ageless Borobudur: Buddhist Mystery in Stone, Decay and Restoration, Mendut and Pawon, Folklife in Ancient Java*. Rev. trans. Wassenaar, Netherlands: Servire, 1976.

Booth, Anne. *The Indonesian Economy in the Nineteenth and Twentieth Centuries: A History of Missed Opportunities*. New York: St. Martin's Press, 1998.

Bosma, Ulbe, and Remco Raben. *Being "Dutch" in the Indies: A History of Creolization and Empire, 1500–1920*. Athens: Ohio University Press, 2008.

Boxer, Charles R. *The Dutch Seaborne Empire: 1600–1800*. New York: Knopf, 1965.

Breman, Jan, ed. *Imperial Monkey Business: Racial Supremacy in Social Darwinist Theory and Colonial Practice*. Casa Monographs, no. 3. Amsterdam: VU University Press, 1990.

Brown, Colin. *A Short History of Indonesia: The Unlikely Nation?* Crow's Nest, New South Wales, Australia: Allen and Unwin, 2003.

Carey, P. B. R. *The Power of Prophecy: Prince Dipanagara and the End of the Old Order in Java, 1785–1855*. Leiden, Netherlands: KITLV Press, 2007.

Casparis, J. G. de. "Some Notes on Relations Between Central and Local Government in Ancient Java." Pages 49–64 in David G. Marr and A. C. Milner, eds., *Southeast Asia in the 9th to 14th Centuries.* Canberra: Australian National University, Research School of Pacific Studies, 1986.

Christie, Jan Wisseman. "Revisiting Early Mataram." Pages 22–55 in Marijke Klokke and Karel R. van Kooij, eds., *Fruits of Inspiration: Studies in Honour of Prof. J. G. de Casparis, Retired Professor of the Early History and Archeology of South and Southeast Asia at the University of Leiden, the Netherlands, on the Occasion of His 85th Birthday.* Groningen, Netherlands: Egbert Forsten, 2001.

Christie, Jan Wisseman. "State Formation in Early Maritime Southeast Asia: A Consideration of the Theories and the Data." *Bijdragen tot de Taal-, Land- en Volkenkunde* (Leiden, Netherlands) 151, no. 2 (1995): 235–88.

Colombijn, Freek, and J. Thomas Lindblad, eds. *The Roots of Violence in Indonesia: Contemporary Violence in Historical Perspective.* Leiden, Netherlands: KITLV Press, 2002.

Cribb, Robert B. *Historical Atlas of Indonesia.* Honolulu: University of Hawai'i Press, 2000.

Cribb, Robert B. "Nation: Making Indonesia." Pages 3–38 in Donald K. Emmerson, ed., *Indonesia Beyond Suharto. Polity, Economy, Society, Transition.* Armonk, New York: Sharpe, 1999.

Cribb, Robert B., ed. *The Indonesian Killings, 1965–1966.* Clayton, Victoria, Australia: Monash University, Centre of Southeast Asian Studies, 1990.

Cribb, Robert B., ed. *The Late Colonial State in Indonesia.* Leiden, Netherlands: KITLV Press, 1994.

Cribb, Robert B., and Colin Brown. *Modern Indonesia: A History Since 1945.* London: Longman, 1995.

Cribb, Robert B., and Audrey R. Kahin. *Historical Dictionary of Indonesia.* 2d ed. Lanham, Maryland: Scarecrow Press, 2004.

Crouch, Harold A. *The Army and Politics in Indonesia.* Rev. ed. Ithaca: Cornell University Press, 1988.

Dick, Howard W., et al. *The Emergence of a National Economy: An Economic History of Indonesia, 1800–2000.* Honolulu: University of Hawai'i Press, 2002.

Dijk, Kees van. *A Country in Despair: Indonesia Between 1997 and 2000.* Leiden, Netherlands: KITLV Press, 2001.

Dreyer, Edward L. *Zheng He: China and the Oceans in the Early Ming Dynasty, 1405–1433.* New York: Pearson Longman. 2007.

Elson, Robert E. *The Idea of Indonesia: A History.* Cambridge: Cambridge University Press, 2008.

Elson, Robert E. *Suharto: A Political Biography.* Cambridge: Cambridge University Press, 2001.

Elson, Robert E. *Village Java under the Cultivation System.* Sydney: Allen and Unwin, 1994.

Emmerson, Donald K., ed. *Indonesia Beyond Suharto. Polity, Economy, Society, Transition.* Armonk, New York: Sharpe, 1999.

Eng, Pierre van der. "The Real Domestic Product of Indonesia, 1880–1989." *Explorations in Economic History* 29, no. 3 (July 1992): 343–73.

Fasseur, Cornelis (Cees). *The Politics of Colonial Exploitation: Java, the Dutch, and the Cultivation System.* Trans., Robert E. Elson and Ary Kraal. Ithaca: Cornell University, Southeast Asia Program, 1992.

Feith, Herbert. *The Decline of Constitutional Democracy in Indonesia.* Ithaca: Cornell University Press, 1962.

Forrester, Geoff, and Ronald J. May, eds. *The Fall of Soeharto.* Singapore: Select Books, 1999.

Frederick, William H. *Visions and Heat: The Making of the Indonesian Revolution.* Athens: Ohio University Press, 1989.

Friend, Theodore. *Indonesian Destinies.* Cambridge, Massachusetts: Belknap Press of Harvard University Press, 2003.

Gimon, Charles A. *Sejarah Indonesia: An Online Timeline of Indonesian History,* 2004. http://www.gimonca.com/sejarah.

Glover, Ian, and Peter Bellwood, eds. *Southeast Asia from Prehistory to History.* London: RoutledgeCurzon, 2004.

Gotō, Ken'ichi. *Tensions of Empire: Japan and Southeast Asia in the Colonial and Postcolonial World.* Ohio University Research in International Studies, Southeast Asia Series, no. 108. Athens: Ohio University, Center for International Studies, 2003.

Graaf, Hermanus J. de, and Theodore G. Th. Pigeaud, trans. *Chinese Muslims in Java in the Fifteenth and Sixteenth Centuries: The Malay Annals of Sĕmarang and Cĕrbon.* Merle C. Ricklefs, ed. Monash Papers on Southeast Asia, 0727–6680, no. 12. Melbourne: Monash University, 1984.

Hall, D. G. E. *A History of South-East Asia.* New York: Palgrave Macmillan, 1981.

Hall, Kenneth R. *Maritime Trade and State Development in Early Southeast Asia.* Honolulu: University of Hawai'i Press, 1985.

Harvey, Barbara S. *Permesta: Half a Rebellion.* Publication no. 57. Ithaca: Cornell University, Southeast Asia Program, Modern Indonesia Project, 1977.

Hauswedell, Peter Christian. "Sukarno: Radical or Conservative? Indonesian Politics 1964–5." *Indonesia* 15 (April 1973): 109–43.

Hefner, Robert W. *Civil Islam: Muslims and Democratization in Indonesia.* Princeton: Princeton University Press, 2000.

Hering, Bob B. *Soekarno: Founding Father of Indonesia, 1901–1945.* Leiden, Netherlands: KITLV Press, 2002.

Hirata, Andrea. *Laskar Pelangi* [Rainbow Warriors]. Yogyakarta: Bentang, 2005.

Hooker, Virginia Matheson, ed. *Culture and Society in New Order Indonesia.* Singapore: Oxford University Press, 1993.

Hunter, Helen Louise. *Sukarno and the Indonesian Coup: The Untold Story.* Westport, Connecticut: Praeger, 2007. (Originally distributed by U.S. Central Intelligence Agency as *Indonesia 1965: The Coup That Backfired,* Washington, DC, 1968.)

Indrayan, D. *Indonesian Constitutional Reform, 1999–2002.* Jakarta: Kompas, 2008.

Ingleson, John. *The Road to Exile: The Indonesian Nationalist Movement, 1927–1934.* Singapore: Heinemann, 1979.

International Institute of Social History. *WWW–VL History Indonesia.* Bangkok, 2009. http://www.iisg.nl/w3vlindonesia/.

Jenkins, David. *Suharto and His Generals: Indonesian Military Politics, 1975–1983.* Ithaca: Cornell University, Modern Indonesia Project, 1984.

Jong, R. C. de. *The Economic and Administrative History of Indonesia between 1500 and 1630.* Leiden, Netherlands: Brill, 1977.

Kahin, Audrey R., ed. *Regional Dynamics of the Indonesian Revolution.* Honolulu: University of Hawai'i Press, 1985.

Kahin, George McTurnan. *Nationalism and Revolution in Indonesia.* Ithaca: Cornell University Press, 1952.

Kartini, Raden Adjeng. *Letters of a Javanese Princess* [1904]. Trans., Agnes Louise Symmers. New York: Norton, 1964.

Kartodirdjo, Sartono. *Modern Indonesia, Tradition and Transformation: A Socio-Historical Perspective.* Yogyakarta: Gadjah Mada University Press, 1984.

Kemp, Herman C. *Annotated Bibliography of Bibliographies on Indonesia.* Leiden, Netherlands: KITLV Press, 1990.

Kingsbury, Damien, and Harry Aveling, eds. *Autonomy and Disintegration in Indonesia.* London: RoutledgeCurzon, 2003.

Kulke, Hermann. "The Early and Imperial Kingdom in Southeast Asian History." Pages 1–22 in David G. Marr and Anthony C. Milner, eds., *Southeast Asia in the 9th to 14th Centuries.* Canberra: Australian National University, Research School of Pacific Studies, 1986.

Kumar, Ann. *Java and Modern Europe: Ambiguous Encounters.* London: Curzon, 1997.

Kumar, Ann, and John H. McGlynn, eds. *Illuminations: The Writing Traditions of Indonesia.* Jakarta: Lontar, 1996.

Kurasawa Aiko. "Propaganda Media on Java under the Japanese, 1942–1945." *Indonesia* 42 (October 1987): 59–116.

Laffan, Michael F. *Islamic Nationhood and Colonial Indonesia: The Umma below the Winds.* School of Oriental and Africa Studies/RoutledgeCurzon Studies on the Middle East. London: RoutledgeCurzon, 2003.

Legge, John D. *Sukarno: A Political Biography.* 3d ed. Singapore: Archipelago Press, 2003.

Lev, Daniel S. *The Transition to Guided Democracy: Indonesian Politics, 1957–1959.* Ithaca: Cornell Modern Indonesia Project, 1966.

Liu Hong. "Constructing a China Metaphor: Sukarno's Perception of the PRC and Indonesia's Political Transformation." *Journal of Southeast Asian Studies* (Singapore) 28, no. 1 (March 1997): 27–47.

Lloyd, Grayson, and Shannon Smith, eds. *Indonesia Today: Challenge of History.* Singapore: ISEAS, 2001.

Locher-Scholten, Elsbeth. "Dutch Expansion in the Indonesian Archipelago around 1900 and the Imperialism Debate." *Journal of Southeast Asian Studies* (Singapore) 25, no. 1 (March 1994): 91–111.

Ma Huan. *Ying-yai sheng-lan: "The Overall Survey of the Ocean's Shores"* [1433]. Trans. and ed., Feng Ch'eng-chün. Hakluyt Society. Extra Series, no. 42. Cambridge: Cambridge University Press, 1970.

Manguin, Pierre-Yves. "Palembang and Sriwijaya: An Early Malay Harbour-City Rediscovered." *Journal of the Malaysian Branch, Royal Asiatic Society* (Kuala Lumpur) 66, pt.1, no. 264 (1993) 23–46.

Manguin, Pierre-Yves. "The Southeast Asian Ship: An Historical Approach." *Journal of Southeast Asian Studies* (Singapore) 11, no. 2 (September 1980): 266–76.

Mark, Ethan. "Appealing to Asia: Nation, Culture, and the Problem of Imperial Modernity in Japanese-Occupied Java, 1942–1945." Ph.D. dissertation. New York: Columbia University, 2003.

McGlynn, John H., et al., eds. *Indonesia in the Soeharto Years. Issues, Incidents, and Images.* Jakarta: Lontar, 2007.

McVey, Ruth T. *The Rise of Indonesian Communism.* Ithaca: Cornell University Press, 1965.

Meilink-Roelofsz, M. A. P. *Asian Trade and Indonesian Influence in the Indonesian Archipelago Between 1500 and About 1630.* The Hague: Martinus Nijhoff, 1962.

Miksic, John N., ed. *Ancient History.* Indonesian Heritage Series, vol. 1. Singapore: Archipelago Press, 1996.

Miksic, John N., and Endang Sri Hardiati Soekatno, eds. *The Legacy of Majapahit.* Singapore: Singapore National Heritage Board, 1995.

Miksic, John N., and Marcello Tranchini. *Borobudur: Golden Tales of the Buddhas.* Boston: Shambala, 1990.

Miller, George. *Meta-Guide to Indonesia: Annotated Bibliography of Post-1990 Bibliographies on Indonesia.* Version 1.5. August 20, 2004. http://coombs.anu.edu.au/WWWVLPages/IndonPages/Meta-Bibliography.html.

Moertono, Soemarsaid. *State and Statecraft in Old Java: A Study of the Later Mataram Period, 16th to 19th Century.* Rev. ed. Ithaca: Cornell Modern Indonesia Project. 1981.

Mortimer, Rex. *Indonesian Communism under Sukarno: Ideology and Politics, 1959–1965.* Ithaca: Cornell University Press, 1974.

Morwood, M. J., et al. "Archaeology and Age of a New Hominin from Flores in Eastern Indonesia." *Nature* (London) 431, no. 7012 (October 28, 2004): 1087–91.

Mrázek, Rudolf. *Sjahrir: Politics and Exile in Indonesia.* Ithaca: Cornell University, Southeast Asia Program, 1994.

Multatuli [Eduard Douwes Dekker]. *Max Havelaar: Or the Coffee Auctions of the Dutch Trading Company* [1860]. Trans., Roy Edwards. Library of the Indies Series. Amherst: University of Massachusetts Press, 1982.

Munoz, Paul Michel. *Early Kingdoms of the Indonesian Archipelago and the Malay Peninsula.* Singapore: Didier Millet, 2006.

Naerssen, F. H. van. *The Economic and Administrative History of Early Indonesia.* Leiden, Netherlands: Brill, 1977.

Nagazumi Akira. *The Dawn of Indonesian Nationalism: The Early Years of the Budi Utomo, 1908–1918.* I.D.E. Occasional Papers Series, no. 10. Tokyo: Institute of Developing Economics, 1972.

Noer, Deliar. *The Modernist Muslim Movement in Indonesia, 1900–1942.* Kuala Lumpur: Oxford University Press, 1973.

Noorduyn, J. "Majapahit in the Fifteenth Century." *Bijdragen tot de Taal-, Land-, en Volkenkunde* (Leiden, Netherlands) 134, nos. 2–3 (1978): 207–74.

Oppenheimer, Stephen, and Martin Richards. "Fast Trains, Slow Boats, and the Ancestry of the Polynesian Islanders." *Science Progress* (London) 84, no. 3 (Fall 2001): 157–81.

Post, Peter, ed. *The Encyclopedia of Indonesia in the Pacific War.* Handbuch der Orientalistik. Section 3, Southeast Asia, 0169–9571, vol. 19. Leiden: Brill, 2009.

Pluvier, Jan M. *Historical Atlas of South-East Asia*. New York: Brill, 1995.

Prapañca, Mpu. *Desawarnana (Nagarakrtagama)* [1365]. Trans., Stuart O. Robson. Leiden, Netherlands: KITLV Press, 1995.

Raben, Remco, ed. *Representing the Japanese Occupation of Indonesia: Personal Testimonies and Public Images in Indonesia, Japan, and the Netherlands*. Amsterdam: Netherlands Institute for War Documentation, 1999.

Ravesteijn, Wim, and Marie-Louise ten Horn-van Nispen. "Engineering and Empire. The Creation of Infrastructural Systems in the Netherlands East Indies, 1800–1950." *Indonesia and the Malay World* (London) 35, no. 103 (November 2007): 273–92.

Reeve, David. *Golkar of Indonesia: An Alternative to the Party System*. Kuala Lumpur: Oxford University Press, 1985.

Reid, Anthony J. S. *Charting the Shape of Early Modern Southeast Asia*. Singapore: Institute of Southeast Asian Studies, 2000.

Reid, Anthony J. S. *The Indonesian National Revolution, 1945–1950*. Melbourne: Longman, 1974.

Reid, Anthony J. S. *Southeast Asia in the Age of Commerce, 1450–1680*. 2 vols. New Haven: Yale University Press, 1988 and 1993.

Reid, Anthony J. S., ed. *Early Modern History*. Indonesian Heritage Series, vol. 3. Singapore: Archipelago Press. 1996.

Resink, Gertrudes J. *Indonesia's History Between the Myths*. Selected Studies on Indonesia, vol. 7. The Hague: Van Hoeve, 1968.

Riantiarno, N. *Time Bomb and Cockroach Opera: Two Plays*. Trans., Barbara Hatley and John H. McGlynn. Jakarta: Lontar, 1992.

Ricklefs, Merle C. *A History of Modern Indonesia Since c. 1200*. 4th ed. Stanford: Stanford University Press, 2008.

Ricklefs, Merle C. *Mystic Synthesis in Java. A History of Islamization from the Fourteenth to the Early Nineteenth Centuries*. Norwalk, Connecticut: EastBridge, 2006.

Ricklefs, Merle C. *The Seen and Unseen Worlds in Java, 1726–1749*. Sydney: Allen and Unwin, 1998.

Ricklefs, Merle C. *War, Culture and Economy in Java, 1677–1726*. Sydney: Allen and Unwin, 1993.

Robison, Richard, and Vedi Hadiz. *Reorganizing Power in Indonesia: The Politics of Oligarchy in an Age of Markets*. London: RoutledgeCurzon, 2004.

Robson, Stuart O. "Java at the Crossroads: Aspects of Javanese Cultural History in the Fourteenth and Fifteen Centuries." *Bijdragen tot de Taal-, Land-, en Volkenkunde* (Leiden, Netherlands) 137, nos. 2–3 (1981): 259–92.

Roosa, John. *Pretext for Mass Murder: The September 30th Movement and Suharto's Coup d'état in Indonesia.* New Perspectives in Southeast Asian Studies Series. Madison: University of Wisconsin Press, 2006.

Sato Shigeru. *War, Nationalism and Peasants: Java under the Japanese Occupation. 1942–1945.* Sydney: Allen and Unwin, 1994.

Schwarz, Adam. *A Nation in Waiting: Indonesia in the 1990s.* Boulder, Colorado: Westview, 1994.

Sedyawati, Edi. "The State Formation of Kadiri." Pages 7–16 in G. J. Schutte, ed., *State and Trade in the Indonesian Archipelago.* Working Papers, Koninklijk Instituut voor Taal-, Land- en Volkenkunde, 0923–5418, no. 13. Leiden, Netherlands: KITLV Press, 1994.

Setten van der Meer, N. C. van. *Sawah Cultivation in Ancient Java: Aspects of Development During the Indo-Javanese Period, Fifth to Fifteenth Centuries.* Canberra: Australian National University, 1979.

Shiraishi Takashi. *An Age in Motion: Popular Radicalism in Java, 1912–1926.* Ithaca: Cornell University Press, 1990.

Simanjuntak, Truman, Bagyo Prasetyo, and Retno Handini, eds. *Sangiran: Man, Culture, and Environment in Pleistocene Times. Proceedings of the International Colloquium on Sangiran, Solo–Indonesia, 21st–24th September 1998.* Jakarta: Yayasan Obor Indonesia, 2001.

Slametmuljana. *A Story of Majapahit.* Singapore: Singapore University Press, 1976

Sneddon, James N. *The Indonesian Language: Its History and Role in Modern Society.* Sydney: University of New South Wales Press, 2004.

Soekmono, R., J. G. de Casparis, and Jacques Dumarçay. *Borobudur: Prayer in Stone.* Singapore: Archipelago Press, 1990.

Suharto. *Soeharto: My Thoughts, Words, and Deeds: An Autobiography.* Trans., Sumadi. Ed., Muti'ah Lestiono. Jakarta: Citra Lamtoro Gung Persada, 1989.

Sukarno. *Indonesia Accuses! Soekarno's Defense Oration in the Political Trial of 1930.* Trans., Roger K. Paget. Kuala Lumpur: Oxford University Press, 1975.

Sukarno. *Nationalism, Islam, and Marxism* [1926]. Trans., Karel H. Warouw and Peter D. Weldon. Ithaca: Cornell University, Southeast Asia Program, 1969.

Sukarno. *Sukarno: An Autobiography as Told to Cindy Adams.* Indianapolis: Bobbs-Merrill, 1965.

Sutherland, Heather. *The Making of a Bureaucratic Elite: The Colonial Transformation of the Javanese Priyayi.* Singapore: Heinemann, 1979.

Swift, Ann. *The Road to Madiun: The Indonesian Communist Uprising of 1948.* Ithaca: Cornell University, Modern Indonesia Project, 1989.

Swisher, Carl C., III, et al. "Age of the Earliest Known Hominids in Java, Indonesia." *Science* 263, no. 5150 (February 25, 1994): 1118–21.

Syahrir, Sutan. *Out of Exile.* Trans., Charles Wolf. New York: Greenwood Press 1969.

Tanter, R., and K. Young, eds. *The Politics of Middle Class Indonesia.* Melbourne: Monash University, Centre for Southeast Asian Studies, 1990.

Taylor, Jean Gelman. *Indonesia: Peoples and Histories.* New Haven: Yale University Press, 2003.

Tur, Pramudya Ananta. *This Earth of Mankind [Bumi Manusia]* [1980]. Rev. ed. Trans., Max Lane. New York: William Morrow, 1991.

Van Niel, Robert. *Java Under the Cultivation System: Collected Writings.* Verhandelingen van het Koninklijk Instituut voor Taal-, Land- en Volkenkunde, no. 150. Leiden, Netherlands: KITLV Press, 1992.

Van Niel, Robert. *The Emergence of the Modern Indonesian Elite.* The Hague: Van Hoeve, 1960.

Veur, Paul W. van der. *The Lion and the Gadfly: Dutch Colonialism and the Spirit of E. F. E. Douwes Dekker.* Verhandelingen van het Koninklijk Instituut voor Taal-, Land- en Volkenkunde, no. 228. Leiden, Netherlands: KITLV Press, 2006.

Vickers, Adrian. *A History of Modern Indonesia.* Cambridge: Cambridge University Press, 2005.

Vos, J. de, and P. Sondaar. "Dating Hominid Sites in Indonesia." *Science* 266, no. 5191 (December 9, 1994): 1726–27.

Wertheim, Willem Frederik. *Indonesian Society in Transition: A Study of Social Change.* 2d rev. ed. The Hague: Van Hoeve, 1959.

Wicks, Robert S. *Money, Markets, and Trade in Early Southeast Asia: The Development of Indigenous Monetary Systems to A.D. 1400.* Studies on Southeast Asia Series. Ithaca: Cornell University, Southeast Asia Program, 1992.

Wild, Colin, and Peter Carey, eds. *Born in Fire, The Indonesian Struggle for Independence.* Athens: Ohio University Press, 1986.

Wolters, O. W. *Early Indonesian Commerce: A Study of the Origins of Srivijaya.* Ithaca: Cornell University Press, 1967.

Zoetmulder, Petrus J. *Kalangwan: A Survey of Old Javanese Literature.* Koninklijk Instituut voor Taal-, Land- en Volkenkunde. Translation Series, no. 16. The Hague: Martinus Nijhoff, 1974.

Zurbuchen, Mary S., ed. *Beginning to Remember: The Past in the Indonesian Present.* Seattle: University of Washington Press, 2005.

(Various Web sites and issues of the following publications also were used in the preparation of this chapter: *Bijdragen tot Taal-, Land- en Volkenkunde* (Leiden) (http://www.kitlv-journals.nl); *Indonesia* (http://cip.cornell.edu/Indonesia); *Journal of Southeast Asian Studies* (Singapore) (http://journals.cambridge.org/action/displayJournal?jid=SEA); and *South East Asia Re-search* (London) (http://www.ingentaconnect.com/content/0967-828X).)

Chapter 2

Akita, T. "Income Inequality in Indonesia." World Bank Development Report, April 2002. http://www.iuj.ac.jp/research/wpdv02-2.pdf.

Arustiyono. *Promoting Rational Use of Drugs at the Community Health Centers in Indonesia.* Boston: Boston University, School of Public Health, Department of International Health, September 1999.

Atkinson, Jane. "Religions in Dialogue: The Construction of an Indonesian Minority Religion." Pages 171–86 in Rita Smith Kipp and Susan Rodgers, eds., *Indonesian Religions in Transition.* Tucson: University of Arizona Press. 1987.

Beatty, Andrew. *Varieties of Javanese Religion: An Anthropological Account.* Cambridge: Cambridge University Press, 1999.

Beeby, C. E. *Assessment of Indonesian Education.* Education Research Series, no. 59. Wellington: New Zealand Council for Educational Research, 1979.

Bemmelen, R. W. van. *The Geology of Indonesia.* The Hague: Martinus Nijhoff, 1970.

Bjork, Christopher. *Indonesian Education: Teachers, Schools, and Central Bureaucracy.* East Asia Series. New York: Routledge, 2005.

Blackwood, Evelyn. "Big Houses and Small Houses: Doing Matriliny in West Sumatra." *Ethnos* (London) 64, no. 1 (March 1999): 32–56.

Bos, Eduard, et al. *Asia Region Population Projections, 1990–91 Edition.* Working Paper Series, no. 599. Washington, DC: World Bank, Population and Human Resources Department, February 1991.

Brenner, Suzanne. "Reconstructing Self and Society: Javanese Muslim Women and 'The Veil.'" *American Ethnologist* 24, no. 4 (November 1996): 673–97.

Chambert-Loir, Henri, and Anthony Reid. *The Potent Dead: Ancestors, Saints, and Heroes in Contemporary Indonesia.* Honolulu: University of Hawai'i Press, 2002.

Cohen, Sarah. "When the Earth Flexes its Muscles." *Atlantic Unbound,* July 10, 2003. Interview with Simon Winchester. http://www.theatlantic.com/doc/200307u/int2003-07-10.

Colombijn, Freek, and J. Thomas Lindblad, eds. *Roots of Violence in Indonesia: Contemporary Violence in Historical Perspective.* Singapore: Institute of Southeast Asian Studies, 2002.

Cribb, Robert B., and Audrey R. Kahin. *Historical Dictionary of Indonesia.* 2d ed. Lanham, Maryland: Scarecrow Press, 2004.

Dobby, Ernest. *Southeast Asia.* London: University of London Press, 1950.

Donner, Wolf. *Land Use and Environment in Indonesia.* Honolulu: University of Hawai'i Press, in association with the Institute of Asian Affairs, Hamburg, 1987.

Family Health International. "Country Profiles: Indonesia." Research Triangle Park, North Carolina, 2006. http://www.fhi.org/en/CountryProfiles/Indonesia+shared+country+ page.htm.

Fealy, Greg. "Islamic Radicalism in Indonesia: A Faltering Revival?" Pages 104–21 in Chin Kin Wah and Daljit Singh, eds., *Southeast Asian Affairs, 2004.* Singapore: Institute of Southeast Asian Studies, 2004.

Geertz, Hildred, and Clifford Geertz. *Kinship in Bali.* Chicago: University of Chicago Press, 1975.

Grimes, Barbara F., ed. *Ethnologue: Languages of the World.* 11th ed. Dallas: Summer Institute of Linguistics, 1987.

Guinness, Patrick. "'Social Harmony' as Ideology and Practice in a Javanese Village." Pages 55–74 in Paul Alexander, ed., *Creating Indonesian Cultures.* Oceania Ethnographies, no. 3. Sydney: Oceania, 1989.

Hawkins, Mary. "Is *Rukun* Dead? Ethnographic Interpretations of Social Change and Javanese Culture." *Australian Journal of Anthropology* (Sydney) 7, no. 3 (December 1996): 283–314.

Heaton, Tim B., Mark Cammack, and Larry Young. "Why Is the Divorce Rate Declining in Indonesia?" *Journal of Marriage and Family* 63, no. 2 (May 2001): 480–91.

Hefner, Robert W. "Hindu Reform in an Islamizing Java." Pages 93–108 in Martin Ramstedt, ed., *Hinduism in Modern Indonesia: A Minority Religion Between Local, National, and Global Interests.* New York: Routledge, 2004.

Hefner, Robert W. *The Political Economy of Mountain Java: An Interpretive History.* Berkeley: University of California Press, 1991.

Heider, Karl G. *Indonesian Cinema: National Culture on Screen.* Honolulu: University of Hawai'i Press, 1991.

Heusken, Franz, and Huub de Jong, eds. *Violence and Vengeance: Discontent and Conflict in New Order Indonesia.* Saarbrücken, Germany: Verlag für Entwicklungspolitik, 2002.

Hill, Hal. *The Indonesian Economy since 1966: Southeast Asia's Emerging Giant.* Cambridge: Cambridge University Press, 2000.

Hon, Priscilla M. L. "Indonesia's Neglected Universities Look Ahead." *Times Literary Supplement* (London), no. 5122 (June 1, 2001): 10.

Howell, Julia Day. "Islam, the New Age, and Marginal Religions in Indonesia: Changing Meanings of Religious Pluralism." Paper delivered at Center for Studies of New Religions Conference, Vilnius, Lithuania, April 10–12, 2003.

Hugo, Graeme J. "Effects of International Migration on the Family in Indonesia." *Asian and Pacific Migration Journal* (Quezon City, Philippines) 11, no. 1 (2002): 13–46.

Hugo, Graeme J. "*Pengungsi*: Indonesia's Internally Displaced Persons." *Asian and Pacific Migration Journal* (Quezon City, Philippines) 11, no. 3 (2002): 297–332.

Hugo, Graeme J., et al. *The Demographic Dimension in Indonesian Development*. Singapore: Oxford University Press, 1987.

Human Rights Watch. "Indonesia: The War in Aceh." August 2001. http://www.hrw.org/reports/ 2001/aceh/.

Human Rights Watch. "Violence and Political Impasse in Papua." July 2001. http://www.hrw. org/reports/2001/papua/.

Indonesia. Central Statistical Office. *Penduduk Indonesia: Hasil sensus penduduk tahun 2000* [Population of Indonesia: Results of the 2000 Population Census]. Series L2.2. Jakarta, December 2001.

Indonesia. Department of National Education. *Rangkuman Statistik Persekolahan 1999/2000* [School Statistics Summary, 1999/2000]. Jakarta, 2000.

Indonesia. Department of National Education. *Statistik Pendidikan Nasional, Tahun 2007/2008* [National Education Statistics, Year 2007/2008]. Jakarta, 2008. http://www.psp. kemdiknas.go.id.

Indonesia. Department of National Education. *Statistik Pendidikan Nasional, Tahun 2008/2009* [National Education Statistics, Year 2008/2009]. Jakarta, 2009. http://www.psp. kemdiknas.go.id.

Indonesia. Department of Transmigration. Directorate General of Settlement Preparation. Regional Physical Planning Programme for Transmigration. *The Land Resources of Indonesia: A National Overview, 1990*. Jakarta, 1990.

International Labour Organisation. *Migration: Opportunities and Challenges for Poverty Reduction*. Technical Briefing Note 11. Jakarta, 2004. http://www.ilo.org/public/english/region/asro/jakarta/download/tbn11.pdf.

Jay, Robert. *Javanese Villagers: Social Relations In Rural Modjokuto*. Cambridge, Massachusetts: MIT Press, 1969.

Jones, David Martin. "Democratization, Civil Society, and Illiberal Middle Class Culture in Pacific Asia." *Comparative Politics* 30, no. 2 (January 1998): 147–58.

Kahn, Joel S. *Minangkabau Social Formations: Indonesian Peasants and the World Economy*. Cambridge Studies in Social Anthropology, no. 30. Cambridge: Cambridge University Press, 1980.

Kevane, Michael, and David I. Levine. "The Changing Status of Daughters in Indonesia." Institute of Industrial Relations, Working Paper Series, no. iirwps–077–00. Berkeley: University of California, November 20, 2000. http://repositories.cdlib.org/iir/iirwps/ iirwps-077-00.

King, Victor T., ed. *Environmental Challenges in South-East Asia*. Man and Nature in Asia Series, no. 2. Richmond, United Kingdom: Curzon Press, 1998.

Koentjaraningrat. "Cultural Diversity and National Development in Indonesia." Lecture presented at the School of Area Studies, Foreign Service Institute, United States Department of State, Washington, DC, 1986.

Kratz, E. U. "Islam in Indonesia." Pages 425–55 in Stewart Sutherland, et al., eds., *The World's Religions*. Boston: G. K. Hall. 1988.

Kroef, Justus van der. "Indonesia." Pages 1–5 in Lee C. Deighton, ed., *The Encyclopedia of Education*. Vol. 5. New York: Macmillan, 1971.

Kuipers, Joel C. *Power and Performance: The Creation of Textual Authority in Weyewa Ritual Speech*. Philadelphia: University of Pennsylvania Press, 1990.

Kusumaatmadja, Mochtar. "The Concept of the Indonesian Archipelago." *Indonesian Quarterly* (Jakarta) 10, no. 4 (October 1982): 14–22.

Li, Tania Murray. *Articulating Indigenous Identity in Indonesia: Resource Politics and the Tribal Slot*. Working Paper no. 7. Berkeley: University of California, Institute of International Studies, January 2000.

MacDougall, John. *Indonesia Publications: Online University Course*. 2009 http://www. indopubs.com/inco.html.

Matthews, Emily, ed. *The State of the Forest: Indonesia*. Washington, DC: Global Forest Watch, 2002.

Milone, Pauline D. *Urban Areas in Indonesia: Administrative and Census Concepts*. University of California, Berkeley, Institute of International Studies, Research Series, no. 10. Berkeley: University of California Press, 1966.

Murray, Thomas. "Indonesian Education: Communist Strategies (1950–1965) and Governmental Counter Strategies (1966–1980)." *Asian Survey* 21, no. 3 (March 1981): 369–92.

Murray, Thomas. "Islamic Revival and Indonesian Education." *Asian Survey* 28, no. 9 (September 1988): 897–915.

"Online University Course: Indonesia." Ohio University and Hamline University, 2006. http://www.indopubs.com/inco.html.

Parrinder, Geoffrey. *Dictionary of Non-Christian Religion.* Amersham, United Kingdom: Hulton, 1981.

Pemberton, John. "The Appearance of Order: A Politics of Culture in Colonial and Postcolonial Java." Ph.D. dissertation. Ithaca: Cornell University, 1989.

Pollack, James L. "Southeast Asian Religions: New Religious Movements in Insular Cultures." Pages 8,652–55 in Lindsay Jones, ed. in chief, *Encyclopedia of Religion.* Vol. 13. 2d ed. Detroit: Macmillan Reference USA, 2005.

Ramstedt, Martin. "Introduction: Negotiating Identities—Indonesia 'Hindus' Between Local, National, and Global Interests." Pages 1–34 in Martin Ramstedt, ed., *Hinduism in Modern Indonesia: A Minority Religion Between Local, National, and Global Interests.* New York: Routledge, 2004.

RAND. Labor and Population Division. "Indonesian Family Life Survey, 2000." IFLS3 Updates, 2005. http://www.rand.org/labor/FLS/IFLS/ifls3.html.

Robison, Richard. *Indonesia: The Rise of Capital.* Southeast Asia Publications Series, no. 13. Sydney: Asian Studies Association of Australia, Allen & Unwin, 1986.

Robison, Richard, and Vedi R. Hadiz. *Reorganizing Power in Indonesia: The Politics of Oligarchy in an Age of Markets.* London: RoutledgeCurzon Press, 2004.

Samydorai, Sinapan. "Indonesia: The Killing Field of West Kalimantan." Human Rights Solidarity, 1997. http://www.hrsolidarity.net/mainfile.php/1997vol07no02/255/.

Satriyo, H. H., Adi Abidin, and Hari Kusdaryanto. "Indonesia Rapid Decentralization Appraisal." Asia Foundation, 2004. http://www.asiafoundation.org/pdf/IRDA4_English.pdf.

Schneebaum, Tobias. *Embodied Spirits: Ritual Carvings of the Asmat.* Salem, Massachusetts: Peabody Museum of Salem, 1990.

Sears, Laurie J., ed. *Fantasizing the Feminine in Indonesia.* Durham: Duke University Press, 1996.

Sen, Krishna, and David T. Hill. *Media, Culture, and Politics in Indonesia.* New York: Oxford University Press, 2000.

Siegel, James T. *The Rope of God.* Berkeley: University of California Press, 1969. Reprint. Ann Arbor: University of Michigan Press, 2000.

Singarimbun, Masri. *Kinship Descent and Alliance among the Karo Batak*. Berkeley: University of California Press, 1975.

Skinner, G. William. "The Chinese Minority." Pages 97–117 in Ruth T. McVey, ed., *Indonesia*. Rev. ed. New Haven: Human Relations Area Files, 1963.

Soetjipto, ed. *Mpu Tantular*. Surabaya: Bagian Proyek Pembinaan Permuseuman Jawa Timur (National Museum of Jawa Timur), 1991.

Sneddon, James N. *The Indonesian Language: Its History and Role in Modern Society*. Sydney: University of New South Wales Press, 2004.

Sundrum, R. M., and A. E. Booth, "Income Distribution in Indonesia: Trends and Determinants." Pages 455–85 in James J. Fox, et al., eds., *Indonesia: Australian Perspectives*. Canberra: Australian National University, Research School of Pacific Studies, 1980.

Suryadinata, Leo A., ed. *Chinese Indonesians: State Policy, Monoculture, and Multiculturalism*. Ethnic Studies Series. Singapore: Eastern Universities Press, 2004.

Suryadinata, Leo A., Evi Nurvidya, and Aris Ananta. *Indonesia's Population: Ethnicity and Religion in a Changing Political Landscape*. Singapore: Institute of Southeast Asian Studies, 2003.

Syamsulhadi, M., and Siswandari. *Menyongsong Perguruan Tinggi Masa Depan* [Welcoming the Universities of the Future]. Jakarta: Lembaga Pengembangan Pendidikan, 2005.

Tan, Jee-pang, and Alain Mingat. *Education in Asia: A Comparative Study in Cost and Financing*. World Bank Regional and Sectoral Studies. Washington, DC: World Bank, 1992.

United Nations Development Programme. Human Development Report Office. *2007/2008 Human Development Report*. http://hdrstats.undp.org/indicators/147.html.

United Nations Educational, Scientific, and Cultural Organization. Institute for Statistics. "Regional Average of Indicators on Teaching Staff by ISCED Level." Quebec, June 20, 2006. http://stats.uis.unesco.org/unesco/TableViewer/tableView.aspx?ReportId=196.

United Nations International Children's Emergency Fund. "At a Glance: Indonesia." New York, 2006. http://www.unicef.org.

United Nations Office of the Recovery Coordinator for Aceh and Nias. *UNORC 2008 Annual Report*. unorc_annual_report[1].pdf found at http://www.unorc.or.id/.

United States. Census Bureau. International Programs Center. "International Data Base, Summary Demographic Data for Indonesia." Washington, DC, 2006. http://www.census.gov/chi-bin/ipc/idbsum.pl?cty=ID.

United States. Department of Health and Human Services. Centers for Disease Control and Prevention. "Indonesia Situation Update—May 31." Atlanta, 2006. http://www. pandemicflu.gov/news/indonesiaupdate.html.

United States. Department of the Interior. Geological Survey. Earthquake Hazards Program. Washington, DC, 2004–10. http://earthquake.usgs.gov/earthquakes/.

United States. Department of State. Bureau of Democracy, Human Rights, and Labor. *International Religious Freedom Report, 2009.* Washington, DC, 2009. http://www.state. gov/g/drl/rls/irf/2009/127271.htm.

United States. Smithsonian Institution. Global Volcanism Program. Washington, DC, 2000–10. http://www.volcano.si.edu/world/.

U.S. Committee for Refugees and Immigrants. "Internally Displaced Persons." Washington, DC, 2006. http://www.refugees.org/countryreports.aspx?id=1315.

Vickers, Adrian. *The City and the Country.* Working Paper Series, no. 56. Hong Kong: City University of Hong Kong, Southeast Asia Research Center, 2003.

Volkman, Toby Alice. *Feasts of Honor: Ritual and Change in the Toraja.* Illinois Studies in Anthropology, no. 16. Urbana: University of Illinois Press, 1985.

Weinstock, Joseph A. "Kaharingan: Life and Death in Central Borneo." Pages 71–97 in Rita Smith Kipp and Susan Rodgers, eds., *Indonesian Religions in Transition.* Tucson; University of Arizona Press, 1987.

Widodo, Amrih. "Consuming Passions: Millions of Indonesians Must Watch Soap Operas." *Inside Indonesia: Bulletin of the Indonesia Resources and Information Programme* (Northcote, Australia), no.72 (October–December 2002): 8–10.

Wolf, Diane L. *Factory Daughters: Gender, Household Dynamics, and Rural Industrialization in Java.* Berkeley: University of California Press, June 1994.

Wolters, Willem. "The Making of Civil Society in Historical Perspective." Pages 131–49 in Henk Schulte Nordholt and Irwan Abdullah, eds., *Indonesia in Search of Transition.* Yogyakarta: Pustaka Pelajar, 2002.

World Bank. Indonesia Office. *Indonesia Environment Monitor: Special Focus, Reducing Pollution.* Jakarta: World Bank Research Reports, 2003.

World Bank Group. "World Development Indicators Online: Indonesia Data Profile," 2004. http://econ.worldbank.org/external/default/main?pagePK=64165259&theSitePK=469372&piPK=64165421&menuPK=64166093&entityID=000160016_20040608153404.

World Health Organization. "H5N1 Avian Influenza: Timeline of Major Events." February 23, 2009. http://www.who.int/csr/disease/avian_influenza/Timeline_09_02_23.pdf.

World Health Organization. "Indonesia." December 2004. http://www.who.int/hac/crises/idn/background/2004/Indonesia_Dec04.pdf.

World Health Organization. "World Health Report, 2006: Working Together for Health." Washington, DC, 2006. http://www.who.int/whr/2006/whr06_en.pdf.

World Health Organization and United Nations Children's Fund. *Coverage Estimates: Improved Drinking Water: Indonesia 2004.* New York, 2004. http://www.wssinfo.org.

World Health Organization and United Nations Children's Fund. *WHO/UNICEF Joint Monitoring Programme for Water Supply and Sanitation Estimates for the Use of Improved Drinking-Water Sources: Indonesia.* New York, March 2010. http://www.wssinfo.org.

World Health Organization and United Nations Children's Fund. *WHO/UNICEF Joint Monitoring Programme for Water Supply and Sanitation Estimates for the Use of Improved Sanitation Facilities: Indonesia.* New York, March 2010. http://www.wssinfo. org.

Wurm, Stephen A., and Shirō Hattori, eds. *Language Atlas of the Pacific Area.* Pacific Linguistics, Series C, no. 66. Canberra: Australian Academy of the Humanities in collaboration with the Japan Academy, Pt. 1, 1981, Pt. 2, 1983.

(Various issues of the following publications also were used in the preparation of this chapter: Indonesia, Central Statistical Office, *Statistik Indonesia* (Jakarta) (http://www.bps. go.id), 2001–6; *New York Times*, 2003; United Nations, *Statistical Year Book*, 1996–2005; U.S. Central Intelligence Agency, *The World Factbook* (https://www.cia.gov/library/publications/the-world-factbook/geos/id.html), 1991–2009; and *Washington Post*, 2006.)

Chapter 3

Alisjahbana, Armida S., and Chris Manning. "Survey of Recent Developments." *Bulletin of Indonesian Economic Studies* (Canberra) 38, no. 3 (December 2002): 277–306.

Arndt, H.W. "Banking in Hyperinflation and Stabilization." Pages 359–95 in Bruce Glassburner, ed., *The Economy of Indonesia: Selected Readings*. Ithaca: Cornell University Press, 1971.

Ashcroft, Vincent, and David Cavanough. "Survey of Recent Developments." *Bulletin of Indonesian Economic Studies* (Canberra) 44, no. 3 (December 2008): 335–63.

Aswicahyono, Haryo, and Hal Hill. "Survey of Recent Developments." *Bulletin of Indonesian Economic Studies* (Canberra) 40, no. 3 (December 2004): 277–305.

Aswicahyono, Haryo, Titik Anas, and Yose Rizal. *The Development of the Indonesian Automotive Industry.* CSIS Working Papers Series, WPS 051. Jakarta: Centre for Strategic and International Studies, 1999. http://ideas.repec.org/p/eab/tradew/53.html.

Australian National University. Indonesia Project. "Indonesia Update Series." Canberra, 2002–8. http://rspas.anu.edu.au/economics/ip/publications.php.

Bank Indonesia. *Annual Report, 2002.* Jakarta, 2003.

Bank Indonesia. *2004 Economic Report on Indonesia.* Jakarta, 2005.

Barichello, Richard R., and Frank R. Flatters. "Trade Policy Reform in Indonesia." Pages 271–91 in Dwight H. Perkins and Michael Roemer, eds., *Reforming Economic Systems in Developing Countries.* Harvard Studies in International Development. Harvard Institute for International Development. Cambridge, Massachusetts: Harvard University Press, 1991.

Barlow, Colin, and Thomas T. Tomich. "Indonesian Agricultural Development: The Awkward Case of Smallholder Treecrops." *Bulletin of Indonesian Economic Studies* (Canberra) 27, no. 3 (December 1991): 29–54.

Booth, Anne. *Agricultural Development in Indonesia.* Sydney: Allen and Unwin, 1988.

Booth, Anne. "Counting the Poor in Indonesia." *Bulletin of Indonesian Economic Studies* (Canberra) 29, no. 1 (April 1995): 53–84.

Booth, Anne. *The Indonesian Economy in the Nineteenth and Twentieth Centuries: A History of Missed Opportunities.* New York: St. Martin's Press, 1998.

Booth, Anne. "Repelita V and Indonesia's Medium Term Economic Strategy." *Bulletin of Indonesian Economic Studies* (Canberra) 25, no. 2 (August 1989): 3–30.

Booth, Anne. "Survey of Recent Developments." *Bulletin of Indonesian Economic Studies* (Canberra) 35, no. 3 (December 1999): 3–38.

Booth, Anne, ed. *The Oil Boom and After: Indonesian Economic Policy and Performance in the Soeharto Era.* Singapore: Oxford University Press, 1992.

Booth, Anne, and Peter McCawley, eds. *The Indonesian Economy During the Soeharto Era.* Kuala Lumpur: Oxford University Press, 1981.

Butcher, John G. *The Closing of the Frontier: A History of the Marine Fisheries of Southeast Asia, c. 1850–2000.* Modern Economic History of Southeast Asia Series. Singapore: Institute of Southeast Asian Studies, 2004.

Chia Lin Sien. "The Development of Marine Transport." Pages 97–132 in Thomas R. Leinbach and Chia Lin Sien, eds., *South–East Asian Transport: Issues in Development.* Singapore: Oxford University Press, 1989.

Conroy, J. D., and P. J. Drake. "Survey of Recent Developments." *Bulletin of Indonesian Economic Studies* (Canberra) 26, no. 2 (August 1990): 5–41.

Deuster, Paul R. "Survey of Recent Developments." *Bulletin of Indonesian Economic Studies* (Canberra) 38, no. 1 (April 2002): 5–38.

Dick, Howard W., and Dean Forbes. "Transport and Communications: A Quiet Revolution." Pages 258–82 in Anne Booth, ed., *The Oil Boom and After: Indonesian Economic Policy and Performance in the Soeharto Era.* Singapore: Oxford University Press, 1992.

Dick, Howard W., et al. *The Emergence of a National Economy: An Economic History of Indonesia, 1800–2000.* Honolulu: University of Hawai'i Press, 2002.

Dickie, Robert B., and Thomas A. Layman. *Foreign Investment and Government Policy in the Third World: Forging Common Interests in Indonesia and Beyond.* New York: St. Martin's Press, 1988.

Elson, Robert E. *Suharto: A Political Biography.* Cambridge: Cambridge University Press, 2001.

Emery, Robert F. *The Money Markets of Developing East Asia.* New York: Praeger, 1991.

Evans, Kevin. "Survey of Recent Developments." *Bulletin of Indonesian Economic Studies* (Canberra) 34, no. 3 (December 1998): 5–36.

Fane, George. "Survey of Recent Developments." *Bulletin of Indonesian Economic Studies* (Canberra) 36, no. 1 (April 2000): 13–44.

Gillis, Malcolm. "Comprehensive Tax Reform: The Indonesian Experience, 1981–1988." Pages 79–114 in Malcolm Gillis, ed., *Tax Reform in Developing Countries.* Durham: Duke University Press, 1989.

Gillis, Malcolm. "Episodes in Indonesian Economic Growth." Pages 231–64 in A. C. Harberger, ed., *World Economic Growth.* San Francisco: Institute for Contemporary Studies, 1984.

Gillis, Malcolm. "Indonesia: Public Policies, Resource Management, and the Tropical Forest." Pages 43–113 in Robert Repetto and Malcolm Gillis, eds., *Public Policies and the Misuse of Forest Resources.* Cambridge: Cambridge University Press, 1988.

Glassburner, Bruce. "Indonesia: Windfalls in a Poor Rural Economy." Pages 197–226 in Allen H. Gelb and Associates, ed., *Oil Windfalls: Blessing or Curse?* New York: Oxford University Press, 1988.

Grenville, S. "Monetary Policy and the Formal Financial Sector." Pages 102–25 in Anne Booth and Peter McCawley, eds., *The Indonesian Economy During the Soeharto Era*. Kuala Lumpur: Oxford University Press, 1981.

Haryoseputro, R. "Sumarlin's Second Drastic Measure." *Indonesian Quarterly* (Jakarta) 19, no. 2 (1991): 96–98.

Heytens, Paul. "Rice Production Systems." Pages 38–57 in Scott Pearson, et al., *Rice Policy in Indonesia*. Ithaca: Cornell University Press, 1991.

Hill, Hal. *Foreign Investment and Industrialization in Indonesia*. East Asian Social Science Monographs. Singapore: Oxford University Press, 1988.

Hill, Hal. "Indonesia: Export Promotion After the Oil Boom." Pages 182–212 in Chris Miller, ed., *Export Promotion Strategies: Theory and Evidence from Developing Countries*. New York: New York University Press, 1990.

Hill, Hal. "Indonesia's Industrial Transformation, Part I." *Bulletin of Indonesian Economic Studies* (Canberra) 26, no. 2 (August 1990): 79–120.

Hill, Hal. "Indonesia's Industrial Transformation, Part II." *Bulletin of Indonesian Economic Studies* (Canberra) 26, no. 3 (December 1990): 75–109.

Hill, Hal. *The Indonesian Economy*. 2d ed. Cambridge: Cambridge University Press, 2000.

Hill, Hal. *The Indonesian Economy in Crisis: Causes, Consequences and Lessons*. Singapore: Institute of Southeast Asian Studies, 1999.

Hill, Hal. *The Indonesian Economy Since 1966: Southeast Asia's Emerging Giant*. Cambridge: Cambridge University Press, 1996.

Hill, Hal, and Pang Eng Fong. "The State and Industrial Restructuring: A Comparison of the Aerospace Industry in Indonesia and Singapore." *ASEAN Economic Bulletin* (Singapore) 5, no. 2 (November 1988): 152–68.

Hunter, Alex. "The Indonesian Oil Industry." Pages 254–314 in Bruce Glassburner, ed., *The Economy of Indonesia: Selected Readings*. Ithaca: Cornell University Press, 1971.

Indonesia. Capital Investment Coordinating Board. *Perkembangan Penanaman Modal/Trend of Investment*. Jakarta: 2006.

Indonesia. Central Statistical Office. *Statistical Yearbook of Indonesia, 2004*. Jakarta, 2005.

Indonesia. Central Statistical Office. *Statistics During 50 Years of Indonesian Independence.* Jakarta, 1997.

Indonesia. Central Statistical Office. *Transportation and Communication Statistics, 2004.* Jakarta, 2005.

Indonesia. Department of Home Affairs. "Departemen Dalam Negeri Republik Indonesia Web Site." September 24, 2008. http://www.depdagri.go.id/index.php.

Indonesia. Department of Transportation. Angkasa Pura. *Statistik Lalu Lintas Angkatan Udara 2001 Edisi Millenium* [Air Traffic Statistics 2001 Millenium Edition]. Jakarta, 2002.

Indrawati, Sri Mulyani. "The Economy: Macro and Micro Reform for Growth." Pages 74–95 in Hal Hill and Thee Kian Wie, eds., *Indonesia's Technological Challenge.* Singapore: Institute of Southeast Asian Studies, 1998.

International Centre for the Study of East Asian Development. *East Asian Economic Perspectives: Recent Trends and Prospects for Major Asian Economies.* Vol. 17, no. 1. Kitakyushu, Japan, 2006.

Kuncoro, Ari, and Budy P. Resosudarmo. "Survey of Recent Developments." *Bulletin of Indonesian Economic Studies* (Canberra) 42, no. 1 (January 2006): 7–31.

Kuo, Chin S. "The Mineral Industry of Indonesia." In United States Geological Survey, *2006 Minerals Yearbook: Indonesia.* Washington, DC, March 2008. http://minerals.usgs.gov/minerals/pubs/country/2006/myb3-2006-id.pdf.

Lewis, Blane D., and Jasmin Chakeri. "Central Development Spending in the Regions Post-decentralization." *Bulletin of Indonesian Economic Studies* (Canberra) 40, no. 3, (December 2004): 379–94.

Lindblad, J. Thomas. "Indonesian Labour and the Challenges of Globalisation (1966–2001)." Pages 177–93 in Alex E. Fernández Jilberto and Marieke Riethof, eds., *Labour Relations in Development.* London: Routledge, 2002.

Lindblad, J. Thomas. "The Petroleum Industry in Indonesia before the Second World War." *Bulletin of Indonesian Economic Studies* (Canberra) 25, no. 2 (August 1989): 53–78.

Lindblad, J. Thomas. "Political Economy of Recovery in Indonesia." Pages 246–64 in Jolle Demmers, Alex E. Fernández Jilberto, and Barbara Hogenboom, eds., *Good Governance in the Era of Global Neoliberalism: Conflict and Depolitisation in Latin America, Eastern Europe, Asia and Africa.* London: Routledge, 2004.

Lindblad, J. Thomas. "Structural Characteristics of Japanese Investment in Indonesia." *Ekonomi dan Keuangan Indonesia/Economics and Finance in Indonesia* (Jakarta) 53, no. 2 (2005): 195–214.

MacIntyre, Andrew. "Political Institutions and the Economic Crisis in Thailand and Indonesia." Pages 142–57 in H. W. Arndt and Hal Hill, eds., *Southeast Asia's Economic Crisis: Origins, Lessons, and the Way Forward*. Singapore: Institute of Southeast Asian Studies, 1999.

Mackie, J. A. C. "The Indonesian Economy, 1950–63." Pages 16–69 in Bruce Glassburner, ed., *The Economy of Indonesia: Selected Readings*. Ithaca: Cornell University Press, 1971.

Manning, Chris. *Indonesian Labour in Transition: An East Asian Success Story?* Cambridge: Cambridge University Press, 1998.

Manning, Chris, and Sisira Jayasuriya. "Survey of Recent Developments." *Bulletin of Indonesian Economic Studies* (Canberra) 32, no. 2 (August 1996): 3–43.

Manning, Chris, and Kurnya Roesad. "Survey of Recent Developments." *Bulletin of Indonesian Economic Studies* (Canberra) 42, no. 2 (August 2006): 143–70.

McLeod, Ross H. "The Economy: High Growth Remains Elusive." Pages 31–50 in Budy P. Resosudarmo, ed., *The Politics and Economics of Indonesia's Natural Resources*. Singapore: Institute of Southeast Asian Studies, 2005.

McLeod, Ross H. "Survey of Recent Developments." *Bulletin of Indonesian Economic Studies* (Canberra) 29, no. 2 (August 1993): 3–42.

McLeod, Ross H. "Survey of Recent Developments." *Bulletin of Indonesian Economic Studies* (Canberra) 36, no. 2 (August 2000): 5–41.

Obidzinski, Kristof. "Legal Logging in Indonesia: Myth and Reality." Pages 193–205 in Budy P. Resosudarmo, ed., *The Politics and Economics of Indonesia's Natural Resources*. Singapore: Institute of Southeast Asian Studies, 2005.

Pangestu, Mari E. "The Role of the Private Sector in Indonesia: Deregulation and Privatisation." *Indonesian Quarterly* (Jakarta) 19, no. 2 (1991): 27–51.

Pangestu, Mari, and Iwan J. Azis. "Survey of Recent Developments." *Bulletin of Indonesian Economic Studies* (Canberra) 30, no. 2 (August 1994): 3–48.

Pangestu, Mari, and Miranda S. Goeltom. "Survey of Recent Developments." *Bulletin of Indonesian Economic Studies* (Canberra) 37, no. 2 (August 2001): 141–71.

Pardede, Raden. "Survey of Recent Developments." *Bulletin of Indonesian Economic Studies* (Canberra) 35, no. 2 (August 1999): 3–39.

Pearson, Scott, and Eric Monke. "Recent Policy Influences on Rice Production." Pages 8–21 in Scott Pearson, et al., *Rice Policy in Indonesia*. Ithaca: Cornell University, 1991.

Prawiro, Radius. *Indonesia's Struggle for Economic Development: Pragmatism in Action*. Kuala Lumpur: Oxford University Press, 1998.

Ramstetter, Eric D. "Survey of Recent Developments." *Bulletin of Indonesian Economic Studies* (Canberra) 36, no. 3 (December 2000): 3–47.

Ray, David J. "Survey of Recent Developments." *Bulletin of Indonesian Economic Studies* (Canberra) 39, no. 3 (December 2003): 245–72.

Robinson, Ross. "Regional Ports: Development and Changes since the 1970s." Pages 133–69 in Thomas R. Leinbach and Chia Lin Sien, eds., *South-East Asian Transport*. Singapore: Oxford University Press, 1989.

Robison, Richard. *Indonesia: The Rise of Capital*. Southeast Asia Publications Series, no. 13. Canberra: Asian Studies Association of Australia, 1986.

Sadli, Muh. "The Indonesian Crisis." Pages 16–27 in Heinz W. Arndt and Hal Hill, eds., *Southeast Asia's Economic Crisis: Origins, Lessons, and the Way Forward*. Singapore: Institute of Southeast Asian Studies, 1999.

Satō, Yuri. "The Palm Oil Industry." Pages 63–94 in Mari E. Pangestu and Yuri Satō, eds., *Waves of Change in Indonesia's Manufacturing Industry*. ASEDP Series, no. 42. Tokyo: Institute of Developing Economies, 1997.

Soesastro, Hadi. "The Political Economy of Deregulation in Indonesia." *Asian Survey* 29, no. 9 (September 1989): 853–69.

Soesastro, Hadi, and M. Chatib Basri. "Survey of Recent Developments." *Bulletin of Indonesian Economic Studies* (Canberra) 34, no. 1 (April 1998): 3–54.

Soesastro, Hadi, and Peter Drysdale. "Survey of Recent Developments." *Bulletin of Indonesian Economic Studies* (Canberra) 26, no. 3 (December 1990): 3–44.

Syahrial, Syarif. "Fiscal Decentralization and Government Size: The Case of Indonesia." *Ekonomi dan Keuangan Indonesia/Economics and Finance in Indonesia* (Jakarta) 53, no. 2 (2005): 177–94.

Tabor, Steven R. "Agriculture in Transition." Pages 161–203 in Anne Booth, ed., *The Oil Boom and After: Indonesian Economic Policy and Performance in the Soeharto Era*. Singapore: Oxford University Press, 1992.

Tambunan, Tulus. "The Role of Small-Scale Industries in Economic Development: A Case of Indonesia." *Social and Economic Studies* (Mona, Jamaica) 40, no. 3 (September 1991): 115–52.

Thee Kian Wie. "The Indonesian Economic Crisis and the Long Road to Recovery." *Australian Economic History Review* (Sydney) 43, no. 2 (July 2003): 183–96.

Tomich, Thomas T. "Smallholder Rubber Development in Indonesia." Pages 250–70 in Dwight H. Perkins and Michael Roemer, eds., *Reforming Economic Systems in Developing Countries.* Harvard Studies in International Development. Cambridge, Massachusetts: Harvard University Press for Harvard Institute for International Development, 1991.

United States. Department of Energy. Energy Information Administration. *The Global Liquefied Natural Gas Market: Status and Outlook.* Report No. DOE/ EIA–0637. Washington, DC, December 2003. http://www.eia.doe.gov/oiaf/ analysispaper/global/index.html.

United States. Department of State. Embassy in Jakarta. *The 1991 Petroleum Report: Indonesia.* Jakarta, 1991.

World Bank. *The East Asian Miracle: Economic Growth and Public Policy.* World Bank Policy Research Report. New York: Oxford University Press, 1993.

World Bank. *Indonesia: From Crisis to Opportunity.* Washington, DC, 1999.

World Bank. *Indonesia: Sustaining High Growth with Equity.* Washington, DC, 1997.

World Bank. *Indonesia in Crisis: A Macroeconomic Update.* Washington, DC, 1998.

(Various Web sources and issues of the following publications also were used in the preparation of this chapter: ASEAN Secretariat (http:// www.aseansecr.org); Asian Development Bank (http://www.adb.org); *Asian Wall Street Journal* (Hong Kong); Bank Indonesia (http://www.bi.go.id), *Report for the Financial Year,* 1984–99; *Bulletin of Indonesian Economic Studies* (Canberra); Capital Investment Coordinating Board (http://www.bkpm.go. id); Central Statistical Office (http://www.bps/go.id); Centre for Strategic and International Studies (http://csis.or.id); *Far Eastern Economic Review* (Hong Kong); National Development Planning Board (http://www.bappenas.go.id); University of Indonesia (http://www.ni.ac.id); and World Bank, *World Development Indicators,* 1998–99.)

Chapter 4

Abuza, Zachary. *Political Islam and Violence in Indonesia.* Asian Security Studies Series. New York: Routledge, 2007.

Alagappa, Muthiah. *Towards a Nuclear-Weapons-Free Zone in Southeast Asia.* ISIS Research Note. Kuala Lumpur: Institute for Strategic and International Studies Malaysia, 1987.

Alves, Dora, ed. *Cooperative Security in the Pacific Basin: The 1988 Pacific Symposium.* Washington, DC: National Defense University Press, 1990.

Anderson, Benedict R. O'G. *Language and Power: Exploring Political Cultures in Indonesia.* Ithaca: Cornell University Press, 1990.

Anderson, Benedict R. O'G., and Audrey R. Kahin, eds. *Interpreting Indonesian Politics: Thirteen Contributions to the Debate.* Ithaca: Cornell University, Southeast Asia Program, Modern Indonesia Project, 1982.

Anwar, Dewi Fortuna. *Negotiating and Consolidating Democratic Civilian Control of the Indonesian Military.* Honolulu: East–West Center, 2001.

Anwar, Dewi Fortuna, and Harold A. Crouch. *Indonesia: Foreign Policy and Domestic Politics.* Singapore: Institute for Southeast Asian Studies, 2003.

Aspinall, Edward. *Helsinki Agreement: A More Promising Basis for Peace in Aceh?* Policy Studies, no. 20. Washington, DC: East–West Center, Washington, DC, 2005.

Azra, Azyumardi. *Indonesia, Islam, and Democracy: Dynamics in a Global Context.* Jakarta: Solstice, 2006.

Barron, Patrick, Samuel Clark, and Muslahuddin Daud. *Conflict and Recovery in Aceh: An Assessment of Conflict Dynamics and Options for Supporting the Peace Process.* Jakarta: World Bank, 2005.

Bertrand, Jacques. *Nationalism and Ethnic Conflict in Indonesia.* Cambridge: Cambridge University Press, 2004.

Blaustein, Albert, and Gisbert H. Flanz, eds. *Constitutions of the Countries of the World*, 7. Dobbs Ferry, New York: Oceana Publications, 1990.

Boland, B.J. *The Struggle of Islam in Modern Indonesia.* The Hague: Martinus Nijhoff, 1971.

Bresnan, John. *Managing Indonesia: The Modern Political Economy.* New York: Columbia University Press, 1993.

Bresnan, John, ed. *Indonesia: The Great Transition.* Lanham, Maryland: Rowman and Littlefield, 2005.

Brundige, Elizabeth, et al. *Indonesian Human Rights Abuses in West Papua: Application of the Law of Genocide to the History of Indonesian Control.* New Haven: Allard K. Lowenstein International Human Rights Clinic, Yale Law School, 2003.

Budiman, Arief, ed. *State and Civil Society in Indonesia.* Clayton, Victoria, Australia: Monash University, Centre of Southeast Asian Studies, 1990.

Butt, Simon "'Unlawfulness' and Corruption under Indonesian Law," *Bulletin of Indonesian Economic Studies* (Canberra) 45, no. 2 (August 2009): 179–98.

Chandler, David P., and Merle C. Ricklefs, eds. *Nineteenth and Twentieth Century Indonesia: Essays in Honour of Professor J. D. Legge.* Clayton, Victoria, Australia: Monash University, Centre of Southeast Asian Studies, 1986.

Crouch, Harold A. *The Army and Politics in Indonesia.* Rev. ed. Ithaca: Cornell University Press, 1988.

Djiwandono, J. Soedjati. *Southeast Asia as a Nuclear Weapons–Free Zone.* Kuala Lumpur: Institute for Strategic and International Studies, Malaysia, 1986.

Effendy, Bahtiar. *Islam and the State in Indonesia.* Singapore: Institute for Southeast Asian Studies, 2003.

Eldridge, Philip J. *NGOs in Indonesia: Popular Movement or Arm of the Government?* Working Paper, no. 55. Clayton, Victoria, Australia: Monash University, Centre of Southeast Asian Studies, 1989.

Eldridge, Philip J. *Non-government Organizations and Democratic Participation in Indonesia.* Kuala Lumpur: Oxford University Press, 1995.

Emmerson, Donald K. "Indonesia in 1983: *Plus Ça Change...*" *Asian Survey* 24, no. 2 (February 1984): 135–48.

Emmerson, Donald K. "Invisible Indonesia." *Foreign Affairs* 66, no. 2 (Winter 1987/1988): 368–87.

Emmerson, Donald K. "Power and *Pancaroba*: Indonesia in a Changing World of States." *International Journal* (Toronto) 46, no. 3 (Summer 1991): 449–74.

Emmerson, Donald K., ed. *Indonesia Beyond Suharto: Polity, Economy, Society, Transition.* Armonk, New York: Sharpe, 1999.

Federspiel, Howard M. "Muslim Intellectuals and Indonesia's National Development." *Asian Survey* 31, no. 3 (March 1991): 232–46.

Federspiel, Howard M. "The Position and Role of Islam in Soeharto's Indonesian New Order at the 21st Year Mark." Paper presented at the Southeast Regional Conference, Association of Asian Studies, Charlotte, North Carolina, January 1988.

Feith, Herbert. *The Decline of Constitutional Democracy in Indonesia.* Ithaca: Cornell University Press, 1962.

Forrester, Geoff, and Ronald J. May, eds. *The Fall of Soeharto.* Singapore: Select Books, 1999.

Geertz, Clifford. *The Religion of Java.* Glencoe, Illinois: Free Press, 1960.

Gunn, Geoffrey L. "Ideology and the Concept of Government in the Indonesian New Order." *Asian Survey* 19, no. 8 (August 1979): 751–69.

Habibie, Bacharuddin Jusuf. *Decisive Moments: Indonesia's Long Road to Democracy.* Jakarta: Ilthabi Rekatama, 2006.

Haseman, John B. "Indonesia: Turbulent Times—From Autocracy to Democracy." Pages 229–47 in Richard J. Ellings, Aaron L. Friedberg, and Michael Wills, eds., *Strategic Asia 2003–04: Fragility and Crisis.* Seattle: National Bureau of Asian Research, 2003.

Haseman, John B., and Eduardo Lachica. *Toward A Stronger U.S.– Indonesia Security Relationship.* Washington, DC: United States– Indonesia Society, 2005. http://www.usindo.org/publications/reports/pdf/Security%20Relations.pdf.

Haseman, John B., and Eduardo Lachica. *The U.S.–Indonesia Security Relationship: The Next Steps.* Washington, DC: United States–Indonesia Society, 2009. http://www.usindo.org/publications/reports/pdf/HASEMAN%20LACHICA%20BOOK%20Final.pdf.

Hefner, Robert W. *Civil Islam: Muslims and Democratization in Indonesia.* Princeton: Princeton University Press, 2000.

Hefner, Robert W. "Islamizing Java? Religion and Politics in Rural East Java." *Journal of Asian Studies* 46, no. 4 (August 1987): 533–54.

Hering, Bob, et al. *New Order Indonesia: Five Essays.* Occasional Paper, no. 27. Townsville, Australia: James Cook University of North Queensland, Centre for Southeast Asian Studies, 1988.

Hiorth, Finngeir. *Timor: Past and Present.* South East Asian Monograph, no. 17. Townsville, Australia: James Cook University of North Queensland, 1985.

Houseman, Gerald L. *Researching Indonesia: A Guide to Political Analysis.* Lewiston, New York: Edwin Mellen, 2004.

International Crisis Group. "Papua: Answers to Frequently Asked Questions." Brussels and Jakarta: *Asia Briefing,* no. 53, September 5, 2006.

Jackson, Karl D., Sukhumbhand Paribatra, and J. Soedjati Djiwandono, eds. *ASEAN in Regional and Global Context.* Berkeley: University of California, Institute of East Asian Studies, 1986.

Joliffe, Jill. *East Timor: Nationalism and Colonialism.* St. Lucia, Australia: University of Queensland Press, 1978.

Kahin, George McTurnan. *Nationalism and Revolution in Indonesia.* Ithaca: Cornell University Press, 1952.

King, Blair A. "Empowering the Presidency: Interests and Perceptions in Indonesia's Constitutional Reforms, 1999–2002." Ph.D. dissertation. Columbus: Ohio State University, 2004.

King, Blair A. *Peace in Papua: Widening a Window of Opportunity.* Council Special Report, no. 14. New York: Council on Foreign Relations, March 2006.

King, Dwight Y., and M. Ryaas Rasjid. "The Golkar Landslide in the 1987 Indonesia Elections: The Case of Aceh." *Asian Survey* 28, no. 9 (September 1988): 916–25.

Klinken, Gerry van. *Communal Violence and Democratization in Indonesia: Small Town Wars.* London: Routledge, 2007.

Koentjaraningrat. *Javanese Culture.* Southeast Asian Studies Program, Institute of Southeast Asian Studies, Singapore. Singapore: Oxford University Press, 1985.

Leifer, Michael. *Indonesia's Foreign Policy.* London: Allen and Unwin for Royal Institute of International Affairs, 1983.

Lev, Daniel S. *The Transition to Guided Democracy: Indonesian Politics, 1957–1959.* Modern Indonesia Project Monograph Series, Ithaca: Cornell University, Department of Asian Studies, Southeast Asia Program, Modern Indonesia Project, 1966.

Liddle, R. William. "Indonesia in 1987: The New Order at the Height of Its Power." *Asian Survey* 27, no. 2 (February 1988): 180–91.

Liddle, R. William. "Indonesia's Democratic Past and Future." *Comparative Politics* 24, no. 4 (July 1992): 443–62.

Liddle, R. William. *Politics and Culture in Indonesia.* Ann Arbor: University of Michigan, Institute for Social Research, Center for Political Studies, 1988.

Liddle, R. William. "Soeharto's Indonesia: Personal Rule and Political Institutionalization." *Pacific Affairs* (Vancouver) 58, no. 1 (Spring 1985): 68–90.

MacDougall, John James. "Indonesian Economic Growth and Political Order." *Current History* 85, no. 510 (April 1986): 172–75, 178–79.

MacIntyre, Andrew. *The Power of Institutions: Political Architecture and Governance.* Ithaca: Cornell University Press, 2003.

Mainwaring, Scott. "Presidentialism, Multipartism, and Democracy: The Difficult Combination." *Comparative Political Studies* 26, no. 2 (July 1993): 198–228.

Manning, Chris, and Peter Van Diermen, eds. *Indonesia in Transition: Social Aspects of Reformasi and Crisis.* Singapore: Institute for Southeast Asian Studies, 2000.

McLeod, Ross H., and Andrew MacIntyre, eds. *Indonesia: Democracy and the Promise of Good Governance.* Singapore: Institute of Southeast Asian Studies, 2007.

Mietzner, Marcus. *The Politics of Military Reform in Post-Suharto Indonesia: Elite Conflict, Nationalism, and Institutional Resistance.* Washington, DC: East–West Center Washington, 2006.

Moertono, Soemarsaid. *State and Statecraft in Old Java: A Study of the Later Mataram Period, 16th to 19th Century.* Modern Indonesia Project Monograph Series. Ithaca: Cornell University, Department of Asian Studies, Southeast Asia Program, Modern Indonesia Project, 1968.

Morfit, Michael. "Pancasila: The Indonesian State Ideology According to the New Order Government." *Asian Survey* 21, no. 8 (August 1981): 838–51.

Mortimer, Rex. *Indonesian Communism under Sukarno: Ideology and Politics, 1959–1965.* Ithaca: Cornell University Press, 1974.

Nordholt, Henk Schulte, and Gerry van Klinken, eds. *Renegotiating Boundaries: Local Politics in Post-Suharto Indonesia.* Leiden, Netherlands: KITLV Press, 2007.

Nyman, Mikaela. *Democratising Indonesia: The Challenges of Civil Society in the Era of Reformasi.* Copenhagen: NIAS Press, 2006.

Orentlicher, Diane F. *Human Rights in Indonesia and East Timor.* New York: Human Rights Watch, Asia Watch Committee, 1988.

Osborne, Robin. *Indonesia's Secret War: The Guerrilla Struggle in Irian Jaya.* Sydney: Allen and Unwin, 1985.

Piscatori, James P., ed. *Islam in the Political Process.* Cambridge: Cambridge University Press, 1983.

Purdy, Susan S. "The Civil Religion Thesis as it Applies to a Pluralistic Society: Pancasila Democracy in Indonesia." *Journal of International Affairs* 36, no. 2 (Fall–Winter 1982–83): 307–16.

Rabasa, Angel, and Peter Chalk. *Indonesia's Transformation and the Stability of Southeast Asia.* Santa Monica, California: RAND, 2001.

Ramage, Douglas. "The Political Function of Pancasila, Indonesia's State Ideology." Master's thesis. Columbia, South Carolina: University of South Carolina, 1990.

Reeve, David. *Golkar of Indonesia: An Alternative to the Party System.* Singapore: Oxford University Press, 1985.

Roeder, O. G. *The Smiling General: President Soeharto of Indonesia.* Jakarta: Gunung Agung, 1969.

Said, Salim. *Genesis of Power: General Sudirman and the Indonesian Military in Politics, 1945–49.* Singapore: Institute of Southeast Asian Studies, 1991.

Said, Salim. *Soeharto's Armed Forces: Problems of Civil Military Relations in Indonesia.* Jakarta: Pustaka Sinar Harapan, 2006.

Savage, David. *Dancing with the Devil: A Personal Account of Policing the East Timor Vote for Independence.* Clayton, Victoria, Australia: Monash University, Asia Institute, 2002.

Smith, Anthony L. *Strategic Centrality: Indonesia's Changing Role in ASEAN.* Singapore: Institute of Southeast Asian Studies, Regional Strategic and Political Studies Programme, 2000.

Suryadinata, Leo A. "Indonesia–Vietnam Relations Under Soeharto." *Contemporary Southeast Asia* (Singapore) 12, no. 4 (March 1991): 331–46.

Suryadinata, Leo A. *Military Ascendancy and Political Culture: A Study of Indonesia's Golkar.* Ohio University Monographs in International Studies, no. 85. Athens: Ohio University, Center for International Studies, 1989.

Tanter, Richard, Gerry van Klinken, and Desmond Ball, eds. *Masters of Terror: Indonesia's Military and Violence in East Timor.* Lanham, Maryland: Rowman and Littlefield, 2006.

Thambapillai, Pushpa. "The ASEAN Growth Triangle: The Convergence of National and Sub-National Interests." *Contemporary Southeast Asia* (Singapore) 13, no. 3 (December 1991): 299–314.

Thoolen, Hans, ed. *Indonesia and the Rule of Law: Twenty Years of "New Order" Government: A Study.* Prepared by the International Commission of Jurists and the Netherlands Institute of Human Rights. London: Frances Pinter, 1987.

Weatherbee, Donald E. "Indonesia: The Consolidation of the Pancasila State." Paper presented at the Asia Society, New York, November 11, 1985.

Weatherbee, Donald E. "Indonesia: The Maturation of a Regional Power." Paper presented at the Southeast Regional Conference, Association of Asian Studies, Charlotte, North Carolina, January 1988.

Weatherbee, Donald E. "Indonesia: The Pancasila State." Pages 133–51 in *Southeast Asian Affairs 1985.* Singapore: Institute of Southeast Asian Studies, January 1985.

Weatherbee, Donald E. "The Indonesianization of East Timor." *Contemporary Southeast Asia* (Singapore) 3, no. 1 (June 1981): 1–23.

Weatherbee, Donald E. *Islam and Politics in Southeast Asia.* East Asia Trends contract report. Washington, DC: U.S. Department of State, 1986.

Weatherbee, Donald E. "Papua New Guinea's Foreign Policy: A Bridge to Indonesian Shores." *Contemporary Southeast Asia* (Singapore) 4, no. 3 (December 1982): 330–45.

Weatherbee, Donald E. "The Philippines and ASEAN: Options for Aquino." *Asian Survey* 27, no. 12 (December 1987): 1223–39.

Weatherbee, Donald E., ed. *Southeast Asia Divided: The ASEAN–Indochina Crisis.* Boulder, Colorado: Westview, 1985.

Wessel, Ingrid, and Georgia Wimhöfer, eds. *Violence in Indonesia.* Hamburg: Abera, 2001.

Wing, John, and Peter King. *Genocide in West Papua? The Role of the Indonesian State Apparatus and a Current Needs Assessment of the Papuan People.* Sydney: University of Sydney, Centre for Peace and Conflict Studies, West Papua Project, 2005.

Winters, Jeffrey A. *Power in Motion: Capital Mobility and the Indonesian State.* Ithaca: Cornell University Press, 1996.

Wurfel, David, and Bruce Burton, eds. *The Political Economy of Foreign Policy in Southeast Asia.* International Political Economy Series. New York: St. Martin's Press, 1990.

(Various Web sites and issues of the following publications also were used in the preparation of this chapter: *Asian Survey; Asian Wall Street Journal* (Hong Kong); *Far Eastern Economic Review* (Hong Kong); Indonesia government Web sites, many of which are listed at http://www.indonesia.gov.id/en/; and *Southeast Asian Affairs* (Singapore).)

Chapter 5

Amnesty International. *Amnesty International Report, 1991.* New York, 1991.

"The Blood Sweet Flower Ceremony at Santa Cruz Cemetery in Dili." *Editor* (Jakarta), November 23, 1991, 27–33.

Bruce, Robert H. "Paramilitary Police as Political Resources in Civil–Military Crisis: The Mobile Brigade Between Sukarno and the Army in Indonesia." *Asian Profile* (Hong Kong) 14, no. 5 (August 1986): 471–78.

Conboy, Kenneth J. *Elite: The Special Forces of Indonesia 1950–2008.* Jakarta: Equinox, 2008.

Conboy, Kenneth J. *Intel: Inside Indonesia's Intelligence Services.* Jakarta: Equinox, 2003.

Conboy, Kenneth J. *Kopassus: Inside Indonesia's Special Forces.* Jakarta: Equinox, 2003.

Cribb, Robert B., and Audrey R. Kahin. *Historical Dictionary of Indonesia.* 2d ed. Lanham, Maryland: Scarecrow Press, 2004.

Crouch, Harold A. *The Army and Politics in Indonesia.* Rev. ed. Ithaca: Cornell University Press, 1988.

Crouch, Harold A. "Military–Civilian Relations in Indonesia in the Late Soeharto Era." Pages 61–66 in Viberto Selochan, ed., *The Military, the State, and Development in Asia and the Pacific.* Westview Studies in Regional Security. Boulder, Colorado: Westview Press, 1991.

Crouch, Harold A. "Patrimonialism and Military Rule in Indonesia." *World Politics* 31, no. 4 (July 1979): 571–87.

Durch, William J. "UN Temporary Executive Authority." Pages 285–98 in William J. Durch, ed., *The Evolution of UN Peacekeeping: Case Studies and Comparative Analysis.* New York: St. Martin's Press, 1993.

Editors, The. "Current Data on the Indonesian Military Elite, September 2005–March 2008." *Indonesia* 85 (April 2008): 79–122.

Embree, Ainslie T., ed. *Encyclopedia of Asian History.* 4 vols. The Asia Society. New York: Scribner's, 1988.

Foss, Christopher F., ed. *Jane's Armour and Artillery, 1991–92.* Coulsdon, United Kingdom: Jane's Information Group, 1991.

Frederick, William H., and A. Kohar Rony. *Indonesia: A Select Reading Guide in English.* Aspects of Indonesian Culture Series. New York: Festival of Indonesia, 1991.

Friend, Theodore. *Indonesian Destinies.* Cambridge, Massachusetts: Belknap Press of Harvard University Press, 2003.

Ghoshal, Baladas. *Role of the Military in Indonesia.* Monograph Series, no. 2. Madras: University of Madras, Centre for South and Southeast Asian Studies, 1980.

Greville, P. J. "Living with Indonesia." *Asia-Pacific Defence Reporter* (Sydney) 17, no. 9 (March 1991): 37–38.

Habib, H. Hasnan. "Indonesia's Defence Industry: Its Role, Mission, and Set-Up." Pages 69–95 in Chandran Jeshurun, ed., *Arms and Defence in Southeast Asia.* Issues in Southeast Asian Security. Singapore: Institute of Southeast Asian Studies, Regional Strategic Studies Programme, 1989.

Harfield, Alan G. *British and Indian Armies in the East Indies, 1685–1935.* Chippenham, United Kingdom: Picton, 1984.

Haseman, John B. "The Dynamics of Change: Regeneration of the Indonesian Army." *Asian Survey* 26, no. 8 (August 1986): 883–96.

Haseman, John B. "East Timor: The Misuse of Military Power and Misplaced Military Pride." Pages 180–91 in James J. Fox and Dionisio Babo Soares, eds., *East Timor: Out of the Ashes: Destruction and Reconstructions of East Timor.* Adelaide: Crawford House, 2000.

Haseman, John B. "Indonesia: Turbulent Times—From Autocracy to Democracy." Pages 229–47 in Richard J. Ellings, Aaron L. Friedberg, and Michael Wills, eds., *Strategic Asia 2003–04: Fragility and Crisis.* Seattle: National Bureau of Asian Research, 2003.

Haseman, John B., and Eduardo Lachica. *Toward A Stronger U.S.–Indonesia Security Relationship.* Washington, DC: United States–Indonesia Society, 2005. http://www.usindo.org/publications/reports/pdf/Security%20Relations.pdf.

Hogg, Ian V., ed. *Jane's Infantry Weapons, 1991–92.* Coulsdon, United Kingdom: Jane's Information Group, 1991.

Human Rights Watch. Asia Watch Committee. *Asia Watch Criticizes Commission Report on East Timor.* New York, January 3, 1992.

Human Rights Watch. Asia Watch Committee. *Injustice, Persecution, Eviction: A Human Rights Update on Indonesia and East Timor.* New York, March 1990.

Indonesia, Department of Defense. "Defense Media Centre." 2006–8. http://www.dmcindonesia. web.id/.

Indonesia. Department of Defense. "Departemen Pertahanan RI." 2006–8. http://www.dephan. go.id/.

Indonesia. Department of Defense and Security. "AKABRI in Highlight." Jakarta, September 1991.

Indonesia. Department of Defense and Security. *Organization and Mission of the Department of Defense and Security.* Jakarta, November 8, 1983.

Indonesia. Department of Defense and Security. *Republic of Indonesia Armed Forces Manual and Dual Functions of the Armed Forces.* Jakarta, June 1, 1982.

Indonesia. Department of Defense and Security. Institute of History. *The Indonesian Armed Forces and the New Order.* Jakarta, 1968.

Indonesia. Department of Information. Directorate of Foreign Information Services. *Indonesia 1992: An Official Handbook.* Jakarta, 1991.

Indonesia. Military Honor Council. *News Conference by the Army Chief of Staff.* Jakarta, February 27, 1992.

Indonesia. National Commission of Inquiry into the 12 November 1991 Incident in Dili. *Advance Report.* Jakarta, December 26, 1991.

Indonesia. National Police. *A Glimpse on Activities of the Indonesian National Police.* Jakarta: Police Information Service, 1976.

Indonesia–Timor-Leste Commission on Truth and Friendship. *Final Report.* Denpasar, Indonesia, March 31, 2008.

International Crisis Group. "Indonesia: Communal Tensions in Papua." *Asia Report* (Brussels) no. 154 (June 16, 2008). http://www.crisisgroup.org/home/index.cfm?id=5485.

Jane's Information Group. *Jane's Sentinel Security Risk Assessments: Southeast Asia.* http://sentinel.janes.com/public/sentinel/index.shtml (subscription required; accessed August 2008).

Jenkins, David. *Suharto and His Generals: Indonesian Military Politics, 1975–1984.* Ithaca: Cornell University, Modern Indonesia Project, 1984.

Jeshurun, Chandran, ed. *Arms and Defence in Southeast Asia.* Issues in Southeast Asian Security. Singapore: Institute of Southeast Asian Studies, Regional Strategic Studies Program, 1989.

Johns, Yohanna. "The PETA Army in Indonesia, 1943–1945." Pages 32–45 in William H. Newell, ed., *Japan in Asia, 1943–1945.* Singapore: Singapore University Press, 1981.

Lee Lai To. "Managing Potential Conflicts in the South China Sea: Political and Security Issues." *Indonesian Quarterly* (Jakarta) 18, no. 2 (April 1990): 154–63.

Leifer, Michael. "Uncertainty in Indonesia." *World Policy Journal* 8, no. 1 (Winter 1990–91): 137–57.

Liddle, R. William. "Indonesia's Democratic Past and Future." *Comparative Politics* 24, no. 4 (July 1992): 443–62.

Lowry, Robert. *The Armed Forces of Indonesia.* St. Leonard's, New South Wales, Australia: Allen and Unwin, 1986.

MacDougall, John A. "Military Penetration of the Indonesian Government: The Higher Central Bureaucracy." *Indonesia Reports*, no. 14 (March 1986): 2–15.

MacIntyre, Andrew, and Douglas E. Ramage. *Seeing Indonesia as a Normal Country: Implications for Australia.* Barton, Australia: Australian Strategic Policy Institute, May 2008.

May, Brian. *The Indonesian Tragedy.* London: Routledge and Kegan Paul, 1978.

Maynard, Harold W. "A Comparison of Military Elite Role Perceptions in Indonesia and the Philippines." Ph.D. dissertation. Washington, DC: American University, 1976.

Maynard, Harold W. "Indonesian and Philippines Military Elites." Pages 123–53 in Sheldon W. Simon, ed., *The Military and Security in the Third World: Domestic and International Impacts.* Westview Special Studies in Social, Political, and Economic Development. Boulder, Colorado: Westview Press, 1978.

McGuire, G., and Bob B. Hering. "The Indonesian Army: Harbingers of Progress or Reactionary Predators?" *Kabar Seberang* (Townsville, Australia), no. 17 (June 1986): 158–75.

McVey, Ruth T. "The Post-Revolutionary Transformation of the Indonesian Army: Part I." *Indonesia* 11 (April 1971): 131–76.

McVey, Ruth T. "The Post-Revolutionary Transformation of the Indonesian Army: Part II." *Indonesia* 13 (April 1972): 147–82.

Mokoginta, Rachmat. "Dual Functions of the Indonesian Armed Forces." Research paper. Carlisle, Pennsylvania: U.S. Army War College, April 1, 1991.

"National Investigation Commission." *Ankatan Bersenjata* (Jakarta), November 20, 1991, 4.

Notosusanto, Nugroho. *The Dual Function of the Indonesian Armed Forces*. Jakarta: Department of Defense and Security, Centre for Armed Forces History, 1970.

Notosusanto, Nugroho. *The National Struggle and the Armed Forces in Indonesia*. 2d rev. ed. Jakarta: Department of Defense and Security, Centre for Armed Forces History, 1980.

Notosusanto, Nugroho. *The Peta Army During the Japanese Occupation of Indonesia*. Tokyo: Waseda University, 1979.

Orentlicher, Diane F. *Human Rights in Indonesia and East Timor*. New York: Asia Watch Committee, 1988.

O'Rourke, Kevin. *Reformasi: The Struggle for Power in Post-Suharto Indonesia*. Crows Nest, New South Wales, Australia: Allen and Unwin, 2002.

Paridah Abdul Samad. "Internal Variables of Regional Conflicts in ASEAN's International Relations." *Indonesian Quarterly* (Jakarta) 18, no. 2 (April 1990): 171–81.

Paridah Abdul Samad. "The Sources of Threat to Domestic Order in the ASEAN States." *Indonesian Quarterly* (Jakarta) 18, no. 4 (October 1990): 332–46.

Pirngadie, Rudi. *Revolution, Political Stability, and the Army in Indonesia: A Soldier's Appraisal*. Manila, 1966.

Prakash, Sanjiv. "Indonesia After Suharto." *Defense and Foreign Affairs* 17, no. 2 (February 1989): 13–14, 32.

Prakash, Sanjiv. "Suharto's Indonesia: In the Spirit of Garuda." *Defense and Foreign Affairs* 17, no. 2 (February 1989): 6–12, 32.

Rabasa, Angel, and John B. Haseman. *The Military and Democracy in Indonesia: Challenges, Politics, and Power*. Santa Monica, California: RAND, 2002. http://www.rand.org/pubs/monograph_reports/MR1599/index.html.

Rieffel, Lex, and Jaleswari Pramodhawardani. *Out of Business and On Budget: The Challenge of Military Financing in Indonesia*. Washington, DC: United States–Indonesia Society, Brookings Institution Press, 2007.

Robison, Richard. *Indonesia: The Rise of Capital*. Southeast Asian Publications Series, no. 13. Canberra: Asian Studies Association of Australia, 1986.

Robison, Richard. "Toward a Class Analysis of the Indonesian Military." *Indonesia* 25 (April 1978): 17–39.

Roff, Sue Rabbitt. *Timor's Anschluss: Indonesian and Australian Policy in East Timor, 1974–1976*. Lewiston, New York: Edwin Mellen Press, 1992.

Rudner, Martin. "The Indonesian Military and Economic Policy: The Goals and Performance of the First Five-Year Development Plan, 1969–1974." *Modern Asian Studies* (London) 10, no. 2 (April 1976): 249–84.

Said, Salim. *Genesis of Power: General Sudirman and the Indonesian Military in Politics, 1945–49.* Singapore: Institute of Southeast Asian Studies, 1991.

Said, Salim. *Legitimizing Military Rule: Indonesian Armed Forces Ideology, 1958–2000.* Jakarta: Pustaka Sinar Harapan, 2006.

Said, Salim. *Soeharto's Armed Forces: Problems of Civil Military Relations in Indonesia.* Jakarta: Pustaka Sinar Harapan, 2006.

Schwarz, Adam. *A Nation in Waiting: Indonesia in the 1990s.* 2d ed. Boulder, Colorado: Westview Press, 2000.

Scott, Margaret. "Suharto Writes His Last Chapter." *New York Times Magazine*, June 2, 1991, 28–67.

Shiraishi, Takashi. "The Military in Thailand, Burma, and Indonesia." Pages 157–80 in Robert A. Scalapino, Seizaburo Sato, and Jusuf Wanandi, eds., *Asian Political Institutionalization.* Research Papers and Policy Studies, no. 15. Berkeley: University of California, Institute of East Asian Studies, 1986.

Suharto. *Soeharto: My Thoughts, Words, and Deeds.* Trans., Sumadi. Ed., Muti'ah Lestiono. Jakarta: Citra Lamtoro Gung Persada, 1991.

Sukma, Rizal. "Jakarta–Beijing Relations and Security Challenges in Southeast Asia." *Indonesian Quarterly* (Jakarta) 18, no. 2 (April 1990): 280–91.

Sundhausen, Ulf. "The Military: Structure, Procedures, and Effects on Indonesian Society." Pages 45-81 in Karl D. Jackson and Lucian W. Pye, eds., *Political Power and Communications in Indonesia.* Berkeley: University of California Press, 1978.

Sundhausen, Ulf. *The Road to Power: Indonesian Military Politics, 1945–1967.* Kuala Lumpur: Oxford University Press, 1982.

Suryadinata, Leo. "Indonesian Policies toward the Chinese Minority under the New Order." *Asian Survey* 16, no. 8 (August 1976): 770–87.

Suryadinata, Leo. *Military Ascendancy and Political Culture: A Study of Indonesia's Golkar.* Monographs in International Studies. Southeast Asia Series, no. 85. Athens: Ohio University, Center for International Studies, 1989.

Taylor, John G. *Indonesia's Forgotten War: The Hidden History of East Timor.* London: Zed Books, 1991.

Transparency International. *Global Corruption Report, 2004*. Berlin, January 24, 2004. http://www.transparency.org/publications/gcr.

United Nations Department of Public Information. *The Blue Helmets: A Review of United Nations Peace-keeping*. 2d ed. United Nations Publication Sales, no. E.90.I.18. New York, 1990.

United States. Arms Control and Disarmament Agency. *World Military Expenditures and Arms Transfers, 1990*. Washington, DC: GPO, November 1991.

United States. Central Intelligence Agency. *The World Factbook, 1991*. Washington, DC, 1991.

United States. Department of State. *International Narcotics Control Strategy Report: Mid-Year Update*. Washington, DC, September 1991.

United States. Department of State. Bureau of Democracy, Human Rights, and Labor. *Country Reports on Human Rights Practices for 2009*. Washington, DC: GPO, March 2010. http://www.state.gov/g/drl/rls/hrrpt/2008/index.htm.

United States. Office of the Director of National Intelligence. National Counterterrorism Center. "Worldwide Incidents Tracking System." http://wits.nctc.gov [Indonesia] (accessed October 5, 2009).

University of Maryland. National Consortium for the Study of Terrorism and Responses to Terrorism. "Global Terrorism Database." http://www.start.umd.edu/gtd (accessed October 5, 2009).

Utrecht, Ernst. *The Indonesian Army: A Socio-Political Study of an Armed Privileged Group in the Developing Countries*. South East Asia Monograph Series, no. 4. Townsville, Australia: James Cook University of North Queensland, Southeast Asian Studies Committee, 1978.

Utrecht, Ernst. *The Military and the 1977 Election*. Townsville, Australia: James Cook University of North Queensland, Centre for Southeast Asian Studies, 1980.

Waldack, Albert C., and John B. Haseman. "Dwi-Fungsi: The Indonesian Army in Civil Affairs." *Military Review* 61, no. 9 (September 1981): 13–19.

Wilson, Donald W. *The Indispensable Man Sudono: The Continuing Journey*. Jakarta: Yayasan Persada Nusantara, 1992.

Yani, Achmed. *The Indonesian Army's Doctrine of War*. Jakarta: Indonesian Army Information Service, 1965.

Zakaria Haji Ahmad, and Harold A. Crouch, eds. *Military–Civilian Relations in South-East Asia*. Singapore: Oxford University Press, 1985.

(Various Web sites and issues of the following publications also were used in the preparation of this chapter: Amnesty International (http://www.amnesty.org/en/region/indonesia); *Asian Wall Street Journal* (Hong Kong); "Current Data on the Indonesian Military Elite," published in Cornell University's journal *Indonesia* (http://cip.cornell.edu/indonesia); Indonesian Department of Defense, Defense Media Centre (http://www.dephan.go.id); *Far Eastern Economic Review* (Hong Kong); *Human Rights Watch* (http://www.hrw.org/en/asia); International Institute for Strategic Studies, *The Military Balance*; U.S. Department of Defense, Defense Security Assistance Agency, *Congressional Presentation*; and *Van Zorge Report on Indonesia: Commentary and Analysis on Indonesian Politics and Economics* (Jakarta) (http://www.vanzorgereport.com/report/index.cfm).)

Glossary

abangan—Refers to people who are nominally Muslim but who are generally followers of *kebatinan* (*q.v.*). The word is derived from the Javanese *abang*, which means "red."

Asian Development Bank—Established in 1967, the bank assists in economic development and promotes growth and cooperation in regional member countries. The bank is owned by its 48 regional member governments, including Indonesia, as well as 18 nonregional members in Western Europe plus the United States.

Association of Southeast Asian Nations (ASEAN)—Founded in 1967 for the purpose of promoting regional stability, economic development, and cultural exchange. ASEAN's founding members were Indonesia, Malaysia, the Philippines, Singapore, and Thailand. Brunei joined ASEAN in 1984, Vietnam joined in 1995, Laos and Burma in 1997, and Cambodia in 1999. Papua New Guinea has observer status, and there are 11 dialogue partners: Australia, Canada, China, the European Union, India, Japan, South Korea, New Zealand, Russia, the United States, and the United Nations Development Programme (UNDP). Timor-Leste has requested to be considered for membership. The ASEAN Regional Forum (ARF) was established in 1994 to foster constructive dialogue and consultation on political and security issues of common interest and concern. In 2009 it had 26 members, including the 10 ASEAN member states, Papua New Guinea, and Timor-Leste.

Bahasa Indonesia—The Indonesian national language, also known as Indonesian; an Austronesian language thought to have its roots in Riau Malay and 80 percent cognate with Standard Malay. The so-called perfected or new spelling of Bahasa Indonesia—*ejaan yang disempurnakan* (EYD)—was adopted in 1972.

Confrontation (Konfrontasi)—In 1963 then-President Sukarno ordered "confrontation" with the emerging new state of Malaysia, in part to distract attention from Indonesia's increasingly dire economic straits. Guerrilla warfare and intelligence operations involving Indonesian forces, British commandos, and the nascent Malaysian armed forces ensued, mostly on both sides of the two countries' land border on Kalimantan; went on for two years; and was only halted after Sukarno lost power in October 1965.

Consultative Group on Indonesia (CGI)—Formed after the March 1992 demise of the Inter-Governmental Group on Indonesia (IGGI; *q.v.*). Except for the Netherlands, the membership was the same as for the IGGI. The Indonesia government disbanded the CGI in 2007.

cukong—A Chinese term from Hokkien dialect, meaning "master" but taken in the Indonesian context to mean a Chinese businessman or middleman cooperating closely with native Indonesian legal license holders, especially the military, during the New Order period.

exclusive economic zone—Per Act No. 3 of 1983, enacted October 18, 1983, the outer strip bordering the Indonesian territorial sea as determined by the law applicable to the Indonesian waters, covering the seabed, the subsoil of the seabed, and the water above it with an outermost limit of 200 nautical miles, measured from the baseline of the Indonesian territorial sea. Within this zone, Indonesia claims sovereign rights to conduct the exploration, exploitation, management, and conservation of the living and nonliving resources on the seabed and in the subsoil thereof, as well as the water above it, including other activities for the purpose of economic exploration and exploitation of the zone, such as the generation of power by means of water, current, and wind.

fiscal year (FY)—Calendar year. Prior to 2001, the fiscal year ran from April 1 to March 31. The change meant that FY 2000 covered only nine months.

Free Aceh Movement (Gerakan Aceh Merdeka—GAM)—A separatist group that fought for Acehnese independence between 1976 and 2005. Also known as Aceh Sumatra National Liberation Front (ASNLF; see table A).

Fretilin (Frente Revolucionária do Timor Leste Independente; Revolutionary Front for an Independent East Timor)—A guerrilla movement that fought for the independence of East Timor. Fretilin was established in 1974, suppressed during the ensuing 25 years, but endured Indonesian occupation and emerged as the first governing party of independent East Timor in 1999.

Gini index—The Gini coefficient expressed as a percentage. The Gini coefficient measures the extent to which the distribution of income (or, in some cases, consumption expenditure) among individuals or households within an economy or society deviates from a perfectly equal distribution. It measures the degree to which two frequency (percentage) distributions correspond. The Gini index is a number between 0 and 1, where 0 means perfect equality (everyone has the same income) and 1 means perfect inequality (one person has all the income, everyone else earns nothing). It was developed by Corrado Gini (1884–1965), an Italian statistician.

Golkar—Originally *golongan karya*, which literally means functional groups within society, such as peasants, workers, and women, but later taken to be Golongan Karya or Golkar (an organization of functional groups), the government party during Suharto's New Order. The Golkar Party, with many changes, is one of many parties in the post–New Order period.

gross domestic product (GDP)—A value measure of the flow of domestic goods and services produced by an economy over a period of time, such as a year. Only output of goods for final consumption and intermediate production are assumed to be included in the final prices. GDP is sometimes aggregated and shown at market prices, meaning that indirect taxes and subsidies are included: when these direct taxes and subsidies have been eliminated, the result is GDP at factor cost. The word *gross* indicates that deductions for depreciation of physical assets have not been made. Income arising from investments and possessions owned abroad is not included, only domestic production—hence the use of the word *domestic* to distinguish GDP from gross national product (GNP; *q.v.*).

gross national product (GNP)—The gross domestic product (*q.v.*) plus net income or loss stemming from transactions with foreign countries, including income received from abroad by residents and subtracting payments remitted abroad to nonresidents. GNP is the broadest measurement of the output of goods and services by an economy. It can be calculated at market prices, which include indirect taxes and subsidies. Because indirect taxes and subsidies are only transfer payments, GNP often is calculated at factor cost by removing indirect taxes and subsidies.

Indonesian Communist Party (Partai Komunis Indonesia—PKI)—Founded in 1913 as the Indies Social-Democratic Association (ISDV), which became the Communist Association of the Indies (PKH) in 1920 and was renamed the Indonesian Communist Party in 1924. The PKI flourished during the Sukarno years of the 1950s and early 1960s. Accused of attempting a coup d'état on September 30, 1965, during which five senior military officers were killed, the party was suppressed in an ensuing pogrom by the armed forces and ordinary citizens. The actual role of the PKI in the September 30 incident is still the subject of historical examination in the wake of the resignation of former president Suharto in May 1998.

Indonesian National Armed Forces (Tentara Nasional Indonesia—TNI)—
This official designation of the Indonesian armed forces was adopted in
April 1999 after the National Police of Indonesia (Kepolisian Republik
Indonesia—Polri) was removed from the armed forces (it had been a co-
equal fourth branch since 1960). The former name for the armed forces,
from 1962 to 1999, was Angkatan Bersenjata Republik Indonesia
(ABRI; Armed Forces of the Republic of Indonesia). TNI was also used
between 1947 and 1962 for the army.

Inter-Governmental Group on Indonesia (IGGI)—An international group of
lenders established in 1967 by the Netherlands to coordinate multilateral
aid to Indonesia. The other members included the Asian Development
Bank (*q.v.*), International Monetary Fund (IMF), United Nations
Development Programme, World Bank, Australia, Belgium, Britain,
Canada, France, Germany, Italy, Japan, New Zealand, Switzerland, and
the United States. In March 1992, Indonesia announced that it was
rejecting further IGGI aid as long as the Netherlands was a member of
the organization. The IGGI was replaced by the Consultative Group on
Indonesia (*q.v.*), with the original members minus the Netherlands.

kebatinan (mysticism)—An amalgam of animist, Hindu-Buddhist, and
Islamic (especially Sufi) mystical elements that combine to form
Javanese mysticism. Not a single body of faith, but an *aliran*, a
"stream" of beliefs held by a number of groups, *kebatinan* is officially
recognized by the government, and its schools are administered by the
Department of National Education rather than by the Department of
Religious Affairs. Also known as *kejawen*, *agama Jawa*, or Javanism.

Konfrontasi—Confrontation (*q.v.*).

Laakso-Taagepera Index—A commonly used measure to determine the
effective number of political parties when parties vary substantially in
their vote or share of seats. It is named after political scientists Markku
Laakso and Rein Taagepera, who developed the index in 1979.

Nonaligned Movement—Established in September 1961 with the aim of
promoting political and military cooperation apart from the traditional
East and West blocs. Indonesia was among the original members; as of
2009, there were 118 members, 15 observers, and 24 guests. Indonesia
held the chair of the Nonaligned Movement from 1992 to 1995.

Organization of the Petroleum Exporting Countries (OPEC)—Founded
in Baghdad, Iraq, on September 14, 1960, by Iran, Iraq, Kuwait, Saudi
Arabia, and Venezuela with the aim of coordinating petroleum
policies of its member countries. OPEC membership increased with
the addition of Qatar in 1961, Indonesia and Libya in 1962, the United

Arab Emirates in 1967, Algeria in 1969, Nigeria in 1971, Ecuador in 1973, Gabon in 1975, and Angola in 2007. Ecuador suspended its membership from 1992 to 2007; Gabon terminated its membership in 1995; Indonesia, when it became a net importer of oil, suspended its membership effective January 2009.

Outer Islands—Older term used by some sources to refer to all islands of the Indonesian archipelago other than Java and Madura. Other sources, however, use the term to refer to all islands except Java, Madura, Bali, and Sumatra; still others say except Java and Bali or exclude Java, Madura, and Bali. The term as translated from Dutch—*buitengewesten*—means outer territories or regions, while a similar term from Bahasa Indonesia (*q.v.*)—*tanah seberang*—means land (or lands) over there, or across the seas. The term is sometimes considered pejorative by those people living on the islands indicated.

Pancasila—State philosophy based on five interrelated principles: belief in one supreme God; just and civilized humanitarianism; nationalism as expressed in the unity of Indonesia; popular sovereignty arrived at through deliberation and representation or consultative democracy; and social justice for all the Indonesian people. The Pancasila was announced by Sukarno on June 1, 1945. From Sanskrit: *panca* (five) and *sila* (principle). It became the country's official doctrine under Suharto, when all military and civil servants were required to attend a course on Pancasila principles. While still a part of the national doctrine, its importance has waned in the post-Suharto years.

pribumi—Literally, an indigene, or native. A term coined in the post-colonial period to replace the Dutch word *inlander*, a term that also meant "native" but which did not refer to Arabs, Chinese, or Eurasians who might have been born in the Indies. The distinction between *pribumi* and non-*pribumi* has had significant implications for economic development policy.

priyayi—Traditional aristocratic, bureaucratic elite of Java.

reformasi—An Indonesian blanket term for democratic reforms initiated and implemented by all elements of government after the 1998 fall of Suharto, up until around 2004.

Repelita (Rencana Pembangunan Lima Tahun)—A five-year economic development plan: Repelita I (FY [*q.v.*] 1969–73), Repelita II (FY 1974–78), Repelita III (FY 1979–83), Repelita IV (FY 1984–88), Repelita V (FY 1989–93), and Repelita VI (FY 1994–98).

rupiah (Rp)—Basic unit of currency. The exchange rate was fixed at Rp415 to US$1 from 1971 to 1978, when the rupiah was devalued to Rp625.

Following two devaluations in 1983 and 1986, the rupiah was gradually depreciated at an average rate of about 5 percent per year up to the financial crisis in 1997–98, when the Indonesian currency was floated, and the exchange rate fell dramatically. During the recovery after the crisis, the rupiah stabilized at a level of about Rp11,000–12,000 per US$1, and in the early twenty-first century it improved to about Rp8,000–9,000 per US$1. At the end of July 2011, the interbank exchange rate was valued at Rp8,481.76 per US$1, or Rp1 = US$0.00012. The rupiah is issued in 1, 25, 50, 100, 200, 500, and 1,000 coins and 1,000, 5, 000, 10,000, 20,000, 50,000, and 100,000 notes.

santri—Orthodox Muslims. In the Javanese context, the *santri* are also sometimes referred to as *putihan* (white ones), an allusion to their purity, especially as contrasted to *abangan* (*q.v.*) in Javanese.

sharia (Arabic; *syariah* in Bahasa Indonesia, *q.v.*)—Islamic canon law. Among Shia (*q.v.*) Muslims, the sharia includes the Quran and the authenticated sayings of the Prophet (*hadith*) and the Twelve Imams.

Shia (or Shiite)—A member of the smaller of two great divisions of Islam. The Shias supported the claims of Ali and his line to presumptive right to the caliphate and leadership of the Muslim community, and on this issue they divided from the Sunnis (*q.v.*) in the first great schism of Islam. Later disagreements have produced further schisms among the Shias. Shias revere 12 imams, most of whom are believed to be hidden from view.

Sufi—From *suf*, the Arabic word for "wool." The term derives from the practice of wearing a woolen robe, a sign of dedicating oneself to the mystical life, known in Islam as becoming a Sufi. Sufis, who seek mystical union with God, have been condemned by some Sunni (*q.v.*) legal schools.

Sunni—From the Arabic *sunna* meaning "custom," with the connotation of orthodoxy or tradition based on the Prophet Muhammad's example. One of the two great divisions of Islam, the Sunnis supported the traditional method of election to the caliphate and accepted the Umayyad line. On this issue, they divided from the Shia (*q.v.*) discipline in the first great schism within Islam.

Supersemar (Surat Perintah Sebelas Maret)—The Letter of Instruction of March 11, 1966, in which Sukarno signed over his executive authority, in the wake of the September 30, 1965, coup attempt, to General Suharto.

Transmigration Program—A voluntary rural resettlement plan that sought to move large numbers of Javanese to Indonesia's underpopulated Outer Islands (*q.v.*); *transmigrasi* in Bahasa Indonesia (*q.v.*).

Contributors

William H. Frederick is Associate Professor of History, Department of History, Ohio University, Athens, Ohio.

John B. Haseman is a retired U.S. Army colonel, former U.S. Defense Attaché in Jakarta, and now a consultant and writer.

Blair A. King is a foreign service officer at the U.S. Agency for International Development.

Joel C. Kuipers is Associate Professor of Anthropology, Department of Anthropology, The George Washington University, Washington DC.

J. Thomas Lindblad is Associate Professor in Economic History and the History of Indonesia, University of Leiden, The Netherlands.

Robert L. Worden is retired chief of and now consultant to the Federal Research Division, Library of Congress, Washington, DC.

Published Country Studies

(Area Handbook Series)

Afghanistan
Albania
Algeria
Angola
Argentina

Armenia, Azerbaijan,
  and Georgia
Australia
Austria
Bangladesh

Belarus and Moldova
Belgium
Bolivia
Brazil
Bulgaria

Burma
Cambodia
Cameroon
Chad
Chile

China
Colombia
Commonwealth Caribbean,
  Islands of the
Congo
Costa Rica

Côte d'Ivoire (Ivory
  Coast)
Cuba
Cyprus
Czechoslovakia

Dominican Republic
  and Haiti
Ecuador
Egypt
El Salvador

Estonia, Latvia, and
  Lithuania
Ethiopia
Finland
Germany

Ghana
Greece
Guatemala
Guinea
Guyana and Belize

Honduras
Hungary
India
Indian Ocean
Indonesia
Iran

Iraq
Israel
Italy
Japan
Jordan

Kazakstan, Kyrgyzstan,
  Tajikistan, Turkmenistan,
  and Uzbekistan
Kenya
Korea, North

Korea, South
Laos
Lebanon
Liberia
Libya

Malawi
Malaysia
Mauritania
Mexico
Mongolia

Morocco
Mozambique
Nepal and Bhutan
Nicaragua
Nigeria

Oceania
Pakistan
Panama
Paraguay
Persian Gulf States
Peru

Philippines
Poland
Portugal
Romania
Russia

Rwanda and Burundi
Saudi Arabia
Senegal
Sierra Leone
Singapore

Somalia
South Africa
Soviet Union
Spain
Sri Lanka

Sudan
Syria
Tanzania
Thailand
Tunisia

Turkey
Uganda
Uruguay
Venezuela
Vietnam

Yemens, The
Yugoslavia
Zaire
Zambia
Zimbabwe

 GPO U.S. GOVERNMENT PRINTING OFFICE: 2012—373-677

wayang (theater)—A dramatic form in several major variations, in which puppets or human performers portray gods, heroes, villains, and other characters in literary epics. The *wayang kulit* is shadow theater using highly decorated flat leather puppets.

World Trade Organization (WTO)—Established in 1994 as successor to the General Agreement on Tariffs and Trade (GATT) and effective from January 1, 1995, the WTO has the goal to provide a forum to resolve trade conflicts between members and to carry on negotiations with the goal of further lowering and/or eliminating tariffs and other trade barriers. The WTO has 153 members, including Indonesia, and 30 observers.

Index